GW00835936

THE CAMBRIDGE COMPANION

RELIGIOUS STUDIES

The Cambridge Companion to Religious Studies is both informative and provocative, introducing readers to key debates in the contemporary study of religion and suggesting future research possibilities. A group of distinguished scholars takes up some of the most pressing theoretical questions in the field. What is a "religious tradition"? How are religious texts read? What takes place when a religious practitioner stands before a representation of gods or goddesses, ghosts, ancestors, saints, and other special beings? What roles is religion playing in contemporary global society? The volume emphasizes religion as a lived practice, stressing that people have used and continue to use religious media to engage the circumstances of their lives. This underlying conviction provides a realistic perspective on religion, and the volume's chapters engage with real-world religious practices. The chapters should prove valuable and interesting to a broad audience, including scholars in the humanities and social sciences and a general readership, as well as students of religious studies.

Robert A. Orsi is Professor of Religious Studies and History and Grace Craddock Nagle Professor of Catholic Studies at Northwestern University. He is the author of several prize-winning books, including *The Madonna of 115th Street: Faith and Community in Italian Harlem, 1880–1950*, 3rd Edition (2010); *Thank You, Saint Jude: Women's Devotions to the Patron Saint of Hopeless Causes* (1996); and *Between Heaven and Earth: The Religious Worlds People Make and the Scholars Who Study Them* (2005).

CAMBRIDGE COMPANIONS TO RELIGION
This is a series of companions to major topics and key figures in theology and religious studies. Each volume contains specially commissioned chapters by international scholars, which provide an accessible and stimulating introduction to the subject for new readers and nonspecialists.

Other Titles in the Series

AMERICAN JUDAISM Edited by Dana Evan Kaplan

KARL BARTH Edited by John Webster

THE BIBLE, 2nd edition Edited by Bruce Chilton

BIBLICAL INTERPRETATION Edited by John Barton

DIETRICH BONHOEFFER Edited by John de Gruchy

JOHN CALVIN Edited by Donal K. McKim

CHRISTIAN DOCTRINE Edited by Colin Gunton

CHRISTIAN ETHICS Edited by Robin Gill

CHRISTIAN PHILOSOPHICAL THEOLOGY Edited by Charles Taliaferro and Chad V. Meister

CLASSICAL ISLAMIC THEOLOGY Edited by Tim Winter

JONATHAN EDWARDS Edited by Stephen J. Stein

FEMINIST THEOLOGY Edited by Susan Frank Parsons

THE JESUITS Edited by Thomas Worcester

JESUS Edited by Markus Bockmuehl

LIBERATION THEOLOGY Edited by Chris Rowland

C. S. LEWIS Edited by Robert MacSwain and Michael Ward

MARTIN LUTHER Edited by Donald K. McKim

MEDIEVAL JEWISH PHILOSOPHY Edited by Daniel H. Frank and Oliver Leaman

MIRACLES Edited by Graham H. Twelfthtree

MODERN JEWISH PHILOSOPHY Edited by Michael L. Morgan and Peter Eli Gordon

MOHAMMED Edited by Jonathan E. Brockup

THOMAS MORE Edited by George M. Logan

POSTMODERN THEOLOGY Edited by Kevin J. Vanhoozer

PURITANISM Edited by John Coffey and Paul C. H. Lim

THE QUR'AN Edited by Jane Dammen McAuliffe

THE TRINITY Edited by Peter C. Phan

KARL RAHNER Edited by Declan Marmion and Mary E. Hines

REFORMATION THEOLOGY Edited by David Bagchi and David Steinmetz

FREIDRICH SCHLEIERMACHER Edited by Jacqueline Mariña

SCIENCE AND RELIGION Edited by Peter Harrison

ST. PAUL Edited by James D. G. Dunn

THE TALMUD AND RABBINIC LITERATURE Edited by Charlotte E. Fonrobert and Martin S. Jaffee

HANS URS VON BALTHASAR Edited by Edward T. Oakes and David Moss

JOHN WESLEY Edited by Randy L. Maddox and Jason E. Vickers

THE CAMBRIDGE COMPANION TO
RELIGIOUS STUDIES

Edited by Robert A. Orsi
Northwestern University

CAMBRIDGE
UNIVERSITY PRESS

CAMBRIDGE
UNIVERSITY PRESS

32 Avenue of the Americas, New York NY 10013-2473, USA

Cambridge University Press is part of the University of Cambridge.

It furthers the University's mission by disseminating knowledge in the pursuit of education, learning, and research at the highest international levels of excellence.

www.cambridge.org
Information on this title: www.cambridge.org/9780521710145

© Cambridge University Press 2012

This publication is in copyright. Subject to statutory exception and to the provisions of relevant collective licensing agreements, no reproduction of any part may take place without the written permission of Cambridge University Press.

First published 2012
Reprinted 2013 (twice)

A catalog record for this publication is available from the British Library.

Library of Congress Cataloging in Publication data
The Cambridge companion to religious studies / edited by Robert A. Orsi.
   p. cm. – (Cambridge Companions to religion)
Includes bibliographical references and index.
ISBN 978-0-521-88391-7 (hardback) – ISBN 978-0-521-71014-5 (paperback)
 1. Religion – Study and teaching. 2. Religion – Research. I. Orsi, Robert A.
BL41.C34 2011
200–dc22   2011010731

ISBN 978-0-521-88391-7 Hardback
ISBN 978-0-521-71014-5 Paperback

Cambridge University Press has no responsibility for the persistence or accuracy of URLs for external or third-party Internet Web sites referred to in this publication, and does not guarantee that any content on such Web sites is, or will remain, accurate or appropriate.

Contents

Notes on contributors   *page* ix
Acknowledgments   xiii

Introduction   1
ROBERT A. ORSI

Part one   Religion and religious studies:
the irony of inheritance

1. On sympathy, suspicion, and studying religion:
    historical reflections on a doubled inheritance   17
    LEIGH E. SCHMIDT

2. Thinking about religion, belief, and politics   36
    TALAL ASAD

3. Special things as building blocks of religions   58
    ANN TAVES

4. The problem of the holy   84
    ROBERT A. ORSI

Part two   Major theoretical problems

5. Social order or social chaos   109
    MICHAEL J. PUETT

6. Tradition: the power of constraint   130
    MICHAEL L. SATLOW

7. The text and the world   151
    ANNE M. BLACKBURN

8. On the role of normativity in religious studies   168
    THOMAS A. LEWIS

9. Translation   186
    MARTIN KAVKA

10. Material religion   209
    MATTHEW ENGELKE

11. Theology and the study of religion:
a relationship   230
CHRISTINE HELMER

Part three   ***Methodological variations***

12. Buddhism and violence   257
BERNARD FAURE

13. Practicing religions   273
COURTNEY BENDER

14. The look of the sacred   296
DAVID MORGAN

15. Reforming culture: law and religion today   319
WINNIFRED FALLERS SULLIVAN

16. Sexing religion   338
R. MARIE GRIFFITH

17. Constituting ethical subjectivities   360
LEELA PRASAD

18. Neo-Pentecostalism and globalization   380
MARLA F. FREDERICK

19. Religious criticism, secular critique, and
the "critical study of religion": lessons from
the study of Islam   403
NOAH SALOMON AND JEREMY F. WALTON

Index   421

Notes on contributors

Talal Asad is Distinguished Professor of Anthropology at the City University of New York (CUNY) Graduate Center. His publications include *Genealogies of Religion: Discipline and Reasons of Power in Christianity and Islam* (Johns Hopkins University Press, 1993); *Formations of the Secular: Christianity, Islam, Modernity* (Stanford University Press, 2003); and, most recently, *On Suicide Bombing* (Columbia University Press, 2007).

Courtney Bender is Associate Professor in the Department of Religion at Columbia University. She is author of *The New Metaphysicals: Spirituality and the American Religious Imagination* (University of Chicago Press, 2010) and *Heaven's Kitchen: Practicing Religion at God's Love We Deliver* (University of Chicago Press, 2003).

Anne M. Blackburn, Associate Professor of South Asian Studies and Buddhist Studies in the Department of Asian Studies at Cornell University, is author of *Buddhist Learning and Textual Practice in Eighteenth-Century Lankan Monastic Culture* (Princeton University Press, 2001) and, most recently, *Locations of Buddhism: Colonialism and Modernity in Sri Lanka* (University of Chicago Press, 2010).

Matthew Engelke is a senior lecturer in anthropology at the London School of Economics. His book *A Problem of Presence: Beyond Scripture in an African Church* (University of California Press, 2007) won the 2008 Clifford Geertz Prize from the Society for the Anthropology of Religion and the 2009 Victor Turner Prize for Ethnographic Writing.

Bernard Faure is Kao Professor in Japanese Religion at Columbia University. His books include *The Red Thread: Buddhist Approaches to Sexuality* (Princeton University Press, 1998); *The Power of Denial: Buddhism, Purity, and Gender* (Princeton University Press, 2003); and *Double Exposure: Cutting Across Buddhist and Western Discourses* (Stanford University Press, 2004).

Marla F. Frederick is Morris Kahn Professor of African and African American Studies and a member of the Committee on the Study of Religion at Harvard University. She is the author of *Between Sundays: Black Women and Everyday Struggles of Faith* (University of California Press, 2003).

R. Marie Griffith is the John C. Danforth Distinguished Professor and Director of the John C. Danforth Center on Religion and Politics, Washington University in St. Louis. Her books include *God's Daughters: Evangelical Women and the Power of Submission* (University of California Press, 1997), *Born Again Bodies: Flesh and Spirit in American Christianity* (University of California Press, 2004), and *American Religions: A Documentary History* (Oxford University Press, 2007).

Christine Helmer is Professor of Religious Studies and Adjunct Professor of German at Northwestern University. She is the author of *The Trinity and Martin Luther* (Zabern, 1999) and has published numerous articles and edited (and coedited) volumes in the areas of Luther studies, Schleiermacher studies, biblical theology, philosophy of religion, liberal theology, and constructive theology, most recently *The Global Luther: A Theologian for Modern Times* (Fortress, 2009).

Martin Kavka is Associate Professor in the Department of Religion at Florida State University. He is the author of *Jewish Messianism and the History of Philosophy* (Cambridge University Press, 2004), which in 2008 was awarded the inaugural Jordan Schnitzer Book Award in Jewish thought and philosophy by the Association for Jewish Studies. He is coeditor of *Tradition in the Public Square: A David Novak Reader* (Eerdmans, 2008) and *Saintly Influence: Edith Wyschogrod and the Possibilities of Philosophy of Religion* (Fordham University Press, 2009).

Thomas A. Lewis is Associate Professor in the Department of Religious Studies at Brown University. His publications include *Freedom and Tradition in Hegel: Reconsidering Anthropology, Ethics, and Religion* (University of Notre Dame Press, 2005); *Religion, Modernity, and Politics in Hegel* (Oxford University Press, 2011); and numerous articles on methodology in the study of religion, religion and politics, liberation theology, and communitarianism.

David Morgan is Professor of Religion at Duke University, with a secondary appointment in the Department of Art, Art History, and Visual Studies. His most recent book is *The Lure of Images: A History of Religion and Visual Media in America* (Routledge, 2007). He edited and contributed to *Key Words in Religion, Media, and Culture* (Routledge, 2008).

Robert A. Orsi is Professor of Religious Studies and History and the Grace Craddock Nagle Professor of Catholic Studies at Northwestern University. His most recent book is *Between Heaven and Earth: The Religious Worlds People Make and the Scholars Who Study Them* (Princeton University Press, 2005), which won the 2005 Award for Excellence in the Study of Religion, Constructive-Reflective Studies Category, from the American Academy of Religion.

Leela Prasad is Associate Professor in the Religion Department at Duke University. Her book *Poetics of Conduct: Oral Narrative and Moral Being in a South Indian Town* (Columbia University Press, 2007) was awarded the 2007 Best First Book in the History of Religions Prize from the American Academy of Religion.

Michael J. Puett is Professor of Chinese History in the Department of East Asian Languages and Civilizations and Chair of the Committee on the Study of

Religion at Harvard University. His books include *To Become a God: Cosmology, Sacrifice, and Self-Divinization in Early China* (Harvard University Asia Center for the Harvard-Yenching Institute, 2002), and he is coauthor, with Adam B. Seligman, Robert P. Weller, and Bennett Simon, of *Ritual and Its Consequences: An Essay on the Limits of Sincerity* (Oxford University Press, 2008).

Noah Salomon is Assistant Professor of Religion at Carleton College, where he teaches courses in Islamic studies and theory and method in the study of religion. He is the author of recent articles on Muslim piety movements in contemporary Sudan and is preparing a manuscript, *In the Shadow of Salvation: Sufis, Salafis and the Project of Late Islamism in Contemporary Sudan*.

Michael L. Satlow is Professor of Religious Studies and Judaic Studies in the Department of Religious Studies at Brown University. Among his books are *Jewish Marriage in Antiquity* (Princeton University Press, 2001) and *Creating Judaism: History, Tradition, Practice* (Columbia University Press, 2006).

Leigh E. Schmidt is the Edward Mallinckrodt University Professor at Washington University in St. Louis. He is the author of numerous books, including *Hearing Things: Religion, Illusion, and the American Enlightenment* (Harvard University Press, 2000), which won the American Academy of Religion Award for Excellence in Historical Studies and the John Hope Franklin Prize of the American Studies Association; and *Restless Souls: The Making of American Spirituality* (HarperOne, 2005).

Winnifred Fallers Sullivan is Professor of Law and Director of the Law and Religion Project at the University of Buffalo. Her publications include *The Impossibility of Religious Freedom* (Princeton University Press, 2005) and *Prison Religion: Faith-Based Reform and the Constitution* (Princeton University Press, 2009).

Ann Taves is Professor in the Department of Religious Studies at the University of California at Santa Barbara and holder of the Virgil Cordano O.F.M. Endowed Chair in Catholic Studies. Her book *Fits, Trances and Visions: Experiencing Religion and Explaining Experience from Wesley to James* (Princeton University Press, 1999) won the 2000 Association of American Publishers Award for Best Professional/Scholarly Book in Philosophy and Religion. Her most recent book is *Religious Experience Reconsidered: A Building Block Approach to the Study of Religion and Other Special Things* (Princeton University Press, 2009).

Jeremy F. Walton is Assistant Professor and Faculty Fellow in New York University's Religious Studies Program. He is currently at work on *Horizons and Histories of Liberal Piety: Civil Islam and Secularism in Contemporary Turkey* and is coeditor of *Anthropology and Global Counterinsurgency* (University of Chicago Press, 2010).

Acknowledgments

I have been fortunate in spending much of my life talking about the challenges of studying religion with an extraordinary community of fellow scholars, many of whom have become friends as the years have piled up and conference has followed conference. I owe a tremendous debt to all of them, for their support, encouragement, and criticism, but most of all for their friendship and for all that I have learned from them.

This book began in a conversation with my wife, Christine Helmer, in a cabin we were renting in Maine for a couple of weeks one summer, with our little son, Anthony, sleeping in the next room, and my father, Mario, doing Italian crossword puzzles on the couch. One of the great delights of our marriage is a shared fascination with religious practice and imagination and the many long dinnertime conversations this provokes. I have learned a great deal about the study of religion from Christine, not least a robust understanding of Friedrich Schleiermacher's centrality to the making of Western religious theory. I am especially grateful to her for encouraging me to take on this project and then for her guidance in seeing it through to the end. Our son Anthony and my daughter Claire are an endless source of joy and sustenance. Claire remains one of my most cherished and trusted intellectual partners.

The conversation continued in the hallways of the Barker Center at Harvard University, when I was chair of the Study of Religion. Here I was fortunate to be part of an invigorating everyday discussion of the issues that found their way into this volume. I owe a particular word of gratitude to Ann Braude, David Hall, Tal Lewis (who since has moved to Brown University), Parimal Patil, Michael Puett (then chair of the Department of East Asian Languages and Civilizations), and Ronald Thiemann. Carole Bundy, Kit Jaeger (and their dogs), and Katherine Kunkle made the Study of Religion a warm and welcoming place. The Committee on the Study of Religion is what serves as a religious studies department at Harvard in the Faculty of Arts and Sciences. The Religion Colloquium in the Study of Religion was a wonderful venue for generating and exploring ideas about religion and religions and about methods and theories. I record here my gratitude to the graduate students and faculty who faithfully participated in these meetings several evenings each semester.

Over the years, students in classes on theory and method in the study of religion, first at Indiana University, then at Harvard, and now at Northwestern University, have challenged and enlightened me on the topic of the study of religion; the learning that took place in these classrooms was always shared. I remain grateful to these successive generations of students. They are now respected scholars and teachers themselves (or on their way to becoming so). May they be as fortunate in their students as I have been in my students, which is to say, as I was (and am) in them. I want to remember and thank here too the extraordinary undergraduates who took my theory and method seminar at Harvard in 2006 as their sophomore tutorial. These students not only brought an exuberant curiosity about religion and an impressive openness to critical inquiry to our conversations, they were among the most gracious and generous group of students I have ever taught. My understanding of the historiography of the study of religion developed over two decades of conversations and many long evenings of food and drink with my good friend Leigh Eric Schmidt. Andy Beck, then an editor at Cambridge University Press, was enthusiastic about this project from the start.

Brian Clites and Matthew Cressler, graduate students in religious studies at Northwestern University, checked and rechecked every citation and quotation in every chapter in this volume, working under time pressure with energy, creativity, and focus. They also helped me assemble the index. Another graduate student at Northwestern, Matthew Robinson, assisted with the initial formatting of the individual chapters.

Finally, I owe my greatest debt to the contributors to the volume. All were involved with major projects of their own when I approached them in e-mails from out of the blue about joining me in putting together this book. I was fortunate that they also believed that it is an exciting and challenging time in the history of the study of religion and I very much appreciate their enthusiasm and their support. I found our back-and-forth exchanges over the months about their chapters exhilarating and inspiring.

Introduction

ROBERT A. ORSI

> Religion is sociologically interesting not because, as vulgar positivism
> would have it, it describes the social order (which, insofar as it does, it
> does not only very obliquely but very incompletely), but because, like
> environment, political wealth, jural obligation, personal affection, and
> a sense of beauty, it shapes it.
>
> Clifford Geertz, "Religion as a Cultural System"[1]

> Religion is more complicated than it sometimes seems.
>
> <div align="right">Nicholas D. Kristof, <i>New York Times</i>, October 9, 2010[2]</div>

The Cambridge Companion to Religious Studies comes at a critical and
challenging time for the academic study of religion in the United States
and around the world. The field of religious studies is at a crossroads, having embarked for the past two decades on a fundamental reexamination
of its most basic ideas and terms, while the world at large has awakened
to the enduring public salience of religion and to religion's importance
to the everyday lives of much of the planet's population. Recent political
events have given an anxious edge to this curiosity about religion, but
religious conflict and violence, important and compelling as these are as
subjects, do not exhaust the place of religion in the contemporary world,
nor do they account completely for the intensified academic interest in
the study of religion across the humanities and social sciences. Rather,
people of the late twentieth and early twenty-first centuries have turned
out to be not nearly as disenchanted as earlier generations of thinkers
about religion had predicted – just the opposite, in fact. The secular and
the sacred are braided together today, sometimes in novel configurations and in unexpected places, and there are those who suggest that

---

[1] Clifford Geertz, "Religion as a Cultural System," in *The Interpretation of Cultures*
(New York: Basic, 1973), 119.
[2] Nicholas D. Kristof, "Test Your Savvy on Religion," *New York Times*, October 9, 2010,
online at http://www.nytimes.com/2010/10/10/opinion/10kristof.html (accessed
May 27, 2011).

we have never been modern, never completely disenchanted. This has invited renewed attention to what religion is and what religion does to and for individuals and communities, social movements, global and national economies, and to the politics of nation-states and the relations between them.

Scholars in the nations of the former Soviet space and China, for example, are asking about the role that religion and religions will play in their respective contexts, amid revolutionary social, economic, and demographic upheaval and transformation. Does religion contribute to national identity or undermine it by redirecting personal allegiance to transnational affiliations (for example, global Islam or world Catholicism) or to ethnic particularity? What does it mean to be Muslim in the rapidly changing social and economic circumstances of post-Soviet Kyrgyzstan or in France, and what does it mean to be Catholic anywhere in the world given the multiple inheritances and diverse interpretations of the Second Vatican Council (1962–5)? No one is certain how these matters will develop or what new shapes religions will take.

Does it make sense any longer to speak of religious "traditions," given what we know of the multifarious and hybrid nature of all religious worlds? How are sacred texts read, and what is the relationship between text and practice in changing social and religious contexts? Are religions inherently violent or inherently peaceful? There is urgency to such questions today because people understand that they need to be able to think clearly about these matters in order to comprehend their turbulent environments and to live with eyes wide open in the modern world.

This convergence of circumstances – the reevaluation of critical terms in the study of religion and the exigent interest in religion in the social, political, economic, and existential environments of the world today – opens a charged but productive space for creative theoretical work. How do we take the theoretical and historical inheritances of the study of religion in the West, so thoroughly deconstructed and criticized of late, and in a constructive manner generate forward-looking theoretical perspectives on religion and religions that will result in research agendas for the twenty-first century? The recognition of this unique moment, with its promise and attendant risks, inspired this volume.

A fundamental commitment of this *Companion* is to pay attention to the genealogies of the issues at stake in each chapter. This follows the recent historicist turn in religious studies. Scholars of religion have become deeply interested in the history of their various subfields (of the study of Buddhism, for instance, or of the philosophy of religion), and it is understood now that scholarship in any area of religious studies must be alert to its genealogy, to the history of the making of its terminology, to the cultural and religious values inscribed in its account of the past, and to the broader social and political context of its judgments. This begins with "religion" itself. Scholars of religion are asking what forces converged to shape particular understandings of "religion" and "religions" as the objects of critical inquiry, primarily in the modern West (where most of the analytical terminology for the scientific study of religion developed), and as the lens through which those objects would be viewed. The past of "religion" is a historical question with theoretical and methodological implications, in other words, for the present and future. "Genealogy," anthropologist Talal Asad has written, is a "way of working back from our present to the contingencies that have come together to give us our certainties."[3] Searching the past of the study of religion is not about rethinking static entities – "religion," "Buddhism," "Hinduism" – but about exploring the dynamic and contingent encounters out of which came both our certainties and the resources with which to challenge them. This is the spirit of this volume.

I. "RELIGIONS" AND "RELIGION" IN THE MODERN WEST

The history of the making of "religion" as the object of critical inquiry and the invention of "religions" to be compared with Christianity and to each other begins in the sixteenth century and was deeply entangled from the start with the social, political, military, and intellectual history of the West in its engagement with the rest of the world. But there is a long prehistory to the modern study of religion that contributed terms, general perspectives and orientations, and judgments to later religious scholarship. Classical philosophers asked where the gods came from, noting the strong similarities between the lives and behaviors of the deities and those of the humans who worshipped them and between the imagined orderings of heaven and social hierarchies on earth (anticipating much later ideas about the social origins and functions of religion). During the medieval period, scholars working within particular religious contexts sometimes thought comparatively about their religious worlds and about religion as a dimension of human life. Reflection on religion and religions became especially necessary at the

---

[3] Talal Asad, *Formations of the Secular: Christianity, Islam, Modernity* (Stanford, CA: Stanford University Press, 2003), 16.

borders where different worlds came into contact with each other. Such meeting places have been rich grounds for the generation of questions (and anxieties) about religion and religions. Many of the words used to talk about religion from early modernity onward were inherited from the ancient world, especially from Christians' encounters with pagans, first in Greek and Roman lands and then in the forests of northern Europe, and from the long and troubled relationship between Christians and Jews. Knowing about how the others worshipped their gods, buried their dead, or honored their rulers could be essential information for intercultural survival and communication, for mutual understanding, as an aid in defining and establishing one's own social and religious identities, and for the purposes of peace or domination.

The impress of this prehistory has been enduring, but it was in modernity, with its own specific concerns and crises, that the critical and comparative languages of religious scholarship acquired the meanings they have today. Four key moments may serve as organizational focuses for this brief historical survey: the geographical discoveries of the fifteenth and sixteenth centuries and the subsequent expansion of European power and presence throughout the world; the breakup of Christendom in the sixteenth century and the terrible protracted internecine religious violence that followed it; the epistemological reorientations of the seventeenth and eighteenth centuries and the rise of the social and natural sciences; and the institution of the first university chairs in the science of religion and comparative religions in the late nineteenth and early twentieth centuries. Each of these points of crisis, transition, and intellectual innovation fundamentally shaped how religion and religions came to be understood, not only in Western contexts but also around the globe.

The discovery of the new world confronted Europe with peoples and ways of life – including religious practices – utterly unknown to ancient authorities. This provoked an epistemic crisis and compelled European thinkers to stretch their inherited conceptions of history, cosmology, law, religion, and anthropology to take into account what was being reported from other lands. The expansion of European trade with Asia brought Christians in contact with ancient religions of rich textual and ritual traditions, while the proximity of Muslim armies kept the fear and fascination of Islam burning in European imaginations. Curiosity about the religions of others and about one's own in relation to these others expanded in this earlier age of globalization. European intellectuals, some of them writing from afar, approached what they identified as the religions of distant people in terms of the religious practices they were familiar with closer to home, developing frameworks for thinking about and comparing religion and religions globally. These reproduced Christian theological assumptions and confirmed their authors' belief in the superiority of Christianity. Later theorists of the emerging science of religion in the nineteenth century drew on accounts of indigenous religions by missionaries, travelers, soldiers, and administrators in developing their understandings of the nature of religion and its role in society and human experience, with reference to the era's new theories of evolution and social development. Sometimes these accounts called the superiority of Christianity into question, but most often they affirmed it.

These efforts to locate unfamiliar religious practices within recognizable categories was further inflected by the hostility between Protestants and Catholics, which endured at varying degrees of intensity in different places from the sixteenth century into the twentieth. Various agents of European nations carried this schism out to the rest of the world, and scholars of religion mapped it onto other peoples, recreating the religious history and contemporary religious practices of Asians, Africans, and South Americans in the image of Protestant/Catholic prejudices. Buddha became the Luther of Asia in the view of Protestant scholars, for example, and Buddhists were cast as Asia's Protestants, in contrast to "Hinduism," which was denigrated in the very process of its invention by Western Protestant scholars because of its alleged resemblance to Catholicism. The devotional practices of Irish laborers in England and the sacred festivities of Sicilian peasants were classified in the racist categories used for the religions of Africa and South Asia and vice versa. Catholics protected themselves from the similarities they perceived (and Protestants pointed out) between Catholicism and indigenous religions around the world by declaring the latter to be the mimetic work of Satan.

Then in the seventeenth century, philosophers and theologians, weary of internecine Christian violence – men and women who were thinking on a pile of bones, in Voltaire's grim image – sought to come up with an irenic religion stripped of its particularities (dogmas, rituals, and hierarchies) and thus acceptable to all reasonable people.[4] Enlightenment philosophers extended this endeavor further by setting religion within

---

[4] Voltaire's vision of a world devastated by religious wars may be found in the anthology edited by Isaac Kramnick, *The Portable Enlightenment Reader* (New York: Penguin Books, 1995), 119–24. It appears as the entry for "Religion" in *The Philosophical Dictionary* published by Voltaire in 1764.

the newly established epistemological limits of rationality. Between the seventeenth and eighteenth centuries, the modern notion of "religion" acquired its shape. Against it other forms of religious practice, not conforming to this norm, in Europe and elsewhere, in the present and in the past, were measured and then recast as premodern, irrational, emotional, magical, superstitious, and "primitive." In the narrative of "religion," these now lower forms of religion were destined either to disappear from history or evolve into modern religions on the model of European and North American Protestantism. "Religion" underwrote new thinking about the organization of society, about freedom of conscience, and about human nature and destiny.

Finally, the separation of the study of religion as an academic enterprise from theological studies in the universities of northern Europe and the United States in the late nineteenth and twentieth centuries brought the study of religion into engagement with the physical and social sciences and the humanities and secured its place in the modern research university. It also instituted a deep and lasting division between the empirical study of religious practices and theological reflection that would deepen over time, to a greater or lesser extent in varying cultural and religious contexts. This grafted onto other distinctions in academic culture, such as those between faith and reason, between scholarship supervised by religious authorities and religious inquiry free of such constraints, between objectivity and subjectivity, and between empathy and detachment as scholarly positions. These polarities continue to bedevil the study of religion, and thinking past them remains a powerful and generative challenge.

Any attempt to address contemporary interest in religions and religion within the academy and outside it must take account of the impact of this history on the making of the discipline. When they talk about *religion*, scholars of religion are referring – or have been referring for more than a century, at least – to three things: (1) a critical, analytical category that aims to name a distinct and universal dimension of human experience as the subject of academic inquiry (about which there has been definitional debate but fundamental agreement that such a dimension exists); (2) a normative discourse about religion deeply enmeshed with the intellectual, political, and military aims of Western nations that proposes how people ought to live and how states ought to be organized and that distinguishes good religion from bad, the tolerable and the intolerable, with northern European and American Protestantism as exemplary forms of the good and tolerable; and (3) the lived practices of men and women around the world. "Religion" and "religions" as terms guiding inquiry have always entailed both descriptive and prescriptive ambitions, inscribing one way of being religious – as developed out of the epochal events and broad shifts in the global reality of the sixteenth and seventeenth centuries – as "religion" itself and measuring other religions against this standard.

At the same time, the past of religious studies and of "religion" is characterized by the irony and inconsistencies common to every area of human history. Devout Christians made fundamental contributions to the critical study of East and South Asian religions. For example, the Oxford translator and interpreter of Confucian texts, James Legge (1815–97), a pious Protestant, found himself regularly denounced by other Christians for his scrupulously fair and relatively nonjudgmental accounts of Confucius's life and teachings and especially for daring to compare Christ and Confucius favorably. Theologians such as Rudolf Otto (1869–1937) and Ernst Troeltsch (1865–1923), working within confessional contexts (in their cases, Lutheranism) and contending with the epistemological and theological legacy of Immanuel Kant (1724–1804), introduced important theoretical terms for religious analysis. A British and American tradition of learned clergy writing popular volumes about other religions, ancient and contemporary, contributed to broadening public knowledge and literacy about the world's religious diversity. One of the finest examples of such texts is Reverend F. D. Maurice's *The Religions of the World and Their Relationship to Christianity* (1847), which originated in a lecture series for a British working-class audience. A great irony of the past of the study of religion is that groundbreaking work on religious traditions other than Christianity was done by scholars who not only had little affinity for these religions, but – as in the case of the influential Sanskrit scholar, Monier Monier-Williams (1819–99) – despised and feared them or translated their texts with an eye toward the conversion of "heathens."

The "heathens" were not silent figures in this story, moreover. Religious scholarship arose in a world in which Europeans and Americans were meeting and talking with real people, with memories and histories of their own. Among the interlocutors of Westerners curious about other religions were figures within these cultures and religious worlds. The efforts of Asian scholars to understand religions in China, Japan, and Korea predated the West's interest, subsequently informed and challenged what Western scholars came to think about these religions, and continued to develop alongside and in communication with Western scholarship. The others pushed back against and corrected the work of Western scholars of religion. Sometimes political actors or religious leaders in other lands used Western analyses for their own ends; on occasion they misled Western agents to protect local religious sources, knowledge, and artifacts. The history of the study of religion is the history of such relationships in specific circumstances evolving over time in varied political, institutional, and religious environments. Religious sources, scholars, and scholarship were all caught up in transactions and exchanges on quite particular historical fields.

II. DEBATES IN CONTEMPORARY RELIGIOUS STUDIES

As the various dimensions of the history of the study of religion have come into sharper focus, its equivocal quality has contributed to a number of critical conversations over the most fundamental theoretical, political, and ethical questions in the contemporary discipline of religious studies. Some historians of the Western study of religion have argued, for instance, that because such scholarship was so central to the imposition of the modern Western political and intellectual project on the rest of the world, religious studies is caught in a relentless solipsism. Modern religious studies, says Daniel Dubuisson, one of the voices in this debate, represent the West's "lonely face-to-face encounter with itself." Why do Westerners study Hinduism? So "we could peer into the past of our own religion in the Indian present," in the words of another scholar.[5]

Because Christian theological assumptions and conceptions have been so foundational not only to the study of religion but also to the construction of "religion" as a modern category, one of the challenges facing the discipline today is to understand this legacy and its implications. Debates over the relationship between theology and religious studies approach the question from two different – indeed, opposing – perspectives, emphasizing two divergent concerns: the introduction of theological perspectives and norms into religious studies, on the one hand, and the rejection of the theological legacy as irrelevant to the study of religion, on the other. Religious studies cannot escape theology, according to some; religious studies as empirical practice has abandoned theological analysis to the flattening, if not the death, of its subject, say others. The relationship between theology and religious studies requires care to clarify its history and critical implications, judicious consideration

---

[5]   Daniel Dubuisson, *The Western Construction of Religion: Myths, Knowledge, and Ideology*, trans. William Sayers (Baltimore: Johns Hopkins University Press, 2003), 69; Ronald B. Inden, *Imagining India* (Bloomington: Indiana University Press, 2000 [1990]), 91.

of the methodological questions attending both empirical and constructive work, and attention to theological engagements with the humanities and social sciences.

The very work of critical self-scrutiny within the discipline in recent decades has aroused suspicion. The denial of the stability and coherence of religious "traditions," for instance, may appear to those with strong commitments to these traditions as a rejection of their deepest beliefs and values and a dismissal of their history and memory. Deconstructions of the entity called "Hinduism," for example, or interpretations that focus on aspects of South Asian myth and imagery that some would prefer to deemphasize have appeared to a number of South Asian intellectuals and public figures as yet another expression of colonial presumption and power, with outsiders once again claiming the authority of determining what is real and what is not about the South Asian religious world.

Who has the right to teach particular religions, in any case? Those who insist that religious traditions are unified, coherent, and authoritative say that only practitioners of these traditions legitimately represent them and that they do so for the purposes of advancing the faith among students who belong to these traditions or of presenting them in a positive light to outsiders. The more radical traditionalists from several religious worlds have disrupted gatherings at the annual meetings of the American Academy of Religion in recent years, threatened scholars "outside" traditions who make arguments that "insiders" find offensive or upsetting, trashed books and derailed careers, obstructed research, and sought to influence hiring decisions in religious studies programs in the United States and in other countries.

Meanwhile, as scholars of religion contend seemingly endlessly with each other over the meanings of their terminology and the limits of their knowledge, often coming to conclusions that emphasize polyvalence and instability of critical terms, people are looking for assistance with the real religious challenges of their local worlds and with their immediate and personal concerns. Religion is fundamentally implicated today in the most challenging areas of contemporary life, such as in making some sense of and living with pain and suffering; in the shaping of historical memories and the political actions that may be provoked by them; in the lives of immigrants, migrants, and refugees; in the generation or contestation of national or ethnic identities; and in the ways that people adapt to new technologies. The eruption of epistemological doubt and the understandable reluctance of contemporary religion scholars to speak in the singular about phenomena that are always "both/and" can appear at times an abandonment or sidestepping of the field's responsibilities to the wider public.

These fault lines seem to be threatening the very existence of the academic study of religion as a distinctive component of liberal education today. But from another perspective, the one taken here, these places of most acute intellectual and public contestation offer opportunities for identifying new research possibilities, introducing theoretical innovations, and addressing the public's urgent questions in relevant ways. It is the assumption of this book that the conversation does not end with the questions that are most roiling the discipline today. It starts with them.

III. *THE CAMBRIDGE COMPANION TO RELIGIOUS STUDIES*

The ambiguous genealogies of "religion" and of the "religions" have been well established. What next? How do we move forward within the discipline? Contributors to *The Cambridge Companion to Religious Studies* respond to this challenge by exploring how the study of religion has lived with and against its multiple inheritances (and its varied encumbrances), with equivocal, instructive, creative, and unpredictable outcomes. The goal is to find a balance between the recognition of the ambiguous historical legacy of the study of religion and engagement with contemporary theoretical innovations and opportunities in the discipline.

The chapters ahead are organized into three parts. The first, "Religion and Religious Studies: The Irony of Inheritance," explores how the inherited terminology of religious studies might be worked with, worked through, or reworked to be of use in developing research agendas moving forward. The second, "Major Theoretical Problems," takes up especially gnarled and contentious issues in the study of religion today, the field's hot spots, to explore where such fierce and focused questioning might or can lead. The final part, "Methodological Variations," addresses theoretical questions in emergent areas of religious inquiry.

It is one of the book's governing commitments that productive and innovative avenues of religious inquiry open up at the intersection of theory and empirical study. Modern theories of religion were developed in relation to assembled evidence of religious practice, narrative, experience, and imagination that was more or less accurate; in some cases, this evidence was obtained directly, either in the archives or the field, while in others it came refracted through intermediaries. But the science of religion has had one foot firmly planted in the world of facts since its earliest days. The point here is not to make a claim for the primacy or transparency of the empirical. Rather, it is to emphasize that religious theorizing at its best tracks back and forth from lived contexts in the present and the past to the issues and questions of contemporary moment in the academic study of religion, and then back again, allowing each – the empirical and the theoretical – to inform, question, and illuminate the other.

The insistence on this intellectual and existential movement between practice and theory permits the men and women we study to contest and resist what we scholars of religion make of them in theory. This is both an epistemological assumption and an ethical position. Religious theorizing is not done *upon* men and women, as if they were specimens in the natural sciences, but in relationship to them. It is done alongside them too, as they struggle to understand themselves and their worlds in the available light of their times. This is one reason that the insider/outsider question – whether a religious world is best (or only) understood by a practitioner of it or by a scholar with no affiliation to it – is so beside the point. All humans are always insiders and outsiders to their worlds, which is what makes research in the humanities and social sciences possible.

Another objective of the volume is to resist the utter unraveling or rejection of key concepts in the study of religion. The point is taken that religion and religions are always to be understood in their local and particular coordinates. But we must have a way to bring these disparate phenomena into relationship to each other in order to know what we are studying, as well as to continue framing and developing comparative understandings of religion and human experience. "He who knows one," said F. Max Müller (1823–1900), a German philologist and Oxford professor who was one of the founders of the modern academic study of religion, "knows none."[6] To say that religion is whatever religion is said to be in any specific place and time is to set an insuperable obstacle to coherence, comparison, and theoretical development in the field. This is why we need to keep working on and thinking through the theoretical nomenclature of the study of religion, in order to continue identifying fruitful avenues and methods of comparison.

[6] Quoted in Eric J. Sharpe, *Comparative Religion: A History*, 2nd Edition (LaSalle, IL: Open Court, 1986), 31, from Friedrich Max Müller, *Introduction to the Science of Religion: Four Lectures Delivered at the Royal Institution in 1870* (London: Longmans, Green, 1873).

Moreover, because this volume takes up problems and questions that are shared in all the disciplinary subfields of the study of religion as well as in the humanities and social sciences generally, there is no necessary correlation between the examination of a particular issue and the geographical area, religious tradition, or historical period of a scholar's specialization. This organization is meant to destabilize the position of Western phenomena as the default objects of religious theorizing. So a scholar of Chinese religions writes about the problem of order/chaos in thinking about religion and religions; a specialist in contemporary African Christianities takes up the theoretical question of "presence" in religious scholarship; a scholar of Jewish religious thought addresses the matter of translation across religious traditions and experiences; and so on.

This comparative focus mirrors the most consequential sociological and demographic change affecting the study of religion in the United States within the past half-century, namely, the arrival in the academy of populations long absent, denied, or excluded. The growing presence in American classrooms of women, African Americans, Catholics, Jews, Latinos and Latinas, and, more recently, East and South Asians and Africans of various religious backgrounds has contributed to the revision of old certainties in religious studies (another instance of the inescapably dialogical nature of all thinking about religion and religions). These students bring with them distinctive life histories, memories, experiences, sorrows, and religious educations and from these perspectives challenge received accounts of their families' religions by American scholars. Family lore and personal experience are not superior or necessarily more trustworthy than other sources or other forms of religious knowledge, but such stories and memories constitute a new empirical and social context for understanding and representing religions other than Christianity and Judaism. This, too, is changing the field.

As a companion, this book differs from other introductions to the study of religion by not being organized by religious tradition or great thinkers. Again, there is a theoretical issue at stake here. Classical and contemporary theorists are engaged throughout, as conversation partners in thinking through problems and questions. They may be searched for in the index. But many of us in the discipline of religious studies have come to understand its subject as the work of men and women in particular times and places engaging the circumstances of their lives in the company of their special beings (saints, gods, bodhisattvas, spirits) and of each other; the memory and ongoing effort to understand and communicate these experiences (in texts, songs, material objects, visions, art, and stories); the implication of religious idioms in the making and contesting of various forms of power; and the development of such practices, narratives, and understandings over time. What is compared are not religious traditions, but occasions of working on the world in the idioms of religion – in times of social crises, within families, in the domains of power and politics, when contending with illness and death, in marking life transitions, and so on – in order to raise questions and develop illuminating perspectives on human life itself.

Religion understood in this way is neither inherently good nor inherently bad. As anthropologist Clifford Geertz wrote:

> One of the main methodological problems in writing about religion scientifically is to put aside at once the tone of the village atheist and that of the village preacher, as well as their more sophisticated equivalents, so that the social and psychological implications of particular religious beliefs can emerge in a clear and neutral light. And when that is done, overall questions about whether religion is "good" or "bad," "functional" or "dysfunctional," "ego-strengthening" or "anxiety-producing," disappear like the chimeras that they are, and one is left with particular evaluations, assessments, and diagnoses in particular cases.[7]

Religions are lived, and it is in their living, in the full and tragic necessity of people's circumstances, that we encounter them, study and write about them, and compare them, in the full and tragic necessity of our circumstances.

---

7   Geertz, "Religion as a Cultural System," 123.

Part one

Religion and religious studies: the irony of inheritance

1   On sympathy, suspicion, and studying
    religion: historical reflections on a
    doubled inheritance
    LEIGH E. SCHMIDT

Wilfred Cantwell Smith opened *The Meaning and End of Religion*, published in 1962 shortly before he took charge of Harvard's Center for the
Study of World Religions, with a conspicuously slanted account of the
scholarly enterprise of studying religion. Privileging experiential faith,
Smith reproached "certain scholars," unnamed, for the vanity of their
empiricism and historicism, for their underlying irreverence and insen-
sitivity. "Such scholars might uncharitably be compared to flies crawling
on the outside of a goldfish bowl," Smith concluded, "making accurate
and complete observations on the fish inside, measuring their scales
meticulously, and indeed contributing much to a knowledge of the subject, but never asking themselves, and never finding out, how it feels to
be a goldfish." Here instead, Smith argued, was a subject that demanded
"imaginative sympathy" and "appreciative understanding," even perhaps
"something akin to awe" and "experiential participation." Only careless
hubris allowed scholars to think that religion was a "field of study" in
which "a would-be surveyor" could draw its bounds and stride confidently
across it: "One must tread softly here," Smith advised, echoing a line from
William Butler Yeats, "for one is treading on men's dreams." Smith insisted
that he wanted to hold onto "the hard-won heritage of scholarship and science" in the academy, alongside "the precious heritage of ultimates at the
heart of the world's faith." Still, when it came to the study of religion, he
clearly wished to put the former in the service of the latter. Critical suspicion and secular scholarship did not measure up well against the higher
ideals of sympathetic appreciation and spiritual cosmopolitanism.[1]

Smith's effort to historicize the category "religion" was a bellwether
move. It augured a whole generation of scholarship in which the skeptical
examination of the discipline's categories has been front and center – not

[1]   Wilfred Cantwell Smith, *The Meaning and End of Religion: A New Approach to the
      Religious Traditions of Mankind* (Minneapolis: Fortress Press, 1991 [1962]), 5–8.

only the invention of "religion" per se, but "Hinduism," "Buddhism," "Shinto," "magic," "animism," "totemism," "world religions," and so on. And, yet, the difference between Smith's aspiration for dismantling the category "religion" and the ambitions of most of the subsequent genealogists could hardly be more pronounced. Smith saw the modern Western reification of "religion" as a threat to the living practices of piety and faith – that is, to being warmly religious rather than being mundanely academic. "The rise of the concept 'religion,'" Smith hazarded, "is in some ways correlated with a decline in the practice of religion itself." He saw the modern construction of the study of religion – the fly's way of observing goldfish – as impeding scholars in the field from contributing to what was most urgently needed in the twentieth century: (1) helping imagine a world community in which different faiths and cultures cohered, and (2) finding existential meaning amid modernity's wasteland. Latter-day genealogists – including Talal Asad, Timothy Fitzgerald, Tomoko Masuzawa, and Russell McCutcheon – have found Smith's underlying theological concerns very much part of what needs to be analyzed, another strong indication of the liberal Protestant norms that have for too long shaped the discipline. From that perspective, Smith's emphasis on "faith" – as opposed, say, to practice – was no less a tool of liberal Protestant misrecognition than the abstracted concept of "religion" has been an instrument of colonial administration. In effect, the latter-day genealogists have hoisted Smith on his own petard.[2]

One of Talal Asad's critiques, in his judicious reading of Smith's classic, is that Smith had been inattentive to the question of secularism, the "Siamese twin" of religion's modern conceptualization. Smith had more to say about "secularism" than Asad acknowledges, not least when it came to seeing religion's reification as a species of secular differentiation and social fragmentation. Smith's wariness of secular methods and separations is not as thoroughgoing as Asad's analysis of secularism's "practical knowledges and powers," but the two theorists are often in sympathy with one another about the vices of the secular. Safe to say the scale-measuring fly on the fishbowl, the stand-in for the enlightened secularist, does not come off well from either of these angles of vision. In the one, it is swatted for missing the heart of the world's faiths; in the other, for refracting every culture through the same modern Western lens.[3]

---

[2]   Smith, *The Meaning and End of Religion*, 19.
[3]   Talal Asad, "Reading a Modern Classic: W. C. Smith's *The Meaning and End of Religion*," *History of Religions* 40, 3 (2001): 205–22; Smith, *The Meaning and End of Religion*, 124–5.

It would be tempting to announce that this chapter comes to the defense of the pesky fly, but that would not be quite right. Instead, it strives to resituate the interpretive tension between sympathetic appreciation and critical suspicion within a longer historical view. Rather than moving forward from Smith's world theology to Asad's postcolonial genealogy, this chapter offers the momentary pause of a backward glance. It looks at the discipline's double inheritance of sympathy and suspicion and explores what those deep-rooted dispositions have bequeathed to contemporary religious studies. An unresolved ambivalence at the heart of the discipline's modern formation, these interpretive postures have been almost endlessly embodied, exemplified, and engaged. Hence, with more than a hint of capriciousness, this chapter takes two nineteenth-century American figures, Thomas Wentworth Higginson and D. M. Bennett, as particularly illustrative of these competing, yet mutually constitutive, perspectives. Both Higginson and Bennett were amateurs, but then so were most learned inquirers in the nineteenth century. Both managed in the fifteen years following the Civil War to make typifying entries into the yet nascent study of religion among American intellectuals. Higginson energetically promoted sympathy as the key to understanding the religions of the world; Bennett advanced freethinking suspicion as the primary instrument for forwarding a natural history of the gods and religions.

I. THE SYMPATHY OF RELIGIONS

In 1871, Thomas Wentworth Higginson – a fiery abolitionist, a respected colonel of an African American regiment during the Civil War, an activist for women's rights, and a voluble essayist – published his most influential piece on religion, "The Sympathy of Religions." He had first focused on the subject during a six-month sojourn in the Azores in 1855–6 as part of a book on the current American religious scene, which he planned to call "The Return of Faith and the Decline of the Churches." (Already Wilfred Cantwell Smith's distinction between living faith and the weight of cumulative tradition has its transcendentalist foreshadowing.) Amid a respite from his abolitionist agitating – a break occasioned by his wife's health – Higginson had used his island encounter with Portuguese Catholicism to stoke his curiosity about religious variety and similarity. He had also found the salubrious climate in the Azores a stimulus to his Thoreauvian side; wandering about the volcanic crags, he was primed to discover religion in "the depth of personal experience," moments of epiphany that he was sure were as likely to come "on a mountain's height" as in church. Once back in New England, Higginson never completed his book on the return of faith, and the project was soon shunted aside in the face of more immediate political concerns and crises.[4]

In the years after the Civil War, Higginson returned to these religious questions for the liberal lecture circuit. In his diary, he noted that he began work on the "Sympathy of Religions" on January 24, 1870, and finished a thirty-page manuscript in less than a fortnight on February 4, just in time to present it two days later at Horticultural Hall in Boston. Of the event, Higginson noted simply in his diary: "Read my lecture 'Sympathy of Religions' which seemed to please people very much." The event had indeed gone well enough that he immediately set out to revise the discourse for publication, and it appeared early the next year in the *Radical*, an important literary nexus for liberal clubs and causes. The Free Religious Association, a post-Christian alliance made up mostly of Unitarian intellectuals, soon embraced the lecture as a charter document and started circulating it in 1876 as a tract for the times – one hundred copies for $3.00. Its influence spread to Chicago, where it appeared in the 1880s as a proclamation of unity and resolve among liberal religionists there, Midwestern heirs of Ralph Waldo Emerson and Theodore Parker. Eventually, it was republished as a philosophical manifesto for the World's Parliament of Religions in 1893, and Higginson himself journeyed to the gathering to give his latest rendition of what was by then a very well-traveled lecture, a banner of "our Liberal Faith."[5]

The essay, republished in London in 1872 and translated into French in 1898, even had international reach and became a respected embodiment of the universalism and cosmopolitanism often evinced in the early science of religions. When, for example, Higginson met F. Max Müller on a trip to England, the latter was thrilled to meet the author of "The Sympathy of Religions" and promptly invited him to Oxford.[6]

---

4 See Leigh E. Schmidt, "Cosmopolitan Piety: Sympathy, Comparative Religions, and Nineteenth-Century Liberalism," in *Practicing Protestants: Histories of the Christian Life in America, 1630–1945*, ed. Laurie F. Maffly-Kipp, Mark Valeri, and Leigh E. Schmidt (Baltimore: Johns Hopkins University Press, 2006), 199, 204, 209. This section of the chapter on sympathy is elaborated from the piece on "Cosmopolitan Piety," in which Higginson's effort to "appreciate" Portuguese Catholicism is critically examined.

5 Thomas Wentworth Higginson (TWH), Diaries, 24 Jan. to 19 Feb. 1870; 5 Jan. 1871, bMs 1162, Houghton Library, Harvard University; TWH, Clippings on "The Sympathy of Religions," in Scrapbooks, bMs Am 1256.2; TWH, *The Sympathy of Religions* (Boston: Free Religious Association, 1876); *Unity Church-Door Pulpit*, 16 June 1885.

6 Mary Thacher Higginson, *Thomas Wentworth Higginson: The Story of His Life* (Boston: Houghton Mifflin, 1914), 328, 411–12.

That invitation was very much in keeping with Müller's deep attraction to these transcendentalist souls: He had already dedicated his *Introduction to the Science of Religion* (1873) to Emerson in honor of the Concord sage's own visit to Oxford. Though Higginson often dwelled on religious topics in the *Atlantic Monthly* and elsewhere, he always took special pride in "The Sympathy of Religions" as his "most learned" achievement. Late in life in annotating a copy of his seven-volume collected works for his secretary, he placed this essay among "the very best things I ever wrote," "the most varied & labored piece of scholarship I ever produced." Certainly, his espousal of sympathy had a long and illustrious afterlife – not only as an expression of a universalistic piety but also as a scholarly aspiration.[7]

Not that Higginson had taken out a patent on sympathy. His appeal to this affection set his essay within long-flowing currents in moral philosophy from Francis Hutcheson, David Hume, and Adam Smith forward. As theorized in eighteenth- and early nineteenth-century discussions of the moral sentiments, sympathy was especially an ethic of fellow-feeling with those in pain or distress. It was the innate human capacity for compassion. (Empathy, it is worth noting, was an early twentieth-century coinage of aesthetic import; it was used initially to connote the viewer's imaginative identification with an object of art. Hence in the eighteenth and nineteenth centuries, sympathy was the term for heart-identifying engagement with the suffering, weak, or sorrowful; it shared no contrastive relation to empathy.) As a social virtue, cultivating sympathy was seen as a way of bridging differences and recognizing common purposes; it was a basis of overcoming isolation through affective connection, of joining people in shared enterprises. Social bonds were formed and sustained through a solidarity of sympathetic emotion – a universal human sentiment more essential to the benign functioning of civic, commercial, and religious life than the particularities of any special revelation.[8] Sympathy, in short, was a richly complex social and moral sentiment, laden with consequence for imagining relational affinities and interconnections. Largely shorn of its prior occult associations with magical healing and astrological

[7] TWH, 15 Dec. 1871, bMs Am 784, Box 6, #1077; Inscribed frontispiece, TWH to Eva S. Moore, in *The Writings of Thomas Wentworth Higginson*, 7 vols. (Boston: Houghton Mifflin, 1900), Houghton Library, *AC85.H5358.C900wb v.7. See also Friedrich Max Müller, *Introduction to the Science of Religion: Four Lectures Delivered at the Royal Institution in 1870* (London: Longmans, Green, 1873)

[8] Sympathy is the subject of a considerable literature, especially in the history of moral philosophy, but particularly helpful and relevant in the context of studying religion is Jennifer A. Herdt, *Religion and Faction in Hume's Moral Philosophy* (Cambridge: Cambridge University Press, 1997).

correspondence, sympathy had come to conjure instead the mysteries of social attachments and affections.

Higginson turned to that sort of moral theorizing as a practical paradigm for dealing with the rapidly growing "knowledge of the religions of the world." His hope was to mold sympathy into a social virtue that would push Christian particularity in the direction of religious openness: "When we fully comprehend the sympathy of religions," he concluded, "we shall deal with other faiths on equal terms." He sought through sympathy to release Americans into a global field of spiritual appreciation, cosmopolitan rapport, and eclectic insight. However it lined up with Protestant moral sentiments, sympathy was in Higginson's liberal, enlightened theorizing intended as a post-Christian virtue.[9]

Higginson's lecture on "The Sympathy of Religions" opened at sea, passing "from island on to island," perhaps a literary residue of his excursion fifteen years earlier to the Azores, where he had first sketched out his ideas on the subject. "The human soul, like any other noble vessel, was not built," Higginson maintained, "to be anchored, but to sail." The global web of commercial shipping, which so much facilitated the accumulation of knowledge that made Higginson's religious collations possible, was also present from the opening lines: "It would be a tragedy," he averred, "to see the shipping of the world whitening the seas no more, and idly riding at anchor in Atlantic ports; but it would be more tragic to see a world of souls fascinated into a fatal repose and renouncing their destiny of motion." It was an instructive image in which the market's unceasing transport of cargo paralleled the movement of religions from "stranded hulks" into the flux of endless exchange. In all that sparkling motion of ships and souls, in the twinned fluidity of religious identities and global markets, Christian devotions were no "more holy or more beautiful" than "one cry from a minaret" or the soft murmuring of "Oh! the gem in the lotus – oh! the gem in the lotus." All sacred incantations were equally conduits of transcendental vision; all were likewise potential commodities for the satisfaction of consumer longing within a global religious bazaar.[10]

Higginson's essay was overflowing with optimism. The fast-growing knowledge of the religions of the world was not ominous or disorienting, but productive of progress, freedom, and concord: "There is a sympathy in religions.... [E]very step in knowledge brings out the sympathy between them," Higginson swore. "They all show the same

---

9   TWH, "The Sympathy of Religions," *Radical* 8 (Feb. 1871): 2, 20.
10   TWH, "Sympathy," 1–2.

aim, the same symbols, the same forms, the same weaknesses, the same aspirations." Certainly, Higginson acknowledged, there were "shades of difference" from one religion to another that were quite recognizable upon "closer analysis," but those differences were nonetheless easy to elide. Indeed, such nuances hardly mattered in the end, for once the learned investigator was alert to all "such startling points of similarity," Higginson asked rhetorically, "where is the difference?" Religions took on the same forms from place to place, and it was the commonality of patterns and not sectarian "subdivisions" that mattered. Religion was not something to put under a microscope; it required instead a sensitive ear in which all religions could be appreciated for their grander harmonies – or, to invoke Wilfred Cantwell Smith's terms, for "the precious heritage of ultimates" that rang through them.[11]

As Higginson saw it, recognizing these points of unity, these universal commonalities, would lift the human spirit above any single institution, scripture, or tradition. From all religions and sacred books, from the Vedas and the Bible, from Chinese Buddhists and African American Christians, Higginson prophesied, will be "gathered hymns and prayers and maxims in which every religious soul may unite – the magnificent liturgy of the human race." The implications of such religious sympathies were manifest: The cosmopolitan inquirer was not merely invited but enjoined to explore widely, to create a composite scripture out of selected sheaves from the vast storehouse of religious inspiration. That might mean gathering the moral gems of Jesus or stringing together luminous passages from Emerson and Whitman or pulling them all into the company of the Buddha. As Higginson grandly proclaimed, "I do not wish to belong to a religion only, but to *the* religion; it must not include less than the piety of the world."[12]

That grand enlargement of piety represented, to Higginson, a triumph of the human spirit; it meant the ultimate undoing of religious exclusion, partiality, and rivalry. No single faith could claim a monopoly on love, truth, devotion, forgiveness, prayer, honesty, or mystical illumination; "all do something to exemplify, something to dishonor them," Higginson wrote, "all other religions show the same disparity between belief and practice, and each is safe till it tries to exclude the rest." Though he still gave more than an occasional nod to Anglo-American Protestant civilization – in its production of "manners,"

[11] TWH, "Sympathy," 2–5; the phrase "the precious heritage of ultimates" is from Smith, *The Meaning and End of Religion*, 8.
[12] TWH, "Sympathy," 3, 22.

"arts," and "energy" – that hardly made his argument more palatable to his orthodox brethren. Christian claims about the soteriological uniqueness and all-sufficiency of biblical revelation would yield the platform to the sympathy of religions, to meeting those of other faiths on common ground. As Higginson concluded bluntly of the exclusion of exclusion at the heart of liberal inclusion, "The one unpardonable sin is exclusiveness."[13]

Higginson's promotion of the sympathy of religions achieved an almost proverbial quality in New England's liberal intellectual circles. It was echoed by one inquirer after another as a basis for a world fellowship of faiths. Yet, that enthrallment did not mean the construct went unchallenged among Higginson's compatriots. William Potter, a colleague in the Free Religious Association, found Higginson's view of sympathy Pollyannaish. At best a partial account, Higginson's lecture was said to require "a companion-picture," one of "the 'Antagonisms of Religions.'" "What makes the special religions," Potter reminded, "is not so much the things in which they agree as the things in which they differ – that is, the claims which are peculiar to each religion." From this perspective, Higginson's optimism about "a common ground-work of ethical and spiritual intelligence" had to be matched by a frank emphasis on the conflicts that were constitutive of divergent religions. Another arch-liberal and sometime Harvard professor, Joseph Henry Allen, offered a more pointed critique along the same lines. Noting the religious animosities that circled the globe – from pogroms in Eastern Europe to Muslim–Hindu bloodshed in India – Allen deemed Higginson's concept to be naïve and colorless: "We have not much encouragement … for any signs of the 'sympathy of religions.' Each of them, so far as we can see, while it is a living force is far from sympathetic. Nay, it is antagonistic and aggressive." By 1897, William Wallace Fenn, one more Harvard liberal who enjoyed dispelling liberalism's illusions, announced that Higginson's "idea of the sympathy of religions" had produced little more than "a huge cloud of thin but amiable sentiment."[14]

[13] TWH, "Sympathy," 16–18.
[14] William J. Potter, "'Sympathy of Religions,'" *Index* 3 (1872): 329; W. Creighton Peden and Everett J. Tarbox, Jr., eds., *The Collected Essays of Francis Ellingwood Abbot (1836–1903), American Philosopher and Free Religionist*, 4 vols. (Lewiston: Edwin Mellen Press, 1996), 1: 321–324; Francis E. Abbot, "A Study of Religion: The Name and the Thing," *Index* 4 (1873): 109; Joseph Henry Allen, "The Alleged Sympathy of Religions," *New World* 4 (1895): 320; William Wallace Fenn, "The Possibilities of Mysticism in Modern Thought," *New World* 6 (1897): 201.

Still, even amid their critiques, it remained difficult for Allen, Fenn, Potter, and company simply to dismiss Higginson's call for sympathetic appreciation. If Higginson had constructed the sympathy of religions as too much a matter of sameness and commonality, they could hardly set aside the parallel aspiration for cosmopolitan affinities and alliances – for a "sympathy of souls." Higginson uneasily pursued two forms of unity: one chased after religious essences and the distillation of common notions; the other emphasized a sentimental ethics of fellow-feeling and intersubjective communication. Sympathy, so conceived, sought both abstracted comparisons and cosmopolitan relationships. Even those self-critical liberals who took apart Higginson's naïve universalism were reluctant to give up on his hopeful cosmopolitanism. "True sympathy," Higginson affirmed, "teaches true largeness of soul." It was, he insisted, the basis for "sympathetic admiration" between people of different faiths, cultures, and races.[15]

The fact that Higginson jumbled these two forms of sympathy together – a difference-erasing universalism and a relational cosmopolitanism – took another generation or more of learned reflection to sort out. By the second decade of the twentieth century, though, liberal theorists of pluralism were effectively shifting ground to the sympathetic appreciation of differences rather than the assimilationist celebration of resemblances. Higginson's virtue of sympathy, in other words, was refigured by liberal theorists themselves as warmly responsive to diversity, not sameness. That reconstruction took time, and was uneven, but that self-critical discussion of sympathy was indicative of the internal elasticity of this liberal intellectual tradition. The virtue of sympathy was reworked to recognize what one early twentieth-century elaborator called "the mutual enhancement of diversities." The only unity of religion worth having, it was now said, was one that respected variety. Higginson's sympathy, in other words, was enriched without being abandoned.[16]

The debate about sympathy, about both universalism and cosmopolitanism, that flowed from Higginson's lecture – the whole extended run of affirmations and refutations – had a formative influence on the scholarly study of religion in American culture. It is easy indeed to hear echoes of that exchange in the founding vision of Center for the Study of World Religions, which Wilfred Cantwell Smith would serve so ably and comfortably: "A sympathetic study of other religions" was expressly

---

[15] Quoted in Schmidt, "Cosmopolitan Piety," 208, 216.
[16] Schmidt, "Cosmopolitan Piety," 219–20.

enjoined; "a fundamental unity and reality back of all religions" affirmed; and "a discipline in spiritual communication" across the "fruitful diversity" of faiths avowed.[17] Here are the contours of a distinct nineteenth-century liberal ambition carried into the middle decades of the twentieth century. Call it romantic cosmopolitanism; call it Unitarian free religion; call it a parliamentary mix of Theosophist, Whitmanite, Vedantist, and ecumenical Protestant dreams. It was a form of liberal universalism, to be sure, but it was also a pedagogy of the moral sentiments, a cultivation of sympathy as an affective disposition. The point, in short, was not to be a disengaged fly on a fishbowl; the point was the capacity to feel like a goldfish felt. The study of religion, it was claimed, would be a hollow, distorting, secularizing enterprise without that intuitive sympathy.

II. CONFRONTING THE GODS

Higginson may have published his lecture in a journal called the *Radical*, but then there was D. M. Bennett's *The Gods and Religions of Ancient and Modern Times*, issued in two volumes in New York in 1880 by the Liberal and Scientific Publishing House and running to 1,792 pages. A tip-off that this was not a run-of-the-mill compilation came in the frontispiece to the second volume, where the author appeared in prison garb. Then, of course, there was the note on the title page that the book had been written in the Albany Penitentiary while Bennett was serving a thirteen-month sentence ostensibly for sending an obscene pamphlet through the mails, but really – so he claimed – "for being an infidel editor and publisher." "The work has been written under some disadvantages," Bennett explained further, "in prison and the hospital belonging thereto, surrounded by sick and dying men of varied nationalities, colors, and crimes; sometimes twenty of us in a single room.... I have not had by me many works I would gladly have consulted.... My imprisonment is simply a piece of religious persecution, instituted by orthodox enemies in consequence of my heterodox opinions." Not many of those who wanted to advance a natural history of religion wrote from prison as Bennett did, but his predicament is a reminder that for those secular freethinkers who pushed for critical suspicion, there was much at stake in taking up (and taking on) religion, not least their own liberty.[18]

---

[17] John B. Carman and Kathryn Dodgson, *Community and Colloquy: The Center for the Study of World Religions, 1958–2003* (Cambridge, MA: Harvard Divinity School, 2006), 11–19.

[18] D. M. Bennett (DMB), *The Gods and Religions of Ancient and Modern Times*, 2 vols. (New York: Liberal and Scientific Publishing House, 1880), 1: ix–x.

DeRobigne Mortimer Bennett – one can see why his name was usually shortened to D. M. – was praised by some as an American Voltaire or latter-day Tom Paine, but he began his life as a Methodist Sunday-School kid in a hard-scrapple farming family in rural New York, sixty miles west of Albany. With his family destitute, having lost their farm and any semblance of cohesion, Bennett ended up leaving home at age fourteen when the Shakers in New Lebanon offered to take him into their community. He lasted thirteen years with the United Society of Believers in Christ's Second Appearing before the Shaker demand for celibacy proved too onerous. He eloped with another member of the community in 1846, but he continued long afterward to have an almost familial regard for these "kindhearted Brethren and Sisters." An apostate adrift, he settled for a time in Louisville, Kentucky, where he set himself up as a druggist and nostrum seller. It was here between 1848 and 1850 that Bennett discovered the literature of infidelity, particularly Paine's *Age of Reason*. For the next twenty-five years, Bennett fit the bill more of a village atheist than a freethought operative. Struggling in one commercial venture after another – in Louisville, Rochester, Cincinnati, and finally Paris, Illinois – he had squabbled over Christianity with local clergymen but had done little more than that. The change came in 1873. After a drought ruined his latest business of seed farming, he decided to start at age fifty-five his own infidel journal, the *Truth Seeker*. The masthead for the new journal seemed literally to say it all:

> Devoted to Science, Morals, Freethought, Free Discussion, Liberalism, Sexual Equality, Labor Reform, Progression, Free Education, and whatever tends to emancipate and elevate the human race. Opposed to Priestcraft, Ecclesiasticism, Dogmas, Creeds, False Theology, Superstition, Bigotry, Ignorance, Monopolies, Aristocracies, Privileged Classes, Tyranny, Oppression and Everything that Degrades or Burdens Mankind Mentally or Physically.

Bennett had belatedly found his métier.[19]

Soon moving his new publishing venture to Manhattan, Bennett created a niche for himself in the surprisingly robust world of infidels, radicals, agnostics, spiritualists, and women's rights activists of the 1870s. He also found trouble in the crisscrossing laws aimed at blasphemy and obscenity. At about the same moment that Bennett had founded the *Truth Seeker*, Anthony Comstock, a young evangelical crusader against

---

[19] See Roderick Bradford, *D. M. Bennett, the Truth Seeker* (Amherst, NY: Prometheus, 2006), 17, 25, 90. I have relied on Bradford for the outlines of Bennett's biography.

all things lewd and lascivious, had incorporated the New York Society for the Suppression of Vice. That Comstock soon managed to obtain federal authority as a special agent of the U.S. Post Office gave his vice society unprecedented police power for an evangelical reform organization. Comstock always had a very full caseload, but he had a particular distaste for liberals and freethinkers, whom he viewed as closet smut peddlers and free-lusters in bed with the sex trades. In November 1877, Comstock and one of his deputies arrived at Bennett's office with a warrant for his arrest. In his society's blotter, Comstock noted that Bennett was guilty of publishing the "most horrible & obscene blasphemies" as well as "indecent tracts that purport to be Scientific." The specific offense was sending "obscene matter through the Mail" – in this instance, Bennett's *Open Letter to Jesus Christ* and a pamphlet on sexual reproduction in marsupials. His lawyer got that case dismissed, but Bennett was arrested again the following year for circulating an infamous free-love tract on marriage reform and "sexual self-government," Ezra Heywood's *Cupid's Yokes*. Earlier that year, Comstock had already imprisoned Heywood himself, the president of New England's Free-Love Association, who, in *Cupid's Yokes*, had mocked the "lascivious fanaticism" of the vice crusader and asked the startling question: "Why should priests and magistrates supervise the sexual organs of citizens?"[20]

This time, no lawyerly intervention helped, and Bennett's case went to trial in March 1879 with freethinkers rallying under a free-speech, free-press banner. That civil-liberties line of argument was at this point no match for the charge of mailing of an obscene, lewd, and indecent book. Bennett was summarily convicted in federal court – a conviction that was then sustained on appeal. His case actually had the effect of significantly strengthening Comstock's legal hand in that a British precedent on obscenity, the Hicklin standard, was now extended to American jurisprudence. A literary work was considered obscene if any part of it was deemed to have a tendency to corrupt the minds of the innocent and chaste. Bennett was sent to the Albany Penitentiary to serve a thirteen-month term, the victim of what he and other free-press defenders were now calling the American Inquisition. There he suffered the wretched indignities of prison life, and certainly his announced infidelity won him no friends among the institution's authorities. "You know," he said to one comrade who visited him at the penitentiary, "I have not been used to being treated and spoken to like a dog."[21]

[20] Bradford, *Truth Seeker*, 117; E. H. Heywood, *Cupid's Yokes: Or, the Binding Forces of Conjugal Love* (Princeton, MA: Co-Operative Publishing Co., 1877), 12, 22.
[21] Bradford, *Truth Seeker*, 181–2, 203, 206.

It was in this setting in these months that he decided to write his really big book on *The Gods and Religions of Ancient and Modern Times*. In all kinds of ways, the two volumes were a mess, a hodgepodge compilation, in which Bennett regularly used long extracts to pad his work and almost randomly inserted encyclopedic tools (for example, an eighteen-page glossary of Norse mythology). Not in a position to have much of a library at hand, he had two kinds of sources from the emergent comparative study of religion at his disposal: The first type was from the Higginson side of the religious spectrum – the works of romantic liberals and Unitarians, including Lydia Maria Child's three-volume *Progress of Religious Ideas* (1855) and James Freeman Clarke's *Ten Great Religions* (1871). The second type was from the works of more secular-minded evolutionists, including freethinker Thomas Inman's *Ancient Faiths and Modern* (1876) and anthropologist E. B. Tylor's *Primitive Culture* (1871). It was from this second set of writers that Bennett took his orientation, boldly positioning himself in the lingering glow of Enlightenment skepticism and the more recent gleam of biological and cultural evolutionism.

Bennett began his natural history of religion with a grand picture of the advancement of geology and paleontology – sciences that he saw foreclosing the biblical account of creation. The opening excursus set up a familiar freethinking opposition: the real knowledge of empirical science displacing the fables and fantasies of religion. "Illusion gives way to reality," Bennett remarked, "and the magic picture disappears." The questions to ask about religion were not theological or exegetical, but evolutionary, social, and psychological: When and why did humans invent religion? Embracing a line of argument familiar from Thomas Hobbes and David Hume, among others, Bennett attributed the primal source of religion to fear and dread, emotional vulnerabilities that were compounded by ignorance of the forces of nature and an anthropomorphizing imagination. Then borrowing another page from Enlightenment histories of religion – the originating power of priestcraft – Bennett postulated that "a special class" emerged to exploit these fears and came to exercise tyrannical control over the common people. "It is this class of self-constituted agents and advisers of the supernal powers," Bennett concluded, "that have invented the almost countless number of creeds and religions which man has been compelled to sustain." In turn, the power of priests had for millennia impeded progress in religion. Though sparks of positive evolutionary development could be discerned – predictably, sun worship was seen as an improvement on fetishism – mostly humanity had awaited the advent of modern science to make any headway against superstition and priestcraft.[22]

The bulk of Bennett's first volume was devoted to the invention of the gods – ancient and modern – in their endless variety from India to Rome, from Africa to North America. The encyclopedic entries went on for hundreds of pages – an undisciplined catalogue that looked well on its way to consuming the first 835-page volume until it finally became evident that all of these other gods were prologue to de-centering and diminishing the Christian God. At best, the Christian faith was but a facsimile of prior mythologies: "JESUS A COPY FROM PAGAN MODELS" read one section head. At worst, Christianity seemed simply to redouble mindless supernaturalism (say, miracles and demons) and oppression (of women and slaves, for example). Perhaps most immediately revealing was Bennett's section on "Bible Obscenity," in which he made a long list of the "coarse narratives" of the scriptures, involving adultery, rape, incest, concubinage, polygamy, and the like. All these lewd and immoral tales made him wonder why he was doing time for mailing a pamphlet on marriage relations in which there was "not one hundredth part of the indecency that the Bible contains." The bottom line for Bennett was this: "The sooner man lets all the gods go to the shades of forgetfulness, ... the better it will be for him and for the world."[23]

The second volume did much the same for the various religious traditions that were organized around the vast pantheon of gods. Here Bennett marched his way through the rites, temples, prayers, and scriptures of the religions of the world in both evolutionary and geographic terms, again culminating in a long and critical account of Christianity. By the end of the 957-page second volume, Bennett had set up a monument to freethought, the most sustained critical history of religion yet produced by an American. Why, when he was simply supposed to be making shoes in a prison factory, did Bennett expend so much effort cataloguing the religions of Phoenicia, Chaldea, Egypt, and Assyria – not to mention Judaism, Christianity, and Islam? Why bother obsessively studying religion, the whole human propensity for "the devising of gods," when one found that proclivity so childish? His compulsion was based on a view of knowledge not so much as power, but as liberation. It was not a cynical project of destruction and mockery – or at least not solely that – but instead a humanistic mission of enlightenment and emancipation. The point was to set the human mind free of religious phantoms and those who manipulate them for their own gain and privilege. Bennett quoted the famed agnostic orator Robert Ingersoll to this effect toward the close of his work: "The doubter, the investigator, the Infidel, have been the saviors of liberty." Bennett undertook his project of disenchantment in that heroic, even salvific, light. To write "this natural history of the gods" was to underscore the bleak history of religious violence, bloodshed, tyranny, and persecution; it was to reveal the fearful, ignorant, oppressive roots of America's own inquisition. Religion, in short, deserved not appreciative sympathy of its transcendental flights; religion demanded instead hard-nosed suspicion of its cunning politics.[24]

III. CONCLUSION

Neither Higginson nor Bennett was a professional scholar. Neither was in danger of being labeled a narrow specialist or succumbing to William James's Ph.D. octopus. As amateurs, neither had anything like the academic standing of that initial generation of university chair-holders in the science of religions, a small handful of whom had been installed by the 1870s and 1880s in Europe and the United States. Yet, the tension between sympathy and suspicion that they dramatized was very much inherited by the emergent discipline. It imbued one formulation after another of what it would mean to cultivate the study of religion in the American university – not as a wing of Protestant theological schools, but as a distinct endeavor within the arts and sciences.

In *The Varieties of Religious Experience* (1902), William James, hoping his lectures might become "a crumb-like contribution" to the new "'Science of Religions,' so-called," confronted this tension directly. On the one hand, he saw this science as having the potential to sift out "a consensus of opinion" and thereby "offer mediation between different believers" – a kind of interreligious diplomacy based on an inductive understanding of the experiential core of religions. The science could conceivably, James suggested, do what Higginson hoped and Max Müller too espoused – that is, help its practitioners discern universal sympathies or ideal essences across religions. On the other hand, James reasoned that this new science might be at cross-purposes with that aspiration; it could well turn out, he remarked, that "the best man at this science might be the man who found it hardest to be personally

---

[24] DMB, *Gods*, 1: 823; 2: 923, 940.

devout." Was there any reason that the science of religions would not fall into line with other materialistic sciences and come to "blunt the acuteness" of "living faith"? "The sciences of nature," James observed, "know nothing of spiritual presences." Understanding the elementary forms of religion – "the purely theoretic attitude," James called it – was fundamentally dissimilar from "living religion." He speculated that "the very science of religions itself" was actually the product of a deeper "antipathy to religion." Was it not finally committed to a view of religion as an anachronism or survival, "an atavistic relapse" that the enlightened have outgrown? Was it not aimed at freeing people of the "groveling and horrible superstitions" that "the cultivator of this science" confronted time and again? In short, James faced at the close of the *Varieties* this troublesome question: Was this new university science one of sympathy or suspicion?[25]

James highlighted these tensions in the "'Science of Religions,' so-called," without resolving them. They lingered. When Princeton University called the philosopher George Thomas to lay the foundation for a Department of Religion in 1940, he gave an inaugural lecture in which the consequences of secularism and naturalism for the study of religion haunted him. "To ask for an impartial, objective study of religion is legitimate and, in a university, essential," he acknowledged. Yet, he insisted, "The rational analysis of religion which we are undertaking should never be allowed to become a substitute for the *living experience* of religion.... The analysis and evaluation from the outside, from the point of view of the observer, must be supplemented by an attempt to penetrate to the heart of it by intuition and to identify oneself with it in feeling." Thomas ended his Harrington Spear Paine Foundation lecture where Wilfred Cantwell Smith began *The Meaning and End of Religion*, with an emphasis on direct insight and sympathetic fellow-feeling trumping secularism and naturalism. Thomas had no crawling fly on a fishbowl, but he did have an image of an aloof observer scrutinizing a rock or crystal and hazarded that any scholar of religion who similarly contemplated religion "from the outside with cool detachment" would never achieve "genuine understanding."[26]

No doubt the pendulum has swung dramatically in the last generation away from the sympathies of Higginson, James, Thomas, and Smith. No doubt the critical study of religion has come to depend more

[25] William James, *The Varieties of Religious Experience* (New York: Penguin, 1982), 433, 455–7, 488–95.
[26] George F. Thomas, *Religion in an Age of Secularism* (Princeton, NJ: Princeton University Press, 1940), 23–8.

and more on cutting through such romantic sentiments rather than cultivating them. "Reverence is a religious, and not a scholarly virtue," Bruce Lincoln has tartly remarked. "The failure to treat religion 'as religion' – that is, the refusal to ratify its claim of transcendent nature and sacrosanct status – may be regarded as heresy and sacrilege by those who construct themselves as religious," Lincoln elaborates, "but it is the starting point for those who construct themselves as historians." Perhaps then critical suspicion has finally carried the day – and rightly. Perhaps the field's romantic past has finally been relinquished, the only reverence left is that for academic excellence and deep learning. Perhaps scholars of religion can now be scholars without apology – historicist, empiricist, unsympathetic, even blasphemous and obscene, letting the chips from their workshop fall where they may. And, yet, it would be surprising if such a fundamental ambivalence had resolved itself so neatly, that, with this liberal Protestant genealogy pinned down, religious studies can now march along a critical scholarly path cleverly exposing one truth regime and knowledge/power nexus after another. After all, secular critique has now turned dramatically on itself, and the return of religion seems everywhere apparent, not least across the humanities.[27]

Even D. M. Bennett, once out of prison, embarked on one last big project, a tour of the globe that he chronicled in a four-volume travelogue entitled *The Truth Seeker Around the World*. Given how he viewed primitives and their gods, his literary traipsing was not a cosmopolitan tour de force. The excursion gave him a chance to visit, as he said, "the numerous god-factories" of other cultures firsthand. Something strange, yet strangely predictable, happened, though, when he got to India: He fell in with Madame Blavatsky, Henry Olcott, and their community of Theosophists, spiritualists, yogis, and Buddhist catechists. He was taken up short by the mysterious phenomena surrounding Olcott in particular, the inexplicable communications from the guide Koot Hoomi, supposedly two thousand miles away in the Himalayas. This was not what his freethinking subscribers back in America were expecting from his globetrotting – a questioning of his own materialism, a slack-jawed amazement at occult powers, a hobnobbing with suspected charlatans. "I am ready to believe Hamlet was right," he claimed, "when he assured his friend Horatio that there was in heaven and earth many things not dreamed of in his philosophy." In 1882, with the backing of Blavatsky

---

[27] Bruce Lincoln, "Theses on Method," in *The Insider/Outsider Problem in the Study of Religion: A Reader*, ed. Russell T. McCutcheon (London: Cassell, 1999), 395–8.

and Olcott, Bennett became a member of the Theosophical Society. It turned out for Bennett, as it has often turned out since then, that transcendental aspirations and romantic sympathies were not so easy to dispel. There he was, the old freethinker and erstwhile Shaker, bedeviled by the same curiosities that had smitten Higginson and company. Bennett, too, had come to ask, and perhaps even to intuit, how it feels to be a goldfish.[28]

Whatever else it implies, Bennett's turn to Theosophy suggests the intimacy of suspicion and sympathy, how quickly liberal secularism could turn into liberal religion, and vice versa. That is the twinned inheritance of the scholarly study of religion: the mirrored reflections of romantic cosmopolitanism and freethinking secularism. Not even in the early twenty-first century, with all our genealogical canniness, is it easy to stand outside that dual legacy or to separate these Siamese twins. Nor is it obvious that we would want to pry them apart if we could and then proceed with one half of the pair over the other. In the charged space between distance and engagement, scholars of religion still make their way: secular, empiricist, historicist, to be sure, but also well aware how limited, fragile, and particular the stance of critical suspicion has been and will be. The science of religions, so-called, was a mixed bag of late nineteenth-century methods, hopes, and perplexities, an untidy merger of transcendentalism and freethought. That mixture was a source not only of contamination and occlusion, but also of curiosity and insight, a crumb-like contribution to the humanistic pursuit of freedom, enlightenment, and cosmopolitanism. Sympathy, it seems only fair to conclude, can now be accorded the discipline's own historical amalgam without sacrificing suspicion.

Select Bibliography

Fitzgerald, Timothy. *Discourse on Civility and Barbarity: A Critical History of Religion and Related Categories.* New York: Oxford University Press, 2007.

   The Ideology of Religious Studies. New York: Oxford University Press, 2000.

Harrison, Peter. *"Religion" and the Religions in the English Enlightenment.* Cambridge: Cambridge University Press, 1990.

Jones, Robert Alun. *The Secret of the Totem: Religion and Society from McLennan to Freud.* New York: Columbia University Press, 2005.

Marchand, Suzanne L. *German Orientalism in the Age of Empire: Religion, Race, and Scholarship.* Cambridge: Cambridge University Press, 2009.

[28] DMB, *A Truth Seeker Around the World,* 4 vols. (New York: Bennett, 1882), 3: 90–4; 4: 396.

Masuzawa, Tomoko. *The Invention of World Religions, or, How European Universalism Was Preserved in the Language of Pluralism*. Chicago: University of Chicago Press, 2005.

McCutcheon, Russell T. *Manufacturing Religion: The Discourse on Sui Generis Religion and the Politics of Nostalgia*. New York: Oxford University Press, 1997.

Smith, Wilfred Cantwell. *The Meaning and End of Religion: A New Approach to the Religious Traditions of Mankind*. Minneapolis: Fortress Press, 1991 [1962].

Styers, Randall. *Making Magic: Religion, Magic, and Science in the Modern World*. New York: Oxford University Press, 2004.

2 Thinking about religion, belief, and politics
TALAL ASAD

Since the closing decade of the millennium, social friction generated by the presence of substantial numbers of Muslim immigrants in Europe, as well as the threat of Muslim terrorists, has given a new impetus to the fear of politicized religion. Violent and intolerant "Fundamentalist movements" have emerged not only in the Muslim world (although these are the most frightening in the West) but also in Israel and the United States. The secular values of liberal democracy are under siege – or so the Western media tell us. Academics who teach religious studies have responded eagerly, seeing in this an opportunity to demonstrate the public relevance of their expertise. What is to be done about the dangers of religious belief to liberal democracies?

More generally one may ask: What are the relations between the secular promise of liberal democracy and the conditions for private belief in transcendence? There is no simple answer to this question, of course, because modern religion has both hindered and aided liberal values and because liberal values are more contradictory and ambiguous than is sometimes acknowledged. But I want to begin with other questions: What *is* "religion"? How has it come to be defined in the ways it has? What are some of the political consequences of making *belief* central to the definition? I will address some of these questions by discussing aspects of Charles Taylor's work *A Secular Age*, whose central argument is that secularization cannot be narrated as a simple subtraction story (that is, as the gradual abandonment of superstition and intolerance), but must take the form of an account of historical remaking in which the choice of belief and unbelief come to have an equal and equally protected status in the liberal-democratic state. This

Earlier versions of this chapter were delivered first as the 2008 Foerster Lecture at Berkeley and then, in December 2008, as the Inaugural Danforth Lecture at Princeton. I thank both audiences for their comments and questions. I am grateful also to the following colleagues who have read versions of the text and offered valuable criticisms: Hussein Agrama, Gil Anidjar, Colin Jager, David Scott, George Shulman, and Jeffrey Stout.

is an important thesis, but I want to think beyond it. I will do so by looking at the ambiguous notion of belief as both Taylor and some anthropologists have dealt with it. I will urge the importance of studying the senses in order to identify ways they can build sensibilities and attitudes that are distinct from beliefs. Then I will turn to a recent ethnographic work that is concerned with the place of listening in the contemporary political scene in Cairo, Charles Hirschkind's *The Ethical Soundscape.* I will conclude with some questions about the connections between sensibilities and politics.

It is by now well known that the modern concept of religion as an object of systematic study is relatively recent. The term *religio* is of course quite old, but it did not have the sense that emerged in early modern times. Roughly from the seventeenth century on, the idea gradually crystallized among European thinkers that in every society people believed in supernatural beings and told stories about the origin of the world and about what happens to the individual after death; that in every society people instituted rituals of worship and deferred to experts in these matters; and that therefore religion was not something only Christians had.

Skeptics have long written about the origin of religion. However, for most of them it was not the *concept* of religion that was puzzling, only its emergence. At least since the Enlightenment, one important approach to understanding religion has consisted in what anthropologists call "the sociology of error." The main question was: What gave rise to such patently false beliefs in the first place? The testing of belief propositions – and thus their falsification – that is presupposed in this question tends to depend on a highly simplified language ideology that predicates both the counterintuitive character of religious belief-statements and the irrational character of religious conviction. "The sociology of error" invented by Victorian anthropologists for understanding religion eventually gave rise to another approach in which a different set of questions was raised: Is religion a universal? What kinds of belief and practice are peculiar to religion? What meanings do religious beliefs and practices give to life? What functions does religion perform? Anthropologists and others sought to explain religion by reference to externalities – that is, by looking for its social function or for its cultural meaning. The concept of religion itself remained virtually unexamined in this approach.

To my knowledge, Wilfred Cantwell Smith's *The Meaning and End of Religion* (1962) was the first book to present a historical sketch of the concept of religion in the West and to suggest that it was relatively recent.[1] Smith argued perceptively against essentialist approaches, yet in the end he didn't quite break free of a residual essentialism himself.[2] He sought to substitute the word "faith" for "religion" in order to avoid the danger of reification, but *this* move led him to an emphasis on religion as an ineffable experience. It's not that there's anything wrong in stressing the importance of experiences that are difficult to articulate when discussing religion. What is questionable is his making a *particular* language game the basis of a *universal* conception of religion as "faith," as when he writes, "My faith is an act that *I* make, myself, naked before God."[3] The latter phrase appears to indicate an unmediated innerness opening up to the divine gaze, so that my faith is at once an enactment (confronting God) and an experience (of an authentic subject) that constitutes that act as an act of faith.

The reason there cannot be a universal conception of religion is not because religious phenomena are infinitely varied – although there is in fact great variety in the way people live in the world with their religious beliefs.[4] Nor is it the case that there is no such thing, really, as religion.[5]

[1] Unfortunately, I had not read it yet when I wrote my 1983 essay on the definition of religion in anthropology ("Anthropological Conceptions of Religion: Reflections on Geertz," *Man*, N.S. 18 [1983]: 237–59) that was eventually republished as Chapter 1 of *Genealogies of Religion* (Baltimore: Johns Hopkins University Press, 1993), and it was therefore unable to benefit from its insights. Jonathan Z. Smith's pioneering volume *Imagining Religion: From Babylon to Jonestown*, Chicago Studies in the History of Judaism (Chicago: The University of Chicago Press, 1982) was also not available to me in time. Since then, other studies have appeared in which the concept of religion has been historicized. Notable among these are Philip C. Almond, *The British Discovery of Buddhism* (New York: Cambridge University Press, 1988); Peter Harrison, *'Religion' and the Religions in the English Enlightenment* (New York: Cambridge University Press, 1990); Daniel Dubuisson, *L'Occident et la religion: Mythes, science et idéologie* (Bruxelles: Éditions Complexe, 1998); and Tomoko Masuzawa's *The Invention of World Religions, or, How European Universalism Was Preserved in the Language of Pluralism* (Chicago: University of Chicago Press, 2005).
[2] See my essay, "Reading a Modern Classic: W. C. Smith's *The Meaning and End of Religion*," in *Religion and Media*, ed. Hent de Vries and Samuel Weber, Cultural Memory in the Present (Palo Alto, CA: Stanford University Press, 2001), 131–47.
[3] Wilfred Cantwell Smith, *The Meaning and End of Religion: A New Approach to the Religious Traditions of Mankind* (Minneapolis: Fortress Press, 1991 [1962]), 191 (emphasis added).
[4] Robert A. Orsi's *Between Heaven and Earth: The Religious Worlds People Make and the Scholars Who Study Them* (Princeton, NJ: Princeton University Press, 2005) depicts with insight and compassion the way the ordinary lives of individuals are shaped by a range of religious emotions, sensibilities, and objects.
[5] Thus, "most anthropologists would now maintain, that there is no such *thing* as religion, other than the somewhat, but only somewhat, similar phenomena one finds in different places, and which remind the observer, in a theoretically insignificant way, therefore, of what we have been brought up to understand by the term."

It is that defining is a historical act and when the definition is deployed, it does different things at different times and in different circumstances, and responds to different questions, needs, and pressures. The concept "religion" is not merely a word: it belongs to vocabularies that bring persons and things, desires and practices together in particular traditions in distinctive ways. This applies also to religion's twin, "secularity," which brings different sensibilities into play in different historical contexts. Thus the institutional practices and psychological responses that define *laïcité* in contemporary France are largely foreign to those that define "the separation of church and state" in today's United States.

To define is to repudiate some things and to endorse others. Defining what is religion is not merely an abstract intellectual exercise; it is not just what anthropologists or other scholars do. The act of defining (or redefining) religion is embedded in passionate disputes; it is connected with anxieties and satisfactions, it is affected by changing conceptions of knowledge and interest, and it is related to institutional disciplines.[6] In the past, colonial administrations used definitions of religion to classify, control, and regulate the practices and identities of subjects. Today, liberal democracy is required to pronounce on the legal status of such definitions and thus to spell out civil immunities and obligations.[7] When definitions of religion are produced, they endorse or reject certain uses of a vocabulary that have profound implications for the organization of social life and the possibilities of personal experience. For this very reason, academic expertise is often invoked in the process of arriving at legal decisions about religious matters.[8] In all these legal functions, liberal democracy

Maurice Bloch, "Are Religious Beliefs Counter-intuitive?" in *Radical Interpretation in Religion*, ed. Nancy K. Frankenberry (Cambridge: Cambridge University Press, 2002), 13. What this nominalism leaves out is how things recognized as "religion" in one place consist of things (including attitudes and practices) that hang together – but differently in different traditions. This "hanging together" is what makes "religion" real, and it poses the theoretically difficult question of how and to what extent one religious vocabulary can be translated into another.

[6] An account of the reconstruction of Sinhala Buddhism through its confrontation with colonial Protestantism is David Scott's fine essay entitled "Religion in Colonial Civil Society" in his *Refashioning Futures: Criticism After Postcoloniality*, Princeton Studies in Culture/Power/History (Princeton, NJ: Princeton University Press, 1999), 53–69.

[7] An example of this is discussed at length in my article, "Trying to Understand French Secularism," in *Political Theologies: Public Religions in a Post-Secular World*, ed. Hent de Vries and Lawrence E. Sullivan (New York: Fordham University Press, 2006), 494–526.

[8] An outstanding study, whose author was called by the courts as an expert, is Winnifred Fallers Sullivan, *The Impossibility of Religious Freedom* (Princeton, NJ: Princeton University Press, 2005).

(whether at home or abroad in its colonies) not only works through secularity, it requires that *belief* be taken as the essence of religiosity. The
ambiguity of this notion of belief needs to be spelled out.

Scholars as well as others usually assume that belief, both private
and public, is expressed in the solemnities of ritual. Thus Victorians,
like evolutionary anthropologists then and now, tend to interpret rites
as "magical" ways of coping with difficulties of the natural environment. Protestant theologians who were also students of "primitive
religion," such as William Robertson Smith, took the view that "true
Christianity" required that it be stripped of "Catholic magic," that is,
of superstition; what mattered was true *belief*. But later anthropologists
saw all this as a methodological mistake.[9] Rituals, they maintained,
were not to be regarded as primitive ways of adjusting to nature and not
as evidence of primitive minds. As actions, rituals had a social function
of their own. Some anthropologists such as Edmund Leach proposed
that rituals were not instrumental actions at all; rituals symbolized
something, communicated cultural meanings. Thus for Victorian evolutionists, as well as for many of their anthropological successors, the
modern notion of "belief" attributed to what used to be called primitive peoples was essential to the concept of ritual. Whether it took the
form of a cosmology or of culturally defined norms, whether it was to
be reconstructed from explanations offered by practitioners or read into
social actions and arrangements by resort to Western theories of signification, the idea of *belief* was central to an understanding of the repetitive activities classified as rites and ceremonies.

"Ritual," as a component of religion, became a distinct theoretical
category of "meaningful action." Whereas John Austin had taught scholars that using words was a way of doing things,[10] the symbolic approach
to ritual took doing things to be expressions of meanings – albeit
embedded pre-reflectively in social imaginaries or systems of symbols.
For anthropologists drawn to a symbolic approach, social imaginaries
might be seen as beliefs that were not (yet) articulated.

Several anthropologists who addressed the question of belief did so
with respect to the universalism-versus-relativism debate in which cognitive and primary attention was paid to implicit meanings in ritual.[11] Thus

9 Some of the most influential British social anthropologists immediately after
World War II were also Catholic converts, including E. E. Evans-Pritchard, Godfrey
Lienhardt, David Pocock, and Victor Turner.
10 J. L. Austin, *How to Do Things with Words* (Oxford: Oxford University Press, 1962).
11 For example, Jean Pouillon, "Remarks on the Verb 'To Believe'," in *Between Belief
and Transgression: Structuralist Essays in Religion, History, and Myth*, ed. Michel

Malcolm Ruel observed in a widely read article that "the performance
of the [Christian] creed is as complex, symbolic and condensed an act of
ritual as any other liturgical act and is consequently as much subject to
the categories developed, for example, by Turner for the analysis of ritual symbolism."[12] The Christian creed, Ruel pointed out, combines two
senses of belief: belief *in* a divine Person (the living Christ) and belief
that a sacred Event had occurred (crucifixion and resurrection). Both were
symbolically united in the ritual utterance (a performance) of the creed, a
particular instance of a general phenomenon.

The anthropologist Maurice Bloch took linguistic performance
itself as the paradigm of symbolic action. Bloch argued that the very
"formality" of oratory (as in the formality of polite manners) was a crucial means of social control and political domination. Formal communication – including religious ritual *and* political oratory – was to be
seen as the *denial of choice* and therefore as submission to traditional
authority.[13] Since traditional authority, in Max Weber's influential view,
was one of the three modes of legitimate domination, this approach to
ritual reinforced the idea that the autonomous subject needed to break
from tradition and from the imitation of the past it demanded from him
or her – and to choose his or her own beliefs.

The claim that ritual had a repressive social function resonated with
the view that liberal religion should primarily take the form of private
belief and with the historic Protestant rejection of Catholic ritualism. It
reinforced the well-known notion that ritual was not only irrational but
also, by virtue of its being symbolic and therefore separated from interiority, antipolitical in the sense of the politics that liberal democracy
values. However, the notion that formality is necessarily an external
form of coercion is questionable, for it is only when forms become elements in a strategy such as those described by Erving Goffman that they

Izard and Pierre Smith (Chicago: University of Chicago Press, 1982 [1979]), 1–8;
Dan Sperber, "Apparently Irrational Beliefs," in *Rationality and Relativism*, ed.
Martin Hollis and Steven Lukes (Oxford: Blackwell, 1982), 149–80; Pascal Boyer, *The
Naturalness of Religious Ideas: A Cognitive Theory of Religion* (Berkeley and Los
Angeles: University of California Press, 1994); Bloch, "Are Religious Beliefs Counter-
intuitive?"

[12] Malcolm Ruel, "Christians as Believers," in *Religious Organization and Religious
Experience*, ed. John Davis (London: Academic Press, 1982), 16–17.

[13] Maurice Bloch, "Symbols, Song, Dance and Features of Articulation: Is Religion an
Extreme Form of Traditional Authority?" *European Journal of Sociology* 15 (1974):
55–81; the argument about formality and domination is elaborated in the Introduction
to his *Political Language and Oratory in Traditional Society* (London: Academic
Press, 1975).

serve as a means of control over others.[14] To the extent that public forms contribute to the making and remaking of the self in a social world, to the cultivation of the self – where, in other words, external forms are part of *developing* subjectivities – the effects of public forms are different. What the embodied subject learns to say and do in that context and how the embodied subject handles behavioral and verbal forms in relationship to others are at the center of its moral potentialities and not merely an external imposition.[15] In short, if one thinks of ritual not as an activity that denies choice by imposing formalities but as aiming at aptness of behavior, sensibility, and attitude, one may see the repetition of forms as something other than a blind submission to authority. For the aptness of formal performance (whether this be politeness or reverence) requires not only *repeating* past models but also *originality* in applying them in appropriate/new circumstances. In other words, although at one level the cultivation of appropriate formality necessary to ethical virtues may not allow *unlimited* choice, it does require the exercise of judgment. Like the rules of grammar, forms are at once potentialities and limits, necessary to original thought and conduct.

It was Marcel Mauss who offered the most fruitful insight into the study of ritual. In his famous essay entitled "Body Techniques" (1934), Mauss ignored the divide between religion and secularity. He had no investment in constructing a category called "ritual" as a component of a universal called "religion." His concern was to explore the way that attitudes, whether sacred or profane, were formed. Most importantly, he asked questions without reference to belief. Mauss's interest was not in the construal of experience and the question of individual choice, but in the mode in which the living human body, as a thing, exists, acts, and is acted upon. His work encourages the thought that secular sensibilities and experiences (such as the religious) require particular "social-psychological-biological" conditions, that the distinctive attitudes and desires underlying secularism as a political arrangement presuppose particular configurations of the senses. At the sociological level, it should be evident that while some culturally valorized senses form part of theorized disciplinary projects, others emerge out of the chance convergence of various political-economic forces and the regulatory strategies to which these give rise – in modern industries, mass markets, cosmopolitan cities,

---

[14] Erving Goffman's dramaturgical sociology has made this theme famous; see his *The Presentation of Self in Everyday Life* (New York: Anchor, Doubleday, 1959).

[15] See Saba Mahmood's important account of this process in *Politics of Piety: The Islamic Revival and the Feminist Subject* (Princeton, NJ: Princeton University Press, 2005).

modern transport and communications, and, not least, modern warfare. So, of course, ideas, including religious ideas, are important for thinking about ethics and politics in modern liberal society, but they are linked to feelings and senses in multiple and unpredictable ways.

Liberal critics and defenders of religion as a universal phenomenon have argued with one another over the implications of religious belief for modern ethics and politics. Central to both sides of the polemics is the notion of "belief" as being at once a privilege (the subject's right to choose his or her belief) and a danger (belief's incitement to violence and intolerance). A first step toward understanding ground shared by both positions is to review John Locke's classical doctrine of religious freedom that set some of the main ideological terms for this continuing argument.

According to a modern argument, belief should not be coerced because that affronts the dignity of the individual person. Perhaps a more common view is that belief cannot – in the sense of impossibility – be coerced. That is the core of Locke's theory of toleration and one part of the genealogy of secularism. The theory rests on a new religious psychology and a new concept of the state that were beginning to emerge in seventeenth-century Europe. These shifts in epistemology and politics allowed Locke to insist that the prince's attempt to coerce religious belief – including belief in the implications of religious practices for salvation – was irrational because it could not be done. All that force could secure was an insincere profession of faith and outward conformity. Therefore – so the argument went, and so the argument still goes – force employed by civil government should be directed only at securing objective public interests: the protection of life, limb, and property. Some liberal philosophers have countered the awkward example of brainwashing by arguing that this merely creates *inauthentic* belief, however *sincerely* it may be held.[16] Authenticity, these philosophers say, consists in the subject's ability *to choose* his or her beliefs and act on them. In this fashion, the idea of belief reinforces the idea of an autonomous subject.

But does the insistence that authentic belief is quite different from a sincere and yet inauthentic one mean that the act of saying something passionately without choosing should be pronounced inauthentic? If someone says that he or she is doing something not because there is

---

[16] For example, Susan Mendus, *Toleration and the Limits of Liberalism*, Issues in Political Theory (Atlantic Highlands, NJ: Humanities Press International, 1989). Mendus borrows this distinction from Bernard Williams.

no logically conceivable alternative but because there is no moral choice (as with Martin Luther's "Here I stand: I can do no other"), what follows for ethics and politics by labeling this act inauthentic?[17]

External forces *can*, in fact, make subjects do or refrain from doing things, of course; they *can* persuade subjects to trust some piece of information as true and to think they are choosing freely. This is what discipline and the organized cultivation of sensibilities (that is, awareness of and responsiveness toward persons and things) do. So although the insistence that beliefs cannot be changed from outside appeared to be saying something empirical about "personal belief" (its singular, autonomous, and inaccessible-to-others location), it was really part of a political discourse about "privacy," a claim to civil immunity with regard to religious faith that reinforced the idea of a secular state and a particular conception of religion.[18]

In *A Secular Age* (2007), Charles Taylor describes the historical formation of modern secular society in which the claim to personal belief can be made and defended. Although there is virtually nothing in this book on the liberal-democratic state as such,[19] Taylor understands that contemporary Western Christianity, with its commitment to the right to choose one's religion – or to reject all religion – depends on it. The fact

[17] A friend has pointed out to me that authenticity may be defined without reference to choice if belief is seen as the *byproduct* of my own inquiries with which I identify but which are not imposed by brainwashing. This nonvoluntarist alternative to the idea of authenticity without invoking choice is appealing, but I am not entirely persuaded by it. What exactly is the relation between "my identity" and "my own inquiries"? Are the assumptions and feelings on which my inquiry depends *mine* even when I have acquired them from others (parents, teachers, advertisers, newscasters, and so on)? And if I have examined them, when can I say that I have done so adequately? Finally, are my beliefs truly mine only when they result from an *intellectual* effort?

[18] That claim has tended to be made against the state, not against the market – where intrusive advertising is typically transmuted into internal compulsion (the desire to consume), which is then rendered a matter of subjective right and individual responsibility. And, of course, the claim cannot be made in a general way against parents or teachers.

[19] Charles Taylor, *A Secular Age* (Cambridge, MA: Belknap Press of Harvard University Press, 2007). There are brief references to the fact that the modern state – and common institutions and practices – are no longer connected to faith in God. This point is spelled out in other texts where Taylor deals with secularism. For example, see Charles Taylor, "The Politics of Recognition," in *Multiculturalism and "The Politics of Recognition,"* ed. Amy Gutmann (Princeton, NJ: Princeton University Press, 1992), 25–73; Charles Taylor, "Modes of Secularism," in *Secularism and Its Critics*, ed. Rajeev Bhargava (Delhi: Oxford University Press, 1998), 31–53; Charles Taylor, *Modern Social Imaginaries* (Durham: Duke University Press, 2004); and also Gerard Bouchard and Charles Taylor, *Building the Future: A Time for Reconciliation* (Abridged Report, Government of Quebec, 2008).

that humans are taken axiomatically to be "self-interpreting animals" –
a view Taylor has elaborated brilliantly in previous publications – helps
to explain why this is first and foremost an intellectual history in the
traditional sense of a history of ideas.[20]

The book's first chapter opens with the following statement: "One
way to put the question I want to answer here is this: why was it virtually impossible not to believe in God in, say, 1500 in our Western society, while in 2000 many of us find this not only easy, but inescapable."[21]
Taylor answers this question by tracing the reform that led to "social
imaginaries" shifting from transcendence to immanence, eventually
giving birth to religious pluralism in which belief can be freely chosen
(or abandoned).

However, the notion of belief that Taylor relies on in this account is
not without ambiguity. To begin with, there is the old question of identifying belief as a state of mind. It was Rodney Needham who first critically examined how Anglophone ethnographers identified the religious
beliefs of the non-Europeans they studied.[22] What exactly, he asked,
is being presented to the reader when the ethnographer claims to be
writing about the interior state of believers? His answer was a skeptical
one: Because these states are necessarily expressed socially – through
language – there are no inner states that are universal. Not everyone
found this answer conclusive, but Needham's study drew attention to
the problematic linguistic relation between *experience and its interpretation*, between the singularity of the material world and the diversity
of language games.

How does one identify belief, especially in "higher religions"
(a nineteenth-century notion invoked by Taylor)? Medieval Christians,

---

[20] This point is stated eloquently in Taylor's essay "Embodied Agency," in *Merleau-
Ponty: Critical Essays*, ed. Henry Pietersma, Current Continental Research 553
(Washington, DC: University Press of America, 1989), 1–21. For example: "Moreover
as a bodily agent I can not only act on things, but *things can act on me*. My field is
not only articulated into zones of accessibility and inaccessibility, but into zones of
threat and security; and these different distinctions are of course closely interwoven: a cliff at my feet delimits not only a zone of inaccessibility but one of danger.
And this because action and suffering are interwoven. My surroundings being relatively encumbered, so that I can't move around easily, I can experience as quasi-
imprisonment" (5; emphasis added). The emphasis here is on the meaning of things
accorded by the embodied agent – almost as though the objective of cliffs was to "act
on me," and my embodied agency recognized that act as meaningful for me. Cliffs
are not acknowledged as indifferent to me.
[21] Taylor, *A Secular Age*, 25.
[22] Rodney Needham, *Belief, Language and Experience* (Chicago: University of Chicago
Press, 1972).

for example, often rejected orthodox doctrines (such as the immortality of the soul, the resurrection, the Incarnation, Virgin Birth, and Purgatory), although it is not clear whether this meant a rejection of religious beliefs as such or the adoption of alternative religious beliefs. The question is this: What are to count as *religious* beliefs? Should beliefs denounced by the Medieval Latin Church as *superstitio* (wrongheadedness) therefore be regarded as secular beliefs? Or should they be pronounced religious on the criteria provided by late-Enlightenment critics for whom all religion was superstition? Is the intention to carry out a particular act always crucial to its religiosity? If so, how and by whom is that to be judged?

Recently, medievalists have come to recognize the problem in translating Latin words we now assume correspond to the modern English *belief* (or French *croyance*).[23] Take the word *infidelitas*, often glossed quite simply as "unbelief." *Infidelitas* was typically used in secular contexts, such as charters, laws, and historical narratives; it usually meant breaking a contract or an oath, acting in a disloyal manner, or breaching someone's trust. *Infideles* were thus not simply those who failed to hold orthodox convictions. They were first and foremost those who acted disloyally in some way, or those who, through acts of treason or misfortune, were no longer a part of the relations that bound together God, Latin Christians, and their king one to another. *Credere*, the Christian Latin word rendered into English as *believe*, usually had an ethical rather than an epistemological sense, meaning "to trust someone" more often than "to be convinced that a proposition was true." Thus Dorothea Weltecke, who has written on this subject, cites the case of Aude Fauré, a young peasant woman who was brought before the Inquisition: she was unable, she said, to *credere in Deum*. What she meant by this, Weltecke points out, emerges from the detailed context. Aude Fauré took the existence of a God for granted. It was because, in her desperation, she could not see in the Eucharist anything but bread and because she found

---

[23] My comments on the medieval Latin usages of what we now translate as "belief" rely heavily on Dorothea Weltecke's excellent "Beyond Religion: On the Lack of Belief during the Central and Late Middle Ages," in *Religion and Its Other: Secular and Sacral Concepts and Practices in Interaction*, ed. Heike Bock, Jörg Feuchter, and Michi Knecht (Frankfurt: Campus Verlag, 2008), 101–14. I have also consulted Rudolf Bultmann and Artur Weiser, *Faith*, trans. and ed. Dorothea M. Barton, P. R. Ackroyd, and A. E. Harvey, Bible Key Words 3 (London: Adam & Charles Black, 1961), especially Part IV, which deals with New Testament usage. Chapter 6 of Wilfred Cantwell Smith's *Faith and Belief* (Princeton, NJ: Princeton University Press, 1979) provides a very useful history of the English word "belief" that is consistent with Weltecke's discussion of the medieval Latin.

herself struggling with disturbing thoughts about Incarnation that she had no hope of God's mercy. It is not clear that the *doctrine* of God's body appearing in the form of bread is being challenged here; what is certainly being expressed is the woman's *anguished relationship* to God as a consequence of her own incapacity to see anything but bread. In short, it is not that our present concept of belief (*that* something is true) was absent in premodern society, but that the words translated as such were usually embedded in distinctive social and political relationships and articulated distinctive sensibilities. They were first of all lived and only occasionally theorized.

Taylor would probably agree with this, but then one would have to say that what is primarily at stake in the story of secularity is change in what Wittgenstein called an entire "way of life," in which the under-standing of everyday experience and behavior does not necessitate inter-pretation. It is not that disbelief was impossible at one point in history and then very possible at another, but that the word "belief" is being used in radically different ways in the two cases, indicating different lived orientations. One may then wonder whether the story of secularity is best told not as a shift from "transcendent" to "immanent" imaginar-ies whose contents are continually being reinterpreted, but as a series of shifts in ways of sensing and living. If one took the latter course, one would have to go beyond the story of how imaginaries such as "deism" *led* to "humanism" or how ideological reforms were improperly carried out. One would have to ask, instead, how the "drive to make over the whole society to higher standards,"[24] how the very urge to total reform, itself originates as a life posture.

Taylor of course is not primarily concerned with beliefs as theo-ries, but with how lived experience acquires its plausibility. He wants to recount how "the whole context of understanding in which our moral, spiritual, or religious experience takes place" is gradually changed. How was it that the premodern "porous self" – which does not dis-tinguish itself from forces in its environment (and therefore confuses internal wish with external cause) – gave way to the modern "buffered self" that assumes "a clear boundary between mind and world, even mind and body"? But this contrast between porous and buffered selves presupposes a transcendent vantage point. These binaries do not cap-ture the complexity of selves in and to the world, to conceptions of inside and outside, to the way the senses work in different cultures, classes, moments, and epochs. It is, says Taylor, when the modern

---

[24] Taylor, *A Secular Age*, 63.

"disenchanted" individual, freed from porousness, attempts to restore something felt as a historical loss, to overcome the "modern malaise" that is an outcome of distorted reform, that he seeks re-enchantment by choosing one of a number of spiritual beliefs on offer. (One may suggest, incidentally, that it is because Taylor is here working with an intuitive definition of religion in terms of *transcendent* – Christian – *beliefs*[25] that he ignores the enchantments imposed on individual life by secular consumer culture – as well as by modern science and technology.[26] If the term *enchantment* is to be understood to refer to being in the grip of "false causes" [superstition], then this is not something that moderns – whether secular or religious – necessarily regard as a loss. On the other hand, understood as a state of rapture and delight, enchantment is still very much present in modern secular life. Disenchantment in the sense of "meaninglessness" is too indeterminate a notion.)

At any rate, at the end of the book one gets the clear sense that for Taylor a reconstituted Christianity would preserve the virtues of liberal modernity without its malaise. One cannot go back because there is no golden age; a true Christianity must be re-imagined. This confidence in the possibilities of *proper* reform may explain Taylor's dismissal of those who regard modern life as having a tragic character – that is, those made cruelly aware of the impossibility of resolving a calamitous human impasse brought about by one's own blind actions, by the uncontrollable things that surround one, and by the treachery of interpretation.[27]

As I understand Taylor, it is precisely the modern individual's *interpreted* experience that leads to its optional character. And although it is true that the idea of belief in Taylor's story does not always have the sense of a proposition, the centrality of the notion of "construal" by the buffered self in this story seems to presuppose something that is capable of being articulated – if not propositionally, then in the form of a narrative.

[25] "So 'religion' for our purposes can be defined in terms of 'transcendence,' but this latter term has to be understood in more than one dimension. Whether one believes in some agency or power transcending the immanent order is indeed, a crucial feature of 'religion' ..." (Taylor, *A Secular Age*, 20). Belief is not all there is to religion, of course, but it *is* a central concern of Taylor's book.

[26] See, for example, Colin Campbell, *The Romantic Ethic and the Spirit of Modern Consumerism* (Oxford: Blackwell, 1987); and Jane Bennett, *The Enchantment of Modern Life: Attachments, Crossings, and Ethics* (Princeton, NJ: Princeton University Press, 2001).

[27] There is nothing "heroic" in this awareness. For a thought-provoking discussion of the modern political predicament as a tragic one, see David Scott's study of the Haitian revolution, *Conscripts of Modernity: The Tragedy of Colonial Enlightenment* (Durham, NC: Duke University Press, 2004).

But before proceeding, I want to make a distinction between sensing and interpreting in order to characterize "believing" (*that* something is the case) as an analytical category. I will do so by drawing on R. G. Collingwood's distinction between feeling and sensing, on the one hand, and thinking (and believing), on the other. Only in the latter case, Collingwood points out, does it make sense to talk of *failure* having occurred, because feeling is not a directional activity.[28] There is nothing in feeling and sensing that can be said to constitute a mistake. Thoughts – and beliefs as thoughts – can contradict each other, but feelings and sensations cannot unless they are made the objects of interpretation (thinking); the two are analytically distinct. One may, of course, be mistaken about the *cause* of what one feels, but in apprehending causes, one is already in the realm of what Collingwood calls "thinking" as opposed to "sensing."

Collingwood reminds the reader that the word *feeling* has been used to refer to a range of body states, including sensations (hot/cold, hard/soft, bright/dark, and so on) and emotions (pain or pleasure, anger, fear, jealousy, and so on), which have been variously classified in more recent literature on the subject. Sense and emotion are not alternatives, as the sensation of seeing or hearing might be; they are structurally combined. Our experience of the world is thus partly sensuous-emotional and partly intellectual, but since mistakes are made only at the level of thinking and interpreting, not at the level of feeling, it seems to me one should not assume that an interpretive frame always and necessarily accompanies sensing and feeling. It is true that we normally see things *as* something, but this does not in itself imply that experience inevitably depends on interpretation. *Where* the subject recognizes herself as "I" (in divinity, in humanity, in animality); the degree to which she seeks an integrated image of herself; what happens when (in consternation) she fails to find herself where she assumed quite naturally that image would be – these are matters that do not necessitate construal on the subject's part.

How does it happen that in modern capitalist society Christians and non-Christians, believers and non-believers, live more or less the same life? Put another way, unless you knew someone well, you could not tell whether she was a believer or not merely from the way she lived.

---

[28] See R. G. Collingwood, *The Principles of Art* (Oxford: Clarendon Press, 1938), especially chapter 8. Collingwood's entire discussion of this topic seems to me more persuasive than Taylor's use of "man as a self-interpreting animal," because the former allows for understanding without interpretation in a way that the latter doesn't seem to.

What does this say about religious belief? One answer may be that religious belief where it exists among moderns is *so* deep that it has at best a very tenuous connection with observable behavior. Sometimes the connection is denied altogether, as in this statement of the prime minister of Ontario, quoted in a local newspaper: "'As premier, I have made decisions that defy the beliefs of my own religion,' Mr. McGuinty said, citing his support for same-sex marriage and abortion. 'My Catholicism, my private faith, does not determine my position.'"[29] This suggests that it is not so much the neutrality of the liberal-democratic state that protects the right to interpret and believe, but the modern disjunction between belief and behavior that permits this kind of neutrality.

It is worth pondering why there is no mention in Taylor's story of the global crises that threaten the world today: climate change, the militarization of space and of disease, increasing poverty and unceasing demand for economic growth, nuclear proliferation, or war and terrorism. The word "crisis" appears in the entire text only in reference to the loss of personal meaning, to the need for salvational belief. But what if liberal democracy, which guarantees Christians and non-Christians alike their right to choose their own beliefs, is unable to confront the global crises – because, as critics have so often said, as a form of government, liberal democracy is permeated by special interests and exceptionally receptive to corporate power because it favors or at least permits the extension of market rationality into all social relations and because its citizens are easily pushed into nationalist paranoia? What if liberal democracy[30] not only impairs the development of virtues necessary for dealing effectively with global crises but also (and more importantly for the present argument) continually disrupts the conditions on which what Taylor calls "the sense of fullness" depends? And what if, paradoxically, it is precisely the continual feeling of disruption, of uncertainty, that feeds both the power of liberal democracy and its promise of continuous reform?

[29] Siri Agrell, "It's Wrong to Fund Private Religious Schools"; online: http://www.theglobeandmail.com/servlet/story/RTGAM.20070917.wlibs0917/BNStory/ontarioelection2007 (accessed December 8, 2008).

[30] I am reluctant to speak here of *"so-called* liberal democracy," for two main reasons. First, I am concerned primarily with the structures that articulate actually existing liberal-democratic societies – capitalist economies depending on unrestrained growth and consumerism – and not with what some citizens believe liberal democracies ought to be. Second, to speak of *so-called* liberal democracy is to assume (mistakenly, I think) that the public language of liberal democracy used by defenders and critics of the political order is clear and unambiguous, that sound argument can fatally undermine the ideological justifications of rulers – and thus dissolve the drives (conscious and unconscious) that are embedded in existing institutional structures.

To explore how religion, belief, and politics are linked to one another, we need to enquire not only into institutional landscapes but also ask a number of questions about the body, its senses, and its attitudes. For this, we need ethnographies of the human body – its attitudes toward pain, physical damage, decay, and death, as well as toward bodily integrity, growth and enjoyment, and the conditions that isolate persons and things from or connect them strongly with others. What architecture of the senses – hearing, seeing, smelling, touching, tasting – do particular embodiments and sensibilities depend on? How (whether through projects or fortuitous developments) do new sensory perceptions take shape and make older ways of engaging with the world and older political forms *irrelevant*? In trying to answer these questions, the researcher will of course need a framework of interpretation to help identify the senses and their expression, but the senses themselves do not *necessarily* require meanings.[31] The researcher will understand that it is possible for someone to encounter something unpredictably that transforms her, to be gripped through her senses by a force (whether immanent or transcendent) *without having to interpret anything*. We need to think about the self in ways that are neither relativist (the world is what the self sees it as) nor reductionist (the self is determined by external and internal causes).

The anthropological historian Alain Corbin has taken up the problem of changing perceptions of the world appropriated by the different

---

[31] The work of Walter J. Ong, S.J., especially *Ramus, Method, and the Decay of Dialogue: From the Art of Discourse to the Art of Reason* (Cambridge, MA: Harvard University Press, 1958), and *The Presence of the Word: Some Prolegomena for Cultural and Religious History* (New Haven: Yale University Press, 1967), is relevant to these questions because he was among the first to trace shifts from the reliance on hearing to primary emphasis on seeing. Ong has rightly been criticized for recounting an overly simple story of historical stages in the development of human communication (from oral culture through alphabet and print to the electronic media). In fact, both in the past and today, orality and writing have been intertwined in complicated ways. Let me give an example from the Islamic scriptural tradition, in which the senses of hearing and seeing, reading and reciting, are closely intertwined. Thus the Qur'an (which means "recitation") is deeply rooted in complex continuities – quite apart from the major schools of interpretation that have provided it with its meanings. The earliest text, written in a primitive seventh-century Arabic script, seems to have been treated as a kind of musical score, a prompt for the oral rendition that depended on memorization through reiteration. Sign and sound went together, but not in any direct or fixed way. It was only because the oral traditions were continuous that they were able to provide an immanent frame for the written text, and thus for its scholarly reception over the centuries. An effort has always been required to abstract the Qur'anic text as an intellectual interpreted object from the relationship between the charged sound and the attentive body with its growing store of memorizations.

human senses – hearing, seeing, touching – without being primarily concerned with interpretation. Thus in *The Foul and the Fragrant*, Corbin traces the densely interwoven discourses on the cramped condition of the urban masses, the conditions of contagious disease, and the practices of individual hygiene in eighteenth- and nineteenth-century French society. One eventual consequence of these conditions, Corbin observes, was an added emphasis on the priority of clear sight. He writes, "there was increased concern for light in private dwellings, as in public space; this was the beginning of the great swing in attitudes that was to give uncontested supremacy to the visual." Corbin points out that it was not always the ideas themselves that immediately changed, rather that the new form of perception made for a "new intolerance of traditional actuality." For example, he notes that up to the end of the eighteenth century, animal-based perfumes (such as musk) had been used by women to emphasize their odor, but in the nineteenth century, with the new concern for personal hygiene, these were discredited in favor of perfumes that would disguise body odor while at the same time evoking discreet intimations of the feminine. These feelings were not interpretations (as sensation and affect, they could not be *mistaken* by the subject: only thinking about them could make them so). But they were, nevertheless, part of what was given to experience – and therefore available for interpretation.[32]

Shifts in sensory perception endow experience of other people and things with complicated emotions (anxieties and pleasures), a function not merely of what is sensed but how it is sensed. The new arrangement of the senses, associated with new patterns of living, contributed to an aspect of modern subjectivity that we might provisionally identify as secular. "Techniques of ventilation," Corbin argues, "insofar as they acknowledged the need for space between bodies and gave protection against other people's odors, brought individuals into a new encounter with their own bodily smells and, as such, contributed decisively to the development of a new narcissism."[33] If Corbin is right, then this narcissism, this love for one's purity and integrity, may have reinforced the thought that one's *private* experiences and beliefs ultimately define who one is in the world.

Smell, unlike vision, is a passive sense. It cannot be switched off at will, as seeing can. This is not to say that the faculty of smell – or,

[32] Alain Corbin, *The Foul and the Fragrant: Odor and the French Social Imagination* (Cambridge, MA: Harvard University Press, 1986), 154–6, 73.

[33] Corbin, *The Foul and the Fragrant*, 95.

for that matter, other senses – cannot be cultivated. My point is that as an involuntary medium of contamination smell may cause anxiety. There is a resonance between some emerging sensory orientations to which Corbin points and arguments made by the anthropologist Mary Douglas in her book *Purity and Danger* (1966).[34] The notion of pollution, she maintained, depended on the transgression or confounding of a system of categories: "uncleanness," in her famous phrase, "is matter out of place." Purity rituals are therefore attempts to restore the triple order of living body, society, and cosmos that has been confounded. Among other things, such rituals instruct the individual in the ways certain sensory experiences should be understood and dealt with. Douglas helps us to see why Corbin's narcissist might have an inclination to paranoia, for it is precisely the anxious search for systematic meaning in a world believed to contain a hidden threat to one's personal purity, and to one's system, that would make him a paranoiac. This may also help us to understand the urge to reform – the drive to alter total systems – as a response to continuous danger.

Corbin's stress on the consequences of new sense perceptions as part of an uncontrolled world of changing things seems to me important because it puts into question the attempt to account for transformations by reference merely to the intention of intellectual reforms or to their unintended consequences. Of course, attitudes and sensibilities are deliberately cultivated in the body by institutions and social movements, and reforms *do* have unintended consequences. But whether deliberately cultivated or unintended, the senses are central to the public life in which people participate, to the ways they promote, resist, submit, or remain indifferent to the forces of political life, not because of what they mean, but because of what they do.

The modern secular state is not simply the guardian of one's personal right to believe as one chooses; it confronts particular sensibilities and attitudes, and puts greater value on some than others. And yet the work of the senses has received less attention than the function of beliefs in the study of politics. What *has* come to be increasingly discussed is discipline: discipline in the cultivation of attitudes as well as in the regulation of individual conduct by authorities. But important though discipline is, the conscious cultivation of behavior and belief is not quite the same thing as the unintended shifts in the sensorium

[34] Mary Douglas, *Purity and Danger: An Analysis of the Concepts of Pollution and Taboo* (London: Routledge, 2002).

described by anthropologists and historians such as Corbin and Leigh Eric Schmidt.[35]

The familiar story about the role of discipline in the formation of civilization too often fails to pursue *all* the disparate effects of discipline, whether intended or not. But assuming, for the sake of argument, that discipline is central to the story, we encounter an intriguing question when we consider so-called fundamentalists in the contemporary Middle East. Thus, although in Euro-America the disciplined subject is said to be the distinctive figure of modernity and its freedom, the presence of discipline in Muslim life generally and Islamic movements in particular is commonly taken in the West as evidence of precisely its opposite. The existence of rules of conduct (of dress, comportment, daily prayers, and so on) and the cultivation of sensibilities (the control of emotion in speech and behavior toward others and reverence towards the sacred voice) are seen as constraint and suppression. This is an example of precisely what arguments for toleration warn against: if political or religious authority imposes norms of conduct and doctrine on the individual, and if this imposition is accepted, then this must be a case of "sincere but inauthentic belief." Yet one difference is that the discipline for pious Muslims is connected to a strong sense of and orientation to divine presence. I suggest, therefore, that instead of approaching such behavior in terms of belief (in this case, of *inauthentic* belief or "false consciousness"), one might enquire into how the bodily senses are cultivated or how they take shape in a world that cannot be humanly controlled, and hence into what politics these formations make possible or difficult.

This leads me to a study by an anthropologist who tried to formulate the questions in his ethnography of pre–Tahrir Square Cairo in just this way, Charles Hirschkind's *The Ethical Soundscape*.[36] Hirschkind's monograph is not in an account of ideas and beliefs, but an analysis of

[35] In *Hearing Things: Religion, Illusion, and the American Enlightenment* (Cambridge, MA: Harvard University Press, 2000), Leigh Eric Schmidt examines the retraining of the ear that was promoted through a range of embodied regimens, by Christians and deists alike. Schmidt's main concern is with changing attitudes of religiosity, but the story he tells about the retraining of the sense of hearing is also crucial to the formation of secular attitudes. Connected to the retraining of hearing is the move from an unreflective acceptance of the senses to one in which all the senses are assessed and disciplined as sources of reliable knowledge. It was through this contrast that the modern meaning of belief as mental assent came to be foregrounded and Christian claims to truth were put on the defensive.

[36] Charles Hirschkind, *The Ethical Soundscape: Cassette Sermons and Islamic Counterpublics*, Cultures of History (New York: Columbia University Press, 2006).

exchanges that belonged to a particular way of life. He asks how the enormously popular practice of listening to sermons in Cairo shaped religious sensibilities and what some of its consequences were for politics. Throughout Islamic history, attending the Friday sermon has been an important part of Muslim subject formation. Hirschkind analyzed the reception of sermons as an active process, one in which the faithful listener cultivated his or her ability to attend. Listening to sermons in modern Cairo is no longer confined to the Friday mosque and it is no longer a one-off experience. Taped sermons can now be heard numerous times, in many urban contexts, without supervision. Hirschkind describes this with the felicitous phrase "undisciplined discipline."

Political oratory and media entertainment have affected sermon styles and so established new connections between practitioners and the institutions of national life, as well as with the transnational Islamic community (the *umma*). This movement grew partly in response to the Hosni Mubarak government's attempts to suppress the Muslim Brotherhood, which constituted the single most serious popular opposition to it prior to the January 2011 uprising in which President Mubarak was ousted.

Hirschkind's account of the movement describes how the practice of cassette listening promoted an acoustic sensibility opposed to the former state's obsession with spatial control, as well as to the nouveaux riches who had withdrawn into their clean, orderly, gated communities. Contained in this opposition was an unending struggle for how "real Islam" is to be lived. What Hirschkind calls a "counter-public" is thus an Islamic space of moral distancing from the hegemonic religious-secular order. Many Islamists, he tells us, regarded the regime of personal discipline as helping to develop a responsiveness that might moderate, if not totally negate, the seductions of a neoliberal consumer culture. The movement is certainly not liberal; it does not promote and defend autonomous individuality in which the subject is always encouraged to make its own choices. Its aim instead is to form moral subjects capable of acting in national politics.

After Hirschkind did his fieldwork for this study, an oppositional movement emerged known as *kifaya!* ("Enough!"). *Kifaya!* overlapped with the counter-public that Hirschkind described, bringing together a variety of social elements – Muslims and Christians, Islamists and secular liberals, men and women, professionals and labor unionists – in a coalition against the authoritarian, neoliberal state. It is not that there is now a happy union of all these elements, but that an irreducible plurality persists as a foundation of political sensibility. What gathered secular liberals and Islamists together – despite a measure of mutual unease – was precisely *not* their belief, but their oppositional attitude, their common feeling that circumstances in Egypt had become intolerable, and more specifically their sense of outrage at the brutality and corruption of the Mubarak regime. They speak of their opposition as something they did not *choose* but were compelled to take up. However, this situation is not merely negative; it also provided a space of daily interaction and negotiation. Discreet and not-so-discreet intrusions by American imperial power, as well as the stranglehold that the regime of Egyptian leader Mubarak had on the political-economic system, make teleology virtually impossible. The religiosity of individual Muslims involved in this movement whom I have encountered is characterized by a mode of being often inwardly unsettled yet outwardly civil. This religiosity seeks the cultivation of feelings attuned to mutual care within the community, and in that sense it can lay claim to a democratic ethos. To what extent this is successfully cultivated among significant numbers of people is of course another matter, but my point is that belief in the sense of private conviction has little to do with it.

I end with a question that needs to be thought about here. It is an old question but one that has not, in my view, been satisfactorily answered: How does *democratic sensibility as an ethos* (whether "religious" or "secular") accord with *democracy as a state system*? The former, after all, involves the desire for mutual care, distress at the infliction of pain and indignity, concern for the truth more than for immutable subjective rights, the ability to listen and not merely to tell, and the willingness to evaluate behavior without being judgmental toward others; it tends toward greater *inclusivity*.[37] The latter – democracy as a state system – is jealous of its sovereignty, defines and protects the subjective rights of its citizens (including their right to "religious freedom"), infuses them with nationalist fervor, and invokes bureaucratic rationality in governing them justly; it is fundamentally *exclusive*. My point is not to make an invidious comparison between sensibility and political systems, nor to insist that the two are finally incompatible. I simply ask whether the latter undermines the former – and if it does, then to what extent.

One might suggest, finally, that the modern *idea* of religious belief (protected as a right in the individual and regulated institutionally) is a

---

[37] See the remarkable work by Stanley Hauerwas and Romand Coles, *Christianity, Democracy, and the Radical Ordinary: Conversations Between a Radical Democrat and a Christian*, Theopolitical Visions 1 (Eugene, OR: Cascade, 2008), which describes some of these attitudes by distinguishing what they call radical democracy from liberal democracy.

critical function of the liberal-democratic nation-state but not of democratic sensibility.

Select Bibliography

Asad, Talal. "Anthropological Conceptions of Religion: Reflections on Geertz." *Man*, N.S. 18 (1983): 237–59.

"Reading a Modern Classic: W. C. Smith's *The Meaning and End of Religion*," 131–47. In *Religion and Media*. Edited by Hent de Vries and Samuel Weber. *Cultural Memory in the Present*. Palo Alto, CA: Stanford University Press, 2001.

"Trying to Understand French Secularism," 494–526. In *Political Theologies: Public Religions in a Post-Secular World*. Edited by Hent de Vries and Lawrence E. Sullivan. New York: Fordham University Press, 2006.

Bloch, Maurice. "Are Religious Beliefs Counter-intuitive?" 129–46. In *Radical Interpretation in Religion*. Edited by Nancy K. Frankenberry. Cambridge: Cambridge University Press, 2002.

Dubuisson, Daniel. *L'Occidente et la religion: Mythes, science et idologie*. Bruxelles: Editions Complexe, 1998.

Hirschkind, Charles. *The Ethical Soundscape: Cassette Sermons and Islamic Counterpublics*. Cultures of History. New York: Columbia University Press, 2006.

Ruel, Malcolm. "Christians as Believers," 9–31. In *Religious Organization and Religious Experience*. Edited by John Davis. London: Academic Press, 1982.

Smith, Jonathan Z. *Imagining Religion: From Babylon to Jonestown*. Chicago Studies in the History of Judaism. Chicago: University of Chicago Press, 1982.

Smith, Wilfred Cantwell. *Faith and Belief*. Princeton, NJ: Princeton University Press, 1979.

The Meaning and End of Religion: A New Approach to the Religious Traditions of Mankind. Minneapolis: Fortress Press, 1991 (1962).

Taylor, Charles. "Embodied Agency," 1–21. In *Merleau-Ponty: Critical Essays*. Edited by Henry Pietersma. Current Continental Research 553. Washington, DC: University Press of America, 1989.

A Secular Age. Cambridge, MA: Belknap Press of Harvard University Press, 2007.

Weltecke, Dorothea. "Beyond Religion: On the Lack of Belief During the Central and Late Middle Ages," 101–14. In *Religion and Its Other: Secular and Sacral Concepts and Practices in Interaction*. Edited by Heike Bock, Jörg Feuchter, and Michi Knecht. Frankfurt: Campus Verlag, 2008.

3 Special things as building blocks of religions
ANN TAVES

Given that religion, religious, and religions are Western folk concepts, that their meaning is unstable and contested, and that they cannot be defined so as to specify anything uniquely, we need to consider broader, more generic ways of characterizing the sorts of things that interest us as scholars of religion. Rather than relying on emically loaded first-order terms, such as sacred, magical, spiritual, mystical, or religious, we can seek ways to translate the disciplinary second-order discourse of religion, religious, and religions into broader, more generic terms when designing research. Instead of stipulating a definition for a key first-order term, such as "religious," and, thus, defining in advance what exactly will count as such, I propose – to borrow a fishing metaphor – that we cast our nets more broadly and then sort through the variety of things that our nets pull in. Identifying a broader set of nets that we can use – singly or in combination – to specify what it is we want to study would not only eliminate the confusion between first- and second-order use of the term "religious," it would also highlight the impossibility of uniquely specifying what is meant by the first-order terms and force us to specify what it is about this constellation of concepts that most interests us.

I. SPECIALNESS AS A GENERIC ATTRIBUTE OF THINGS CONSIDERED RELIGION-LIKE

The idea of specialness is one broader, more generic net that captures most of what people have in mind when they refer to sacred, magical, spiritual, mystical, or religious, and then some. We can consider specialness both behaviorally and substantively, asking whether there are behaviors that tend to mark things off as special and whether there are particular types of things are that are more likely to be considered special than others.

The approach I am suggesting can be and indeed has been derived fairly directly from a certain reading of Émile Durkheim. Durkheim defines "a religion" (not "religion") as "a unified system of beliefs and practices relative to sacred things, that is to say, things set apart and forbidden." While Durkheim is not entirely consistent, he makes a clear distinction between *religions* and the elementary phenomena that constitute them. Sacred things (things set apart), religious beliefs (beliefs about sacred things), and rites (rules for behavior in the presence of sacred things) can all exist apart from religions. Sacred things and beliefs and rites related to them are separable from religions and at the same time provide the fundamental raw material that people use to construct "religions."[1]

Durkheim's concept of "sacred things as things set apart and forbidden" can be used to generate a generic second-order concept of "specialness," if care is taken to avoid certain pitfalls:

- Given the many meanings attached to the sacred, some of them highly problematic, we can consider the sacred an emic term and refer simply to "things set apart and forbidden," where "thing" can literally mean *anything*, whether event, person, behavior, object, experience, or emotion.
- Things are always set apart relative to other things in a class. Setting something apart in this way marks it as special; we can refer to this process as one of "singularization."[2]
- We can locate "things set apart and forbidden" at one end of a continuum that runs from the ordinary to the special, with things that are so special that people set them apart and protect them with prohibitions or taboos at one extreme. In doing so, we can avoid Durkheim's problematic claim that religious thought divides the world "into two domains, one containing all that is sacred and the other all that is profane," and refer simply to things that are more or less special, things understood to be singular, and things that people set apart and protect with prohibitions.[3]

We can use the idea of *specialness* to identify a set of things that includes much of what people have in mind when they refer to things as sacred, magical, mystical, superstitious, spiritual, and/or religious. Whatever else they are, things that get caught up in the web of relations marked

---

[1] Émile Durkheim, *The Elementary Forms of Religious Life*, trans. Karen E. Fields (New York: Free Press, 1995), 44 (emphasis added), 38.
[2] Igor Kopytoff, "The Cultural Biography of Things: Commoditization as Process," in *The Social Life of Things: Commodities in Cultural Perspective*, ed. Arjun Appadurai (Cambridge: Cambridge University Press, 1986), 64–91.
[3] Durkheim, *Elementary Forms*, 34.

out by these terms are things that someone or some group has granted some sort of special status. Whether or not particular things should be considered special is typically a matter of dispute and leads different individuals and groups to position things differently in relation to the web of related concepts. Although neither the specific Western terms nor the web of relationships that they constitute correspond precisely to distinctions made in other cultural contexts, the concept of specialness, insofar as we can operationalize it in terms of behaviors, provides a more promising starting point for crosscultural, cross-temporal, and perhaps even cross-species research. Such a starting point will most likely capture more than what scholars might normally (that is, from our culturally located perspective) consider religious, spiritual, magical, and so on. Rather than viewing this as a cause for concern, this gap will allow us to view ourselves and what we tacitly consider religious, spiritual, magical, and such in a more reflexive light.

II. SPECIAL THINGS AS THINGS SET APART

In what follows, I want to consider a series of questions about specialness: first, whether there are particular behaviors that can help us to identify things that people consider special; second, whether there are some kinds of things that people are more likely to consider special than others; and third, what methods are needed in order to interact with these things.

In the first section, I am going to come at the issue from a formal or functional perspective, using Durkheim's definition of sacredness as "things set apart and protected by taboos" as a starting point. By specifying various prohibitions commonly used to set things apart as special, we can identify formal marks of specialness that should be usable across cultures and time periods. In the second section, I will approach the matter of specialness more substantively, asking whether we can identify more substantive characteristics of things that tend to be set apart as special. Here I will suggest that both anomalous and ideal things may tend to stand out for people and that much of what we traditionally associate with religion (for example, spiritual beings and abstract concepts such as transcendence, ultimate concern, and nirvana) can be interpreted as either anomalous or ideal. In the third section, I will consider the special methods required to interact with special things insofar as (1) they are set apart by prohibitions that preclude interaction and (2) they or their special qualities are evanescent. Insofar as people do not care to attend to special things, such methods are not necessary. The discussion of special methods (for example, practices, rituals, prayer, chanting, and divination) for engaging with special things will require us to distinguish between simple ascriptions (things deemed special) and composite ascriptions (methods deemed efficacious for engaging with things deemed special).

Throughout, I will reflect – albeit quite tentatively – on the question of why humans singularize things. Distinguishing between simple and composite ascriptions of specialness allows us to identify basic building blocks that can be incorporated into more complex sociocultural formations. Comparison of humans across cultures and with other animals may allow us to consider the interplay between things that humans are biologically primed to view as special, on the one hand, and culturally primed to view as special, on the other.

In looking at the concept of specialness formally, substantively, practically, and comparatively, I am not attempting to create a new, more embracing definition of religion. Instead, I am breaking down what we have generally meant by "religion" into "religious things" and "religions" and then positioning both within a larger, more encompassing framework of special things and the methods deemed efficacious for engaging with them.

III. MARKS OF SPECIALNESS

Durkheim's definition does not provide a precise sense of what researchers should look for if they seek to identify things that people consider special and in more extreme cases set apart and protect with taboos. Drawing from classical debates over commodities (Karl Marx, Georg Simmel), fetishes (Marx), the sacred (Durkheim), and gifts (Marcel Mauss), scholars in various disciplines have proposed ways to operationalize these prohibitions in relation to wider discussions of where value is or ought to be placed in relation to concrete objects, relationships, and abstractions. These discussions are typically framed against the backdrop of economic exchange and identify various prohibitions as protecting forms of valuation that exist alongside or in opposition to economic exchange value.[4]

---

[4] Durkheim, *Elementary Forms*; Karl Marx, *Capital: A Critique of Political Economy*, edited by Friedrich Engels (New York: International Publishers, 1970); Georg Simmel, *The Philosophy of Money*, 3rd Edition, edited by David Frisby (New York: Routledge, 2004); Marcel Mauss, *The Gift: The Form and Reason for Exchange in Archaic Societies*, trans. W. D. Halls (New York: W. W. Norton, 2000).

Building on Durkheim, Igor Kopytoff introduced the idea of "singularization" as one method that people or groups use to "set apart a certain portion of their environment, marking it as 'sacred.'" As defined by
Kopytoff, singularities are things that individuals, groups, or societies
refuse to commodify, implicitly marking them as priceless. Societies
typically have a set of things – "a symbolic inventory" – that they consider singular, such as public lands, historic monuments, state museums, and symbols of office, from government buildings to artifacts, and
that they refuse to exchange. Nations, groups, and individuals do not
necessarily agree on what counts as singular, as we can see, for example,
in disputes between native peoples and the governments of the United
States and Canada over lands that native peoples consider sacred or
debates over what events should be memorialized and in what fashion.[5]

Although some people may understand singularity to inhere in
the thing itself, things often pass from one status to the other and
back. Many religious traditions have prescribed methods for sacral-
izing (consecrating) and desacralizing (deconsecrating) objects. In the
ancient Near East and in India, elaborate rituals transformed human-
made statues into cult objects in which deities resided. More recently,
anthropologists have reported on Thais who have singularized trees by
"ordaining" them (wrapping them in the saffron-colored cloth associated with Buddhist monks) and by photographing them in order to prevent their destruction. Although singularities are usually highly valued,
they may also be completely shunned, as in the case of things viewed as
demonic or evil.[6]

Things are not necessarily either completely singular or completely
commodified. U.S. flags are technically commodities, but are nonetheless considered special. Flag etiquette requires that the flag should not
touch the ground, should be illuminated at night, and should be destroyed
respectfully if damaged. There have been numerous attempts to pass a
flag desecration amendment to the U.S. Constitution. Other things that
are set apart may be traded within a very narrow sphere of exchange or
only under certain conditions. The U.S. government allows logging in

[5] Kopytoff, "Cultural Biography," 73–5, quotes on 73; David Chidester and Edward
T. Linenthal, eds., *American Sacred Space* (Bloomington and Indianapolis: Indiana
University Press, 1995).

[6] On the animation of statues, see Michael B. Dick, ed., *Born in Heaven Made on
Earth: The Creation of the Cult Image in the Ancient Near East* (Winona Lake, IN:
Eisenbrauns, 1999). On the singularization of trees, see Peter Vail, "Making the
Mundane Sacred Through Technology: Mediating Identity, Ecology and Commodity
Fetishism," *Visual Communication* 3, no. 2 (2004): 129–44.

national forests under certain conditions and generally prohibits it in national parks. Whether drilling for oil should be allowed in the Arctic National Refuge is hotly debated. Other commodities, such as papal indulgences, medicines, and certain forms of software, are intended for their original user; they can be sold once, but cannot be resold.

There are often intimate connections between singularity and identity, whether individual or collective. Anthropologist Annette Weiner introduced the idea of inalienable possessions, that is, possessions that have histories that are carried in the object whether they are kept or circulated to others as gifts, loans, or copies and, as a result, establish an "emotional lien upon the receiver." Patrick Geary has shown how medieval Christian relics, as physical remains of special (that is, saintly) dead people, were normally given as gifts, thus retaining their ties to the donor, establishing a lien on the receiver, and constituting networks of ecclesial patronage. Relics that were stolen or sold were alienated from the giver and escaped these patronage relationships.[7]

Some scholars have questioned the value of Durkheim's definition of the sacred as things set apart, arguing that his understanding is overly dichotomous and cannot account for the ways in which sacred things are embodied materially and exchanged commercially. Colleen McDannell, for example, has made this argument with respect to the international distribution of holy water from the Catholic shrine at Lourdes and Suzanne Kaufman, drawing on McDannell's critique, in relation to the commercial activities surrounding the shrine itself.[8]

Although they rightly criticize the idea of two distinct and comprehensive domains of the sacred and profane, it is clear from McDannell's account that the holy water was not actually sold. Distributors were given the water from the shrine in return for donations. Water was distributed from replicas of Lourdes in the United States and elsewhere, again in return for donations instead of payments. Lourdes water currently on sale on the Internet would seem to belie this point, but at least one site is careful to state, "We do not sell the water but sell the container to offset import costs."[9] Although this may seem like a technical

[7] Annette B. Weiner, "Inalienable Wealth," *American Ethnologist* 12, 2 (1985): 210–27; Patrick Geary, "Sacred Commodities: The Circulation of Medieval Relics," in *The Social Life of Things*, ed. Appadurai, 169–91.

[8] Colleen McDannell, *Material Christianity: Religion and Popular Culture in America* (New Haven: Yale University Press, 1995), 4–8, 132–62; Suzanne K. Kaufman, *Consuming Visions: Mass Culture and the Lourdes Shrine* (Ithaca, NY: Cornell University Press, 2005), 7–9.

[9] http://ourladyoflourdescatholicgifts.com/LourdesWater.html (accessed May 12, 2008).

nicety, it is a technicality that matters at least to the more devout. From a scholarly perspective, it is a subtle but crucial boundary that sets the water apart as a gift, not a commodity. As long as this boundary is honored, everything else can be commodified: representations of the visionary, Bernadette Soubrious; bottles for the water; souvenirs of Lourdes; package tours; and so on – all can be sold.

The Catholic tradition, which enshrines precise rules regarding the treatment of holy objects in canon law, may lead Catholics to make distinctions that others would not. Commercial activity associated with other shrines may offer more support for the idea that specialness and commodification are not necessarily opposed. Nurit Zaidman's research on the religious objects sold at Jewish pilgrimage sites and New Age shops in Israel indicates that there are many things that people consider special, yet not so special that they cannot be bought or sold.[10]

In the case of the shrine at Lourdes, however, most Catholics do not consider the holy water special in its own right, but by virtue of its association with an alleged appearance of the Virgin Mary to Bernadette. The primary thing that was set apart, in other words, was not an object (the water), but an event (a series of visionary experiences). While prohibitions against selling or trading are commonly used to set objects apart, people often use other, more abstract prohibitions to set apart more abstract and ephemeral things. In his research on "sacred values," psychologist Philip Tetlock highlights the importance of taboos against mixing and comparing for setting apart more abstract and ephemeral things.[11] Thus, to return to the examples of Lourdes, Bernadette's visionary experience was not set apart by means of prohibitions against selling it (or accounts of it, which definitely were sold), but by precluding comparisons between it and other similar experiences. When the claims of competing visionaries threatened to undermine the specialness of Bernadette's experience, her backers responded by discrediting her competitors' visions as inauthentic. In doing so, they reasserted the singularity of her visions and set them apart from others they deemed inauthentic.[12]

---

[10] Nurit Zaidman, "Commercialization of Religious Objects: A Comparison Between Traditional and New Age Religions," *Social Compass* 50, no. 3 (2003): 345–60.

[11] Philip E. Tetlock, Orie V. Kristel, S. Beth Elson, Melanie C. Green, and Jennifer S. Lerner, "The Psychology of the Unthinkable: Taboo Trade-offs, Forbidden Base Rates, and Heretical Counterfactuals," *Journal of Personality and Social Psychology* 78, no. 5 (2000): 853–70.

[12] Sandra L. Zimdars-Swartz, *Encountering Mary: From La Salette to Medjugorje* (Princeton, NJ: Princeton University Press, 1991), 57–67; Ruth Harris, *Lourdes: Body and Spirit in the Secular Age* (New York: Penguin Compass, 1999), 91–109.

If we think more carefully about what is involved in attaching a price to something, we can see how pricing, mixing, and comparison are related. First and most basically, setting a price means specifying the value of a thing in relation to other things. If something is priceless, it cannot be compared with other things in this way because doing so reduces it to something that can be bought and sold. Indeed, the mere thought of attaching a price to things such as friends, children, or country sparks feelings of outrage in most people. This powerful emotional response to the idea of putting a price on something priceless points to a second, less rational aspect of pricing. Comparing something of infinite value to something of finite value does not simply reduce the value of the former in a purely rational economic sense. Emotionally, the reduction of a priceless thing to something that can be bought and sold degrades it in the most literal sense of the term. By extension, something of infinite value is polluted and contaminated when it is mixed with or even compared to things of finite value. While there may be some things that literally cannot be sold, anything, however abstract, is potentially subject to degradation by means of mental mixing or comparison. Prohibitions against mixing and comparison thus provide the most comprehensive means of setting things apart, whether they are objects, persons, events, experiences, or ideas. Framed positively, prohibitions against trading, mixing, and comparing allow people to set things apart as priceless, pure, and incomparable.

Where Tetlock expands the price/priceless binary to include comparable/incomparable and mixable/unmixable, anthropologist David Graeber suggests three alternative measures of value (proportionality, ranking, and presence/absence) that intersect with those proposed by Tetlock. Proportional value refers to value relative to other things and thus involves price, comparison, and implicitly mixing with other things. Things that can be compared but not priced can be ranked. Thus, in some frames of reference, Jesus can be ranked more highly than the saints, Allah more highly than jinn, celibacy more highly than marriage, the aristocracy more highly than the bourgeoisie, Brahmins more highly than Kshatriyas, and so on. Even when things cannot be priced, mixed, or compared, Graeber points out that "there is still the difference between having them (or otherwise being identified with them) and not."[13] So, for example, in the wake of the California Supreme Court decision allowing same sex couples to marry, Pope Benedict XVI stated

---

[13] David Graeber, *Toward an Anthropological Theory of Value: The False Coin of Our Own Dreams* (New York: Palgrave, 2001), 75.

that heterosexual marriage should not be confused with or compared to
other types of unions, thus setting heterosexual marriage apart as special. Although the Pope held up heterosexual marriage as unique and
incommensurate, people must still decide whether to hold to or identify
with this value or not.[14]

Much of the complexity that surrounds the setting apart of objects
applies as well to the setting apart of things such as behaviors, experiences, and events. Thus, a society's symbolic inventory is not limited
to tangible places, structures, and objects, but may also include events,
experiences, and ideas that may be recounted in narratives and embodied
in beliefs. These more ephemeral things, like objects, may be set apart
as singularities or placed on a level with other events, experiences, and
behaviors. As is the case with objects, the value of the thing set apart in
this way does not have to be positive; things with an infinitely negative
value – for example, things that are evil or absolutely disgusting – may
also be set apart. Some people, for example, set apart the Holocaust as
a uniquely horrifying event that cannot be compared to other events
without compromising it.[15]

Although singularity may seem to inhere in certain events and
experiences, here too things often pass from one status to the other and
back, whether in the minds of individuals or within or between groups.
Thus, while adherents understand key events as singular (for example,
the giving of the tablets to Moses on Mount Sinai, the revelation of
the Qur'an through the Prophet Muhammad, the Incarnation of God in
Christ, or the Enlightenment of the Buddha), competing traditions and
secular methods of study can and do cast them in terms that effectively
desingularize them and make them more ordinary. As with singular
objects, we can expect to find that other sorts of singularities are also
bound up with matters of identity and that they can be transmitted (or
circulated) in ways that preserve that identity more or less intact or in
ways that alienate them from meanings that people have ascribed to
them in the past. Thus, people are more likely to recount events they
consider singular as narratives and reenact them in rituals than to
use historical, critical methods to study them alongside other similar
events. Competing notions of how past events should be remembered

14 Philip E. Tetlock, "Thinking the Unthinkable: Sacred Values and Taboo Cognitions.
Trends in Cognitive Science 7, 7 (2003): 320–4; Graeber, *Toward an Anthropological
Theory of Value.*
15 Edward T. Linenthal, "Locating Holocaust Memory: The United States Holocaust
Memorial Museum," in *American Sacred Space,* ed. Chidester and Linenthal,
220–61.

can lead to intense controversy over how memories should be enshrined in memorials, as was the case, for example, with the Holocaust Museum in Washington, D.C.[16]

In light of this expanded understanding of the ways things can be set apart, we can interpret the *sui generis* approach to religion as one that sets religion apart and protects it with taboos. In asserting that religion is *sui generis*, advocates of this approach assert their belief that religion is inherently special. The disciplinary axiom that prohibits "reducing" religion to something else protects religion from comparison with *nonreligious* things and from explanations that cast it in *nonreligious* terms. Thus, those who view religion as *sui generis* set it apart from other objects of study and protect it – typically without any further justification – from profanation by means of the taboo against reductionism.

When people set something apart and protect its specialness with prohibitions against selling, trading, mixing, or comparing it with ordinary things, they assume that violating those prohibitions will cause something bad to happen. Narrowly conceived, this assumption leads people to fear that human violation of the taboo will make the special thing ordinary; broadly conceived, the assumption leads them to fear that breaking the taboo will cause everything the special thing represents to collapse (that is, specific relationships and, by extension, potentially the whole social and cosmic order). In the case of the *sui generis* approach to religion, scholars seem to fear that violating the taboo against reductionism will destroy "religion" or at least deprive it of its specialness. If religion is not special and set apart, this in turn may lead some to question the need for special departments devoted to its study and thus, by extension, threaten the "cosmic order" of the university (or at least a small corner of the humanities). These fears, however, presuppose a binary relationship between special/ordinary analogous to Durkheim's binary opposition between sacred and profane. If special and ordinary are viewed on a continuum, violation of a taboo might simply make a very special thing a little less special without necessarily making it ordinary.

If violating taboos causes things to happen, so too does setting things apart, as Durkheim recognized, configuring social relations in certain ways. When a woman sets apart a particular infant as hers, she constitutes a mother-child bond between herself and that infant. Should she violate the taboo against exchanging her infant for any other infant,

---

[16] Linenthal, "Locating Holocaust Memory," 220–61.

she violates the taboo that sets her infant apart from all other infants and destroys the mother-child bond between them. Violating the taboo that sets the thing apart thus does more than make the thing in question "profane," it also destroys the singular relationship between the thing and those who set it apart. The thing set apart can play an entirely passive role in this process and thus does not need to be an agent in its own right. The only agency required is that of the individual or group that sets something apart and observes the taboos surrounding it. In doing so, the ones setting the thing apart constitute the thing as special and constitute their own special relationship with the thing. If the ones who set the thing apart violate the taboo associated with the special thing, they allow it to become an ordinary thing and cause their special relationship with that particular thing to disappear.

Whether we view specialness as inherent in some things or as ascribed to them, it would appear that the tendency to set some things apart as special is a deeply rooted human characteristic. Although there has not been a great deal of attention given to the biological foundations of specialness as such, some researchers have suggested that the inviolability of sacred things is rooted in relationships (for example, parent-child, mate, or leader-follower) that are essential to the formation and stability of groups (such as family, herd, or tribe). If this is correct, it would suggest that the ability to set things apart is not simply a human characteristic but a mammalian one rooted in the mother-infant bond and extended by some mammals to relationships between mating pairs and hierarchical relations between leaders and followers.[17] If, as this line of reasoning suggests, the idea of set-apartness is implicit in relationships common to primates and other mammals, then we can assume that it is extended by analogy both to objects and linguistic abstractions that are linked in some way to relationships, whether these are basic relationships or more complex ones.

Within such a theoretical framework, one expects that people would not only view some relationships as inviolable but that they would also ascribe more value to objects or abstractions associated with inviolable

[17] For theorists who root the inviolability of sacred things in relations, see, in addition to Durkheim, *Elementary Forms*, James W. Dow, "A Scientific Definition of Religion," *Anpere: Anthropological Perspectives on Religion*, online at http://www. anpere.net/2007/2.pdf, 8 (accessed 25 May 2011); Graeber, *Toward an Anthropological Theory of Value*, 521; Lee A. Kirkpatrick, *Attachment, Evolution, and the Psychology of Religion* (New York: Guilford Press, 2005), 246–7. On the creation of mother-infant bonds in animals and their extension to other social relations, see Jaak Panksepp, *Affective Neuroscience: The Foundations of Human and Animal Emotions* (New York: Oxford University Press, 1998), 246–60.

relationships than to those with no such associations. This enhancement of value is evident in what economists refer to as the "endowment effect," which refers to the tendency of people to attribute a higher price to an object they have been given than to an identical object they could purchase in a store. In a series of experiments, researchers found that the disparity increased dramatically (from 2:1 to 8:1) when the objects in question were acquired via communal or family rituals. Moreover, when the objects were acquired from intimate partners, people were often unwilling to assign any price to them at all.[18] Although further research on this is needed, it may be that the value of the things that people set apart in this way is derived directly or indirectly from relationships that humans as a species need to survive and which, for that reason, people tend to view as inviolable.

IV. TYPES OF SPECIALNESS

In the discussion thus far, we have looked at specialness as a function of value, such that singular things are things whose value cannot be specified relative to other things. Value is not the only way to think about specialness, however. As a formal feature of specialness, it tells us more about the form that specialness takes (its set-apartness) than about specialness per se. Now we need to consider whether there are some types of things that are more likely to be considered special than others. Are there characteristic features that tend to make some things stand out as special regardless of whether people consider them so special that they set them apart with prohibitions? While this is ultimately a matter for empirical research, we can further such efforts by distinguishing between two logically distinct types of singularity: ideal things and anomalous things. We can locate both on continua from the ordinary to the special and consider what happens when people consider them so special that they set them apart and protect them with prohibitions.

IV.1. Ideal things
Let us begin by considering things that stand out as special because they seem ideal, perfect, or complete. They may stand out in this way in a relative sense or, if they are thought to approach an ultimate horizon or limit, they may signal an ideal in an absolute sense. As absolutes,

---

[18] For a summary of this research, see Philip E. Tetlock, "Thinking the Unthinkable: Sacred Values and Taboo Cognitions," *Trends in Cognitive Science* 7, 7 (2003): 320–4.

they are no longer on a continuum with limited things, however special such things might be, but are fully set apart. Many of the qualities that we use to designate something as special – for example, true, real, good, beautiful, pure, natural, or bad – can be transformed into absolutes. English speakers often turn these qualities into absolutes by nominalizing and capitalizing them. Thus, for example, "beautiful" may be used to designate a flower as special ("a beautiful flower") or transformed into an absolute by nominalizing and capitalizing it as "Beauty." Many other qualities that we use to mark things as special can be turned into absolutes in the same way, including Transcendence, the Infinite, Reality, Truth, Good, Evil, Purity, Perfection, Nature, and Ground of Being. The language of specialness and things set apart thus allows us to distinguish between terms that designate something as special (for example, beautiful) and terms that set things apart as absolutes (Beauty, for example).

The language of specialness and things set apart also allows us to sidestep the question of whether an absolute, such as "Beauty," is a philosophical or a religious concept in order to focus on the features that distinguish it as an absolute from a quality that simply marks something as special. The chief feature of the fully set-apart absolute, I want to suggest, is its (postulated) existence apart from human perception and imagination. If we describe a flower as beautiful, we perceive a quality in the flower and mark the flower as special – in this case, beautiful. If the perceived beauty of the flower evokes a response in us and we attribute the flower's ability to evoke this response to Beauty manifesting itself in the flower, then we have transformed a perceived quality into an absolute. If people believe that an absolute exists in itself, they can search for it, cultivate it, recognize it, respond to it, and attribute causality to it. People can conceive of an absolute, in other words, that exists in itself (is not created by them) and causes things to happen in a purely passive sense (without intentional agency).

Alternatively, people may view themselves as creating something in which the absolute can manifest itself. Thus, for example, artists often create things that they and others consider beautiful. Even though everyone acknowledges that artists create works of art, artists and others may feel that the standards of beauty used to judge their work are absolute. Wassily Kandinsky, for example, characterized the artist as the "priest of beauty." Beauty was to be sought in "the principle of the inner need," which springs from the soul, and allows for the "ever-advancing expression of the eternal and objective in terms of the periodic and subjective."[19] Here beauty as eternal and objective is fully set apart from the periodic and subjective even though it is expressed through it.

Philosopher Owen Flanagan's recent attempt to articulate a non-dualistic, nontheistic spirituality oriented toward good, truth, and beauty rejects what I am calling fully set-apart absolutes in favor of absolutes that are not completely set apart from the ordinary, natural world. While Plato's unchanging Forms (such as the Good, the True, and the Beautiful) are fully set apart from the flux and change of the material world, Flanagan recasts the Platonic ideals in light of his scientific, evolutionary perspective as natural goals toward which humans orient themselves. As such, they are not fully set apart from the natural, but nonetheless still partake functionally of the character of absolutes by virtue of a human desire for transcendence and a human ability to imagine absolutes.[20]

Flanagan suggests that these ideals are the outgrowth of a natural disposition to make sense of things, which he roots in the evolution of the moral emotions. Although still at a preliminary stage, research on emotions – both the primary emotions common to all animals and the more elaborated moral emotions shared to some degree by primates and humans – is potentially suggestive in this regard. Thus, for example, Jonathan Haidt and others upend the Platonic view of reason as ruler of the passions and identify five affective foundations, each with separate evolutionary origins, upon which they believe human cultures construct moral communities. These psychological foundations, they argue, give rise to intuitions having to do with harm and fairness; in-group and out-group dynamics and loyalty; social hierarchy, authority, and deference; and bodily defilement and purity.[21] Their research suggests that all of these moral intuitions can be caught up in culturally divergent processes of meaning making and formulated as absolutes.

Haidt and others have also argued for a family of awe-related emotions, which they suggest are evoked by a sense of vastness that cannot readily be accommodated within existing frames of meaning. Vastness

---

[19] Wassily Kandinsky, *Concerning the Spiritual in Art* (Boston: Museum of Fine Art, 2006), 63, 40.

[20] Owen Flanagan, *The Really Hard Problem: Meaning in a Material World* (Cambridge, MA: Massachusetts Institute of Technology Press, 2007), 39–44, 187.

[21] Flanagan, *The Really Hard Problem*, 197–8; Jonathan Haidt, "The Moral Emotions," in *Handbook of Affective Sciences*, ed. R. J. Davidson, K. R. Scherer, and H. H. Goldsmith (Oxford: Oxford University Press, 2003), 852–70; Jonathan Haidt, "The New Synthesis in Moral Psychology," *Science* 316 (2007): 998–1002.

can take various forms and can be elicited by powerful individuals, nature, and art. In a more recent study, Michelle Shiota, Dacher Keltner, and Amanda Mossman found that awe is elicited by a heterogeneous set of experiences, the most common of which are experiences of natural beauty, artistic beauty, and exemplary or exceptional human actions or abilities.[22]

Although Flanagan attempts to locate a capacity for transcendence, defined as a latent capacity for meaning making, at the level of the moral emotions, it may be that the urge to make sense of things is rooted more basically than that. Focusing on primary rather than moral emotions, neuropsychologists Jaak Panksepp and Douglas Watt identify two basic clusters of emotions (a social connection cluster and an organism defense cluster), as well as a "seeking system" that drives organisms to engage with other living things in order to meet their essential emotional and biological needs. Flanagan's notion of transcendence might have its biological roots in something like Panksepp's "seeking system."[23]

IV.2. Anomalous things

Anomalies are things that people consider special because they are strange or unusual or in some way violate people's ordinary expectations. Whether people consider something anomalous may be highly contextually dependent or it may not. With naturally occurring events, such as hurricanes or earthquakes, geography plays a part in shaping what people consider anomalous. What might seem anomalous to people in California (hurricanes) would not seem so strange to people in Florida. Some experiences, such as spirit possession, may be considered strange or unusual in one culture but not in another. Comparisons across time, culture, and species can help us to identify things that are widely perceived as anomalous and things that people perceive as anomalous only in particular contexts.

[22] Jonathan Haidt, "The Positive Emotion of Elevation. *Prevention and Treatment*, 3, 3 (2000): 1–5; Dacher Keltner and Jonathan Haidt, "Approaching Awe, a Moral, Spiritual, and Aesthetic Emotion," *Cognition and Emotion* 17, 2 (2003): 297–314; Michelle N. Shiota, Dacher Keltner, and Amanda Mossman, "The Nature of Awe: Elicitors, Appraisals, and Effects on Self-Concept," *Cognition and Emotion* 21, 5 (2007): 944–63.

[23] Panksepp, *Affective Neuroscience*, 144–63; Jaak Panksepp, "Affective Consciousness," in *The Blackwell Companion to Consciousness*, ed. Max Velmans and Susan Schneider (Malden, MA: Blackwell, 2007), 114–29; Douglas Watt, "Toward a Neuroscience of Empathy: Integrating Affective and Cognitive Perspectives," *Neuro-Psychoanalysis* 9, no. 2 (2007): 119–72; Douglas Watt, "Attachment Mechanisms and the Bridging of Science and Religion," in *Ways of Knowing: Science and Mysticism Today*, ed. Chris Clarke (Charlottesville, VA: Imprint Academic, 2005), 70–89.

As with our discussion of ideal things, we can consider anomalous things as special, locating them somewhere on a continuum from ordinary to very special, without necessarily considering them so special that they are set apart with taboos against comparison. In discussing anomalous things, we can further distinguish between anomalous things (whether events, places, objects, or experiences) that do not involve anomalous agents and anomalous experiences (that is, perceptions, sensations, or feelings) that suggest the presence of an unusual agent. We can begin with anomalous things that do not involve anomalous agents since they are similar in many ways to ideal things. Here, as in the case of ideal things, we have things – whether events, places, objects, or experiences – with anomalous characteristics that cause them to stand out. Their anomalous characteristics attract people's attention and make it more likely that people will consider them special. Just as qualities associated with ideal things can be absolutized and set apart, so too qualities associated with anomalous things can be reified and set apart.

People often use the terms "mystical" and "spiritual" to mark events, places, objects, or experiences as very special and, depending on what they mean by the terms, sometimes to signal that they consider the thing in question so special that it cannot or should not be compared to other, less special things. People may use these terms to mark things as belonging to another realm or manifesting a different sort of energy or exemplifying a higher aspect of reality that is not just special, but so special that it cannot be compared to more ordinary things.

We can take as an example the anomalous experience in which the boundary between self and world seems to dissolve. Most people would probably consider such an experience unusual and thus special to some degree. Some philosophers of religion characterize such experiences as mystical and in so doing mark them as very special, tacitly asserting that they cannot or should not be compared with experiences that are not viewed as such.[24] Viewed in this way, mystical or spiritual refers to qualities that manifest themselves in (anomalous) things; people recognize and respond to these qualities as existing apart from themselves, even when they are manifest through their own bodies. Insofar as these qualities are not considered agents, neither the mystical nor the spiritual acts intentionally. Insofar as people believe that they can be manifest in themselves and other things, however, they can search for them, cultivate them, recognize them, respond to them, and attribute

---

[24] See, for example, Caroline Franks Davis, *The Evidential Force of Religious Experience* (Oxford: Oxford University Press, 1989), 176–7, 190–1, 233.

causality to them in a passive sense, without viewing themselves as creating them. When they respond to such qualities, people believe they respond because the qualities exist apart from themselves and have the power to passively elicit a response in them.

Although anomalous events, places, objects, and experiences characterized as mystical or spiritual are not experiences *of* an agent, people may still attribute them *to* an agent, if they believe that there are agents who can and do cause such things to occur. We can distinguish, in other words, between things that are attributed to the action of an agent, that is, things people believe were caused by an agent, and feelings, sensations, and perceptions *suggestive of agency*. In the first instance, an agent is presumed to exist and something is attributed to the presumed agent based on people's knowledge of or beliefs about the agent in question. In the second instance, we have feelings, sensations, and perceptions that are suggestive of agency. On the basis of this type of experience and the beliefs they hold about it, people may postulate the presence of an agent to whom they *then* can attribute the power to act and effect things.

We can extend this distinction between agents and suggestions of agency to situations in which people postulate the presence of anomalous agents and report feelings, sensations, or perceptions suggestive of anomalous agency.[25] Claims regarding the actions of anomalous agents presuppose their existence and are based on what people believe such agents are likely to do. Claims of the second sort can and do exist apart from beliefs about the existence of anomalous beings. Beliefs about

---

[25] As is generally so in the case of anomalies, some kinds of agents may be widely perceived as anomalous and others as anomalous only in particular contexts. Cognitive scientists of religion, who have focused attention on beings of this sort, use the concept of "counterintuitiveness" to identify anomalies that that they think humans recognize as such across cultures. This concept is premised on the discovery that regardless of culture, people divide things into the basic categories of persons, animals, plants, natural objects, and tools. These researchers describe something as counterintuitive when it includes features that violate the characteristics that humans normally associate with these basic categories. Counterintuitive agents, in this view, are constructed through the reshuffling of attributes in ways that modestly violate what we are naturally prepared to expect. Pascal Boyer, *Religion Explained: The Evolutionary Origins of Religious Thought* (New York: Basic, 2001); Justin L. Barrett, "Coding and Quantifying Counterintuitiveness in Religious Concepts: Theoretical and Methodological Reflections," *Method and Theory in the Study of Religion* 20, 4 (2008): 308–38. Based on this research, things can become counterintuitive agents in one of two ways: agents (i.e., persons and other animates) can acquire some counterintuitive property (minds without bodies, omniscience, etc.), or nonagents (i.e., spatial entities, solid objects, and things that do not appear to be self propelled) can acquire attributes of humans or other animates (e.g., the ability to talk, feel, move, or think) and, thus, the ability to act as agents.

anomalous agents often play a considerable role in determining whether experiences suggestive of anomalous agency are transformed into claims about the presence of anomalous agents.

The movement from *suggestions of anomalous agency* to *postulated anomalous agents* is a key step on the continuum of specialness. Thus, anomalous experiences suggestive of agency are likely to be considered special, but not exceedingly so as long as the suggestions of agency are not taken to be signs of the actual presence of an anomalous agent. Thus, for example, most people would consider a vivid experience of an unseen "felt presence" as unusual and thus to some degree special. Some philosophers of religion characterize such experiences as numinous and in so doing mark them as very special.[26] Although some people might view the experience as, say, a hallucination, we can assume that in many cases the *feeling* of presence (the intimations of agency) will be attributed to the *actual* presence of an invisible agent. In such cases, the assumed presence of a real entity that is capable of performing intended actions would lead most people to consider the experience more unusual and thus more special. When people interpret feelings, perceptions, or sensations that are suggestive of agency as evidence of the presence of an actual agent, they attribute the experience to an external source.

People will in turn consider signs of the actual presence of an anomalous agent more or less special depending on the beliefs they hold about them. If people believe in the existence of anomalous agents, such as spirits, ancestors, ghosts, demons, fairies, and deities, then the specialness of signs of the actual presence of an anomalous agent will depend on which agent is presumed to be present and how special that agent is considered to be. People clearly do not consider all anomalous agents so special that they set them apart with taboos. If the unseen presence were thought to be a ghost, people would not consider it nearly as special as if it were thought to be a divinity.

Responses to Bernadette's vision of Mary illustrate the role of beliefs about anomalous agents in determining how special people consider an event to be. Devout Catholics considered the apparition to Bernadette very special not only because it was Mary who appeared, but also because she referred to herself as the "Immaculate Conception." In doing so, she confirmed Pope Pius IX's definition of the doctrine of the Immaculate Conception, promulgated in 1854, and contributed to the general mystique (or aura of specialness) surrounding the papacy in the run-up to the declaration of papal infallibility in 1870. Skeptics,

---

[26] Davis, *The Evidential Force of Religious Experience*, 176–7, 190–1, 233.

however, viewed the apparition as a hallucination. In the eyes of the latter, it was still anomalous, in the sense that waking hallucinations are somewhat unusual, but not particularly special.[27]

Scholars have developed several theories to explain the widespread crosscultural tendency to postulate the existence of anomalous (or, more technically, counterintuitive) agents, all of which have been derived from experimental research into the workings of the human mind viewed in an evolutionary perspective. Of these theories, which are complementary, two are cognitive and the third is affective. The first cognitive explanation theorizes that human beings ascribe counterintuitive agent-related properties to objects because they have a basic tendency to overattribute agency, particularly in situations of ambiguity. These theorists speculate that this tendency to attribute agency so capaciously has evolutionary adaptive value. When leaves rustle, for example, it is a better bet to assume that an unseen predator is lurking than to assume it is just the wind and thus risk getting eaten.[28]

The second cognitive explanation, which emerges out of developmental psychology, suggests that humans are readily able to conceive of agents (spirits, souls, deities, ancestors, ghosts) without bodies or agents who inhabit others' bodies because we naturally distinguish between objects (bodies) and persons. Whatever a consistent metaphysics might suggest, the default mode for human beings, according to this research, is an intuitive or commonsense dualism grounded in two parallel, weakly integrated cognitive systems for perceiving bodies (objects) and persons. These cognitive characteristics predispose people to postulate counterintuitive agents, especially in contexts in which ambiguous stimuli and cultural presuppositions would support such conclusions.[29]

These cognitive dispositions can be grounded in turn in affective dynamics, including attachment processes, kinship relations, and hierarchical relations of dominance and subordination that are common to most primates. Veneration of ancestors, which is found is nearly all

---

[27] Thomas A. Kselman, *Miracles and Prophecies in Nineteenth-Century France* (New Brunswick, NJ: Rutgers University Press, 1983), 92–4; Zimdars-Swartz, *Encountering Mary*, 55–67; Harris, *Lourdes*, 91–109.

[28] Boyer, *Religion Explained*, 137–67; Justin L. Barrett, *Why Would Anyone Believe in God?* (Walnut Creek, CA: AltaMira Press, 2004); Scott Atran and Ara Norenzayan, "Religion's Evolutionary Landscape: Counterintuition, Commitment, Compassion, Communion," *Behavioral and Brain Sciences* 27, 6 (2004): 713–70.

[29] Paul Bloom, *Descartes' Baby: How the Science of Child Development Explains What Makes Us Human* (New York: Basic, 2004); Emma Cohen, "What Is Spirit Possession? Defining, Comparing, and Explaining Two Possession Forms," *Ethnos: Journal of Anthropology* 73, 1 (2008): 101–26.

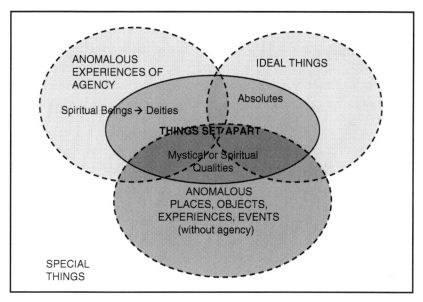

Figure 3.1. Various kinds of special things.

cultures, may build on a combination of cognitive and affective processes to extend the attachments that individuals have with parents or other close kin believed to live on as unseen agents after their death.[30]

I can sum up this discussion of special things diagrammatically. The box shown in Figure 3.1 represents the set of all special things. I have discussed two kinds of things that are often considered special (ideal things and anomalous things) and have distinguished between anomalous agents and anomalous things that lack agency. In each case, I suggested that these special things fall along continua of specialness ranging from the ordinary to the very special, with some things considered so special that they are set apart and protected by taboos. In the diagram, spiritual beings run the gamut from moderately to very special, with deities offered as examples of anomalous agents that may be considered so special that they are set apart and protected by taboos; absolutes are offered as a generic descriptor of ideal things that tend to be set apart, and mystical and spiritual as qualities that can be ascribed to anomalous things lacking agency in order to set them apart. The potential overlap between these things in practice is represented schematically by the overlap between the circles, such that, for example,

---

[30] Kirkpatrick, *Attachment*, 247–8; Lyle B. Steadman, Craig T. Palmer, and Christopher F. Tilley, "The Universality of Ancestor Worship," *Ethnology* 35, 1 (1996): 63–76.

deities (agents) with ideal properties and mystical characteristics are represented at the center of the diagram.

Whether people ascribe specialness to things consciously or unconsciously, the specialness of the thing is usually evanescent unless steps are taken to preserve it. The absolute may manifest in something, but only those who are there will know it. A spiritual being may cause an event, but again, only those who are there will witness it. If the thing or event is deemed so special that it is set apart and protected by taboos, its set-apartness makes it impossible for people to engage with it in ordinary ways. Something more is needed if people want to engage with these evanescent and/or set-apart things on a more continuous basis.

V. WAYS OF ENGAGING SPECIAL THINGS: SIMPLE VERSUS COMPOSITE ASCRIPTIONS

In the discussion so far, I have been envisioning special things as elementary phenomena standing on their own. Individuals or groups, however, can also incorporate special things into more elaborate formations that provide means for people to engage them on a more regular or continuous basis. These in effect institutionalize the special things, which in this way take on the formal characteristics that in some contexts we associate with religions or spiritualities. Simple ascriptions of specialness as such are not *religions* or *spiritualities*, but rather the basic building blocks that people use to construct them.

Without implying that this is the only way that simple ascriptions are taken up into more complex formations, I want to suggest that the *path* is a basic concept that individuals and groups routinely use to transform religious ascriptions into protoreligions and spiritualities. Scholars from disparate disciplines have suggested the utility of the notion of the path in thinking about religions.[31] Drawing on the path concept, we can distinguish between *special things* and *special paths*, where special paths are defined as sets of practices that individuals or groups view as effective in attaining goals associated with special things.

The idea of a path implies both a goal and a means of getting to the goal. In contrast to the simple ascriptions already discussed, the idea

---

[31] See, for example, Robert E. Buswell and Robert M. Gimello, eds., *Paths to Liberation: The Marga and Its Transformations in Buddhist Thought* (Honolulu: University of Hawaii Press, 1992), 2–3; and Kenneth I. Pargament and Annette Mahoney, "Sacred Matters: Sanctification as a Vital Topic for the Psychology of Religion," *International Journal for the Psychology of Religion* 15, 3 (2005): 179–98.

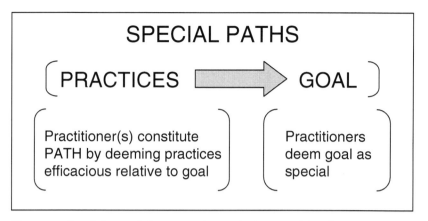

Figure 3.2. Breakdown of the composite ascription: special paths.

of the path contains two ascriptions, one associated with the goal and the other with the means of getting to the goal. Practitioners deem the goal toward which the path aims as special in one or more of the basic ways already discussed, that is, by association with things set apart, spiritual beings, or limitless absolutes. For a path to be a path, however, practitioners must also agree on *means* that they consider efficacious for getting from where they are to the goal. We can characterize the means of getting to the goal – the things people can do to get there – as practices. The distinctive feature of a path is the linkage between the practices and the goal; this linkage is constituted when people ascribe efficacy to practices relative to a goal. When the goal of a path has to do with special things, the path incorporates the simple ascription into a composite formation made up of two ascriptions. The first ascription deems the path – or more specifically, the goal toward which the path leads – as special. The second ascribes efficacy to practices in relation to the goal (see Figure 3.2).

The linkage that the practices constitute between the starting point and the goal may vary depending on the way the starting point is conceived, the nature of the special thing, and the way that practitioners want to engage it. If the special thing is set apart and protected by prohibitions, the practices will need to allow for engagement while at the same time maintaining the prohibitions that set the thing apart as special. If the special thing is an event associated with one or more spiritual beings, the practices may re-create the event or otherwise allow for reengagement with the spiritual being. If the special thing is an absolute, the practices may prepare things (humans, animals, places, objects, and so on) to manifest the absolute. However the practices constitute the linkage between the point of origin and the goal, practitioners must agree that that the practices are capable of doing so, that is, that they are efficacious.

The path concept, with its source-path-goal structure, highlights the explicitly stated goals of practitioners and the means they view as effective for achieving them. It provides us with a basic schema for analyzing more complex behaviors from the point of view of practitioners. We can contrast it with definitions that highlight indirect effects that subjects most likely would not view as the goal or purpose of their behavior. Thus, for example, when Durkheim defines "a religion" as "a unified system of beliefs and practices ... which unite into one single moral community called a Church, all those who adhere to" those beliefs and practices, he identifies an indirect effect of performing practices relative to sacred things.[32] While this is an important effect, people normally do not hold to beliefs and perform practices in order to unite themselves into a single moral community; they hold the beliefs because they think they are true and perform the actions because they think they will achieve some goal.

VI. CONCLUSION: A BUILDING-BLOCK APPROACH

Things that strike people as special are (among) the basic building blocks of religion. Things that stand out as ideal or anomalous tend to draw people's attention and so are more likely to be considered special. Ascriptions of specialness may take place below the threshold of awareness; when this happens, it tends to make things seem inherently special. People can decide, upon reflection, that things that seem special are more or less special than they initially seemed. In the process of reflection, special things may be caught up in preexisting systems of belief and practice, may generate new or modified beliefs and practices, or may lose their specialness and become ordinary. Whether people consider a special thing as (say) religious, mystical, magical, superstitious, spiritual, ideological, or secular will depend on the preexisting systems of belief and practice, the web of concepts related to specialness, and the way that people position themselves in a given context.

Why do humans singularize? I have suggested that the basic tendency is rooted in the special relationships that humans and perhaps some other animals need to survive. If that is the case, we may be biologically primed to see some things as special. Obviously, however,

[32] Durkheim, *Elementary Forms*, 44.

humans have elaborated this tendency in complex ways, infusing this biological priming with sociocultural particularities that may enhance or undercut them. Thus, we are quite capable of deciding upon reflection that something that seems special is not really so special after all and to experience some things as special for us, even if they are not for others. Indeed, the very idea of specialness suggests that what each of us considers special (for example, my child, my country) strikes us as inherently more special than the things others consider special, even if we know rationally that that is not the case.

The tendency to singularize may be primal, but it is not limited to small-scale societies. Both small-scale and complex societies manifest tensions between special things and commodities and incorporate special things into more elaborate formations so they can be engaged on a regular basis. The crucial difference between the two types of societies, according to Kopytoff, is the vast proliferation of competing schemes of valuation and singularization in complex societies.[33] The challenge for researchers, particularly in studying more complex societies, thus lies in deciding how to cut into this vast proliferation of competing schemes in order to further their own research agenda. Disaggregating "religion" into special things and special paths, each of which can be specified in particular ways, is intended as a strategy that will allow us to design research projects that probe the innumerable competing schemes of valuation and singularization in complex societies in more precise ways and, we may hope, with more cumulative effect. The various ways in which people singularize things and under some circumstances incorporate them into more elaborate formations give researchers many options when setting up an object of study.

If specialness strikes others as a plausible generic framework within which to consider culture-specific webs of religion-like concepts, this idea could be tested and further refined historically and crossculturally. I have identified several marks of specialness – prohibitions against trading, mixing, and comparing – and two types of things likely to be considered special: ideal things and anomalous things. I hope that scholars will continue to refine these marks and types and add others as needed to reflect what they find in various contexts. In the process, we should try to distinguish between culturally specific distinctions and underlying types of distinctions that may reflect basic affective and cognitive processes common to humans and perhaps to other animals as well. Scientists, borrowing a culinary metaphor, speak of carving various

---

[33] Kopytoff, "Cultural Biography," 79–80.

domains (such as linguistics and biology) at their joints, by which they mean making conceptual distinctions that reflect underlying evolutionary and developmental processes and which are, in that sense, nonarbitrary. By comparing the way humans across time and cultures identify and mark things as special and by extending our comparisons, where relevant, to other species, we may find ways to carve specialness at its joints. In doing so, we would dramatically refine our understanding of one of the building blocks commonly used to create what we think of as religions or spiritualities.

This building-block approach has several implications for scholars of religion in departments of religion or religious studies. First, I don't think we need to worry so much about defining "religion." I think we can simply consider it an abstraction that many use to allude to webs of overlapping concepts that vary from language to language and culture to culture. I have suggested that the concepts that we (as scholars) associate with these webs are associated with things that people view as special and often, but not always, connect with special beliefs and special practices. Conceiving of "religion" in this way allows scholars to examine what things people consider special and how they position them in relation to these webs of concepts. Second, I don't think scholars of religion have a monopoly on special things, since there are lots of special things that do not have religion-like connotations, but I think it is quite possible that the more special people consider something to be, the more likely they and others are to place it under some religion-like heading (for example, religious, sacred, magical, superstitious, and so on). If that is the case, departments of religious studies might want to conceive of themselves as loci for studying special things and the ways people incorporate them into and perpetuate them by means of larger sociocultural formations, such as religious traditions, spiritual disciplines, and other assorted paths. An underlying focus on specialness and processes of singularization would not provide religious studies with an exclusive franchise, but rather with a focus on processes that are integral to and exemplified in the formation of religions and spiritualities and, at the same time, extend well beyond them. A focus on such processes would provide a bridge to other disciplines across the humanities and the sciences.

Select Bibliography

Atran, Scott and Ara Norenzayan. "Religion's Evolutionary Landscape: Counterintuition, Commitment, Compassion, Communion." *Behavioral and Brain Sciences* 27, 6 (2004): 713–70.

Barrett, Justin L. *Why Would Anyone Believe in God?* Walnut Creek, CA: AltaMira Press, 2004.

Boyer, Pascal. *Religion Explained: The Evolutionary Origins of Religious Thought.* New York: Basic, 2001.

Davis, Caroline Franks. *The Evidential Force of Religious Experience.* Oxford: Oxford University Press, 1989.

Flanagan, Owen. *The Really Hard Problem: Meaning in a Material World.* Cambridge, MA: Massachusetts Institute of Technology Press, 2007.

Kirkpatrick, Lee A. *Attachment, Evolution, and the Psychology of Religion.* New York: Guilford Press, 2005.

Pargament, Kenneth I. and Annette Mahoney. "Sacred Matters: Sanctification as a Vital Topic for the Psychology of Religion." *International Journal for the Psychology of Religion* 15, 3 (2005): 179–98.

Tetlock, Philip E. "Thinking the Unthinkable: Sacred Values and Taboo Cognitions." *Trends in Cognitive Science* 7, 7 (2003): 320–4.

Tetlock, Philip E., Orie V. Kristel, S. Beth Elson, Melanie C. Green, and Jennifer S. Lerner. "The Psychology of the Unthinkable: Taboo Trade-offs, Forbidden Base Rates, and Heretical Counterfactuals." *Journal of Personality and Social Psychology* 78, 5 (2000): 853–70.

4 The problem of the holy

ROBERT A. ORSI

> Holiness is the great word in religion;
> it is even more essential than the notion of God.
>
> Nathan Söderblom[1]

> What is the subject of our thought? Experience! Nothing else!
> And if we lose the ground of experience then we get into all
> kinds of theories.
>
> Hannah Arendt[2]

I. INTRODUCTION

Many (not all) scholars of religion become restive sooner or later with
the simple sufficiency of explanations of religious phenomena and experiences in terms of the social and psychological. It is not that these
scholars of religion propose foregoing social explanations. It is that they
recognize that such accounts fall short of the realness of the phenomena
they purport to describe and explain in people's experience. And not just
this: social accounts that pretend to be exhaustive distort those experiences and diminish them, *precisely as* historical and cultural phenomena. Such explanations are empirically insufficient, in other words. The
famous epistemic "bracket" of religious studies, which is the practice of
setting aside questions about the ontological realness of religious phenomena as a condition of research – we are not interested in whether
or not the Blessed Mother *really* appeared to Bernadette at Lourdes, we

[1] Nathan Söderblom, "Holiness," in *Encyclopedia of Religion and Ethics*, ed. James
   Hastings (New York: Charles Scribner's Sons, 1914), vol. 4: 731–41; quote on 731.
[2] Hannah Arendt, "On Hannah Arendt," in *Hannah Arendt: The Recovery of the
   Public World*, ed. Melvyn A. Hill (New York: St. Martin's Press, 1979), 308.

Robert Ford Campany and Christine Helmer read earlier drafts of this chapter and gave me
the most helpful critical commentary. I also benefited from the coincidence of the preparation of this chapter with the invitation to offer a faculty seminar at the University of
Minnesota on method and theory in the study of religion. A particular note of gratitude in
this context is due to Professor Jeanne Kilde.

84

say, thus immediately making the seer into a psychotic – begins to seem false or inadequate. These scholars have witnessed something in their fieldwork or historical study, close to home and across the globe, which they want to name and without which theories of religion seem to be beside the point. They have seen, for example, how Jesus is a real figure in a Pentecostal woman's everyday experience, as real to her as the other people around her, as real as her kitchen table and her arthritis. She does not "believe in" Jesus. Jesus is present to her. Moreover, this woman's Jesus has an existence that is greater than the sum of her intentions, desires, needs, hopes, and fears, and that cannot be completely accounted for with reference to her social circumstances. He has a life of his own in her life.

Such criticism of the limits of the social or psychological explanations is not exclusive to scholars of religion. Contemporary historians, anthropologists, and psychologists share it as well. But given the special place that such explanations of religious phenomena – of biblical miracles, for example, the resurrection of Christ or religious visions and ecstasies – occupied in the very making of modern knowledge, scholars of religion confront these limits inescapably and with particular intimacy, anxiety, and urgency. Our struggle with them, as a result of this history, holds special promise for knowledge across the disciplines. It is here that the discipline of religious studies may make a distinctive theoretical contribution to modern ways of thinking about culture, self, and society.

The term most commonly associated with this apprehension of the really real in the discipline of religious studies is "the holy." But "the holy" has also been one of the most contentious concepts in the field and it is currently in disrepute. "The holy" has the musty smell of late nineteenth and early twentieth-century bourgeois European piety about it, of the canon's study and the don's lecture hall. It appears to be hopelessly entwined with highly technical Western philosophical debates and categories that mean little to anyone anymore. As it was developed at the turn of the twentieth century, moreover, the concept of "the holy" was implicated in the European ideology of Western superiority that underwrote the colonial project, because invariably the most perfect experience of the holy was judged to be the modern European Protestant Christian. In the contemporary academic context, the very aim of the holy as a concept – to name the really realness of religious phenomena independent of cultural and social coordinates – seems jejune.

Yes, but – the holy still seems to me to name both a reality and an approach to religion that scholars of religion ought to think about.

For one thing, people all over the world and in different historical periods have experienced something out of the ordinary in certain persons, places, or things, and they know what they mean, or enough of what they mean, to use the word "holy" (or one like it), even feel compelled to use it, as the only possible word for what they have experienced. This is the empirical warrant for continued interest in the term. "In whatever language they resound," the early twentieth-century theorist of the holy, Rudolf Otto, wrote, "these most exalted words [Hebrew *Kadosh*, Latin *Sanctus*, and Russian *Swiat* are the ones he mentions] that have ever come from human lips always grip one in the depths of the soul, with a mighty shudder exciting and calling into play the mystery of the other world latent therein."[3] The holy is apprehended as immediately and undeniably real. This is what people who have experienced the holy in different times and places report and this was Otto's understanding (working from these accounts and reflecting as well on his own experiences). People do not say "this seems holy to me," or, "we are told this is holy," nor is the holy taken as the sign of a reality that is elsewhere; it is not a metaphor or a symbol. The holy is here, in fact, before me, otherwise it is not holy. As American writer Flannery O'Connor replied to an acquaintance who had just remarked that a consecrated communion wafer, which O'Connor as a Catholic took to be the flesh and blood of Jesus Christ, is a symbol, "well, if it's a symbol, to hell with it."[4] The holy stands apart from the person experiencing it, as real as bread and blood and water. Contemporary pilgrims to the mouth of the Yamuna River in northern India told religious studies scholar David L. Haberman that they were there to have *darśan* (visual communion) of the goddess of the river, Yamuna-ji. They had come to a place made holy by the goddess, and were there to see her and to be seen by her. Scholars of religion in earlier times (and some still today) collected many such examples of the experience of the holy around the world.[5]

For another thing, rethinking the holy can contribute to the recovery of experience as a key category after years of its displacement in religious studies, as in other disciplines of the humanities and social sciences, by language, social structure, and power. With the (re)introduction of experience comes renewed interest in the agency of the subject

3 Quoted in Philip C. Almond, *Rudolf Otto: An Introduction to His Philosophical Theology* (Chapel Hill and London: University of North Carolina Press, 1984), 18.
4 Flannery O'Connor, "To A," Milledgeville, 16 December [19]55, in *Collected Works*, ed. Sally Fitzgerald (New York: Library of America, 1988), 977.
5 David L. Haberman, *River of Love in an Age of Pollution: The Yamuna River of Northern India* (Berkeley: University of California Press, 2006).

of experience, with issues of freedom, action, and limitations; in the multiple sources of experience, such as the imagination (collective and individual), memory, family contexts, emotions, and the unconscious, which are never simply identical to the world as it is given (in authorized versions of "reality," for example, in facts or in ordinary consciousness), and how these contribute to the making of the really real; and in the relational grounds of experience, including dimensions of intersubjectivity other than the verbal or the conscious (meaning touch, intuition, and the erotic in its most capacious meaning).

Was Otto's contemporary and fellow theorist of the holy Nathan Söderblom correct in thinking (as quoted in the epigraph to this chapter) that some notion of the holy is necessary for the study of religions? This remains to be seen. But the term has been so encrusted with meanings accreted over the past century in bitter and contentious debates that it requires reconsideration, even rehabilitation, before it can be used again. This is what I aim to do here, because to take up Söderblom's charge in a somewhat different spirit, I believe that the holy, reexamined, is potentially the opening to fresh questions, lines of research, and perspectives in the study of religion.

What follows is a discussion of the holy as it was developed by Otto and others at the turn of the twentieth century; a review of the major criticism of the concept; and a consideration of what a restored notion of the holy contributes to the analysis of religious phenomena. But I want to begin with the personal grounds of my own interest in the question, by way of clarifying the stakes of a debate that may otherwise seem abstract.

II. MY PROBLEM WITH THE HOLY

I spent a lot of time as a boy growing up in the Bronx in the company of an uncle who had cerebral palsy. Often I went along with him on outings organized by New York Catholic organizations with a special mission to "shut-ins" and "cripples," in the language of the time. The word "holy" was much in the mouths of the volunteers helping out on these days and of the priests in the sponsoring parishes, who found themselves unexpectedly standing before an unusual congregation of men and women with twisted limbs, who had difficulty speaking, and who needed assistance with the most basic life functions – eating, drinking, going to the bathroom. Cripples are holy people, the well-intentioned ambulatory announced to the "cripples," who nodded their heads but kept their thoughts mostly to themselves, although my uncle occasionally made his amusement at being cast in the role of holy object known to me by subtle signs. This is holy ground, the priests asserted, meaning the church hall now filled with cripples.[6] My uncle was looking forward to the cold beers piled in great sweating heaps in ice chests and the lunch we could smell cooking in the church cafeteria, but talk of the holy droned on and on.

What did "holy" mean in this context? Otto called the cruel torture and death of the innocent Jesus on Golgotha the holiest *fact* (his word and emphasis) in the world's history.[7] This great mystery of the cross marks physical distress, especially the suffering of the innocent, in a special way in Christian culture. Images of Jesus's broken body, of his weeping mother, and of martyrs with great raw and gaping wounds in their flesh surrounded us in the churches we visited on those days in the Bronx and established the repertoire of the holy. Talk of "holy" cripples drew on these associations. It is what made being close to crippled bodies so exciting. But if we step back from the immediacy of the event and its visual and theological context, we can see that "holy" was also the word for the uneasiness and embarrassment of the priests and the volunteers, many of whom were unaccustomed to being around people with disabilities, and for what they felt when they saw how much could go wrong with the human body. The word "holy" on these days was spoken with a dreadful combination of sentimentality, horror, titillation, awe, and disgust.

Moreover, the "holy" was a way of asserting control over my uncle and his friends, over their bodies. Being "holy" meant that they were not like the rest of us, that they did not have the same needs and desires we did, and so they did not have to be treated in the way we expect to be treated ourselves. They could be moved from here to there in their wheelchairs without being asked, for example, or they could be told they were done with lunch when they wanted to linger with their friends.

[6] I cannot use the more appropriate and acceptable term "persons with disabilities" here because it was the very sound of the word "cripple," with all its brutality, that evoked the power and presence of the holy. This discussion of my uncle's experience draws on "'Mildred, Is It Fun to Be a Cripple?' The Culture of Suffering in Mid-Twentieth Century American Catholicism," in *Between Heaven and Earth: The Religious Worlds People Make and the Scholars Who Study Them* (Princeton, NJ: Princeton University Press, 2005), 19–47.

[7] Rudolf Otto, *Religious Essays: A Supplement to the "Idea of the Holy,"* trans. Brian Lunn (London: Oxford University Press, 1931), 50; also *The Idea of the Holy: An Inquiry into the Non-Rational Factor in the Idea of the Divine and Its Relation to the Rational*, trans. John W. Harvey (London: Oxford University Press, 1923), 172–3. In the latter, Otto writes, "it is in the Passion and death of Christ that the objects of the strongest religious intuition must be sought" (172).

"Holy" especially meant that the cripples did not have sexual desires, so that "holy" also became the medium of denial. "Holy" made my uncle and his friends into freaks, unlike us, but in our control.

So "holy" and "holiness" are deeply suspect terms in my lexicon; the demythologization of these words in religious studies, which I discovered later in life, confirmed my childhood experiences with my uncle and his friends. When I hear someone or something called holy – when rich prelates or first world theologians declare that the poor are God's special people, or when adults say that children are especially gifted spiritually, I am on the lookout for domination, denial, and exploitation. "Holy" crowds out the lived realities of the people so designated, rendering them at once alien and empty, and preparing them to be filled up and possessed by the fantasies of the ones calling them "holy." "Holy" marks the limit of human empathy, identification, and justice. Figures designated "holy" have stopped being recognizably who they are in actuality. The sound of "holy" is the sound of the satisfaction of the complacent and powerful. In the context I am describing, "holy" is a term of appropriation and domination.

If all I knew was that the "holy" made my uncle and his friends into freaks or that it transformed the suffering and dying people on the streets of Benares into saints in the self-indulgent fantasies of Western pilgrims, there would be no "problem" of the holy. I would agree that it is a term to be deconstructed, despised, and dismissed. But calling my uncle and his friends "holy" was also a powerful antidote to the everyday cruelties inflicted on them in their homes and neighborhoods, even though it arose out of these cruelties. One of their southern Italian neighbors on New York's Lower East Side called my uncle a "diseased piece of meat" and demanded that my grandmother keep him off the building's stoop, where he liked to sit as a boy watching people go by. My uncle reported similar stories and worse about his friends, whose families beat and ridiculed them and hid them away in airless rooms in shame. Amid such realities, the ground designated "holy" was a place where my uncle and his friends could be free of violence and humiliation, at least temporarily, and find some respect, even if it came in dubious and questionable (to me) terms. Or if this seems too much, "holy" meant that my uncle and his friends were seen, that they were brought out into the world (these were outings away from home, after all), and that attention was paid to them, that they were acknowledged and called special. I have to admit that while my uncle seemed mostly amused or irritated on such occasions by the volunteers, he appeared to accept in an odd sort of way what was being said about him and his friends as his due, or at least as better than the alternatives. The holy opened a crack in the givenness of the social world. It made possible for my uncle and his friends, as well as for the people around them, other experiences besides those mandated by social discourses in an environment that was otherwise mostly cruel and dismissive of persons with handicaps.

It was also the case that however formed or disciplined the priests, nuns, and volunteers hovering around the holy cripples on these days were by Catholic culture to experience persons with disabilities as avatars of the broken and redemptive body of Christ – the beds on which cripples lay were often identified in Catholic popular devotional writing with the hill of Calvary on which Jesus suffered and died, for example – the ambulatory were having a religious experience. This was not an innocent experience (but what religious experience is innocent?); aspects of it were deeply troubling (not unusual for religion); its implications for the lives of persons with disabilities were equivocal (at best); and it is politically and psychologically suspect. But it is a religious experience of a certain kind that the persons involved called an experience of "the holy" and of "holiness." To insist that this experience is not *sui generis* (and I agree that it is not) is not to have said very much about it. To explain it as a function of cultural formation (which it is) does not adequately take into account how the people having the experience of the holy described it or how it acted upon them. Contemporary religious studies wants to stop with the sociological formation of the holy, but this is really only the beginning of understanding this human experience that earlier generations of religious theorists named "holy." How is "the holy" experienced as really real and what does this mean for people's lives and for the social world?

The experience of my uncle and his friends as "holy" cripples and the lived implications of this underscore the importance of a phenomenology of the holy. The figure of the holy cripple was a powerful, if unpredictable, agent of – and at the same time, a powerful, if unpredictable, wedge of destabilization and otherness to – the authority of the world in which the holy cripple arose and was experienced. To give just one example of what I mean here, the holy cripple endorsed certain norms of the good body, of physical wholeness, while it subverted them too, by recasting the body with disabilities as numinous (in Otto's term). This was so in part because holiness in this context was lived relationally, on a particular social field, among persons with disabilities and others. This is the ground of my own ambivalence with the project of the demythologization of "the holy."

My uncle's things, crammed into a small cardboard carton, came to me after his death. These consisted of many chewed and broken cigarette holders; prayer books stuffed with brightly colored holy cards and bound with wide, red rubber bands; scores of Polaroid photographs of the very many pretty girls he had flirted with over the years at various summer camps for handicapped people; purple mimeographed copies of short essays he had written for different newsletters, mostly on the experience of having cerebral palsy; and an incredible number of rosaries. Among his possessions was also a small statue of Blessed Margaret of Città di Castello, a thirteenth-century figure born with multiple handicaps, who was rejected and abandoned by her family (after being locked away in a room by them for years), adopted by the local Dominicans, and proclaimed a saint by the people of Umbria after her death. Today Blessed Margaret is internationally recognized as a patroness of the handicapped and of the anti-abortion movement (because had she been born today, my uncle once told me, "she would have been an abortion"). My uncle discovered "little Margaret," as she is known, later in his life, and she became one of his favorite saints. Going through his possessions, all jumbled together and smelling sweetly of tobacco, after his death, I got a glimpse of how living in a world focused on the broken body of God understood as a sacred gift, of how being in relation to holy figures like little Margaret within the wider web of his intimacies and associations, may have opened up to my uncle deeper possibilities of love and joy – and, above all, for connectedness – that otherwise might have been closed to him. Holiness – the holiness imputed to him, the holy figures he engaged, the holiness of Jesus's suffering, the holy ground beneath his wheelchair, the holiness that others experienced in his proximity – fundamentally and really transformed his world. It has prevented me from being able simply to dismiss the term "holiness" in the study of religion, unstable and treacherous as it is in experience and flawed and problematic as it is as a concept. This is my deeper problem with the idea of the holy, the place I come to after critical analysis and deconstruction. Holiness describes something real in culture and history, with real, if ambivalent, effects. I do not mean something unequivocally good or bad, nor do I mean something free of time and place, at least in its inception (I think it *becomes* free of time and place, a topic I will return to). Rather, I mean something that is more than the sum of its social parts and that comes to have a life of its own independent of the humans out of whose imaginations, inheritances, and circumstances it emerged.

III. THE ~~IDEA OF THE~~ HOLY

Rudolf Otto was not the only one thinking about the holy, or what he called the numinous (his neologism), in the early twentieth century, but his name has become virtually an ideogram for the subject in religious studies. Otto's 1917 book on the holy, *Das Heilige*, published in German and quickly translated into many languages, found a receptive global audience. It was an international phenomenon. But the problem with the holy is evident already in the translation of Otto's title: the switch from the straightforward realism of "the holy" to the psychological "idea of the holy" is a shift from the objective to the subjective, just the opposite of what Otto had intended. That the realness of the holy was in the mind of the practitioner rather than out there in the world (which is what Otto meant) was evidently the only way that this would be tolerable to certain English readers. For the early twentieth-century northern European theorists who developed it as a theoretical idea, the holy was the solution to the dilemma created for thinking about religion in human experience by the epistemology of Immanuel Kant. Kant situated religion within "the limits of reason," by which he meant within the coordinates of human space and time. This is the ground of social explanations of religion. But theorists of "the holy," who were likewise working within this Kantian framework, added that in the single instance of this distinctive religious experience or feeling the ontologically real was directly encountered and known as such. The English title throws the holy back into the realm of interiority.

Otto maintained that religion originated in the feelings of awe, terror, and desire that humans experience in encounter with the numinous, which he also named the *mysterium tremendum* (another neologism). "It first begins to stir," he writes, "in the feeling of something 'uncanny,' 'eerie,' or 'weird.'" The holy is experienced as "something which has no place in our scheme of reality but belongs to an absolutely different one," as absolutely objective, and as existing outside of the self. It is "wholly other." The feelings aroused by the mysterium tremendum are "awefulness," amazement, and an unearthly terror, but the numinous is fascinating (*fascinans*, again Otto's coinage) and compelling too. Such feelings are evidence of the objective reality of the numinous. Its evidentiary ground, he said, was "the symptom of 'creeping flesh.'"[8]

---

[8]   The phrase "creeping flesh" is from Otto, *The Idea of the Holy*, 16; the first stirring of the experience of the holy is described on 14.

There is no question here, in other words, of the numinous being a bit of undigested gravy, as Dickens's Scrooge desperately asserted in order to naturalize and protect himself from the mysterium tremendum of Marley's ghost. It was precisely against such naturalizing and rationalizing (and self-protecting) explanations of religious phenomena that Otto set his notion of the holy. "With all its great qualities," Otto writes of the philosophy of "the enlightenment," it offered "an intensely one-sided appreciation of human nature," valuing "man essentially as a being thinking according to the laws of intelligence and acting according to the laws of morality, as the creature of 'theoretic' and 'practical' reason." Otto and the other theorists of the holy understood themselves to be working within the intellectual traditions of the Enlightenment. It was the decadence of these ways of knowing that they objected to, the distortions, aggrandizement, and misapplication of enlightened critical reason, and the epistemological pretensions of those whom Otto called "minor champions of the enlightenment." Otto's criticism of the abuse of modern reason thoroughly captures the spirit of the theorists of the holy and its adversarial impulse. "The intellectualism of the *rationalismus vulgaris* of the age," Otto writes, "was reduced to a bald matter-of-fact complacency; world, nature, history became commonplace; the desire for explanation left no mystery, nothing that was wonderful or inexpressible, no profound riddle in the universe; the hidden springs were to be sealed up; the riddles of history, past and present, were to be rationalized by the trivial explanations of a meager pragmatism." The idea of the holy in this way belongs to the Romantic reaction against the broad and exclusive claims of modern rationalism.[9]

The holy is transhistorical (but not evolutionary). These feelings of awe and terror appeared first in the history of the species as "daemonic dread," according to religious theorists, the fear of ghosts or the forest's darkness. Other theorists at the time working in a similar psychological vein as Otto called this "the threshold of religion" (the phrase was R. R. Marett's).[10] This was not religion, in other words, but imminent pre-religion. The experience of the mysterium tremendum did not develop in an evolutionary fashion *out of* the fear of ghosts (although there was a strain of religious theorizing, associated with the famous theorist of animism, Edward Burnett Tylor, that maintained this). For Otto and other likeminded theorists of the holy, the shudder in the night

[9] Otto, *Religious Essays*, 70–1.
[10] See R. R. Marett, *The Threshold of Religion* (London: Methuen, 1909); and Andrew Lang, *The Making of Religion* (London: Longmans, Green, 1898).

belongs to humans' natural endowment; it may even have played a role in the species' evolution.[11] The religious feelings of "awefulness" and fascination in the encounter with the mysterium tremendum, on the other hand, *have nothing to do with anything in this world.* The holy is "non-natural" and "supernatural." The feelings associated with the mysterium tremendum are not analogous to other emotions (such as ordinary fear). This is the reason for Otto's neologisms: the feeling of the numinous is not like all the other emotions for which we have names, so we need a new vocabulary for it. It was not a feeling of "utter dependence," as German theologian Friedrich Schleiermacher, who otherwise had a profound influence on Otto, maintained. Rather, it was what Abraham felt in the hands of the living God, or Job standing in the ruins of his life before the enormity of God. It was to feel oneself "dust and ashes" or as "absolute profaneness." The feeling of the numinous is not a moral intuition, either. "The supernatural is not moral or immoral," R. R. Marett wrote, "but simply unmoral," and this was Otto's position too.[12]

Although everyone has a predisposition or faculty of receptivity toward the numinous, which Otto called *divination,* most people cannot produce religious feelings by themselves. Nor does the numinous feeling arise spontaneously in response to some external stimulus in the sensual world. Otto rejected such materialistic, psychologistic, and sensate views of religion. Rather, the feeling of the holy is "induced, incited, and aroused" in ordinary folk by "the instrumentality of other more highly endowed natures," which Otto also called "divinatory natures." "Faith, in the deepest sense of the word," he wrote, "can only be kindled." This was the work of seers and prophets and other religious virtuosi. As Otto puts it, "to each *numen* is assigned a seer and there is none without one." He called these seers "numinous persons." For Otto and other European theorists working in the broad environment of pietism and within the boundaries of Kant's phenomenal world, the experience of the holy is interpersonal (a dimension of Otto's holy that I will return to later in this chapter). Otto's exemplum of numinous sociality was the relationship that Jesus shared with his Apostles.[13]

---

[11] On this latter idea, see Stewart Elliott Guthrie, *Faces in the Clouds: A New Theory of Religion* (New York: Oxford University Press, 1995). Tylor's major work is the two-volume *Primitive Culture: Researches into the Development of Mythology, Philosophy, Religion, Art and Custom* (London: J. Murray, 1871).

[12] Marett, *The Threshold of Religion,* 114.

[13] *The Idea of the Holy* is the source for the phrases "induced, incited, and aroused" (60); "the instrumentality of other more highly endowed natures" (177); "'divinatory' natures" (150); "to each *numen* is assigned a seer" (122); and "numinous persons" (152). The comment about faith being kindled is from *Religious Essays,* 15.

Otto's insistence on the absolutely *sui generis* nature of "deeply-felt religious experience" and his insistence on the role of seers in the experience of the numinous are what led him famously (or infamously) to assert on the eighth page of the English translation of his text that if a reader had not had such a numinous experience, he or she would not understand the book and should put it down. These assumptions determined the book's poetics. "It will be our endeavor," he writes early in *The Idea of the Holy*, "to suggest this unnamed Something to the reader as far as we may, so that he may himself feel it." The holy cannot be defined, taught, handed down, or described, Otto maintained. The reader "must be guided and led on by consideration and discussion of the matter through the ways of his own mind, until he reach the point at which 'the numinous' in him perforce begins to stir, to start into life and into consciousness." Otto did not so much develop the notion of the holy (he did append to the text a second volume of philosophical elaborations) as evoke it. Others in this tradition of religious theory and in the psychology of religion (including William James) chose to display the holy in numerous biographical instances rather than define it, to offer glimpses of the holy flickering in certain lives and historical moments.[14]

Otto was clearly working in a Christian vein, yet he believed that his idea of the holy provided the grounds for a genuinely comparative study of religions at the deepest level. This included comparison between "primitive" and modern religion. The question of the relationship between "primitive" and modern minds was a vexed one in European theory. Was there any enduring connection between the religious worlds of "savages" (in the era's language) and the great world religions, in particular Christianity? "*Religion is itself present at its commencement*," was Otto's response to this question (the emphasis is his), "religion, nothing else, is at work in these early stages of mythic and daemonic experience." The most surprising fact in the history of religion, he writes, is that "beings, obviously born of horror and terror, become *gods* – beings to whom men pray, to whom they confide their sorrow or their happiness, in whom they behold the origin and the sanction of morality, law, and the whole canon of justice." Otto used the Kantian term *schematization* for the process of development by which the numinous came to be ever more clearly apprehended and increasingly charged with ethical content. He believed this proceeded differently in different cultures and religions. The work of comparative

14 Otto, *The Idea of the Holy*, 6–7.

religion was tracking and assessing these developments. But even at its most advanced (this is Otto's perspective), the numinous feeling was still marked by its primitive antecedents. Even when daemonic dread has reached the level of the worship of the gods, "these gods still retain ... something of the 'ghost' in the impress they make on the feelings of the worshipper." Still, it was Otto's view that Christianity represented the highest development of the numinous feeling.[15]

This exaltation of Christianity was one reason that social scientists and scholars of comparative religion rejected Otto's theoretical framework. But Otto's mysterium tremendum regularly slipped the bounds of his historical typology and became something more generous and genuinely comparative. The very idea of the holy as a theoretical lens for thinking about religion generally came to him in the first place when he was visiting a North African synagogue as a young man. Otto believed forever after that attention to the numinous brought him into the living heart of religions, the "primitive" and "savage" as well as the "higher," as it disclosed the common experiential ground of the planet's tremendous religious diversity (which Otto prized for what it disclosed about the multiple possibilities of the holy). Otto muses in *The Idea of the Holy*, what was it like to be among those who walked with Jesus? What did this *feel* like? The way to know, he proposes, is not by historical scholarship on the early Christian community, nor by looking at "the staled feelings and blunted sensitivity" of the modern church (the sort of comment that did not make Otto any ecclesiastical friends), but by finding "living instances of the thing as it may still be found today," in "remote corners of the Mohammedan and Indian world ... in the streets of Mogador and Marrakesh," where "religion shows itself alive as a naïve emotional force, with all its primal quality of impulse and instinct."[16]

IV. THE PROBLEM OF THE HOLY

Despite its popular success (maybe even because of it, academic jealousy being what it is), *The Idea of the Holy* was a scholarly failure, and since Otto's death in 1937 his idea of the holy has suffered "a more than usually severe vilification," in the words of historian Eric Sharpe. Criticism in Otto's day and after came both from Christian theologians

---

[15] Otto's comment about "religion" being present at the creation is from *The Idea of the Holy*, 132; so is the observation that beings originally born of terror become gods, 136–7; schematization is discussed on 45–9; and the enduring impress of the ghost in the gods is on 17.

[16] Otto, *The Idea of the Holy*, 157.

and from scientists of religion. The former found Otto insufficiently Christian; the latter accused him of imposing a Christian construct on other religions. Liberal Protestants faulted him for overemphasizing the emotional dimension of religion at the expense of the ethical and the rational; conservative Protestants did not like his openness to other religions. Otto's psychological emphasis looked like subjectivism – although this was a gross misunderstanding of his work – and seemed to diminish the objective realness of God (he meant it to do just the opposite). The fate of the holy also got bound up in Otto's biography, specifically his silence during the early days of National Socialism. As Gregory D. Alles puts it starkly in the second edition of the influential *Encyclopedia of Religion*, Otto "did not actively oppose the Nazi regime." This evident compliance seemed to link the idea of the holy with the dark and decadent late-romantic irrationalism out of which National Socialist ideology and imagery developed.[17]

Within the field of religious studies, the enduring problem of the "holy" has to do with Otto's assumptions about the nature of human experience, in particular the relationship between experience and culture (including language, ways of knowing, patterns of memory, the structures of power and authority, and so on). The fate of "holiness" as a concept and Otto's standing as a theorist have been bound up in the twentieth century with what Martin Jay calls the "demise of experience" as the result of the pervasive assumption of the "already always mediated nature of cultural relations."[18] In his resolute emphasis on the *sui generis* nature of the numinous feeling, "which has no place in the everyday world of natural experience," and its universal identity (before it is taken up into the cultural particularization of schematization), Otto located the reality of the holy – and by extension, religion itself – outside of history and culture. But in modern ways of thinking about culture and psychology, there is no "out of" history and culture, no place antecedent to or outside of the social circumstances, relationships, and ways of thinking about and imagining the world and of understanding the self into which humans are born. Would someone not Hindu or not already a devotee of the goddess Yamuna-ji experience the Yamuna River as numinous? Would the cripples in the church

[17] Eric J. Sharpe, *Comparative Religion: A History*, 2nd Edition. (LaSalle, IL: Open Court, 1986), 167; Gregory D. Alles, "Otto, Rudolf," in *Encyclopedia of Religion*, 2nd Edition, ed. Lindsay Jones (Detroit: Thomson Gale, 2005), Vol. 6: 6928–31, quote on 6929.

[18] Martin Jay, *Songs of Experience: Modern American and European Variations on a Universal Theme* (Berkeley: University of California Press, 2005), 3.

cafeterias have been experienced as holy without the cultural surround
of imagery and theology that gave a special and privileged meaning to
the broken body? If the answer to these questions is no (as anyone must
surely acknowledge who has seen tourists in t-shirts and shorts milling
about in a decidedly unholy manner in holy places not their own), then
we are drawn back across the epistemological divide, as in the translated
title. The Yamuna River is a goddess for those who believe the Yamuna
River is a goddess. This is not a matter of objective or subjective, real or
imaginary; it is a matter of culture and history. *Homo religiosus*, as historian of religion J. Z. Smith has written, is "preeminently, *homo faber*."
The "holy" is a construction; it is a made thing.[19]

There are other problems. A woman who throws an image of a saint
onto the backseat of her car to punish him for not answering her prayers
for her husband to find work – as modern Catholic women did to Saint
Jude, Patron Saint of Hopeless Causes – is not feeling the mysterium
tremendum. That is the numinous, upside down on the floor of an old
Chevy! Numinous beings and ordinary people move back and forth quite
familiarly in most religious contexts and engage in many different kinds
of exchanges. Saying that such common religious forms are characteristic of lower stages of religious life is prejudice, not critical theory. Awe
and terror are not the only feelings people have in religious contexts, as a
visit to any shrine will immediately show (if there is anything universal
in human religiousness, it is this: that people will behave in all kinds
of ways in the company of their gods). Discounting these other feelings
and practices as "not religious" is to shut out and deny whole dimensions of human experience and of religion. Otto's fervent rhetorical style
vis-à-vis the holy – "the feeling of it may at times come sweeping like a
gentle tide ... it may burst in sudden eruption up from the depths of the
soul with spasms and convulsions, or lead to the strangest excitements,
to intoxicated frenzy ... it has its wild and demonic forms and can sink
to an almost grisly horror and shuddering ... it may become the hushed,
trembling, and speechless humility of the creature in the presence of –
whom or what?" – contributed to an enduring strain of romanticism in
religious studies. What this has meant in the history of the discipline
is that religious others (savages and primitives, children and women,
Native Americans, peasants and pagans, and so on) become alluring avatars of the antimodern, endowed with a holiness that makes that available for fantasy and appropriation, as we saw with my uncle. Holiness

[19] Jonathan Z. Smith, "The Unknown God: Myth in History," in *Imagining Religion: From Babylon to Jonestown* (Chicago: University of Chicago Press, 1982), 89.

was a treacherous pivot on which fantasies and realities of domination, desire, and destruction spun around each other.[20]

V. THE TRADITION OF THE MORE

Some of these criticisms are to the point (Otto really did believe in the superiority of Christianity and thus contributed to a hierarchical and Western-centered view of global religion); others are misinterpretations of the theoretical tradition of the holy, sometimes by failing to see it in its necessary Kantian context. But we can acknowledge the problems with it and still recognize that the theoreticians were embarked on an important and necessary project, which we understand more fully now. They wanted to account for the really realness of religion in such a way that complicated and called into question the absolute authority of naturalistic explanations, and they did so in a comparative frame that brought a vast array of events and experiences from around the world and across time to the theoretical table. These theoreticians belong in their aims to a wider current in modern Western intellectual culture. Borrowing an expression from William James, who was very interested in this $2 + 2 = 5$ factor of religious experience, I will call this trajectory of scholarship in religion the *tradition of the more*. It arose in protest against the sterility of materialist, positivist, and naturalist analyses of culture generally, religions in particular, and against the bourgeois theological insistence that the holy was primarily a moral category, and it is marked by a strong contrarian and even subversive impulse.

Often scholars in the tradition of the more approach their subject in small and hesitant steps, because they have internalized the authority of social explanations of religious phenomena. One way they do so is by intensifying the language they use to describe the realness of religious effects. "Religion without interiority, without some 'bathed in sentiment' sense that belief matters," anthropologist of religion Clifford Geertz wrote, for instance, "and matters terribly, that faith sustains, cures, comforts, redresses wrongs, improves fortune, secures rewards, explains, obligates, blesses, clarifies, reconciles, regenerates, redeems, or saves, is hardly worthy of the name."[21] With his insistent proliferation of verbs, the rolling out of phrases emphasizing the literalness and the urgency of religious phenomena, Geertz seems to want to enact or

[20] Otto, *The Idea of the Holy*, 12–13.
[21] Clifford Geertz, *Available Light: Anthropological Reflection on Philosophical Topics* (Princeton, NJ: Princeton University Press, 2000), 178.

to perform for readers the realness of religion and its efficacy in culture, and in this I see him gesturing toward what it was the theorists of the holy also wanted to name.

Theorists in the tradition of the more have given various names to their visions of phenomena in culture that exceed reality as it can be accounted by totaling up psychological and social factors. Early nineteenth-century philosopher Jacob Friedrich Fries, another interpreter of Kant and an influence on Otto, called it *Ahndung*, by which he meant an intuition of the overplus. French historian Michel de Certeau spoke of "the unanticipated" in history, of the "nocturnal" that is "outside or below ... history's law" erupting into broad daylight. (Such spatial designations are common in this tradition: the 2 + 2 = 5 is *outside* and breaks *into*, at the same time that it is always *inside*.) Michel Foucault imagined "subjugated knowledges" circulating disruptively through normative culture. Contemporary phenomenologist and theologian Jean-Luc Marion refers to "saturated phenomena," exemplified by the wafer become the real body and blood of Christ in the Catholic sacrament. British psychoanalyst D. W. Winnicott wrote of "transitional" phenomena that are neither inside (in the imagination or consciousness) nor outside (in the social environment), but in-between, on the border (another instance of spatial metaphors). Christopher Bollas, working in the research tradition associated with Winnicott, talks of "the unthought known" and of human consciousness having "a separate sense that reaches through the barriers exercised by the limits of consciousness." Anthropologist Stanley Tambiah describes a way of being in the world he calls "participation" that occurs "when persons, groups, animals, places, and natural phenomena are in a relation of contiguity, and translate that relation into one of existential immediacy and contact and shared affinities." Tambiah cites as instances of participation "the bonding and relation between parents and children, between kinsmen by the ties of blood and amity; the transmission of charisma or *metta* through amulets and talismans between a Buddhist saint and his followers; or between Thai royalty and their subjects; the Indian concept of *darśan* of a deity whose eyes fall upon the worshippers as much as the worshippers view their diety." (I would add to this the relations among pilgrims at shrines or at apparitional sites.) Anthropologist Gananath Obeyesekere writes of "hypnomantic states" and cultures, wherein "a pathway is established between id and ego" and "fantasy can come out into open consciousness and the superego can tolerate its presence." Philosopher Franz Rosenzweig identified his methodology as "absolute empiricism," which Rosenzweig scholar Eric Santner elaborates as the "attunement to the surplus of the real within reality." Walter Benjamin distinguished an experience of memory he called *Erfahrung* in which images from an individual's past, "combine[d] with material of the collective memory," inflected by "accumulated ... unconscious data," come to have vivid and compelling immediacy in the present. Dipesh Chakrabarty has challenged fellow historians to think of historical time as "out of joint with itself" so that they will be able to recognize that "gods and spirits are existentially coeval with the human," a history he identifies as "radically heterogeneous."[22]

To be sure, the thinkers cited were working in different philosophical contexts and academic disciplines; the problems they encountered in their research and theory and the solutions they proposed were inflected in distinctive ways by these particular inheritances. I take liberties in bringing them together under a common rubric. But I am less interested in identifying a coherent intellectual history than I am in pointing to a common spirit or ambition, for however important their divergences, the figures I have listed share the determination to approach the 2 + 2 = 5 from within but at the very limits of the analytical frameworks of their respective disciplines.

---

[22] Otto discusses Fries in *The Idea of the Holy*, 146. Quoted or referenced in this paragraph are Michel de Certeau, *The Possession at Loudon*, trans. Michael B. Smith (Chicago: University of Chicago Press, 1996), 1; Michel Foucault, *Power/Knowledge: Selected Interviews and Other Writings, 1972–1977*, ed. Colin Gordon, trans. Colin Gordon, Leo Marshall, John Mepham, Kate Soper (New York: Pantheon, 1980), 81–2; Jean-Luc Marion, *In Excess: Studies of Saturated Phenomena*, trans. Robyn Horner and Vincent Berraud (New York: Fordham University Press, 2002), 29–53; D. W. Winnicott, *Playing & Reality* (London: Tavistock/Routledge, 1971), 1–25, 104–10; Christopher Bollas, *The Shadow of the Object: Psychoanalysis of the Unthought Known* (New York: Columbia University Press, 1987); the reference to a "separate sense" is from Bollas, *Cracking Up: The Work of Unconscious Experience* (New York: Routledge, 2002 [1995]), 47; Stanley Jeyaraja Tambiah, *Magic, Science, Religion, and the Scope of Rationality* (Cambridge: Cambridge University Press, 1990), 107–8; Gananath Obeyesekere, *Medusa's Hair: An Essay on Personal Symbols and Religious Experience* (Chicago: University of Chicago Press, 1981), 167; Eric L. Santner discusses absolute empiricism in *On the Psychotheology of Everyday Life: Reflections on Freud and Rosenzweig* (Chicago: University of Chicago Press, 2001), 118; a rich discussion of Benjamin's view of time and memory is David Gross, *Lost Time: On Remembering and Forgetting in Late Modern Culture* (Amherst: University of Massachusetts Press, 2000), 46–7; Dipesh Chakrabarty, *Provincializing Europe: Post-Colonial Thought and Historical Difference* (Princeton, NJ: Princeton University Press, 2000), 46. Also in this tradition of the "more" is the work of scholar of religion Jeffrey J. Kripal; see, for example, *Roads of Excess, Palaces of Wisdom: Eroticism and Reflexivity in the Study of Mysticism* (Chicago: University of Chicago Press, 2001), and *The Serpent's Gift: Gnostic Reflections on the Study of Religion* (Chicago: University of Chicago Press, 2007).

VI. 2 + 2 = 5: TO FATHOM THE HOLY

It remains to give a sense of the coordinates of the 2 + 2 = 5, which I am using as another phrase for the holy, as it is experienced in space and time, to express what marks out the 2 +2 = 5/holy as the really real to those who experience it and to suggest some of the implications of this critical question for religious studies.

But here I come up against an internal uneasiness. To provide a catalogue of the characteristics of the more so that it can be recognized in nature like a rare species of bird or mammal seems to be just the sort of reductive naturalizing move that the tradition I have identified eschews. This is why writers in this tradition have most often sought to describe the holy in the biographies of religious virtuosi (as James did), in the lived experience of patients (Bollas and Winnicott) or historical agents (Chakrabarty), or preferably to evoke it (as Otto attempted to do and Benjamin succeeded). So here it is useful to remember that the tradition of the more is deeply analytical in its intellectual commitments. The point of describing (or evoking) the holy in religious studies, writes theorist Daniel Gold (who calls it the "sublime"), is not the "pious appreciation of a religious object," which is the work of religious practitioners, but "a simultaneous attempt rationally to *fathom* it: to discern from it something humanly important, to calculate at last some aspect of the potentially incalculable significance it may hold." Scholars of religion can account for how such experiences come to have the power that they do in culture and in people's lives, how the holy comes to be really real and what this means, Gold continues, "by providing intellectual perspective as well as imaginative sensibility." Scholars of religion stand at the interface of the powerful work of the imagination and the imperative of intellectual perspective. So as religious theorist J. Z. Smith says (echoing Plato), "classify we must."[23]

Classify I will. The holy is experienced as "objective and outside the self" (in Otto's phrase), according to its theorists. It is known as objectively real, not as delusion or fantasy. It is what James called "the reality of the unseen" (although very often it is seen, too, in visions, objects, and persons). It is radically other, extraordinary, and utterly different; the fact that the holy is encountered as really real *here* does not diminish – in fact, it accentuates – its sheer apartness. Even when what

[23] Daniel Gold, *Aesthetics and Analysis in Writing on Religion: Modern Fascinations* (Berkeley: University of California Press, 2003), 75–6; Jonathan Z. Smith, *Relating Religion: Essays in the Study of Religion* (Chicago: University of Chicago Press, 2004), 174.

is experienced is recognizable from the cultural repertoire – Roman Catholics in the nineteenth and twentieth centuries, for example, were familiar with persons marked by Christ's wounds and with Marian apparitions – it comes as shocking, extraordinary, and unexpected. It is experienced as *happening to* the ones experiencing it. The experience is relational, intersubjective; holiness happens among people present in an immediate and direct way to each other. Bollas writes of transcendent moments characterized by "a reciprocally infinite falling of oneself into another." (Otto himself described how the experience of the numinous is shared by means of "a penetrative imaginative sympathy with what passes in the other person's mind."[24]) In turn, the experience intensifies this connectedness. It is among people so peculiarly connected that the really realness of the phenomena is determined, known, and affirmed, and in which it takes on its life. The realness of the holy is extensive: it moves out to transform objects, persons (beginning with the persons most immediate to the experience), places, and categories of person (rulers, saints, healers). A scholar of the civil rights movement described to me the experience of Montgomery during the bus boycott as holiness flowing out into the streets. Ordinary metrics of space and time do not count in such experiences. Water taken from the miraculous healing spring at Lourdes is brought away by pilgrims to distant places and then the power of the place is said to be there too where the holy water is. The holy is excessive. In response to the excessive holy, humans generate rituals and stories. As all the theorists of the holy insisted, the experience is not about morality; it does not present itself in nor can it be encapsulated by the categories of good or bad. The key category of the holy is its realness. The holy takes on a life and efficacy of its own. To return to an earlier example, even if Marley were the product of intestinal distress, he confronted Scrooge as something substantive outside of himself, a ghost with its own aims and intentions. The $2 + 2 = 5$ of holiness inserts a wedge of unpredictability into history and society, of the unforeseeable and unaccountable. Finally, the holy marks those who have experienced it. Without exaggerating this or rendering it into an ethical imperative (and recognizing that there is no single enduring religious state, like awe or reverence), the holy remains existentially present. It becomes the pivot of social and personal narrative.

---

[24] Christopher Bollas, *Cracking Up: The Work of Unconscious Experience* (New York: Routledge, 1997), 28. Bollas writes, "One person's direct effect on the other – unconscious to unconscious – cannot be witnessed by consciousness. It is a discordant symphonic movement of a reciprocally infinite falling of one self into another." Also quoted in this paragraph is Otto, *The Idea of the Holy*, 60.

Note that the words "believe in" or "have faith in" have not appeared here. This is because the holy is met as the really real and this renders otiose such terms that in their modern meanings connote subjective experience on a stark subjective/objective grid. The experience of the holy blurs certain boundaries of the real as moderns conceive it: between here and there, for instance, the past and the present, or between one person and another. It also unsettles boundaries dear to modern ways of knowing: between academic disciplines (psychoanalysis and history, for instance); between accounts of conscious knowing and the unconscious; and especially between the imaginary and the real. It requires a new theoretical vocabulary, which is why the experience was so generative of neologisms and what I have resorted to the 2 + 2 = 5.

VII. CONCLUSION

The idea of the holy fell victim, as we have seen, to seismic shifts in the understanding of culture, self, and society, and in the nature of knowledge itself, in epistemology and phenomenology. But intellectual history is a long dialectical conversation and there is evidence that a "rediscovery of experience," as historian and philosopher F. R. Ankersmit puts it, is under way, "a shift away from language toward experience." "The difficult ... future task of the historical theorist," Ankersmit goes on, is "to liberate the history of historical experience from the heavy and oppressive weight of (the historian's) language and to unearth experience from the thick sedimentary strata of language covering it."[25] The same is true for contemporary religious studies and the experience of the holy, the really real, or the 2 + 2 = 5. The liberation that Ankersmit is calling for from domination by the structures of modern knowledge has been the aim of theorists of the holy all along. As Söderblom said, what we have seen of human experience in the present and the past impresses on us the need for a concept of the holy; the concept has gone through the most intense and prolonged critical fires now for decades; and the changing shape of knowledge across the humanities and social sciences opens the prospect of restoring some version of it to our critical lexicon. The theorists of the holy recognized right from the start that this requires of scholars of religion intellectual generosity, a thoughtful and self-aware empathy, an epistemological skepticism, and a capacious imagination.

[25] F. R. Ankersmit, *Sublime Historical Experience* (Stanford, CA: Stanford University Press, 2005), 2, 1, 14.

Select Bibliography

Alles, Gregory D. "Otto, Rudolf." In *Encyclopedia of Religion*. Edited by Lindsay Jones. 2nd Edition. Detroit: Thomson Gale, 2005. Vol. 6: 6928–31.

Almond, Philip C. *Rudolf Otto: An Introduction to His Philosophical Theology*. Chapel Hill and London: University of North Carolina Press, 1984.

Lang, Andrew. *The Making of Religion*. London: Longmans, Green, 1898.

Marett, R. R. *The Threshold of Religion*. London: Methuen, 1909.

Otto, Rudolf. *The Idea of the Holy: An Inquiry into the Non-Rational Factor in the Idea of the Divine and Its Relation to the Rational*. Translated by John W. Harvey. London: Oxford University Press, 1923.

  Religious Essays: A Supplement to the "Idea of the Holy." Translated by Brian Lunn. London: Oxford University Press, 1931.

Söderblom, Nathan. "Holiness." In *Encyclopedia of Religion and Ethics*. Edited by James Hastings. New York: Charles Scribner's Sons, 1914. Vol. 4: 731–41.

  The Living God: Basal Forms of Personal Religion. London: Oxford University Press, 1933.

Part two

Major theoretical problems

5 Social order or social chaos

MICHAEL J. PUETT

I. INTRODUCTION

Max Weber, writing during a period that he felt marked a shift into a new world of modernity, described that world as follows:

> The fate of our times is characterized by rationalization and intellectualization and, above all, by the "disenchantment of the world." ... To the person who cannot bear the fate of the times like a man, one must say: may he rather return silently, without the usual publicity build-up of renegades, but simply and plainly. The arms of the old churches are opened widely and compassionately for him.[1]

The emergence of modernity has entailed a loss of the enchanted cosmology that defined traditional societies. Weber characteristically viewed such a rationalization of the world in ambivalent terms. It has led to the recognition that the world is governed by humans, not gods, and it has allowed us to make a rational science of human society. These were, to Weber, overall good things, and the resulting disenchantment of the world ought thus to be thought of as something we must learn to bear as the flip-side of the same coin. Those too weak to face this shift can always return to the churches – the remnants of the traditional world.

This tradition–modernity distinction has dominated not only the field of religious studies but also commonsensical views in the West for the past two centuries concerning religions in general. Humans before the modern period believed themselves to be living in a world created and controlled by gods; according to this framework, in which the cosmos was therefore structured, humanity had a predefined place and purpose for existence, and human societies were given order through religious beliefs and institutions. Such a world was cohesive, harmonious, and

---

[1] Max Weber, "Science as a Vocation," in *From Max Weber: Essays in Sociology*, ed. Hans H. Gerth, trans. C. Wright Mills (New York: Oxford University Press, 1946), 129–56, quote on 155.

unified, and religion was the glue that held it together. The dramatic shift in human history, according to this narrative, thus occurred in the modern world, when a loss of belief in the religious sphere led to fragmentation and alienation. Humans no longer had a defined place and purpose in the cosmos and human society no longer had a force leading to harmony and cohesion.

The lessons drawn from this narrative have varied. Some have argued that we need to return to a traditional world of religion so that we can be saved from our fragmented lives, or that we at least need to find some functional equivalent of religion for the modern age. Others have celebrated the shift to modernity without ambivalence, seeing the overthrow of the religious sphere as a good thing, allowing human agents to approach their sociopolitical world as humanly constructed and thus as changeable. And perhaps most have been like Max Weber, arguing that we must learn to accept this existential situation, even as we hold a clear nostalgia for what has been lost.

Regardless of the lessons one draws, however, the narrative has been surprisingly stable over the past two centuries, and underlying the narrative is a remarkably stable view of religion: religion is the force that brings order and cohesiveness to a human world that is otherwise contingent, fragmented, and bereft of higher meaning. Indeed, this definition of religion has been so stable that even those thinkers in the past few decades who have rejected evolutionary readings of human history still continue to define religion as that which gives order to an otherwise contingent and meaningless world.

What are the implications of such a view of religion? Why has it been so recurrent over the past two centuries? And, perhaps most significantly, is such a view empirically correct? If not, are there other ways to frame our understandings of religion – not to mention our narratives of the modern world?

To answer these questions, it will be helpful to first explore some of these arguments in a bit more depth.

II. THE CHAOS OF HUMANITY

Weber positioned himself (albeit not always happily) as a modernist – as someone who understands that the world is in fact governed by humans rather than gods. The social science that Weber championed would thus serve, among other goals, to unmask the traditional, religious assumptions about the way the world operates. Thus, for example, Weber saw one of the roles of religion in traditional societies to be that of legitimating authority – presenting the contingent world of human politics as having sacred force:

> The validity of a social order by virtue of the sacredness of tradition is the oldest and most universal type of legitimacy. The fear of magical evils reinforces the general psychological inhibitions against any sort of change in customary modes of action. At the same time the manifold vested interests which tend to favor conformity with an established order help to perpetuate it.[2]

The contingent social worlds of humanity were legitimated in traditional societies by making them appear to be sanctioned by sacred powers, and thus as immutable and timeless.

Such a claim of unmasking was a dominant motif in social scientific writings in the nineteenth and early twentieth centuries. Émile Durkheim went so far as to argue that the very notion of the divine was a misguided understanding of society:

> Society in general, simply by its effect on men's minds, undoubtedly has all that is required to arouse the sensation of the divine. A society is to its members what a god is to its faithful. A god is first of all a being that man conceives of as superior to himself in some respects and one on whom he believes he depends.[3]

Society itself defines humans. In traditional cultures, humans, not able to grasp the power of society, mistakenly came to believe in divine powers that were guiding the world. Only the modern social scientist can see that in fact it is society itself that created the notion of the divine.

But, of course, one can hold the same view of religion and reverse both the valuation and the analytic stance. If the social sciences largely took the view that the modern debunking of religion was correct (even if psychologically difficult to accept), several highly influential figures in the early development of the field of religious studies took the opposite view. Mircea Eliade, one of the most influential figures in the development of the field of religion, also defined his analyses in terms of a fundamental distinction between the contingent, human projects in the

---

[2] Max Weber, *Economy and Society: An Outline of Interpretive Sociology*, 2 vols., ed. Guenther Roth and Claus Wittich (Berkeley: University of California Press, 1978), vol. 1: 37.

[3] Émile Durkheim, *The Elementary Forms of Religious Life*, trans. Karen E. Fields (New York: Free Press, 1995 [1912]), 208.

profane world and the timeless ones of the sacred world, but with the opposite valuation.

For Eliade, what he calls "religious man" sees the world as having been created by divine powers. The world, "has a structure; it is not a chaos but a cosmos, hence it presents itself as creation, as work of the gods."[4] Indeed, the sacred is what is real and significant and humans participate in this true reality by imitating the divine:

> Whatever the historical context in which he is placed, *homo religiosus* always believes that there is an absolute reality, *the sacred*, which transcends this world but manifests itself in this world, thereby sanctifying it and making it real. He further believes that life has a sacred origin and that human existence realizes all of its potentialities in proportion as it is religious – that is, participates in reality. The gods created man and the world, the culture heroes completed the Creation, and the history of all these divine and semi-divine works is preserved in myths. By reactualizing sacred history, by imitating the divine behavior, man puts and keeps himself close to the gods – that is, in the real and the significant.[5]

Humans do not legitimate their actions by appeal to the sacred but rather, in their attempts to create order, are in fact imitating the gods. The sacred, in other words, precedes us, and we imitate it. The sacred models are embedded in the cosmos and when humans construct order in their own social worlds, they do so by following these sacred models.

Although the general framework – the sacred world as eternal and ordered, and the human world as contingent – is almost identical to what we have seen in the preceding, the valuation is clearly altered. The real is not the contingent world of humanity that is mistakenly legitimated by way of the sacred. The real is the sacred.

And the contrast continues. Like so many figures before him, Eliade contrasts this traditional world of belief in a sacred order with a modern loss of such a belief. But note again the shift in valuation:

> It is easy to see all that separates this mode of being in the world from the existence of a nonreligious man. First of all, the nonreligious man refuses transcendence, accepts the relativity of "reality," and may even come to doubt the meaning of existence. The great cultures of the past too have not been entirely without nonreligious

4 Mircea Eliade, *The Sacred and the Profane: The Nature of Religion*, trans. Willard R. Trask (New York: Harcourt, 1959 [1957], 116–17.
5 Eliade, *The Sacred and the Profane*, 202.

men, and it is not impossible that such men existed even on the archaic levels of culture, although as yet no testimony to their existence there has come to light. But it is only in the modern societies of the West that nonreligious man has developed fully. Modern nonreligious man assumes a new existential situation; he regards himself solely as the subject and agent of history, and he refuses all appeal to transcendence. In other words, he accepts no model for humanity outside the human condition as it can be seen in the various historical situations. Man *makes himself*, and he only makes himself completely in proportion as he desacralizes himself and the world. The sacred is the prime obstacle to his freedom. He will become himself only when he is totally demysticized. He will not be truly free until he has killed the last god.[6]

If the world of religious man is impregnated with the sacred, the societies of the modern West refuse the transcendental. The sacred is still there; but modern man no longer listens.

Despite these different valuations among Weber, Durkheim, and Eliade – three of the most influential theorists on twentieth-century studies of religion – the frameworks are almost identical. Traditional societies believed in a structured, harmonious cosmos controlled by gods, and they believed these gods to be the source of authority in the human realm as well. And the belief in such a structured, harmonious cosmos has been rejected in the modern world, such that humans now believe themselves to be the makers of their own history. Theorists may debate whether this is a good or bad thing, whether the sacred really exists or is just a misunderstanding of human society or a means of legitimating political authority, but the framework is strikingly similar.

III. FRACTURED COSMOLOGIES

But, then, what about the empirical fact that so many religions simply do not posit such a structured cosmos? Throughout much of twentieth-century thought, the answer was simple: any such religious tendency was a precursor to modernity. Indeed, many of Weber's studies of religions throughout the world came in part to rest on the question of the degree to which they did or did not posit a tension between humans and the cosmos. To the extent that they did, they were seen as moving closer on the scale of rationality toward modernity; to the extent that they did not, they were posited as inhibiting that development.

---

[6] Eliade, *The Sacred and the Profane*, 202–3.

For example, Weber read religions in China as emphasizing the necessity of humans adjusting to the larger harmony of the ordered cosmos:

> Confucianism meant adjustment to the world, to its orders and conventions.... The cosmic orders of the world were considered fixed and inviolate and the orders of society were but a special case of this. The great spirits of the cosmic orders obviously desired only the happiness of the world and especially the happiness of man. The same applied to the orders of society. The "happy" tranquility of the empire and the equilibrium of the soul should and could be attained only if man fitted himself into the internally harmonious cosmos.[7]

Weber contrasts this with the tensions in Protestantism that would ultimately generate a desire among humans to master and transform the world:

> From the relation between the supra-mundane God and the creaturally wicked, ethically irrational world there resulted ... the absolute unholiness of tradition and the truly endless task of ethically and rationally subduing and mastering the given world, i.e., rational, objective "progress." Here, the task of the rational transformation of the world stood opposed to the Confucian adjustment to the world.[8]

Protestantism, by creating a tension between humans and God, thus helped to usher in the modern world. In other words, premodern religions are categorized according to the degree to which they emphasize cosmic harmony or begin to push against such harmony by positing a tension with the cosmos. In the latter case, the religions would be pointing toward modernity.

This paradigm has had a long history in twentieth-century scholarship, as various scholars have argued where the significant breaks from the more primordial world of harmony and continuity occurred. K. C. Chang, for example, the leading twentieth-century archaeologist of China, gives a variant of Weber's model, arguing that the shift occurred with the emergence of civilizations in the Near East. To set up the argument, Chang asserts, very much like Eliade, that primitive religion was based upon an assumption of a continuity between humans and the rest

---

[7]   Max Weber, *The Religion of China: Confucianism and Taoism*, trans. Hans H. Gerth (New York: Free Press, 1951), 152–3.
[8]   Weber, *The Religion of China*, 240.

of the cosmos: "... continuity between man and animal, between earth and heaven, and between culture and nature." What is distinctive about China, according to Chang, is that this primordial religion of continuity was maintained. As he writes, "the first civilized society of China carried on many essential features of its savage and barbarous antecedents." In contrast, this primordial continuity between heaven and earth was broken in the West. Chang thus defines "... the Chinese pattern as one of *continuity* and the Western pattern as one of *rupture*."[9]

Chang's distinction is between China and the West, rather than tradition and modernity, but the terms of the argument are by now quite familiar: continuity and harmony are more primordial, and the central question is when and why was this broken. The latter is associated with modernity, or with the West more generally.

As is clear from just these two examples, China came to play a significant role in twentieth-century theories of religion precisely because it seemed to exemplify the dominant claims of the time concerning the nature of traditional cosmologies. For the same reason, those cosmologies that arose in premodern periods that appeared to posit a tension between humans and the cosmos drew a significant amount of interest as being possible precursors to modernity. We have already seen the significance Weber granted to Protestantism. Another such religion that generated tremendous interest in twentieth-century theories of religion was so-called Gnosticism, the name given to a number of texts from the Mediterranean late antiquity that claimed the cosmos to have been created by an ignorant or even evil demiurge and that argued true liberation accordingly consisted of transcending this created cosmos.

Hans Jonas's formulations concerning Gnosticism were particularly influential on twentieth-century thought. Jonas describes the modern condition of nihilism in the following terms:

> This is the human condition. Gone is the cosmos with those immanent logoi my own can feel kinship, done the order of the whole in which man has his place. That place appears now as a sheer and brute accident.... The utter contingency of our existence in the scheme deprives that scheme of any human sense as a possible frame of reference for the understanding of ourselves.[10]

9 Chang Kwang-Chih, "Ancient China and Its Anthropological Significance," in *Archaeological Thought in America*, ed. C. C. Lamberg-Karlovsky (Cambridge: Cambridge University Press, 1989), 155–66, quotes on 165, 161.

10 Hans Jonas, *The Gnostic Religion: The Message of the Alien God and the Beginnings of Christianity*, 2nd Edition (Boston: Beacon Press, 1963), 323.

And, for Jonas, this is precisely the view one finds in Gnosticism:

> There is one situation, and one only that I know of in the history
> of Western man, where – on a level untouched by anything resem-
> bling modern scientific thought – that condition has been realized
> and lived out with all the vehemence of a cataclysmic event. That is
> the Gnostic movement, or the more radical ones among the various
> Gnostic movements and teachings, which the deeply agitated first
> three centuries of the Christian era proliferated in the Hellenistic
> parts of the Roman Empire and beyond its eastern boundaries.[11]

Gnosticism, in short, presages the modern, nihilistic view of humans
not having a pre-given place within a structured cosmos.

Jonas is not claiming that Gnosticism led to modernity; absent here
are the causal arguments about the emergence of modernity from cosmologies that posit a tension between humans and divinities. But clearly
at work is the notion that such tension-based cosmologies involve a
break from earlier, structured cosmologies, and that they are akin to
modern ones. This reading of Gnosticism would subsequently spawn
an entire body of literature equating Gnosticism with various aspects of
the modern condition.[12]

Cosmic order or tension with the world. Most of these frameworks
(with the exception of Jonas) were either overtly or implicitly based
upon evolutionary frameworks. A religious world based upon cosmic
harmony is repeatedly seen as the more primordial conception, while in
contrast the modern world is cast as one of discontinuity, contingency,
and tension with the cosmos. The question then comes down to when
the crucial shifts away from this more primordial sense of cosmic order
occurred: was it with the emergence of transcendental gods, with the
emergence of Gnosticism, with the emergence of Protestantism, or elsewhere? But the paradigm remains the same.

IV. STRUCTURE AND COGNITION

Throughout much of the twentieth century, however, critics have
questioned these evolutionary frameworks. Even among these critics,
however, one finds amazing constancy in the basic framework and

---

[11] Jonas, *The Gnostic Religion*, 325.
[12] See, in particular, Eric Voegelin, *The New Science of Politics: An Introduction*
(Chicago: University of Chicago Press, 1987); Eric Voegelin, *Science, Politics, and
Gnosticism* (Chicago: H. Regnery, 1968); Cyril O'Regan, *Gnostic Return in Modernity*
(Albany: State University of New York Press, 2001).

definition of religion. A recent debate among two leading theorists will help underline the point.

Clifford Geertz, perhaps the most influential anthropologist of the twentieth century, was deeply concerned with emphasizing the importance of the interpreter respecting the beliefs of each culture under study. He thus rejected any reductionistic readings of those religious beliefs and opposed any framework that would lead the interpreter toward such reductionism.

Geertz was equally opposed to Eliade's concern with discovering universal religious archetypes that archaic humanity shared. Geertz on the contrary was hoping to study the cultural assumptions of each society, very much under the claim that these assumptions would be radically different in each society. And, perhaps most significantly, for Geertz, the religious sphere is embedded in an entire belief system, thus rendering a distinction between the sacred and the profane meaningless.

Yet pervasive in Geertz's arguments concerning religion is a distinction between the disordered and contingent nature of human experience and the order conferred by religion. For Geertz, humans live in a world of chaos, and religion serves to give meaning to humans in such a world:

> There are at least three points where chaos – a tumult of events which lack not just interpretations but *interpretability* – threatens to break in upon man: at the limits of his analytic capacities, at the limits of his powers of endurance, and at the limits of his moral insight. Bafflement, suffering, and a sense of intractable ethical paradox are all, if they become intense enough or are sustained long enough, radical challenges to the proposition that life is comprehensible and that we can, by taking thought, orient ourselves effectively within it – challenges with which any religion, however "primitive," which hopes to persist must attempt somehow to cope.[13]

Without religion, our life is chaotic, meaningless, and lacking in any ethical justifications. Religion thus serves to give our lives a fundamental order:

> How is it that the religious man moves from a troubled perception of experienced disorder to a more or less settled conviction of fundamental order? Just what does "belief" mean in a religious context?

[13] Clifford Geertz, "Religion as a Cultural System," in *The Interpretation of Cultures* (New York: Basic, 1973), 100.

> ... It seems to me that it is best to begin any approach to this issue with frank recognition that religious belief involves not a Baconian induction from everyday experience – for then we should all be agnostics – but rather a prior acceptance of authority which transforms that experience.[14]

By accepting the authority of religious belief, we allow ourselves to deny our everyday experience and instead accept the existence of an ordered cosmos.

Given his insistence that religion provides order to an otherwise meaningless and chaotic existence, it is perhaps not surprising that Geertz consistently finds in his analyses of religious beliefs a harmonious, ordered world, often based in eternal cycles and a structured cosmos. Whether discussing notions of time in Bali or the nineteenth-century Balinese royal court, Geertz consistently portrays a religious sphere of harmony and order.[15]

It is the status of such religious beliefs that concerned Maurice Bloch, another leading anthropologist who criticized Geertz's arguments.[16] Bloch turned his attention in particular to Geertz's study of the Balinese, who Geertz claimed had a fundamentally cyclical notion of time.[17] Bloch's argument was that Geertz had developed his claims by looking only at materials from ritual contexts, and was then taking such ritual claims as being assumptions of Balinese culture in general. Bloch's argument in contrast was that for all humans, the everyday experience of time is linear. Cyclical time is part of a ritual context, associated with religion, and as such it is removed from our everyday lives. Geertz's mistake, according to Bloch, was in reading claims made within a ritual context and then taking these as general beliefs in the culture at large.

At issue here is a significant debate as to whether all humans fundamentally think alike (as Bloch argues) or have fundamentally different assumptions about the world (Geertz). But note immediately that both thinkers in the debate still assert the same distinction between everyday life and religion, here reasserting it at the level of cognition. The only question was whether the religious sphere leads people to think

---

[14] Geertz, "Religion as a Cultural System," 109.

[15] Clifford Geertz, "Person, Time and Conduct in Bali," reprinted in *The Interpretation of Cultures*, 360–411; Clifford Geertz, *Negara: The Theatre State in Nineteenth-Century Bali* (Princeton, NJ: Princeton University Press, 1981).

[16] Maurice Bloch, "The Past and the Present in the Present," *Man* 12, 2 (1977): 278–92; reprinted in Maurice Bloch, *Ritual, History and Power: Selected Papers in Anthropology* (London: Athlone Press, 1989), 1–18.

[17] Geertz, "Person, Time, and Conduct in Bali."

differently – in this case, whether the ritual claim concerning cyclical time results in people actually believing in cyclical time outside of a ritual context.

The definition of religion, in other words, remains the same. The religious sphere is timeless and orderly; it is contrasted with a world of contingency and change. The debate within the various frameworks thus comes down to whether this religious sphere fully informs people's thinking or not. This is a tremendously important question, but the fundamental definition of religion remains unchanged.

But if religious claims should be read as general assumptions, then how should they be understood? For Bloch, ritual language is based upon a claim of timeless (either unchanging or cyclical) order precisely because it serves the function of providing transcendental sanction to an otherwise contingent human world, the argument formulated so strongly by Weber. Social hierarchies may be a product of power, but if hierarchies are seen by those on whom they are exercised as simple oppression, they will not tend to last for very long – those on the lower rungs will seek to remove those on the upper. Legitimization of such hierarchies thus involves, according to Bloch, the attempt to make the hierarchies seem to be an immutable aspect of ordered cosmos. In other words, religion legitimates the contingent world of humans by making that world appear as divinely sanctioned:

> In the political context the elder has to fight off rivals. However, in the role of religion this is not necessary any more. Indeed one can say that a political event becomes religious when individual power struggles have become unnecessary. Formalization thus not only removed what is being said from a particular time and particular place, it has also removed it from the actual speaker, and thus created another supernatural being which the elder is slowly becoming or speaks for. The creation of this other supernatural being is best seen in possession, where the notion that two beings are present, one supernatural and one natural, is explicit. The elder is transformed into an ancestor speaking eternal truth; this transformation seems to me the articulation between traditional authority and religion.[18]

The world humans live in is contingent, always changing, and based upon immediate struggles with other humans and ever-changing configurations of power. The sphere of religion, on the contrary, is timeless,

---

[18] Maurice Bloch, "Symbol, Song, Dance and Features of Articulation: Is Religion an Extreme Form of Traditional Authority?" in Bloch, *Ritual, History and Power*, 44–5.

based upon eternal moral principles, and run by deities removed from the contingent world of humanity. Traditional authority is based in religion.

So much is this so that religion itself probably had its origins in this need to legitimate authority in traditional societies:

> The significance of this is that we should perhaps see the origin of religion in this special strategy of leadership, the use of form for power, which we have found in a lesser form in our study of communication of traditional authority, we would then see the performance of religion as serving a special form of authority.[19]

Religion sanctifies an otherwise contingent world, precisely the view we have seen in other forms throughout the twentieth century. Instead of reading the dualism of a timeless cosmic order and contingent human action within an evolutionary framework, Bloch has placed it within a structured distinction between a ritual order and universal world of everyday human cognition. But the definition of religion remains the same.

Thus, even among those thinkers who reject an evolutionary approach, we see a set of endless permutations concerning the status and nature of religious belief, but all surrounding a common assertion about the role that religion plays in positing an ordered, structured, timeless cosmos in opposition to the chaotic contingency of human life.

V. SHIFTS IN THE PARADIGM

Early in his career, University of Chicago historian of religion Jonathan Z. Smith worked with a variant of this paradigm as well. Smith posited a distinction between what he called "locative" religions and "utopian" religions. Focused as he was at the time on shifts in the Near East and Mediterranean regions from the ancient period to late antiquity, Smith's arguments at first glance sound similar to those of Hans Jonas. For Smith, the locative view, which dominated the Mediterranean and Near Eastern world "for some two thousand years," was based upon a belief in a "cosmic order," created by the gods, in which humans had a defined place.[20] Within such an order, there can be no sustained tension between humans and the cosmos:

[19] Maurice Bloch, "Symbol, Song, Dance and Features of Articulation," 45.
[20] Jonathan Z. Smith, *Map Is Not Territory: Studies in the History of Religions* (Chicago: University of Chicago Press, 1978), 132.

There may be periods of tension (such as the myth of the theft of the tablets of destiny by the Zu bird or the imprisonment of Marduk during the New Year festival), but the "reliable" and "unalterable" structures of destiny will ultimately win out. They will be victorious because they are real, having been established by the gods.... Man's responsibility becomes one of discovering, of knowing his place.... Man is charged with the task of harmonizing himself with the great rhythms of cosmic destiny and order.[21]

Such a description is almost identical in wording to Eliade's description of primordial religions or Weber's description of traditional cosmologies.

Referring to Hans Jonas, Smith argues that the emergence of Gnosticism in the Hellenistic period marked a moment when a "radical revaluation of the cosmos occurred."[22] The emphasis shifted from one of order to one of liberation – a "utopian" vision, in Smith's terminology. Another example of a utopian vision rejecting an earlier locative one would be the modern world: "Such a locative view of the cosmos seems foreign to our tendency to idealize openness and mobility."[23]

This certainly sounds like the evolutionary framework we have seen before, with a belief in cosmic order being the primordial position for humanity and with rejections of that position being precursors to modernity. However, Smith explicitly opposes any attempt to see one of these as more primordial then the other:

Is the material Eliade describes best organized under the categories "archaic" and "modern"? ... Whatever terminology is employed, we must be careful to preserve a sufficient sense of the experiential character of this dichotomy and resist imposing even an implicit evolutionary scheme of development "from the closed world to the infinite universe" (to borrow the title of Alexander Koyré's well-known work). This requires our resisting as well the frequent tendency to identify the centripetal-closed-locative view with primitive, archaic society and the centrifugal-open-utopian with the modern. Both have been and remain coeval existential possibilities which may be appropriated whenever and wherever they correspond to man's experience of the world.[24]

[21] Smith, *Map Is Not Territory*, 133. The words "reliable" and "unalterable" are taken from Heidel's translation of the *Enuma elish*: Alfred Heidel, *The Babylonian Genesis*, 2nd Edition (Chicago: University of Chicago Press, 1951).
[22] Smith, *Map Is Not Territory*, 138.
[23] Smith, *Map Is Not Territory*, 137.
[24] Smith, *Map Is Not Territory*, 100–1.

If the locative is not more primordial than the utopian, then it would follow that the entire attempt to posit a shift from a primordial, locative vision of the world to a modern viewpoint is mistaken.

And, just as importantly, it would follow that religious orientations do not necessarily posit a cosmic order. Thus, for example, Bloch would agree that at any given time, one could posit either a claim of cosmic order or a lack thereof. But for Bloch this would amount to a distinction between a ritual order versus the world of everyday experience. For Smith, however, a claimed lack of cosmic order can be every bit as religious as its claimed existence.

Smith went on to develop his critique. Noting the degree to which the field of religious studies had been built out of a basic claim concerning the primordiality of religions that emphasize harmony, continuity, and order (the "locative," in Smith's terminology), Smith pointed out that the field has therefore largely failed to deal with those religions that do not fit this paradigm:

> It strikes me that historians of religion have been weakest in interpreting those myths which do not reveal a cosmos in which man finds a place to dwell and on which he found his existence, but rather which suggest the problematic nature of existence and fundamental tension in the cosmos. I have in mind such traditions as dualistic creation myths, Earth-diver traditions, Tricksters, or the complex narratives of Corn or Rice Mothers who create by "loathsome" processes (e.g., rubbing the dirt off their bodies, by defecation, secretion). Clearly these mythologies, many of which are extremely archaic, point to a different spiritual horizon than that described by Eliade as the fundamental "archaic ontology."[25]

By treating religious conceptions not based on placing humans within a structured and harmonious cosmos as later reactions against a more primordial worldview pointing toward the modern world or as part of a universal world of everyday experience outside of the ritual sphere, our understandings of a substantial body of religious phenomena have been greatly impoverished.

VI. THE HISTORICAL AND ETHNOGRAPHIC RECORD

Smith's point should be amplified. As we have seen, the study of religions has been dominated for roughly two centuries by essentially one

[25] Smith, *Map Is Not Territory*, 100.

definition: the sacred is consistently portrayed as being based on a vision of cosmic order. In a modernity narrative, world history is then read as a shift from a traditional world, in which religion provided order to the contingent struggles of humanity, to a modern world, in which the loss of religious faith has resulted in – for better or worse – a loss of that grounding in a higher order. Even those figures – such as Geertz and Bloch – who opposed such evolutionary claims (and disagreed strongly among themselves about the status of religious beliefs) still defined the religious sphere in much the same way.

It is rare when one finds a view concerning religion so constant and so universally agreed upon – not just in the field of religious studies but throughout the social sciences as well. And this theoretical unanimity is made all the more remarkable when one considers the fact that, in the ethnographic and historical record, this is, to put it politely, a very one-sided view of the religious sphere. Yes, one can certainly find example after example of places where the religious sphere is presented as a timeless or cyclical cosmic order. Political leaders have certainly throughout history legitimated their rule through appeals to divine powers and a stable cosmic order. But alternative religious views and practices, as well as modes of dealing with the divine, are at least as common. And yet, despite their constant presence in our ethnographies and historical works, it is striking how rarely religious views and experiences that contradict the accepted definition are discussed in our theoretical literature – unless that literature is directed to explicating shifts related to the rise of modernity or to distinctive features of Western civilization.

Moreover, even many of the cosmologies presented as what Smith has called locative are perhaps still being misdescribed. Claims of cosmic order are rarely as seamless and lacking in tension as they are so often presented in our theoretical discussions.

An example will help to underline the point. Mention was made previously concerning the recurrent claim that, prior to the twentieth century, the divine sphere in China was seen as harmonious and structured, with humanity having a predefined place and role. Such a claim has played a dominant role in theoretical and comparative claims concerning traditional China. We saw previously Weber's argument that such a cosmology resulted in the Chinese not developing the kind of tension with the world that one sees with the rise of Protestantism and that became (he claimed) so dominant in modernity, as well as K. C. Chang's argument that China maintained the kind of continuous cosmology found in primitive religions.

And, yet, as historical research has clearly shown, claims of harmony were only one possible way the divine sphere could be seen. Moreover, and tellingly, such claims tended to be associated not with common practice but rather with millenarian movements set in opposition to contemporary practice.

The first example in our extant corpus of a group claiming the divine world to be hierarchical, structured, and morally just, providing a place and role for humanity in the larger cosmos, are the Mohists, a utopian, antiritual movement that began in the fifth century BCE. Comparable cosmologies are found consistently throughout Chinese history among millenarian movements. But all of these movements were opposed to common religious practice, which consistently saw the divine sphere as populated by dangerous and highly capricious demons and ghosts. Humans were thus constantly undertaking an endless number of sacrifices aimed at mollifying the demons or transforming them into ancestors and gods who would then be called upon to work on behalf of humanity. Much of religious practice throughout Chinese history can be characterized as an endless domestication of the divine sphere – trying to take a highly dangerous corpus of spirits and transform it into a hierarchical pantheon that would help human endeavors. Far from a harmonious, structured cosmos that was then available to sanction to human authority, the divine sphere was consistently seen as inherently dangerous and capricious, in need of dramatic transformation so that humans could thrive. Indeed, the domestication of the divine sphere was often compared with the domestication of the natural world through agriculture and the domestication of human emotions through ritual.[26]

When the human domestication of the divine was successful, the result would be a cosmos much like that often described in the theoretical literature: a structured cosmos run by a hierarchically arranged pantheon of gods and ancestors organized much like a patriarchal lineage structure. But such a pantheon was seen as the ideal result of human domestication: it is not that humans were modeling themselves on or accommodating themselves to a structured, harmonious cosmos but the precise opposite. And, at least as importantly, the domestication of the divine sphere – like the domestication of the natural world and the

---

[26] Michael J. Puett, *To Become a God: Cosmology, Sacrifice, and Self-Divinization in Early China* (Cambridge, MA: Harvard University Asia Center, 2002); Michael Puett, "The Offering of Food and the Creation of Order: The Practice of Sacrifice in Early China," in *Of Tripod and Palate: Food, Politics, and Religion in Traditional China,* ed. Roel Sterckx (New York: Palgrave Macmillan, 2005), 75–95.

domestication of human emotions – is never complete. The deities are more powerful than the human domesticating rituals, so they often do not act according to those categories. The gods and ancestors always tend to revert to being demons and ghosts haunting humanity, just as dangerous human emotions continue to emerge against other humans and just as droughts and floods (the parts of nature humans cannot domesticate) continue to cause hunger and starvation.

This is most certainly not a utopian vision, but it is also not a loca-tive vision, at least not in the sense of positing a cosmic order to which humans must accommodate themselves. On the contrary, the perceived tension here between humans and the cosmos is quite extreme. But our paradigms concerning religious order have led to a consistent misunder-standing of the practices in question.

Similar points can be made concerning the entire issue of legitimi-zation, to which figures such as Weber and Bloch devoted so much atten-tion. One of the terms used by rulers in China was "Son of Heaven." This was certainly a claim to the legitimacy of the ruler's position by reference to the high god in Heaven. But it was clearly understood to be a ritual claim: no one ever claimed that Heaven had actually given birth to the ruler. (When a shift in dynasties occurred, the new ruler would be able to take the title only after performing the proper rituals. He certainly never claimed in retrospect to have been born from Heaven.) And the ritual claim was that Heaven would, it was hoped, act like a proper (that is, properly domesticated, with dangerous emotions kept under control) father, just as it was hoped that the ruler would act like a proper son.[27] But, of course, neither tended to actually do so on a con-sistent basis. Heaven would send down disasters for no reason, and the ruler would often act arbitrarily. So, yes, it was legitimization, but it was also an attempt to domesticate both the divine and the human – and was always seen as an endless process that could never fully succeed. And explaining such legitimization through a distinction between rit-ual and everyday cognition would also miss the point. It is not that participants in ritual contexts believed that Heaven was a moral deity operating in an ordered cosmos and then thought differently outside of those ritual contexts. Heaven was seen as dangerous and capricious in both contexts, and the goal of ritual was to domesticate both Heaven and human alike.

[27] Michael Puett, "Human and Divine Kingship in Early China: Comparative Reflections," in *Religion and Power: Divine Kingship in the Ancient World and Beyond*, ed. Nicole Brisch (Chicago: Oriental Institute of the University of Chicago, 2008), 199–212.

Ancestor worship went along the same lines. Recent scholars, building out of the same theoretical concerns we have been discussing, have argued that humans in traditional China thought of themselves as existing "under the ancestor's shadow," trying to follow the wishes of the ancestors.[28] In fact, deceased humans were seen as dangerous ghosts, and one of the goals of the rituals was to form these dangerous ghosts into ancestors who it was hoped would then act on behalf of the living, just as it was hoped that the living would then behave better as well by thinking of themselves as descendants. But here too the ancestors would often revert to being ghosts and would inflict illnesses upon the living and the living would have to continue trying to form them into ancestors.

In short, there certainly was never an assumption in China that the divine world was naturally harmonious. When one reads a statement from China that the world is harmonious, one needs to see the tremendous agony that underlies such a claim and the tremendous effort expended in trying (and in the long run always failing) to create such a unified system. Accommodating oneself to a pre-given cosmos of harmony is hardly an accurate description.

And, of course, the implicit violence does not simply lie on the side of the undomesticated world of human emotions, wild animals, and dangerous ghosts. The point of critique of the various millenarian movements in China that have arisen in opposition to these practices of domestication is precisely that human efforts to transform the divine and human worlds simply create yet more violence, as they often did. In other words, domestication leads to as many horrors as a lack of domestication. It is, to paraphrase Geertz, violence all the way down.

In short, it is not just that we have failed to account for utopian, antilocative movements in religion. We have also mischaracterized the religions that have been treated as locative, as assuming cosmic order. Many of the common examples pulled from China to show that it is a culture that emphasized the importance of imitating the cosmic order of the divine (ancestor worship, the title of the ruler as a "Son of Heaven," and so on) reveal a very different set of religious concerns.

These examples from China can be multiplied throughout the world. Our theories posit traditional or archaic humans as assuming a harmonious cosmos, but such a claim is rarely anything but one claim

---

[28] The phrase comes from Francis L. K. Hsu, *Under the Ancestors' Shadow: Kinship, Personality, and Social Mobility in China* (Stanford, CA: Stanford University Press, 1967).

among many concerning the divine; it is usually posited as the ideal
(and by definition never to be fully realized) end point of ritual action.
A world of harmony would be the ideal result of these rituals, an ideal
that by definition would never be achieved. Yet it is this ideal that has
been consistently treated by scholars as an assumption, as, indeed, a
prototypical example of a traditional religious order.

VII. THE RELATIONSHIPS OF RELIGIONS

A more promising approach would be to shift away from frameworks
focused on the end point of human action and instead focus on the processes of religious life themselves. As Robert A. Orsi has written:

> Religious theories that emphasize meaning focus on the end-prod-
> uct, a story that is said to link heaven and earth, but the solidity
> and stability of this dissolves if you focus instead on the processes
> of religious meaning-making. What we see if we do this is the
> wounding; in this devotional world, as in others, meaning making
> is wounding.[29]

Such a focus on meaning-making operates, as Orsi notes, in the "register
of the tragic."[30] Even for those religions that call for the creation of an
order linking humans to the larger cosmos – the religions that Smith
would define as locative – the process of trying to create such an order is
inevitably painful and very often filled with violence. As Orsi describes
his grandmother's relationship to Saint Gemma Galgani:

> What the saint seems to have offered was companionship on a bit-
> ter and confusing journey – bitterness and confusion to which the
> saint's own stories had contributed. My grandmother asked no
> grace of Gemma other than that of accompaniment, no miracle
> beyond the recognition of shared lives. But the sharing was costly.
> As Gemma's and Giulia's stories teach, in between a life and the
> meanings that may be made in it, for and against that life is the
> wound. Meaning making begins in wounding, and the process of
> meaning making is wounding.[31]

Orsi's approach thus shifts the focus from the end points of religious
practice (the ideal creation of a perfectly harmonious world with humans

[29] Robert A. Orsi, *Between Heaven and Earth: The Religious Worlds People Make and the Scholars Who Study Them* (Princeton, NJ: Princeton University Press, 2005), 144.
[30] Orsi, *Between Heaven and Earth*, 170.
[31] Orsi, *Between Heaven and Earth*, 145.

properly situated in a defined cosmic order) to the endless dynamic of relationships. Relationships always veer between order and chaos. They can be both loving and abusive; filled with care, yet equally filled with angers, jealousies, and resentments. And so it is with gods and goddesses, with ghosts, with ancestors. Pain is very often present in these relationships. At times, the relationships become so fraught that the situations degenerate into horrific violence – not always, perhaps not even often, but the potential is always there.

Those involved in these relationships may claim that the bonds, whether with other humans or with gods and ghosts, are stable, orderly, and morally clear. And from particular points of view, they can sometimes be described as such, but only by willfully ignoring most of what actually goes on in the relationships. Such claims are very interesting and very telling, but they are hardly an accurate vision on which to base our theories of religion.

To return to the religious practices in China: are the divine powers moral gods or dangerous ghosts, and are the humans moral agents or violent creatures? The answer, of course, is all of the above. Neither humans nor divine powers are either inherently orderly or chaotic. The dynamics of the relationships are such that both are always present to varying degrees. And it is almost never the case that only one side in the relationship is creating all of the violence. The violence is a product of the dynamics of the relationships themselves.

What would be the implications of shifting the focus away from our commitment to the claim that religions create social order – giving up, in other words, one of our most cherished, even if empirically indefensible, claims about religion? It would mean allowing ourselves to study, analyze, and theorize the complex dynamics of relationships through which religions operate without resorting to the frameworks of harmony and coherence that have so dominated our analyses and so limited our understandings. It would mean accepting that there is no clear order or coherence in religions except as claims made by participants in certain circumstances – claims that must then be analyzed as such. And it would mean recognizing that the dynamics of these relationships – the dynamics on which and through which meaning construction and ritual action take place – involve a potential to create violence at every level.

It would mean, in short, ending our distinction between contingent human action and timeless religious order (along with the various evolutionary and functionalist frameworks in which the distinction has been employed) once and for all, and focusing instead on the complex and difficult processes by which humans attempt to work through the relationships of their lives and the tensions and potential violence that emerge from this work.

Select Bibliography

Durkheim, Émile. *The Elementary Forms of Religious Life.* Translated by Karen E. Fields. New York: Free Press, 1995 (1912).

Eliade, Mircea. *The Myth of the Eternal Return: Cosmos and History.* Translated by Willard R. Task. Princeton, NJ: Princeton University Press, 1954. (The original French version appeared in 1949.)

Geertz, Clifford. "Religion as a Cultural System." Reprinted in *The Interpretation of Cultures: Selected Essays.* New York: Basic, 1973.

   Negara: The Theatre State in Nineteenth-Century Bali. Princeton, NJ: Princeton University Press, 1981.

Orsi, Robert A. *Between Heaven and Earth: The Religious Worlds People Make and the Scholars Who Study Them.* Princeton, NJ: Princeton University Press, 2005.

Smith, Jonathan Z. *Map Is Not Territory: Studies in the History of Religions.* Chicago: University of Chicago Press, 1978.

Weber, Max. *Economy and Society: An Outline of Interpretive Sociology.* Edited by Guenther Roth and Claus Wittich. 2 vols. Berkeley: University of California Press, 1978.

6 Tradition: the power of constraint

MICHAEL L. SATLOW

To Valerius Maximus, the fawning author of *Memorable Doings and Sayings*, dedicated to the Roman emperor Tiberius sometime between 14–37 CE, it was self-evident that Roman religious practices were profoundly traditional. "Our ancestors (*Maiores*)," he states at the very beginning of his tract in his discussion of "On Religion" (*De religione*), decreed the very foundations and institutions of Roman religion. The "ancients" (*antiques*) zealously sought both to observe and to expand religion, and Valerius Maximus reports approvingly of several rituals and auguries that were performed "in the way of our ancestors," the *mos maiorum*.[1]

It is generally not wise to rely on the testimony of Valerius Maximus, a man who, as one classical scholar writes, "possessed neither sharpness of intellect nor clarity of style."[2] In this case, however, Valerius Maximus accurately reflected not only the common Roman belief about their own religion but also a sentiment widely shared throughout the circum-Mediterranean and Near East. Piety, defined by Cicero (first century BCE) as "justice towards the gods," meant in part honoring ancestral customs. One of the primary reasons that Romans looked askance at early Christians was that Christians rejected the customs of their ancestors.[3] Nor were Romans alone in their insistence on preserving ancestral practices. In the face of immense social, economic, political, and religious challenges, Egyptians in late antiquity tenaciously held to traditional religious practices. Jews, of course, maintained their

---

[1] Valerius Maximus, *Memorable Doings and Sayings, Books I–V*, trans. D. R. Shackleton Bailey, Loeb Classical Library 492 (Cambridge, MA.: Harvard University Press, 2000), 1.1a–1b, 15. Cf. 1.4.3.

[2] Clifford Ando, *The Matter of the Gods: Religion and the Roman Empire*, The Transformation of the Classical Heritage 44 (Berkeley: University of California Press, 2008), 2.

[3] Cicero, *The Nature of the Gods*, trans. Horace C. P. McGregor (Harmondsworth, UK: Penguin, 1972), 1.116–17; Robert Louis Wilken, *The Christians as the Romans Saw Them*, 2nd Edition. (New Haven, CT: Yale University Press, 2003), 62–7.

own "chain of tradition": "Moses received Torah and transmitted it to Joshua, Joshua to the elders, the elders to the prophets, and the prophets transmitted it to the men of the Great Assembly." One passage in the Palestinian Talmud goes so far as to maintain that when religious law derived from a process of judicial reasoning (that is, *halakah*) conflicts with ancestral custom, the latter takes precedence. Islamic legal jurisprudence similarly ascribes authority to custom. The extreme emphasis placed on filial piety in ancient China – whether the parent is alive or dead – points in the same direction: religion was seen as constituted out of traditions of the ancestors.[4]

Modernity, on the other hand, has been unkind to the notion of "tradition." For a variety of reasons, beginning in the Enlightenment period (or perhaps even earlier, during the Protestant Reformation), "tradition" took on an increasingly negative connotation. Modern scholarship has largely discounted or even disparaged the notion of tradition; the social sciences in particular have largely neglected it, both as a topic and as a practice. As historian Mark Salber Phillips notes, scholars have been far more interested in examining how traditions change or are "invented" than in exploring the aspects that ground the concept.[5] Hence, Edward Shils's ambitious treatment of tradition emphasizes malleability:

> A process of industrial production is not a tradition.... The product is not a tradition. An act of exercise of authority is not a tradition.... The performance of a ritual action, whether it is an act of communion or the celebration of an anniversary or loyal toast to a monarch, is not a tradition: it is a set of words and physical movements expressive of a state of sentiment and belief.
>
> None of these states of sentiment of mind is a tradition, none of these physical actions and social relationships is a tradition. None

---

4 David Frankfurter, *Religion in Roman Egypt: Assimilation and Resistance* (Princeton, NJ: Princeton University Press, 1998); Mishnah *Avot* 1:1; cf. Elie Bikerman (Elias Bickerman), "La chaine de la tradition pharisienne," *Revue Biblique* 59 (1952): 44–54; Palestinian Talmud *Bava Metzia* 7:1, 11b; Gideon Libson, "On the Development of Custom as a Source of Law in Islamic Law," *Islamic Law and Society* 4 (1997): 131–55; Judith E. Tucker, *In the House of the Law: Gender and Islamic Law in Ottoman Syria and Palestine* (Berkeley: University of California Press, 1998), 11–22; Donald Holzman, "The Place of Filial Piety in Ancient China," *Journal of the American Oriental Society* 118 (1998): 185–99.

5 Mark Salber Phillips, "What Is Tradition When It Is Not 'Invented'? A Historiographical Introduction," in *Questions of Tradition*, ed. Mark Salber Phillips and Gordon Schochet (Toronto: University of Toronto Press, 2004), 3–29. Cf. Eric Hobsbawm and Terence Ranger, *The Invention of Tradition* (Cambridge and New York: Cambridge University Press, 1983).

of these ideas is a tradition. None of them in itself is a tradition. But all of them can in various ways be transmitted as traditions; they can become traditions. They nearly always occur in forms affected or determined in varying degrees by tradition. They recur because they are carried as traditions which are reenacted. The reenactment is not the tradition: the tradition is the pattern which guides the reenactment.[6]

Shils goes on to describe "religious knowledge" as comprised of "patterns of symbols which uphold and keep on the right track the presentation and reception of cognitive religious beliefs, popular and learned." This approach to tradition strongly echoes Clifford Geertz's symbolic anthropological definition of religion as an inherited "system of symbols."[7]

Recent philosophical approaches to tradition share much with this anthropological one. Alasdair MacIntyre and his interlocutors best exemplify this orientation. MacIntyre succinctly defines a "living tradition" as "an historically extended, socially embodied argument, and an argument precisely in part about the goods which constitute that tradition." Princeton ethicist Jeffrey Stout, although otherwise strongly critical of MacIntyre for putting the notion of tradition in opposition to "modernity," is content to define tradition as "a discursive practice considered in the dimension of history," with "pragmatic considerations" governing the individuation of traditions. Tradition, in this way of thinking, is a (somewhat) bounded but always changing discursive field.[8]

There is much that is attractive in these anthropological and philosophical approaches to tradition, especially as applied to the academic study of religion. At the same time, though, both approaches share three deficiencies that lessen the usefulness of tradition so defined as an *analytic* category. First, as Phillips notes, both emphasize dynamism over continuity. There is certainly no requirement that modern critical (that is, second-order) categories of analysis conform to the meanings given to words within religious communities (that is, first-order usage), but in this case it seems to me that by subtly adopting the invidious distinction between "tradition" and "modern," we lose the wherewithal to appreciate a critical, nearly universal characteristic of religion, because almost every religious community maintains traditions that it

6   Edward Shils, *Tradition* (Chicago: University of Chicago Press, 1981), 31.
7   Shils, *Tradition*, 96; Clifford Geertz, "Religion as a Cultural System," in *The Interpretation of Cultures: Selected Essays* (New York: Basic, 1973), 91–4.
8   Alasdair C. MacIntyre, *After Virtue: A Study in Moral Theory* (Notre Dame, IN: University of Notre Dame Press, 1981), 222; Jeffrey Stout, *Democracy and Tradition*, New Forum Books (Princeton, NJ: Princeton University Press, 2004), 135.

regards as ontological givens. Second, neither the philosophical or the anthropological approach is very good at differentiating between the discrete practices that are actually transmitted from one generation to another and the larger "tradition" (that is, the "system," "pattern," or "discourse") that is supposed to be the sum of these practices. Finally, both approaches devalue "ritual" practices in and of themselves, unless they are integrated into some larger system of meaning. They privilege the broad structure – which in any case they struggle to find the appropriate language to describe – over the various bits of transmitted cultural bricolage.

In this chapter, I want to suggest that an analytic category that emphasizes continuity in religion can be useful to scholars both as an explanatory model and as a means to make fruitful comparisons. Toward that end, I submit a tentative, working definition of "tradition":

> *(I.) static (II.) resources that (III.) individuals, communities, and institutions understand as (IV.) authentic and regard as (V.) authoritative.*

I devote the rest of this chapter to unpacking and providing nuance to this formulation. The definition is broad and can be tested outside of the academic study of religion, although my examples and my attempts to illustrate how the definition might be useful are confined to this field. As I am a scholar of early Judaism with comparative interests, my examples primarily reflect my own comfort zone, and even that I have pressed. As will become clearer in the sections that follow, my focus is on the smaller, discrete traditions rather than "the traditions" (or "religions") writ large.

I. STATIC

Traditions and the discourses that rationalize and justify them change, sometimes rapidly and radically. Religious actors frequently modify existing practices and then frame new practices, meanings, and combinations as "traditional." The Jewish ultra-Orthodox movement and the Mormons come to mind as particularly striking examples of this impulse. It is thus not with a little hesitation that I use a term that emphasizes continuity over change.[9]

---

[9] Michael K. Silber, "The Emergence of Ultra-Orthodoxy: The Invention of Tradition," in *The Uses of Tradition: Jewish Continuity in the Modern Era*, ed. Jack Wertheimer (New York: Jewish Theological Seminary of America, 1992), 23–84; Jan Shipps, *Mormonism: The Story of a New Religious Tradition* (Urbana: University of Illinois Press, 1987 [1985]).

Yet it is continuity – or more precisely, the perception of continuity – that stands at the heart of tradition. The word *tradition*, after all, comes from the Latin word *traditio*, meaning to hand over or transmit, and *traditum*, the thing being handed over. What deserves emphasis here is not the actual, objective evaluation of the authenticity of the tradition (to be discussed in section IV), but the conviction of those receiving the tradition that the "practice" (a loose term discussed in section II) should or must be preserved.

Traditions are the things that we think are worth preserving, whether we like them or not. They are the things that until recently in human history we did not deliberately manipulate. I am not suggesting that prior to modernity there were no "invented traditions," only that for the most part in religious contexts such a term would have seemed baffling, and that the inventions and manipulations were more subtle and organic than intentional and functional. Today, the tendency among Western religious actors is to choose and modify traditions, but in most societies and times, traditions constrain.[10]

Traditions are static because they are understood to exercise a *constraining force*. Traditions are the inheritances or the innovations with which we *must* deal. How we do so – that is, the exact understanding and power of that constraining force – is a question of authority, which itself is highly negotiable (as discussed later in this chapter). At this juncture, it is only important to emphasize that a traditional practice is "traditional" and static because religious actors feel either that the resource is valuable or that they have no choice but to preserve it. It is a definitional issue: in this sense, by definition, traditions constrain.

Understanding traditions as static practices (or resources) that constrain encourages scholars to think about the *strategies* by which religious actors contend with that constraining power. A religious actor who receives a sacred text that contains an attitude or idea that conflicts with prior commitments (moral, ethical, or otherwise) might, for example, *interpret* the text to convey a different meaning, but the option of neglecting or changing the text is not open. Religious actors tend to *harmonize* or *prioritize* traditions that they perceive as containing conflicting norms. There are many such strategies for dealing with tradition while maintaining it, and the compilation and comparison of them are a desideratum.

Two oversimplified and brief examples might better illustrate these strategies. First is the Christian ritual of the Eucharist. During the period

---

[10]   Robert N. Bellah, *Habits of the Heart: Individualism and Commitment in American Life* (Berkeley: University of California Press, 1985), 219–49.

of the Protestant Reformation and its aftermath, many Christians preserved what they regarded as the essential elements of the ritual even as they radically reinterpreted the meaning of this practice. The understanding of the practice was secondary to the practice itself. A second example is the emphasis placed over time and in different locales on competing notions of *jihad* among modern Muslims. Traditional Islamic texts contain both inward (that is, internal and psychological) and outward (that is, holy war) applications of this concept; different Muslim communities "choose" which strain to emphasize. Few Muslims, though, would completely abandon the notion of *jihad*.[11]

Both of these examples can be used to illustrate how traditions transform. But emphasizing the static elements of traditions together with their constraining force makes it possible to reframe the inquiry into the meaning of "tradition." Instead of inquiring about the reasons for change (for example, to what extent has it stayed the same, or why was there a historical shift?), we might instead ask about the specific strategies that religious actors employed to work with their traditions in different environments. In the example of *jihad*, we might ask who, when, how, and why Muslims emphasize one notion of *jihad* over the other rather than trying to make implicitly normative judgments about the "authenticity" of one understanding over another.

II. RESOURCES

By the term "resources," I mean both to clarify the mode by which a practice becomes a tradition and to sharpen what has been to this point my vague use of the term "practice" for the actual content of traditions.

In his learned and capacious entry on "Tradition" in the *Encyclopedia of Religion*, Paul Valliere states that, "A general theory of the formation of religious traditions has eluded scholars of tradition." He locates the source of this lacuna in the tension between historical analysis, which emphasizes the cultural specificity of the origins of tradition, and "the religious concept of tradition as a body of inviolate sacred canons transcending time and change." Indeed, there is a long tradition of historical scholarship that understands traditions as "formed by elites as a means of legitimating power and privilege."[12]

---

[11] Lee Palmer Wandel, *The Eucharist in the Reformation: Incarnation and Liturgy* (Cambridge and New York: Cambridge University Press, 2006); Bernard Kenneth Freamon, "Martyrdom, Suicide, and the Islamic Law of War: A Short Legal History," *Fordham International Law Journal* 27 (2003): 299–369.

[12] Paul Valliere, "Tradition," in *Encyclopedia of Religion*, ed. Lindsay Jones (Detroit: Macmillan Reference USA, 2005), vol. 13: 9272–3, quotes on 9272.

Valliere's emphasis on origins is misplaced, however. Whatever the origins of traditions, what actually makes them "traditions" is that they are preserved as such by a later generation. The determination and commitment to preserve follow from a large range of factors, such as a tradition's political utility to an institution or simple inertia (for example, "I do this because my parents did it"). At the heart of preservation, though, is the issue of usefulness.

I want to suggest that many, perhaps even most, religious traditions exercise a constraining force because religious actors find such traditions useful. They are the *resources* from which and around which these actors construct meanings. A resource becomes a tradition and exercises constraining force only once it is preserved. Somebody has to think that it is worth preserving. The search for a "theory of origins" is thus misdirected. Traditions are created not when particular practices first arise, but when they are received and preserved by the next generation. A culture produces a fluid, complex, and vast number of practices; cultural life is, as Claude Lévi-Strauss claims, a bricolage. Traditions are the preserved and transmitted elements of this bricolage.

The productive and critical questions are thus not those of origins but of preservation. Why, out of all the possibilities, did this particular religious actor at this time find that this particular practice was worth preserving? Why did the next generation attribute a constraining force to it? This is the true origin of a tradition: the point of transmission across time and sometimes space.

Understanding traditions as resources for specific religious actors also helps to account for the distinctiveness of what we often call "religions" or the "traditions." Such abstractions (for example, Judaism, Christianity, Islam, Buddhism, and Hinduism) are normally defined by belief, "discourse," or pattern and structure of meaning. Yet from both a theoretical and an empirical perspective, such definitions are problematic. Theoretically, belief-centered approaches to the definition of religion force us into normative and essentialist judgments. That is, the student of religion has two choices. Either he or she can accept the essentialist definition offered by a particular religious community (which, of course, is but one of many communities identifying with a particular religion, such as Southern Baptists or Shi'ite Muslims), thus uncritically transforming a first-order claim of priority ("this is what Christians believe") into an analytical category, or he or she can create a new definition that must also adjudicate claims about which religious manifestations are "authentic." Empirically, though, it is all but impossible to specify which beliefs, discourses, and structures of meaning occur among all communities (not to mention individuals) that identify with a specific religion. Jewish communities, for example, might express allegiance to a concept of "monotheism," but the term is often stretched and manipulated to include belief in angels, demons, and other supernatural powers that regularly occur in sacred texts, not to mention the multifaceted God of the Zohar.[13] Scholars, both within and outside the Jewish community, have developed ways of harmonizing the creedal assertion with the empirical evidence, but the result here, as in most similar cases, leads to an expansion of the meaning of the assertion (for example, Judaism is monotheistic) to the point where it becomes vague and analytically less useful.

Rather than being defined primarily by its beliefs, a religion might better be seen as a heuristic abstraction that accounts for the family resemblance among religious actors, each responding in different ways to more or less the same set of traditions. That is, what is at the core of "a religion" is neither a symbolic system that remains constant through space and time nor an extended argument, but a set of discrete static resources to which religious actors attribute a constraining force. Shi'a and Sunni Muslims are linked less by common beliefs (although there certainly are some) than by their shared veneration of the Qur'an *hadith* and some extratextual practices. Understanding "a religion" as a diverse set of responses to the same or linked *resources* explains both the similarities among the historical communities that create these responses and the differences among different "religions."

To elaborate further, these resources are of three general types: narratives, objects, and practices. *Narratives* are stories and other verbal artifacts (including creeds and law codes); *objects* are material things such as an icon, crucifix, or totem; and *practices*, in a more precise sense than used heretofore, refer to activities, many of which we might call rituals. Each warrants some brief discussion.

II.1. Narratives

Many religious actors regard narratives of origin as foundational. These narratives, which are transmitted in oral or written form, account for the creation of the natural order and establish a particular group's identity and preeminence. Narratives (stories) of origins are usually referred

[13] Michael L. Satlow, "Defining Judaism: Accounting for 'Religions' in the Study of Religion," *Journal of the American Academy of Religion* 74, 4 (2006): 837–60.

to as "myths," although that term is innately fuzzy and carries with it centuries of value-laden connotations.[14] Hence I prefer the term *narratives of origin*.

Narratives of origin are resources. They are almost always either cryptic or contradictory, and thus they almost always become objects of interpretation. When the Jewish philosopher Philo (first century BCE to first century CE), for example, read the biblical account of the creation of Eve (Gen 2:21), he rejected a literal interpretation out of hand. "These words in their literal sense are of the nature of a myth," he wrote. "For how could anyone admit that a woman, or a human being at all, came into existence out of a man's side?"[15] The accounts of Jesus's life in the New Testament gospels are likewise so various in narrative detail that they have engendered a great corpus of Christian commentary that attempts to harmonize them, to privilege one account over the others, or to find theological significance in the variations. Narratives of origin are pregnant with meanings, and the consumers of these stories have to make choices about which particular meaning(s) to highlight.

Here the concept of memory is useful. In one sense, narratives of origin are "memories"; they are ways in which people choose to remember the past, apart from what we might call "historical veracity." Because these narratives are always undergoing interpretive readings, however, the narrative tradition that constitutes the memory is itself less constraining than is any single particular reading of the narrative. The living memory is the way a narrative is understood over time by a particular person or group.

The distinction here among tradition, history, and memory is important. History is a specific intellectual and narrative practice with its own set of hermeneutical rules. Although narrative traditions, including narratives of origin, tell stories of the past that involve continuity and change over time, they are not histories. They follow different sets of hermeneutical rules. Religious actors have of course long recognized this, largely shunning historical critical readings of their narratives. They have instead actualized these narratives as memory, a useful vision of the past that serves (in part) to create group identities among those who subscribe to it. Over the past two centuries in the West, these distinctions have increasingly blurred, with historians

---

[14] Bruce Lincoln, *Theorizing Myth: Narrative, Ideology, and Scholarship* (Chicago: University of Chicago Press, 1999).

[15] Philo, *Allegorical Interpretation of Genesis*, 2.19, trans. F. H. Colson and G. H. Whitaker, Loeb Classical Library 226 (Cambridge, MA: Harvard University Press, 1929), vol. 1: 237–9.

attempting to mine traditional narratives for historical data, often criticizing their historical accuracy in the process, and religious actors seeking to "defend" these narratives against such historical criticism. This conflict over meanings is certainly not new, but it has come increasingly to characterize the modern cultural discourse about religion and religious traditions.[16]

Religious narratives are linked to issues of scripturalization and canonization. Traditional religious narratives can be oral or written (there is often a rather fluid relationship between the two). The traditional narratives that have become part of foundational religious scriptures have commonly emerged from oral performances. The transformation of an oral narrative tradition regarded as sacred into a written one might be termed the process of scripturalization. Canonization, on the other hand, usually refers to the processes by which religious actors and authorities give a narrative (or set of narratives, usually written) an imprimatur. Canonical narrative traditions are those that have been officially approved, although the fact of canonization alone does not necessarily indicate how "non-official" religious actors understand or impute authority to canonical traditions. An authority's claim about the canonicity of a tradition or text might be accepted, rejected, or modified, whether by other authorities or larger religious groups.

There are other types of textual narrative traditions. The Babylonian Talmud, for example, is a complex text that weaves together ancient stories, interpretations, legal reasoning, and law itself. Creeds and legal codes themselves may be traditional narratives. They function, however, just like other narratives: they are resources that exercise a constraining force, the nature of which can vary.

II.2. Objects

Religious objects are traditional in two senses. They may be actual material objects (or structures or places) that are preserved and venerated; or they may be a form or pattern – a template – for the creation of such objects. In the first class are objects such as relics and icons; costumes, masks, crucifixes, prayer beads, and phylacteries fall into the latter category. Although each one might be subject to stylistic and

---

[16] Angelika Rauch, *The Hieroglyph of Tradition: Freud, Benjamin, Gadamer, Novalis, Kant* (Cranbury NJ: Associated University Presses, 2000), 23–65; Yosef Hayim Yerushalmi, *Zakhor: Jewish History and Memory*, The Samuel and Althea Stroum Lectures in Jewish Studies (Seattle: University of Washington Press, 1982), 5–26; Lincoln, *Theorizing Myth*, 47–137.

artistic creativity, the objects are recognizable and are typically used in a religious context.

Relics and icons stand at one end of the spectrum of traditional objects, preserved and guarded within communities. They are often housed in religiously marked spaces and treated in a ritually approved manner. Objects, however, also may be preserved and reverenced in other contexts. Many places of worship have preserved objects that they display and use only at certain times. Families too pass down religious objects, using and displaying them in various ways. It is a tad ironic that today such objects are frequently housed in secular museums.

Like narrative traditions, traditional religious objects *carry no innate meaning*. The object exercises constraining force, but its "meaning" may or may not be fixed. Religious actors may connect particular objects to particular narratives – at times using institutional authority to justify these connections – but these associations also frequently shift over time and place. An object might be tightly or loosely integrated into a larger "discourse" or "pattern of meaning" for some practitioners or hardly at all for others. Like narratives and practices, objects are resources that religious actors use in ways that are not always predictable.

II.3. Practices

Practices are patterns or forms of human activity. Near the beginning of this chapter, I used the term "practices" broadly to include also discursive acts (such as narratives), but here it will be useful to tighten the term. Practices in the sense of patterns or forms of human activity might include manner of dress, cuisine, modes of worship, celebration of festivals, and other acts intended to propitiate, ward off, or bribe supernatural agents to do or not to do something.

Ritual is one category of practices. As discussed by the late Catherine Bell, the ritual theorist, "ritual" is a notoriously difficult category to pin down. Bell understood rituals as acts that are formal, traditional, invariant, rule-governed, and performed. These features probably require more specification than Bell provides – who sets the rules, for example, and how are they monitored? – but they do point to sets of practices that have assumed formal dimensions. Such ritualized practices are often transmitted not only mimetically, but also via articulated (oral or written) codes and scripts, and are frequently connected to explanatory narratives.[17]

---

[17] Catherine Bell, *Ritual: Perspectives and Dimensions* (New York: Oxford University Press, 1997), 138–69.

Defined as highly patterned, closely monitored, and officially authorized performances, rituals constitute but one kind of traditional religious practice. Many religious practices that people inherit and use are much less scripted and formalized. Sometimes institutional codes do formalize these practices, but sometimes they do not – whether such a code is the family cult of a saint or the use of a particular color on the outside of a house to ward off evil powers.[18] Traditional practices can be local, confined to certain congregations or even to particular families.

Like religious objects, practices are in a key sense inherently *meaningless*. Meanings often accompany practices (particularly in the case of institutionalized rituals), but the words and stories that explain the meanings of a practice are most often subordinate to the practice itself. Put differently (and explained in more detail later in this chapter), the narrative of meaning generally carries less *authenticity* and *authority* than the traditional practice itself. I might do something because my parents and community do it, as (I believe) their ancestors did it originally, but I might have to adjust how I understand what I am doing in order to have it make sense to me and others. Practices, no less than narrative traditions (for example, scripture), constitute parallel, additional sources of tradition and authority within a religious world.

In most cultures and at most times, practices transmitted by mimesis – that is, by imitation and embodiment – are a more transparent window into popular religious life than narrative traditions and institutions. This is because religious practices respond to a variety of human needs – health, love, prosperity, fertility, and domestic harmony, to cite just some of the everyday issues that bedevil people – which are sometimes of only marginal interest to the small (usually elite male) cohort that controls the "official" religious institutions. Although such "unofficial" practices and the understandings attached to them have been called the "little tradition," such traditions – including, for example, the festivals of women in ancient Greece or the extra-ecclesial and improvised worship idioms of nineteenth-century American slaves – are no "smaller" or less authentic than any other tradition.[19]

---

[18] Robert A. Orsi, *Between Heaven and Earth: The Religious Worlds People Make and the Scholars Who Study Them* (Princeton, NJ: Princeton University Press, 2005), 110–45.

[19] Robert Redfield, *Peasant Society and Culture: An Anthropological Approach to Civilization* (Chicago: University of Chicago Press, 1956); Ross Shepard Kraemer, *Her Share of the Blessings: Women's Religions Among Pagans, Jews, and Christians in the Greco-Roman World* (New York: Oxford University Press, 1992), 22–49; Albert J. Raboteau, *Slave Religion: The "Invisible Institution" in the Antebellum South* (New York: Oxford University Press, 1978).

III. INDIVIDUALS, COMMUNITIES, AND INSTITUTIONS

It bears emphasizing, although it may strike some readers as obvious, that tradition, traditions, and religions have no agency. Traditions do not do things in the world; religions do not act. It was not Islam that brought down the World Trade Center on September 11, 2001, but particular Muslims, acting in conformity to traditions they deemed imperative and authentic. To the extent that traditions, and more broadly, religions, exercise a constraining force, they do so only because humans attribute such authority, necessity, and efficacy to them. Religious actors themselves, of course, may well feel that such a force is externally (perhaps divinely) imposed, but as a second-order category, traditions and religions acquire their power through and in their human agents.

The term "religious actors" likewise conflates realities that might be more profitably distinguished. Individuals, communities, and institutions all do things with traditions, and the dynamics that typify those interactions differ. At the same time, these interactions do not occur in isolation. A societal understanding of a tradition might stand in tension to those of an institution or individual.

Most discussions of "tradition" in religious contexts focus on institutional use – what traditions mean to particular religious communities. I understand "religious institution" capaciously, on the other hand. It can include the Roman Catholic Church, an Islamic school of law, a cultic site, or a local Buddhist monastery. All of these *institutions* utilize traditions to justify their authority; they often put great effort into preserving and controlling these traditions. The canonization of narrative traditions by institutions thus can serve political purposes, as we well know.[20]

Institutions also do things with traditional objects. Sometimes these objects are intrinsically and organically related to the institution. A priest may perform miracles under the auspices and with the approval of his church (as was the case with the southern Italian stigmatic Padre Pio), and upon dying, his body may made into a sacred relic (again as happened with Padre Pio, who is now Santo Pio). At other times, the relationship between the institution and the object is more intricate, even equivocal. Objects considered holy by some may generate distinctive cults and practices, which other institutions might later absorb and reinterpret.

[20] Benedictus de Spinoza, *Theological-Political Treatise*, trans. Michael Silverthorne and Jonathan Israel (Cambridge and New York: Cambridge University Press, 2007), 68–80.

The use of the pre-Muslim Kaaba by Muslims is an example of this phenomenon. Traditional holy objects might also serve as sites of popular resistance to the very institutions that are trying to appropriate them.

It is usually in the political realm that communal traditions become most visible, especially when they are in tension with the authorities, political and religious. As mentioned previously, narrative historical traditions ("memory") provide justification for political communities and their actions, and, similarly, the role of ritual in the civil order has been discussed extensively.[21] Tradition and its control became a key issue in the battle between the "secular" authorities in England and the Roman Catholic Church in the sixteenth century, for example, which ultimately led to Henry VIII's break with the papacy and the foundation of the Church of England.

Most communal religious traditions, however, do not have such a visible, let alone explosive, political dimension. Local communities develop and preserve distinctive local religious traditions. The mode of transmission is usually mimetic rather than didactic. These local religious practices are no less persistent or important for religious actors than those more formally preserved by institutions. Religious traditions frequently emerge within local communities before institutions appropriate (or oppose) them. Individuals and their families likewise create and transmit religious traditions. Many families have their own customs or places of worship. The *pūjā* is an excellent example of this phenomenon: a shrine located within the Hindu household, each of which is supposed to contain certain items. The *pūjā* is thus a domestic shrine that allows for individual and familial variation while at the same time identifying practitioners with broader South Asian sacred traditions.

Ancestor worship is similarly a family matter. At the same time, within many cultures, there are inherited, regionally similar practices of ancestor worship, although the ancestors to be worshipped – now supernatural beings – are specific to individual families. For the Tellensi, a tribe in Ghana, faithful observance of the ancestor cult "is the bridge between the internal presence and the external sanctity of parental authority and power." Idiosyncratic traditions, narratives, objects, and practices (rituals) continue to play an important role in the religious lives of most modern Western families.[22]

---

[21] Robert N. Bellah, "Civil Religion in America," *Daedalus* 96 (Winter 1967): 1–21.
[22] Elizabeth Bloch-Smith, *Judahite Burial Practices and Beliefs about the Dead*, JSOT/ ASOR Monograph Series 7; JSOT Supplement Series 123 (Sheffield: JSOT Press, 1992); Meyer Fortes, "Pietas in Ancestor Worship," *Journal of the Royal Anthropological Institute of Great Britain and Ireland* 91, 2 (1961): 187.

The assignation of meaning highlights the complicated interplay of institution, community, and individual. Many institutions create formal meanings for traditions, but whether communities or individuals adopt these meanings is variable. An individual might accept an institution's explanation of a tradition; he or she might misunderstand (intentionally or not) an institutional meaning script, appropriating it in unpredictable ways; or else he or she might reject or otherwise ignore the meanings given to the tradition by others. Individuals, in complex negotiations with the social units to which they belong, make the links between practices and a variety of diverse (and not always predictable) texts that create meaning.

Emphasizing the role that human agency plays in tradition necessarily (and properly) raises the issues of politics and power (discussed later in this chapter), but explaining the creation and persistence of traditions entirely as vehicles of power is far too reductionist. Religious actors subscribe to traditions for many reasons. Traditions establish and reinforce communal identities; they help to maintain proper relationships with supernatural beings; and they provide psychological succor. Traditions are sometimes maintained out of inertia and a simple fear of change. In all cases, though, people give traditions their constraining force, even when they inherit a tradition as given.

IV. AUTHENTIC

What makes an "invented tradition" authentic? Until recently, the question would have been unthinkable. Religious actors at most times and in most places have gauged the authenticity of tradition – to the extent that the issue would have occurred at all – by three criteria: accuracy, antiquity, and its privileged source. While not every tradition claims all three grounds of authentication, most religious actors use some combination of them in assessing (however subtly or inarticulately) the authenticity of their traditions and thereby the authority they ascribe to them.

A tradition must be believed to be accurate in order to be believed in. If it is an object, it must be the real thing: Catholics make distinctions among relics, for example, distinguishing actual pieces of a saint's body (first-class relics) from articles of clothing (second class) and cloth touched by the bones of the saint (third class). Power in this case is extensive – a third-class relic is as real and efficacious as a first-class one – but is referenced back to a real object. The historical details of a narrative of origins might not be accurate, but the words of the narrative themselves must be.

A paraphrase of the Hebrew Bible is different from the Bible itself, whether as a narrative or even as a physical object. For many Jews and Muslims, scriptures written in their original languages (Hebrew and Arabic) have a very different status than translations, however faithful they may be. To be efficacious, it is widely thought, most rituals need to be performed precisely.

The Islamic "chain of tradition," the *isnad* that came to preface every *hadith* (a tradition or story about Muhammad and his circle), illustrates an explicit religious recognition of this issue. The Islamic scholars who collected these various stories in the early Middle Ages assigned to *hadith* an *isnad*, an account of who heard or saw it first, to whom the tradition was passed, and other such authenticating details. The importance of the *isnad* becomes clearest in the realm of law (*fiqh*). Given the large number of sometimes conflicting *hadith*, Islamic scholars developed a sophisticated science for evaluating the relative authenticity of a tradition based on the names of its transmitters. Accuracy of the text here has legal consequences.

A tradition need not be ancient to be considered authentic, but it helps, even when a tradition is relatively recent. Many traditions, particularly narratives, assert their own antiquity. Although such claims are usually false (or at least unverifiable) from the perspective of modern historical practice, religious actors recognize some authority in them. Many *isnads*, for example, are fictive, in the sense of constructed, and the Torah dates itself prior to its actual historical period of formation and compilation. A large number of the noncanonical tracts now known as "the Old Testament Pseudepigrapha" were written in the Hellenistic period or later, but they are attributed to biblical characters. The Zohar claims a second-century CE dating, although the tracts were almost certainly compiled in the thirteenth century.

The role that antiquity plays in assessing authenticity might best be seen in the cases where it is missing. From its origins, the Book of Mormon was derided by many Christians in part due to their skepticism about its assertions to its own antiquity. Likewise, the transformation of aspects of "ancient" and traditional worship (although most often these were modern innovations) made by the Roman Catholic Church at Vatican II was (and continues to be) met with some resistance. At the same time, though, the religious actors who accept these "new" traditions almost never see them as "new." They are justified on the basis of even mistaken attributions. Roman Catholic reformers, both at Trent and at Vatican II, understood themselves to be restoring ancient traditions. Institutional support might help to establish and nurture new traditions, but ultimately it is simple staying power that will over the accumulated years increase their authenticity.[23]

Individuals, communities, and institutions have always created resources that would later become traditions, but perhaps nowhere is this done with the frequency, intention, and valorization as in modern America. The scholarly focus on invented traditions is indicative of a broader cultural Zeitgeist that values innovation over tradition. Religious actors in America today routinely create new rituals and modes of worship; the notion of "antiquity" can be much compressed. The bat mitzvah, for example, a ritual (and celebration) noting a Jewish woman's coming of age analogous to the bar mitzvah (which itself dates to the Middle Ages), apparently was first publicly celebrated in America in 1922. Although if remains rare in Europe and Israel, it is common in America today even among Orthodox groups (although in a different form) and has achieved the status of the "traditional."[24]

Accuracy, antiquity, and source largely constitute the areas of intrareligious battle for the authenticity of tradition. Religious groups often frame their differences in terms of tradition, as in, "We have and follow authentic traditions and you do not." When early modern Protestants attacked the Roman Catholic Church, for example, they focused their theological criticism on the inauthenticity of its traditions and the Church's betrayal or abandonment of what Protestants deemed authentic primitive Christian traditions. The attack was thus directed at the faithfulness of its traditions; their antiquity; and their source (common, even venal, human beings).[25] The battle over the authenticity of tradition is not the only cause of intrareligious strife or its only outcome, but when such disagreements arise, they are prominent.

While accuracy, antiquity, and source tend to be the criteria by which many religious actors regard a tradition as authentic, the presence of these three criteria alone hardly accounts for the acceptance of traditions. Nearly every canonical collection excluded texts that met all three criteria. In most cases, the selection process and criteria remain obscure. The Book of Jubilees, written in the third century BCE (earlier than the canonical Book of Ecclesiastes, parts of Daniel, and

---

[23] Richard L. Bushman, *Joseph Smith and the Beginnings of Mormonism* (Urbana: University of Illinois Press, 1984).

[24] Ivan G. Marcus, *The Jewish Life Cycle: Rites of Passage from Biblical to Modern Times*, The Samuel and Althea Stroum Lectures in Jewish Studies (Seattle: University of Washington Press, 2004), 105–16.

[25] Jaroslav Pelikan, *The Christian Tradition: A History of the Development of Doctrine*, vol. 4, *Reformation of Church and Dogma (1300–1700)* (Chicago: University of Chicago Press, 1984), 304–31.

some Psalms in the Hebrew Bible) and purporting to be an ancient revelation from God, was accepted as authentic by the authors of some of the Dead Sea Scrolls, although it did not enter the canon of the rabbis (ca. first to sixth centuries CE) and later Jewish communities. The Church fathers did not accept as canonical the gospels found at Nag Hammadi. Religious actors tend to take these criteria seriously, but ultimately their decisions (whether on an institutional, communal, or individual level) incorporate many other, inchoate factors.

V. AUTHORITATIVE

Most contemporary theoretical discussions of tradition take authority to be constitutive of and fundamental to the concept. Edward Shils, for example, writes that for some religions, tradition, particularly sacred scriptures, acquired an "intrinsic authority."[26] The authority of tradition is a given, to theorists as well as to theologians (recognizing that the two are not always distinct).

By contrast, I have argued, traditions exercise a constraining force. For religious actors, this force is self-evident. At the same time, though, these same religious actors frequently ascribe different levels of authority to their traditions. "Authority" here might be fine-tuned. Traditions, of course, frequently claim their own authority, as we have seen. Narratives most typically make such claims explicitly. An object's claim to authority is more indirect, often by means of a long-established cult that cares for it. Similarly, long-observed practices, especially those that a community feels are efficacious, claim authority in and of themselves.

Whether and how any religious actor actually believes the tradition's claim is another question entirely. Individuals, communities, and institutions make choices about whether to ascribe authority to a particular resource, developing a logic that rationalizes these judgments. But such assessments are not entirely rational. Many factors play a role in a religious practitioner's "decision" to attribute authority to a traditional resource. Inertia, social pressure, idiosyncratic psychological needs, or even coercive power might influence such decisions. Religious institutions, on the other hand, often go to great pains to articulate the reasons behind their attribution of authority to a tradition. Most religious persons, coming to terms with their traditions, fall between these two poles of the contingent and the intentional.

---

[26] Shils, *Tradition*, 95.

The kind of authority attributed to a tradition also varies widely. At the minimum for my definition is the notion of a resource having enough authority to warrant its preservation and transmission and exercising a constraining force. This rather low bar draws attention to the mass of cultural resources that are not even able to achieve this relatively modest status. Many religious actors, of course, assign far greater levels of authority to traditions. Some religious actors, conflating tradition and memory with history, attribute literal truth to narratives of origin (such as modern "creationism"). Others view such narratives as *essentially* true and subscribe to the major concepts (as they understand them) illustrated or performed by such narratives while rejecting the historical truth of their details. An individual Jew might understand herself as biologically connected to other Jews while rejecting the biblical account of Abraham's existence. The difference between these two approaches to narrative traditions is more an issue of quality than quantity.

Narrative traditions also include codes of conduct. Individuals, communities, and institutions might differ about both the content and authority of these traditions. Like common law, religious law ascribes an "authority of the past," but individuals demonstrate a wide range of stances on their acceptance of this authority.[27] Communities and religious institutions have occasionally found themselves at odds with the authority of a tradition, sometimes with fatal consequences. The articulated imprimatur of a religious institution confers a clear authority, but, again, the authorized tradition actually contains only as much authority as other religious actors give it.

Varying amounts and kinds of authority are ascribed to different religious objects and practices. The relic of a Buddhist saint has a different value than does the shrine at Mecca. In the eyes of religious institutions, ancient, long-standing practices commonly used by individuals to ward off evil beings often possess less authority than accepted practices, even though individuals might reverse that evaluation on particular occasions.

Authority also has a coercive dimension. Religious actors may try to impose normative traditions on others. Coercion takes many shapes. Communities use a wide variety of "technologies," to borrow Michel Foucault's key word, in order to impose "discipline" upon its members, whereas only some involve the actual use of force. Religious institutions may or may not be able to use force. As Stalin famously said about the moral threat of the Vatican, "How many divisions does the Pope

---

[27] Anthony T. Kronman, "Precedent and Tradition," *Yale Law Journal* 99, 5 (1990): 1044.

have?" Still, the mutual slaughter of Protestants and Catholics in early modern Europe and their brutal internal campaigns to maintain orthodoxy and fidelity provide an example of religious violence on behalf of the authority of traditions. In contemporary Iran, religious coercion has been, until very recently, exercised more subtly, often by means of paramilitary groups with shadowy ties to official religious institutions and leaders.[28]

Most contemporary religious institutions, though, do not have the authority or ability to impose their will by force. They rely on persuasion. In its "soft" version, persuasion means convincing religious actors that there is more good in adhering to a tradition than not. "Hard" persuasion works by convincing them that ignoring the traditions will result in grave, perhaps eternal, punishment. Both, though, promote actively the authority of tradition.

VI. CONCLUSION

The primary goal of this chapter has been to "rehabilitate" the concept of "tradition," not as a philosophical, theological, ethical, or psychological category, but as a non-normative analytic category useful for the study of religion. In much scholarship, the concept of "memory," which emphasizes subjectivity and change, has largely supplanted tradition. While memory remains an important and useful concept, I have argued that a robust understanding of tradition can provide significant insights. The definition submitted here is meant provisionally and heuristically. Whether it is a "good" one ultimately depends on its usefulness.

A definition of an analytic category should do two things: open new avenues of investigation and fresh questions and locate the balance between the general and specific so as to allow useful comparisons. The purpose of the category is to allow for meaningful and fruitful comparisons between data that might, in their respective native contexts and languages, seem incommensurate.[29] Valerius Maximus and his contemporaries, of course, had something entirely different in mind when they invoked the concept of *mos maiorum*, but a traditional view

[28] Carlo Ginzburg, *The Cheese and the Worms: The Cosmos of a Sixteenth-Century Miller*, trans. John and Anne Tedeschi (Baltimore: Johns Hopkins University Press, 1980); Farhad Kazemi, "Civil Society in Iranian Politics," in *Civil Society in the Middle East*, ed. Augustus Richard Norton (Leiden and New York: Brill, 1995), vol. 1: 119–52.

[29] Michael L. Satlow, "Disappearing Categories: Using Categories in the Study of Religion," *Method and Theory in the Study of Religion* 17 (2005): 287–98.

of tradition, with some important modifications, might continue to serve us as well as it did them.

Select Bibliography

Bell, Catherine. *Ritual: Perspectives and Dimensions.* New York: Oxford University Press, 1997.

Geertz, Clifford. "Religion as a Cultural System," In *The Interpretation of Cultures: Selected Essays.* New York: Basic Books, 1973, 87–125.

Hobsbawm, Eric and Terence Ranger, eds. *The Invention of Tradition.* Cambridge and New York: Cambridge University Press, 1983.

Lincoln, Bruce. *Theorizing Myth: Narrative, Ideology, and Scholarship.* Chicago: University of Chicago Press, 1999.

MacIntyre, Alasdair C. *After Virtue: A Study in Moral Theory.* Notre Dame. IN: University of Notre Dame Press, 1981.

Rauch, Angelika. *The Hieroglyph of Tradition: Freud, Benjamin, Gadamer, Novalis, Kant.* Cranbury, NJ: Associated University Presses, 2000.

Satlow, Michael L. "Defining Judaism: Accounting for 'Religions' in the Study of Religion." *Journal of the American Academy of Religion* 74, no. 4 (2006): 837–60.

Shils, Edward. *Tradition.* Chicago: University of Chicago Press, 1981.

Stout, Jeffrey. *Democracy and Tradition.* New Forum Books. Princeton, NJ: Princeton University Press, 2004.

Valliere, Paul. "Tradition." In *Encyclopedia of Religion.* Edited by Lindsay Jones. Detroit: Macmillan Reference USA, 2005. Vol. 13: 9267–81.

7 The text and the world

ANNE M. BLACKBURN

I. INTRODUCTION

In 1455, King Tilokaraja of Chiang Mai, a northern kingdom in what we now know as Thailand, began to build a new Buddhist temple in imitation of the Maha Bodhi temple at Bodh Gaya (India), which marks the site of Sakyamuni Buddha's enlightenment. After first installing a *bodhi* tree – a devotional reminder of the Buddha's enlightenment – transferred from one of Chiang Mai's most powerful existing Buddhist sites, Tilokaraja continued to sponsor work at the new temple for years to come. Spaces for the veneration of Sakyamuni Buddha were constructed, along with a pavilion for the recitation of Buddhist texts and a monastic library. This temple in Chiang Mai, the Seven Spires Monastery, later housed a large gathering of Buddhist monks invited by the king to purify and recite the contents of canonical Buddhist texts.

The labor, wealth, and royal support required for this temple and its editorial assembly, as well as the importance of both to subsequent Thai Buddhist memory, remind us that the texts central to religious traditions and communities of practitioners are – and long have been – alive in the world. Such texts are performed in liturgy and ritual. They are references used in sophisticated intellectual debate, as well as tools for basic education. Celebrated within religious communities, texts also shape the world of material culture, guiding the creation of statues and paintings and providing descriptive models for the construction of spaces for ritual and devotion. Those books or manuscripts deemed transformatively powerful are drawn into the work of magic and protective ritual. To possess religious texts, or to support their production, is often (especially in a manuscript culture) a display of wealth and power.

In such ways, texts are often central to vital human activities that take place within institutions and contexts of practice we now call

I am grateful to Robert A. Orsi for his comments on earlier versions of this chapter.

religious. However, it requires trained vision and analytical imagination to see the centrality of texts and their multiple purposes with
fullness and clarity. In our historical moment, such training requires
that we recognize and consciously attempt to overcome the constraints
posed by two influential strands of reflection on the place of texts in the
study of religions that have developed over the past century and a half
or more. The first we might call *reductive textualism* and the second
critical post-textualism.

II. REDUCTIVE TEXTUALISM

Early scholars of comparative religions (understood then more often as
comparative religion) worked in a cultural-intellectual space marked
by the intersection of the new field of historical philology as well as
modern Protestant theology and biblical criticism. Within certain
modern Protestant traditions, especially those associated with university scholars, an important inheritance from the Reformation shaped
the approach to religious texts and histories taken by many scholars
of religion. This was the assumption that religious traditions were
most authentically and fully represented by their scriptures. In other
words, the texts historically closest to a tradition's temporal origin and
Urmoment of revelation, prophecy, or meditative realization were considered the surest testimony to the heart of that tradition. Although
this was by no means the only notion of scripture to be found in early
modern and modern Europe and America, it came to dominate the academic study of religion, thanks to the intellectual influence of biblical
critics who sought to understand the history and meaning of Jewish and
Christian scriptures.

   These intellectual developments continue to exert a powerful sway
on the scholarly study of religions, as well as on the ways we express our
curiosity about other religions more widely. After September 11, 2001,
for example, people debated whether the Qur'an did or did not endorse
violence, as if this were the sole guide to Muslim understanding and
behavior. Within American religious institutions, interreligious dialogue often focuses on the comparison of ideas expressed in scriptures,
with much less attention to other influential religious texts or to the
character of lived religious practice. Despite recent critical rejoinder
by some scholars of religion, the claim that there are "religions" with
"essences" or "cores" accessible through their "scriptures" is built into
the DNA of religious studies. And, therefore, even dedicated scholars
and highly motivated critical readers outside the academy often neglect

the many other works that have been produced within religious communities as companions and rejoinders to authoritative foundational texts. This neglect comes at a high price, for one then misses valuable witness to the restless creativity of generations of intellectuals and practitioners. For decades and centuries, women and men faced the inspiration and limitation of their textual and liturgical moment, and then – in words and deeds – exceeded it, vitalizing their communities of belonging and shaping the textual heritage of future generations.

Textual reductionism extends beyond the narrow range of texts examined to include the ways in which one engages the texts themselves. Moderns tend to read texts silently and alone. We often take for granted that one's relationship to a text is a matter of eye and mind, forgetting the long history of reading aloud alone or in groups that was often central to devotional textuality. We rarely smell our texts, run our fingers over the distinctive texture of manuscript leaves and papers, examine critically calligraphic style, or look for the marks and emendations of former readers and scribes. All this was, and sometimes remains, a commonplace in the textual culture of many practitioners. Scholars of religion do not generally honor or revere the texts we are trained to read critically, or handle them as precious objects, although many others who inhabit modern religious worlds continue to engage religious texts with such devotion. We scholars meet these texts mostly with our mental faculties, and those too are distinctive to our own milieu as scholars in a modern (or perhaps postmodern) university setting. While we hope the texts we read will transform our scholarly work, most of us rarely expect or hope that they will transform and protect us in our present circumstances or after death. We use them in social practice, but according to logics distinctive of our milieu. Our handling, reading, and interpretation of texts linked to religious traditions are shaped by our own moment in time, place, and discourse, and the kinds of collective belonging most alive to us. This is understandable, yet it also poses dangers for our scholarly work and comprehension of other texts and reading practices. It may abet anachronistic analysis and promote the failure to imagine richly other times and places of textual practice linked to religious traditions and communities.

III. CRITICAL POST-TEXTUALISM

In recent decades, scholars of religion have devoted considerable attention to the textual reductionist attitude just mentioned, exploring its roots in the intellectual histories of European modernities. This exploration has identified the imperial and colonial histories of Britain and Europe as a crucial context for the rise of the academic study of religion, one that fundamentally shaped the discipline's approach to historical and lived religions. Central to this account is a critical investigation of the ways in which scholarly research and writing on the cultures and histories of colonized territories fed and was fed by the political-institutional demands of colonial rule. On this view, still most famously associated with Edward Said's classic study *Orientalism*, European intellectual exploration of then relatively new analytical frameworks such as "race," "ethnicity," "culture," "nation," and "religion" (themselves partly the product of new information about distant locales generated by European trade and colonization) shaped the terms within which the persons and social worlds of colonized territories were recognized and translated for use in scholarly discourse and colonial administrative practice. The academic study of religion developed within networks stretching across oceans, as colonial bureaucrats, university professors, private scholars, the local religious leaders of colonized territories, and Christian missionaries converged (albeit often for diverse and competing purposes) to investigate forms of belief and practice perceived as at least partly analogous to the more familiar Abrahamic traditions of Eurasia. In this process, the distinctive approaches to religious textuality characteristic of modern European theological, ecclesiastical, and scholarly communities shaped the terms through which study of devotional, ritual, and intellectual practices within colonized territories were translated into data for the emergent "science of religion." So did the interpretive perspectives of local religious leaders and intellectuals, who served as translators and informants for their foreign interlocutors. Such local intermediaries emerged as influential voices in rapidly growing local print media and educational institutions.

A striking result of these complex global exchanges was the creation of a new understanding of religion and of religious traditions within the colonized territories among local religious practitioners, even as information about these newly conceived traditions was exported to the colonial metropolises. In Asia, for instance, congeries of ritual, devotional, aesthetic, and intellectual practices clustered around the figure of Buddha, or Śiva, or Vishnu – practices present in recognizably similar form across substantial geographic space – were interpreted within a new and encompassing European taxonomy as the *religions* of Hinduism and Buddhism. The earliest stratum of texts associated with these traditions, respected for their age as well as the "classical" greatness of their language (Sanskrit, classical Chinese, Pali, and so on), became associated with the essence of each religious tradition. As these religions took their shape as objects of investigation and then as traditions for affiliation, early or "original" practice (discerned from authoritative foundational texts, typically read as descriptive accounts rather than as ideals and exhortations) was valued above medieval or contemporary forms considered degenerate.

During the last three decades, the discipline of the academic study of religion has undergone a postcolonial self-criticism, linked to wider intellectual currents within postcolonial studies as well as to moves within the humanities and social sciences to investigate the institutional and intellectual histories of these modern disciplines. In addition to developing histories of the academic study of religion, especially in its eighteenth- and nineteenth-century guises, to which this chapter and earlier chapters of this book refer, the field has witnessed a methodological reaction against the highly textualized character of its own formative moment, as the categories of "religion" and "tradition" have undergone historical deconstruction. Contemplating the dizzying arguments that there is no natural entity or phenomenon matching what we call "religion," that the term and some of its accompanying "-isms" (such as Hinduism, Confucianism, Buddhism, and Taoism) are of historically and culturally limited recent vintage, and that the emphasis on scriptures and historical origins in the study of religion might be characterized as a politically and intellectually suspect continuation of colonial forms of knowledge and Eurocentrism, some scholars of religion have sought refuge in the study of practice rather than text, ritual rather than doctrine, and contemporary contexts rather than those of the past. Such intellectual moves have been made yet more natural and attractive by increasingly close ties between scholars of religion and anthropology after World War II (partly in the context of shared postcolonial criticism), as well as a growing awareness that the religious character of contemporary life deserves careful study in the face of failed theories of secular modernization.

Such new developments in the academic study of religion constitute a valuable contribution in themselves. There is a danger, however, that the turn to studies of ritual and everyday life, especially in the context of an apologetic retreat from the study of texts, leaves scholars of religion in an intellectually untenable position. We may fail to recognize the often profoundly influential connections between texts and devotional practice, for example, and to neglect the very high value accorded to textual composition, transmission, and interpretation within the communities we seek to understand. Moreover, in retreat from the study of texts, we ignore crucial evidence of the processes by which religious collectivities have renewed and transformed themselves, and continue to do so. There is a need to rehabilitate the study of texts within the study of religion. Scholars of religion require a more capacious space for collaboration between those who read texts closely, edit them, and translate them and those who would ask questions about the place of such texts in the lives of persons, collectives, and traditions. Without this, we risk losing the valuable scholarly resources made possible by the discipline's historic investment in philology, language, and literature. Moreover, we would marginalize textualists and their materials from the work of historical and ethnographic writing, occluding from view the ubiquitous presence of texts and textuality in religious worlds, past and present.

Scholars of religion have begun to grapple with these problems. There is already increased vitality among those who engage textual materials with reference to histories (and to some extent ethnographies) of religions. As we might expect from a discipline that has always renewed itself in interdisciplinary conversation while contributing to the development of these other disciplines, new directions are emerging in the contact zones between the academic study of religion, anthropology, social and intellectual history, and philosophy. Manifest in diverse forms, there is a shift in emphasis from the study of texts to the study of textual practice, looking at how texts are taken up by persons and communities for particular reasons, in distinctive ways. There is also the recognition that religious communities may be studied fruitfully as literary cultures, characterized by location- and period-specific patterns of argument, social patronage, aesthetic expectations, and textual forms. In the following sections, working with several examples, I sketch some modes of description and analysis rooted in the turn to the study of textual practice and literary cultures that may allow us to avoid the doubled danger of textual reductionism and critical post-textualism.

IV. TEXTUAL HERITAGE, VALUE, AND EFFICACY

Why did the Chiang Mai king Tilokaraja undertake the massive act of Buddhist patronage described at the beginning of this chapter? When authoritative foundational texts are brought to life in a public setting and linked to the highest authority of polity, what is the logic of such a move? What attitudes toward foundational authoritative texts made natural a move to publicly edit and perform a Buddhist canon? How were such texts valued in performance? A moment in which a given text or set of texts enters social action is for scholars of religion potentially a precious opening onto the analysis of how and why men and women choose to remain invested in the textual heritage of their religious affiliation. What are the values and understandings of efficacy attributed to texts that make such texts the focus of creative human labor?

Tilokaraja's reign was fraught with difficulty, as he strove to secure his position among rival factions in the Chiang Mai region. Acceding to the throne after the deposition of his father, he struggled to affirm his local leadership. At the same time, he was challenged from the south, militarily and diplomatically, by the growing power of his rival Trailokaraja at Ayutthaya.[1] Each king sought to develop networks of military control, with access to labor and revenue, in what is now northern and central Thailand. The Pali Buddhist texts that Tilokaraja sought to purify and promulgate were valued not only for their declarative content that offered access to liberating knowledge. Many of these texts were also understood to contain powerful words and syllables, potent Buddha-speech with transformative properties. In Tilokaraja's milieu, Buddhist texts could be deployed through chant or as written talismans to access the superhuman power of Sakyamuni Buddha. Such power could be used to protect the realm and its subjects, the king and his army. The Buddhist editorial assembly held at the Seven Spires Monastery drew on a repertoire for royal action in the pursuit of magical power and protection.

The construction of the Seven Spires Monastery and the celebratory performance of authoritative foundational texts were actions quite tightly implicated within the micropolitics of Buddhist Chiang Mai as well as struggles for regional primacy. Yet, simultaneously, through these acts Tilokaraja expressed his devotional engagement with Buddhist teachings and institutions. He sought protection not only for himself, his throne, and his realm in the sphere of immediate and mundane concerns but also for Buddhist teachings. These were understood to be at risk with the passage of time, within a process of degeneration that eventually strips the world of access to the salvific discourse of the

---

[1]   Editorial constraints do not permit full textual citations for the research on which this and subsequent sections draw. See the works cited in Anne M. Blackburn, "Writing Histories from Landscape and Architecture: Sukhothai and Chian Mai," *Buddhist Studies Review* 24, 2 (2007): 192–225, and Anne M. Blackburn, *Buddhist Learning and Textual Practice in Eighteenth-Century Lankan Monastic Culture* (Princeton, NJ: Princeton University Press, 2001). In this chapter, I have omitted diacritical marks for all proper names except the names of texts. See Blackburn, "Writing Histories" and *Buddhist Learning* for specialist transcriptions.

teachings. To protect Buddhist texts, the teachings they contained, and the practices they made possible – through editorial consolidation and performance – was seen as an act of devotional generosity to those living in the present era and those to come. By offering this gift, Tilokaraja improved his prospects for rebirth and his continued progress along the Buddhist path, thanks to the karmic merit made in such patronage. The king's engagement with the authoritative foundational texts of his Buddhist world thus drew on his understanding that the defense of these particular texts was a spectacularly powerful devotional act.

Tilokaraja's interest in foundational authoritative Buddhist texts, and their celebrated proclamation in Chiang Mai, is instructive well beyond the social and institutional history of Buddhism in Thailand. Reading the textual and material evidence from Chiang Mai, and attentive to the ideas of technology and ritual, vulnerability, and protection that informed royal acts of Buddhist patronage, *we begin to recognize that texts live in religious worlds according to historically particular expectations of textual value and efficacy.* These expectations are part of what we must understand if we wish to comprehend the long history through which authoritative foundational scriptures have remained central to practitioners and communities. The ways in which texts are written and performed, attributed value, and celebrated as powerful is a matter for investigation. In such research, the study of sacred texts becomes partly a study of the mentalities within which texts figure. One explores the expectations that surround texts, and how such attitudes influence patterns in the institutionalization of text production, reception, and use. Tilokaraja recognized that these Pali texts contained important didactic contents for Buddhist practitioners. However, it was for him at least as important, if not more so, that the texts could be performed in order to improve his material and physical circumstances, his prospects after death, and the safety of his realm. These texts were drawn into ritual transactions, not as historical traces of early Buddhist practice or as doctrinal compendia, but as a corpus infused with the power to protect present and future lives of a patron and his subjects.

V. TEXTUAL MODELS FOR ACTION

Tilokaraja and Trailokaraja, rivals for regional territorial control, acted in a distinctively Buddhist imperial idiom, aspiring to recognition as righteous rulers on a cosmic scale. They sought to act in public and dramatic ways like the exemplary kings celebrated by earlier Buddhist narratives, those carried by foundational authoritative and early historical texts. That is, they sought to instantiate in real time the literary models of the *cakkavattin* king described in early *sutta* texts, whose power was linked to their support for cosmic order, as well as that of the Indic king Asoka (third century BCE), glorified in Buddhist historical narratives as a model ruler and religious patron. In such narratives, Asoka is celebrated for his dramatic midcareer expression of confidence in the Buddha, his rule according to *dharma*, the purification of Buddhist teachings in an editorial assembly, and royal resolution of fierce intramonastic disputes. In his rivalry with the southern power of Ayutthaya, and in the unstable arena of Chiang Mai itself, Tilokaraja cultivated what we might think of as an Asokan persona[2] in the work of claiming and performing rightful rule. The editorial council held at the new Seven Spires Monastery, and commemorated within Chiang Mai Buddhist histories, formed an important part of that persona. King Tilokaraja attempted to show his subjects and rivals, near and far, that he had the power, the wealth, and the meritorious karmic fortune from past lives to do as King Asoka had done nearly two thousand years before: sponsor the redaction and recitation of authoritative Buddhist texts to secure the well-being of those with confidence in the teachings of the Buddha.

Acting in accordance with celebrated depictions of kingship transmitted by Buddhist texts, and seeking to anchor properly and publicly foundational authoritative Buddhist texts in the world, Tilokaraja made good use of his Seven Spires Monastery for the performance of kingship to local and regional audiences. The editorial assembly and textual recitation generated social capital. That is, the editorial assembly and recitation were a means through which the king could accumulate marks of status and authority. They were partly maneuvers within a social space marked by Buddhist monastic rivalries at home, an unstable royal court, and expansionary politics.

Texts associated with religious traditions live in the world partly as repositories of the memory of things past, which often include celebratory stories about how others have served these traditions. In other words, *they often model styles of human action and character that inform the imagination, action, and interpretation of those who read, see, or hear them.* Tilokaraja's Buddhist world was constituted in part by such stories and models, carried within the prized body of Buddhist

---

[2] John Clifford Holt, *The Religious World of Kīrti Śrī: Buddhism, Art, and Politics in Late-Medieval Sri Lanka* (London: Oxford University Press, 1996); James S. Duncan, *The City as Text: The Politics of Landscape Interpretation in the Kandyan Kingdom* (Cambridge: Cambridge University Press, 1990).

texts brought to Chiang Mai through monastic networks originating in Lanka (now Sri Lanka). The ways in which he made and remade Chiang Mai as a Buddhist and royal space, through construction and ritual, owed much to these texts, within which the model of Asoka and the image of the *cakkavattin* king held powerful place. The very possibility that a certain kind of performance – sponsoring an editorial assembly and reciting celebrated texts – could occur as a strategic move in social relations depended on the participation of patron, rivals, and audience within a shared literary world. *Shared access to the models of cakkavattin kingship and Asokan rule – through texts, sermons, and visual images – shaped the contours of human relations within which expressions of authority and eminence, as well as valued manifestations of devotion, were accumulated and recognized.* This was a regional Buddhist space in which aspirations to imperial kingship were expressed not only through military might but also in acts informed by narrative models. Influential narratives such as these may be carried within authoritative foundational texts, but also within a wider corpus of written and visual material, including sermon collections, histories, and commentaries.

VI. TEXTUAL PROWESS

In the mid-eighteenth century, a Buddhist monk in Lanka was invited by his king to compose a commentary in Sinhala, a local literary language, on a collection of canonical Buddhist texts in the language of Pali. These texts were valued as Buddha-speech and believed to have the power to protect those who heard them. Since the protective power of these texts lay in the proper recitation of their Pali language form, there was no need to translate them to Sinhala or to comment upon them in this local language in order to maintain or improve their magical efficacy. However, the Buddhist monk Valivita Saranankara composed a lengthy word-gloss treatment on the texts. The resulting commentarial text, *Sarārthadīpanī (Illuminator of Essential Meaning)*, became one of the scholarly projects for which he was best known. When he composed *Illuminator*, he was a suitor for royal favor, as the leader of a new monastic group in the up-country Kandyan kingdom of Lanka. He and his monastic colleagues criticized rivals in Kandy, seeking royal backing for the introduction of a new monastic ordination line that would reorganize the local monastic administration in their favor.

There may seem, at first blush, no obvious connection between Valivita's monastic political concerns and his composition of a bilingual commentary on Buddhist protective recitations. Yet the connections were powerful, and the nature of their power tells us something about religious texts and the world well beyond the life of Buddhist monks in early modern Asia. In medieval and early modern communities oriented by devotion to the Buddha, as in many other religious communities of that time in Asia and beyond, ritual specialists and religious intellectuals sought the favor and patronage of aristocrats and members of the royal court. Private patronage of schools, monasteries, compositions, and publications was the order of the day. In such elite worlds, those of high rank also expressed and defended their social status by offering patronage to scholars. Supporting the production and performance of texts valued for their intellectual and transformative power was a way to demonstrate, or to claim, wealth and power. In Kandy, Valivita's royal patron held sway over a multilingual and multireligious court within which ritual specialists and religious intellectuals were part of the entertainment. The patronage of such scholars, and support for their compositions and public performances of erudition, was a mark of a ruler's superior judgment and social prowess. For the ambitious scholar, access to the king or an elite circle of patrons required the careful use of social contacts as well as the ability to demonstrate publicly erudition and literary acumen. When we seek to understand the relationship between texts, religious traditions, and human worlds, an important area for consideration is the culture or cultures of patronage, composition, and performance within which texts were and are produced and reproduced, orally and in writing. Examining these arenas for textual practice reveals much about elite culture, including aesthetic expectations and the specific values attributed to literacy and textual skill. *In ways that vary somewhat from place to place and across time, the demonstration of textual prowess by scholars and their patrons reveal to us interlocking expectations and experiences of pleasure, power, and learning.* The interpenetration of such expectations and experiences in textual practice often reveals much about how the domains we sometimes separate analytically as "religion," "politics," and "entertainment" were, and are, bound together through the work of texts. The texts important to such forms of textual practice in spheres linked to religious affiliation may indeed be authoritative foundational texts. Typically, however, they will extend beyond such canonical materials to include scriptural commentary and compendia, as well as poetry, theological and philosophical treatises, expert witness on the privileged sciences (that is, grammar, astrology and astronomy, literary theory, hermeneutics, medicine, and so on), and stories of saints, teachers, and heroes.

VII. THE SOCIAL POWER OF LANGUAGE AND GENRE

The form of a text may be crucial to the value it is accorded in its context and to the difference it can make as an object, or act, within social relations. Valivita's *Illuminator* accomplished much for its author because of the languages it used and the genre in which it was composed. Commenting upon foundational authoritative recitation texts in Pali language demonstrated Valivita's access to the earliest texts of his tradition, to Buddha-speech, and to the cosmopolitan Buddhist milieu of Pali language use that stretched from Lanka to southeast Asia. At the same time, by providing local language access to these texts in Sinhala, in order to make them suitable for preaching and monastic education, the commentarial project helped shape an image of Valivita as a dedicated teacher and agent of monastic reform. Meanwhile, Valivita and his colleagues criticized their local monastic competitors on grounds of impure monastic practice and ignorance of Buddhist textual traditions. The case of Valivita and his *Illuminator* underscores the fact that in multilingual contexts, linguistic choices are powerful ones. *What language is used when, by whom, and to what purpose? What are the social meanings attributed to a specific language? What is the symbolic power of language and language choice?* In religious communities that stretch across large territories and many local language groups, the public use of a translocal cosmopolitan literary language in recitation, inscription, or composition is typically a social act that asserts high status and direct access to the most highly privileged textual materials. Pali was a language with deep social resonance, like Sanskrit, Arabic, Persian, Latin, and classical Chinese.

Valivita used two languages for his commentary. Like the Pali, the Sinhala also communicated far more than verbal content. By the time he wrote his commentary, Sinhala too had a long history of literary associations. Certain styles of Sinhala language, and certain genres of Sinhala composition, were associated with specific historical periods and with particular social and religious groups. Valivita was well aware of this. His *Illuminator* inaugurated a return to an earlier Sinhala commentarial genre associated with a thirteenth-century literary renaissance and with "pure" and ascetic forms of Buddhist monastic life. By offering his composition to the king in that genre and linguistic combination, at that juncture, Valivita laid claim to a set of positive associations within the Lankan Buddhist world, positioning himself as the heir to highly desirable monastic traditions. Indeed, the genre reintroduced by his commentary became the "signature line"[3] of Valivita's monks when they came to dominate the Lankan Buddhist world as the newly formed Siamese Order.

Thus, languages and genres do not carry and convey only the verbal meaning contained in texts. Language and textual form carry historical and symbolic associations. In a given textual community oriented by religious affiliation, clusters of associations related to power, purity, devotion, knowledge, and privilege develop around particular languages and genres. *Acts of textual composition and performance lay claim to these associations on behalf of authors and performers.* The extratextual associations of genres and languages help authors, redactors, and performers to accomplish social ends through texts. To discern better the social lives of texts, we may seek an understanding of these extratextual associations that augment the declarative or documentary content[4] of the texts we study. Like the models for action referred to earlier, some of these associations are carried within authoritative foundational and historical texts. They also accrue in a wider body of textual production, including the biographies and hagiographies of literati that create, sustain, and rework the semipublic history of a textual culture. Each textual culture is characterized by distinctive patterns in the attribution of symbolic power and historical associations to specific languages, genres, and modes of performance. Discerning such patterns, and analyzing the ways in which the formal features of texts acquire and express meaning beyond the verbal declaration of their contents, is a way to enter the long histories of religious traditions as they have been constituted by their participants in various moments and brought to bear on the enjoyment and negotiation of human relations.

VIII. TEXTUAL COMMUNITIES

Each of the last four sections offers a way to think about the social locations of texts connected to religious affiliation: how human engagement with such texts is a practice that conditions and is conditioned by social relations, as well as context-specific notions of what makes texts and their composition and performance good, desirable, powerful,

---

3 Blackburn, *Buddhist Learning;* Georges Dreyfus, "Where Do Commentarial Schools Come From? Reflections on the History of Tibetan Scholasticism," *Journal of the International Association of Buddhist Studies* 28, 2 (2007): 235–40.
4 Dominick LaCapra, *Rethinking Intellectual History: Texts, Contexts, Language* (Ithaca, NY: Cornell University Press, 1983).

and efficacious. Throughout I have emphasized human uses – both self-conscious and otherwise – of texts in the world. If we are to understand the power of texts connected to religious affiliation and their effects in the world, however, it is helpful to isolate more clearly another fundamental dimension of the relations among texts and their authors and audiences implicit in these earlier discussions. This is that the texts we use also constitute us in powerful ways as individuals and collectives. They shape the horizons of our imagination, our vision of what is good or precious in intellect and action, our sense of those with whom we share experience and affiliation and those from whom we differ. *Those who participate in shared practices of reading, writing, listening, interpretation, and performance, with reference to the same body of texts (perhaps, but not necessarily, a formal curriculum), may be said to constitute a textual community.*[5] The textual practices of such a community may be oral, literate, or both. They may be rooted in print or electronic media, or manuscripts, or combined technologies. Heuristically, we may distinguish two kinds of textual communities in the context of the study of religion. The first are smaller collectives within a larger religious community defined by forms of devotion, ritual, protective practice, assent to authoritative foundational texts, and so on. Monastic and clerical orders form such textual communities by virtue of their educational formation, for instance, as do preachers, ritual specialists, academic theologians, and those trained for apologetics and religious debate. Nonspecialist practitioners may also form textual communities of this kind, to the extent that they share distinctive textual practices – reading, hearing, copying, and viewing the same corpus of texts. In other cases, including scholastic and philosophical practice directed both to adherents and outsiders, a textual community may cut across lines of religious affiliation. This was common in most of the elite literate worlds of medieval and early modern Eurasia, in the philosophical and theological debate cultures that unfolded in Sanskrit, Latin, Persian, Arabic, and classical Chinese.

One way of conceptualizing the medieval history of Buddhism in southern Asia is as the development of an ever-larger textual community

[5] Blackburn, *Buddhist Learning*; Michael W. Charney, *Powerful Learning: Buddhist Literati and the Throne in Burma's Last Dynasty, 1752–1885* (Ann Arbor: University of Michigan Center for South and Southeast Asian Studies, 2006); Stanley Fish, *Is There a Text in This Class?: The Authority of Interpretive Communities* (Cambridge, MA: Harvard University Press, 1980); and Brian Stock, *The Implications of Literacy: Written Language and Models of Interpretation in the Eleventh and Twelfth Centuries* (Princeton, NJ: Princeton University Press, 1983).

oriented by Pali language texts[6] that originated in the Indic world and then reached the southeast Asian mainland largely through the flow of monks and monastic lineages from Lanka. These men, and the locally based monastic ordination lineages they inaugurated, shared forms of meditative and ritual practice, devotional style, conceptions of history, standards for learned performance, approaches to textual hermeneutics, and expectations of courtly culture and polity. Their shared orientations were rooted in the literate and oral encounters with a common body of textual materials, although the libraries of any single community differed somewhat in emphasis. This textual corpus was not limited to foundational authoritative texts, but was formed crucially through commentary, compendia, histories, hagiographies, and the like. Closer to our own era we note the continued importance of this translocal textual community, which shaped a variety of Buddhist responses to colonial rule and Christian missionary projects in Asia. In the nineteenth century, for instance, Lankan and Burmese monks corresponded with one another about how Pali Buddhist scriptural and other texts could be used to answer Christian missionary attacks on Buddhist teachings, presuming a shared textual world for religious reflection and interreligious debate. At the same time, Sinhala, Burmese, and Thai manuscript copies of these texts and their commentaries were compared by Lankan monks who sought to purify of error the canon from which they would rebut Christian attacks on Buddhist texts during the religious polemics that figured so prominently in the oral debate and print culture of the period. By the late nineteenth and early twentieth centuries, the rise of locally owned Sinhala-language printing presses made possible a new textual community comprising nonmonastic as well as monastic Buddhists. They debated matters of proper devotional practice, ritual offerings, monastic decorum, education, and textual interpretation with reference to printed extracts from a wide range of earlier texts in Pali, Sinhala, and Sanskrit.[7]

Thinking of texts and the world through the idea of textual communities is one way in which to extricate ourselves from the double-bind of textual reductionism and a critical post-textual stance. A textually reductionist position isolates only a small body of texts as worthy of consideration and then reads them with an anachronistic understanding of their intent and the context of their composition. The post-textual

---

[6] Steven Collins, *Nirvana and Other Buddhist Felicities* (Cambridge: Cambridge University Press, 1998).

[7] On these examples, see further Anne M. Blackburn, *Locations of Buddhism: Colonialism, and Modernity in Sri Lanka* (Chicago: University of Chicago Press, 2010).

position renders problematic any confidence that the terms "religion" or "religious tradition" match any historical phenomenon before the projects of Enlightenment and colonialism, or that the texts identified as central to traditions by early scholars of religion are a representative point of entry from which to understand complex histories of devotion, protective ritual, philosophy, apologetics, and so on. Looking for, and at, textual communities, however, allows scholars of religion to look into the long histories of such past and contemporary practice by examining what texts – oral, written, and visual – are in play in a particular setting, who uses them, and how they use them. In this way, the misleading homogeneity and temporal stasis of reference to "traditions" may be set aside for many purposes, in favor of efforts to see and understand at a more modest and representative scale how groups of people are joined and separated by the texts that they engage. To which texts do they assent and from which do they demur? What are the styles of their engagement with and distancing from such texts and their interlocutors? If their textual practice isolates "us" from "them," what are the terms of reference for such a distinction? This broader and more dynamic analytical perspective helps reveal the internal dissent and pluralism characteristic even of large groups that share an allegiance to a body of authoritative foundational texts, and that may agree on many matters of liturgy and performance. Further, the study of textual communities changing across time reveals to us shifts both sudden and gradual in the ways that what we now refer to as religions or religious traditions are, and have been, constructed and recognized by their participants. Instead of discovering religions defined by their essences, we find diverse and historically distinctive communities of textual practice and interpretation.

Select Bibliography

Boyarin, Jonathan. Ed. *The Ethnography of Reading*. Berkeley: University of California Press, 1993.

Chartier, Roger. *The Order of Books: Readers, Authors, and Libraries in Europe Between the Fourteenth and the Eighteenth Centuries*. Translated by Lydia G. Cochrane. Stanford, CA: Stanford University Press, 1994.

Dagenais, John. *The Ethics of Reading in Manuscript Culture: Glossing the Libro de buen Amor*. Princeton, NJ: Princeton University Press, 1994.

Irvine, Martin. *The Making of Textual Culture: 'Grammatica' and Literary Theory*. Cambridge: Cambridge University Press, 1994.

Levering, Miriam. Ed. *Rethinking Scripture: Essays from a Comparative Perspective*. Albany: State University of New York Press, 1989.

McDaniel, Justin. *Gathering Leaves and Lifting Words: Histories of Buddhist Education in Laos and Thailand*. Seattle: University of Washington Press, 2008.

Messick, Brinkley. *The Calligraphic State: Textual Domination and History in a Muslim Society*. Berkeley: University of California Press, 1993.

Pollock, Sheldon. Ed. *Literary Cultures in History: Reconstructions from South Asia*. Berkeley: University of California Press, 2003.

    Ed. *The Language of the Gods in the World of Men: Sanskrit, Culture, and Power in Premodern India*. Berkeley: University of California Press, 2006.

Smith, Jonathan Z. *Imagining Religion: From Babylon to Jonestown*. Chicago: University of Chicago Press, 1982.

8   On the role of normativity in religious studies

THOMAS A. LEWIS

Like other fields across the humanities and social sciences, religious studies grapples with the complex and often hidden relationships between descriptions and normative presuppositions and implications – roughly, between claims about what is and about what ought to be. For reasons concerning both its subject matter and the particular history of the field, however, debates about these issues in religious studies are particularly charged as well as particularly illuminating. Here, the issues have largely arisen in the context of larger debates over the appropriate substance, methods, and approaches in the academic study of religion. These debates, in turn, have often been framed in terms of the relation between religious studies and theology. Critics have repeatedly charged that the field remains tainted, that it has not yet escaped the die cast by its largely Protestant theological roots. For these critics, the field thus functions as a kind of liberal Protestant – or, at best, ecumenical – apologetics. Where earlier debates were concerned with obviously theological work being done in religious studies, recent scholarship has highlighted the more subtle endurance of Protestant presuppositions even in supposedly more pluralistic conceptions of the study of religion.[1] From the other side, theologians decry an exclusion that they see as based in models of objectivity and rationality that are no longer defensible. Some

---

[1] See, for example, Timothy Fitzgerald, *The Ideology of Religious Studies* (New York: Oxford University Press, 2000); Jonathan Z. Smith, *Drudgery Divine: On the Comparison of Early Christianities and the Religions of Late Antiquity* (Chicago: University of Chicago Press, 1990); Daniel Dubuisson, *The Western Construction of Religion: Myths, Knowledge, and Ideology*, trans. William Sayers (Baltimore: Johns Hopkins University Press, 2003); Tomoko Masuzawa, *The Invention of World Religions, or, How European Universalism Was Preserved in the Language of Pluralism* (Chicago: University of Chicago Press, 2005); and Russell T. McCutcheon, *Critics Not Caretakers: Redescribing the Public Study of Religion* (Albany: State University of New York Press, 2001).

I would like to thank Stephen Bush, Robert A. Orsi, John P. Reeder, Jr., Jonathan W. Schofer, and Aaron Stalnaker for invaluable suggestions on earlier drafts of this contribution.

of these theologians seek to transmute postmodern critiques of reason into tickets for readmission to the guild.[2]

In much of this debate, a crucial background assumption – sometimes stated but often not – is that whereas theologians make normative claims, religious studies scholars should refrain from doing so. Rather, scholars in religious studies should distinguish themselves from theologians precisely by striving for some type of distance, neutrality, or objectivity in relation to their subject matter, where this is understood to entail analysis regarding what is rather than claims about what ought to be. The account of this relationship might be formulated in a variety of ways, some more modern, some with a postmodern aspect. At times, for instance, those who do normative work are contrasted with historians, who are presumably investigating an object with a degree of openness to the data and determination to abstain from judging that is seen as lacking in the normative thinker. In other cases, the "normative" work of theologians is contrasted with the "analysis" that should distinguish religious studies.[3]

In considering this debate, it bears noticing that work in a number of other disciplines regularly makes explicitly normative claims without arousing suspicion that such claims do not belong. Philosophy and political science provide some of the most obvious examples. Apparently, explicitly normative claims associated with religion provoke greater suspicion than normative claims in other areas. This inequality of suspicion, I want to suggest, points us toward hidden assumptions largely responsible for the intractability of this debate. Normativity is viewed differently in relation to religion because of a pervasive assumption that religion cannot be argued about – that it is, in essence, "reason's other." In this view of religion, normative claims related to religion cannot be argued about but are fundamentally matters of "faith." This I take to be the most problematic theological presupposition that continues to

[2] Variations of this strategy are a recurrent motif in the March 2006 *Journal of the American Academy of Religion* on the theme, "The Future of the Study of Religion in the Academy." See, for instance, Ellen T. Armour, "Theology in Modernity's Wake," *Journal of the American Academy of Religion* 74, 1 (2006): 7–10, and Gavin D. Flood, "Reflections on Tradition and Inquiry in the Study of Religions," *Journal of the American Academy of Religion* 74, 1 (2006): 48. Robert Orsi notes this broader tendency as well: Robert A. Orsi, *Between Heaven and Earth: The Religious Worlds People Make and the Scholars Who Study Them* (Princeton, NJ: Princeton University Press, 2005), 194.

[3] Orsi's use of "normative" in Orsi, *Between Heaven and Earth*, chapter 6, sometimes carries the former sense. McCutcheon's language often contrasts the "analysis" that he sees as appropriate to religious studies with the "normative" claims that are not (e.g., McCutcheon, *Critics Not Caretakers*, 134–5).

haunt discussions of religion – a presupposition shared by many writers on both sides of the debate.

More precisely put, the drive to define religious studies largely through the contrast with theology too often rests on two closely related, highly problematic presuppositions: first, of those writing on religion, only the theologians make normative claims; and, second, normative claims related to religion are fundamentally a matter of faith, where faith is juxtaposed with reason. While the latter supposition is undoubtedly valid for many normative religious claims that are made, it is not for all. As we think about how to construct of the discipline of religious studies, it is essential that we not build this presupposition into its foundations. We should not exclude such views, but neither should they be fundamental to the conception of the discipline.

With these concerns in mind, I want to argue that our discussions about the distinctiveness of the academic study of religion should be recast from debates about religious studies versus theology or descriptive versus normative work to a focus on normativity and the justification of normative claims. My point is not to include every kind of writing on "religion" as appropriate for religious studies but to reframe the discussion in order to provide more defensible and coherent criteria for inclusion or exclusion. Let me stress that the concern here is with the boundaries of religious studies, not the particular approaches I find most convincing; there are of course many approaches that I find unproductive or based on mistakes that I nonetheless do not want to exclude from the discipline. Framing the debate in terms of theology and religious studies, however, is ultimately neither intellectually defensible nor heuristically productive. The term "theology" covers too much that is too diverse in crucial respects; it occludes by eliding differences. Shifting the frame should help to dissolve a number of pseudo-arguments and illuminate the substantive intellectual issues – issues that are shared with many disciplines across the university.

Focusing on the issue of normativity, I want to begin with a rather simple claim: normative claims are inevitable in the study of religion (as in most if not all disciplines). What is important is not to try somehow to exclude normative claims but rather to be willing to offer justification for the norms that we invoke. Participants in the academic study of religion must be willing to bring the norms themselves into debate and subject them to critical inquiry. The shift of attention I propose, then, is ultimately to the justification offered for particular norms. The moves that exclude one from the discipline are appeals to an authority that is claimed not to require justification, appeals to an authority conceived as unquestionable, and appeals to private forms of justification – that is, justifications for which, in principle, no argument can be given.

I. THE INEVITABILITY OF NORMATIVITY

In speaking of normativity, I have in mind claims – whether made explicit or remaining implicit – regarding the way we ought to act or think. In describing ethical claims as "normative," Christine Korsgaard writes, "They make *claims* on us; they command, oblige, recommend, or guide. Or at least, when we invoke them, we make claims on one another.... Concepts like knowledge, beauty, and meaning, as well as virtue and justice, all have a normative dimension, for they tell us what to think, what to like, what to say, what to do, and what to be."[4] Focusing on the breadth of the term, Jonathan Dancy writes, "our 'ought' here is not particularly a moral ought, nor even just a practical ought.... For the notion of value (good and bad) is held to be as normative as the notion of the right."[5] Normativity need not be limited to deontological conceptions of morality, in which the central ethical issue concerns the choices we make and these are evaluated in terms of adherence to a formal moral norm rather than their results. Rather, normativity as a whole concerns a wider range of judgments of value. It is in play any time judgments of value are made, whether implicitly or explicitly.

Attending to the broad scope of normativity will enable us to appreciate its role even in empirical research where it is least suspected. With regard to the subject at hand, this attention to judgments of value is particularly relevant: it simultaneously points to what many have objected to in the work of scholars defending a particular tradition over others and enables us to identify normative claims made by many of the most vocal critics of the role that theology has played in the field. Conceiving of normativity broadly in this manner in itself leaves a great deal open regarding the different ways in which norms are understood to be grounded.

As broad as this conception is, however, I do want to focus on normative judgments of the material or people that a scholar studies. It is *also* the case that scholars presuppose norms for scholarship itself. In fact, it is precisely these norms that we are debating. But the point

[4] Christine M. Korsgaard, *The Sources of Normativity* (Cambridge: Cambridge University Press, 1996), 8–9.
[5] Jonathan Dancy, "Editor's Introduction," in *Normativity*, ed. Jonathan Dancy (Oxford: Blackwell, 2000), vii. For a similar focus on "ought," see Ralph Wedgwood, *The Nature of Normativity* (Oxford: Clarendon Press, 2007), 1.

here is that in addition to presupposing or defending norms for the practice of academic work itself, scholars also inevitably make normative judgments regarding the materials and people they are studying. One could also treat views on what counts as a good justification in terms of epistemic normativity, but I am making a more focused claim about normative value judgments of the subjects being studied.

For the present purposes, a few relevant examples will be more helpful than further theorizing of the concept of normativity.[6] To make the case as persuasive as possible, I have chosen representative examples spanning a range of approaches, some of which are among those that seem least likely to be normative. The most obvious examples of normative claims are those that explicitly invoke the language of "should" or "ought." Kant's categorical imperative, "act only in accordance with that maxim through which you can at the same time will that it become a universal law," provides a classic example.[7] Much scholarship in ethics – whether philosophical or religious – falls into this category, as in arguments about the morality of abortion, the war in Iraq, or social justice.

Although such claims might be explicitly religious, they need not be. Drawing on Aristotle, the philosopher Martha Nussbaum argues that we can identify "sphere[s] of universal experience and choice," such as "bodily appetites and their pleasures," "distribution of limited resources," and so forth.[8] In each of these spheres, human beings are necessarily faced with choices about how to act: "If it is not appropriate, it is inappropriate; it cannot be off the map altogether. People will of course disagree about what the appropriate ways of acting and reacting in fact *are*. But in that case, as Aristotle has set things up, they are arguing about the same thing, and advancing competing specifications of the same virtue."[9] The virtues, such as moderation and justice, are simply

---

[6] For a concise treatment of important philosophical discussions of the relation between description and normativity, see Hilary Putnam, "Objectivity and the Science-Ethics Distinction," in *The Quality of Life*, ed. Martha C. Nussbaum and Amartya Sen (Oxford: Clarendon Press, 1993), 143–57. For an important recent contribution to this still lively philosophical debate, see Robert B. Brandom, *Between Saying and Doing: Towards an Analytic Pragmatism* (Oxford and New York: Oxford University Press, 2008).

[7] Immanuel Kant, *Groundwork of the Metaphysics of Morals*, in *Practical Philosophy*, The Cambridge Edition of the Works of Immanuel Kant, ed. Mary J. Gregor and Allen W. Wood and trans. Mary J. Gregor (Cambridge: Cambridge University Press, 1996), 73.

[8] Martha C. Nussbaum, "Non-Relative Virtues: An Aristotelian Approach," in *The Quality of Life*, ed. Nussbaum and Sen, 246. Although Nussbaum currently holds appointments in the University of Chicago Law School, the Philosophy Department, and the Divinity School, I identify her principally as a philosopher.

[9] Nussbaum, "Non-Relative Virtues," 247.

ways of talking about what it is to choose appropriately in each sphere. Nussbaum is concerned here to highlight the way that this approach frames the issues so that competing ethical views can be understood as competing arguments about a common topic; but that point should not let us lose sight of the normative force of the competing specifications of each virtue – the kind of specification in which Nussbaum engages in greater detail in other parts of her corpus.[10] Significantly, though she is explicitly normative, her being so does not raise questions about whether she belongs in a secular university.

Though these works in ethics are obviously normative, other projects reveal these not to be a special case. We are also making normative claims when we interpret a particular religious practice as an expression of a universal human need – for community or solidarity, for instance. Such theories typically, if often implicitly, make the satisfaction of such needs normative for human beings. Value is attributed to the practice by virtue of its satisfaction of this need.

Take, for example, the work of historian of religion Robert A. Orsi. Orsi has been deeply concerned with how religion should be studied academically and with the ongoing influence of Protestant theology on the field. Even he, however, makes important normative claims. One example comes from his book *Between Heaven and Earth*. The background for this passage is his research for an earlier book, *Thank You, St. Jude*, on devotion to the patron saint of hopeless causes. One of the women he interviewed had asked him whether he had ever prayed to St. Jude. At a later point, he did not exactly pray to St. Jude but he did something that he viewed as comparable: "Instead of actually praying to Saint Jude I tried to find some analogue to this act in my own emotional and behavioral repertoire."[11] As a result of this experience and its impact on him, he writes, "what I learned as I tried to take Clara's challenge seriously is that we were alike nonetheless in our need, vulnerability, and risk."[12] Here, Orsi is claiming a "common humanity," characterized by need and vulnerability, and discussing the value of a variety of responses to this human predicament. Crucially, his understanding of Clara's action in these terms (with the normative claims entailed) determines his characterization of her action. More generally, any time we claim – explicitly or implicitly – that human behavior can be explained

---

[10] See, for instance, Martha C. Nussbaum, *Women and Human Development: The Capabilities Approach* (Cambridge: Cambridge University Press, 2000), especially chapter 1.

[11] Orsi, *Between Heaven and Earth*, 172.

[12] Orsi, *Between Heaven and Earth*, 173.

in a particular way – as the pursuit of economic interests or cultural capital, for instance – we are making controversial claims about the nature of human existence with important consequences for how we should live. And as Orsi's example indicates, even a scholar who rejects strongly reductionist accounts of religion will invoke normative claims as soon as he or she moves past the most superficial levels of description. Even the question of what merits explanation – for example, men possessing more power than women in a given society – depends in part of normative commitments. These claims too, then, are normative.

Lest the normativity in the preceding example be attributed to apologetics on Orsi's part, however, it will be helpful to consider scholars even more critical of their subjects' self-understanding. Timothy Fitzgerald is an ardent critic of the discipline of religious studies, largely on the grounds of the pervasiveness of an "ecumenical liberal theology [that] has been disguised (though not very well) in the so-called scientific study of religion." In *The Ideology of Religious Studies* (2000), he seeks to expose the way in which the resulting conception of "religion" as a generic concept has not only corrupted much – though by no means all – of the work done in the field, but also underwritten major political projects: "The construction of 'religion' and 'religions' as global, crosscultural objects of study has been part of a wider historical process of western imperialism, colonialism, and neocolonialism. Part of this process has been to establish an ideologically loaded distinction between the realm of religion and the realm of non-religion or the secular." My point here is neither to critique nor to defend the claims that Fitzgerald is making – though I think that he does provide valuable insights on the conceptualization of religion in the modern West. Rather, the point is that his project – to transform religious studies in part by ridding it of pervasive theological presuppositions – is itself thoroughly normative and concerns more than the norms of inquiry itself. While the scholar must be "freed" from this "ideological construct," the stakes are not merely academic. Fitzgerald is not concerned only with the norms of the discipline. Rather, the conception of religion developed and perpetuated by theologians, religious studies scholars, and others has played an important role in the legitimization of "the modern ideology of individualism and capitalism."[13] Given Fitzgerald's rhetoric, then, at stake are practical consequences for billions of people. These are normative judgments, making extensive claims about what ought to be – and what ought not to be.

---

[13] Fitzgerald, *Ideology of Religious Studies*, 7–8.

Finally, we make normative claims whenever we try to identify "what is really going on here." To describe an experience as delusional or as transcendent, for instance, is to make a claim about the nature of reality. And such claims are normative in the relevant sense: they have strong consequences for how we should act.[14] This point comes out in a fascinating manner in Edward Slingerland's treatment of reductionism. Slingerland pursues the implications of what he describes as the "'embodied' approach to the study of culture," which sees "the human mind and its products as part of the physical world...."[15] Against the social constructivists he criticizes, he holds that "this body-brain is no more than a very complex physical thing, a product of millions of years of evolution. Human thought is not a ghostly, disembodied process, but rather a series of body-brain states – a series of physical configurations of matter – each causing the next in accordance with the deterministic laws that govern the interactions of physical objects." At some level, we should adopt a physicalist perspective, not just as scholars, but as human beings: "Physicalism matters because it simply works better than dualism, and – once the reality of this superiority is fully grasped – this is an irresistibly powerful argument for creatures like us."[16] The tremendous achievements of modern medicine, based in this kind of physicalism, demonstrate this point.

Yet Slingerland's position is more interesting precisely because it argues against one set of normative implications that the "hard-core physicalists" (Slingerland's term for scholars such as Daniel C. Dennett) have claimed to find in this physicalism. Where they take this physicalism to entail that we should abandon all beliefs that depend on notions such as free will, Slingerland draws on a physicalist argument to avoid that particular normative claim. He views human beings as having been genetically "designed" to hold on to precisely the kinds of beliefs that hard-physicalists want us to abandon. Thus, the hard physicalists are trying to fight precisely the kinds of biological mechanisms that they generally want to champion. Instead, Slingerland proposes living

[14] There is a question whether a certain conception of discourse as nothing more than a language game can abstain from making the kinds of normative claims that I have in mind here. While that might be possible, were we to limit academic discourse to language conceived in this way, we would have to exclude most of what currently happens in the academy – particularly in the natural and social sciences – from the university.

[15] Edward Slingerland, "Who's Afraid of Reductionism? The Study of Religion in the Age of Cognitive Science," *Journal of the American Academy of Religion* 76, 2 (2008): 378.

[16] Slingerland, "Who's Afraid of Reductionism?" 382–3, 402.

with a "dual consciousness, cultivating the ability to view human beings simultaneously under two descriptions: as physical systems and as persons."[17] Slingerland thereby claims that humans are right to hold on to – at one level – the beliefs that involve free will and to act accordingly. Admittedly, we might well ask whether Slingerland has given us any reason to think that we *should* cultivate a dual consciousness rather than face the perhaps Sisyphusian task of trying to live without the "illusions" of viewing other human beings as persons and thinking we have a free will (as Slingerland's Dennett enjoins us) or whether the question is even coherent once one accepts an entirely deterministic view. (Slingerland's references to Kant, for instance, suggest that he has not grasped the challenge that Kant poses to efforts to ground normativity in the way that Slingerland implicitly does.[18]) My point here, however, is that Slingerland makes these normative claims – particularly, that we are right to adopt this dual consciousness.

Perhaps more importantly, in his discussion of hard-physicalists he highlights the normative entailments of undermining someone's reasons for acting in a certain manner. Typically, if a belief in a transcendent being or a particular moral code can be shown to be caused by factors that the agent herself cannot recognize as constituting a good reason (such as a genetically based illusion), she should give up the belief. Insofar as I show someone's reasons for action to be based on a falsehood, I have thereby argued that she has no reason to act in that way – unless some other justification is given. Slingerland then takes it upon himself to provide this other justification, one grounded in physicalism itself. But the broader point is that much work in religious studies is normative precisely in undermining people's reasons for acting as they do. In doing so, it enjoins them – whether implicitly or explicitly – not to act in this way (unless an alternative justification can be found).

The latter kinds of normativity highlight that we are not only making normative claims when we declare, "This is good," "This is orthodox," or "This is an abomination." The work of Nussbaum, Orsi, Fitzgerald, and Slingerland, for instance, is no less normative than the work of many theologians whose work might be considered suspect or inappropriate in religious studies. They offer examples of normative claims that seem clearly to belong within secular academia, but they are not necessarily radically different from the work of a "theologian"

---

17 Slingerland, "Who's Afraid of Reductionism?" 393, 402.
18 See, for instance, Slingerland, "Who's Afraid of Reductionism?" 385, 402–3. My thinking on these matters in Kant is greatly indebted to conversations with Wesley Erdelack.

analyzing Augustine's account of original sin as a distinctly Christian formulation of a universal human condition of finitude and a response of pride. Like those of that particular Augustinian "theologian," the various claims described earlier in this section presuppose (and sometimes make explicit) strong claims about the nature of human existence – and/or reality more generally – and have important consequences for how we should live. I focus on these kinds of claims because they strike me as precisely the type that are often given as grounds for excluding theology from the academic study of religion. Too often, we distinguish those who are explicitly doing normative work – ethicists, theologians, and philosophers of religion, for instance – from those who are doing more descriptive work – such as many historians. Instead of viewing this distinction as the difference that makes a difference, I believe we should read it as shorthand for a relatively minor distinction: All are making normative judgments; much of what distinguishes them is that those in the first category are *more likely* to be reflecting explicitly on the justification for their normative claims, whereas those in the second are more likely to focus their energy elsewhere.

II. PRESUPPOSING RELIGION AS REASON'S OTHER

Be that as it may, however, the fact remains that many are much more comfortable with Nussbaum and Slingerland in the secular academy than with the Augustinian. This contrast should provoke us to ask, Why do explicitly religious thinkers making normative claims raise so much more suspicion about their place in the modern, pluralistic university than a philosopher such as Nussbaum? This question returns us to the second of the presuppositions I identified previously: that normative claims regarding religion are fundamentally matters of "faith" and not subject to reasoned argument. Much of the reason normative claims that are explicitly "religious" raise this suspicion while others do not is that much of our academic as well as other public discourse is shaped by a conception of religion as reason's other. Many of our discussions take for granted that religion is not something about which one can argue rationally. It is fundamentally about a "faith" that one either has or does not. This view finds powerful expression in the opening pages of Rudolf Otto's *The Idea of the Holy*.[19] With everything resting on that, all

---

[19] Rudolf Otto, *The Idea of the Holy: An Inquiry into the Non-Rational Factor in the Idea of the Divine and Its Relation to the Rational*, 2nd Edition, trans. John W. Harvey (Oxford and New York: Oxford University Press, 1958), 1–11. See my further discussion of Otto later in this chapter.

subsequent argument is futile and/or trivial. Without a doubt, religion has often functioned in this way, and this arational strand has a long history in Christianity. But this conception received a significant boost in the wake of Enlightenment challenges to religion. Facing these challenges, one of the most prominent Protestant responses was a division of territory – a kind of noncompetition agreement.[20] Religion would dominate – but be confined to – a realm that reason could not reach. Friedrich Schleiermacher is a crucial figure in this tradition, though it seems to flow more from an oversimplification of his views than from his own vision. This tradition arguably lies behind much of the discourse on religion as *sui generis*, yet it is not limited to followers of Otto and Mircea Eliade.[21] William James's *The Varieties of Religious Experience*, for instance, easily has a similar effect: directing our attention to a "branch" of religion occupying a sphere that reason cannot reach.[22]

Though few would defend this conception of religion in the simple form I have sketched it here, it nonetheless seems to have a surprising degree of influence – at least in the United States. It is used to justify excluding "religion" as a whole from the university as well as to defend religious claims from rational criticism. It is the hidden, shared presupposition in many disagreements between religion's critics and its defenders. I suspect it also operates in the work of a number of contemporary continental philosophers whose call for a return to religion appears motivated in part by their views on the limits of reason. If reason fails, turn elsewhere – that is, to religion. And it is both powerful and dangerous in our public political discussions: it frequently leads us to presuppose that meaningful, reasoned debate on topics such as reproductive freedom or gay rights is impossible and consequently not worth attempting. On both sides, positions are further polarized by an unwillingness to search for common ground that would enable reasoned exchange. For some, appeals to "faith" function as a trump card that purportedly excuses them of the need to provide arguments. As noted previously, this is one of the most significant ways in which discussions

[20] For an extended treatment of a competing Protestant response, see Thomas A. Lewis, *Religion, Modernity, and Politics in Hegel* (Oxford and New York: Oxford University Press, 2011).

[21] For an excellent discussion of related matters in terms of the "sacred/profane" dichotomy, see Robert A. Orsi, "Everyday Miracles: The Study of Lived Religion," in *Lived Religion in America: Toward a History of Practice*, ed. David D. Hall (Princeton, NJ: Princeton University Press, 1997), 3–21, especially 5–7.

[22] Of course, there are serious questions regarding the adequacy of that interpretation of James's project. I am grateful to Matthew Bagger for discussions on this point.

of religion continue to be shaped by an unacknowledged but specific Protestant theological vision.

In arguing that this conception of religion should not be foundational to the discipline, it is important to demonstrate the ways in which this conception is inadequate. The focus on norms and their justification illustrates this inadequacy well. If we frame the discussion in terms of normativity, the crucial issue becomes whether someone is willing to offer an argument or justification for a norm – and, accordingly, what counts as offering an argument. There can and should be much debate about what counts as "giving an argument" in the context of the academic study of religion. I suggest that in thinking about the discipline as a whole, we should conceive of this process broadly enough to encompass a wide range of justificatory strategies. For instance, arguments need not conform to a foundationalist epistemological model – a view in which, to be justified, a belief must be shown to be derivable from foundations that are not themselves derived or inferred from other claims. Conceiving of the possibilities broadly does not mean one has to agree with them all, but we should not necessarily exclude people from the field just because we do not agree with the arguments they offer in favor of their positions. Broadly speaking, then, I propose that we navigate between the Scylla of an overly stringent demand for arguments conforming to a very narrow model (that would exclude pragmatism, for instance) and the Charybdis of the notion that all views ultimately depend upon equally arbitrary and indefensible presuppositions.

As we seek to illuminate what it can mean to offer an argument for a position, it is vital to emphasize the breadth of possibilities. One set of strategies includes various forms of foundationalism, arguments that seek to trace the justifications for any given claim back to a noninferential claim that is considered basic. Though different, appeals to purportedly universal human experiences – of the sort that Nussbaum argues for – also enter the realm of debate. We can argue, for all kinds of reasons, against the universality of these experiences, and it is this space for argument that is essential.

In the neopragmatist tradition, Jeffrey Stout has sought to bring our attention to the diversity of argumentative strategies that we use in our everyday discourse on public matters, including religion, in pluralistic societies. Rejecting the idea that once we come to the topic of religion, all argument stops – that is, that religion is a conversation stopper – Stout stresses the important role of immanent criticism, in which we start with the other person's own viewpoint and argue that in some respect it contradicts itself and/or should lead to another conclusion than the person thinks.[23] Championing the pervasiveness and power of immanent criticism over John Rawls's conception of public reason, Stout writes:

> Immanent criticism is both one of the most widely used forms of reasoning in what I would call public political discourse and one of the most effective ways of showing respect for fellow citizens who hold differing points of view. Any speaker is free to request reasons from any other. If I have access to the right forum, I can tell the entire community what reasons move me to accept a given conclusion, thus showing my fellow citizens respect as requesters of my reasons. But to explain to them why *they* might have reason to agree with me, given their different collateral premises, I might well have to proceed piecemeal, addressing one individual (or one type of perspective) at a time.[24]

The nonconfessional university is a public forum in just this sense, and immanent criticism will be one important way in which we argue with others in this context. Perhaps more importantly, it is a context in which "[a]ny speaker is free to request reasons from any other." That sentence expresses well a basic feature of this setting: no claim is beyond questioning.

In a different intellectual lineage, despite the challenges he seeks to pose to the modern academy through his championing of tradition, Alasdair MacIntyre offers another model of providing argument in support of a position. Rejecting what he sees as the Enlightenment ideal of arguments standing free of tradition and appealing to a universal audience, MacIntyre articulates and defends a model of reason as necessarily borne by – rather than an alternative to – tradition. His argument that traditions are frequently incommensurable poses grave challenges to rational dialogue among those who do not share a tradition.[25] Though

---

[23] Stout's work is particularly relevant because one of his significant targets is the claim – made but subsequently disavowed by another neopragmatist, Richard Rorty – that religion is a conversation stopper. See Richard Rorty, "Religion as Conversation-stopper," in *Philosophy and Social Hope* (London: Penguin, 1999), 168–74. Rorty has revised his position in "Religion in the Public Square: A Reconsideration," *Journal of Religious Ethics* 31, 1 (2003): 141–9.

[24] Jeffrey Stout, *Democracy and Tradition*, New Forum Books (Princeton, NJ: Princeton University Press, 2004), 73.

[25] Alasdair MacIntyre, *Whose Justice? Which Rationality?* (Notre Dame, IN: University of Notre Dame Press, 1988), chapter 19. I have treated MacIntyre on these issues at greater length in Thomas A. Lewis, "On the Limits of Narrative: Communities in Pluralistic Society," *Journal of Religion* 86, 1 (2006): 55–80.

such reasoned exchange between those not sharing a tradition is possible, it requires learning the other tradition as a "second first language" and then providing an account of the other tradition as a whole. Providing a rational argument to the other person will often require demonstrating that one's own tradition can explain the other tradition – its successes as well as its failures – more effectively than it can explain itself.[26] While argument across traditions is possible, then, it requires a level of engagement that will be rare; for the most part, the best we can do is to face the world from within a coherent tradition, relinquishing the universalistic hope of providing arguments that can appeal to everyone.

The folly of the modern university is closely tied to its failure to recognize this difficulty. MacIntyre takes the modern secular academy to be largely based upon an ultimately indefensible conception of reason as standing independent of traditions of inquiry.[27] And yet, over the course of several books and many articles, he develops a complex and widely influential argument for his position.[28] He seeks to undermine the coherence of alternative conceptions of reason and to demonstrate that to appeal to tradition in the manner that he does is not irrational. He demonstrates that latter point at greatest length in *Whose Justice? Which Rationality?*, where he argues that we must understand a tradition at any given point in time in terms of the dilemmas and perplexities whose resolution gave rise to it. Reflecting the power of MacIntyre's arguments to appeal to and persuade many people who did not previously share a tradition with him, MacIntyre's thought has won great attention and acclaim in precisely the academic context that he holds generally lacks the practices necessary to support the model of inquiry that he defends. Despite MacIntyre's stated rejection of the Enlightenment goal of appealing to a universal audience, then, it would be misleading to suggest that MacIntyre is unwilling to offer arguments to defend the normative claims he makes – arguments that appeal to more than limited community.

Because I discuss these examples so briefly, some may appear unconvincing. One might contend, for instance, that MacIntyre has abandoned – in theory and practice – the goal of making an argument

[26] Alasdair MacIntyre, *Three Rival Versions of Moral Enquiry: Encyclopedia, Genealogy, and Tradition* (Notre Dame, IN: University of Notre Dame Press, 1990), 117–21.
[27] MacIntyre, *Three Rival Versions*, especially 216–36.
[28] See, in particular, Alasdair MacIntyre, *After Virtue: A Study in Moral Theory*, 2nd Edition (Notre Dame, IN: University of Notre Dame Press, 1984); *Whose Justice? Which Rationality?*; and *Three Rival Versions*.

that appeals to more than a limited community sharing a set of practices that are not shared by the modern academy as a whole. There is
certainly room for argument. But that is the point: there is room for
argument. And the arguments can be made without appealing to transcendent authority and without presupposing "faith."

To say that a scholar must be willing to provide reasons for any particular claim or position, however, does not entail that she must do so
in every piece of writing or even that every scholar must count doing so
as within her areas of specialization. Just as an economist might make
use of game theory without providing an extensive justification of its
validity, so scholars of religion may produce works that take certain
claims for granted within that context. Doing so becomes problematic
only when the scholar declares those presuppositions to be illegitimate
objects of enquiry. Part of the academic enterprise is that, when pressed,
a scholar should admit the importance of being able to offer such a
defense. We do not need to write a philosophical treatise every time we
use the word "cruel," but we need to be willing to accept the concept
of "cruelty" as a legitimate issue for enquiry. (It is likely the case that
scholars of religion encounter claims that a particular authority or experience is beyond question more frequently than scholars in many other
disciplines, but I suspect that the same dynamic is common in other
fields as well.)

In defining broadly what it means to offer justification for our normative claims, I seek to define religious studies inclusively. I would err
on the side of inclusiveness with regard to the kinds of arguments that
might be offered. We might not agree with the arguments, but as we try
to conceive of the field as a whole, we should be slow to rule arguments
simply out of bounds.

Yet even if this broad conception of offering an argument provides us
with a generally irenic conception, there is also a rub. The vision of the
study of religion that I am proposing does require everyone to be willing
to debate – and in doing so to submit to critique and criticism – their
normative claims. No claim or canon can stand as unquestionable or as
free of the need for justification of its authoritative status. To cordon off
a set of texts or body of doctrines as simply "givens," whose normative
status requires no justification or cannot be argued about, is to remove
oneself from this discussion. So is attaching authority to holders of a
particular office simply by virtue of their holding that office.

Perhaps more significantly in the present context, appeals to
anything like private revelation or unique experiences do not allow
much basis for conversation if this is the only justification someone

is willing to offer. Take the opening of the third chapter of Rudolf Otto's *Idea of the Holy*:

> The reader is invited to direct his mind to a moment of deeply-felt religious experience, as little as possible qualified by other forms of consciousness. Whoever cannot do this, whoever knows no such moments in his experience, is requested to read no farther; for it is not easy to discuss questions of religious psychology with one who can recollect the emotions of his adolescence, the discomforts of indigestion, or, say, social feelings, but cannot recall any intrinsically religious feelings.[29]

When an author makes this rhetorical move, he or she removes himself or herself from a discussion in which claims are arbitrated through argument, for to make this move is to step out of the practice of giving and asking for reasons and to appeal to the purported givenness of an individual experience. "I had a feeling" is no more relevant as evidence in the study of religion than in the study of literature or economics. If we have not had this experience, then Otto – at least in this passage – claims to have nothing to say to us: he has no argument to offer.

Of course, many believers from many religions make these kinds of moves. I am not claiming that they should not. But in making claims of this sort, individuals remove themselves from the realm of academic discourse. They are not basing their claims on grounds that are in any sense subject to constructive debate by a larger community.

Focusing on normativity and the arguments brought to defend normative claims shifts the debate over the work appropriate to the academic study of religion from the theology-versus-religious-studies standstill – which too often leaves us wondering exactly how far the debate has come since the 1960s and 1970s – to more promising ground. And because debates about the nature of reason and argument are by no means unique to the study of religion, doing so also demonstrates that the substantive issues genuinely at stake here in the study of religion are the same as those in many other departments around the university. In showing that our problems are not unique but are rather the same as those in many other fields, this shift can help us to better articulate the ways in which we do belong in the secular university.

At the same time, this shift leaves space for diverse approaches within religious studies. Too often, our discussions of what is proper in the study of religion sound as if there should be one way of doing

---

[29] Otto, *The Idea of the Holy*, 8.

religious studies. Against such presuppositions, I think the strength of the discipline derives in large part from the plurality of types of investigations we conduct and questions we ask.

Finally, with an eye toward broader issues, let me close with what is perhaps the most practically significant – not "merely academic" – reason for reframing the debate in this manner. The simple juxtaposing of theology and religious studies is too often premised on an assumption that religion is fundamentally nonrational. Whether understood as an irrational superstition, as based in feeling and intuition, and/or as an irreducibly personal experience, religion understood in this manner becomes something about which reasoned exchange is impossible. In accepting this picture and portraying theology as antithetical to reasoned inquiry, adamant secularists unwittingly join forces with anti-intellectual adherents of religious traditions in supporting the idea that we cannot engage religious ideas constructively. One of the greatest costs of allocating religion such a small role in public and secular education in the United States is that it results in broad swaths of the population – including many educated elites – who never question that faith is some primordial given about which it is impossible to reason. The public discourse about religion that results is remarkably uninformed and uncritical. Ultimately, then, one of the most important reasons for recasting the theoretical issues at stake in defining the academic study of religion in the secular university is that it educates people to think more critically about religious claims.

Select Bibliography

Brandom, Robert B. *Between Saying and Doing: Towards an Analytic Pragmatism.* Oxford and New York: Oxford University Press, 2008.

Dancy, Jonathan. Ed. *Normativity.* Oxford: Blackwell, 2000.

Fitzgerald, Timothy. *The Ideology of Religious Studies.* New York: Oxford University Press, 2000.

Korsgaard, Christine M. *The Sources of Normativity.* Cambridge: Cambridge University Press, 1996.

MacIntyre, Alasdair. *Whose Justice? Which Rationality?* Notre Dame, IN: University of Notre Dame Press, 1988.

Nussbaum, Martha C. "Non-Relative Virtues: An Aristotelian Approach." In *The Quality of Life.* Edited by Martha C. Nussbaum and Amartya Kumar Sen. Oxford: Clarendon Press, 1993, 242–69.

Orsi, Robert A. *Between Heaven and Earth: The Religious Worlds People Make and the Scholars Who Study Them.* Princeton, NJ: Princeton University Press, 2005.

Putnam, Hilary. "Objectivity and the Science-Ethics Distinction." In *The Quality of Life*. Edited by Martha C. Nussbaum and Amartya Kumar Sen. Oxford: Clarendon Press, 1993, 143–57.

Slingerland, Edward. "Who's Afraid of Reductionism? The Study of Religion in the Age of Cognitive Science." *Journal of the American Academy of Religion* 76, no. 2 (2008): 375–411.

Stout, Jeffrey. *Democracy and Tradition*. New Forum Books. Princeton, NJ: Princeton University Press, 2004.

9 Translation

MARTIN KAVKA

In times of geopolitical conflict, attempts to translate religion are often attempts to heal. After the attacks of September 11, 2001, Muslims in Western nations, as well as U.S. President George W. Bush and other non-Muslim Westerners, engaged strenuously in an effort to translate: "Islam is peace," or "Islam means peace."[1] This was not the first attempt

[1] For a list of sources, the reader is encouraged to search through the 112 listings for "Islam means peace" and 360 listings for "Islam is peace" for 2001 alone at http://news.google.com; there are 15 listings for "Islam means peace" and 2 listings for "Islam is peace" for the calendar year 2000. (Some of these listings may be duplicates of wire stories running in various American newspapers.) In the index of major newspapers available through the LEXIS/NEXIS database, there are 6 occurrences of "Islam means peace" in 2000, and 40 in 2001; there are 9 occurrences of "Islam is peace" in 2000, and 80 in 2001. For Bush's first use of "Islam is peace" on September 17, 2001, see http://georgewbush-whitehouse.archives.gov/news/releases/2001/09/20010917-11.html (accessed May 25, 2011).

My thanks to Kathryn Lofton, Mark Jordan, Gregory Alles, and Robert A. Orsi for comments and conversations while I was at work on this chapter, to Orsi again for the bounty of his editing skills, and to those who attended a faculty–student colloquium in the Department of Religion at Florida State University at which I presented a draft of this chapter. Special thanks to my sister Misha Kavka for calling my attention to the queer/*quer* link, to her partner Stephen Turner for his thoughts on Mâori pragmatism, and to both of them for conversations about Mâori culture that we had after attending the 2007 Hokianga Film Festival at Moria marae.

I dedicate this chapter to the memory of Tessa Bartholomeusz, a scholar of Buddhism in Sri Lanka and my colleague in the Department of Religion at Florida State University, who died of cancer in the spring of 2001. When I interviewed for my current position in January of 2000, she asked me why I depended upon translations so extensively in my dissertation (which she had read thoroughly), and made no bones about the fact that if I had been a scholar of Asian religions who depended on translations in such a manner I would have been laughed out of the field. We had a tense and exciting conversation about scholars' assumptions about the fungibility of English and Western European languages, during which I miraculously managed to avoid bursting into tears. During the summer of 2001, I retranslated all of my citations (and often made significant changes to my arguments as a result) while preparing the final version of *Jewish Messianism and the History of Philosophy* (Cambridge: Cambridge University Press, 2004). I thought of Tessa all that summer and I miss her charm and rigor as intensely now as I did then.

to defuse crisis through religious translation. The rise of religious studies as a discipline is intertwined with the belief that *this discipline
itself* could bring about peace through its acts of translation. But this is
a myth scholars of religious studies ought to protest strenuously.

The notion that religious studies can avert or relieve social and cultural crises goes back to the early days of the organization of the field
in the United States. In his 1949 lecture on "The History of Religion in
the Universities," for example, George F. Thomas, chair of Princeton's
Department of Religion at the time, noted that religious studies is a
difficult discipline to organize pedagogically, for "our students are now
being moved to take our courses in religion not only by intellectual
curiosity but also by religious need." In the context of the Cold War,
"the religious and moral confusion of our time and the threat of secularism to our civilization have made it necessary for us to find our
way back to the wellsprings of faith that have given meanings to the
lives of our fathers."[2] But Thomas knew that religious studies does not
lead back *only* to the wellsprings of the traditions in which Princeton
students had been inculcated. Departments of religion, he suggested,
must do more than allow students to reclaim their Christian (or Judeo-
Christian) heritage – even at a private institution such as Princeton. So
Thomas cautioned against a strictly Christian curriculum in departments of religion, claiming that "any open-minded study of the higher
religions of the Orient is bound to convince one that there are religious
and ethical insights in them which Christians can ill afford to neglect."[3]
Such attention to the "'general revelation' in other religions" is not
threatening to Christian belief; it might indeed strengthen the religious
identity of the Christian student. Translation would thus serve not only
the receiver of the translation (the Christian student who becomes more
deeply Christian), but also the translated tradition, for the "Orient"
becomes less "other" as a result. Still, Thomas evinced an anxiety about
being understood as offering a perennialist view of religion or a notion

Bush's speech on this date is also an attempt to determine more precisely the class
of America's enemies, as "terrorists" and not "Muslims." This is not about healing
per se – after all, it maintains inimical relations – but about healing relations with
one set of persons (Muslims) who suddenly feared that they were being classed as
enemies, in part because of Bush's association with the war on terrorism with the
language of "crusade" in remarks made on September 16, 2001. See "Bush Warns of
a Wrathful, Shadowy, and Inventive War," *New York Times* (September 17, 2001);
online at http://query.nytimes.com/gst/fullpage.html?res=9506E6DA173BF934A257
5ACoA9679C8B63 (accessed May 25, 2011).

2 George F. Thomas, "The History of Religion in the Universities," *Journal of Bible
and Religion* 17, 2 (1949): 103.

3 Thomas, "The History of Religion," 104.

of ethics as the common core of religious traditions. Translation has its limits. Comparison was the culprit here, in Thomas's view, because it held the danger of "superficiality and distortion ..., it is all too easy to fall into error when one takes the Buddha's teaching about love out of its context in his teachings as a whole and compares it with Jesus' teaching about love of neighbor."[4]

Note what happens in Thomas's essay. The actual public translation of one discourse into another – the act of comparison – is threatening, because it raises the possibility that "general revelation" might be *essentially* superficial and distorting. Yet translation ought to occur, within the heart of the Christian student, hidden away there from other students, professors, and administrators. As a result, translation is never to articulate itself. If translation were to articulate itself, the mangling of Buddhist notions of love would show that the desire to translate is an unfulfillable desire, and that the belief in an entirely adequate translation (a translation in which one religious tradition would not lose anything by being expressed in the language of another tradition) is an unverifiable one. It is this very anxiety about religious studies as a practice that distorts that drives Thomas's essay – and much of religious studies today too. Why should we have such anxiety? To be blunt, it is because the visible act of translation – right there, on the page – can end up looking ridiculous.

Take this passage from Rudolf Otto's *The Idea of the Holy*, published during World War I, a recollection of a conversation he had while traveling in India in 1911:

> I recall vividly a conversation I had with a Buddhist monk, who had been lavishing upon me his *theologia negativa* and the arguments for his doctrines of *anātman* and emptiness in dogged succession. But when he came to an end, I asked him what nirvana itself might be. After a long pause the single answer, faint and restrained, finally came [in English]: "Bliss – unspeakable!" And in the faintness and restraint of the answer – in the solemnity of his voice, mien, and gestures – what was meant became more clear than in the words. This was an acknowledgment [*Bekenntnis*] of the *mysterium fascinans* and said in its own way what Rumi speaks in his fashion: "the essence of belief is only amazement, not in order to look away from God, but to cling drunkenly to The Friend, entirely lost in him." And the *Gospel of the Hebrews* speaks the same

---

4   Thomas, "The History of Religion," 105.

unusually deep words: "But who has found, will be amazed, and being amazed will be King."[5]

These last two sentences were added by Otto in the mid-1920s to *Das Heilige*, originally published in 1917. They are included in current German editions of the work, but not in the English edition that was published by Oxford University Press as *The Idea of the Holy*. This translation, by John W. Harvey, first appeared in 1923. It was reissued in 1950 with a new preface by Harvey, but without its main text being altered. Harvey evidently refused to translate Otto's references to the thirteenth-century Sufi mystic Rumi, as well as the second-century *Gospel of the Hebrews* (a document now lost, but quoted in writings by Clement of Alexandria and other early Church fathers). The reasons for this refusal are obscure and I must speculate. Perhaps Harvey found it difficult to render Rumi's rhyming-couplet scheme in English (a scheme that Georg Rosen's 1913 German translation, which Otto cited, had retained) and eliminated the reference to the early Christian text accordingly. But whatever Harvey's motives, he is excused by another refusal to translate, Otto's own. There is the matter of Otto's rendering the Buddhist monk's words in English. "Bliss – unspeakable!" remains inscrutable to his non-English-speaking German readers, as few as they may have been. Yet Otto's refusal to translate these words is immaterial. Nothing is lost in the refusal to translate. This refusal belongs to the strategy of pushing language to the wayside in the religious scholar's project of narrating the sense of a religious speech-act. Religious language, whether written or oral, is secondary for Otto because its sense has nothing to do with the culturally conditioned vocabulary used to communicate that sense. What Otto's Buddhist interlocutor was trying to communicate was entirely nonlinguistic. The translation of "bliss – unspeakable!" is unnecessary, even irrelevant, because Otto had *already translated* everything that a reader needs. The faintness of the monk's voice and the gravity of his bearing, the "hushed restraint of that answer" (to cite Harvey's translation), are the crucial details, because they communicate more than any syntagm ever could. By this logic, the citations to Rumi and the *Gospel of the Hebrews* thereby become expendable in any translation of Otto. (This would be true *despite* Otto's own conviction that his text required this addition.) Tone and bodily comportment are

⁵ Rudolf Otto, *Das Heilige* (Munich: C. H. Beck, 1963), 51–2. Translation mine, corresponding and adding to *The Idea of the Holy*, trans. John W. Harvey (Oxford: Oxford University Press, 1923), 39. For the original 1917 text, see Rudolf Otto, *Das Heilige* (Breslau: Trewendt und Granier, 1917), 43.

sufficient to come to the conclusion that Otto has already set out for the reader in his previous paragraphs. Nirvana is a *"fascinans* that can bring its adherents to rapture,"[6] just as "alluring and seductive"[7] to the Buddhist as the *numen* is for Christians such as Jonathan Edwards, Jakob Böhme, and the believers whose testimonies are detailed in William James's *The Varieties of Religious Experience.*[8] To invoke the lingo of a contemporary American celebrity-obsessed magazine, "Buddhists – they're just like US!"[9]

Otto made an all-too-hasty assumption about the set of inferences that readers will make from his encounter with the Buddhist monk. But readers with different sensibilities could easily make others. For what we have in the conversation between Otto and the Buddhist monk is a scene in which two men, together, disrobe language and discover the divine. This is not anything that they could do separately, each on his own. It is impossible to think of their intimacy with the supernatural apart from the intimacy of their conversation. Because Otto's yearning for a glob-ally valid definition of the holy is so tightly bound with his view of the monk's body – its demeanor and gestures – the conversation is at least homoerotic. And so one might be inspired, following Susan Sontag's comment in "Notes on Camp," that "camp is as well a quality discover-able in objects and the behavior of persons,"[10] to think of other intimate conversations, other scenes of hushed restraint, in which awe is shown to another, in which words serve only as obstacles to the expression of what two men feel deep inside – the imaginary soundtrack swells – and the audience is treated to a sexual montage. Or the screen fades to black as a couple's lips come ever nearer to each other. One might also want to describe this moment with a word that offers a more negative connota-tion, because what Otto has done, in communicating the monk's view of nirvana as unspeakable, is deprive the monk of the opportunity to speak. Otto renders this monk simply as a mute body. I want to suggest, especially given the homoerotic overtones of the conversation, that an

---

6 Otto, *Das Heilige*, 51; see Otto, *The Idea of the Holy*, 39.
7 Otto, *Das Heilige*, 42; see Otto, *The Idea of the Holy*, 31.
8 Otto, *Das Heilige*, 50; see Otto, *The Idea of the Holy*, 37–8.
9 See also the opening paragraph of "Buddhism and Christianity – Compared and Contrasted": "Both Christianity and Buddhism can be classified in the one common category that we call religion.... [T]here is something similar here that moves people in each case under different names." Rudolf Otto, "Buddhism and Christianity – Compared and Contrasted," trans. and introd. Philip C. Almond, *Buddhist-Christian Studies* 4 (1984): 89.
10 Susan Sontag, "Notes on 'Camp'," in *Against Interpretation* (New York: Farrar, Straus & Giroux, 1966), 277.

apt word to get across the risible aspects of the conversation is "gay," in its contemporary popular use as a predicate adjective that communicates disparagement (for example, "homophobia is so gay"). The mark of this scene's gayness is its culmination, when the two men discover the fullness of each other, in the transcendence of the unspeakable and in the silence that represents perfect understanding and love.

Let us call this *the silence that accompanies pure translation*, for translation is nothing more (and nothing less) than an instantaneous, unspoken mutual understanding.

To ridicule such an account of silence and its importance is merely call attention to the fact that such fantasies of adequacy, immediacy, and purity as Otto's are no longer dominant in the humanities and the social sciences, thankfully. Yet scholars are still entranced by silence. This is so in part because of an assumption that if the scholar keeps his or her silence, this serves to maximize the power of the stories of the people about whom the scholar writes, the power of their lives. In his justly famous book on the Rwandan genocide, *We Wish to Tell You That Tomorrow We Will Be Killed with Our Families: Stories from Rwanda*, for example, Philip Gourevitch writes early on that after the genocide, "there were only people's stories."[11] This frames Gourevitch not as the author of a narrative, but as a compiler of narratives to which he has *listened* silently. This stance as listener gives heft to his criticisms of the moral platitudes that come out of the mouths of politicians who merely assert their commitment to oppose genocide, but do not act as if they mean for their assertions to have any political force.[12]

In the contemporary practice of the study of religion, one of the most notable defenders of the moral salience of silence is the anthropologist

---

[11] Philip Gourevitch, *We Wish to Tell You That Tomorrow We Will Be Killed with Our Families: Stories from Rwanda* (New York: Picador, 1998), 21.

[12] Gourevitch, *We Wish to Tell You*, 151–2: "In May of 1994, I happened to be in Washington to visit the United States Holocaust Memorial Museum.... Waiting amid the crowd, I tried to read a local newspaper. But I couldn't get past a photograph on the front page: bodies swirling in water, dead bodies, bloated and colorless, bodies so numerous that they jammed against each other and clogged the stream. The caption explained that these were the corpses of genocide victims in Rwanda. Looking up from the paper, I saw a group of museum staffers arriving for work. On their maroon blazers, several wore the lapel buttons that sold for a dollar each in the museum shop, inscribed with the slogans 'Remember' and 'Never Again.' The museum was just a year old; at its inaugural ceremony, President Clinton had described it as 'an investment in a secure future against whatever insanity lurks ahead.' Apparently, all he meant was that the victims of future exterminations could now die knowing that a shrine already existed in Washington where their suffering might be commemorated."

Michael Jackson, who has since 2005 held the post of "distinguished professor of world religions" at Harvard Divinity School. Jackson did most of his field work in Sierra Leone. In a 2004 article, Jackson passes on the narrative of a Sierra Leonean woman named Fina Kamara about the attack on her village in 1998 (during the civil war that raged in Sierra Leone between 1991 and 2002), as a proof text of sorts for an argument that "the practice of silence" is a fitting response to the suffering of others.[13] His response begins with a literal translation. Fina Kamara's story appears in her own words, translated by Jackson from their interview conducted in the Kuranko language. The contrast between her voice and Jackson's own style of writing could not be greater. Jackson's prose is involved in a passionate love affair with dependent clauses and their concomitant commas and em dashes, while his translation of Fina's narrative consists of simple sentences. "The RUF [Revolutionary United Front] came suddenly. They shot many people. They stacked the bodies under the cotton tree. Then they grabbed us. Their leader said they were going to kill us too. But then they sent their boys to bring a knife. My daughter Damba was six. They took her from me and cut off her hand. After that they cut off all our hands."[14] Two years later, Damba was separated from her mother by an American aid agency and taken to the United States to be fitted with a prosthetic limb.

As Jackson points out, this separation of Fina and Damba can and should be understood as involving a robust claim to know the good on the part of the aid agency. The source of this knowledge of Fina and Damba's best future, however, is unclear. Jackson argues that what has happened is that the aid agency has refused to let the supernatural remain supernatural. That which is properly beyond being, the good, has become immanent, with destructive results. Jackson writes:

> I had no way of knowing how this unidentified agency had justified such a prolonged separation of mother and daughter. Perhaps the overriding consideration had been rescuing Damba from the brutality of war, and giving her a prosthetic limb, rather than the bond between her and her mother. In her despair, Fina had no option but to look to God. Yet, in our complacency, have we not arrogated the power of God to ourselves, and as a consequence placed people like

---

[13] Michael Jackson, "The Prose of Suffering and the Practice of Silence," *Spiritus: A Journal of Christian Spirituality* 4, 1 (2004): 44–59. See also Michael Jackson, "Whose Human Rights?" in *Existential Anthropology: Events, Exigencies, and Effects* (Oxford: Berghahn, 2005), 159–80, and *The Politics of Storytelling: Violence, Transgression and Intersubjectivity* (Copenhagen: Museum Tusculanum, 2002), 129ff.

[14] Jackson, "The Prose of Suffering," 45–6.

Fina in the invidious position of having to look to us for what we may not have the means to do?[15]

The aid agency, in deciding what must be done, claimed a religious mantle for itself, made itself the agent, if not the instantiation, of God on earth. The falsity of this claim could only lead Fina to search for God elsewhere, to call upon supernatural forces that were not represented in the political life of Sierra Leone during its civil war. Given the lack of any external institutional power to relieve the effects of the destruction, Fina, in an "awareness of her own powerlessness,"[16] develops a disinterest in punishing the perpetrators of the attack on her, her daughter, and the others in her village, or in any kind of working through of the past.

The dominant emphasis that Jackson found among the residents of Sierra Leone upon his return there after the civil war was on the need for them – all of them – to rebuild the country's infrastructure. "Even explaining, judging, and blaming are luxuries one cannot afford. This is why theodicy is not an issue."[17] Standing in solidarity with Sierra Leoneans, Jackson recommends that ethnographers not use their ethnographies as a means of speaking truth to power. He finds this latter aim unbearably narcissistic, reflecting more the superior social position of the ethnographer than anything else. Rather,

> ...we should learn the value of silence, seeing it not as a sign of indifference or resignation, but of respect. This is not shocked silence – as when one is struck dumb by events that beggar belief, or cannot be narrated – but silence as a deliberate choice. For there are certain events and experiences of which we choose not to speak. Not because they hold us in thrall, freezing the tongue. Not because we fear they might reveal our flaws or frailty. Still less because we feel our words can never do them justice. Silence is sometimes the only way we can honour the ineffability and privacy of certain experiences.[18]

If we cannot translate another's pain without taking it up for our own ends, if a translator's narrative of someone else's suffering ends up saying more about the translator than about the sufferer whose pain is being translated, then perhaps it is best to translate as minimally as possible, if at all. One should simply narrate the facts (as Jackson does

---

[15] Jackson, "The Prose of Suffering," 47.
[16] Jackson, "The Prose of Suffering," 53.
[17] Jackson, "The Prose of Suffering," 52.
[18] Jackson, "The Prose of Suffering," 56.

in his translation of Fina's narrative from the Kuranko) and not gussy it up with anything that attempts to give it meaning or seeks to go beyond what the sufferer has actually said. And then one should remain quiet.

Let us call this *the silence of impossible translation*.

These two options cannot be the end of what there is to say about translation in the field of religious studies. In addition to these silences, is there any possibility for *speaking*? After all, we scholars talk for a living and we scholars of religion in particular usually find ourselves talking about religious cultures, about religious lives, experiences, and understandings that are unfamiliar to our students. How many lectures in a semester can one fill with variants of "bliss – unspeakable!" or with calls to let others' voices take precedence over one's own, without producing silence (or snoring) among students? Is there no possibility that our talk about others might be able to do some good?

To begin to answer this question, it is necessary to follow the story of what happened to Fina and Damba after Jackson's encounter with Fina in the early 2000s. In the spring of 2006, Damba, still in the United States, sent a video about herself to Oprah Winfrey. She and the producers of *The Oprah Winfrey Show* then spent four months tracking down Fina in Sierra Leone and arranging a visa for her. They flew her to Chicago in early November of that year as part of a special "Dream Day" episode of the show, surprising Damba as well as the studio audience for that afternoon's taping.[19] The *Washington Post* profiled Damba on the same day that the episode aired. The article ends with Damba stating that "sometimes I cry, thanking God that she's finally here after six years." Whether Damba identified the proper object of her gratitude remains an open question. In the logic of Oprah, the power accrued through capitalism – the ability to amass resources that can then be expended on finding a single woman, cutting through bureaucratic red tape, and arranging transcontinental airfare for several people – can solve the problems that neither the anthropologist Jackson nor any other finite institutional body could solve. Oprah's reach is infinite, as befits the religious overtones of her show and her persona. Religion

---

[19] "A Daughter's Dream Come True," *Washington Post* (November 8, 2006), B1; online at http://www.washingtonpost.com/wp-dyn/content/article/2006/11/07/AR2006110701413.html (accessed May 25, 2011). See also the description of this episode of *The Oprah Winfrey Show* entitled, "A Mother's Love," on its website: http://www.oprah.com/slideshow/oprahshow/oprahshow1_ss_20061107/ (accessed May 25, 2011). Damba was also profiled in several newspapers in late 2000, including the *New York Times* ("For Maimed War Victims, a Tenuous Respite in Staten Island," [December 17, 2000], A55), after she arrived in the United States. She also appears in George Packer, "The Children of Freetown," *New Yorker* (January 13, 2003), 50ff.

scholar Kathryn Lofton has written about Oprah in an analysis of the relationship between self-making and capitalism on *The Oprah Winfrey Show*: "the only way religion or religious belief works for Oprah is if it is carefully coordinated with capitalist pleasure. Thus, the turn to 'spirituality': the non-dogmatic dogma that encourages an ambiguous theism alongside an exuberant consumerism."[20] The segment of *Oprah* that reunited Damba and Fina replicates and extends this logic. For Oprah, and for the millions of American women (and not a few men to boot) who view her as a role model, the consumerism made possible by capitalism can also buy goodness, bringing those for whom one does good to give thanks to God. Yet although the reach of consumerism is given a moral spin in this episode, the ambiguity that Lofton describes persists. Who has brought Fina and Damba together: God or Oprah? Damba cannot tell the difference, but this is not because she is blind or stupid. Rather, Damba has intuited the fact that many Americans seem to know already, that God and Oprah are structurally identical, both fully human and fully divine.

Placing *Oprah*'s narrative of Fina and Damba side by side with Jackson's creates some difficulty and dissonance. Most importantly, the summary of the segment on *Oprah*'s website gives the impression that Fina willingly ceded the care of Damba to the aid agency, the Friends of Sierra Leone. This conflicts with Jackson's description of Fina as in "despair" over the loss of her daughter. But regardless of whether Jackson is in this case indeed truly speaking for Fina, it remains the case that his critique of engaged action and his vision of ethnography as "trying not to escape into consoling intellectualizations, sympathetic identifications, or political actions that reduce the other to a means for advancing a career, or demonstrating what a compassionate person one is, or changing the world,"[21] in effect powerfully places Oprah and Oprah-ism in its sights. For Oprah's narrative of Fina and Damba finally turns back to herself and to her acolytes. At the end of the segment, the focus shifts from Fina and Damba to the production staff of *The Oprah Winfrey Show*, who talk about their efforts in bringing Fina to Chicago. Per the summary of the segment on the show's website, "this joyous reunion wasn't just a dream come true for Damba and Fina – it was a dream for *Oprah*'s producers too.... Along the way, producer Veronica says they ran into nearly every roadblock imaginable.... 'All we had was

---

[20] Kathryn Lofton, "Practicing Oprah; or, the Prescriptive Compulsion of a Spiritual Capitalism," *Journal of Popular Culture* 39, 4 (2006): 616.
[21] Jackson, "The Prose of Suffering," 54.

hope,' [production staffer] Jill says."[22] This is not the segment's coda. It is its pinnacle, for it serves to verify Oprah's, *Oprah*'s, and the audience's belief that consumerism could never be falsified by the inability to reunite a mother and daughter who had been kept apart for six years by war and its consequences. I – either Oprah or the audience member – must remain secure in my self-image as compassionate and able to make a difference in the world, while I hand a credit card to a cashier at the mall. If I spend it, she will come. She must.

Let us call this kind of speech *the speech that is translated through consumption*.

Are there any other discursive possibilities for speech that do not fall into the egoism that will go to any length not to be threatened in its choices? Or are we doomed, again, to silence? I would like to argue, to some extent against Jackson despite my appreciation for his critical voice, that there are other possibilities. I will call this alternative *the speech that knows not where translation begins or ends*. This kind of speech views translation not as an attempt to carry across an idea, or an -ism, from one culture to another. Rather, it sees translation as the process of articulating and negotiating the boundary between one person and another, or one group and another. It consists in the giving and taking of reasons for an action or an identity, for placing the boundary *here* and not *there*, or for drawing it thickly and not thinly. Most importantly, it is an open-ended process. We do not decide to translate. We find ourselves translating simply because we live among varied and varying communities. We find ourselves translating in different ways at different times because the others among whom we live change. The aim of translation therefore cannot be some permanent mapping of concepts onto one another. The meaning of those concepts will change over time, so translation will never exhaust itself.

Where can we find examples of such speech? I suggest that the canon of modern Jewish philosophy offers such examples. This is not to privilege this one canon over others; it is simply the one in which I am most expert. Furthermore, I am not sure that the major figures in that canon consciously intend to offer such examples of translation as process; rather, my reading those figures as representatives of inconclusiveness is more likely the result of my exposure to other scholars' second-order reflection upon their work. Let me try to explain this with reference to

---

[22] "A Mother's Love," online at http://www.oprah.com/slideshow/oprahshow/oprahshow1_ss_20061107/4 (accessed May 25, 2011).

two figures: the French Jewish philosopher Emmanuel Levinas (1906–95) and the German Jewish philosopher Moses Mendelssohn (1729–86).

Much of the ink that has been spilled about Levinas's writings in the last several decades has taken up the relationship between the categories of "Jew" and "Greek" in his thought. To what extent can the singularity of the "Jew" relate to the universal order that "Greek" philosophy marks? As Robert Gibbs took care to point out in his 1992 *Correlations in Rosenzweig and Levinas*, Levinas himself seemed to change his mind on this issue. In essays dating from the late 1950s and early 1960s, Levinas seemed to argue that the classical Jewish tradition, specifically the conversation between ancient rabbis about law and theology contained in the Babylonian Talmud (redacted in the sixth century CE), contained a kind of wisdom that was opposed to the universalist order of philosophy, which silenced the singular voice and thus might either unwittingly or wittingly support those totalitarian practices that enact that silencing by reducing an individual to the pure substance of either blood or ashes. Most famously, in the 1964 essay "The Temptation of Temptation," Levinas argued that the heteronomous commitment to God implicit in the Israelites' statement "we will do [the divine teachings of the Torah] and we will [then] hear it (*na'aseh ve-nishma'*)" (Exodus 24:7) serves to temper the instrumentalization of reason that Greek philosophy inevitably becomes, on account of its lionization of autonomy.[23] On the other hand, no philosopher would describe the relation between "Jew" and "Greek" as one of pure difference, for in this case, "Jew" and "Greek" would speak radically incommensurable languages. And so Levinas must admit that there is a "Greek" parallel to the valuation of heteronomy in Jewish texts, namely Plato's notion of the transcendent good beyond being in the seventh book of the *Republic*. Here Levinas comes close to the classic identification of God and the good (and explicitly identifies the Torah with the good).[24] This intimacy

[23] Emmanuel Levinas, *Quatre Lectures Talmudiques* (Paris: Minuit, 1968), 67–109; Emmanuel Levinas, *Nine Talmudic Readings*, trans. Annette Aronowicz (Bloomington: Indiana University Press, 1990), 30–50; Robert Gibbs, *Correlations in Rosenzweig and Levinas* (Princeton, NJ: Princeton University Press, 1992), 155–75. (The English *Nine Talmudic Readings* comprises the four essays in *Quatre Lectures Talmudiques* as well as the five in *Du Sacré au saint* [Paris: Minuit, 1977].) I have expanded on these remarks in my "Is There a Warrant for Levinas's Talmudic Readings?" *Journal of Jewish Thought and Philosophy* 14, 1–2 (2006): 153–73. See also Oona Eisenstadt, "Levinas Versus Levinas: Hebrew, Greek, and Linguistic Justice," *Philosophy and Rhetoric* 38, 2 (2005): 145–58.

[24] Levinas, *Quatre Lectures Talmudiques*, 100; Levinas, *Nine Talmudic Readings*, 46.

between "Jew" and "Greek" deepens further in later essays. Levinas's mature position, as articulated in several essays written in the 1980s, is necessary for Judaism to articulate its own singularity. In an essay from 1983 entitled "The Translation of Scripture," Levinas approvingly quotes a pun in the tractate Megillah of the Babylonian Talmud (folio 9b) made by Rab Hiyya bar Abba, supporting Rabbi Shimon ben Gamliel's authorization of the translation of scripture into Greek, in interpreting Genesis 9:27 ("May God enlarge [*yaft*] Japheth"; the descendents of Noah's brother Japheth are traditionally understood to include Greeks). The word *yaft* is a form of the root *p.t.h*, to make wide or open, and thus the verse is a wish for prosperity. The pun imagines that the word is to be read *yofuto*, a form of the noun *yafut* (from the root *y.f.t*), beauty. And so Rab Hiyya bar Abba translates the verse as "May God give his beauty to Japheth," and comments, "Now, what is most beautiful in the descendents of Japheth is Greek; may it reside in the tents of Shem." Levinas adds that this text acknowledges "the value of the clarity of the Greek language, of the Greek genius."[25] Nevertheless, Levinas does not abjure his earlier opposition between Judaism and the Greek. (Indeed, he also affirms in this essay the many criticisms of Greek wisdom that are also to be found in the Talmud.) The resulting situation is oh-so-slightly dizzying:

- Judaism lies in need of Greek aesthetics, the clarity that comes in the intuition of beauty, in order to articulate itself. Nevertheless, at present, the link between the ethnic Greekness of Noah's son Japheth and beauty is already posited, whether or not any translation is taking place.
- Those universalisms that are described in shorthand as "Greek" lie in need of Judaism's critical energies. Nevertheless, these critical energies have parallels in Greek philosophical texts – for example, Plato – whether or not any translation is taking place.

In other words, translation is *both* something to occur in the future *and yet* something that has already occurred. There could never have been any pure intuition either of "Judaism" or "Greek philosophy." They already exist as historically inflected by each other. The work of translation would thus involve the imaginary unweaving of history and the positing of pure essences *that can never be shown to have existed*, in order to reweave *that which already exists as woven together*, but now in a new fashion, for a new purpose (in Levinas's case, an ethical

---

[25] Emmanuel Levinas, "La traduction de l'écriture," in *A l'heure des nations* (Paris: Minuit, 1988), 64; Emmanuel Levinas, "The Translation of the Scripture," in *In the Time of the Nations* (Bloomington: Indiana University Press, 1994), 53.

one). Translation continues. Since we cannot locate its starting point, all that we can say is that it has always been. But why would it need to continue? If it has already taken place, wouldn't that be the mark of its success? It appears that we must also say that because translation has been continual, translation is also constantly failing. We acknowledge that mistranslations have occurred in the past, so translation must begin again. Our ideas have not yet been made clear. Our acts have not truly instantiated a logic of the universal.

Of course, it would be wrong to reduce the canon of modern Jewish philosophy to a single thinker, much less a recent one. Yet this inconclusiveness about the results of translation, all while it is happening, also occurs at the arguable beginning of this canon, with Moses Mendelssohn's *Jerusalem* (1783). This is a text that translates the Jewish tradition into Enlightenment language, in response to interlocutors who doubted Mendelssohn's claim to be an Enlightenment Jew and wanted to cast him either as a closet atheist or a closet Christian.[26] By arguing that Judaism does not truck with revealed dogma but simply legislates practices that produce happiness, Mendelssohn avoids postulating the Torah as another kind of reason (which would lead to charges of "dual loyalty"). Instead, he describes it as a culturally specific path by which Jews come to assent to the same set of rational claims as all other enlightened folk. Much of the scholarship on *Jerusalem* asserts that it is an incoherent book – a bad translation, if you will. A dear friend once described Mendelssohn to me as an "Uncle Tom," and while that epithet appears only once in the scholarly literature to my knowledge,[27] claims that Mendelssohn does not affirm classical Judaism or that he does not really mean what he says abound in the literature. For the former, one can point to David Novak's *The Jewish Social Contract*, which argues that Mendelssohn sees "religion is a matter of free will, which is what one is persuaded – not commanded – to do,"[28] thus vitiating the Jewish tradition of the force of its commands/*mitzvot*. For the latter, one might point to Kenneth Seeskin's claim that Mendelssohn makes little sense because, "despite beginning with a defense of autonomy, Mendelssohn

---

[26] For the most recent summary of the arguments of *Jerusalem* and their historical context, see Aamir R. Mufti, *Enlightenment in the Colony: The Jewish Question and the Crisis of Postcolonial Culture* (Princeton, NJ: Princeton University Press, 2007), 56–69. For a lengthier account, see Jonathan M. Hess, *Germans, Jews and the Claims of Modernity* (New Haven, CT: Yale University Press, 2002), 25–135.

[27] Stanley Nash, *In Search of Hebraism: Shai Hurwitz and His Polemics in the Hebrew Press* (Leiden: E. J. Brill, 1980), 65.

[28] David Novak, *The Jewish Social Contract: An Essay in Political Theology* (Princeton, NJ: Princeton University Press, 2005), 170.

ends up supporting a version of heteronomy at least as far as Jewish law is concerned," since he states – at least exoterically – that Jews are obligated to observe the *mitzvot* simply by virtue of being born into the Jewish people.[29]

Both of these sorts of claims are simply false, in my opinion, in part because they depend upon an essentializing of "Judaism" and "Enlightenment" as heteronomous and autonomous, respectively, and in part because they also depend upon a notion of "Jewish philosophy" that involves itself only with the abstract realm. Mendelssohn's intent throughout *Jerusalem* is to throw a spanner in the works of the Judaism/Enlightenment/heteronomy/autonomy analogy. This intent succeeds not because of any abstract theologizing about "commandedness" or the purity of the will, but because of the *sensuousness* of his theologizing – the very aesthetics that Levinas thought was purely the province of the "Greek." There is quite a well-known passage in Part II of *Jerusalem* about the attractiveness of the Torah:

> The more you search in it [Torah], the more you will be astounded at the depths of insight which lie concealed in it. At first glance, to be sure, the truth presents itself therein in its simplest attire, and as it were, free of any pretensions [*ohne Anspruch*]. Yet the more closely you approach it, and the purer, the more innocent, the more loving and longing is the glance with which you look upon it, the more it will unfold before you its divine beauty, veiled lightly, in order not to be profaned by vulgar and unholy eyes. But all these excellent propositions [*Lehrsätze*] are presented to the understanding, submitted to us for consideration, without being forced upon our belief.[30]

Now, the last sentence of this passage expresses precisely the diminution of heteronomy or commandedness that seems puzzling or non-Jewish, even Uncle-Tom-ish, to scholars working on Mendelssohn. Nevertheless, the process by which the Torah is presented to the understanding is a complex one; it is by no means clear that the individual's understanding is always in control of the situation. Take the second sentence in

[29] Kenneth Seeskin, *Autonomy in Jewish Philosophy* (Cambridge: Cambridge University Press, 2001), 140. For Mendelssohn's claim, see *Jerusalem, oder über religiöse Macht und Judentum*, in *Gesammelte Schriften: Jubiläumsausgabe* [JubA], ed. Felix Bamberger et al. (Stuttgart: F. Frommann, 1971), vol. 8:198; Moses Mendelssohn, *Jerusalem, or on Religious Power and Judaism*, trans. Allan Arkush (Hanover, NH: University Press of New England, 1983), 133.
[30] Mendelssohn, *Jerusalem* in JubA, 8:166; *Jerusalem*, trans. Arkush, 99–100.

the preceding passage. The phrase that Allan Arkush translates as "free of any pretensions" is *"ohne Anspruch."* Reading this as equivalent to *anspruchslos*, or "modest," makes literal sense in the context of the preceding clause describing the Torah in its simplest attire (*einfachsten Bekleidung*). Yet Mendelssohn's text too has layers of clothing. It is legitimate to see the talk of the garments of the Torah as rhetoric for talking about the process by which the Torah comes to make a *demand* or a *claim* – an *Anspruch* – upon the reader.

Reading *"ohne Anspruch"* as "without claim" or "without demand" leads us to recast the opening sentences of the preceding quotation as asserting that a glancing encounter with the Torah is an encounter with a book that makes no claims upon the reader. As the passage continues, however, it becomes apparent that Mendelssohn believes that more significant encounters with the text do lead the reader to acknowledge its commanding stature, and that this is because of the text's "divine beauty, veiled lightly." Here, then, would lie the introduction of something like heteronomy into the argument of *Jerusalem*. The ground of the will's acceptance of the *mitzvot* of the Torah as binding is something outside reason – the feeling of aesthetic pleasure – and not the pain of the moral feeling that Kant associates with autonomous reason.[31] But if this is the case, then how is it that Mendelssohn can end the paragraph by stating that "all these excellent propositions [in the Torah are] submitted to us for consideration"? It would seem that heteronomy, the mark of an authentically Jewish worldview, would appear in *Jerusalem* only to slink away embarrassedly in the following sentence.

The resolution of this conundrum requires a move to the end of this paragraph in *Jerusalem*, where Mendelssohn writes:

> Commandment and prohibition, reward and punishment are only for actions, acts of commission and omission which are subject to a person's will and which are guided by ideas of good and evil and therefore, also by hope and fear. Belief and doubt, assent and opposition, on the other hand, are not determined by our power of desire, by our wishes and longings, or by fear and hope, but by our knowledge of truth and untruth.[32]

Reading this block quote along with the previous one, one might say that Mendelssohn is here creating a taxonomy by which one can make

[31] Immanuel Kant, *Kritik der praktischen Vernunft*, in *Werke* (Berlin: de Gruyter, 1968), vol. 5:72ff; Kant, *Critique of Practical Reason*, in *Practical Philosophy*, ed. and trans. Mary J. Gregor (Cambridge: Cambridge University Press, 1996), 198ff.
[32] Mendelssohn, *Jerusalem* in JubA, 8:167; *Jerusalem*, trans. Arkush, 100.

a distinction between two kinds of responses to the Torah. On the one hand, there are responses to the assertions of the Torah; *Lehrsätze* would here have the sense of "dogmas." On the other hand, there are responses to the commandments; here, *Lehrsätze* would have the broader sense of "propositions," including both matters of belief and matters of legislated action. Only the former are independent of the appetites or material principles. To the extent to which the Torah is a set of assertions to which our understanding can give or withhold approval, it makes no claims upon the reader. Belief in those rational dogmas is determined by the subject's independent knowledge of a set of true claims. But this is not all that the Torah is. In the case of our response to those propositions of the Torah that are commands, these are guided by what Mendelssohn here, using a standard term in eighteenth-century German aesthetic theory, refers to as the "power of desire" (*Begehrungsvermögen*). How does this guidance work? In an essay from 1761 entitled "Rhapsody," Mendelssohn notes, again in opposition to Kant's cordoning of the emotions off from ethics, that "emotions and sensuous sentiments are so often mightier than reason,"[33] especially when the impulse produced by an emotion aims at an object that contains a greater magnitude of perfection. Mendelssohn expands as follows: "Reason's distinct concepts cannot have the liveliness or array of features that befit a sensuous concept. They are also not present to our soul as constantly, and must be pondered for some time. Thus, for all their certainty, they have a slighter effect on the power of desire."[34] So an emotion can have a greater role in determining the shape of an individual's desire and thereby be more effective in determining her or his striving for perfection. The greater the perfection that causes the emotion, the more effective the striving. And this striving is not divorced from a regimen of life. Mendelssohn goes on to discuss how striving requires "constant practice," which both "transforms" the capacities of the self into skill sets and maintains one's ability to be aroused by "quick sentiment" as opposed to "slow rational inferences."[35] Finally, the surest motor for such effective knowledge is beauty. Near the opening of the 1757 "On the Main Principles of the Fine Arts and Sciences," Mendelssohn waxes rhapsodically: "Yet are

---

[33] Moses Mendelssohn, "Rhapsodie, oder Zusätze zu den Briefen über den Empfindungen," in JubA, 1:415; Moses Mendelssohn, "Rhapsody, or Additions to the Letters on Sentiments," trans. Daniel O. Dahlstrom, in *Philosophical Writings* (Cambridge: Cambridge University Press, 1997), 161.

[34] Mendelssohn, "Rhapsodie," 416; Mendelssohn, "Rhapsody," 161.

[35] Mendelssohn, "Rhapsodie," 421; Mendelssohn, "Rhapsody," 165.

there any phenomena that move every impulse of the human soul more than the effects of the fine arts do? Beauty is the self-empowered mistress of all our sentiments, the basis of all our natural drives, and the animating spirit which transforms speculative knowledge of the truth into sentiments and incites us to active decision."[36]

Reading these claims back into the sentences on the attractiveness of the Torah in *Jerusalem*, what Mendelssohn there claims is that the perfectly beautiful object, the Torah, determines the faculty of desire in such a way that ensures its reader's effective striving for perfection and further ensures that the understanding's conceptual knowledge is vitalized through the very set of practices that the Torah legislates. The will is not sovereign. If it were, it would have less confidence that its knowledge could actually be transformed into action, that is, that the power of desire would be effected. Thus, the law is valid for Jews neither because it is rational, nor because of any historical chain of testimony about what is demanded of Jews, but because it is beautiful. The perfect beauty of the Torah gives rise to a pleasure that makes one delighted to obey the *mitzvot*. The essence of scripture is thus neither its propositional content nor some ineffable feeing to which its content gives rise (poetics, after all, allows readers of the Torah to "eff the ineffable," *pace* Otto and the Buddhist monk). Instead, it is its motivating force to govern and inspire a life. Our choices are our own, but the power of our choices is not necessarily grounded in us.

We find in *Jerusalem*, as we did in Levinas, an act of translation that both "others" Judaism – renders it in the jargon of eighteenth-century German moral and aesthetic theory – and claims that "Judaism" signifies the ideal in the target language. Judaism is othered, insofar as "law" is recast as "beauty." Judaism is not othered at all, insofar as Judaism, as the ideal, is something that philosophy expresses. Philosophy is othered, insofar as its path of moving from opinion to truth is relativized with respect to that of Judaism. Philosophy is not othered at all, insofar as it teaches how to interpret Judaism most productively.

Is this "Jewish" or is this "Greek"/"Enlightenment"/"Western"? Who knows? And, truly, on what grounds, apart from the egotistic ones of power politics and/or the maintenance of intellectual authority, can anyone be bothered to care to decide once and for all? There is no answer available here, no moment of pure "philosophy" or "Judaism"

---

[36] Moses Mendelssohn, "Ueber die Hauptgrundsätze der schönen Künste und Wissenschaften," in JubA, 1:427–8; Moses Mendelssohn, "On the Main Principles of the Fine Arts and Sciences," in *Philosophical Writings*, 169–70.

that becomes purely something else or remains purely selfsame when it is translated into the other. All we have is the history of negotiations of this issue, in which one philosopher explicitly or implicitly calls another to task by offering a reason against the other's. The conversation will continue, with new parties and new partners, without solving the conundrum of "Jewish philosophy" or "Jew versus Greek." And in this continuation, history will repeat itself again and again.

What the story of modern Jewish philosophy teaches us to do is to doubt the validity of the kinds of essentialism that underlie the customary translation work that scholars of religion (and others too) do (for example, "Islam is peace"). There is no moment at which the scholar will be able to cognize a tradition or a figure as a whole. Rather, scholarship builds upon and intervenes in the sedimented accounts that are handed down to us: traditions. They change because we take them up, and we are historical beings. As Charles Sanders Peirce wrote in 1868, "The point here insisted on is not this or that logical solution of the difficulty [of the origin of cognition], but merely that cognition arises by a *process* of beginning, as any other change comes to pass."[37]

What this account of translation allows us to do is both to affirm a boundary between cultures and at the same time acknowledge that the boundary is contingent. It allows for translation – cultures are neither incommensurable (making translation impossible) nor identical (making it unnecessary) – and at the same time it acknowledges that at various historical moments, the ways in which we want to translate might change. It authorizes both our freedom and the freedom of those whom we study – to describe ourselves, themselves, and each other – in ways that contemporary scholarship does not always allow. In the last chapter of his 2007 book *Excursions*, for example, Michael Jackson tells a story about the suspicion of biogenetic technologies found among Māori in Aotearoa/New Zealand, on the basis of the Māori belief that "transferring genetic material across species boundaries constitutes a dangerous, unprecedented, and irreversible intervention in the natural order of things."[38] Reporting a conversation with Manuka Henare,

[37] Charles Sanders Peirce, "Questions Concerning Certain Faculties Claimed for Man," in *The Essential Peirce: Selected Philosophical Writings*, vol. 1, *1867–1893*, ed. Nathan Houser and Christian Kloesel (Bloomington: Indiana University Press, 1992), 27. Emphasis in the original.

[38] Michael Jackson, "A Critique of Colonial Reason," in *Excursions* (Durham, NC: Duke University Press, 2007), 246.

a professor at the University of Auckland, Jackson concludes that the Mâori objection to biogenetic technologies is not necessarily fixed in a cultural worldview. It is possible, he says, to leave worldview behind and take a more "pragmatic" view of the matter:

> He described to me a Mâori gathering at which he asked people to raise their hands if they were diabetic and using insulin. As he had expected, a large number of people raised their hands. He then asked how many people were against genetic engineering. All of them were. Manuka then told his audience that insulin was produced through genetic engineering. How many people, he now asked, would continue using insulin? All said they would. If it was [sic] a life-and-death issue, Manuka said, one would set aside one's ideological objections to genetic engineering.
>
> This kind of pragmatism struck a chord in me, for I had long been critical of the view that the way human beings live their everyday lives is wholly determined by the views they espouse or the beliefs they hold.[39]

It is impossible for Jackson to consider the possibility that "pragmatism" might indeed be part of a "worldview." "Pragmatism" is a term that is simply untranslatable into Mâori, or perhaps into the language of any culture.[40] On what grounds is this true? On what grounds is philosophy only metacultural and not something that picks out – even while othering – elements in a worldview? When observant Jews suspend divine laws, such as Sabbath observance or dietary restrictions, in the interest of extending or saving life, as they are commanded to do in accordance with the Talmudic principle of *pikuach nefesh* ("saving of a life"), are Jews being "Jews" or "pragmatists"? The question is malformed. The refusal of such a distinction is a mark of at least one work of Mâori scholarship on *tikanga Mâori*, the Mâori customs of right that govern the practices of Mâori life. In Hirini Moko Mead's *Tikanga Mâori: Living by Mâori Values*, some *tikanga* are described as possessing, of

---

[39] Jackson, "A Critique of Colonial Reason," 249.
[40] It is unclear whether Henare believes this himself. In an article, coauthored by Henare, on the cultural politics of genetic modification among the Mâori, the authors describe Mâori culture as "pragmatic." Elsewhere in that article, the authors distinguish between "pragmatic considerations" and "cultural considerations." See Mere Roberts et al., "Whakapapa as a Mâori Mental Construct: Some Implications for the Debate over Genetic Modification of Organisms," *Contemporary Pacific* 16, 1 (2004): 1–28, especially 17–18.

their own accord, a "pragmatic aspect"[41] and the entire worldview is detached from any intuition of its foundations:

> It is important to note that what we see happening when tikanga is put into practice is not necessarily the ideal manifestation of that tikanga. It is true that precedents have been set and what we witness may well be a perfect example of an interpretation of the concept, but we have no way of knowing this. Other examples have to be seen to identify the essential features, and with this information judgements can be made about the concept.... It is also true that without the practice and performance aspects of tikanga we would not know about the ideas, concepts and background knowledge that underpin them. One can work backwards from the practice to the idea and the reasons for it.[42]

So ideas have no meaning without their performance, in which they are revised, further determined, and made true in a vital sense. What could be more pragmatist than Mead's claim here, namely that truth is verification (in this case, through cultural practices)?[43] And on what grounds could one possibly argue that Mead's claim is completely exterior to the cultural practices that serve as its ground?

All of this is to say that worldviews and traditions are conceptually rich and manifold. Within a "worldview," there is a giving and taking of reasons[44] about what practices mean and whether practitioners have good reasons to do what they do. And so such a giving and taking of reasons – translation – can take place between those within that worldview and those outside of it.[45] Translation can be discursive – indeed, must be discursive, because it is only through discourse that we can come to know what is at stake in our practices. It is true that discourse is not necessarily a means of peace; it might be a means to determine why a relationship with another or others might be inimical. But to enter into discourse without any expected aim – to let translation go where it will

---

[41] Hirini Moko Mead, *Tikanga Māori: Living by Māori Values* (Wellington: Huia Publishers, 2003), 17.

[42] Mead, *Tikanga Māori*, 18–19.

[43] See William James, *Pragmatism and Other Writings*, ed. Giles Gunn (New York: Penguin, 2000), 87–104.

[44] The phrase comes from the work of Robert B. Brandom. See his *Making It Explicit: Reason, Representing, and Discursive Commitment* (Cambridge, MA: Harvard University Press, 1994), and its appropriation for religious studies in Jeffrey Stout, *Democracy and Tradition* (Princeton, NJ: Princeton University Press, 2004).

[45] See John R. Bowlin and Peter G. Stromberg, "Representation and Reality in the Study of Culture," *American Anthropologist* 99, 1 (1997): 123–34.

and to be open to the contingency of the current mapping of concepts – is to open oneself up to critique, and this is perhaps enough to lessen, if not to eradicate, geopolitical conflict. There is good reason to believe that we can do more when we give up the goal of contented silence.[46]

In "Some Versions of Homer," Jorge Luis Borges comments that, unlike *Don Quixote*, Homer's *Odyssey* is a panoply for him, "a library of works in prose and verse" in multiple translations, on account of the fact that Borges does not read Greek. "The rich and even contradictory variety of this library" is rooted in "the impossibility of knowing what belonged to the poet and what belonged to the language."[47] Who would know how to translate Homer, to sing in tune with him? A translator cannot but ask questions of the text and cannot but offer answers that invariably rip Homer out of the ninth century BCE. This is a betrayal. Something will always go awry. And something goes awry whenever we relate with each other, whenever we ask each other to justify why we do what we do. Our answers will be oblique, for there will be no adequate justification. A German might translate this going awry by the phrase *"quer gehen."* But if such going awry is necessary, then religious studies, as a human science, must be a *quer* science. Only by participating in a *quer* science – a queer science[48] – can a scholar deepen the narratives of the range of the differences between us. And only as participants in a queer science can we leave Rudolf Otto's gay (in the pejorative sense used earlier in this chapter, on account of its proclivities to silence others) vision of the study of religion behind.

Select Bibliography

Bowlin, John R. and Peter G. Stromberg. "Representation and Reality in the Study of Culture." *American Anthropologist* 99 (1997): 123–34.

Jackson, Michael. "The Prose of Suffering and the Practice of Silence." *Spiritus: A Journal of Christian Spirituality* 4, 1 (2004): 44–59.

James, William. *Pragmatism and Other Writings*. Edited by Giles Gunn. New York: Penguin, 2000.

[46] For an example of the profits of this kind of sacrifice, see Gourevitch, *We Wish to Tell You*, 349, reporting the words of a Rwandan friend: "I think of your country. You say all men are created equal. It's not true and you know it. It's just the only acceptable political truth. Even here in this tiny country with one language, we aren't one people, but we must pretend until we become one."

[47] Jorge Luis Borges, "Some Versions of Homer," *PMLA* 107, 5 (1992): 1134–8.

[48] For the *quer*/queer link, see Eve Kosofsky Sedgwick, *Tendencies* (New York: Routledge, 1994), viii. See also the comments at José Esteban Muñoz, *Disidentifications: Queers of Color and the Performance of Politics* (Minneapolis: University of Minnesota Press, 1999), 127.

Levinas, Emmanuel. "The Translation of the Scripture," 33–54. In *In the Time of the Nations*. Translated by Michael B. Smith. Bloomington: Indiana University Press, 1994.

Lofton, Kathryn. *Oprah: The Gospel of an Icon*. Berkeley: University of California Press, 2010.

Mendelssohn, Moses. *Jerusalem, or on Religious Power and Judaism*. Translated by Allan Arkush. Hanover, NH: University Press of New England, 1983.

Mufti, Aamir R. *Enlightenment in the Colony: The Jewish Question and the Crisis of Postcolonial Culture*. Princeton, NJ: Princeton University Press, 2007.

Otto, Rudolf. *Das Heilige: Über das Irrationale in der Idee des Göttlichen und sein Verhältnis zum Rationalen*. Munich: C. H. Beck, 1963.

  The Idea of the Holy: An Inquiry into the Non-Rational Factor in the Idea of the Divine and Its Relation to the Rational. Translated by John W. Harvey. London: Oxford University Press, 1923.

Thomas, George F. "The History of Religion in the Universities." *Journal of Bible and Religion* 17, 2 (1949): 102–7.

10 Material religion

MATTHEW ENGELKE

I. INTRODUCTION

All religion is material religion. All religion has to be understood in relation to the media of its materiality. This necessarily includes a consideration of religious things, and also of actions *and* words, which are material no matter how quickly they pass from sight or sound or dissipate into the air. But the difficult part comes in understanding what precisely constitutes the *materiality* of material religion, what makes religious materiality either significant or religious, and according to whom.

Within religious studies and the human sciences more broadly, there has been a growing interest in what the study of materiality offers for our understanding of the lived experience and practices of religion. The move to materiality allows us to reconsider (and resuscitate) the very concept of *religion* itself, for one thing, which has long been recognized as Protestant idealism masquerading as a neutral analytic.[1] "Religion" is not always about belief or the problem of meaning, nor can religion always be recognized as something discrete in culture and society. (This is the paradox of the modern understanding of religion: religion is immaterial but treated always as a distinctive entity apart from everything else.) Approaching "religion" as "material religion" allows us to consider the material as part and parcel of our interests and of the religious worlds of the people we study. The materiality of religious life is not incidental. As Talal Asad writes, "the materialities of religion are integral to its constitution."[2] A number of philosophical and theoretical

[1] See, for example, Talal Asad, *Genealogies of Religion: Discipline and Reasons of Power in Christianity and Islam* (Baltimore: Johns Hopkins University Press, 1993); also Jonathan Z. Smith, "Religion, Religions, Religious," in *Critical Terms for Religious Studies*, ed. Mark C. Taylor (Chicago: University of Chicago Press, 1998), 269–84.
[2] Talal Asad, "Reading a Modern Classic: W. C. Smith's *The Meaning and End of Religion*," *History of Religions* 40, 3 (2001): 206.

I would like to thank Amit Desai, C. J. Fuller, and Robert A. Orsi for their helpful comments on and suggestions for this chapter.

inheritances have contributed to the renewed interest in religious materiality, among them Hegel, Marx, and Charles Peirce, as well as more
recent thinkers such as Bruno Latour. More generally, phenomenology,
the anthropology of the senses, and even cognitive science have also
been used to frame religion as, in one way or another, something that
could be called material.

Material culture has never been truly absent from religious studies.
Take the work of anthropologist Edward Burnett Tylor, whom the historian of the study of religion J. Samuel Preus[3] has rightly recognized
as a key ancestor in the field. Tylor contributed significantly to debates
on the origin and development of religion, notably in his discussions of
animism and the soul in his magnum opus, *Primitive Culture*. Tylor's
evolutionary classifications hinged on these discussions of questions of
materiality. This was evident in his assumption that "religion" could
be treated as an isolatable object. But more interestingly, as I want to
suggest, Tylor's work points to how materiality was used to index belief.
In Tylor's view, stages of mental development were tied directly to the
ways in which material objects were understood to have immaterial
properties.

Victorian social evolutionism was underwritten by the idea that
material culture was a stable source of evidence for determining any
given society's complexity. As the anthropologist Franz Boas argued,
evolutionists proceeded as if a part-for-part comparison of societies
could tell us something about the nature of society itself, as if, for example, we should be comparing Zulu drums with Italian violins to assess
the relative attainments and establish the appropriate ranking of the
two cultures. When it came to religion, this concern with material culture extended beyond the catalogue of fetishes that could be provided
by Tylor's correspondents. (Tylor made a trip to the Caribbean and to
Mexico as a young man that had a serious and enduring impact on his
thinking, but most of his writings were based on secondary sources,
including personal correspondence.) Despite the implicit irony, materiality was a key factor in Tylor's idealist and now (in)famous definition of
religion as "the belief in Spiritual Beings."[4] Things, and what we do with
things, furnished the evidence of ideas and of "things unseen."

---

[3] J. Samuel Preus, *Explaining Religion: Criticism and Theory from Bodin to Freud*
(New Haven, CT: Yale University Press, 1987), 131–56.

[4] E. B. Tylor, *Collected Works of Edward Burnett Tylor*, vols. 3–4, *Primitive Culture:
Researches into the Development of Mythology, Philosophy, Religion, Art, and
Custom* (London: John Murray, 1871), 383 (all citations to this work from vol. 3).

Tylor assumed an inverse relationship between the materiality of spiritual beings and the level of civilization a believer in them
had achieved. Among the "rude races," spirits and the soul had an
"ethereality" or "vaporous materiality." This disappeared the higher
up the ladder of civilization one climbed; among civilized Protestant
Christians, who stood at the apex of religious evolution, spirits would
have no physical presence. Immaterial religion, then, both as a theoretical construct and as a moral norm, was a product of modernity. As
Tylor said, a "metaphysical notion of immateriality could scarcely have
conveyed any meaning to a savage."[5]

Tylor produced a version of what we might call crypto-Protestantism
as a theory of religion that shaped much late nineteenth-century social
thought. By crypto-Protestant, I mean that his scientific outlook was
shaped by currents of religious thought dominant in his life and times.
The fact that these were Protestant currents is not incidental, although
it is important not to place too much emphasis on Protestantism per se,
for the issues in play are, as I will go on to argue in this chapter, part of a
more basic intellectual dynamic of modernity. Still, we might note that
Tylor came from a Quaker family in south London and that his understanding of metaphysics – in particular, the premium he placed on the
immaterial – reflects these roots, even as he severed his connections
to Quakerism in his pursuit of natural science and natural law. Tylor's
brand of science – and the modernity it came packaged with – was meant
"to show that the human soul, the hope of immortality, and the very
idea of God were products of human reason gone astray."[6] For Tylor, the
immateriality that characterized any metaphysics eventually ought to
evaporate completely. True enlightenment comes when we realize that
belief in spiritual beings is a misrecognition altogether. Religion is to
be replaced in the end by a concrete knowledge of that which actually
exists, above all the natural laws that govern humans as much as they
do the rotation of the planets around the sun. Social science *was* natural
science for Tylor. He saw "no impediment to the attainment of perfect
'positive knowledge'."[7]

Tylor's work is a good example of how theologically influenced
Protestant approaches to materiality have shaped social thought and

[5] Tylor, *Primitive Culture*, 412.
[6] George W. Stocking, Jr., *Victorian Anthropology* (New York: Free Press, 1987), 195.
[7] Greg Schrempp, "The Re-Education of Friedrich Max Müller: Intellectual
Appropriation and Epistemological Antinomy in Mid-Victorian Evolutionary
Thought," *Man* 18, 1: 97, in Stocking, *Victorian Anthropology*, 307.

theories of religion,[8] as well as the master narratives of modernity to which these theoretical traditions belong and contribute, in which the fantasy of subject and object is their purity (that is, the idea that subjects and objects can be wholly distinct from one another).[9] It is possible to trace the ways that such conceptions of the material have shaped other approaches to religion – Tylor's is not the only one. But Tylor's work is useful for framing a discussion of material religion because it raises two important issues.

First, it reminds us of the shortcomings of the armchair approach to culture and religion. Tylor belonged to the last generation of anthropologists who worked deductively with impunity, locked away from the stuff of life in their studies. Tylor's concern with the material culture of religion took no account of its materiality in the experience and practice of the people he was writing about, no matter how civilized or rude. The second issue, which underscores the irony I noted previously, is that, even as Tylor contributed to the crowning of "belief" as the essence of religion, his work suggests how even the most idealist view of religion continually invites and relies upon the workings of the material. The fact is that essence needs stuff; spirit demands matter.

The new interest in material religion addresses these issues in part by a focus on lived experience. The recent concern with religious materiality is connected to the broader historical and cultural turns within the human sciences and hammers another nail into the coffin of deductive methods. For scholars of religion, as for their colleagues in other disciplines, there is no single way in which lived experience is shaped or unfolds. The nature of lived experiences, including lived religion, depends on the particularities of time and place and the exigencies of tradition; it also depends, inevitably, on arguments within traditions. In important ways, recent approaches to materiality point beyond persistent analytical bifurcations in the study of religion, all of which we know from experience will fail us: subject/object; spirit/matter; transcendence/immanence; tradition/modernity.

Because lived experience always has a material dimension, the explicit focus on material religion provides an opportunity to consider common issues, problems, and dynamics that surface in the world's

8 Webb Keane, *Christian Moderns: Freedom and Fetish in the Mission Encounter* (Berkeley: University of California Press, 2007), 92–6; also Peter Pels, "The Modern Fear of Matter: Reflections of the Protestantism of Victorian Science," *Material Religion* 4, 3 (2008): 264–83.

9 Bruno Latour, *We Have Never Been Modern*, trans. Catherine Porter (Cambridge, MA: Harvard University Press, 1993).

faiths. The study of material religion allows for "generalizing without universalizing," to adapt a phrase.[10] One of these generalizable issues is what I call the problem of presence.[11] Materiality is the stuff through which "the religious" is manifest and gets defined in the first place: how God, or the gods, or the spirits, or one's ancestors can be recognized as being present and/or *represented*.

God's presence is a formative concern – and problem – within Christianity. Just how God's presence is recognized and experienced differs among Christian traditions, and in different times and places. The Incarnation – God become human in Jesus Christ – is the definitive expression of divine presence in Christianity, but the Incarnation is the beginning of the matter of presence in Christian thought and experience. Presence has been recognized and experienced – re-presented, as it were – within Christianity in a wide variety of ways, including viewing icons, touching statues and relics, telling rosary beads, hearing the Bible read aloud (or reading it silently to oneself), and being filled with the Holy Spirit. Within Christianity, in other words, presence, as recognized in a variety of forms, becomes the reality through which the authority, power, and meaning of God are apprehended (if never fully comprehended). This approach to presence runs throughout the other Abrahamic faiths as well, although there are differences within and among them as to how God's proximity and distance can and should be figured.

But presence also constitutes a problem for religions that do not posit an absolute difference between the human and the divine. Within Hinduism, there is no such absolute difference, yet even in this context being able to recognize and experience divine presence is not a foregone conclusion. As anthropologist C. J. Fuller notes, in many contexts it may be unremarkable for a Hindu to declare that he or she is divine, so that divinity is understood to be not only *within* but *of* the person.[12] But generally, in the act of worship (*pūjā*) there are technologies and modes of recognition that require careful practice and attention. The oft-discussed Hindu concept of *darśan* – "seeing and being seen" via divine "images" – is a key to the experience of presence. The Hindu "image"

[10] Maurice Bloch, "Truth and Sight: Generalizing without Universalizing," in *The Objects of Evidence: Anthropological Approaches to the Production of Knowledge*, ed. Matthew Engelke (Oxford: Wiley-Blackwell, 2009), 21–30.

[11] Matthew Engelke, *A Problem of Presence: Beyond Scripture in an African Church* (Berkeley: University of California Press, 2007).

[12] C. J. Fuller, *The Camphor Flame: Popular Hinduism and Society in India* (Princeton, NJ: Princeton University Press, 1992), 31.

is not necessarily iconic; rocks can be images of the divine as much as elaborate statues or chromolithographs are. According to Fuller, what makes an image significant in the Hindu context is that "unlike an ordinary container, [it] is defined precisely by what it contains – the power of a particular deity – so that in the final analysis there can be no absolute distinction between an image and its corresponding deity."[13] The centrality of *darśan* within Hindu thought and practice points to the importance of vision in this religious world, but as I will explain, the material properties of the image are significant as well. It might matter if the "container" is a statue in good or bad repair, for example.

These brief sketches of Christianity and Hinduism make the key point that problems of presence are problems of representation. Study of the materiality of religion allows us to explore crucial representational and communication aspects of religious thought and practice, not as free-floating signs that reveal meaning, but as indices, identities, and other markers that are inextricably linked to, dependent upon, and subject to the contingencies of the material world. To develop this point, I will need to fill out the sketches of Christianity and Hinduism. Before I do, however, let me unpack my claim about representation/communication and material religion by returning to Tylor's work.

II. CONNEXIONS: TYLOR ON THE PROPRIETY OF REPRESENTATIONS

Tylor's work has always been recognized as important, but almost always as a closed chapter in the history of the modern study of religion. But read against the grain, Tylor's reflections on the materiality and immateriality of "Spiritual Beings" offer a provocative point of departure for considering how the problem of presence occurs in both religious life and in its analysis.

The story Tylor tells in his work on animism and religion is one of a move away from the material into the realm of the immaterial. Tylor was driven by what anthropologist Peter Pels calls "the Protestant fear of matter" that Victorian science parlayed into its own "project of abstraction." Pels uses this latter term to emphasize the separation of ideas from the material world. The modern project of abstraction reached its nadir in the semiology of Ferdinand de Saussure, says Pels, in which linguistic signs are riven from any material base or trace of materiality.[14]

---

[13] Fuller, *The Camphor Flame*, 31.
[14] Pels, "The Modern Fear of Matter," 266, 278–9.

Saussure famously describes the character of signs as "negative": they have no positive content and their functions emerge out of relationships to other signs. As theorist Mladen Dolar emphasizes,[15] for Saussure, even sound should not be understood as part of language proper.[16]

> ... it is impossible that sound, as the material element, should in itself be part of the language. Sound is merely something ancillary, a material that language uses.... Linguistic signals [signifiers] are not in essence phonetic. They are not physical in any way. They are constituted solely by differences which distinguish one such sound pattern from another.[17]

As the material culture specialist Daniel Miller has pointed out, one problem with Saussure's work and more generally with semiology – or the science of signs – has to do with the extent to which its undeniable productivity "took place at the expense of subordinating the object qualities of things to their word-like properties."[18] Dolar's interest in the voice takes this point a step further: in pure Saussurean form, the chief property of words is their lack of properties.

Saussure never treated his main interest (language) as anything other than "a virtual system of denotations."[19] Tylor, on the other hand, approached his main interest (culture) *as if* it were material, but only as a means to the end of uncovering the abstract categories of thought it indexed.[20] This makes sense if we recognize Tylor's anthropology of religion as, at core, an approach to the more general issue of representation.

To understand this point it is helpful to begin with Tylor's own views on language. Tylor argued that the capacity for language was universal and natural. Each language represents "substantially the same intellectual art,"[21] a point that reflects his commitment to the "the psychic unity of mankind." The psychic unity thesis was central to his

---

[15] Mladen Dolar, *A Voice and Nothing More* (Cambridge, MA: Massachusetts Institute of Technology Press, 2006), 15–19.

[16] Ferdinand de Saussure, *Course in General Linguistics*, trans. Roy Harris (LaSalle, IL: Open Court, 1983), 24–5.

[17] Saussure in Dolar, *A Voice and Nothing More*, 18. (The square brackets in the block quote are Dolar's.)

[18] Daniel Miller, *Material Culture and Mass Consumption* (Oxford: Blackwell, 1987), 95–6. See also, Daniel Miller, ed., *Materiality* (Durham, NC: Duke University Press, 2005).

[19] Keane, *Christian Moderns*, 22.

[20] Pels, "The Modern Fear of Matter," 277.

[21] Tylor, *Primitive Culture*, 238.

monogenist and developmentalist views and absolutely crucial for the kind of comparative project he wanted to develop. (Societies could not be ranked in relation to one another, in Tylor's view, if humans could be understood as fundamentally different; perhaps paradoxically, there was an antiracist sentiment in his approach.) Tylor also argued that advances in human knowledge and rational thought came through the evolution of the human ability to use language as a tool for understanding the world. This understanding, in turn, develops in part by means of layer upon layer of metaphorical predications – meaning that humans make sense of what they do not know in terms of what they do. An English-speaker is more sophisticated, in Tylor's understanding, than, say, a Bororo-speaker because of the depth and breadth of the former's ability to use language as a sign system, through which the workings of the world may be more fully accounted. But the difference is one of degree, not of kind:

> The language by which a nation with highly developed art and knowledge and sentiment must express its thoughts ... is no apt machine devised for such special work, but an old barbaric engine added to and altered, patched and tinkered into some sort of capability. Ethnography reasonably accounts at once for the immense power and the manifest weakness of language as a means of expressing modern educated thought, by treating it as an original product of low culture, gradually adapted by the ages of evolution and selection, to answer more or less sufficiently the requirements of modern civilization.[22]

I have noted that in Tylor's opinion one of these "requirements" was that of moving beyond religion altogether. It was not enough, in his view, to treat the spiritual as immaterial, however sophisticated the concept becomes. In Tylor's history of religion, the spiritual would eventually disappear altogether.

Making religious thought disappear was dependent in part on using language "properly," as it were. As with others of his time, Tylor understood so-called savages as being unable to distinguish between a representation and the object it stands for. Savages produced a stunted sign system, by this account; they lived as if all language was literal, governed by what anthropologist Lucien Lévy-Bruhl called the law of mystical participation.[23] Their cognitive reasoning produced a

---

[22] Tylor, *Primitive Culture*, 216–17.
[23] Lucien Lévy-Bruhl, *How Natives Think*, trans. Lillian A. Clare (Salem, NH: Ayer, 1984).

"confusion of objective with subjective connexion," in Tylor's words.[24] By "objective connexion," Tylor meant "such a connexion as there is between the bucket in the well and the hand that draws it up." It is the *literal* or *material* connection between an agent and an object. A "subjective connexion," on the other hand, exists in the portrait of a man, for example. There is no literal connection in this case, as Tylor sees it, "for what is done to the man has no effect upon the portrait, and *vice versâ*."[25] The portrait is a representation; it is not what it stands for. As Tylor argued, savages were unable to understand this distinction, thinking instead that, just like the bucket in the hand, there is a literal connection between the portrait and the man depicted.

It is out of the confusion between objects and representations that belief in spiritual beings emerged and endures, according to Tylor. Most of his examples of this confusion in *Researches into the Early History of Mankind* are drawn from "the superstitious beliefs and practices of the untaught man."[26] People's beliefs about the qualities and properties of material culture – how they recognize it as being "religious" – become the litmus test for the maturity of their rationality. At one point in his discussions, Tylor makes a claim that is particularly relevant to the arguments here:

> The strong craving of the human mind for a material support to the religious sentiment, has produced idols and fetishes over most parts of the world, and at most periods in its history; and while the more intelligent, even among many low tribes, have often seen clearly enough that the images were mere symbols of superhuman beings, the vulgar have commonly believed that the idols themselves had life and supernatural powers.[27]

We get another glimpse in this passage of the assumptions that inform Tylor's understanding of religious representations. Chief among these is the "craving" for an objectifiable confirmation ("material support") of an essentially cognitive disposition ("religious sentiment"). Religion is an idea, a belief, a sentiment. It is immaterial. But for the less sophisticated, the insecurity that accompanies immateriality is understood to be embodied in physical artifacts, to be present *things*.

---

[24] E. B. Tylor, *Researches into the Early History of Mankind and the Development of Civilization* (London: John Murray, 1865), 127.
[25] Tylor, *Researches into the Early History of Mankind*, 117.
[26] Tylor, *Researches into the Early History of Mankind*, 148.
[27] Tylor, *Researches into the Early History of Mankind*, 121.

Tylor's assertion about "the strong craving of the human mind" tells us more about the roots of his own worldview than it articulates a universal truth. It is the kind of deductive thinking for which he was criticized and the reason that his theories were ultimately rejected. Yet we should not throw the baby out with the bathwater. We do not need a theory of human nature or of rationality to explain the intimate connections between persons and things. The things humans do and the sentiments they have are inextricably linked to the material world. Whether or not we have a "craving" for that world (and if so, why) may be an interesting philosophical issue, but it is beside the point in making sense of lived experience.

If we can distinguish Tylor's primary observation from the Protestant and naturalist logics in which it is embedded, it is possible to retain a core insight of his work. Tylor was on to something in his concern with the relationships between materiality and immateriality. His mistake was in insisting on the absolute difference between the material and the immaterial in the first place, compounded by his assumption that the latter is superior to the former. When it comes to religion, there is not a one-way flow from substance to sentiment; nor can we know, without attention to particular cases, what distinguishes the material from the immaterial in the first place. Distinctions such as these are made in culture; they are not given in the nature of the human or of religion.

III. MATERIALITY AND SEMIOSIS

One leading approach to the materiality of religion has been developed by anthropologist Webb Keane, in his thinking on what he calls semiotic ideologies. Keane has worked for over twenty years among the Sumbanese of Indonesia, tracing the relationships between "traditionalist" and Dutch Calvinist understandings of spirit and matter. It is on the basis of this research, coupled with a strong theoretical training in historical anthropology and linguistics, that Keane has developed his ideas. A semiotic ideology, in Keane's account, is an assumption (and often argument) about the kinds of things that things are, what things can stand for, and how, within an ordered and usually hierarchical system, things relate to one another. By "things," I am referring to objects, artifacts, images, gestures, words, ways of speaking, and everything else that can be taken to communicate a message – everything, in other words, which is or can be recognized as a *semiotic form*. For

Keane, the important point in any semiotic analysis is to acknowledge that "the materiality of semiotic form is inescapable."[28] In this regard, he takes his cues from American philosopher Charles Sanders Peirce rather than from Saussure. Peirce's semiotic model considers not only the materiality of signs but also the extent to which the materiality of signs plays a role in the process of signification. A well-known example of this phenomenon is a sign's indexicality: smoke signals fire. There is a material connection here. Keane has emphasized how not only the material properties of certain signs, but also the contingencies of their physicality, are central to what particular signs communicate. These contingencies – what a particular sign looks like, whether it is corroded or new, and so on – are not always predictable or controllable. A Bible is printed on paper; paper is flammable: this does not mean Bibles are meant for burning, although they can be and this can matter. As another anthropologist has shown, following Keane's ideas, even such qualities as "age" can inform the meaning of things and their authority. In modern-day Georgia after Communism, "old" Orthodox churches have become especially significant within the post-Soviet social imagination, to the extent that "new" churches are not always considered churches at all.[29]

Another key aspect of the idea of a semiotic ideology is the extent to which any such organization of the meaning of things involves argumentation. Semiotic forms are often loaded with, or denied, importance, by persons or groups with competing or simply different interests – political, social, moral, metaphysical – including those who share the same social world. Burning a Bible, for example, can be a way of triggering an "argument. "You think there is some spiritual force in this thing," the argument might go, "but I say it's *just a book.*" Such an exchange is an argument about semiotic forms. When Tylor insisted on the difference between subjective and objective connections, he was also making such an argument about the meaning of signs and revealing something of the semiotic ideology that informed his analysis. To say that a portrait of a person is an inanimate object – a "mere symbol" – is to make a clear statement about the nature (indeed, the ontological status) of pictorial representations, as Tylor was indeed doing.

---

[28] Keane, *Christian Moderns,* 24.
[29] Paul Manning, "Materiality and Cosmology: Old Georgian Churches as Sacred, Sublime, and Secular Objects," *Ethnos: Journal of Anthropology* 73, 3 (2008): 327–60.

Tylor argues a painting is just a painting. This brings us back not only to his understanding of primitive mentality, but also to some long-standing Christian theological debates. Tylor writes:

> … it is emphatically true of a large part of Christendom, that the images and pictures, which, to the more instructed, serve merely as a help to realize religious ideas and to suggest devotional thoughts, are looked upon by the uneducated and superstitious crowd, as beings endowed not only with a sort of life, but with miraculous influences.[30]

It was not far, in Tylor's estimate, from Amazonia to Rome. From his (post)-Protestant/naturalist perspective, Roman Catholics suffered an inability like that of primitives to distinguish between the representation and the thing. Understanding the Eucharist as being the body and blood of Christ – rather than a representation of the body and blood of Christ – is a strong argument about the potentials and promises of material things to deliver presence. Likewise is the idea that a particular statue or painting of the Virgin Mary brings you into her proximity.

Roman Catholicism often places a strong emphasis on presence in representations, and this emphasis is indexed in a richly developed material culture. But it would not be enough to point to the obvious difference between a Catholic cathedral and a Quaker meeting house to make this case. Tylor's crypto-Protestant approach to materiality was not confined to Protestant or post-Protestant semiotic ideologies or traditions of thought. That the normative modernist understanding of religion as immaterial had Protestant roots should not prevent us from recognizing that debates over the proper relations between the material and the immaterial, as well as what these are in the first place, are easy to find elsewhere. Robert A. Orsi's work on the Catholic Church in the United States shows that within a national tradition that might otherwise serve as a foil for Protestantism or modernity, there are ebbs and flows in what constituted acceptable levels of materiality in the faith. In the 1960s, modernizers embarked on a "season of iconoclasm," writes Orsi, in which "devotions were derided as infantile, childish, or as exotic imports from Catholic Europe, alien and inappropriate in the American context."[31] Churches were thinned of the religious stuff they contained in an effort to dislodge the pull of devotionalism in the minds

---

[30] Tylor, *Researches into the Early History of Mankind*, 121.
[31] Robert A. Orsi, *Between Heaven and Earth: Religious Worlds People Make and the Scholars Who Study Them* (Princeton, NJ: Princeton University Press, 2005), 56.

of ordinary Catholics, particularly as expressed in relation to the Virgin Mary. Orsi shows that this effort to convert "presence ... into senescence" had the paradoxical effect of concretizing "Mary's thereness."[32] In the terms I have been developing, the season of iconoclasm was an effort at reforming the semiotic ideology that governed the laity. As with many ideological struggles, this one was met with resistance and did not result in the end anticipated by reformers.

IV. PRESENCE AND PROTESTANTISM

Even after the semiotic reforms of the 1960s, the material culture of American Catholicism could be seen as more elaborate and elaborated – more present – than within most Protestant traditions. One way to understand the difference is with reference to the intellectual and ideological inheritances of the Protestant Reformation (in all its historical and regional diversity): the break with tradition; the turning inward of faith; and the elevation of the Word, in scripture and in liturgy, as the preeminent medium of presence. This is to sketch with broad strokes, admittedly, but it underscores one of the primary ways that Protestantism came to distinguish itself, tendentiously and not always with due recognition of the actual practices of ordinary Protestants, from Roman Catholicism: as immaterially religious.

But the details of actually existing Protestant traditions over the centuries – from Anglo-Catholicism to Prosperity Gospel Pentecostalism in Ghana – complicate this claim. Given my argument that all religion – including early modern and modern Protestantism – is material religion, it will be helpful to focus on a particular Protestant tradition with a strong commitment to immateriality. Here I turn to my field work in a small African church in Zimbabwe that had such a strong immaterial commitment.[33] What makes this church so provocative in relation to my claim that all religions are material and so productive of theoretical reflection is that its members would deny every aspect of my central thesis. This is a group of Christians for whom *no* religion is (or, at least, ought to be, if it is to be authentically Christian) material religion.

The Friday Apostolics have their origins in the preaching of Shoniwa Peter Masedza. In 1932, while working as a migrant worker around colonial Salisbury in southern Rhodesia, Shoniwa got sick and began to

---

[32] Orsi, *Between Heaven and Earth*, 56, 60.
[33] See Engelke, *A Problem of Presence.*

have dreams in which he was told by God that he was Johane Masowe, "Africa's John the Baptist." Over the next two years, Johane preached where he could, often barely ahead of colonial agents, who were looking for a reason to deem his preaching illegal. One of Johane's earliest pronouncements, one that his "Friday" followers took especially to heart, was to call on all Christians to reject the Bible. On at least one occasion, Johane went as far as to urge the burning of Bibles, although this did not become a common practice. True Christians, as Johane's followers now say, do not need the Bible because they apprehend the presence of God "live and direct" – in the persons of prophets filled with the Holy Spirit; in the congregation's song; and by living according to the tenets *(mutemo)* of faith. Presence comes via a strong sense of here-and-now embodiment. This theology is complemented by a minimalist ritual life. The Apostolics wear simple white robes; they meet under the open sky; they maintain no altars or other focal points of religious observance; and, in their healing rites, the Apostolics rely largely on simple remedies and ordinary things to harness themselves to the power of God.

The rejection of the Bible in part had to do with colonial politics (and is why the authorities were interested in Johane). It was a rejection of the written word, which missionaries had presented as the defining element of both Christianity and civilization; as historians and anthropologists of colonialism have shown, writing served as a tool of social control. Caught up with these political implications, the Apostolics' understanding of the Bible also spoke back to dominant European and mainstream African Christian concerns about how things ought to matter. Many missionaries working in Africa relied on – and emphasized – the thingness of the Bible in their daily lives and writings and in their interactions with Africans. But they almost never directly conceptualized the Bible's physicality in itself. Christianities of the Word – those based on the primacy of scripture – are often projects of abstraction, in which the Word's materiality is made as irrelevant as voice was for Saussure or the museum inventory for Tylor. The ethnographic record in Africa regularly describes how local peoples were indeed attuned to the Bible's thingness, in part because in the initial stages of encounter the particular kind of immateriality the Bible was said by Europeans to exemplify was based on the ability to read. From a nonliterate perspective, the book cannot but be a thing.

In the Apostolics' view, the written word is always only a thing. They talk about the written word as a Protestant reformer in the sixteenth century might have talked about a golden crucifix or as a modernizing American Catholic priest might have talked about the devotional displays in the living rooms of his older parishioners in the later 1960s and 1970s. The most striking and memorable comment on the Bible's materiality I heard during my field work came from a prophet who suggested it could be used as toilet paper. The book is fated to fall apart one day, so why not use it for this most mundane of necessities? Certainly not all Apostolics spoke about the Bible this way (and I saw no evidence of it being used in this way), but the comment captures the dominant attitude toward the Bible as a thing among Apostolics.

The Apostolics' insistence on the Bible's materiality exemplifies what American religious historian Colleen McDannell has discussed in another context as the way in which Protestants can make the Holy Book akin to "religious furniture," despite their intellectual commitment to its immaterial truths.[34] The materiality of semiotic form is inescapable, even when it goes unrecognized. Like other Christians, the Friday Apostolics argued and made claims about how, when, where, and in what sorts of objects one might find the divine; and, again like other Protestants, the Apostolics understand these indices of presence to be defined by immaterial qualities. But thingness is inescapable; commitment to immateriality has to be expressed through *some thing*. What the Apostolics end up guarding against is not only the deadness and degradability of a book, in their view, but also the liveliness of their prophets. Some of these prophets have asserted or suggested identity with the divine, such that they – in their bodies – become controllers of, rather than conduits for, presence. In some instances, in fact, Apostolic prophets have demanded a personal fealty that is at odds with the community's ideal of direct and living contact with the spirit of God. The moral of the story is clear, even among a religious group whose main tenet is the immateriality of the spirit: all religion is material religion. The challenge is in understanding what constitutes the materiality of a religion and for whom it is so material.

V. PRESENCE IN HINDUISM

For argument's sake, let us say – adopting a tone like that of media theorist Marshall McLuhan – that Protestantism is a "religion of the ear."[35]

---

[34] Colleen McDannell, *Material Christianity: Religion and Popular Culture in America* (New Haven, CT: Yale University Press, 1995), 15.

[35] See Walter J. Ong, S.J., *The Presence of the Word: Some Prolegomena for Cultural and Religious History* (New Haven, CT: Yale University Press, 1967); Leigh Eric Schmidt, *Hearing Things: Religion, Illusion, and the American Enlightenment* (Cambridge, MA: Harvard University Press, 2000).

Such a claim is tenable because of the emphasis within the Abrahamic faiths on sound and hearing, which in Protestantism (or in Sunni Islam, to take another example) is often accompanied by a distrust of images and seeing. Sound: what first drew my attention to the Apostolics was their singing. An utterly compelling sound emanates from their make-shift groves. But ritual life in the church is not limited to sound; it is a full sensory experience. Apostolic ritual gains its depth from the spec-tacular look of the congregants' white robes, the smell of approaching rains or the heat of the sun, and the taste of "medicines" (substances the Apostolics use in their spiritual therapies). Nevertheless, in this Protes-tant sensorium, as in many others, hearing often takes pride of place.

In contrast, Hinduism might be understood as a "religion of the eyes." Hindus strive for *darśan*: to see and be seen by the deities. But South Asianist Diana Eck[36] notes that Hindu worship likewise makes full of the full sensorium: the smell of incense or camphor flames, the crush of bodies in a temple, the touch of an image, the taste of food exchanged with the gods, and the sound of mantras. All of these matter, especially mantras, as sound in the Vedas is taken to be primary.[37] But it is sight that organizes and undergirds Hindu religious experience as a whole. It could be argued, indeed, that *darśan* has its own metasensorial logic, since "seeing" the image is understood as "touching" the image. Anthropologist Christopher Pinney[38] calls this ritual synesthesia the corpothetics of *darshan*, its "sensory, corporeal aesthetics." "*Darshan*," Pinney writes, "can be thought of as a physical relationship of visual intermingling."[39] Also notable is the fact that the materiality of Hindu images – their thingness – raises important analytical (and metaphys-ical) problems within the tradition. Although Hindus are comfortable with the materiality of divine presence (while asserting at the same time that divinity is "eminently visible"[40] in everything), this does not mean the physical properties of the image are either irrelevant or inci-dental. Careful attention to an image's material form is often required to make sure the omnipresent is present, at least properly so.

---

[36] Diana L. Eck, *Darśan: Seeing the Divine Image in India* (Chambersburg, PA: Anima, 1981), 11.

[37] C. J. Fuller, personal communication.

[38] Christopher Pinney, "The Indian Work of Art in the Age of Mechanical Reproduction: Or, What Happens When Peasants 'Get Hold' of Images," in *Media Worlds: Anthropology on New Terrain*, ed. Faye D. Ginsburg, Lila Abu-Lughod, and Brian Larkin (Berkeley: University of California Press, 2002), 359.

[39] Pinney, "The Indian Work of Art," 364.

[40] Eck, *Darśan*, 10.

Take the case of the 1995 renovation rituals at the Minaksi Temple in Madurai, for example, which Fuller observed as part of long-standing research on the Hindu priesthood. In his account of the rituals, Fuller[41] notes that the renovation was undertaken with support from the pro-Hindu government of Tamilnadu and the growing middle class. It was also seen as "a notoriously good way of spending 'black' money accruing from corruption and tax evasion."[42] (These are material facts in themselves!) The Minaksi Temple renovation followed a similar form to other renovation rituals, albeit with an unusually high number of 250 priests involved. The rituals took twelve days to perform, for a part of which the Temple was closed so that craftsmen could do the repairs.[43] Needless to say this example cannot be taken as representative of "Hinduism" as a whole; the overarching term "Hinduism" is undeniably problematic.[44] I use it here only as a point of departure, to emphasize that the particular configuration of presence within a particular religious world may look quite different in, say, devotionalist or ascetic practices.[45]

Renovation rituals are called "water-pot bathing rituals" because they culminate by pouring water "charged" with divine power over a temple's tower and images. To carry out renovation, the priests had to empty the towers and images of divine power; transfer the power of the towers into small pictures, then transfer the power of the images into water pots, which contained not only water but special ingredients, such as the smoke from burning ghee and certain leaves. The water pots were in some cases bound with cotton thread "as if it were holding the power tightly inside."[46] These transferences were accompanied by rituals of protection, celebration, pacification, and preparation, because the process of transference is "potentially extremely dangerous."[47] Drawing out the deities' powers also often involved the chanting of mantras and wafting incense into the pots, containing the smoke by capping the water pots with mango leaves and coconuts. With the transfer completed,

---

[41] C. J. Fuller, "The Renovation Ritual in a South Indian Temple: The 1995 *Kumbhabhiseka* in the Minaksi Temple, Madurai," *Bulletin of the School of Oriental and African Studies, University of London* 67, 1 (2004): 40–63.

[42] Fuller, "The Renovation Ritual," 40.

[43] Fuller, "The Renovation Ritual," 52.

[44] For discussion, see David N. Lorenzen, "Who Invented Hinduism?" *Comparative Studies in Society and History* 41, 4 (1999): 630–59.

[45] See, for example, Peter Van der Veer, *Gods on Earth: The Management of Religious Experience and Identity in a North Indian Pilgrimage Centre* (London: Athlone Press, 1988).

[46] Fuller, "The Renovation Ritual," 50.

[47] Fuller, "The Renovation Ritual," 51.

the priests began *yagapuja*, "sacrifice-worship," for the pots, centered around small camphor-fed fires, ladled with ghee, particular special woods, and foodstuffs. On the final day of renovation, priests carried the pots into the temple and up the towers, in front of a crowd of some half a million people, including a number of distinguished guests. With the "vast simultaneous affusion" of water, the crowds cheered. Those close enough tried to touch the water as it flowed past. "By pouring the water, all the power within it was transferred back to the Temple," not only restoring it but having "enhanced divine power located in it."[48]

The spectacle of renovation is intrinsic to the point.[49] It provides a series of arresting visual displays – not only the cascading water, but also the *yoga pūjā* fires and the consumables that are burned within them. The scale of the spectacle underlines a simple but potentially elusive point: visuality here is defined by materiality. But how does materiality matter?

Fuller notes that despite its elaborateness, the "logic and purpose" of renovation "are fairly straightforward."[50] The rituals involve the restoration and augmentation of divine presence. We might say the temple became that which it already was, only more so. As Fuller points out, this creates a paradox that I think we can call a Hindu problem of presence. How can an omnipresent deity be taken out of one thing and transferred to another, much less be made "more present" through reinstallation? Where the Agamic texts (scriptures) remark upon this question in respect to Śiva, we are told, "Śiva is indeed present everywhere, but in some places he is more present than others."[51]

The priests involved in the temple renovation disagreed over how presence should be understood. Fuller's ethnography suggests this disagreement hinged on an understanding of how materiality and immateriality were conceived in relation to the divine. As he notes elsewhere, Hindu worship is marked by the "impermanence of almost all the main materials used."[52] In the renovation rituals, this point is relevant for understanding the significance not only of the water and fires but also of the images as objects. It was in regard to the latter that Fuller observed disagreements among priests. Some argued

[48] Fuller, "The Renovation Ritual," 58.
[49] Fuller, "The Renovation Ritual," 61.
[50] Fuller, "The Renovation Ritual," 59.
[51] Richard H. Davis, *Worshiping Siva in Medieval India: Ritual in an Oscillating Universe* (Princeton, NJ: Princeton University Press, 1991), 119; Fuller, "Renovation Ritual," 60.
[52] Fuller, *The Camphor Flame*, 75.

that the images' deterioration and pollution over time compromised their divine status. In this view, presence is linked to materiality quite closely, such that there is identification between god and thing. Other priests rejected this view, insisting that a deity's power exists "independent of any material constraints."[53] Poorly kept images, according to this camp, pose a problem for their human caretakers, not for the gods. Still others deferred to the Agamic conclusion that omnipresence exists in degrees, so that while to humans this might not make sense, humans are ultimately ignorant about divine workings. In these latter two views, materiality is reduced to the role of medium, although in the first view it is still medium with causality. This whole debate among ritual specialists within a religious context is an example of what I referred to earlier as the arguments inherent to the articulation of a semiotic ideology.

VI. CONCLUSION

This chapter has woven analytical approaches together with case studies to suggest why it is important to take the materiality of religious worlds and practices seriously. Advances in the study of semiotics have been a productive component in this effort, not only for what they reveal about material religion but also because they help rescue the field of semiotics from its associations with idealism. I have mentioned several other literatures and interests that have, alongside a semiotics attentive to material culture, pushed material religion to the fore. Lack of space has prevented me from exploring these various approaches to religious materiality in detail, and interested readers will have more to explore than what is presented here. (The bibliography is meant as an introductory guide to this further examination.) But in a nod to what else comes into view when religion is conceptualized materially, let me close by opening another window.

Another way to approach material religion (and, incidentally, the problem of presence) is to frame *materiality* in terms of *media*. Scholars of religion have long paid attention to media in the commonly understood sense of a particular technology of communication (the printed book, for instance, the mass produced image, or the transmitted voice). Increasingly, however, religious media studies are taking account of media in their wider sense as "middle grounds": something *through which* something else is communicated, presented, made

---

[53] Fuller, "The Renovation Ritual," 60.

known – whether that something is a book or a pair of eyes.[54] This is Dolar's point about the "metaphysics of the voice," in which the voice serves as the "vanishing mediator."[55] The voice, however, is also always a material medium, as revealed in my preceding discussion of the Friday Apostolics.

Some scholars of religion have begun to emphasize religion and media as two sides of the same coin. Good examples of this new scholarship on religious media can be found in Hent de Vries and Samuel Weber's *Religion and Media*,[56] in which one contributor simply notes, "the history of religions is ... the history of the media."[57] Materiality plays a fundamental role in this double history of religion and media. Take the materiality of circulation, for instance, which is a key axis in Charles Hirschkind's 2006 volume on the popularity of cassette sermons in contemporary Egypt. The cassettes belong to the *al-da'wa* movement, inspired by the Muslim Brotherhood. The recorded sounds are intended to foster greater piety and to counter the influence of secularism. The material aspects of the circulation of recorded sound inform Hirschkind's analysis in several ways. As small, inexpensive, and easily reproducible objects, cassettes generally escape state regulation. The classical emphasis on sermon audition within Islam, moreover, which is central to the cultivation of ethics, is reconfigured in relation to the cassettes, a redirection of auditory practice that Hirschkind calls "a history of the pious ear in modern Egypt."[58] Thus through media studies we get a further sense of the sensuality of religious experience and practice, another instance of the "religion of the ear."

These brief sketches are only an indication of how media studies, too, can help make sense of the materiality of religion. It is fitting here, in conclusion, to reflect back on the discussions in this chapter's various sections, not in relation to semiotics but in terms of the idea of media as

---

[54] For general discussion, see Dominic Boyer, *Understanding Media: A Popular Philosophy* (Chicago: Prickly Paradigm Press, 2007).

[55] Dolar, *A Voice and Nothing More*, 15.

[56] Hent De Vries and Samuel Weber, eds., *Religion and Media* (Stanford, CA: Stanford University Press, 2001).

[57] Haun Saussy, "In the Workshop of Equivalences: Translations, Institutions, and Media in the Jesuit Re-formation of China," in *Religion and Media*, ed. Weber and de Vries, 163–81; see also Birgit Meyer and Annelies Moors, eds., *Religion, Media, and the Public Sphere* (Bloomington: Indiana University Press, 2006); Birgit Meyer, "Religious Revelation, Secrecy and the Limits of Visual Representation," *Anthropological Theory* 6, 4 (2006): 431–53.

[58] Charles Hirschkind, "Hearing Modernity: Egypt, Islam, and the Pious Ear," in *Hearing Cultures: Essays on Sound, Listening, and Modernity*, ed. Veit Erlmann (Oxford: Berg, 2004), 131–52.

"middle grounds." For as we can see, in doing so, while problems of presence are problems of representation, they can equally be understood as problems of mediation. What matters in so much religious thought and practice is the precise constitution of these middle grounds: whether the middle grounds are books or ancient churches, images of the Hindu god Minaksi, or smoke-infused water, and whether it is through the ears or the eyes that one is best able to apprehend the divine. It is in such specificities that we can challenge the analytical bifurcations of which I have discussed in this chapter, and in relation to which that we should understand how all religion is material religion.

Select Bibliography

Engelke, Matthew. *A Problem of Presence: Beyond Scripture in an African Church.* Berkeley: University of California Press, 2007.

   "Religion and the Media Turn: A Review Essay." *American Ethnologist* 37, no. 2 (2010): 371–9.

Keane, Webb. *Christian Moderns: Freedom and Fetish in the Mission Encounter.* Berkeley: University of California Press, 2007.

McDannell, Colleen. *Material Christianity: Religion and Popular Culture in America.* New Haven, CT: Yale University Press, 1995.

Miller, Daniel. Ed. *Materiality.* Durham, NC: Duke University Press, 2005.

Morgan, David. Ed. *Religion and Material Culture: The Matter of Belief.* London: Routledge, 2009.

Orsi, Robert A. *Between Heaven and Earth: Religious Worlds People Make and the Scholars Who Study Them.* Princeton, NJ: Princeton University Press, 2005.

Pels, Peter. "The Modern Fear of Matter: Reflections of the Protestantism of Victorian Science." *Material Religion* 4, 3 (2008): 264–83.

Schmidt, Leigh Eric. *Hearing Things: Religion, Illusion, and the American Enlightenment.* Cambridge, MA: Harvard University Press, 2000.

CHRISTINE HELMER

Even the most cursory glance at works written by a number of contemporary religious studies scholars reveals a disturbing use of the term "theology," at least to this theologian. "Theology" is usually (and unfortunately) mentioned in a pejorative sense. Often "theology" appears as the negative foil to the study of religion. Lived religion is opposed to abstract dogmatic propositions; the empirical study of devotional practices is contrasted with the prescriptions of religious authorities far removed from the reality of religion and everyday life; and the value-neutral academic study of religion is preferred to the subjective imposition of theological doctrines.

Given the agreement among some – if not most – religious studies scholars that theology must be decisively disciplined, the presence in this particular book of a chapter on theology and religious studies might raise a few eyebrows, if not elicit a few groans. Is it not the contemporary consensus that the two disciplines, religious studies and theology, are best seen in the disjunctive terms of "either/or"? Is religious studies not premised on its liberation from theology, which is also its ticket to acceptance in the secular academy?

When a theologian cannot recognize herself in descriptions of her discipline by scholars of religion, then she must address the challenge of the disjunction. The aim of this chapter is twofold: first, to set up the historical terms in which the fraught relationship between theology and the study of religion has come to be; and, second, to make a case for a way of doing theology that can be productive for the study of religion.

By way of a preliminary comment on the theological terms that might facilitate a future relationship with religious studies, I turn to the

I owe a debt of gratitude to Matthew Robinson, Matthew Cressler, and Kate Dugan, graduate students at Northwestern University in my seminar on theology and religious studies in the spring quarter of 2010, who were my conversation partners in developing the ideas in this chapter.

nineteenth-century theologian Friedrich Schleiermacher (1768–1834), whose speeches compiled in *On Religion* are regarded as one of the most influential apologies for religion in the West. Schleiermacher begins the first speech by situating his audience, the cultured despisers of religion, firmly in view. He asks his hearers not to regard him as representative of his (despised) guild of theology, but as an individual who speaks from the "inner, irresistible necessity of my nature," and in a spirit of irony he invites them to think with him in a new way about religion in order for "you to be properly informed and thoroughgoing in that contempt [of religion]."[1] Following Schleiermacher's lead in building a bridge from theology to religion, it is my aim in this chapter to imagine ways in which theology might be understood as a necessary and stimulating conversation partner to religious studies. At the ironic least, scholars of religious studies ought to be "properly informed and thoroughgoing" in their characterizations of theology. If you're going to scorn theology, it is best to do so in a learned manner! Theology is not necessarily a "normative" discipline that prescribes propositions for belief on the grounds of divine revelation. Rather, theology may be understood as a discipline that describes that which is referred to as the reality of religion and the ways in which that reality is experienced and known in particular communities of practitioners, thereby opening up additional possible discourses for making sense of the subject matter that we call "religion." Schleiermacher will be my primary conversation partner in the pages that follow, precisely because he so richly theorized the relationship between theology and religion at the very origins of the modern discipline of religious studies.

There are three parts to my exploration in this chapter of "a once and future relationship" between theology and religious studies. The first treats two historical moments in the relationship that I think have contributed to the contemporary bifurcation between the two disciplines. I intend my historical analysis to open up possibilities for revision in order to clarify lingering misunderstandings that currently intensify the bifurcation. The subsequent sections are constructive, meaning that they articulate the task and method of theology in such a way as to show how theology can contribute to the study of religion. The constructive part of the chapter begins in section II with a proposal for considering the reality of religion to be the common subject matter for

---

[1] Friedrich Schleiermacher, *On Religion: Speeches to Its Cultured Despisers*, trans. and ed. Richard Crouter, Cambridge Texts in the History of Philosophy (Cambridge: Cambridge University Press, 2000), 4, 11 (speech 1).

both theology and religious studies. I discuss theology's interest in the question of reality to be precipitated by metaphysical concerns to situate religious experience in history. Further, I discuss the mechanism by which the reality of what is called "religion" is generated in history for further examination by theology and religious studies. The second constructive proposal for theology raises the epistemological issues at stake in the articulation of claims to knowledge. In this section, I look at theology's task in explaining how experience and reason work and how claims to knowledge can be made. The theological perspective in explaining the mechanisms of religious perception and articulation is, I argue, helpful to viewing an important dimension of the phenomenon known as religion.

I. HISTORICAL CONSIDERATIONS OF A COMMON SUBJECT MATTER

The current distance between theology and religious studies has served to erase the intense proximity of their past relationship, even in the work of those most determined to break up the relationship. Theology has always viewed religion as its distinct subject matter; religion has always been theorized theologically. From Plato to Schleiermacher, theology was regarded as the critical discipline of religion. Plato used theology to articulate attributes of deity that were metaphysically more stable than the fickle gods of Greek myths, while Schleiermacher saw theology's task as being to select and organize into a coherent system religious ideas and morals as they are expressed and lived in particular religious communities. Religion as an object of critical inquiry might be approached from a theological perspective by comparing the varieties of Christianity in relation to non-Christian religions, for example. Protestant Orthodox theologians of the seventeenth and eighteenth centuries, to take another example, distinguished between general revelation in all religions and special revelation in Christianity. Religion could also be taken in the same way by both modern liberal theologians and contemporary scholars of religion. Liberal theology shares with the modern study of religion the basic assumption that religion is a historical, cultural, social, and political phenomenon.

Yet there have been moments in the history of the West in which the intimate relationship between theology and the study of religion has been shaken. One was the European Enlightenment of the seventeenth and eighteenth centuries. Although the Enlightenment can be distinguished geographically by region – whether Italy, England, Scotland,

France, or Germany – and confessionally – Lutheran, Reformed, Roman Catholic, or Jewish – the common element of enlightenment is generally seen as the critical use of reason in matters of politics, academic study, and religion. Reason, both in its self-reflective capacity and in its applications in the public sphere, is regarded as the adjudicator of truth and the producer of knowledge. Reason sets the terms for empirical and rationalist knowledge and provides the conditions for experience and morality. Any claim to metaphysical knowledge that falls outside the parameters set by reason is deemed illegitimate on epistemological grounds.

The Enlightenment is often characterized as reason's assault on religion. Reason's limits and powers apply a critical function to religious experience and knowledge; superstition and dogma are exorcised from religion, while theology is purified of appeals to sources and authorities above and beyond reason. Yet care must be taken when applying the historical claim of reason's undermining of religion to the entire Enlightenment. The application is convenient. Religion is understood to be unlike other arenas of public accountability in appeals to the supernatural to support its existence and truth claims.[2] Yet this does not do justice to the complex relationships among religion, culture, society, and politics, on the one hand, and reason's permeation of all of these interrelated spheres, on the other hand. New research on the Enlightenment is noticing the complicated relationship between religion and reason as it developed in this period. Scientists, among them Isaac Newton and Francis Bacon, rather than discounting inherited notions of divine providence, struggled to harmonize their ideas about religion with empirical claims. Philosophers – for example, Gottfried Leibniz – appealed to reason in order to argue for the divine love that is destined to adherents of all religions. So, reason cannot be simply consigned to the role of deconstructing religion in the inheritance of the Enlightenment. Rather, reason as understood in the Enlightenment should be taken as productive of new ways to understand religion. The interpretation of foundational religious texts by lower and higher criticism, for example, an enterprise initiated by the Enlightenment, opened the possibility of regarding religion as a set of historical, experiential, and linguistic factors.

Theology is also oriented by the Enlightenment's emphasis on reason's role in requiring public accountability of religion. According to one view, theology is forced into adopting accommodationist and

---

[2]   Immanuel Kant, was, after all, called "the all-destroyer" ("der Alleszermalmer") by Moses Mendelssohn for dismantling the theoretical proofs for the existence of God.

defensive strategies to prop up its supernatural claims even as historical study deconstructs these claims. The eighteenth- and nineteenth-century historical study of the Bible, as the story of modernity goes, exposed an illegitimate speculative use of reason that underwrote doctrines affirming the divine inspiration of the Bible. The construction of this familiar story of the Enlightenment's rout of theology ironically brings together in the contemporary intellectual context the unlikely bedfellows of historians, pundits, and philosophers who would prefer to see the Enlightenment as destroying religion, on the one hand, and some conservative theologians who like to see (and then entirely reject) the Enlightenment as a massive assault on Christian doctrine, on the other. The consequence of this odd union of intellectual opposites is that any theology articulated in response to reason's increasing authority is doomed to failure, either because theology is a deeply misguided endeavor or because theology is based on alien categories that taint its claims to truth. The complex interrelationship among reason, religion, and theology bequeathed to moderns by the Enlightenment is undone by this interpretation, and theology finds itself excluded from the contemporary academic study of religion.

What is needed to correct the prejudices embedded in this story of the modern Western antithesis between reason and religion since the Enlightenment is a revisionist account of the trinity of reason, religion, and theology as reciprocally related and mutually enriching. Each term in this triad must be fundamentally reconceptualized in relation to the other two. If theology is seen as historically part and parcel of the way that religion is expressed in history, then theology too will acquire a new meaning that better reflects the particular religious experience and practices of men and women in history and society. If the study of religion is better able to understand theology as a critical, rational discipline, then religious scholarship will be enriched as well.

The second historical moment that shook the relationship between theology and religious studies is tied up with the history of theological education and its place in (or outside of) the modern university. The blueprint for the modern study of *Theologie* – in the extended German sense of the term, which includes the three areas of philosophical, historical, and pastoral theology – was established by Schleiermacher with the founding in 1809 of the first modern university, the University of Berlin. Schleiermacher conceived of a theory of knowledge that he intended would serve as the theoretical foundation for the organization of the university. He distinguished the real sciences (*Wissenschaften*), by which he meant the arts and the sciences that pursued "knowledge for knowledge's sake," from the positive sciences, by which he meant the three disciplines of theology, jurisprudence, and medicine that pursued "knowledge for the sake of application" in institutions outside the academy, namely, religious institutions, government, and medical practice.[3] Theology, like the other two positives sciences of law and medicine, was connected to the real sciences by virtue of specific methodologies that established the scientific criteria for all disciplines in the university. The real sciences also provided knowledge for the positive sciences, and the positive sciences in turn recast and developed that knowledge from their respective viewpoints. In the case of theology, Schleiermacher appealed to the fields of what he termed "ethics" – which is more akin to the sociology of history in modern terms – and the "philosophy of religion" – again, meaning what we would call today comparative religion – as informing theology's distinctive approach to the religious dimension to the human person. The eventual bifurcation, at least in North America,[4] between theology and religious studies took place according to Schleiermacher's blueprint. Theology as a "positive science" was allocated to divinity schools attached more or less to universities or to confessional or demominational theological seminaries. This arrangement prepared the way for religious studies in due time to emerge as one of the "real sciences" in departments situated within faculties of arts and sciences.[5]

Although the institutional bifurcation took place gradually over the second half of the twentieth century, it was further complicated by the

---

[3] See Friedrich Schleiermacher, *Occasional Thoughts on Universities in the German Sense with an Appendix Regarding a University Soon to Be Established* (1808), trans. Terrence N. Tice with Edwina Lawler (Lewiston, NY: Edwin Mellen Press, 1991 [2005]).

[4] The contemporary bifurcation between the two disciplines in Europe differs somewhat from its North American counterpart. In some Western European countries – for example, in Germany – departments of theology are almost always departments in universities. These departments are, in some cases, being converted into religious studies departments or, in other cases, they coexist with newly established religious studies departments.

[5] It is beyond the scope of this chapter to document in detail the history in North America of theological institutions, either as university divinity schools or as seminaries, and their relation to the emergence of religious studies departments. To begin the discussion from the Protestant theological perspective, see Edward Farley, *Theologia: The Fragmentation and Unity of Theological Education* (Philadelphia: Fortress Press, 1983; reprint: Eugene, OR: Wipf & Stock, 2001); Peter C. Hodgson, *God's Wisdom: Toward a Theology of Education* (Louisville, KY: Westminster John Knox Press, 1999), 132–40; David Kelsey, *From Athens to Berlin: The Theological Education Debate* (Grand Rapids, MI: Eerdmans, 1993).

reception in theology of early twentieth-century theologian Karl Barth's (1886–1968) evaluation of the theological legacy inherited from the nineteenth century. Barth began wrestling seriously with this theological inheritance as he sought to articulate a critical theological perspective in the aftermath of the First World War. Barth's sincere admiration for Schleiermacher was tempered by his shock that German Christian theology was impotent to address the crisis first of world war and then of the National Socialist cooption of the *Deutsche Christen*. Barth assigned (some) responsibility to nineteenth-century "liberal theology" as taught in Protestant seminaries for political developments in Germany.[6] This theology was so indebted to a notion of religion as a historical-cultural phenomenon, Barth argued, that it was unable to assume a critical position outside of history and culture forceful enough to separate religious-cultural falsity from theological truth.

Barth's criticism of the liberal theology of his predecessors was conceptually linked to his constructive theological moves in epistemology and Christian doctrine. He understood epistemology on exclusively theological terms (rather than on the grounds marked out by philosophy since the Enlightenment); theology must be obedient to God and must listen to God's transcendent word in order to pronounce a judgment on the Christian religion that had so perniciously merged with political ideology. As a result of Barth's intervention, theology's truth by revelation came to be pitted against religion's corrupt alliance with culture and politics. Barth's powerful theological proposal, which had tremendous influence in European and North American seminaries, would radically change the direction that theology had been taking since the nineteenth century. Before Barth, theologians had studied the history of religions and comparative religion as integral to their work; consider here, for instance, the fundamental theoretical contributions to religious studies of Rudolf Otto (1869–1937) and Ernst Troeltsch (1865–1923), as well as, a little further back in history, of the Lutheran churchmen C. P. Tiele (1830–1902) and W. Brede Kristensen (1867–1953). As Tiele wrote in the first volume of his *Elements of the Science of Religion*:

> He who wishes to study the science of religion must survey the whole region, and must have traversed it in every direction; he must know what the researches of anthropologists and historians, and the discoveries of archeologists, have yielded for the history of religion,

---

[6] Christine Axt-Piscalar, "Liberal Theology in Germany," in *The Blackwell Companion to Nineteenth-Century Theology*, ed. David Fergusson (West Sussex, UK: Wiley-Blackwell, 2010), 468, 481.

what is merely probable, and what is still uncertain or positively false. In short, he must be master of the material with which he has to work although others have discovered it for him.[7]

After Barth, the attention of many European and American systematic theologians turned exclusively to the word of the triune God.

The path that Barth mapped out for theology set the bifurcation between theology and religion on theological terms, paralleling and ironically endorsing the bifurcation established by the story of the Enlightenment as the slayer of theology. Recently, the Barthian direction has been challenged by theologians who aim to help theology regain its connection to the concept of religion and to religious studies.[8] Several contemporary theological research programs developed out of this revisionist spirit. A Schleiermacher renaissance taking place over the past three decades, for instance, has focused attention on the intimate relations between the concept of religion and theology that Schleiermacher had established for modern thought. The ongoing research in process thought and theology (based on the legacy of philosopher Alfred North Whitehead) and the emergence of liberal theologies that are recontextualizing the legacy of nineteenth-century German Protestant thought in a global context are likewise both contributing to the theological recovery of religion as its subject matter. These diverse liberal theological traditions are interested in the ways in which social, cultural, and historical factors have shaped and continue to shape religious experience. A review and appropriation of liberal theologies can help to reset theology as a critical discipline that can serve as the condition for any future relationship with the study of religion.

My brief look at two historical moments that shook up the relationship between theology and religious studies reveals the need of both disciplines to move beyond the rhetoric of opposition that flattens out or completely denies the complex history of an intimate relationship between them. Theology can no longer be superficially dismissed as the enemy of reason, and lived religion cannot be rejected as a human endeavor at war with God's word. A careful historical look at the shaping of both disciplines in relation to each other, within the relevant

---

[7] C. P. Tiele, *Elements of the Science of Religion* (Edinburgh and London: William Blackwood and Sons, 1899), vol. 1, 19.

[8] Garrett Green has recently translated a text by Barth on religion that might help to more carefully nuance Barth's understanding of religion. See Karl Barth, *On Religion: The Revelation of God as the Sublimation of Religion*, trans. Garrett Green (Edinburgh: T & T Clark, 2006).

cultural, political, and academic contexts, will help develop an awareness of both as critical disciplines. With a clearer understanding of its
connectedness to theology, the study of religion can be more critical
of its own methodological ideologies and less resistant to appealing to
theology in order to help better understand the content of religion. With
a clearer understanding of how the contemporary bifurcation between
neo-orthodoxy/postliberal theologians on the one hand and liberal theologians on the other hand came to be, theology might also seek to bridge
the conceptual disjunction between its work and religion, recapture its
own legacy in the study of religion, and imagine ways in which it could
offer an irreducible interpretative dimension to religion. I now turn to
my constructive proposal regarding three ways in which a theology
attentive to lived religion can contribute a unique critical and interpretative perspective to the study of religion.

II. REALITY OF RELIGION

The search for subject matter is a perennial task of all academic disciplines. Academic fields are circumscribed by the distinctive ways that
they carve out particular areas of reality for description and analysis.
Given the common subject matter of religion for both theology and religious studies, the fate of both depends on their combined efforts to specify the reality of religion that both can study.

The quest for subject matter is particularly important for theology
today. Theology has traditionally privileged the speculative, conceptual,
and prescriptive approach to religion. Yet the turn after Barth toward
viewing God's word as theology's sole subject matter, accompanied by a
dismissal of, if not downright hostility to, the lived religious practices
of real men and women, has led to a turning away from religion as a historical, social, and cultural reality. At the same time, religious studies
seems oddly to be similarly experiencing a loss of its subject matter. This
loss is precipitated in this case by the exclusive attention paid to the historical, social, cultural, and political contexts in which religion is lived
and expressed. Yet when religion is absorbed by the historical and the
social, as opposed to being viewed in its unique (albeit not independent)
place in history, the subject matter is erased. The way ahead for both
theology and religious studies would be to admit the "special things"[9]
of religion that resist being reduced to any other human phenomenon

---

[9] See Ann Taves's contribution to this book in Chapter 3, "Special Things as Building
Blocks of Religion."

or biological condition. It is to Schleiermacher I turn now to show how a recovery of religion's unique status among human operations can lead to a recovery of the reality of religion, the realness of religion in human historical experience.

II.1. History and Metaphysics

The case for theology to have, as its subject matter, historical religious beliefs and practices as lived out in communities was first made by Schleiermacher, who is regarded as the founder of modern theology because he established theology's primary concern to be with historical religion. The reality of religion can be ascertained only by studying history, Schleiermacher taught. With this conviction, he moved theology away from its classic eighteenth-century task as ectypal theology which was to represent speculatively the perfect archetypal theology God's knowledge of God's self and the world, and he replaced this with theology "done on earth." Theology's task would be oriented to religion as lived out in communities in history. Its tools would be restricted to the "bounds of mere reason."

Religion as a historical reality entailed for Schleiermacher some presuppositions concerning human agency as such.[10] The reality of human endeavors – whether in religion, politics, academy, or "free sociality," as he called intellectual friendships – is the historical-cultural expression of human being in the world. Descriptions of human institutions, such as religious communities, require explanation in terms of human psychology. Human agency is responsible for history, and its study calls for a complex interweaving of historical, psychological, sociological, and cultural factors.

---

[10] My reconstruction of Schleiermacher's intellectual commitments is based on a number of primary sources, including *The Christian Faith (1830/31)*, trans. D. M. Baillie et al., ed. H. R. Mackintosh and J. S. Stewart (Edinburgh: T & T Clark, 1999); *Lectures on Dialectic* (1811–33), available at present only in the orginal German: *Vorlesungen über die Dialektik*, 2 vols., ed. Andreas Arndt, in *Kritische Gesamtausgabe*, Part II, vol. 10/1–2 (Berlin: De Gruyter, 2002); *Hermeneutics and Criticism and Other Writings*, trans. and ed. Andrew Bowie, Cambridge Texts in the History of Philosophy (Cambridge: Cambridge University Press, 1998 [1811–34]); *Brief Outline of Theology as a Field of Study*, 3rd Edition, rev. trans. of 1811 and 1830 editions with essays and notes by Terrence N. Tice (Louisville: Westminster, 2011); and *Lectures on Philosophical Ethics*, trans. Louise Adey Huish, ed. Robert B. Louden, Cambridge Texts in the History of Philosophy (Cambridge, Cambridge University Press, 2002 [1812–17]). For a more detailed treatment of Schleiermacher's thought, see my essay, "Schleiermacher," in *The Blackwell Companion to Nineteenth-Century Theology*, 31–57.

Historical reality also required the identification of "rules" governing historical development. Schleiermacher believed that any historical trajectory created by human agency had distinct rules that related to human psychology. If human agency assumes specific psychological characteristics, then its historical expressions can be measured by those same psychological markers. Particular histories, like individual human persons, have particular origins, moments identified with a powerful experience that result in a creation of a discourse focused on the original experience. History, again like the human individual, then proceeds through a period of development that extends these original formative impulses into different cultural and linguistic arenas in order to be contextualized there. In other words, to do history generally, religious history especially, one has to do psychology.

Historical development, for Schleiermacher, presupposed a reality that remained consistent throughout change. Similar to human psychology, history requires a self-identical "essence" that accounts for a selfsame identification throughout numerous changes and multiple recontextualizations over time and space. The "inner" side of history is grasped by a speculative – in other words, conceptual – hypothesis regarding the selfsame characteristics of a historical entity that changes through time. The "outer" side of history is studied by empirical reason. Both the inner and outer together constitute the reality of history. Both together are always a product of tentative human reason that itself is articulated by a scholar living in a specific moment in history.

The historical religion on which Schleiermacher focused his theology was Christianity. According to Schleiermacher, Christianity's origin was precipitated by the historical appearance of Jesus of Nazareth. Experiences of Jesus of Nazareth's powerful work and redemptive person are recorded in written form in the texts of early Christianity, although the continuous experience of Jesus of Nazareth by men and women in different times and places is required in order for Christianity to be a living historical religion. This dynamic view of Christianity from its origins to its present state permitted Schleiermacher to articulate a hypothesis regarding the "whole" (though yet not complete) historical trajectory of Christianity, and to hold in tension identity and multiplicity. Scheiermacher articulates his Christian apologetics, or in other words, his hypothesis regarding the inner characteristic that qualifies every outer moment of Christianity's change in time, in this way: "Christianity is a monotheistic faith ... that in it everything is related to the redemption accomplished by Jesus of Nazareth."[11] At least until his own present, although with no absolute certainty for the future, Schleiermacher understands the historicity of Christianity in terms of the extension of the experience of Jesus of Nazareth into many different areas of culture and history. The reality of the Christian religion, like any other human reality, must be evaluated in the same historical terms informing any other historical reality. Yet the uniqueness of the specific historical reality of Christianity is consistently attributed to all experiences of redemption caused by the single individual, Jesus of Nazareth. Schleiermacher adapts his general assumptions concerning human agency in history to the particularities of Christianity, thereby identifying Christianity in terms of a unique and irreducible reality.

Schleiermacher's historical understanding of the Christian religion can serve as an example for how the reality of religion can be grasped. If theology and the study of religion are to have religion as their common subject matter, then these two disciplines must be able to articulate the assumptions about the reality of particular religious worlds in order to then frame the appropriate methodology to study these various realities. The issue at this juncture is not whether or not Schleiermacher's model must be adopted for contemporary work, but how his vision provides a multifaceted and rich picture of religion as a historical reality produced and shaped by human beings. Schleiermacher's understanding of religion presupposes and entails claims that regard reality as fundamentally historical. As historical, human reality is produced and shaped by varied expressions of human existence. Psychological, sociological, linguistic, cultural, and personal dimensions of human existence inform the ways in which humans are agents of history. History in an empirical sense, and a metaphysic of history in a speculative sense, are required in order to describe adequately the existence of a reality that changes while remaining identifiable as such a reality through its different historical forms. The topic of how reason can make claims to knowledge concerning the reality of religion will be treated in section III of this chapter, when I turn to epistemology. At this point, suffice to say that the question of reality, assumptions, and claims is at stake when the recovery of the subject matter of theology and religious studies is the issue at hand.

---

[11] Schleiermacher, *The Christian Faith*, §11, proposition (52). (Page references noted in parentheses.)

II.2. Experience and Expression

If the reality of religion is to be the subject matter of both theology and religious studies, then its availability for these disciplines must be explained. Reality, like all other important concepts, is a term that has a diversity of meanings. What is meant by the term must be negotiated if both disciplines are to agree about their common subject matter. In this section, I address the way in which theology tends to approach the question of reality and then turn again to Schleiermacher in order to tease out the particular reality of religion so that it can be the common subject matter for both theology and religious studies.

Theology appeals to the Western philosophical tradition in order to describe and explain the reality that it studies. This tradition goes back to Aristotle, who designated the highest science to be the preoccupation with "Being qua being." By "highest science," he meant metaphysics, which he considered equivalent to theology. Metaphysics, as the title of Aristotle's lectures also goes, is the philosophical discipline that studies the reality of beings. Since turning to historical religion as the reality it studies, theology has brought the historical dimension of reality into metaphysics. Historicity, at least since the nineteenth century, is constitutive of Western metaphysics. Twentieth-century theology also participated in the philosophical turn to language as part of the question concerning reality. Contemporary theology then addresses the question of the reality of religion as the relation between history and language. The conversation between theology and religious studies can begin with the question concerning the reality of religion in history as expressed and shaped by culturally specific language.

The question concerning the reality of religion is one that Schleiermacher addressed. I turn to Schleiermacher's model not because it is the only viable proposal for the reality of religion, but because it is a comprehensive model that attempts to do justice to the way in which the reality of religion exists in history and the way in which religious understanding is produced in history. Schleiermacher's contribution to the discussion of religion for theology concerns how the conditions for theology are themselves produced by lived religion. The mechanism underlying the production of religion in history is the same mechanism explaining how religion generates the possibility of reflection on religion. Theology is set up on the same ground of reality that produces religion.

Religion for Schleiermacher is a human reality that has to do with the transition from experience to expression, and conversely with how expression shapes experience. A theory of human consciousness and its relation to language undergirds Schleiermacher's understanding of how religion generates linguistic expression.[12] Human consciousness consists of a number of distinct psychological aspects that operate together in the unity of a human individual. When one aspect is "stimulated" by a reality occurring outside the individual, that psychological stimulation aims for expression. The impulse from inner experience to outer expression is constituted by an anthropological structure that necessarily binds individuality to intersubjectivity. Humans bring experiences to expression by virtue of their desire to let others know. Although Schleiermacher's understanding of the experience of religion is based on a particular psychological theory concerning self-consciousness, it too is governed by the same rule pertaining to the externalization of experience in expression, from gestures to language. This transition from inner to outer furthermore constitutes intersubjectivity. Any time communication is available, community is created. The historical reality of religion is produced by humans as they express their particular religious experiences, while conversely, the production of religion shapes particular experiences that are held in common by a religious community. Consciousness and language are integrated to give an explanation of how the reality of religion is located in historical communities.

The description of religion's reality occurs right at the beginning of Schleiermacher's designation of the theological task. Schleiermacher begins his description of the task and method of theology in his significant book *The Christian Faith* (1830–1) with an account of how religion is part of particular historical communities. He appeals to specific academic disciplines, such as psychology, history, and philosophy of religion, in order to help circumscribe religion's reality. In his own context, Schleiermacher proposed new disciplines – for example, the philosophy of religion – to help with the task (at the time, these disciplines did not exist). The process of defining the reality of religion as the first part of theology involves relating religion to other disciplines that study human individuality and intersubjectivity in relation to experience and to the communication of that experience. Religion is a particular reality that is related to the reality of human experience and its expression. Its availability to theology and religious studies opens up both conceptual and empirical methods to study it.

The significance of Schleiermacher's description of religion's reality is that it is grounded in human reality. Religion is central to what

---

[12] The following discussion of the experience-expression mechanism is my interpretation of Schleiermacher, *The Christian Faith*, §§ 2–6 (3–31).

it is to be human. Being human entails anthropological, psychological, and intersubjective structures that explain human agency in history. Yet religion has "its own province"[13] in the human soul. Religion is an irreducible element of human experience and expression. Its explanation locates a distinct area of human consciousness in relation to the experience of a distinct religious reality. Its production is historically, culturally, and linguistically situated. Religion's historical reality in religious communities becomes the explanation for the further production of ideas about that religion. Theology presupposes the mechanism explaining how religion is produced and furthers this production by selecting and organizing the content of expressions into representations of the major ideas circulating in distinct religious communities. The importance of this connection has to do with the legitimacy of reflection on historical religious communities. The reality of religion produces the conditions for reflection on that reality. The human activities of "theology and religious reflection" are generated by the same mechanisms governing the production of religion in the first place.

This reconstruction of the mechanism underlying the reality of religion and its reflection is, of course, speculative.[14] But before a speculative account of religion and its reflection is dismissed outright for the fact that it is other than empirical, let us review its primary objective. The question of reality drives – or should drive – the study of religion in history. The speculative dimension to the question of reality adds explanatory power to religion's appearance in history. Speculative explanations demonstrate the necessary objectivity of religion in the face of efforts to expose religion to be an aberrant or utterly socially determined aspect of human society. They complement empirical descriptions of religion by tightening claims as to the *sui generis* dimension of religion located in history and culture while also showing that religion is constitutive of human experience. Speculative framing of the empirical can open the empirical to conceptual possibilities that can in turn reframe the way the empirical is observed. New descriptive possibilities enter into the empirical repertoire. Theology has classically had this role of conceptual

---

[13] Schleiermacher, *On Religion*, 17 (speech 1).

[14] I deliberately appeal to the term "speculative" in the nonpejorative sense of its etymology. The Latin noun *speculum* means "mirror," while the verb *specere* means "to look closely." The Latin sense dovetails with the Greek sense of *theoria*, which means "to look into the essence of things," which is knowledge. Speculative or theoretical knowledge has been constitutive, together with practical knowledge, of the Western sense of knowledge. On *theoria*, see Hannelore Rausch, *Theoria: Von ihrer sakralen zur philosophischen Bedeutung*, Humanistische Bibliothek Reihe I: Abhandlungen 29 (Paderborn, Germany: Wilhelm Fink, 1982).

framing, and has deployed a distinct vocabulary in order to open up possibilities of describing the reality of religious experience. The discourse of mysticism, for example – the proximity of erotic to spiritual discourse – is framed by a metaphysic that brings the temporal and physical into union with the eternal and spiritual. The aim in my appeal to Schleiermacher's reconstruction is to show how religious expression is *metaphysically* connected to experience. The reality of religion informs the production of religion as well as reflection on that reality that has the speculative potential to open new descriptive possibilities.

II.3. The Reality of God

The reality of history and metaphysics, in Western intellectual thought, refers to the highest being or ultimate reality.[15] The two disciplines of theology and metaphysics have both been concerned with God as the most real being (*ens realissimum*) and the highest good (*summum bonum*). Theology and metaphysics tend to intersect on the question of how the system of being is related to its cause; theology and history tend to intersect on the question of how a personal God is related to self and world. From metaphysical perspectives, God is the highest reality – God is the Being upon whom all other beings exist. God is uncaused, whereas all other beings depend on their causation from God. From a historical religious perspective, God is the personal reality to whom "we are to look for all good and in which we are to find refuge in all need."[16] If religious studies is interested in the question of reality, then it must be interested in the metaphysical and historical questions of the highest being in relation to thought and action.

Theology and philosophy have tended to take human questions exhibiting the "lure of ultimate reality" as a point of departure. Humans ask questions concerning the origins and goal of both personal and world experience. Where have we come from? Where are we going? These questions are oriented to ultimate reality from the perspective of causation. Human existence, like the world's existence, is not self-caused. Rather, the cause of all contingent existence in the world, both efficient and final, must be attributed to an external cause that exists by necessity. The most real being (*ens realissimum*) exists by virtue of the necessity

---

[15] I thank Marilyn McCord Adams and Robert Merrihew Adams for this suggestion concerning theology's contribution to the study of religious reality: personal conversation, April 26, 2010, in Chapel Hill, NC.

[16] Martin Luther's "Explanation to the First Commandment" in his *Large Catechism* (1529), found in *The Book of Concord*, trans. Charles Arand et al., ed. Robert Kolb and Timothy J. Wengert (Minneapolis: Fortress Press, 2000), 386, line 2.

of its own being; God's essence is to exist, as the Scholastics agreed. Schleiermacher's own modern psychological foundation for theology appeals to this argument in terms of the specific question of causation posed by "immediate self-consciousness." The question concerning the relation of the world to its source orients consciousness to the feeling of a "Whence of the feeling of absolute dependence." Only in the second edition of his *Christian Faith* from 1830–1 does Schleiermacher explicitly specify the content of this feeling. The feeling of the "Whence" is the feeling of being "in relation to God" that orients human psychology to metaphysical questions at the most primary level of human consciousness. Schleiermacher's earlier 1820 version of § 4,4 of *The Christian Faith* aimed to detract Christian rationalist interpretations of the "feeling of utter dependence" by using the new and nontheological terminology of the "Whence." And by this formulation, the emphasis is on causation rather than on revelation from a personal deity, to orient the speculative question concerning the ground of human existence in an ultimate reality.

The metaphysical question concerning ultimate reality is a philosophical way of querying the cause for human existence that has been appropriated and fleshed out by theologians. Theologians following in Thomas Aquinas's footsteps have sought to bridge the philosophy–theology divide by correlating the ultimate reality with the personal God of historical revelation. By this move, theologians gain in concretion the determination of the historical God who leads God's prophets and people. Metaphysical characteristics, such as "omnipotence" and "omniscience," give way to concrete attributes that are taken as descriptions of God by people who experience God's acts in history. "God is love," is the metaphysical claim found in 1 John 4:18 of the New Testament. In Psalms 103 of the Hebrew Bible, the Psalmist asks the congregation to recall the narrative of God's faithfulness in the past in order to address the situation concerning God's response to present distress. When evil is encountered, the question concerning God's providential goodness becomes most radical. God's permissive will becomes the object of despairing questioning, while God's ordained will becomes the metaphysical assurance that love conquers all, even evil. Reality is not only what is presented in the ambivalent relation between the pain and pleasure of the present tense. It is also available in the questions, prayers, and cries of those who seek the divine face in the future on the basis of a relationship with God in the past.

Perhaps the most radical way of formulating the metaphysical and theological contributions of "ultimate reality" to human discourse is the move undertaken by twentieth-century Catholic theologian Karl Rahner at the beginning of his *Foundations of Christian Faith*. Rahner approached questions of theology with a meditation on what would happen to language, and by extension humanity, without talk about God. He concluded that human reality would be significantly impoverished to the point of annihilation. "The absolute death of the word 'God,' including even the eradication of its past, would be the signal, no longer heard by anyone, that man himself had died."[17] What Rahner's thought experiment points to is that transcendence is constitutive of human reality. Human reality, even the reality of religion, points to the suspension of reality elsewhere. Theology uses this ultimate reality in order to frame conceptually the ways in which human reality is understood. Time is suspended in eternity; human existence is created by an infinitely imaginative and passionate God; death meets its own death in the confrontation with the living God. Theology's contribution to the question of religion's reality is to take God as the "measure" of human reality into account. Its conceptual framing and vocabulary for transcendence is its métier.

III. EPISTEMOLOGY

If reality is to be perceived with the purpose of knowing, then it must be somehow rendered for human perception and reflection. Modernity was the epoch that imposed this restriction on claims about reality. Since the eighteenth century, human knowledge claims about reality must be justified both on the level of scientific criteria regarding the object under investigation, but also on a meta-level. This meta-level specifies that claims about reality must be checked back with human reason's capacity to make the claims in question. The field of epistemology is the study of how humans can claim to know on the basis of reason's capacities and limitations. The reflection of reason upon itself, as Immanual Kant specified in his three *Critiques* – *Critique of Pure Reason* (1781/1787), *Critique of Practical Reason* (1788), and *Critique of Judgment* (1790) – results in the identification of reason's capacities for empirical knowledge, practical knowledge, and aesthetic judgments. But any claim that transcends these capacities – for example, claims about God's being in eternity – is deemed illegitimate. Modernity's requirement concerning the accountability of reason led

---

[17] Karl Rahner, S.J., *Foundations of Christian Faith: An Introduction to the Idea of Christianity*, trans. William V. Dych (New York: Crossroad, 2002), 49.

to adjustments in the speculative disciplines, classically rational theology, rational psychology, and rational philosophy. Theology in particular had to make the move that Schleiermacher and Rahner made: all theologically speculative claims concerning God's being, the unity of the self and the unity of the world, required epistemological grounding. Claims could be made about God through human understanding, but not blank claims referring directly to the transcendent. Knowing is a thoroughly human enterprise, even knowing God.

When the issue of epistemology is raised for theology and religious studies, the contemporary shaping of epistemology's questions by Kant's *Critique of Pure Reason* must first be acknowledged. The contemporary difficulty with assessing the distinctly "religious" in experience goes back to Kant's establishment of the parameters of knowledge of reality to justify the validity of rationality in relation to the rise of Newtonian science in modernity. For Kant, human knowing is limited to the objects of experience, and by "experience," Kant meant sense perception. The experiences of self, world, and God were not considered experiences in the sense of "sense perception." Knowledge of these three metaphysical "ideas" was available only as a function of the unifying function of reason, *Vernunft*. If *Verstand* is the capacity of reason that unites the appropriate category of the understanding with the data of sense perception in order to yield knowledge of an object of experience, then *Vernunft* effects the structuring of the transcendental ideas of self, world, and God on the grounds of the unifying function of reason at a level of reason that transcends *Verstand*. Thus aspects of reality – and we can include much experience in religion, intersubjective intuition, or aspects of the immediacy of the self-relation, as Schleiermacher claimed – "fall between the cracks" of Kant's epistemology. On Kantian terms, these aspects of reality cannot be cognized in such a way that they yield knowledge in Kant's sense of the term. This modern epistemological dilemma continues to affect modern disciplines that treat experience in terms wider than those to which Kant restricted sense experience.

Studies of religion since the late eighteenth century sought to overcome the restrictions Kant posed on reason by extending the arena of human experience to include particular dimensions of religious experience – human affections, intuitions, imaginations, and perceptions. Schleiermacher's bold apology for religion provided another blueprint for stretching religion beyond its culturally approved limitations. "Religion is neither metaphysics nor morals but a sense and taste for the infinite," Schleiermacher wrote in 1799[18] and subsequently worked out in

---

[18] Schleiermacher, *On Religion*, 34 (speech 2).

his theological and philosophical work an epistemological apparatus in order to account for religious experience. Since Schleiermacher, scholars have proposed what "religion" might mean, particularly locating religious phenomena and experiences at the limits of human consciousness, as William James did, or at the level of specific emotional responses to divinity, as Rudolf Otto did, or at the ontological level of the "actual occasion," as Charles Hartshorne did, following process thinker Alfred North Whitehead's lead.[19]

Contemporary theology too has sought to address religious experience, although constructive proposals tend to move in two different directions. One strand, self-identified as postliberal, erases the reality of nondiscursive experience completely and views religion in terms of the discourses that competent speakers deploy. Theology is then an analysis of the constitutive grammar of religious discourse. Another strand insists that experience is crucial to the shaping of theological claims and constructs notions of specifically contextualized experiences that are constitutive of distinct groups. Women's ways of knowing, for example, are claimed as alternative religious paths and represented by particular ideas and vocabularies that are contrasted with men's ways of discursive and rational knowing. The search for an epistemology that is able to discern the reality of religion and then propose an adequate descriptive vocabulary continues.

The constructive question thus concerns how modern epistemology can be stretched in a direction that permits "religion" to appear in reality for the purpose of critical description and analysis. In this regard, theorists of religion might follow Schleiermacher's precedent by revamping a standard Kantian epistemology to make room for distinctive subjective contributions to the discerning and description of religious "specialness."[20] By stretching the subjective conditions for experience to include aspects of perception that are not reducible to

[19] William James, *The Varieties of Religious Experience*, ed. and with an introduction by Martin E. Marty (New York: Penguin, 1985); Rudolf Otto, *Das Heilige: Über das Irrationale in der Idee des Göttlichen und sein Verhältnis zum Rationalen*, Beck'sche Reihe 328 (Munich: C. H. Beck, 1997); Charles Hartshorne, *Reality as Social Process: Studies in Metaphysics and Religion* (New York: Hafner, 1971 [1953]); Alfred North Whitehead, *Process and Reality*, corrected ed. by David Ray Griffin and Donald W. Sherburne (New York: Free Press, 1985).

[20] The move made by Schleiermacher to see religion as something "more" than metaphysics and morals is such an endeavor. Other ways have also been proposed. The Kantian tradition, for example, sees religion in transcendental terms in order to avoid the category mistake that religion be confused with "experience" in Kant's empirical sense of the term. Reformed epistemologists, to refer to another example, argue that beliefs about God are properly basic; it is not required in their view that theistic beliefs have some "foundation" in evidence.

sense perception in the narrow sense of the term, a revision opens possibilities for the "religious" aspect of reality. A revision in the epistemological understanding of possible experiences can help prepare the scholar of religion to hear what people describe through the vocabulary of the ecstatic, of relationality with a transcendent other, or of the demonic.

Schleiermacher's example shows that an expansion of Kant's epistemology required a revision of the psychological-philosophical theory of the self to include "immediate self-consciousness" as the distinct "province" for religion. The new concept of the self as constituted by the unity of immediate self-consciousness with sensible self-consciousness was able to explain how religious experiences could be identified as "total impressions."[21] The distinctive religious phenomenon was grasped by human consciousness as the experience of a totality that transcends the sum of the distinct parts. Religion is about the "whole." It is a "feeling and intuition." Schleiermacher uses both terms together with the terminology of immediate self-consciousness to get at what he means – of a sense of reality that is greater than what is available solely by sense perception and cognized exclusively by discursive reason. There is something special about religion that is constituted as special by a distinct psychological apparatus. What makes Schleiermacher's apology for religion so helpful is that he identifies religion's "province" at the core of human subjectivity, thereby showing that religion is not only unique and distinct because of its relationship to other dimensions of reality, but that it is also necessary to human identity and existence.

Whether Schleiermacher's lead is taken in this constructive-epistemological direction is not the crucial point. Rather, Schleiermacher might be taken as a serious precedent for showing how epistemology can be constructed in order to suit the reality of religion. The disciplines in the academy can help propose epistemologies that may be applied to the subject matter of religion, but it is up to both theology and religious studies in critical conversation with each other to determine an epistemology that is particularly suited to making knowledge claims about the reality of religion. In this regard, theology has historically kept open possible conceptualities and vocabularies for describing religious realities. The categories of revelation and "God's word" have traditionally made possible the framing of the causality of experiences that are inexplicable in exclusively human – meaning exclusively sociological

---

[21] Schleiermacher, *The Christian Faith*, § 99, postscript (423).

or historical – terms. The terms *real presence* and *mystical union* refer to possibilities of intimate relationship between metaphysically binary opposites. Even erotic discourse is privileged in the history of spirituality and theology as a descriptive possibility of human language closest to ecstatic love to describe religious experience. And the veneration paid by religious traditions to foundational texts can be viewed from the perspective of originally powerful religious impulses. Original experiences are expressed in particular languages and cultures in ways that create novel expressions; in turn, new combinations of language reveal unique aspects of reality. The construction of epistemologies adequate to the subject matter requires paying careful attention to language, concepts, and novel linguistic combinations that in turn provide the conceptual and explanatory resources for further describing and analyzing religion.

One key epistemological challenge in the study of theology and religion has been the location of the "subjective" aspect to knowledge claims. Theology has usually been seen as the problem, tainting "objective" knowledge with personal faith or uncritical assent to doctrine. In this regard, the challenge lies in a critical revision and expansion of dominant epistemologies underwriting the "objectivity" of knowledge. An admission that the subjective or individual element is not a dimension that requires excision, but is a necessary aspect of human knowing, perhaps especially so in relation to religious practices and imaginings, is the place to begin thinking about how the subjective aspect can or should not shape knowledge. Kant's insight was to show how subjectivity constitutes knowledge (albeit as universally and objectively valid). And Schleiermacher developed Kant's "hermeneutics of the self" by showing how individuality is related to knowledge by virtue of the dialogical constitution of knowledge. Knowledge is a process that is necessarily located in intersubjective relationship and debate. By virtue of the individuality of interlocutors, the subjective dimension cannot be erased; rather, it must be epistemologically and methodologically accounted for. Subjective items, such as personal investment, empathy, subjective faith, or particular affinity for the object of study, are all part and parcel of epistemologies that play key roles in constructing claims to knowledge. The challenge of critical inquiry, therefore, consists of a critical evaluation of and creative use of the subjective dimension in knowledge that is inevitably constructed by people, not its denial on the grounds of a narrowly conceptualized "objectivity."

The focus on the objectivity of knowledge requires taking stock of relevant epistemological understandings in the history of Western philosophy. In broad Kantian terms, knowledge includes both empirical and conceptual aspects. Knowledge that makes claims to objectivity requires the contributions of empirical content and the conceptual framing of that content. Both the empirical and the conceptual are related to the subjective dimension of knowledge; both are determined to a certain degree by individual ways of seeing and individually expressed linguistic descriptions. Both the empirical and the conceptual also affect the claims to knowledge about the object. The conceptual in Kantian terms has objective and universal validity by virtue of the structure of pure reason that Kant determined was the same in all people. Kant's notion of pure reason has been challenged by arguments showing how the particular – for example, language and embodiment – necessarily affects reason, thereby infusing the objectivity claim with a subjective dimension. Yet the claims to objectivity do not necessarily need to be dismantled by individual determinations of reason. Rather, the conceptual work in knowledge requires a specific degree of universality if empirical work is to be communicated and understood. It needs conceptualization. And further, the conceptual helps to provide working concepts with some degree of transreligious applicability. If the empirical is focused on the particular, then the conceptual helps to frame the particular in such a way that it can produce knowledge and, as such, so that it then has the potential for comparative purposes.

Perhaps the greatest challenge, personal and academic, for scholars of religion is that of truly paying attention to reality. Psychological self-examination with the tools of modern analysis helps clarify prejudices and emotional inheritances that unfairly determine reality, while critical inquiry helps expose methodological blindspots that skew human knowing in the direction of ideology. The challenge for both theology and religious studies is to build bridges toward a common appreciation of each other's work so that both disciplines might better see religion's reality. With a common subject matter in view, both theology and religious studies might rise to the epistemological challenge of constructing ways to make claims more suited to particular knowledge concerning religion. A common epistemological goal might take the shape of looking seriously at the subjective and objective requirements and contributions of both disciplines, as well as the empirical and conceptual requirements and contributions of both disciplines. The aim of expanding current academic epistemologies from the perspectives of theology and religious studies would clarify contributions of each discipline not only to each other, but also to the arts and sciences. If what we call "religion" is part of human nature, thought, and reality, as all part empirical evidence suggests it is, then its study should benefit the enterprise of human knowing, if not being.

IV. CONCLUSION

The contemporary bifurcation between theology and religious studies does not need to stand. The current, at times fierce, rhetoric of opposition does not need to continue. I have argued in this chapter that theology, if taken in the direction I have specified, and religious studies not only can be but ought to be in discussion with each other, in order better to produce knowledge about religion and religions, which, after all, is the goal of our scholarship. For creative and accurate production of knowledge to take place, however, historical and conceptual blindspots must be clarified vis-à-vis the other discipline. Theology must seek to understand religion in the empirical terms of living relationships, while religious studies must seek to understand the conceptual as a crucial dimension to understanding the reality that it studies. Theology must strive to examine its own presuppositions about knowledge and power critically, while religious studies must critically study its own ideological, often tendentious, positioning against "Western" alliances between the study of religion and theological authority. Both disciplines might seek to work out in dialogue the fundamental assumptions of the reality of religion, an appropriate epistemology to investigate the reality, and sites at which knowledge from one field can critically complement the other field. A pivotal figure such as Schleiermacher can help inspire crucial topics of keen interest to both disciplines that might clarify the issues of this fraught relationship in order to open the possibility of a more productive future.

There is much at stake in this relationship for the future of both disciplines. If theology continues its work in an empirical vacuum, then its insights will be radically diminished, if not falsified, by its abstractions. Theology is impoverished when it is solely attuned to abstract doctrines and authoritative ideas. At the same time, if religious studies continues to voice its opinion about theology without historical or conceptual evidence, then its polemic becomes a hollow challenge to an opponent who does not exist. The historical contingency of the relation between theology and the study of religion is far too complicated, enmeshed, and intriguing, while the complementary possibilities are far too rich to be tossed aside by dismissing the other discipline. Religious studies and theology need to be in relationship with each other. In the pursuit of knowledge about religion(s), each provides a point of critical perspective on the other; together the two contribute to a better understanding of religion; and in this critical engagement, each is challenged by the other to refine its methods and approaches. As such, both can join forces to show that religion offers a distinctive and significant perspective to the academy and the world. Religion is part of human life; the reality of religious experience adds an important dimension to understanding humanity in relationship with its environment. This is the goal of any self-critical discipline: to move beyond the ideological and get to the truth of what it means to be human.

Select Bibliography

Farley, Edward. *Theologia: The Fragmentation and Unity of Theological Education*. Philadelphia: Fortress Press, 1983; reprint: Eugene, OR: Wipf & Stock, 2001.

Fergusson, David. Ed. *The Blackwell Companion to Nineteenth-Century Theology*. West Sussex, UK: Wiley-Blackwell, 2010.

Ford, David F. "Theology," 3–26. In *Shaping Theology: Engagements in a Religious and Secular World*. Malden, MA: Blackwell, 2007.

Hodgson, Peter C. "Paideia in Religious and Theological Studies," 132–40. In *God's Wisdom: Toward a Theology of Education*. Louisville, KY: Westminster John Knox Press, 1999.

Schleiermacher, Friedrich. *Occasional Thoughts on Universities in the German Sense with an Appendix Regarding a University Soon to Be Established (1808)*. Translated by Terrence N. Tice with Edwina Lawler. Lewiston, NY: Edwin Mellen Press, 1991 [2005].

   The Christian Faith (1830/31). Translated by D. M. Baillie et al. Edited by H. R. Mackintosh and J. S. Stewart. Edinburgh: T & T Clark, 1999.

   On Religion: Speeches to Its Culture Despisers. Translated and edited by Richard Crouter. Cambridge: Cambridge University Press, 2008.

Sockness, Brent W. and Wilhelm Gräb. Eds. *Schleiermacher, the Study of Religion, and the Future of Theology: A Transatlantic Dialogue*. Theologische Bibliothek Töpelmann 148 (Berlin: Walter de Gruyter, 2010).

Troeltsch, Ernst. *Der Historismus und seine Probleme (1922)*. Kritische Gesamtausgabe Ernst Troeltsch 16. Edited by Friedrich Wilhelm Graf with Matthias Schlossberger. Berlin and New York: Walter de Gruyter, 2010.

Part three

Methodological variations

12 Buddhism and violence

BERNARD FAURE

With the rise of religious fundamentalisms, religion has had rather bad press. Yet this feeling of suspicion has apparently not yet reached Buddhism, which is usually presented as a nonviolent teaching founded on compassion.[1] This is in large part owing to the influence of such figures as the Dalai Lama and the Vietnamese monk Thich Nhat Hahn, who are beloved by the media and who command large Western followings. It is also a result of the attempt among some scholars but more often among Western practitioners to differentiate Buddhism from other religions (and from religion in general) by claiming for it the title of "spirituality." For that very reason, Western adherents of Buddhism see in it a teaching particularly needed for our time. Even when it is described as a religious phenomenon, Buddhism is considered to be the exception among the world religions. It is said to have had no crusades or holy wars, unlike Christianity or Islam. It is allegedly not attached to holy places, out of which it has expelled others, such as Judaism or militant Hinduism. Its name was not associated with an expansionist military ideology, such as Shinto.

The Sinhalese scholar Walpola Rahula is one of the Buddhist apologists who claim that there never was a "Buddhist war." In a popular book entitled *What the Buddha Taught*, Rahula writes: "That spirit of tolerance and compassion has been one of the most highly regarded ideals of the Buddhist culture and civilization from the outset. This is why there is not one single example of persecution or one drop of blood shed either in the conversion of people to Buddhism or in the spread of Buddhism over its two thousand five hundred year history."[2] Ironically,

---

[1] Things are beginning to change, however. See Brian Victoria, *Zen at War* (New York: Weatherhill, 1997); Michael Zimmermann, ed., *Buddhism and Violence* (Wiesbaden: Dr. Ludwig Reichert Verlag, 2006); Bernard Faure, *Bouddhisme et violence* (Paris: Le Cavalier Bleu, 2008); and Michael Jerryson and Mark Juergensmeyer, eds., *Buddhist Warfare* (Oxford: Oxford University Press, 2010).

[2] Walpola Rahula, *What the Buddha Taught* (New York: Grove Press, 1974).

Jesuit missionaries made a similar claim regarding Christianity when trying to convert the Chinese.

This image of Buddhist pacifism, widely promulgated by the media, endures in spite of obvious counterexamples. Buddhism is still largely exempted from the kind of scrutiny leveled at other religions. It is only with the civil war in Sri Lanka that questions have begun to be raised. Nonviolence, compassion, and tolerance are often linked in discussions of Buddhism. Precisely because Buddhism has made these virtues its trademark, it is important to examine its complicated relations with violence.

Two types of violence – direct and indirect – should be distinguished. Direct violence is by far the most visible; it is the kind of physical violence, for example, that occurs in conflict situations leading to the use of armed force. Indirect violence includes symbolic violence, whose effects are sometimes very real. It finds its expression in mythology, iconography, ritual, and predication. It can also be structural, systemic, or institutional violence, which often remains ignored even from those who suffer from it. In that sense, monastic discipline itself can be described as a kind of institutionalized violence.

Buddhist scriptures clearly condemn violence – and above all killing. Nikāya or early Buddhism made no distinction between good and bad violence: any violence, whatever its motivation, only feeds the infernal cycle of violence. To kill is to commit an evil act, which leads to a lower rebirth for the person who commits it (and possibly also for the person who is its victim). One must therefore not kill others, or incite them to violence or allow them to kill. Killing is one of the five *pārājika* rules whose transgression leads to exclusion from the Buddhist community. In the *Samyuttanikāya*, when a military leader asks the Buddha about the common belief that a soldier who dies on the battlefield goes to paradise, the Buddha replies that such a soldier goes to a special hell because of his evil state of mind, manifest in his desire to kill or wound the enemy.[3] The Buddha's view was in direct opposition to the beliefs of his time, which made it a duty for a member of the warrior caste to fight and consider death on the battlefield an honor.[4] In Nikāya Buddhism, however, killing comes as third in the list of the *pārājika* rules, after illicit sex and theft, whereas in the Great Vehicle, it comes first. As the Buddha puts it in the *Brahmā Net Sūtra*, "If a child of Buddha himself

---

[3] See the *Samyuttanikāya*, quoted in Michael Zimmermann, "Only a Fool Becomes a King: Buddhist Stances on Punishment," in *Buddhism and Violence*, ed. Michael Zimmermann (Wiesbaden: Dr. Ludwig Reichert Verlag, 2006), 213–42.

[4] On this question, see Michael Zimmermann, "War," in *Encyclopedia of Buddhism*, ed. Robert E. Buswell, Jr. (New York: Macmillan Reference USA, 2003), 893–7.

kills, or goads someone else to kill, or provides with or suggests means for killing, or praises the act of killing, or, on seeing someone commit the act, expresses approval for what that person has done, or kills by way of incantations, or is the cause, occasion, means, or instrument of the act of inducing a death, he will be shut out of the community."[5] According to the *Treatise on the Great Perfection of Wisdom*, "Murder is the worst of all sins."[6]

I. BUDDHISM AND SOCIETY

Whereas early Indian Buddhist monks were able to preserve a certain degree of independence from the political sphere, in the rest of Asia, Buddhist monks became actively involved in political struggles. While metaphysical and philosophical Buddhist teachings may have exerted their influence on East Asian rulers, the latter perceived Buddhism first and foremost as an instrument for the protection of the state. Tantric or esoteric Buddhism, in particular, possessed a rich arsenal of rituals to defeat enemies, who were assimilated to demons. In countries where Buddhism became the official ideology, it often supported the government in its wars. This is still true today of the Buddhists of Sri Lanka, who have been openly engaged in the struggle against Tamil freedom fighters. Very few of them – if any – have protested against the massive killings that marked the end of the Tamil rebellion in 2009.

In Japan, during the Second World War, all the sects of Japanese Buddhism – and in particular Zen – were actively involved in the war effort. This holds equally true for other national or nationalist forms of Buddhism. Japanese Buddhism's "drift" to militarism may not have been simply an aberration, a deviation from the timeless message of Gautama, the warrior-prince who, once he became the Buddha, preached nonviolence. We are not simply dealing here with a gap between a nonviolent theory and a more ambivalent practice.

The relationships between Buddhism and war are admittedly complex.[7] While the very concept of "just war" is originally Christian

---

[5] Quoted in Bernard Faure, "Buddhism and Violence," David Jacobson, transl., *The Ilankai Tamil Sangam Association of Tamils of Sri Lanka in the USA* (2003), online at http://www.sangam.org/articles/view/?id=118 (accessed May 26, 2011).

[6] See Étienne Lamotte, trans., *Le Traité de la Grande Perfection de Sagesse* de Nagarjuna (Mahaprajnaparamitasastra), 3 vols. (Louvain-la-Neuve: Publications de l'Institut Orientaliste, 1944), vol. 2: 790.

[7] On this question, see Paul Demiéville, "Le bouddhisme et la guerre: post-scriptum à l'*Histoire des moines-guerriers du Japon* de G. Renondeau," in *Mélanges publiés par l'Institut des Hautes Etudes Chinoises*, vol. 1 (Paris: Collège de France, 1957): 347–85.

and cannot be automatically applied to other religions, it remains useful for discussing certain elements shared by Christianity and other religions. Indeed, the notion seems to resurface whenever it is necessary to justify war against an ethics that condemns violence. Even though Buddhism has no clear-cut concept of a "just" or "holy" war, it was often led to legitimize military violence, and so just war theory offers a lens for comparative reflection.

The discourse of Sinhalese Buddhists constitutes perhaps the closest Buddhism came to an apology for holy war. Admittedly, Sinhala Buddhism is a particular kind of fundamentalism, inasmuch as it is based on ethnic identity rather than on a sacred text, but the *Dīpavamsa* (Chronicle of the Island) and the *Mahāvamsa* (Great Chronicle) have in fact come to play the role of sacred texts. One of the main heralds of the Sinhala cause was Walpola Rahula, the same person who, as we have seen, claimed that Buddhism has never shed a drop of blood.

While Buddhism usually supported the state ideology, in some cases it also provided a counterideology, inspiring, for instance, millenarian revolts centered on the future Buddha, Maitreya. The beginning of the sixth century was marked by the emergence in northern China of a millenarian sect that called itself "Great Vehicle" (not to be confused with the Buddhist movement of the same name). Its founder, Faqing, announced the imminent coming of the future Buddha Maitreya and was able to recruit more than fifty thousand followers in his fight against the forces of evil. Considering that the world was the kingdom of Māra, the Evil One, he advocated the killing of all of "Māra's followers" as the only means to purify the world and prepare for the return of Maitreya. He included among the "demons" the members of the Buddhist clergy, and he even established a scale of merits based on the number of demons killed. Such merits allowed the adepts to be reborn as bodhisattvas. This rebellion was eventually crushed in blood. In most cases, however, Buddhist messianism remained pacific and was relatively well tolerated by the authorities.

As Buddhism became another feudal power in medieval Japan, major Buddhist monasteries, having become quasi-autonomous, fought at times against the imperial court and the military rulers, as well as against other monasteries. The medieval period witnessed the rise of a new type of monsatic, the so-called warrior-monks (*sōhei*). These "monks," who were often not fully ordained, behaved actually more like warriors than like monks – carrying weapons, riding horses, and beheading their enemies.[8]

[8]   On this question, see George Renondeau, "Histoire des moines-guerriers du Japon," in *Mélanges publiés par l'Institut des Hautes Etudes Chinoises*, vol. 1 (Paris: Collège de France, 1957): 158–344.

Also around that time, new sects (Jōdo, Shinshū, and Nichiren) appeared whose populist and sectarian tendencies led to the emergence of "states within the state." It was only at the end of the sixteenth century, after a long civil war, that military leaders crushed the power of the great monasteries at long last.

This state of things was not limited to feudal Japan. Warrior-monks were also found in China and Korea, although the trend never developed to the same extent as in Japan. The Shaolin monks in China, in particular, were (and still are) famous for their martial skills.[9] During the Japanese invasions of Korea (1592–8), some Korean Buddhist leaders organized monks into guerilla units. Even within recent times, recurrent fights between armed factions rent the Buddhist sangha. In 1998, for instance, monks of the Purification and Reform Committee (PRC), protesting against the impending reelection of the leader of the Chogye order, occupied by surprise Chogye-sa, the order's headquarters in Seoul, and they had to be dislodged by police forces. Some of them, evoking a famous Vietnamese Buddhist monastic precedent, went so far as threatening to commit self-immolation by fire. This episode was only one in a long series of eruptions of violence in Korean Buddhist monasteries, reflecting the schism of the Korean sangha during the postwar period.

During the Mongol invasions of Japan in the thirteenth century (which were themselves legitimized by the Buddhist preceptors of Khubilai Khan), Japanese priests invoked the "divine winds" (*kamikaze*) that destroyed the enemy armada. They also put forward the notion of Japan as a divine land (*shinkoku*), a notion that continued to play a prominent role until the first half of the twentieth century. During the Second World War, Buddhists supported without flinching the war effort, putting their rhetoric at the service of the imperial mystique. The Buddhist theory of selflessness served to justify giving one's life for the emperor, while the notion of the Two Truths (conventional and ultimate) was used to explain the apparent contradiction between the principle of respect for human life and the martial requirements of patriotic duty.

Buddhists often went beyond the call of duty, however, confusing the Buddhist *dharma* with reasons of state and with patriotism. Medieval Japanese Buddhists, for instance, argued that the law of the Buddha and the kingdom's law were identical. Nationalism or patriotism thus surreptitiously replaced the ideal of monastic detachment toward worldly

---

[9] On the history of the Shaolin monks, see the recent book by Meir Shahar, *The Shaolin Monastery: History, Religion, and the Chinese Martial Arts* (Honolulu: University of Hawai'i Press, 2008).

values. Buddhist doctrine became at times a quasimagical device to acquire peace of mind and for the protection of the body during battle.

With the rise of Asian nationalisms, Buddhism was increasingly confronted by fundamentalist tendencies. Buddhist fundamentalism can be defined simply as participation in a nationalist mystique based on a mytho-history. In that sense, one can call fundamentalist the adhesion of Japanese Buddhists to the myth of Japan as "land of the gods," of Tibetan Buddhists to the myth of Tibet as Kingdom of Shambhala, and of Sinhalese Buddhists to the myth of Sri Lanka as Island of the Dharma.

But there is a tension between the national and transnational aspects of Buddhism. When Buddhist nations have gone to war with each other, Buddhists in the respective countries, in spite of their presumed "internationalism," have never hesitated to assert their patriotism. Indeed, it was only with the Western "rediscovery" of Buddhism in the nineteenth century, and largely in reaction to colonialism, that Buddhists came to think of themselves as participants in a transnational movement. Even then, the perceived affinities among Buddhists of all sides did not prevent national bonds from superseding religious affiliations. Only recently have Buddhists leaders in exile – such as the Dalai Lama and Thich Nhat Hanh – obtained a spiritual status that transcends their national origins (although the Dalai Lama still remains an eminent symbol of Tibetan nationalism).

Buddhism in its various regional instantiations constantly evolved in relation to its sociopolitical contexts. While this co-evolution accounts for a part of the Buddhist discourse on war and violence, contextual explanation rapidly reaches its limits. Yet scholars have for some reason been reluctant to consider the idea that a certain form of violence could be intrinsic to Buddhism, in other words, that the non-dual *dharma* itself could encompass division and violence. Until this question, which raises the specter of a Buddhist fundamentalism, is seriously considered, the relation between Buddhism and violence cannot be fully grasped.

II. JUSTIFICATIONS OF VIOLENCE

As noted previously, most commentators are content to equate Buddhism with compassion and tolerance. Contrary to Christianity, Buddhism is said to extend its compassion to all beings. The Buddhist Golden Legend is thus full of edifying stories in which the bodhisattva (the future Buddha) gives his life to save other beings, human or animal. In virtue of the principle of karmic transmigration, animals are perceived as former or future humans and as potential buddhas. Because they are linked to us humans by bonds of kinship, it seems natural to extend our concern to them.

With Mahāyāna, compassion is said to have come to the forefront – becoming an indispensable element for achieving awakening (*bodhi*). Compassion now represents the ideal of the bodhisattva, this "being of awakening," who, unlike the Buddha himself, postpones his entry into nirvāna in order to save all beings. Compassion no longer needs any karmic justification: it is simply a manifestation of the buddha nature immanent in all beings. It is not a moral virtue, but an ontological characteristic.

Actually, the bodhisattva's compassion is of a very specific kind: while it extends to all beings, it is based on the realization that these beings, like the bodhisattva himself, are ultimately empty, devoid of any reality – and so, therefore, their suffering is also devoid of any reality. Another important caveat is in order. Commentators usually fail to realize how self-serving Buddhist compassion can be. To say this is not to align Buddhism with the sociobiological view according to which altruism is a form of behavior developed in the course of human evolution for the survival and propagation of the species. From a purely Buddhist viewpoint – that of Mahāyāna orthodoxy, as expounded for instance in the *Dazhidu lun*, a work attributed to Nāgārjuna – it is only the bodhisattva who has reached the eighth stage (*bhūmi*) of his path (the non-return point, as it were), who can practice a form of compassion that benefits other beings. Practitioners who have not reached that stage may practice compassion, but it is for their own benefit. Because they are not yet fully enlightened, their compassion has no effect on others.[10]

Paradoxically, compassion is sometimes invoked to justify killing. In Nikāya Buddhism, it was in principle impossible to kill with compassion.[11] A person who develops inner compassion can no longer contemplate killing, because the evil roots of hatred and ignorance that allowed the intention to kill no longer exist in him or her. In Mahāyāna, on the other hand, compassion seems to have lent itself to the oxymoronic notion of "compassionate killing." Compassionate violence thus becomes possible, inasmuch as it can benefit others – even if it harms

---

[10] See Lamotte, trans., *Le Traité de la Grande Perfection*, vol. 3: 1705.

[11] See Rupert Gethin, "Can Killing a Living Being Ever Be an Act of Compassion? The Analysis of the Act of Killing in the Abhidhamma and Pali Commentaries," *Journal of Buddhist Ethics* 11 (2004): 167–202, online at http://blogs.dickinson.edu/buddhistethics/2010/04/27/can-killing-a-living-being-ever-be-an-act-of-compassion-the-analysis-of-the-act-of-killing-in-the-abhidhamma-and-pali-commentaries/ (accessed May 27, 2011).

the person who commits it, the bodhisattva who in any case is supposed to postpone his or her own salvation in order to save all beings. Thus, in the *Bodhisattvabhūmi* and in other texts, the bodhisattva kills a bandit in order to save a group of merchants, but also to save the bandit himself from the karmic consequences of his planned act.

Buddhism is also often praised for its spirit of tolerance, a claim that is based on the fact that Buddhist history does not show the kind of fanatic and inquisitorial excesses on behalf of "orthodoxy" familiar in the histories of Christianity and Islam. While opponents of the "historical" Buddha are sometimes labeled "heretical masters," the accusation of heresy in Buddhism rarely led to physical purges. In China, the teaching of the School of the Three Stages (*sanjie jiao*) was suppressed merely for political reasons. In Japan, the "heretical" Tachikawa branch of the Shingon school was eventually forbidden in the fifteenth century and most of its texts were destroyed in an auto-da-fé. Here again, while the pretext invoked was the sexual nature of its teachings, meaning an ideological difference, the main reason seems to have been political. Other cases of Buddhist intolerance include the denunciation of the new Pure Land school of Hōnen (1133–1212) by the other Buddhist schools, leading to Hōnen's exile in 1207 and the profanation of his grave after his death. Also relevant here are the sectarian antics of Nichiren (1222–82), the founder of the Nichiren sect, who liked to compare the priests of other schools to dogs wagging their tails in front of their masters and to mice afraid of cats. Nichiren barely escaped execution and was also sent into exile. One of his successors, Nichiō (1565–1630), launched the *fuju fuse* (not giving, not receiving) movement, which required his adherents to forsake all relationships with people outside the sect. Their intransigence led his disciples to refuse allegiance to the *shōgun* and to go underground. The Nichiren sect is also well known for its coercive conversion methods (*shakubuku*). Perhaps in part because of this, it is one of the most powerful Buddhist sects in Japan today. Be this as it may, these cases are the exceptions that prove the Buddhist rule, and they underscore the contrast with the practices of the Inquisition in Christianity.

What then of the third fundamental Buddhist virtue, nonviolence? We noted that Nikāya Buddhism strongly condemned all violence. Things did not stay like this, however, and soon the idea emerged that certain forms of violence were permitted, like backfires used to stop the spread of a wildfire. Justifications of violence proliferated and were put in the service of sectarian causes and militarist propaganda, down to the present day. Not only did violence become legitimate in certain cases; it became practically a duty – in the name of Buddhism as well as in the name of patriotism. This was not simply a deviation caused by some concrete circumstances, but rather a central tendency of the Mahāyāna teaching, a tendency that cannot simply be glossed over.

Reasons for bending the principle of nonviolence were never wanting. Some were mainly theoretical – moral, ontological, theological. Others were of a practical nature. The notion of a cosmic fight between the forces of good and evil, which seems to have been borrowed from the Hindu myth of the fight between the Devas and the Asuras, endowed Buddhism with an eschatological dimension that it seems to have lacked in the beginning. This notion, which emphasizes the need to preserve a cosmic balance, lent itself to the development of a kind of theory of the "just war."

The end sometimes justifies the means. When Buddhism is threatened, it is necessary to ruthlessly fight the forces of evil – while preserving, of course, inner compassion. In other words, it is allowed to kill for the *dharma*. Kill them all, and the Buddha will recognize his own. Killing demons is euphemistically called "liberation," since these demons will be released from their harmful ignorance and will be able to obtain a better rebirth than they would have otherwise. Various other theories resort to a similar casuistry, arguing, for instance, that it is just – or charitable, or compassionate – to kill someone to prevent him or her from committing evil. The *Mahāparinirvāna-sūtra*, for instance, claims that the true defenders of the *dharma* should be armed to the teeth to protect the pure monks who observe the Precepts (including the one against killing). According to the same text, the Buddha himself encouraged his disciples to kill those who slander the *dharma*.

This doctrinal reference was put to good use. The text in question was used for sectarian purposes, condoning violence toward the supposed enemies of Buddhism. In medieval Japan, monks came to call "enemies of the Buddha" all the people who resented paying taxes to the monasteries. To attack a monk, furthermore, no matter how corrupt or venal he may have been, was tantamount to attacking the Buddha himself. In esoteric Buddhism, the enemies of Buddhism are labeled *icchantika* (beings who lack a buddha nature) and are consequently cursed. Although one incurs karmic retribution for killing an insect, killing an *icchantika* remains morally neutral.

To defend the *dharma* is to defend the country in which it thrives, and to identify oneself with the buddhas and with bodhisattvas who have walked that path before. One such "bodhisattva" is the Japanese Prince Shōtoku (574–622), who is said to have established Buddhism as his nation's official religion. In the hagiographic tradition, Prince Shōtoku's enemies are described as demons intent on destroying the *dharma*. The bloody episode in which Shōtoku himself crushed his "demonic" enemies became the lens through which all later religious conflicts came to be perceived.

Another oft-invoked justification is the Buddhist notion of emptiness (*śunyatā*). How can one kill another person when in truth everything is empty? The man who kills with full understanding of this fact, having realized that both he and his enemy are devoid of self, actually kills no one. This idea is not specific to Buddhism, since it is also asserted in a classic Hindu scripture, the *Bhagavad Gita*. In China, a Chan (Zen) text, the *Jueguan lun* (Treatise on Absolute Contemplation), similarly states that, if the act of killing is perfectly spontaneous, it is in essence similar to a natural event, and thus entails no responsibility.[12] This sort of casuistry can still be found in the writings of modern Zen apostles such as D. T. Suzuki.[13]

III. INDIRECT VIOLENCE

Violence is usually described as affecting others physically. Physical violence is not always directed at others, however. Well-ordered violence begins with oneself. The Buddha allegedly condemned violence both toward others as well as toward oneself. Suicide, however, is not formally forbidden in the early canonical literature.[14] Even when it is, a distinction is established between self-centered suicide and altruistic self-sacrifice (like that of the bodhisattva sacrificing his life to save others). The distinction is not always clear in practice.

Buddhism also remains ambivalent toward the interiorized form of violence that is asceticism. Chinese monks, to show their determination, would sometimes mutilate themselves – cutting off or burning one or more of their fingers. Self-denial could in some cases extend to self-immolation by fire. We still recall the disturbing image of the Vietnamese monks who, during the Vietnam War (known in Vietnam as the "American war"), chose this form of death as a sign of protest. Many such cases have been recorded in the course of Chinese Buddhist history.[15] Paradoxically, one of the main scriptural sources for that form

12 See Tokiwa Gishin, trans., *A Dialogue on Contemplation-Extinguished* (Kyoto: Institute for Zen Studies, 1973), 14.
13 See Victoria, *Zen at War*, 124.
14 See, for instance, Martin Delhey, "Views on Suicide in Buddhism: Some Remarks," in Zimmermann, ed., *Buddhism and Violence*, 25–63.
15 See Bernard Faure, *The Rhetoric of Immediacy: A Cultural Critique of Chan/Zen Buddhism* (Princeton, NJ: Princeton University Press, 1991); John Kieschnick, *The*

of sacrifice is the Chinese apocryphal *Fanwang jing (Brahmā-Net sūtra)*, a disciplinary text that most vehemently condemns any direct or indirect participation in murder. When this kind of violence is motivated by a scriptural authority or by community pressure, it is no longer clear whether we are dealing with a voluntary suicide or self-sacrifice or with a sacrifice in the traditional sense. At any rate, this kind of violence was institutionalized.

Other less extreme forms of institutional violence in Buddhism are less visible. Monastic discipline, the aim of which is to form an obedient body and mind, can also be seen as a kind of muted violence against oneself. Another important aspect of institutional violence that has come to light is the Buddhist discrimination against women. Despite the theoretical equality between genders asserted by Mahāyāna, Buddhism has always been and remains a largely misogynistic tradition. Even in the twenty-first century, nuns in most Buddhist countries have a subaltern status that largely derives from the eight "strict rules" (*gurudharma*) allegedly laid down by the Buddha. The media reported the case of a Thai nun who was physically attacked by some monks for requesting an improvement of that status. A discussion of this form of violence, however, is beyond the scope of this chapter.[16]

What of violence toward animals? Indian Buddhism is often said to have distinguished itself from Brahmanism by its rejection of animal sacrifice. In the Vinaya, the interdiction to kill extends to the killing of animals. The latter, however, constitutes only a minor offense. Indian Buddhist monks were not entirely motivated by compassion in this matter; they were more concerned with the ritual "impurity" caused by the killing of living beings. Furthermore, in the case of lay Buddhists, killing an animal entailed a negative karma and thus a lower rebirth. Many stories are told of people who, having killed animals, are themselves reborn into the animal realm, or worse, into hell.

The rejection of animal sacrifice is usually linked with the Buddhist rule of vegetarianism.[17] Yet it does not appear that the first Buddhists were strict vegetarians. The question is still debated whether the

---

Eminent Monk: Buddhist Ideals in Medieval Chinese Hagiography (Honolulu: Kuroda Institute, University of Hawai'i Press, 1997); James A. Benn, *Burning for the Buddha: Self-Immolation in Chinese Buddhism* (Honolulu: Kuroda Institute, University of Hawai'i Press, 2007); Reiko Ohnuma, *Head, Eyes, Flesh, and Blood: Giving Away the Body in Indian Buddhist Literature* (New York: Columbia University Press, 2007).

[16] For a detailed discussion, see Bernard Faure, *The Power of Denial: Buddhism, Purity, and Gender* (Princeton, NJ: Princeton University Press, 2003).

[17] See Klaus Vollmer, "Buddhism and the Killing of Animals in Premodern Japan," in Zimmermann, ed., *Buddhism and Violence*, 195–211.

Buddha himself was a vegetarian. Various canonic sources such as the *Lankāvatāra sutra* and the *Mahāparinīrvana sūtra* emphasize that he never ate meat. A stubborn tradition, however, claims that he died from indigestion due to the consumption of pig meat. Much ink has been spilled over that tradition; commentators have attempted to attenuate the scandal of a meat-eating Buddha by arguing that the term wrongly translated as "pork meat" actually referred to a mushroom dish.[18]

At any rate, the Buddha seems to have had a rather moderate attitude regarding meat eating. Among the five rules that his rigorist cousin Devadatta wanted him to adopt was the interdiction to eat meat or fish. The Buddha, however, refused to do so, contenting himself to limit the interdiction to ten kinds of meat, which were already forbidden by the society of his time. Monks and nuns, furthermore, could eat meat as long as they did not know that the animal had been killed especially for them. The three conditions required for this (having neither seen, nor heard, nor suspected that the animal had been killed for oneself) are problematic, since that kind ignorance is impossible to confirm. In Mahāyāna, meat eating seems to have been perceived as more of a problem than in early Buddhism. But the Buddhist tradition is very nuanced and complex on this question. If vegetarianism and the related concept of nonviolence gradually took hold in India, the credit seems to belong to Jainism rather than to Buddhist ascetics.

The Buddhist position on eating meat (and so toward the killing of animals) depends in a large part on the cultural and demographic contexts in which the question was raised. Unable to impose a total vegetarianism in meat-eating societies such as Tibet, China, Korea, and Japan, Buddhism tried to implement days of abstinence. In such societies, a less strict clergy also sought to eradicate its sins through grand rites that set fish and birds free (*fangsheng*). Here again, these rituals were not simply motivated by compassion; they also had significant sociopolitical functions. The condemnation of eating meat, however, had a strong social impact in China and Japan. But here again, the reason invoked was not in all cases simply compassion: monks were to abstain from horse and elephant meat, for instance, because these animals were royal symbols. In some circumstances, Buddhist teaching provided on the contrary a convenient excuse for animal sacrifice and meat eating. In the rituals of Suwa Shrine, for instance, animal sacrifice and the consumption of meat

---

[18] On this question, see Arthur Waley, "Did the Buddha Die of Eating Pork?" in *Mélanges chinois et bouddhiques*, vol. 1 (Brussels: l'Institut Belge des Hautes Études, 1932), 343–54; and G. Gordon Wasson and Wendy Doniger O'Flaherty, "The Last Meal of the Buddha," *Journal of the American Oriental Society* 102, 4 (1982): 591–603.

were justified by the belief that the animals were thus able to share in the karmic merits of the humans who ate them. The lamb eaten by a lion becomes lion, and so the lamb eaten by a Buddhist becomes human, moving one step closer to buddhahood.

IV. ICONOGRAPHY, MYTH, AND RITUAL

Another indirect form – usually neglected by textual scholars – of violence is *symbolic* violence, as expressed in particular through iconography, myth, and ritual.

Images often speak louder than words and they do not always say the same thing as words. Iconography is usually taken as illustrating and reinforcing orthodox teaching. But this crucial visual dimension of Buddhism contradicts at times the claims of normative discourse. Tantric Buddhist imagery, in particular, reveals a form of symbolic violence that, once perceived, is recognized as pervasive within the Buddhist tradition. If compassion is well expressed by serene images of meditating buddhas, the wrathful deities of Tantric Buddhism partake, conversely, in a puzzling symbolic violence. In Mahāyāna, buddhas and bodhisattvas manifest their great compassion and convert all beings by adapting to their capacities. In the case of evil beings or demons, however, the preaching of the law does not suffice to convert them; they need to be coerced (or even "delivered," that is, killed). *Dura lex sed lex.*

A case in point is the myth of Tibet's pacification by Padmasambhava. Padmasambhava, owing to his wondrous powers, is said to have subjugated all the local "demons" of that land (actually, they were the former gods). The metaphor behind the conversion of local deities is often that of sexual submission. In all of these tales, Buddhism is fundamentally male, whereas the local cults are often feminized. Prior to Padmasambhava's conquest, for example, we are told that the first Tibetan king, Songtsen Gampo, subdued the telluric powers symbolized by a demoness, Srinmo. The Tibetan king subdued the female demon, whose body covered the Tibetan territory, by "nailing" her down to the ground. He did so by erecting *stūpas* that served as so many metaphoric nails driven into the twelve points of her body. The Jokhang Temple in Lhasa, the most holy place of Tibetan Buddhism, is asserted to be the nail driven into the central part of the female demon's body, her genitalia. The rape imagery could hardly be more explicit.

A recurring motif in Buddhist iconography is the image of Buddhist deities trampling demons under foot. Such images can be traced back to myths such as that of Vajrāpani's subduing of the Hindu god Śiva (Maheśvara) – the Lord of the Three Worlds – and his consort. Vajrapāni tramples them to death because they refused to yield to the new Buddhist order. This myth constitutes the Tantric paradigm of the submission of Hindu gods (assimilated to demons) to Buddhism.

Most commentators take at face value the interpretation of Maheśvara's subjugation as an expression of Buddhist compassion based on nonduality. Admittedly, this myth, like all myths, can be read in several registers. Yet the interpretation of Vajrapāni's behavior as a form of "ruthless compassion" cannot erase the impression of hubris produced by that scene. Vajrapāni's humiliation of the Hindu gods makes it difficult to accept that this episode simply illustrates the ultimate identity of good and evil. It seems rather intent on proving the overwhelming superiority of Buddhism.

This type of imagery pervades esoteric Buddhist rituals, which are not merely protective, but are also often unmistakably aggressive. The line between defensive and offensive rituals, or, as some would say, between "white" and "black" magic, is difficult to draw in Buddhism (as in other religions) and is at any rate easily crossed, if only because the party that feels – rightly or wrongly – threatened sees his preemptive strike as a defensive action, whereas the other party tends to see it as offensive.

While these rituals of subjugation may not fit our modern definitions, in the premodern period they were seen as real and efficacious violence. The *Brahmā Net Sūtra* clearly condemns the fact of "killing through incantations." Such rituals could have a considerable political impact, moreover, and political rulers took them very seriously, imprisoning or exiling anyone who was suspected to have sponsored or performed them.

One may, however, consider that the violence contained *in* the ritual is also contained *by* it. Symbolic or ritual violence can be a way to channel and control a greater, physical violence. Ritualized, legitimate violence may serve as protection against illegitimate, random violence. Yet it remains a form of violence that cannot without some hypocrisy be explained away as nonviolence. While the ritualist conception of Brahmanical sacrifice, according to which "to kill is not to kill," was initially denounced by Buddhism, it returned – with a vengeance – in Tantric Buddhism. Does this symbolic violence mark a return of the repressed impulses, an outlet for real violence, or is it, on the contrary, its mirror image – indeed, its underlying cause? The question must remain open.

V. CONCLUSION

From this rapid survey, it should be clear that Buddhist violence has various origins and expressions – theological, sociological, political, ethnic, and cultural. Buddhist scholars – and Buddhists in general – ought to question seriously the nature and function of Buddhist violence instead of trying to deny its existence and perpetuating the notion that Buddhism is a religion based on nonviolence and compassion. While significant, the circumstantial collusion between Buddhism and the state cannot explain everything. Inasmuch as Buddhism constitutes what Jan Assmann calls a "counter-religion" that claims to supersede local polytheisms, it shows from the outset a certain tendency toward intolerance. This tendency was fortunately tempered by a great doctrinal flexibility and the strategic need to take local religions into account.

In an extreme case such as that of the ethnic conflict in Sri Lanka, what seems to have triggered an aggressive, militant intolerance is the combination of the idea of the "protection of the *dharma*" – which developed originally in a depoliticized context where Buddhist monks, having in principle renounced the world, did not often leave the secluded atmosphere of their monasteries – with a new, politicized situation where Buddhism, having become an official, engaged religion, identified itself with a recent nationalism and increasingly with an ethnic particularism that carries a heightened awareness of the threat of Tamil separatism. This sociopolitical explanation, however, goes only so far. Theological ideas may also have played a role in creating this violent environment – for instance, the notion of a Buddhist world constantly besieged by the forces of evil, or again, the apparently nonviolent concept of a "pure" Buddhism, which leaves little room for compromises.

There is no denying the existence, at the heart of Buddhism, of an ideal of peace and tolerance. This ideal is reflected in many canonical sources. Unfortunately, other sources – just as canonical – allow violence and war under certain circumstances, in particular when the *dharma* is threatened. This is why there have been, and will again be, "Buddhist wars," and Buddhism's superiority over other religions in this regard is entirely relative. Yet, on the whole, Buddhism remains more resistant to fundamentalism than the other great religions and ideologies. In every age, the Buddhist clergy's will to power and its complicity with violent powers have been counterbalanced by the Buddhist ideals of compassion and nonviolence. Yet the Buddhist doctrine, in order not to remain dead letter, must take account of the violence inherent in the human heart, in society, and in Buddhism itself.

Select Bibliography

Faure, Bernard. *Bouddhisme et violence*. Paris: Le Cavalier Bleu, 2008.

Jerryson, Michael and Mark Juergensmeyer. Eds. *Buddhist Warfare*. Oxford: Oxford University Press, 2010.

Victoria, Brian. *Zen at War*. New York: Weatherhill, 1997.

Zimmerman, Michael. Ed. *Buddhism and Violence*. Wiesbaden: Dr. Ludwig Reichert Verlag, 2006.

13 Practicing religions
COURTNEY BENDER

I. INTRODUCTION

"It is not easy to speak of practice other than negatively," Pierre Bourdieu writes.[1] Like many such key words, *practice* might be better thought of as a term that invokes several loosely bound, historically developed debates. One does not need to delve too far into religious studies before noting the ubiquity of discussions surrounding *practice* and the word's wide semantic field. *Practice* can, for example, signal interest in the things religious people do (praying, singing, meditating, and reading, to name just some of the things religious people do) within the genealogies and traditions associated with these activities. *Practice* also signals a theoretical and conceptual turn to religion that emphasizes embodiment, habit, and daily activity as much as earlier generations emphasized belief, texts, and orthodox theologies proper.[2] Discussions of *practice* also engage debates about the normative and ethical impact of certain modes of action, linking studies of religion to questions of virtue, its proper cultivation, and of the relation of religious virtues to civic, democratic, or political practice.[3]

[1] Pierre Bourdieu, *The Logic of Practice* (Stanford, CA: Stanford University Press 1990), 80.
[2] See Talal Asad, *Genealogies of Religion: Discipline and Reasons of Power in Christianity and Islam* (Baltimore: Johns Hopkins University Press, 1993); Talal Asad, *Formations of the Secular: Christianity, Islam, Modernity* (Stanford, CA: Stanford University Press, 2003); David D. Hall, ed., *Lived Religion in America: Toward a History of Practice* (Princeton, NJ: Princeton University Press, 1997); Michael D. McNally, *Ojibwe Singers: Hymns, Grief, and a Native Culture in Motion* (New York: Oxford University Press, 2000).
[3] Alisdair MacIntyre, *After Virtue: A Study in Moral Theory* (Notre Dame, IN: University of Notre Dame Press, 1981); Jeffrey Stout, *Ethics After Babel* (Boston: Beacon Press, 1988).

The author thanks Rosemary Hicks, Robert A. Orsi, David Smilde, and students in the 2009 Contemporary Religious Identity seminar for very helpful comments on earlier drafts; Andrew Perrin for helpful discussions about trains and strangers; and Rajiv Sicora for assistance with manuscript preparation.

Invoking *practice*, in other words, signals "particular formations of meaning – ways not only of discussing but at another level of seeing many of our central experiences," as cultural critic and historian Raymond Williams put it.[4] With this in mind, we can venture that the common-alities among divergent uses of practice center on the "everyday" living expressions of religions and on investigations of religion's power and authority unfolding in habitual and embodied actions.[5] Religious stud-ies' current focus on the everyday provides a way for scholars to argue that hybridity, pastiche, and "making do" are the constitutive aspects of religion and that these are likewise appropriate places to begin discus-sions of ethics and norms. When practice theorists discuss orthodoxy, for example, they portray it in terms of specific modes of transmission to students, translation, and interpretation techniques. They tend to focus on the processes by means of which historical continuity and authority are reproduced, against the background of other interactions in daily life that not only tell a much more complex and heterogeneous story, but that also actively intersect within the story of orthodoxy itself. Practices may have long histories and accrue enormous power through their embeddedness in various social settings and their repeated, habit-ual uses (as Michael L. Satlow argues in Chapter 6 of this book). Yet every time a practice is "practiced," there is always also the potential for instability, change, or alteration. Practice theories thus elaborate the processes where certain religious concepts and structures appear nor-mal and natural, while simultaneously highlighting their fragility and their uncertainty in particular iterations. This emphasis on the practi-cal, ongoing, and habitual reveals both the naturalness of the relation-ships reproduced in embodied practices and the ever-present possibility of change and reinterpretation of those practices as they are put to use in specific contexts.[6]

No one can dispute the impact of these understandings on religious studies. Yet insofar as the study of practice in the field centers on things (*practices*) rather than on processes (*practicing*), the discipline has left a number of analytical trajectories unexplored. In this chapter, I consider the prospects of an analytical shift to "practicing," as well as some of

[4] Raymond Williams, *Keywords: A Vocabulary of Culture and Society* (New York: Oxford University Press, 1983), 15.
[5] Pamela E. Klassen, "Practice," in *Key Words in Religion, Media and Culture*, ed. David Morgan (London: Routledge, 2008), 136–47.
[6] See Sherry B. Ortner, "Theory in Anthropology Since the Sixties," *Comparative Studies in Society and History* 26, 1 (1984): 126–66; Catherine Bell, *Ritual Theory, Ritual Practice* (New York: Oxford University Press, 1992).

the problems of such a move. At a very basic level, this shift redirects attention from the things or objects that appear to be self-evidently "religious" and turns it instead toward the processes that *make* certain things (activities, ideas, institutions) recognizably religious. Our current challenge is to consider the consequences of such a shift, where "practicing religion" indicates stronger attention to the ways that religion takes shape consciously and unconsciously, entwined in the "lived practice" of law, economics, family, and so on.

Norbert Elias's complex historical examination of the emergence of European civility, *The Civilizing Process*, might serve as an excellent example of what it means to make such a shift.[7] Elias concentrates great attention in his book on the changing uses of forks and knives and related topics. But he develops his argument by connecting a close reading of Erasmus's *De civilitate morum puerilium* (a handbook instructing young men in proper behavior) to a range of interlinked texts and practices. Civility, Elias argues, is inhabited as much as it was conceptualized and imposed; it can best be understood as a calibration of various emergent, interlinked concepts and practices. The "norms" of civilization take on the quality of something normal, natural, and found in the world.

Elias's interests in cutlery, nose blowing, and bedroom behaviors are entertaining. But he is seriously intent on demonstrating how Europeans' sense of self was refashioned not only in new juridical rules, philosophies, and economic interactions, but also through dynamics taking shape in shifting social status markers, inhabited in manners and comportment, commonplace interactions, and even courtly love. These apparently disparate elements of social life, reproduced in various social settings, work together to naturalize a new experience of civilized selves within transformed fields of distinction and power.

Elias's methodological play suggests what a shift from a focus on practices to practicing religion might allow in religious studies. He engages the traces of complex interactions, refusing to cordon off the "lived" experiences of eating and romance from the "lived" experience of decisions affecting relations among European states or the juridical and scientific shifts that were also taking place. Manners are not iterations of structures or rules that are determined from above. Nor do they bubble up from some place below or beyond such structures. The language of levels of macro- and micropractices is absent in his discussion. Instead, Elias investigates changing relations between practices played

---

7 Norbert Elias, *The Civilizing Process* (Oxford: Blackwell, 1994).

out in a wide range of connected social institutions. This example raises a number of possibilities for future analyses of religious practice.

Taking Elias's work as an example, we might consider both the practices that shape religion within religious communities and likewise the broader array of social spaces that are frequently "beyond" the scope of scholarly focus on religion itself to investigate their role in shaping religious practice. And, with Elias's example in mind, we can pursue this by investigating how interconnected and disparate practices across a range of settings produce and normalize taken-for-granted conceptions of religion, embedding interlocutors and the religious traditions they observe or participate within in a range of habits and social spaces that make particular kinds of religious practices visible (or invisible) to various social actors. A story will help flesh out some of the issues and possibilities of pursuing this approach to practicing religion.

II. STRANGERS ON A TRAIN

On a spring morning in 2005, a heavyset white woman in her early thirties boarded a train in Newark, New Jersey, bound for Philadelphia and points farther west in Pennsylvania. She settled into the seat next to a man about her age, immediately across the aisle from where I was sitting with my sleeping one-year-old daughter. The woman was dressed in loose-fitting sweatpants, a long-sleeved, white shirt, and white sneakers. She wore a bandana on her head, covering her hair. Her seatmate wore sunglasses, sneakers, jeans, and a t-shirt and vest that identified him as a member of a train worker's union. The woman was chatty and the two struck up a conversation. The train man was reticent to talk at first, until he discovered that they were both traveling to neighboring towns in the mountains outside of Pittsburgh. He still lived in western Pennsylvania and worked for the railroad. The woman resided with her children and husband in Jersey City and was on her way to her nephew's high school graduation. After a few minutes of their discussion, I gave up trying to concentrate on my dull reading material and idly listened to them. They talked with increasing familiarity about their hometowns and the rise of drug- and gang-related violence there, which they both attributed to the arrival of Mexican immigrants. The woman then commented how much she liked traveling by train, as it provided her a good opportunity to nap. "Trains are so relaxing," she said, "not like on planes, so uncomfortable and the seats are too small! It all makes me nervous."

Her conversation partner concurred. "No way you could get me on a plane now," he said, with all those "crazies – terrorists and such."

The woman replied, without missing a beat, "My husband's Muslim – you know not all of them are like that." The man blinked, but then quickly agreed, saying, "Oh, yeah, of course they're not all terrorists. Everybody's got their crazies." She seemed oblivious to his stammered tone and the worried look that passed quickly over his brow, and continued with the same tone. "That's what my husband says, he's from Tunisia. That's in Africa – northern Africa he says. And you know they all call each other 'brother.' His friends say, you know, 'Thanks, *Brother Osama*, for ruining it for all the rest of us.'" She then told her seatmate that after September 11, 2001, her husband had been picked up and was in jail for three weeks, "just because he didn't have a paper filed." He had a job, he had the right to be here, she said, but they put him in jail. The man replied incredulously, "They put him in jail? That's just not right!"

Without being asked, she related how she had met her husband (working at a restaurant) and how she hadn't realized that he was Muslim when they started dating. When they decided to get married, he asked her if she would cover her hair in a veil. "I wouldn't have, if he'd made me, but he asked, so it was my choice. Now I wear my hair covered. This is the half *hijab*, this is what I usually wear," she said, pointing to the bandanna on her head. Her seatmate repeated the unfamiliar word. "*Hijab?*" She answered as if it were the most normal thing in the world. "Yeah, you know, the veil. The *hijab*. This is a half *hijab*. It covers my hair."

Without waiting for her seatmate to say anything, she added that her Catholic family had not been concerned that her husband was Muslim. "The only thing they really cared about is how he treated the kids, and me." He was such a good husband that he had joined her on her diet even though "he's pretty skinny, and I'm pretty fat!" She was on the South Beach diet and the man asked, "How does that diet work, since you can't eat meat?" She laughed and said, "Oh no, we eat a lot of meat, just not pork." She admitted that she still had weakness for bacon, but since her husband did all the cooking, she didn't eat it at home anymore.

They continued to talk about diets. The man had also tried the South Beach plan, but it hadn't worked. They moved on to other topics, and soon afterward both stopped talking and the man took a nap.

Interchanges like this are not regularly part of the material that religious studies scholars draw upon to discuss or analyze religious practice. This discussion takes place not in a religious organization or institution but in a "public" exchange between strangers (overheard in a public space by a third stranger). The man and the woman were not praying or reciting scripture; they were not engaged in deep theological discussion. Neither was unambiguously religious. The woman identified her husband as Muslim and wore a "half *hijab*," but she made no definitive remark about her belief or identity; the man remained significantly silent on his own religious proclivities or affiliations throughout. Yet the seatmates' conversation positioned them both (as well as the various others who populated their discussion) in relationships where specific religious distinctions resonated and where particular ideas about religion and religions were clearly reproduced. This conversation was marked and shaped by "religion's" varied relations to different domains of practice and social life: the state, global politics, domestic life, race and gender relations, and diet. The interchange was fleeting and relatively insignificant in the scheme of things (though of course, it is impossible to know what kind of impact this event had on either participant; perhaps they told these stories again as I am doing now). Nonetheless, it demonstrates nicely just how interlinked and resonant even a fleeting and everyday conversation about religion is, with various parts of social and political life.

We can say that the pair was *practicing* religion. Their exchange illuminates numerous ways that religion is practiced as they switched among various idioms and speech genres.[8] The rapidity and seamlessness of these switches suggest the availability of shared, dispersed genres that were familiar (or familiar enough) to both speakers. These organized and shaped the conversation as it unfolded, positioning the two people in explicit and implicit relations not only to religion (or Islam) but also to other aspects of social and political practice.[9]

[8] I address the similarities between Mikhail Bakhtin's concept of speech genres and Bourdieu's theories of social practice in *Heaven's Kitchen: Living Religion at God's Love We Deliver* (Chicago: University of Chicago Press, 2003). See M. M. Bakhtin, *The Dialogic Imagination: Four Essays*, trans. Caryl Emerson and Michael Holquist, ed. Michael Holquist (Austin: University of Texas Press, 1981); Mikhail Bakhtin, *Problems of Dostoevsky's Poetics*, trans. Caryl Emerson (Minnesota: University of Minneapolis Press, 1984); M. M. Bakhtin, *Speech Genres and Other Late Essays*, trans. Vern W. McGee, ed. Caryl Emerson and Michael Holquist (Austin: University of Texas Press, 1986).

[9] On strangers and publics, see Michael Warner, *Publics and Counterpublics* (New York: Zone, 2005). Warner's exposition contrasts with a more widely held implicit view that public spaces such as train compartments elicit "less inhibited" and freewheeling discussions that get to the heart of individuals' "true" opinions. See Jeffrey K. Olick, "Collective Memory and Nonpublic Opinion: A Historical Note on a Methodological Controversy About a Political Problem," *Symbolic Interaction* 30, 1 (2007): 41–55.

The question that a scholar focused on practicing religion will ask is, primarily, how this pair came to speak about religion. What social conditions make it possible, or necessary, to engage religion in this moment, on this train, and how did the social conditions that preceded it (or that resonate around such conversations) shape the subjectivities and future possibilities for both? Questions put to practicing, then, are not only about the content but also about the orientation of the event as it unfolds. Or, as Bourdieu states:

> [T]he shift from the practical scheme to the theoretical schema, constructed after the event, from practical sense to the theoretical model, which can be read either as a project, plan or method... lets slip everything that makes the temporal reality of practice in process. Practice unfolds in time and it has all the correlative properties, such as irreversibility, that synchronization destroys. Its temporal structure, that is, its rhythm, its tempo, and above all its directionality, is constitutive of its meaning.[10]

We can briefly observe that this conversation "about" religion was elicited by the invocation of terrorism and by the woman's subsequent intervention, invoking her husband's Muslim voice in agreement with her seatmate's distaste for terrorists. Marshalling her husband's ironic and critical tone ("thanks, *Brother* Osama") shines a light on the limits of her seatmate's (presumed) linkage of terrorism and Islam. It also reinforces it. Her complaint about the intervention of immigration authorities (and the response, "That's just not right!") raises the question of where Islam in the United States is located in the jurisdiction of the state. The switch that followed, as the woman pointed to her head covering ("half *hijab*"), further complicates her story by refocusing attention on family life and domestic negotiations, a topic that they had broached before. The *hijab*, she said, was a choice rather than an act of submission to her husband (or, for that matter, to Allah or to Islam's tenets). However else she might describe or experience her head covering in other interactions, in this moment her *hijab* and its "halfness" linked Islam to customs and traditions that were choices rather than commands, regulated within the inner, private workings of domestic spaces, thus marking out a kind of living Islam (Islam as a "religion") that seemed to set a contrast to the spectral, surveilled Islam linked to violence and the state.

[10] Bourdieu, *The Logic of Practice*, 81.

Whatever else we might say about this interaction, we can see that it reproduces religion not through specifically religious practices but through discursive acts that build upon and play off of distinctions and articulations of domesticity and the family, the state, and so on. The practices engaged here embed both of the interlocutors in a set of relations to each other as they situate different "religions" in relation to nonreligious aspects of contemporary American social life. These likewise have consequences for how religious identities come to attention or disappear from view. The story of the strangers on the train focuses our attention on the ways that social practices shape subjectivities rather than vice versa. Given that we "know more culture than we use,"[11] we cannot simply presume that what a person does or says is a simple emanation of their central views or ideas or the simple reproduction of embodied habits. Rather, the social practices that we live within calibrate with the various habits, meanings, and concepts that inhabit us and are put to use in particular situations. This raises analytical questions about how religious practice is socially distributed.

In other words, while religious practices are embodied, a theory of practice nonetheless suggests that we move away from a view that it is religious people or individuals (or groups) that are keepers or containers of religion who then mobilize or play out "religious practice" in an unmarked social landscape. Instead, we consider how both the self and the social world are constitutively interlinked, made for and by the other. ("Practice" thus also provides an avenue to evaluating the social processes through which we have come to consider religion as something "contained" in individuals rather than as a set of shared and varied social practices, distributed throughout social interactions.[12]) Religious and all other practices are thus socially embodied: "knowing" culture involves habituation and participation in heterogeneous social settings.[13]

These webs of relations mark a dynamic, ever-shifting, religious field[14] that includes both religious practices and institutions (churches,

[11] Ann Swidler, *Talk of Love: How Culture Matters* (Chicago: University of Chicago Press, 2001).

[12] Elias, *The Civilizing Process*, 214–15.

[13] See John R. Hall, "The Capital(s) of Cultures: A Nonholistic Approach to Status Situations, Class, Gender and Ethnicity," in *Cultivating Differences: Symbolic Boundaries and the Making of Inequality*, ed. Michele Lamont and Marcel Fournier (Chicago: University of Chicago Press, 1992), 257–86; and Bruno Latour, *Reassembling the Social: An Introduction to Actor-Network-Theory* (New York: Oxford University Press, 2005).

[14] On field theory, see John Levi Martin, "What Is Field Theory?" *American Journal of Sociology* 109 (2003): 1–49.

religious groups, movements, and so on) and nonreligious ones (those that organize, regulate, or impinge upon it). An analytical shift to practicing religion concentrates on the connections between the various daily, routine, and unconsciously reproduced habits that shape and reproduce this field and its inhabitants. Many recent studies of religious practice have not strongly engaged the concept of the religious field, and there are some issues that rise to the surface as we begin to do so. Before discussing this further, we should briefly highlight some of the key tensions and issues that the study of religious practice has already moved to the center of many of our inquiries.

III. RELIGIOUS PRACTICES

The event on the train allows us to consider several aspects of practice as they relate to the study of religion. A first point worth noting is that religious studies scholars most frequently describe religious practices as relatively discrete sets of operations and activities. We observe, read about, and write about things like prayer, meditation, and writing as religious practices, for example. We trace their histories (or genealogies) and see their work in the world, whether they are consciously undertaken or habitually enacted. In addition to observing these activities, we can also include a broader array of activities with genealogies, such as the kind of talk that took place on the train. While these speech practices "about" religion might arguably be different from "religious practices," most would probably agree that they are linked, albeit in complex ways. Religious studies scholars have to date focused primarily on the first kind of practice, namely, those activities that are intentionally articulated or acknowledged by religious groups as religious practices or that scholars note are embedded in modes of religious reproduction. They have focused much less attention on the variety of religious practices "about" religion. This has consequences for our understanding of religion, a point to which I will return.

A second dynamic revolves around "lived" or "everyday" religions. Most scholars of religion are quick to point out that the "everyday" and the "lived" do not mark out distinct arenas of social life, contrasted with some other kind of life or living. A cardinal point made by those studying religious practice is precisely that social life is practiced; authority and orthodoxy are no less "practiced" than popular religions. As religious historian David D. Hall makes clear, "[these case studies] are not built around a structure of opposition. Nor [does the study of lived religion] displace the institutional or normative perspectives on practice."

A focus on practice helps us see that clergy were "complicitous in the ways of thinking and doing that [lived religious studies] map, complicitous because they, too, were caught up in the same dilemmas."[15]

To open up the frame of this analysis further, however, means to develop attention to the ways that the institutional authority of religion (or lack thereof) is figured within various religious and nonreligious institutional settings. Winnifred Fallers Sullivan's analysis of a federal court case in Florida demonstrates how a judge drew upon tacit, practiced, and naturalized conceptions of religion (weighing them against the testimony of expert witnesses) when deciding on an appeal relating to religious free exercise.[16] While we might argue that the practices shaping judges' decisions have more social impact than the practices that shape the interaction on the train (or vice versa), the more important point for our purposes is that both sets of practices refer to and to some degree depend upon the other. These practices resonate within a field of operations that reproduce what it means to be religious, to talk about religion, and to be able to recognize religion.

The question of the everyday always engages issues of social power, in particular the ways that "daily" practices (from the most fleeting to the most central) reproduce and naturalize systems of distinction and domination. Here power does not adhere in concepts, however, but in orientations (processes) that direct people toward certain kinds of interactions and lead them to anticipate the particular kinds of responses and relationships that take place within them. Practices are necessary to our very capacity to interact with others; in other words, we act through practices rather than think about them. Practices orient our action: we "know" how to act because of our experiences of their use in the past.[17] This is precisely what "causes practices, in and through what makes them obscure to the eyes of their producers, to be *sensible*, that is, informed by a common sense. It is because agents never know completely what they are doing that what they do has more sense than they know."[18] It all seems so natural! Even a simple exchange between strangers on the train shows both how practices can reinforce social and

---

[15] David D. Hall, ed., *Lived Religion in America* (Princeton, NJ: Princeton University Press. 1997), ix.

[16] Winnifred Fallers Sullivan, *The Impossibility of Religious Freedom* (Princeton, NJ: Princeton University Press, 2005).

[17] See Jeffrey K. Olick and Joyce Robbins, "Social Memory Studies: From 'Collective Memory' to the Historical Sociology of Mnemonic Practices," *Annual Review of Sociology* 24 (1998): 105–40; and Michael J. Lambek, *The Weight of the Past: Living with History in Mahajanga, Madagascar* (New York: Palgrave Macmillan, 2002).

[18] Bourdieu, *The Logic of Practice*, 69.

religious norms, but also open up a range of possible responses, including ones that would demand or require further reflection.

Numerous beautiful, fine-grained analyses have elaborated these topics as they engage questions about religious and social agency within devotional communities. Such studies pay close attention to the ways that religious practices structure the conditions of possible action and opportunities for individuals who have embodied those religious ideals through practice. This is a consequential point in both R. Marie Griffith's *God's Daughters* and Robert A. Orsi's *Thank You, Saint Jude*.[19] The authors' respective renderings of Pentecostal and Catholic women's devotional lives focus on the possibilities available within the social and religious positions that their (primarily female) devotees occupy. Both authors illuminate the religious lives made possible from within specific horizons of understanding, thus articulating a sense of the varied and uneven positions that subjects occupy. Neither Orsi nor Griffith argues that women's choices could be effectively analyzed through a lens that implicitly compares their horizons of meaning with an idealized "free" rational agent. Their work thereby presses scholars to consider how religious agency – and indeed all social agency – is shaped in practice and must be analyzed from within the space of social possibilities made possible through practice.[20]

A further issue drawn from practice theory involves the question of religious embodiment. Practice works by linking cognition to embodied states. Bourdieu writes: "[p]ractical belief is not a 'state of mind,' still less a kind of arbitrary adherence to a set of instituted dogmas and doctrines ('beliefs'), but rather a state of the body.... Enacted belief, instilled by the childhood learning that treats the body as a living memory pad, an automaton that 'leads the mind unconsciously along with it,' and as a repository for the most precious values...."[21] Habit, comportment, language, emotion, and so on are naturalized through the ongoing, daily disciplining of the body in specific ritual events and in multiple social

---

[19] R. Marie Griffith, *God's Daughters: Evangelical Women and the Power of Submission* (Berkeley: University of California Press, 1997); Robert A. Orsi, *Thank You, St. Jude: Women's Devotion to the Patron Saint of Hopeless Causes* (New Haven, CT: Yale University Press, 1996).

[20] Saba Mahmood extends and deepens this theoretical and political critique in *The Politics of Piety: The Islamic Revival and the Feminist Subject* (Princeton, NJ: Princeton University Press, 2005); and David Smilde radicalizes the question of agency in belief in *Reason to Believe: Cultural Agency in Latin American Evangelicalism* (Berkeley: University of California Press, 2007). See also Mustafa Emirbayer and Ann Mische, "What Is Agency?" *American Journal of Sociology* 103, 4 (1998): 962–1023.

[21] Bourdieu, *The Logic of Practice*, 68.

interactions. The thoroughly socialized body inhabits a world in which it knows how to move, and does so in such a way that its movements appear thoroughly natural and transparent. We are given practices "in almost the same way that we are given our native language, which we master fluently long before we begin to study grammar."[22] This observation leads to new ways to consider how traditions are carried in embodied forms and dispositions, as much as in theologies, discourse, institutions, and objects.[23]

These trajectories have been enormously influential, yet we should return to the consequences of our first observation that most recent empirical studies focus on the practices of clearly defined, self-aware religious groups, institutions, or traditions. Our collective framework for engaging questions about religious practice remains circumscribed by methodological choices (and practices) that identify religion as taking place primarily within religious groups.[24]

While we do not want to lose sight of such formative settings, it nonetheless bears noting that scholarly emphases and predilections reproduce the widely held understanding religious practice is most meaningfully reproduced in religious settings or collectives. This focus on specific "religious" sites of production shows a marked contrast to research on other social practices (for example, the reproduction of race, class, and gender distinctions through daily practice) that extend across numerous social fields and situations. The scholarly norms that reproduce the space for religious practices within religious institutions make it difficult to build vocabularies or tools to investigate the reproduction of religion in situations like the one I presented earlier. Instead, scholars often either reproduce problematic narratives that religious people carry their religious practice with them into secular settings, or they make a priori distinctions between practices of secularism and religion. Both approaches smooth over vital questions about how religions and religious practices are at work in the world.

[22] Bakhtin, *Speech Genres and Other Late Essays*, 78.
[23] See, for example, Laurie F. Maffly-Kipp, Leigh E. Schmidt, and Mark Valeri, eds., *Practicing Protestants: Histories of Christian Life in America, 1630–1965* (Baltimore: Johns Hopkins University Press, 2006); Pamela E. Klassen, *Healing Christians: Liberal Protestants and the Pathologies of Modernity* (Berkeley: University of California Press, 2011); Christopher G. White, *Unsettled Minds: Psychology and the American Search for Spiritual Assurance, 1830–1940* (Berkeley: University of California Press, 2009); and Charles Hirschkind, *The Ethical Soundscape: Cassette Sermons and Islamics Counterpublics* (New York: Columbia University Press, 2006).
[24] R. Marie Griffith's *Born Again Bodies: Flesh and Spirit in American Christianity* (Berkeley: University of California Press, 2004), is an exemplary text in this regard.

Our ability to explore the questions that a shift from religious practice to practicing religion opens up will depend in part on whether we can adequately work through the questions of religious practice that much of our empirical work and almost all classical theorizing on religion have hitherto avoided. The question that "practicing" puts before religious studies scholars is whether we can approach religious practice in such a way that does not *require* its self-recognition or self-identification as *religious* (within a particular differentiated social field) in order to operate. If we can, we then identify a broader range of sites where we can understand the shaping of religious selves and the making of the social worlds where such selves are singularly possible.

IV. PRACTICING RELIGION

Do we practice religion without knowing it? The answer for Bourdieu and many social scientists writing up through the late 1990s appears to be no. Bourdieu's most extensive discussions of religion focuses not on a broad field of intersecting institutions and conscious and unconscious practices embedded throughout social life, but rather a delimited and identifiable set of religious institutions. In contrast to Elias's analysis of the multiply sited shaping of civility or Bourdieu's discussion of class distinction and domination, Bourdieu's discussion of the "religious field" in modern society focuses explicitly on the Catholic Church.[25] The questions that Bourdieu asks broadly about practice in organizing and reproducing social life and its multiple distinctions seem unrelated to his considerations of religion. Bourdieu does not consider, for example, how religious difference is reproduced within nonreligious settings or how a person's religious identity becomes visible or invisible, troubling or soothing, in public or private life.

Bourdieu's view of religion in modern France is shaped by processes of secularization, where the differentiation of religion from other aspects of society and its decreasing legitimacy and power in social life (its privatization) make it less consequential for social life generally.[26]

---

[25] Pierre Bourdieu, "Genesis and Structure of a Religious Field," *Comparative Social Research* 13 (1991): 1–44. Others have noted problems with Bourdieu's discussion of religion; see Bradford Verter, "Spiritual Capital: Theorizing Religion with Bourdieu Against Bourdieu," *Sociological Theory* 21, 2 (2003): 150–74; David Swartz, *Culture and Power: The Sociology of Pierre Bourdieu* (Chicago: University of Chicago Press, 1997); Michele Dillon, "Pierre Bourdieu, Religion, and Cultural Production," *Cultural Studies/Critical Methodologies* 1, 4 (2001): 411–29.

[26] Bourdieu, "Genesis and Structure of a Religious Field"; Craig Calhoun, "Habitus, Field, and Capital: The Question of Historical Specificity," in *Bourdieu: Critical*

Differentiation and privatization have resulted in religion's loosening influence across multiple social fields in modern life. Within this framework, "practicing religion" is not viable in the way that "practicing gender" or "culture" remains. Instead, the focus turns to religious practices as recognized, recognizable activities (with histories and practical impact) that do not influence or help organize the basic distinctions and social frameworks in which moral, political, and cultural life takes root. The unraveling authority of religion takes place through institutional differentiation. Its impact is felt most acutely for those who focus on practicing as Elias does. The power of constitutively and habitually enacted religious distinctions embedded and articulated across a number of social settings dissipates; religion becomes more identifiable and specific, but loses its capacity to operate in the capillary and practical ways in which other social practices continue to operate.

It is clear that the modern world has not cooperated with this narrative of religion's decreasing impact or its restriction to its own distinct field. Be that as it may, the possibility that religious practices still operate and resonate within a social field of distinctions (or has perhaps "recovered" its position) sits uneasily with many in the social sciences. The recent emergence of the field of secular studies, or the formations of the secular, is, in some respects, a response to the perplexing issue of whether modern people can be religious without knowing it. Noting the historical emergence of secular formations that powerfully shape and reshape religion, scholars have turned their attention to the development of the secular, its formations, and its practices. It is at this point where we find a "field" influencing and inflecting social life broadly. This secular field – tensile, dynamic, and open ended in the ways that practice theory suggests – demonstrates how religious differences continue to operate in this changed modern circumstance. We can be secular without knowing it. Secularism links unconscious and conscious practices and develops in and reproduces a range of institutions that also shape and order the religious in modern life. Thus Talal Asad writes that what is "distinctive about 'secularism' is that it presupposes new concepts of 'religion,' 'ethics,' and 'politics,' and new imperatives associated with them."[27]

Perspectives, ed. Craig Calhoun, Edward LiPuma, and Moishe Postone (Chicago: University of Chicago Press, 1993), 61–88), provides a helpful narrative of structural differentiation as it relates to Weber's and Bourdieu's theories of secularization and practice.

[27] Asad, *Formations of the Secular*, 1–2.

Notwithstanding the value of engaging secularism as an embedded, embodied set of practices, one might caution against the overly quick leap from practicing religion to practicing secularism. One example of the problem that inheres emerges in Charles Taylor's argument that the modern secular age has transformed religion in such a way that the "naïve belief" of religiousness that was once widely dispersed through European practices and institutions is now impossible to sustain.[28] Religion in the contemporary world is utterly changed: it is a choice now, something that one cannot naively enter into, given shifts in social practices and the position of religion's authority. One can, however, be a naïve secularist too.[29] From within the framework of this approach, the pair on the train was practicing secularism. They were reproducing secular articulations of religion that in turn shaped socially comprehensible grounds on which religious belief and subjectivities took shape. The naiveté of the secular field makes reflexive religiosity possible, that is, it makes religion something that one chooses. But an unreflexive, unrecognized practice of religion is not possible in this understanding. Religion becomes identified as recognizable practices and institutions that take shape and are transformed; its operations in social life are different from those of the secular on precisely these grounds. Taylor's stronger argument is that the conditions of secularity require a certain intentionality and awareness of religious belief. Practicing religion is distinguished from practicing secularism on precisely this point.

There may be good reason to describe the couple on the train as practicing secularism rather than practicing religion. Their discussion did not touch directly on personal belief; they did not mention devotional practices, ritual content, or theology. We might say that their discussion mapped out spaces in relation to religion, as part of a secular frame. But on the other hand, doing so simplifies and neatens part of the complexity of their interaction, where issues of belief, identity, and belonging were at times invoked and at other times hovering. It likewise suggests that the field that was operating for both of the interlocutors was in fact secular, built and developed habitually outside of

---

[28] Charles Taylor, *A Secular Age* (Cambridge, MA: Belknap Press of Harvard University Press, 2007).

[29] Similar arguments about the unreflexive cultivation of reflexivity within "modernity" appear in Peter Berger, Brigitte Berger, and Hans Fried Kellner, *The Homeless Mind: Modernization and Consciousness* (New York: Random House, 1973); and Paul Sweetman, "Twenty-First Century Dis-ease? Habitual Reflexivity or the Reflexive Habitus," *Sociological Review* 51, 4 (2003): 528–49.

any particular religious community, without engaging (in ways that we might on further reflection) how Muslims in the United States (or others) build such practices and develop them within their own communities as well. Indeed, I would argue that enormous purchase remains in beginning with the language of "practicing religion" to speak of and about such situations. The quick move to the secular leaves certain qualities of living religion unnoted at best, and at worst turns our attention from the shifting, altering social conditions where religion is reformed and transformed through various social fields and institutions, including those that are often marked as secular.[30] Here, scholarly focus on the everydayness of religion might be marshaled to illuminate the ways that religions flourish in multiple sites, or the ways that religion in its practice is frequently messy, problematic, and not given to easy conceptual framing. To do so, we must employ vocabularies that allow us to consider religious practices and religious fields in the same terms that have recently been given to the secular. That is, we need to investigate the practices that render religious activity unrecognized and unmarked, and ask what kinds of powers religion gains as a result.

V. STRANGERS IN A CAR

Traveling to a conference in early 2009, I rode from the airport to my hotel in a shared car service with a well-dressed middle-aged man and his teenaged son. As we pulled out of the airport, the father commented (by way of introduction) about the tricked-out interior of our shared limo, which sported black windows and multicolored halogen lights. He was a talkative man and I soon learned that he was on his way to a convention. I noted that I was on my way to a conference also, and he asked my profession. I responded that I was a professor who wrote on sociology and religion in America.

I caught a gleam in his eye as he extended his hand and introduced himself. Matt was an organizational and financial consultant traveling to a national conference of financial officers at major corporations. His business was to help financial organizations and their leaders think through their business priorities; his particular angle was to teach his clients about the spiritual aspects of business and of life more broadly. In this economic downturn, he said, a lot of people are rethinking

---

[30] Talal Asad, "Responses," in *Powers of the Secular Modern: Talal Asad and His Interlocutors*, ed. David Scott and Charles Hirschkind (Stanford, CA: Stanford University Press, 2006), 209.

things – is there more to life than turning a profit? There must be. He hastened to add that he helped businesses in the financial sector think about how they could be more profitable: the two went together.

Slipping almost without thinking into my interviewing mode, I asked him what kind of spiritual aspects he meant, since it could mean a lot of different things. Was he spiritual like Deepak Chopra (whose new book was prominently displayed in the airport bookstores that morning) or was he talking about spirituality in a more Christian sense? "That's a good question!" he said, and offered that he understood spirituality from a Christian perspective, an assertion he followed with a brief lecture how the three aspects of the Trinity correspond to different aspects of human psychology and to different relationships in business. He added that he was a trained psychologist, an ordained minister, and also a Christian mystic.

Having just completed work on a book on self-described mystics and spiritual practitioners, my curiosity was piqued. "What denomination were you ordained in?" I asked. He paused just briefly before saying, "My life journey has taken me in many different directions," he said. "I am ordained Southern Baptist. But – well, I like to say that I'm a recovering Southern Baptist." I chuckled and observed, "I imagine that there are a lot of those." Matt's son laughed and nodded.

So, I said, what about being a Christian mystic? What does that mean? Matt looked at me with a more piercing, focused gaze and said, "It means that I talk to God. And God talks back to me. I have been talking to God since I was four years old." Matt described to me in detail his morning meditation and prayer practice of waking up, sitting in prayer, and then going into a deep meditation. During the meditation, he talks with God about his plans for the day, for his business, and for his life. He finished his description by adding that he was not a remarkable person. "Everyone can have the kind of access I do – that kind of relationship – and feel that power."

Perhaps to give me a sense of the power of his relationship with God, he added then that "just that morning," after finishing his meditation, he had sat down and written an article in "twenty-two minutes that should have taken four hours." My book included a discussion of the relationships between writing and divine presence, and I heard myself asking Matt to explain what he thought happened when he was writing. Was God still present when he was writing or was it the power of the meditation that had given him the ability to write so rapidly and effectively? Matt's look of puzzlement suggested that I had proceeded with my questions too quickly, but he gamely described his process.

Before going to bed the previous night, he had read through a stack of books on various business practices in preparation for writing his own list of effective skills that business people should manage. He thought he would get up in the morning and synthesize what he had anticipated would be twenty-five principles for his clients. When he woke in the morning, he practiced his meditation, and then, on finishing, he sat down to write. There, he said, the Holy Spirit instructed him, and he drew together a list of twelve principles synthesizing all of what he had read the night before into a new creation. He was still rather in awe of how everything came together, as he admitted that writing usually was difficult: "You know, you draft and redraft and redraft." I said I knew that very well.

Matt then asked me a number of questions about my research and we continued to talk until we reached the hotel. He asked for my card and suggested that we might have professional things to talk about, and that he would ring me up the next time he came to New York. He chuckled, "You know – everything happens for a reason!" I shook his hand and then his son's hand. I realized then that he had been taking notes on his computer as we had talked. I wished them well, and the son called out several times, "Bless you, Courtney. Bless you."

This conversation reminded me of the many interviews I had conducted in Cambridge, Massachusetts, where I had done the field work for my book. Matt had ongoing experiences with the divine and participated in a number of settings where those interests could be explored and expressed. His own brief narrative highlighted this way of thinking, as he emphasized his "journey" and invoked the language of spirituality rather than religion. Despite the multiplicity of places where Matt located his "spiritual" life, he had not abandoned Christianity. His invocation of the Trinity, his wry smile when I suggested that there were "many ways" to be a recovering Southern Baptist, and his son's benedictory cadence ("Bless you!") suggested ongoing saturation of a particular kind of Christian practice. At the same time, Matt's "spiritual" interests traced out along institutional paths that he considers spiritual and that many others consider secular. Psychology, business (finance), and the self-help (and "life coach") circuits unquestionably are nonetheless shaped by, and shape, religious aspirations, ideas, and practices.[31]

---

[31] See T. J. Jackson Lears, *Fables of Abundance: A Cultural History of Advertising in America* (New York: Basic, 1994); Roland Marchand, *Advertising the American Dream: Making Way for Modernity, 1920–1940* (Berkeley: University of California Press, 1985); Robert C. Fuller, "American Psychology and the Religious Imagination," *Journal of the History of the Behavioral Sciences* 42, 3 (2006): 221–35.

Matt's description of writing presents one opening through which to consider how "secular" institutions continue to build and reproduce within them practices that Christian mystics, spiritual practitioners, and others regard as central to their experiences. Although I did not have time to inquire how Matt learned to write as he did, the practices Matt described are taught as "free writing" in composition classes at the high school and college level and outlined in popular self-help books on artistic freedom and also in Sunday school books on "spiritual journaling" published by conservative Christian denominational presses. In addition, psychologists use free writing to jump-start group therapy sessions. In other words, one can encounter and learn these writing practices in a variety of venues. Manuals, classes, and personal accounts teach people writing practices, highlighting the importance of "catharsis," "inspiration," or letting one's inner voice develop and move upon the page. In some books and classes, these practices are linked more specifically with religious or spiritual terms, encouraging readers that writing will be easier once they stop fighting or worrying and let God (or divine spirit) take control. The passive writer becomes the medium for either one's inner truths to emerge or for God's words and work to move upon the page.

The practices of free writing, cathartic writing, or automatic writing are put to quite different purposes than taking dictation from the Holy Spirit, yet also draw in and reproduce concepts that make them amenable to their retranslation and shifting use in religious and spiritual settings.[32] These widely dispersed practices, resonant and pregnant with past uses, link catharsis to divinity, the self to God, and passivity to a certain kind of presence. They nonetheless are often unmarked and unregistered as practices (religious or otherwise). It may well be that part of their current power and allure is their position and reproduction in social settings that are at best tangential to the "religious" and that we most frequently imagine as secular, having rid themselves of practices that might enchant one's writing or relations with others.

While we may have difficulty talking about religious practices in these respects, this does not mean that others lack such capacity. If

---

[32] Courtney Bender, *The New Metaphysicals: Spirituality and the American Religious Imagination* (Chicago: University of Chicago Press, 2010), chapter 3; Courtney Bender, "How Does God Answer Back?" *Poetics* 36 (2008): 476–92. Various histories of communication mark another range of practices and attendant technologies; see John Durham Peters, *Speaking into the Air: A History of the Idea of Communication* (Chicago: University of Chicago Press, 1999); and Leigh Eric Schmidt, *Hearing Things: Religion, Illusion and the American Enlightenment* (Cambridge, MA: Harvard University Press, 2000).

Matt is anything like the people I met in Cambridge, he may very well understand that his experiences while writing and meditating originate in divine sources that are ever-present, if beyond the capacity of human understanding to explain or to trace. My respondents in Cambridge consider the trace of the divine or of Spirit (or catharsis) on the page to be experience and not practice. They do not ask about the history of their activities or about the traces of the past that might influence their current uses. As such, people like Matt (and often the scholars who engage people like Matt) lose the trail of their own historicized practices as such practices enter the "secular" realm. Yet such practices, continue to operate, carrying past resonances and memories of past uses with them; they also carry the capacity to surprise, perplex, or exhaust those who engage in them.

That said, it is not the scholar's task to be surprised or perplexed at the apparent irruptions of the sacred into daily life. We can investigate how these irruptions take place and the ways that the unfinished, unfinalized movement of some practices from religious to "secular" sites enables the religious to be found rather than practiced. In so doing, we need to embrace the possibility that both scholarly and lay discussions of secular life continue to make space for the operations of practices like Matt's that are transformed into irruptive, enchanted practices in the process. But such an embrace will require broadening our analytical framework to include a wider range of spaces where religion is actively produced and practiced, extending our analysis in ways that engage the divine and supernatural agents with whom our subjects interact.[33]

VI. CONCLUSION: ANOTHER TRAIN

A few years ago, I was traveling on the uptown Broadway express during rush hour, holding my infant daughter on my lap. The train became increasingly packed, and I was grateful for a seat as others' bodies pressed against me. As we left the Seventy-Second Street station, I heard the door at the end of the car open, followed by the croak of a plaintive voice, "Help me, please someone help me!" The voice cut through

---

[33] See Karen A. Cerulo, "Nonhumans in Social Interaction," *Annual Review of Sociology* 35 (2009): 531–52; Webb Keane, "Religious Language," *Annual Review of Anthropology* 26, 1 (1997): 47–71; Dipesh Chakrabarty, *Provincializing Europe: Postcolonial Thought and Historical Difference* (Princeton, NJ: Princeton University Press, 2000); Robert A. Orsi, *Between Heaven and Earth: The Religious Worlds People Make and the Scholars Who Study Them* (Princeton, NJ: Princeton University Press, 2005).

the hum and clatter in the car, repeating over and over. Soon she came into my line of sight. Her clothes practically fell off her thin frame, her lips were chapped, and her face was riddled with sores. Desperation and exhaustion hung about her. I clutched my daughter and felt a wave of revulsion and embarrassment pass through me. The woman's body brushed against one person, then another. She stumbled forward as she passed and the woman sitting next to me reached out her arms to catch her. But we quickly observed that the stumble was intentional. As she fell I caught sight of a habit's hem, and as bodies parted to make room, I saw that she had thrown herself at the feet of two young, diminutive nuns. The crowd of teenagers that had shielded the pair from my view pushed out of the way as the woman said, "Pray for me, sisters, bless me."

Without hesitation, the nuns reached for what appeared to be a small bottle of water and for the crosses that hung on long chains around their necks. They touched her and prayed, hands clasped together, in voices not meant for me. Above the rattle of the tracks, I heard a trace of their supplication, offered in French. The teenagers used indifference, a practice honed to a polish by the rub of the daily commute, to press farther into those standing near them. They opened up a surprisingly large space on the subway floor, shaping a human shield beyond which mundane subway life continued: crossword puzzles marked, romance novels read, advertisements overhead scanned one more time.

The prayers were brief and so the quick genuflecting motion of one of the teenagers was easy to miss. The nuns helped the woman to her feet, the space that had opened up closed back around the nuns, and the woman continued into the next car as we pulled into the Ninety-Sixth Street station.

What puts French-speaking nuns on a New York City subway headed to the Bronx? What brings homeless and ill people into the subway? What practices of indifference make religion visible in that moment or conceal it? What emotions are unleashed, what moral indignation or lack thereof? What memories? What healing does it effect and for whom? The coordination of this event, its very being, is made singularly possible through the calibration of seemingly uncoordinated actions that took shape across the space of a regular subway car on a regular day. Its impact is likewise traced in capillary effects, in stories or habits slightly reshaped in its wake.

It should not escape attention that the anecdotes in this chapter are in fleeting, temporary social settings and that they take place between strangers. Beginning in these spaces sets the coordinates of our discussion about religious practice differently than when it begins within churches, communities, or the like, where we imagine that practices are jointly crafted and meaningful because of individuals' participation within an identifiable group. These examples, I hope, call attention to a different order of relations between various fields of habit, practice, and interaction that also shape religion and religious identity. I have likewise approached these as interactions where religion is produced in practice, through which a religious field is likewise reproduced. These events are not neutral with regard to distinction, power, and force. They are not without their own histories or past uses. Every living experience is shot through with the reach of habits and routines that reinforce social distinctions. This is no less the case for conversations between strangers in trains or for those who pray in subways. These examples call attention to the expansiveness of religious practices' contingent and complex organization within social actions and interactions, their signal ubiquity, and their ability to operate as practices do – without theorization, recognition, or trace.

The study of processes, or practicing, draws attention to the capillary working of power in and through our bodies and speech, normalizing and naturalizing the relations that make our worlds. At this moment, the questions of how far religious fields extend, how webs of relations among religious and other practices (including what we now call the secular or spiritual) shape aspects of our shared and unshared religious and secular futures, are again reopened to argumentation, debate, and investigation. They are vital questions, no less so because of all social practices' power to mystify and confound the social processes that we seek to understand.

Select Bibliography

Bakhtin, Mikhail. *Problems of Dostoevsky's Poetics.* Edited and translated by Caryl Emerson. Minneapolis: University of Minneapolis Press, 1984.
   Speech Genres and Other Late Essays. Translated by Vern W. McGee. Edited by Caryl Emerson and Michael Holquist. Austin: University of Texas Press, 1986.
Bourdieu, Pierre. *The Logic of Practice.* Stanford, CA: Stanford University Press, 1990.
   "Genesis and Structure of a Religious Field." *Comparative Social Research* 13 (1991): 1–44.
Cerulo, Karen A. "Nonhumans in Social Interaction." *Annual Review of Sociology* 35 (2009): 531–52.
Elias, Norbert. *The Civilizing Process.* Oxford: Blackwell, 1994.
Griffith, R. Marie. *Born Again Bodies: Flesh and Spirit in American Christianity.* Berkeley: University of California Press, 2004.

Hall, David D. Ed. *Lived Religion in America: Toward a History of Practice.* Princeton, NJ: Princeton University Press, 1997.

Hirschkind, Charles. *The Ethical Soundscape: Cassette Sermons and Islamic Counterpublics.* New York: Columbia University Press, 2006.

Klassen, Pamela E. "Practice," 136–47. In *Key Words in Religion, Media and Culture.* Edited by David Morgan. London: Routledge, 2008.

Latour, Bruno. *Reassembling the Social: An Introduction to Actor-Network-Theory.* New York: Oxford University Press, 2005.

Orsi, Robert A. *Thank You, St. Jude: Women's Devotion to the Patron Saint of Hopeless Causes.* New Haven, CT: Yale University Press, 1996.

Ortner, Sherry B. "Theory in Anthropology Since the Sixties." *Comparative Studies in Society and History* 26, no. 1 (1984): 126–6.

14 The look of the sacred

DAVID MORGAN

Whatever else it means, to see or be seen is to enter into a relationship, even if doing so involves practices as different as ignoring those who glare at us, returning the gaze of a lover, or cherishing the photograph of a lost family member. Different as they are, each of these behaviors is an example of the many kinds of relatedness that constitute interaction with images. I say "interaction" because it becomes clear upon inspection that a viewer's action toward objects, images, or people is often far more than unilateral. Each looks back; sometimes they even see us before we see them. Of special interest here is how images of the living and the dead, of gods, or of mythic heroes connect to the viewer's body. Seeing bridges the gap separating seer and seen, connecting the two in some way. Representation vanishes in the way that a tool in one's hand fades from consciousness as a sign in the midst of using it. Before use, the tool only signifies what it might actually do. In use, the tool ceases to be separate from the body and becomes instead a physical extension of it. Likewise, when they join viewers to those they love, fear, or hate, images are organic projections of the eyes, material forms of beholding. It is this tangible look, the look of the sacred, that reveals the role of the body in vision, and that will be the subject of this chapter.

If we are to understand the "look of the sacred" robustly, we must recognize in the reports of those who experience images as the presence of the person or thing itself. Images offer the other to viewers, for imploring, touching, kissing, hearing, reviling, and fearing, propelled by the deeply felt assumption that the other will respond accordingly. An image is a signifier, but also more than that since it can become the thing to which it also refers. There is a dual operation of presentation and representation in which the former rivals and sometimes even eclipses the latter. For example, when devotees of Mary speak of their love for her as they gaze upon an image of her, they do not say, "I adore the person pictured here." They say, "I adore her." At one level, they realize that she is not her picture. But at another, it *is* her. More than a sign that stands *for* something, the image may also be the material mediation of a viewer, other viewers, and what stands *in* the image. Images are more than *symbols* of belief. To insist that the image is only a symbol is to disenchant it, to rationalize it as a sign, to make it indifferent toward its reality. The result is a severing of the felt relation between believer and sacred reality. It is what happens when I place the tool on the bench and regard it disinterestedly; no longer is it the organic extension of my body, but something separate, a sign that draws its meaning from what is now absent. When an image becomes an arbitrary symbol, it is rendered inert, becoming a placeholder for thought or words. But for many believers, even many for Protestants, Jews, and Muslims, images and objects operate much more intimately to embody (not only to signify) divine–human relations.[1]

In an influential study on this subject, David Freedberg argued that art historians tend to ignore the other-than-rational power of images evident, for example, in images that speak or move, that perform healings, and that arouse fear or desire.[2] People who believe that images do so are dismissed by some scholars as superstitious, hysterical, hallucinating, captive to the enchantments of magic or occultism, or fueled by fears or impulses that are unseemly, even obscene. The devout viewer is drawn to an image like the bloody body of Jesus (see Figure 14.1) not only to admire its beauty or craft, but for the unreasonable promises it makes to someone driven by needs or interests that are not governed by high-brow taste or professional decorum. Art historians, Freedberg complained, prefer to turn a blind eye to these visual relations. Some seeing is not worth seeing. As the objects of contemplation, beauty and skill defuse the viewer's relationship with the image, substituting the demands of connoisseurship for those of practical use.

For scholars of lived religion, however, the power of indecorous images and how people use them are of great importance because for many people these visual relations constitute religion in its everyday social and personal reality. Robert A. Orsi has made the case for understanding religion "as a web not of meanings but of relationships

---

[1] See, for instance, Kalman P. Bland, *The Artless Jew: Medieval and Modern Affirmations and Denials of the Visual* (Princeton, NJ: Princeton University Press, 2000); Allen F. Roberts and Mary Nooter Roberts, *A Saint in the City: Sufi Arts of Urban Senegal* (Los Angeles: UCLA Fowler Museum of Cultural History, 2003); and David Morgan, *Visual Piety: A History and Theory of Popular Religious Images* (Berkeley: University of California Press, 1998).

[2] David Freedberg, *The Power of Images: Studies in the History and Theory of Response* (Chicago: University of Chicago Press, 1989).

Figure 14.1. Hans Mack, hand-tinted print of *The Flagellation*, 1585, from Albrecht Dürer's *Engraved Passion*, 1513, engraving © The Trustees of the Chester Beatty Library, Dublin.

between heaven and earth."³ The assertion marks a subtle but portentous shift from the long dominance of Clifford Geertz's definition of religion as "a system of symbols."⁴ Orsi aptly stresses the view that religion

³ Robert A. Orsi, *Between Heaven and Earth: The Religious Worlds People Make and the Scholars Who Study Them* (Princeton, NJ: Princeton University Press, 2005), 5.
⁴ Clifford Geertz, "Religion as a Cultural System," in *The Interpretation of Cultures* (New York: Basic, 1973), 90–1. In another famous essay in the same volume, Geertz

materializes the transcendent, defining it as "the practice of making the invisible visible, of concretizing the order of the universe, the nature of human life and its destiny, and the various dimensions and possibilities of human interiority itself ... [making them] present to the senses in the circumstances of everyday life."[5] This approach to religion is much friendlier to materiality, regarding it as constitutive in the world-making, felt, and embodied activity of belief as practice.

The study of images benefits from complementing the semiotics of the sign, which turns on the emptiness of the signifier and the absence of the signified, with an approach that scrutinizes the possibility of presence. Scholars of religion need a way of thinking that is not grounded in the rationality of the symbol. This is not to ignore the importance of signs that absent the sacred in order to preserve its transcendence. But rather than regarding an image as principally a visual code or iconographical message, scholars of lived religion are inclined to refocus on what the image does in terms of the relationships it mediates. Religious seeing consists of practices that engage images to *structure* such relationships as devotion, contrition, or humiliation rather than merely illustrating or referring to nonvisual "meanings." The image is less signifier (though it certainly remains one) than it is agent in constructing and negotiating relations among different parties – heaven and earth, but also, as Orsi intends, individuals, groups, places, things, and institutions.[6]

The power of images to mediate important relationships in religious life is apparent in a travel account written by the Reverend Henry Ward Beecher after he had visited art galleries in England in 1850. Gazing raptly at pictures of religious subjects in colleges at Oxford, Beecher was struck by their ability to transport him. The paintings, he wrote,

> cease to be pictures. They are realities. The canvas is glass, and you look through it upon the scene represented as if you stood at a window. Nay, you enter into the action. For, once possessed with the spirit of the actors or of the scene, all that the artist thought lives in you. And if you are left, as I was once or twice, for an hour quite alone, in the halls, the illusion becomes memorable. You know the personages. You mingle in the action as an actor. You gaze upon the Apostles of Guido [Figure 14.2], and it is not the ideal head that

---

followed Weber's understanding of culture, endorsing the view that "man is an animal suspended in webs of significance he himself has spun" (*The Interpretation of Cultures*, 5).

[5] Orsi, *Between Heaven and Earth*, 73–4.

[6] I have examined the operation of seeing as the structuring of devotion in Morgan, *Visual Piety*, 1–5.

Figure 14.2. Guido Reni, *The Apostle St. Mark Writing His Gospel*, 1630s, oil on canvas. Courtesy of the Bob Jones University Museum and Gallery.

you see, but the character, the life, the career, extend in shadowy length before you. At last you are with them! No longer do you look through the eighteen hundred years at misty shadows. The living men have moved down toward you, and here you are face to face! I was much affected by a head of Christ; not that it met my ideal of that sacred front, but because it took me in a mood that clothed it with life and reality. For one blessed moment I was with the Lord. I knew Him. I loved Him.[7]

The images turn into windows or theatrical stages that allow Beecher to mingle in the action on stage, to see the "living men" face to face, to glimpse Jesus and recognize him. One might regard this as a literary conceit, the sort of dramatic evocation that Victorian travel literature offered its readers. But confining the passage to this reading would mean missing its curious transcendence of time. The account was not published until five years after the events described took place, yet Beecher wrote the text in the present tense, as if he were standing there and the distance and time that literally separate the reader from the pictures were not in force. Not only did the images he saw traverse time to bring him to the sacred past-as-present, so did Beecher's text, crossing space and time to deposit one in what might be called the *somatic present*. I will return to this term shortly in relation to the work of Maurice Merleau-Ponty, but it may be defined here at the outset as the situation in which presentation eclipses representation.

Beecher longed to convey a striking and novel experience of presence that had befallen him in the galleries at Oxford. Gazing upon Guido Reni's portraits of the Apostles, he felt he had joined their presence. The Baroque painter's art was of course designed to invite the experience of immediacy. Guido placed St. Matthew close to the picture plane separating viewer and Apostle and cropped the angel's wing at the left, thus projecting it through the transparent plane so that it crosses into the space of the viewer standing before the image, thereby enhancing the sense of the viewer's presence at the sacred event of the Apostle's revelatory writing. The author, or rather amanuensis, listens carefully to the speaking angel, who articulates sacred truths with the careful enumeration of his fingers in order to deliver every word of divine speech, which the dutiful evangelist transcribes word for word in the bound book of the Bible *avant la lettre*, as it were. What could have been more reassuring to a Protestant preacher of Calvinist descent regarding the authority of the Apostle's image than a portrait of him authoring the biblical text? (Such literalism must have appealed to the American fundamentalist

---

[7] Henry Ward Beecher, *Star Papers; or, Experiences of Art and Nature* (New York: J. C. Derby, 1855), 52. Beecher's view of images of Jesus was complex. Whereas in the passage quoted he was deeply moved by the unnamed picture of Jesus that he saw in Oxford, on the same trip he came to express dissatisfaction with the portraits of Christ he saw.

Bob Jones when he acquired the painting for his eponymous university's collection of sacred art during the 1950s.)

Viewing Guido's images of the apostles in the majestic silence of the famous European university only enhanced Beecher's response to them. He opened his narrative with the observation that being there, "ranging through these historic places," summoned up in him "the keen and fine excitement [that] ... is precisely of the kind favorable for the appreciation of pictures." Theatrical himself, given to the creative sentiments of dramatic preaching and writing, Beecher nevertheless reminds us about the direct relevance of place to the operation of seeing. Seeing always happens somewhere, in a particular time and place, such that people see things in one instance and not in another, depending on the setting. Place contributes to the conditions of visibility.

Seeing, it becomes clear, is driven by desire, conditioned by place, shaped by culture, memory, and history, and bodily engaged by the gaze of the other. Beecher's remembered experience at Oxford suggests that some visual relations can trump the divide separating viewers from what they long to behold, that is, if place and desire combine with image to allow visual disclosure, an iconic form of vision. He holds up for us the constituents of seeing through which we readily note the importance of the enfleshed, spatial, temporal, and cultural coordinates of the viewer. Understood as the matrix or medium of seeing, the body clearly performs a fundamental role in putting vision to religious work.

This argues for grounding the study of images in the experience of the body. The likeness many believers discern between image and referent, which consists of their shared being rather than simply conventional forms of reference, extends a phenomenological account of human embodiment. Maurice Merleau-Ponty provided an influential and insightful description of embodiment in his *Phenomenology of Perception* (1945). Discussing gesture as communication, Merleau-Ponty claimed that it was more like communion. "The gesture," he contended, "*does not make me think* of anger, it is anger itself."[8] The reason for this somatic immediacy rather than the signification of meaning (gesture as symbol of anger) is the common embodiment of viewer and gesticulator. "It is as if the other person's intention inhabited my body and mine his.... The identity of the thing through perceptual experience is only another aspect of the identity of one's own body throughout exploratory

8   Maurice Merleau-Ponty, *Phenomenology of Perception*, trans. Colin Smith (London: Routledge, 1962), 214.

movements; thus they are the same in kind as each other."⁹ By rejecting what Charles Taylor has since called the "mediational epistemology," in which thought is understood as the interior representation of an exterior world to which thinking otherwise has no access, Merleau-Ponty looked to the body as the continuity of thought and world.¹⁰ The body is the matrix of perception that is not fundamentally separate from the world, but part of it: "I become involved in things with my body, they co-exist with me as an incarnate subject."¹¹

Merleau-Ponty distinguished between two selves or forms of consciousness: sensible and intellectual. There is a sensible self and a cogito, the sentient subject and the thinking subject.¹² He did not intend by this a dualist split in the human self, but, on the contrary, he was aiming at the integration of mind and body. The cogito cannot operate without the sensible self, which is the intimate connection or interface of the human organism and its material environment. Without the cogito, however, humans would not be the robustly conscious beings that they are. Perception and abstraction belong on a single cognitive continuum that constitutes human consciousness. The task is to recognize how body and mind are integral aspects of a single organism, though arrayed differently according to culture, society, and history. Body and mind operate both together and at odds with one another, each with its own sovereignty: the one autonomic, involuntary, and confined to the present; the other voluntary, reflective, and dwelling on the past and the future. It is these aspects of the human self that correspond to the tension between presentation and representation that I have mentioned.¹³ The cogito operates at a distance from the world, contemplating it as a disembodied eye, whereas the sensible self discerns an organic continuity between body and world.

---

⁹ Merleau-Ponty, *Phenomenology of Perception*, 215.

¹⁰ Charles Taylor, "Merleau-Ponty and the Epistemological Picture," in *The Cambridge Companion to Merleau-Ponty*, ed. Carman Taylor and Mark B. N. Hansen (Cambridge: Cambridge University Press, 2005), 26–49.

¹¹ Merleau-Ponty, *Phenomenology of Perception*, 215.

¹² For these terms and related ideas, see Merleau-Ponty, *Phenomenology of Perception*, 248–50, 277–80, 373–4, 419.

¹³ This distinction and Merleau-Ponty's treatment of the continuity of mind and body correspond to the strongly nondualist approach that Antonio Damasio takes in distinguishing what he calls "core consciousness," the brain's apprehension of the body's state with regard to the mapping of an object of perception and limited to the here and now, from "extended consciousness," which constitutes the personal or "autobiographical self" in memory and the future mode of expectation and planning. See Antonio Damasio, *The Feeling of What Happens: Body and Emotion in the Making of Consciousness* (San Diego, CA: Harcourt, 1999), 169, 195–6.

Perception constitutes a physical, organic participation in the world, which Merleau-Ponty strikingly compared to Eucharistic communion. He described the experience of color and, by extension, any form of perception as follows:

> ... suddenly the sensible takes possession of my ear or my gaze, and I surrender a part of my body, even my whole body, to this particular manner of vibrating and filling space known as blue or red. Just as the sacrament not only symbolizes, in sensible species, an operation of Grace, but is also the real presence of God, which it causes to occupy a fragment of space and communicates to those who eat of the consecrated bread, provided they are inwardly prepared, in the same way the sensible has not only a motor and vital significance, but is nothing other than a certain way of being in the world suggested to us from some point in space, and seized and acted upon by our body, provided that it is capable of doing so, so that sensation is literally a form of communion.[14]

Perception is an enfolding of organism and environment, an embodied participation that amounts to a form of consciousness or subjectivity that Merleau-Ponty did not wish to subordinate to abstraction, but regarded as working in tandem with it. The body does more than gather sense data to be processed by reason. Perception is a way of knowing distinct from the cogito. According to Merleau-Ponty, for example, "sight and movement are specific ways of entering into relationship with objects," which results in assembling the many different elements within an experience, "not by placing them all under the control of an 'I think' [cogito], but by guiding them toward the intersensory unity of a 'world'." The body, he stated, "is our general medium for having a world."[15]

By giving the body its due, Merleau-Ponty's phenomenology of perception allows us to recognize with greater keenness how images operate in religious experience. When images speak, move, bleed, heal, or reveal the presence of the sacred, they do not merely *appear* to do so to duped, illiterate, or superstitious minds, underdeveloped cogitos, as it were. The embodied perception of images acting nonrationally serves to reveal an animated reality that the cogito or thinking subject may in turn affirm, ignore, or deny. Yet the reality of the perceived event

---

[14] Merleau-Ponty, *Phenomenology of Perception*, 246.

[15] Merleau-Ponty, *Phenomenology of Perception*, 159, 169. For consideration of the relationship of Merleau-Ponty's views to subsequent work on emotions, learning, and other cognitive operations, see Hubert L. Dreyfus, "Merleau-Ponty and Recent Cognitive Science," in *Cambridge Companion to Merleau-Ponty*, 129–50.

persists in the domain of the embodied self, whose relation to it is not one of abstract signification but physical communion. In other words, according to Merleau-Ponty's analysis of perception, images may be said to act on the sensible self in one way, and on the rational subject in another, achieving a sense of the somatic present even as abstract thought, the operation of the cogito or thinking self, is compelled to dis-enchant it. This distinction allows scholars of lived religion to recognize the important and powerful cultural work performed by the discourse of the cogito, which is commonly authorized by the dominant classes as male, educated, clerical, enlightened, secular, or scientific. The body must be disciplined or trained by that discourse, which reduces what the body perceives to signs or symbols. Theology allegorizes the body and its impulses in order to subordinate the sensible self to the abstract cogitations of the thinking self. The challenge is that perception seems to happen instantaneously, below the level of conscious control: we turn our eyes on the world and there it is, immediate and already in place. The sensible self autonomically performs its work, as processes that are involuntary, operating without the intervention of consciousness. Rational thought has long been tutored by philosophers and moralists alike to regard these processes as impulsive, unruly, and belonging to the less noble domain of the body. Sensation, not to mention desire, pleasure, fear, or anger, arises from below, as it were, and needs to be tested and controlled. Culture consists in one important respect as the protocols and strictures for doing so.[16]

But cultures are more than forms of repression. The life of feeling is more subtle than that. A material-culture approach to the study of religion is attuned to the nuanced range of felt life as it takes shape in the senses and the often unconscious career of the senses in ordering fields of human experience. If they are unconscious to those who live by them as well as to those who study religion, it is often because believers take their sense perceptions at face value, the better to take the world as given, and because scholars have been inclined to give greater credence to texts and philosophical constellations of ideas as the "real" nature of religions. But approached visually, religion begins with the datum that images act on human beings. They do so through the medium of the human body formed within a cultural setting (as Merleau-Ponty's use of the Christian Eucharist to characterize the physical immediacy

---

[16] An informative and concise treatment of phenomenology's relevance for the study of material culture is Julian Thomas, "Phenomenology and Material Culture," in *Handbook of Material Culture*, ed. Christopher Tilley et al. (London: Sage, 2006), 43–59.

of perception as "communion" clearly suggests). If the gesture that Merleau-Ponty described as the experience of anger works with that immediacy, it is because the gesture is seen through the medium of a common culture. The gesture is not an abstract signifier, but the felt unity of two historically constructed bodies, the one that gestures and the one experiencing the gesture, though in fact the gesture is apprehended within the matrix of the latter's historical formation. The one experiencing the gesture does not see a symbol to be decoded, but rather experiences the emotion that motivates the gesture. The body's knowledge operates as resonance or repetition rather than as representation.

Driven by the desire to understand how images and visual practices construct and maintain the worlds in which believers live, the visual study of religion is especially interested in what images do, which, as Merleau-Ponty's account of perception would urge, turns on the role the body plays in apprehending the world and discovering in it a sacred presence. Recall Beecher's embodied responses to sacred imagery at Oxford: he stood enthralled before the paintings, projected himself into their scenes, and witnessed the appearance of sacred persons in them. These responses highlight several different moments in which body and image engage one another, which are not, I believe, limited to the Christian construction of embodiment. In the first instance, an image situates the bodies of believers before it. Then it invites viewers to project their bodies into it. Finally, the image evokes bodies beyond or incarnate within it. Three general modes of embodiment may be said to comprise the visual construction of the sacred: the body before the image, the viewer's body entering the image, and the transcendent body materializing within the image. Each of these outlines a key instance of the devout viewer's relationship with the sacred as mediated by the image.

What I have in mind by the first, the *body before the image*, is the spatial setting of images, their display, their physical relation to viewers, and their deployment in visual practices. Think of the power of amulets and charms worn on the body. I once asked a man in Tokyo about his Buddhist medallion (see Figure 14.3), which he told me brought him good luck in his business of selling souvenirs to tourists near a major shrine to Kannon. He wore the amulet on his belt, hanging against his body. It was necessary that the amulet touch him, he explained, because it acted as a relay between himself and the spirit-deity it pictured. By touching the proprietor, the amulet conveyed the good fortune to him. His body was his sensible self, the face of his cogito. The act of beholding is seeing with the longing to hold, to touch, to cancel the difference between the body now and the desired body.

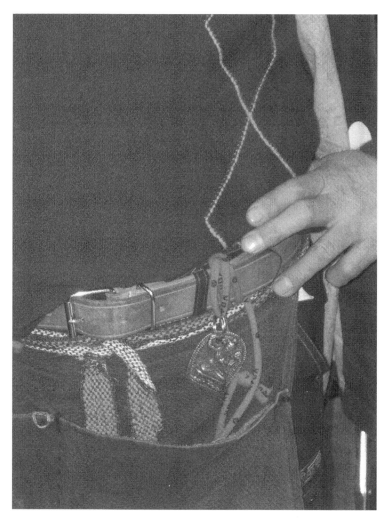

Figure 14.3. Buddhist amulet on antique proprietor's belt, Tokyo, 2004. Photo by author.

Images enable people to revise or re-vision their own bodies and therefore to come into a new relationship with themselves. By positioning themselves before images, people use images to help them imagine alternative versions of themselves. As an example of what I mean here, in a photograph by Lauren Greenfield, entitled *I Approve of Myself* (see Figure 14.4), a woman envisions a new self by relying on both a photograph and a mirror to perform a transformative act of imagination. The photograph captures a visual instance of modern self-help therapy,

Figure 14.4. Lauren Greenfield, *I Approve of Myself*, 2002, photograph. Courtesy of the photographer.

which, if not explicitly religious in this instance, is deeply involved in the personal spirituality of millions of American consumers today, which, as fans of Oprah Winfrey know, is a spirituality of personal empowerment that is particularly important to many women. Greenfield's photograph reflects this as it powerfully captures the practice of constructing personal identity from the resources of mass-produced imagery. With one hand, the woman, a portion of whose face we glimpse in the mirror, holds the image of a fashion model's face, touching what she wants to become. Printed on the piece of paper in the lower left is the message of personal affirmation: I approve of myself. The body before the image is a pliable and transformable self seeking in its relationship to the imaged other a rebirth that can be compelling for the hope and self-empowerment it offers.

By the *body in the image*, I have in mind the intimate fit between the body and an image such that the image welcomes the habits, feelings, and expectations that a body brings to it as a way of inhabiting the image, which is to say, to know it corporally. This fit takes place by means of two broad operations, empathy and anthropomorphism. Both are ways of intuiting what another body feels, thinks, or intends, although they operate in rather different fashions. In 1585, Hans Mack of Nuremberg, a professional colorist of prints, tinted an engraving of the scourged Christ by Albrecht Dürer (see Figure 14.1), accenting the abused body with flicks of red, which is also visible on the column. The two tormenters exert themselves with wild gestures as Jesus meekly submits. On the far right, a well-dressed man bearing the features of Dürer himself quietly gazes directly at viewers. The connection with onlookers outside of the picture was likely intentional. The hand-painted print, reflecting a common practice among devout Catholic and Lutheran Germans in the sixteenth century, customized the suffering of Jesus for the viewer's empathetic devotion.[17]

The image recalls the cover illustration from a sermon of 1519 by Martin Luther on the contemplation of the passion of Christ.[18] Luther engaged the listeners of his sermon in just this sort of visceral participation in the redeemer's suffering, addressing his audience as if the image of the scourged and crucified Jesus were before them. "When you see nails piercing Christ's hands," Luther preached, "you can be certain that it is your work. When you behold his crown of thorns, you may rest assured that these are your evil thoughts."[19] The body in the image is not a lifeless symbol, but the body one touches imaginatively, shamefully in this case, and therefore touches one's own body in turn. As a kind of recrimination, the image touches the convicted viewer, thereby placing the viewer's self in relation to the humiliated Jesus. We note in Figure 14.1 that the tormenter of the left does not bear the malevolent expression that his counterpart does, suggesting perhaps that he stands in for Luther's audience and every devout viewer of the image. To look at this image, then, is to be drawn into a wave of gazes: one looks upon Christ and the tormentor looking pitifully upon him even as the artist looks askance at the viewer. The believer's presence is implicated in this image. Seeing is not dispassionate viewing from afar, but prickling, visceral engagement in the suffering of Jesus. On this point, we might return to Greenfield's photograph (Figure 14.4) to regard the eye within the image, which returns

---

[17] An insightful study of hand-colored sixteenth-century prints is Susan Dackerman, *Painted Prints: The Revelation of Color in Northern Renaissance and Baroque Engravings, Etchings and Woodcuts* (University Park: Pennsylvania State University Press, 2002).

[18] Individually published pamphlets of the sermon, which first appeared in Wittenberg, carried a Cranach print of the crucifixion, or, as in the case of an edition from Nuremberg that appeared in 1521, a copy of a Dürer engraving of the Ecce Homo. For a discussion, see Dieter Koepplin, "Lutherische Glaubensbilder," in *Martin Luther und die Reformation in Deutschland*, ed. Gerhard Bott (Frankfurt am Main: Insel, 1983), 352–3.

[19] Martin Luther, "A Meditation on Christ's Passion," in *Luther's Works American Edition*, vol. 42, ed. Martin O. Dietrich (Philadelphia: Fortress Press, 1969), 9.

the unseen sitter's gaze as the body within the image that is both her own and the one that she is making, and being made by.

The second domain of examples of the body in the image consists of the anthropomorphic response to images. We see human forms in all kinds of things, projecting our own forms and feelings onto other human beings, as well as onto animals and onto inanimate objects such as rocks, trees, and television sets. It is, anthropologists and cognitive psychologists tell us, one of the most common ways in which human beings make sense of the world around them; "to make sense" in this context means seeking out what is important to them and evaluating a thing's relevance for them.[20] We tend to see what matters to us, and faces matter to human beings because they are dense semantic fields that register a nuanced range of feelings and intentions. But making sense is a process that occurs squarely within particular cultures. As Marcel Mauss argued in a seminal essay entitled "Techniques of the Body," which has been widely commented upon by anthropologists, the body is trained and disciplined in distinctive habits that reflect its cultural formation.[21] This means that we each carry within us the dispositions we acquired sitting at the table; competing in sports; and watching our parents and siblings sit, move, talk, laugh, and worship. We rely on this lexicon of techniques to construct and maintain our life-worlds, for feeling our way through the world, for seeing, and for evaluating whatever happens about us. These body habits are not forms of analysis, but ways of ordering ourselves and our environment into recognizable or familiar terms.

So it is not so strange, perhaps, that many people driving by a billboard in Atlanta several years ago morphed a forkful of spaghetti into the face of Jesus.[22] Why Jesus? Because in the Christian imaginary that face looms large. It is a face with currency, keyed to deeply rooted feelings of compassion, guilt, shame, strength, and hope. Seeing that face is something Christians are predisposed to do. In other religious cultures, smears and smudges won't be morphed into gaunt, bearded male faces recognized as Jesus, but as someone else.[23] Children animate dolls

[20] On anthropomorphism, see Stewart Elliott Guthrie, *Faces in the Clouds: A New Theory of Religion* (New York: Oxford University Press, 1993); on empathy, see Ellen Dissanayake, *Homo Aestheticus: Where Art Comes From and Why* (Seattle: University of Washington Press, 1995 [1992]), 140–93.

[21] Marcel Mauss, "Techniques of the Body," *Economy and Society* 2 (1973): 70–88. The essay originally appeared in 1935.

[22] The billboard image is reproduced in Guthrie, *Faces in the Clouds*, Fig. 5–37.

[23] A fascinating example is the discernment of Qur'anic text in images of the Sufi Shaykh Amadou Bamba of Senegal; see Roberts and Nooter Roberts, *A Saint in the City*, 55–59. I have examined variant interpretations of images embedded in a popular image of Jesus, in Morgan, *Visual Piety*, 124–51.

and toys and sticks and stones. But so do grown-up children. Adults stroke objects, hit them, push them away, talk to them, shout at them, and presumptuously address them as versions of themselves. Adults do this not because they are infantile, but because, as Merleau-Ponty noted, the sentient self regards the world as calling to it, as beckoning the body's response. Perception is a kind of colloquy between body and environment.[24] Not only are images alive, they actively direct themselves to us, if inchoately, inviting our engagement with them in what he called a "vague beckoning." One thinks of Roland Barthes's notion of each photograph exerting or projecting a *punctum* that punctures the body of the viewer.[25] But this power of the image to wound the viewer is hardly limited to photographs. Images act on us physically by reaching out to touch us, even to hurt us. The relationship is not abstract, but embodied; it is not conscious and intentional, but visceral, all but unconscious, requiring the viewer to struggle with the image's allure or menace as a vague but undeniable presence.

Consider, for example, the many pictures of Jesus, Mary, and the saints in the Christian tradition or deities and holy persons in Hindu sacred imagery who gaze directly and fixedly at the viewer.[26] Sufi Shaykh Amadou Bamba has been painted countless times by devoted artists who produce iconic imagery that is prized by his followers, the Mourides, for its direct gaze (see Figure 14.5). His images are displayed, kissed, and touched for the *baraka*, or blessing, of the saint that may issue from such intersensory tactile acts of visual piety.[27] These gazes charge the image with a presence that is felt in the bodies of viewers as a penetrating look that establishes an immediate relationship with viewers, so immediate that the image is experienced as more than a representation. Whether a Christian icon, a Sufi devotional image, or a Hindu

[24] Merleau-Ponty takes as an example the sensation of color or feeling an object: "It is my gaze which subtends colour, and the movement of my hand which subtends the object's form.... Thus a sensible datum which is on the point of being felt sets a kind of muddled problem for my body to solve. I must find the attitude which will provide it with the means of becoming determinate, of showing up as blue; I must find the reply to a question which is obscurely expressed" (Merleau-Ponty, *Phenomenology of Perception*, 248–9).

[25] Roland Barthes, *Camera Lucida: Reflections on Photography*, trans. Richard Howard (New York: Hill and Wang, Noonday Press, 1981), 27.

[26] For studies of *darīan* in Hindu popular imagery, see Diana L. Eck, *Darśan: Seeing the Divine Image in India*, 3rd Edition (New York: Columbia University Press, 1998); Christopher Pinney, *"Photos of the Gods": The Printed Image and Political Struggle in India* (London: Reaktion, 2004); and Kajri Jain, *Gods in the Bazaar: The Economies of Indian Calendar Art* (Durham, NC: Duke University Press, 2007).

[27] On the blessing afforded by images of Bamba, see Roberts and Nooter Roberts, *A Saint in the City*, 21–8.

Figure 14.5. Alioune Sow, *Sheik Amadou Bamba*, 2004, painting on glass. Collection of the author.

divine image enabling *darśan*, the image compels a response from the devout viewer that becomes part of the experience of a material presence of the sacred.

Both empathy and anthropomorphism are obviously projective human activities. But I do not wish to ignore the much more interactive relationship that people experience with the world around them. The meaning they find is not purely subjective projection. Human beings evolved in tandem with the habitats in which they have existed.

Moreover, human beings may be said to court the world with beauty, form, style, or design in order to secure a place within it, to identify a welcoming niche within the natural world, a world both of their own building and a world that in a very real sense builds them. We project our feelings and thoughts, but we also attend to what we encounter, opening ourselves to the touch and presence of the physical world, to its ability to move us, nurture us, and provide what we need to survive. All forms of material culture are an intermediate way of belonging to the world, of finding an enduring place within it. Empathy and anthropomorphism are therefore only half of a relationship. They are aesthetic overtures, culturally varying ways of hailing the world and preparing to receive its reply.

Finally, I mean by *body beyond the image* the collective corpus, the public or social body, the nation, clan, divine or sacred community, the larger historical entity or tradition into which viewing an image places viewers. This body originates from beyond the image, but is evoked by the viewer's relationship with the image, which brings the viewer into relation with the transcendent. This form of visual presence may be temporary or enduring. Cult images, objects, or spaces may hold the presence of the deity in an abiding way or the sacred may be temporally evoked in ritual performance. Such images establish the viewer's relation to ethereal entities such as apparitions, dreams, the mythic past, or the apocalyptic future; or they evoke essentially noncorporeal realities such as nations, peoples, or spirit beings. Patriotic ceremonies, which readily become sacred phenomena in civil religion or nationalistic cultus, offer an example of the performative image's embodiment of the immaterial. American citizens are fond of their national flag because it evokes "nationhood." To exercise and display flag veneration, they commonly will organize into reverent rows and salute; crowds will arrange themselves in color-coded configurations that represent the image of the flag; solemn audiences will stand at attention at sports events; and millions of American school children will participate in the morning ritual of the Pledge of Allegiance (see Figure 14.6). The abstract and immaterial nation becomes incarnate in the correctly disciplined bodies of the patriotic such that the image beyond the body and the image before the body merge into a single ritual body. The gathered corpus of patriots forms the collective presence of nationhood in the ritual of civil religion. The spiritual body dissolves when the rite concludes, but has been secured by means of the daily rite.

Embedded in these forms of embodiment is the dynamic relationship of three fundamental ingredients of vision, which might be considered

Figure 14.6. Frances Benjamin Johnston, *Pledge of Allegiance to the Flag*, 1899, Washington, DC. Photo courtesy of the Library of Congress, LC-USZ62-14693.

the primary conditions of visibility: artifact, practice, and paradigm. The three fit together very closely, so snugly that to see an image is for a believer to see the referent in an immediate and compelling way. The image, or *artifact*, is looked at, adored, fondled, used in teaching, hated, avoided, even destroyed; these are all *practices* enacting epistemological, perceptual, moral, and aesthetic dispositions. These dispositions, in turn, are *paradigms* that direct behavior, confirming the rightness or wrongness of a practice and the credibility or repugnance of an image. A practice may be a carefully scripted, institutionally enforced ritual such as venerating an icon on an altar, or it may be an unprecedented, spontaneous act like tearing an offensive image from the wall and pitching it into a waste can. Visual practice is the action done with the image, an action that has efficacy precisely because it does something to, through, or by means of an image.

As an example of how paradigms function, consider the way in which a hypothetical viewer might respond to Hans Mack's image of Jesus (see Figure 14.1). A paradigm performs epistemologically like a list of questions and answers, the kind of interrogation that Merleau-Ponty argued is the nature of perception, a "vague beckoning" to which one is drawn to engage and to reply.[28] Human beings are inclined to regard an object as exhibiting a certain kind of potency, which must be properly classified in order that we might recognize the object's value. Knowing what something is begins with determining its relevance for us or its attitude toward us. So the very first concerns that occupy us when encountering something are manifestly existential. We wish to know whether the object is alive or dead, harmful or benign, spiritually charged or inert, menacing or nutritious, alluring or repellant. We proceed to determine the object's existential register by looking at it, by imagining its softness or hardness, by denoting its fragrance or odor, by attending to any sounds that it makes. Sight is especially useful for this purpose because it may commence the paradigmatic query at a protective distance; then, having determined it is safe or compelling to do so, human vision accommodates moving closer for more detailed inspection.

The initial paradigmatic determination proceeds as a series of rudimentary queries, which may be largely unconscious, intuitive, and instantaneous. I have compared them to questions, but they are actually visceral inquiries, felt or intuitive ponderings. Merleau-Ponty described perception as just such a colloquy with objects. What does this object want, the viewer wishes to know. These ponderings seek answers to compelling concerns about the nature of an object as the viewer's culture inclines one to inquire: Is this object alive? Does it pose a threat to me? Can I eat it? What will happen if I grab it? Asking the questions I do and answering them in the way that I do invokes paradigmatic dispositions that I share with all humans by virtue of biology and with many but not all by virtue of culture and history. All human beings will want to know whether the object can physically harm them, but in asking what will happen if I take the object, I betray my participation in a particular culture that apprehends the object within an ecology composed of such things as ownership, control, property, and authority.

Once I feel satisfied that the object does not pose a threat to me and is no good for eating, I may ask "What does it mean?" At this point, my inquiry shifts from the preponderance of the sensible self to greater engagement with the cogito. The two realms are rarely completely isolated from one another, though it is not difficult to imagine where each dominates. But as the shift takes place, the object begins to change from a motivated sign to an arbitrary one. Corresponding to this change, the symbol bears less visceral relation to the body of its users and therefore

---

[28] Merleau-Ponty, *Phenomenology of Perception*, 248.

plays a less intimate role in the construction and experience of the self. Symbols operate more discursively than icons, charms, talismanic objects, or works of art. They command less presence and enjoy less focus as objects of thought or feeling, the better to serve as the medium for thinking and discourse, which is the business of the cogito. In service to abstraction, the symbol vanishes. Its users are interested in what it means, not what it is.

In the realm of the cogito, belief pertains insofar as I hold the image qua symbol to signify correctly or to signify a doctrine I believe to be true. But this belief is no longer the visceral disposition of the sensible self that finds in the image the material presence of the sacred. Belief as assent is the cogito's affirmation of truth, not the body's relationship with a living reality. Religion is both – integrating body and reason in affirming the same thing.

The argument here has been that religion happens materially in relationships prompted by encounters with images. Seeing images draws the viewer into imagined forms of embodiment, connecting to the sacred other via empathy or interacting with it by means of anthropomorphism. The viewer also participates in the physical creation of a collective or social body, the perceived or imagined community of believers. Rather than regard the sacred as a transcendent or spiritual reality that must be mediated in order to be grasped, I propose that the study of the felt life of religion commence with the body's engagement with images and other artifacts. It is too easy for the body to be forgotten when religion is framed as an intellectual matter or as the volitional act of affirming a dogma. If the body is not included from the outset in the analytical framework, it is quickly dismissed as irrelevant, or worse, as an unruly distraction. The better strategy is to examine how a group produces its own weave of feeling, thought, volition, sensation, emotion, and action. The point is not to subordinate reason or discourse, but to determine how the cogito contributes to the apprehension of the sacred that takes form in sensible experience. Often the very "techniques of the body" enter the repertoire of the child with rationale and discourse attached to them. Why one genuflects, why one takes a particular posture in prayer, why father and mother sit where they do at the dinner table – all of these practices are imbued with reasons, participate in an ideology of everyday life. The gesture is not a symbol, but an amalgamation of body and symbol. Presentation and representation are affixed to one another. Sometimes they conflict with each other; sometimes one is clearly subordinated to the other; often the two are intricately joined in a way that only long cultural histories can make possible. But embedded in these hierarchies, tensions, and unresolved competitions are the embodied cultures of belief that we seek to understand.

The study of lived religion benefits from scrutiny of the *aesthetic* operation of belief in order to explore how perception and feeling inter-mingle with abstraction and other forms of consciousness to render belief much more than an intellectual assent to doctrines. By aesthetic, I do not intend the exercise of taste as the disinterested judgment of the beautiful, as the term has come to mean since the eighteenth cen-tury. Instead, I have in mind the older etymological sense of the word, as recent scholarship has reminded us: *aesthetic* was coined from the Greek word *aisthesis*, which means perception.[29] Aesthetic knowledge is intuitive or felt, constituting a mode of consciousness that corresponds to Merleau-Ponty's sentient subject. Attending to this aspect of religion means focusing on popular practices, on the arts, on ritual performance in informal as well as formal settings, on all aspects of the materiality of belief – images, food, dress, the built environment, the soundscape, and the landscape. These all convey the daily rhythms of activity that form children and adults in the sensuous life of a religion, shaping, coloring, and organizing their relations with one another and with the divine. It is there, at work in the dramas of everyday life, in the visual communion of the body and world, unfolding in the intersecting gazes of eye meeting eye, that the look of the sacred happens.

Select Bibliography

Bland, Kalman P. *The Artless Jew: Medieval and Modern Affirmations and Denials of the Visual*. Princeton, NJ: Princeton University Press, 2000.

Damasio, Antonio R. *The Feeling of What Happens: Body and Emotion in the Making of Consciousness*. San Diego, CA: Harcourt, 1999.

Dissanayake, Ellen. *Homo Aestheticus: Where Art Comes From and Why*. Seattle: University of Washington Press, 1995 [1992].

Eck, Diana L. *Darśan: Seeing the Divine Image in India*. 3rd Edition. New York: Columbia University Press, 1998.

Freedberg, David. *The Power of Images: Studies in the History and Theory of Response*. Chicago: University of Chicago Press, 1989.

---

[29] See S. Brent Plate, ed., *Religion, Art, and Visual Culture: A Cross-Cultural Reader* (New York: Palgrave Macmillan, 2002), 19–26; Jojada Verrips, "Aisthesis & An-aesthesia," in *Off the Edge: Experiments in Cultural Analysis*, ed. Orvar Löfgren and Richard Wilk (Copenhagen: Museum Tusculanum Press, 2006), 29–37; Birgit Meyer and Jojada Verrips, "Aesthetics," in *Key Words in Religion, Media, and Culture*, ed. David Morgan (London: Routledge, 2008), 20–30; and David Morgan, ed., *Religion and Material Culture: The Matter of Belief* (London: Routledge, 2009).

Guthrie, Stewart Elliott. *Faces in the Clouds: A New Theory of Religion*. New York: Oxford University Press, 1993.

Jain, Kajri. *Gods in the Bazaar: The Economies of Indian Calendar Art (Objects/Histories)*. Durham, NC: Duke University Press, 2007.

Merleau-Ponty, Maurice. *Phenomenology of Perception*. Translated by Colin Smith. London: Routledge, 1962.

Morgan, David. *Visual Piety: A History and Theory of Popular Religious Images*. Berkeley: University of California Press, 1998.

  Ed. *Key Words in Religion, Media and Culture*. London: Routledge, 2008.

  Ed. *Religion and Material Culture: The Matter of Belief*. London: Routledge, 2009.

Pinney, Christopher. *"Photos of the Gods": The Printed Image and Political Struggle in India*. London: Reaktion, 2004.

Plate, S. Brent. *Religion, Art, and Visual Culture: A Cross-Cultural Reader*. New York: Palgrave, 2002.

Roberts, Allen F., Mary Nooter Roberts, Gassia Armenian, and Ousmane Guèye. *A Saint in the City: Sufi Arts of Urban Senegal*. Los Angeles: UCLA Fowler Museum of Cultural History, 2003.

15 Reforming culture: law and religion today

WINNIFRED FALLERS SULLIVAN

I. INTRODUCTION

Law, like religion, is a virtually universal feature of human society –
law, that is, understood in its simplest sense, as the organizing structure for collective life. All societies have law. Law, like religion, is also
enormously varied across space and time and has been variously theorized throughout history. Indeed, there is much evidence that, as with
religious pluralism, legal pluralism is a better description of the natural
state of the case than the singular "rule of law" now often imagined and
celebrated as a unitary and ahistorical *desideratum*.[1] We may learn more,
in other words, about what the great legal comparativist Karl Llewellyn
called "law-stuff,"[2] in all societies, by assuming multiplicity, whatever
the structure of official power, than by accepting the narrow positivist
reading of law employed by most scholars today. Yet law continues to
be understood by many to derive its authority and definition exclusively
from the sovereign modern state, pushing to the side and to the past
many rival normative structures – including religion.

The nature of law is, of course, the subject of an extensive literature.
I begin with law in the context of this book because it seems often to

---

[1] For a classic account of the ways in which human societies constantly generate
and destroy norms, and the narratives that carry them, see Robert M. Cover, "The
Supreme Court, 1982 Term – Foreword: *Nomos* and Narrative," *Harvard Law Review*
97, 1 (1983): 4–68. See also John R. Bowen, *Islam, Law, and Equality in Indonesia: An
Anthropology of Public Reasoning* (Cambridge: Cambridge University Press, 2003), for
an ethnographic account of how legal pluralism works in practice.
[2] Karl N. Llewellyn and E. Adamson Hoebel, *The Cheyenne Way: Conflict and Case
Law in Primitive Jurisprudence* (Norman: University of Oklahoma Press, 1941).

I am grateful to my colleague Dianne Avery and to Barry Sullivan for their careful comments
on the chapter and to my colleagues at the University at Buffalo Law School who participated in a workshop discussion of the FLDS case that forms the main example in this chapter. I am also grateful to Susan Mangold for helping to educate me about child welfare laws.
An earlier version of part of this chapter was published on *The Immanent Frame*: http://
www.ssrc.org/blogs/immanent_frame/2008/06/26/reforming-culture/.

be the case that scholars of religion who see religion as multiplicitous and variously embedded in cultures nonetheless accept modern law's account of itself as lacking those qualities, notwithstanding overwhelming evidence to the contrary. One's model of law, as of religion, necessarily affects how one understands the interaction of law and religion and, importantly, the possibility of their separation.

On the modern statist model, law and religion occupy separate realms, and law is understood to be "naturally" secular. The intermingling of law and religion is, on this account, primitive or premodern. There are varying explanations as to how this modern division was achieved, but the division is arguably central to our understanding as moderns.[3] Religion, under this modern dispensation, is that which is not law, and the notion of religious law, an oxymoron.[4]

Various social and political changes, including a new openness to reconsideration of the inevitability – even the fact – of secularization, as well as the increasing salience and presence of Islam, among other factors, are challenging this notion. For Islam and Judaism, law is evidently explicitly and formally central to religious practice and self-understanding, but all religious ways of life supply anthropologies and cosmologies, "narratives," on Robert Cover's reading,[5] that both underlie the "secular" law of their host societies and generate norms that challenge the secularity of law. The secularization of law under these conditions is best seen thus as both a deliberate and an incomplete project, one that was in many ways coterminous with the invention of the modern state.[6]

[3]   For example, for Henry Maine, the great Victorian comparativist, progressive society was famously achieved in the movement from status to contract. See Henry Sumner Maine, *Ancient Law* (New York: Cosimo, 2005 [1861]). For another account of how this separation came to be, see Bruno Latour, *We Have Never Been Modern*, trans. Catherine Porter (Cambridge, MA: Harvard University Press, 1993).

[4]   One result of understanding religious law to be an anomaly is that it prevents comparison of the legal aspects of religious law and secular law. Lawrence Rosen argues, in this connection, that the category "religious law" lumps together legal systems that have very little in common, other than that of being politically denied the status of real law on the ground that they derive their authority beyond the social contract. Rosen himself sees *qadi*-administered Muslim law as legally very much like the common law, and therefore distinct from the code law of continental Europe and its legal diaspora. This insight allows one to see both the religiousness of the common law and the legalness of Islamic law. Lawrence Rosen, *The Anthropology of Justice: Law as Culture in Islamic Society* (Cambridge: Cambridge University Press, 1989). See Peter Goodrich, *Oedipus Lex: Psychoanalysis, History, Law* (Berkeley: University of California Press, 1995), for a reading of religious themes in the history of the common law.

[5]   See Cover, "The Supreme Court, 1982 Term – Foreword: *Nomos* and Narrative."

[6]   For an account of this history, see Winnifred Fallers Sullivan and Robert A. Yelle, "Law and Religion: Overview Article," in *Encyclopedia of Religion*, ed. Lindsay Jones, 2nd Edition (Detroit: Thomson Gale, 2005), vol. 8: 5325–32. See also Robert A. Yelle,

Americans, for the most part, understand the modern division of labor between law and religion to be definitively and foundationally structured and governed by the religion clauses of the First Amendment to the United States Constitution. For the most part, they also believe that the text of these clauses effectively guarantees both the separation of church and state and virtually complete religious freedom.[7] Indeed, Americans believe themselves to enjoy both a healthy democratic politics and a flourishing and vital religious life because of the First Amendment separation of church and state and the guarantee of the free exercise of religion. For both ordinary citizens and most scholars of the United States, what is most distinctive about American religion is that it is untainted by association with the state or with law. It is American limited government and deregulation at its best, many would say.

Although the Supreme Court has been the chief interpreter of the First Amendment religion clauses over the last sixty years or so, its record on this subject has long been deeply unsatisfying to many people across the political and religious spectrum, perhaps even to the Court itself.[8] The Court's forays into this area necessarily involved it in the often messy business of distinguishing religion and nonreligion. Recent cases suggest, however, that the Supreme Court, always reluctant to define religion, is now getting itself out of the business of deciding what religion is legal and what religion is not legal. The Free Exercise Clause is now understood to mean only that laws must be neutral and universal,

---

"Bentham's Fictions: Canon and Idolatry in the Genealogy of Law," *Yale Journal of Law & the Humanities* 17 (2005): 151–79; and Winnifred Fallers Sullivan, Robert A. Yelle, and Mateo Taussig-Rubbo, eds., *After Secular Law* (Palo Alto, CA: Stanford University Press, 2011).

[7] The text of the First Amendment begins: "Congress shall make no law respecting an establishment of religion or prohibiting the free exercise thereof...." These words are known as the "religion clauses." While it is today popularly understood that some religious practice is not protected, that set is understood to be very small, encompassing only extremely antisocial religious practices. The United States, according to this popular myth, has never known religious persecution, although there is much contrary evidence.

[8] Significantly, it was not until 1940 that the religion clauses of the First Amendment, which on their face are directed to "Congress," were applied to the states. In 1940, in its decision in *Cantwell v. Connecticut*, 310 U.S. 296, the Supreme Court held that the Fourteenth Amendment – intended, among other things, to guarantee due process to citizens of the states after the Civil War – "incorporated" the religion clauses. Before the resulting federalization of law governing religion in 1940, religion in the United States was largely regulated by state and local law and state constitutions. For a celebratory account of what she calls the "popular constitutionalism" that drove the post 1940 religion clause litigation in the U.S. Supreme Court, see Sarah Barringer Gordon, *The Spirit of the Law: Religious Voices and the Constitution in Modern America* (Cambridge, MA: Harvard University Press, 2010).

not discriminatory. No special judicial exemptions to laws of general application will be given to those who claim religious motivations for their actions.[9] With respect to the Establishment Clause, the school voucher and faith-based initiative decisions suggest that no particular disability is to be laid on religious institutions in their dealings with the government just because they identify or are identified as religious.[10]

There are a variety of ways to interpret this recent move by the Court. Most importantly, in my view, the new jurisprudence reflects a deep and very American commitment to equality, but it also reflects a real pragmatism with respect to the impossibility of drawing such lines. Both factors underlie what is, in effect, a constitutional withdrawal from the business of distinguishing Americans on the basis of their religious commitments, or lack thereof, whether for the purpose of ensuring free exercise or to effect disestablishment. The new jurisprudence may also reflect a change in the phenomenology of religion in the United States. The churches (and their counterparts for other religious communities) no longer occupy the place they once did. Religious authority is increasingly understood to have shifted decisively from institutions to individuals. Without a "church" in the traditional sense, the "state" arguably has no body from which to separate itself. Disestablishment is impossible. Without churches, there are also no longer religious authorities to determine orthodoxy for the purposes of defining an "exercise of religion" and religious freedom is impossible.[11]

To legal and political theorists, of course, deregulation – or disestablishment, as it is called in the church–state area – does not mean the absence of law or the absence of regulation. It means a different kind of law and a different kind of regulation. Because activities or industries are not actively regulated by top-down, direct government agency does not mean that they are not governed and shaped by law in myriad ways. What is sometimes called "soft law" or "the new governance" today encompasses a wide variety of private regulatory activity and private–public partnerships that set standards and police activity across many domains, domestically and internationally, including food and drug protection, environmental efforts, business and trade practices, manufacturing standards, labor and employment, financial activities, and social customs,

9 *Employment Division v. Smith*, 494 U.S. 872 (1990).
10 *Zelman v. Simmons-Harris*, 536 U.S. 639 (2002). The court has also ended special standing for cases brought under the establishment clause. *Hein v. FFRF*, 551 U.S. 587 (2007).
11 See Winnifred Fallers Sullivan, *The Impossibility of Religious Freedom* (Princeton, NJ: Princeton University Press, 2005).

among others. In the absence of formal church–state negotiation, religion is being shaped and changed by such law. "Lived law," one might say, continuously acts on "lived religion."[12]

Deregulation of religion is not a uniquely American phenomenon, of course. The shift in religious authority from institutions to individuals, and the resulting naturalization of religion into the rest of the social and cultural field managed by government and its private partners, can be seen across the world.[13] But deregulation takes a particular form in the U.S. context because of its distinctive history.[14]

If one shifts one's attention, then, from the Court and its opinions – the high priesthood and scriptural commentary of American constitutionalism – to the ways in which religion is actually managed – "disciplined" by law, one might say – in the United States on a daily basis, one can see the legal shaping of religion at other sites of legal regulation, formal and informal. A different understanding of the intersection of law and religion becomes apparent. Documenting the formative effect of these other kinds of law on the phenomenology of religion is a large and complex task. In this chapter, I will illustrate some of the possibilities of taking such an approach using, as an example, the legal regime evident in the 2008 raid on the Yearning for Zion ranch in Texas.

II. YEARNING FOR ZION

In early April 2008, the Texas Department of Family and Protective Services (DFPS), responding to an anonymous phone call reporting the sexual abuse of a teenaged girl,[15] began "the largest child protection case documented in the history of the United States."[16] Over the course of

---

[12] Or, rather, religion is affected by "law in action," as it is known to some legal sociologists. This phenomenon is not entirely new. Religion has arguably always been more radically disestablished in the United States than most other places, and therefore has been subject to the shaping effect of such "horizontal" regulation.

[13] See David M. Engel and Jaruwan S. Engel, *Tort, Custom and Karma: Globalization and Legal Consciousness in Thailand* (Palo Alto, CA: Stanford University Press, 2010), for a fascinating account of the changing nature and relationship of legal and religious subjectivities in contemporary Thailand.

[14] Exemplary historical studies of the interaction between legal and religious formations in the United States are Mark de Wolfe Howe, *The Garden and the Wilderness: Religion and Government in American Constitutional History* (Chicago: University of Chicago Press, 1965), and Sarah Barringer Gordon, *The Mormon Question: Polygamy and Constitutional Conflict in Nineteenth Century America* (Chapel Hill: University of North Carolina Press, 2002).

[15] This call was later determined to be a hoax.

[16] Texas authorities published a report of this event in December 2008: "Eldorado Investigation: A Report from the Texas Department of Family and Protective Services

three days, child welfare employees and Texas state troopers entered the Yearning for Zion ranch near Eldorado in western Texas, searched and questioned its inhabitants, and took into protective custody all of the more than four hundred children on the ranch. DFPS then initiated court proceedings to convert the emergency custody into permanent foster care arrangements – foster care arrangements that were intended to facilitate the conversion of those children to what was termed "mainstream culture."

What, exactly, was wrong, according to the Texas authorities, with the Yearning for Zion ranch – home to a group that identifies itself with the Fundamentalist Church of Jesus Christ of Latter Day Saints (FLDS)[17] – as a place to raise children? Under current federal and state law, although parents in the United States have wide-ranging rights to raise children as they see fit, it is plain that the State of Texas had the right, even the duty, with respect to any child for whom there was reason to believe that there was ongoing physical abuse, to intervene. Experts in child custody law now estimate that such legally defensible reasons for intervention might have existed for a few of the teenaged girls at the ranch. But what about the more than four hundred other children, boys and girls, ranging in age from under a year to seventeen, who were removed from the ranch in that early-April raid? Generally, children in the United States cannot be removed from their families unless there is an immediate risk of physical harm. Indeed, federal law now provides that even in cases of

December 22, 2008," available for download on their website: http://www.dfps.state. tx.us/about/news/2008/eldorado/default.asp (accessed May 30, 2011).

[17] The Fundamentalist Church of the Latter Day Saints is the name given to itself by one of the groups that broke away from the Church of Jesus Christ of Latter Day Saints at the end of the nineteenth century at the time of the Manifesto. The Manifesto proclaimed a new revelation that prohibited the practice of plural marriage within the LDS community. That revelation is regarded by many as having been closely tied to and motivated by the demands being made on the Mormon community by the federal government in connection with the campaign for Utah statehood. Several groups left the LDS Church at that time, declaring themselves to be faithful to the earlier revelation affirming plural marriage and, significantly, declaring their leaders to be competent to seal such marriages. (The claim to such competence, in Mormon terms, depends on disputed accounts of the existence of an unbroken apostolic succession.) Several such groups continued to practice plural marriage, mostly in the states of the intermountain West, although elsewhere in the United States as well. (For a history of FLDS marriage practices, see Marianne T. Watson, "The 1948 Secret Marriage of Louis J. Barlow: Origins of FLDS Placement Marriage," *Dialogue: A Journal of Mormon Thought* 40 [2007]: 83–136.) With the decline in prosecution of extramarital cohabitation generally in the United States, whether through bigamy laws or through laws against fornication and adultery, such arrangements are increasingly tolerated by local law enforcement and thus, if not formally licensed, are permitted as long as the "marriages" are all between consenting adults.

prior physical abuse, there should be a presumption against placement outside the home.[18] Other interventions, including in-home counseling, are now preferred when officials have reason to believe that children are suffering from abuse.

How did Texas authorities justify such a massive intrusion into the private lives of families, an intervention that eerily reminded many onlookers of both the disastrous Waco, Texas, raid on the Branch Davidians fifteen years earlier, and the Short Creek Raid against Mormon polygamists some fifty years before in northern Arizona, both of which were also instigated to protect children?[19] Texas authorities said they were worried about the "culture" at the ranch. At the subsequent court hearing, a mandated follow-up hearing in the case of any emergency intervention, DFPS, lacking direct evidence of any physical abuse, relied upon the testimony of the investigating social workers that "there is a *culture* of young girls being pregnant by old men." The Supreme Court of Texas, in its May 29 decision ordering the return of the children, described the state as being concerned that the ranch had "a *culture* of polygamy and of directing girls younger than eighteen to enter spiritual unions with older men and have children."[20] State authorities repeatedly said during the hearings that the danger to all of the children, but even to the children who were not adolescent girls, derived from the "culture." It is dangerous, they said, to raise children of any age or sex in a culture that is committed to polygamous and underage marriage.

What is a *"culture* of polygamy"? Is it separate from or the same as the rest of the culture of the Yearning for Zion ranch? How is it related to what Texas authorities called "mainstream *culture"*? What legal authority does Texas have to regulate *culture*? And why are they talking about culture anyway? The word *culture* performed an amazing amount of

---

[18] Child welfare laws have changed over the course of American history. Such law always reflects the joint effort of legislators and academic experts, who in turn reflect changing understandings of developmental and behavior psychology – and religion – and changing notions of the capacity of government agencies to provide adequate care.

[19] For a comparison between the Yearning for Zion raid and the 1953 "Short Creek raid," written by an expert in child custody law, see Linda F. Smith, "Kidnapped from that Land II: A Comparison of Two Raids to Save the Children from the Polygamists," *Children's Legal Rights Journal* 30 (Spring 2010): 32–61. Smith explains that "[t]he Short Creek raid occurred before the advent of statutes requiring investigations of suspected child abuse. Instead, the raid was planned by the Arizona governor and investigated by a Los Angeles detective agency pretending to be a movie company scouting the site and looking for 'extras' thus photographing everyone in the community" (42).

[20] *In re Texas Department of Family and Protective Services, relator.* Texas Supreme Court No. 08-0391 (May 29, 2008) (emphasis added).

work in the course of the various efforts to construct a narrative about these events and to justify the state's activities.[21]

While the Texas authorities were condemning the ranch for its "culture," they were at the same time at pains to demonstrate that they were respecting the children's religious freedom and accommodating what they termed their "unique" cultural needs. During the time that the Yearning for Zion children were in the state's care – first held as a group with some of their mothers in a sports arena in San Angelo, Texas, and subsequently in individual foster homes – the Texas Department of Family and Protective Services quickly produced draft documents to guide childcare personnel who had custody of the children, documents which they posted on their website: "Cultural Awareness Guide for Children from Eldorado" and "Model for Care for Children from the Yearning for Zion Fundamentalist Latter Day Saints Sect."[22] These two documents suggest that Texas believes children need to have culture; they just need the right culture.

The norms of the official Texas childcare guides developed for the children of Yearming for Zion are a curious hybrid, deriving both from the regulatory authority of the State of Texas and from an essentialized version of FLDS norms or customary law.[23] The "law" contained in them was binding on foster care families as well as on the FLDS children. The "Cultural Awareness Guide" describes the "culture," "behaviors," "living conditions," "education," "health care," "recreation," "home environment," and "religious beliefs" of the FLDS community as fearful, insular, communal, and patriarchal. Yet the "Model for Care for Children from the Yearning for Zion Fundamentalist Latter Day Saints Sect" also reminds foster care providers that, "[e]very effort must be

---

[21] Constitutional scholar Marci A. Hamilton of the Cardozo Law School believes that DFPS did the right thing. Like DFPS, she thinks the case is about culture: "So how does the system permit children to be returned to living within an entrenched culture, for which there is documentation that 25% of pubescent girls are forced into child bigamy and childbearing? The answer is: Through the distortion of both message and meaning. We want to believe these insular religious groups are loci of goodness and piety. We want to believe that religious liberty is always good. And we want to have these beliefs even if the facts dictate very much otherwise." Marci A. Hamilton, "Taking Stock of the 2008 Intervention at the Texas Fundamentalist Latter-Day Saints Compound on Its One-Year Anniversary: The Lessons We Must Learn to Effectively Protect Children in the Future," *FindLaw*, online at http://writ.news.findlaw.com/hamilton/20090416. html (accessed May 30, 2011).

[22] The DFPS was remarkably open about the entire event, posting frequent updates on its website.

[23] Much like colonial authorities codified the customary law of subjugated peoples, U.S. legal authorities "codify" the norms and practices of religious communities when they either protect or condemn them.

made to understand, respect, and incorporate their religious beliefs and social practices as much as possible, as the children are gradually introduced into mainstream culture." Texas authorities went to the extent of eliminating the color red entirely from state facilities where the children were staying out of respect for the community's apparent aversion to the use of the color before the coming of Christ, who will be robed in red. Foster care providers were reminded of what the state took to be FLDS rules: no alcohol or tobacco; no TV; only organic food; and modest clothing. Natural foods, pioneer style clothing, and low-tech entertainment are stressed.

Having insisted on such respect for FLDS culture, they were also coached on how to convert FLDS children to "mainstream culture." Instructions to foster parents included the following:

- Younger children especially may be interested in snacks, sweets, candy, etc; introduce these slowly and with more limitations than usual.
- Allow for appropriate privacy, but also be aware that respectful adults may observe and interact, and this can be an opportunity to bond with them.
- Be aware of their culture of communal living and acting as a group; this can be an asset at times, but they will also need *gradual* guidance in independence, decision making, and making choices. These opportunities should be part of their daily routine and should not be artificial or contrived.
- Organized recreational activities should be part of the daily schedule, and can, over time, be a good way to begin integration with general population.
- Help children adjust to our expectations even if different from what they are accustomed to.
- Do not contribute to any false hope about returning to home/parents, but be empathetic and re-focus on how they can get through this difficult time.
- Help them think through any confusion that results from the confrontation between what they have been taught about the outside world and what they are experiencing first hand. Help them develop ability to draw their own conclusions (this will be a long term process).

Characteristic of the mainstream culture to which they were being introduced, according to Texas authorities, is consumption of snacks, interaction with respectful adults, independence, integration with the general population, adjustment, and the absence of false hope and confusion. In their periodic online news briefs, the department assured the public that the children would not be "exposed to mainstream culture too quickly"; that they "would be allowed to worship freely"; and that the department "respect[s] and value[s] their strong sense of faith." Common American parenting practices, idealizations of pioneer life, and the need for "a clear and consistent daily routine" and household chores were mixed with state modifications and codifications of distinctive FLDS ways.

Interestingly, in making its case to the Texas courts for continued state custody of the more than four hundred children, DFPS relied upon the same psychiatric expert it had used to examine the children seized in the raid on the Branch Davidians in Waco, Dr. Bruce Perry.[24] Linda Smith describes his testimony in the Yearning for Zion case:

> While Texas claimed to be intervening to protect teen girls from sexual abuse, its extreme approach of removing all the children and its experts' explanations suggested a larger agenda – rescuing children from an authoritarian religion. Dr. Perry, testifying as to why the children, even pre-teen boys, should not be returned to their mothers, said:
>
> If they return ... to that ... environment, it reinforces this belief that they hold about the community and God and so forth. And so I think that ... the more their life before this happened is replicated, the

---

[24] At the Yearning for Zion trial, this witness, Dr. Perry, was formally legally qualified as an expert on the children of "cults" in the following exchange:

Q. [attorney for the state]: "Dr. Perry, could you continue telling the Court what your specialized experience is in this area?"

A.: "Yes. So – because of my expertise in trying to help children who have been impacted by trauma, I was contacted by the State and asked to help with the children who were removed from the Branch Davidian Compound just after the assault and I ended up going up to Waco and leading a clinical team that worked with those children and their families for many, many weeks, and some of the children after that.... Because of that experience, I learned a little bit about the children who grew up in environments that were by some people called 'cults,' by other people called 'psychologically destructive environments.' And as a result, people started to refer individuals who had come from different types of environments such as that to me. And over the years I developed an expertise, to some degree, in understanding some of the challenges of leaving a – a close-knit group like that; understood a little bit about how some of the beliefs and practices that were atypical to the main secular population would impact the development of these children and their functioning as – as young adults. So over the years I've ended up working with children – people who have come out of Children of God, the Moon Group, Posse Comitatus, a number of smaller fundamentalist separatist groups so forth." *In the Interest of a Child*, Trial Court Cause Nos. 2779 through 2903 (District Court, 51st Judicial District, Schleicher County, Texas), transcript, 55–6.

more they'll believe like they did before the experience. The major source of authority in the community are [sic] the men, the father of the household and the elder of the community. And when they are not around those individuals, then the formal presentation of those elements of the belief system are not as powerfully reinforced. Wherever these kids go, they can't be in traditional foster care. It needs to … have incredible training about the FLDS community, about issues of trauma maltreatment, about creating opportunities for these children to be exposed to similar but not destructive belief systems so they can begin to have an opportunity to create free choice about a variety of things.[25]

Dr. Perry, testifying for the state in the FLDS hearing, gave his expert opinion that the lives of those children had been determined by their authoritarian environment. The goal of the state should be, he says, children who have free choice.

Mothers of the Yearning for Zion children protested immediately and vehemently to anyone who would listen. Attorneys for the children in the mandamus proceeding argued that the mass hearing to extend the emergency protective custody denied FLDS members due process of law and that the only conceivable basis for the court's order was the unconstitutional goal of altering the children's religious training. On appeal, first the Court of Appeals, and then the Supreme Court of Texas, ordered that all of the children be returned to their families on the ground that DFPS had not had legal reasons for removing them.

In December 2008, DFPS issued a lengthy report regarding the "Eldorado Investigation," made available on its website. The report indicated that it had identified twelve girls who were victims of sexual abuse because they had been "spiritually married" between the ages of twelve and fifteen. DFPS's website defends the raid and asserts that the FLDS children "are safer today" due to its efforts, including mandatory education of FLDS mothers and girls about sexual abuse. In explaining itself, DFPS comments that

DFPS consulted with state and national experts with a diverse background to better understand this community and identify information needed by DFPS and providers to best meet the needs of these

[25] Smith concludes: "While mental health professionals attest that 'authoritative' parenting is healthier than 'authoritarian' parenting, this hardly justified removing custody from authoritarian parents or from parents who belong to authoritarian religious communities." Smith, "Kidnapped from That Land II," 51.

children.... Additionally, providers took steps to ensure dietary and clothing needs were met according to the children's background.

For the Department of Family and Protective Services, the Yearning for Zion case is about sexual abuse of girls and children who were taught that underage marriages are a way of life. It is about parents who condoned illegal underage marriages and adults who failed to protect young girls – it has never been about religion.

The report further indicates that the costs to DFPS of the entire proceedings totaled over $12 million.

Why did the State of Texas frame its concerns in cultural terms? The FLDS children were said to have needed both to be rescued from their culture and to be "affirmed" in their culture. Foster parents who cared for the FLDS children during the period of separation spoke eagerly and admiringly to the press about the FLDS children's piety, work ethic, respectful attitudes toward adults, and modest and mature behavior. These children seemed to epitomize attitudes that the rest of America yearns for. At the same time, there was much fevered speculation in the press about the strange sexual practices of the FLDS, echoing similar prurient speculation about the nature of polygamy throughout Mormon history.[26] The appearance of the FLDS children was a double one – they were latter-day inhabitants of *The Little House on the Prairie* and freaks of nature at the same time.

Culture, it appears, was both part of the problem and part of the solution. Children need culture, but they need the right culture. The word "culture" is used throughout the Texas filings and reports, and throughout the public commentary on the event, seemingly indispensable to the situation. Why culture? Tomoko Masuzawa has reminded us in her essay on "culture" that the term has had many meanings since it first appeared in its modern sense in the eighteenth century.[27] It is, she says, "dangerously capacious, semantically vague and confused, and finally taken as a whole, inconsistent." And yet, she acknowledges, it is also "remarkably serviceable," even foundational to our sense of reality, and "thoroughly naturalized in our everyday discourse." Culture has,

[26] See Gordon, *The Mormon Question*. Martin Guggenheim, in his article on polygamy under U.S. law, argues that the "derivative neglect" theory underlying the Yearning for Zion raid reflected a view of the ranch community as akin to a criminal enterprise. He would have authorities focus on danger to the children rather than the lives of the parents. Martin Guggenheim, "Texas Polygamy and Child Welfare," *Houston Law Review* 46, 3 (2009): 101–51.
[27] Tomoko Masuzawa, "Culture," in *Critical Terms for Religious Studies*, ed. Mark C. Taylor (Chicago: University of Chicago Press, 1998), 70–93.

over these two centuries, also strangely and ambiguously been linked to "religion," as Masuzawa discusses. Sometimes religion is the same as culture; sometimes it is a part of culture; sometimes it precedes culture; sometimes it comprehends culture.

The word has arguably only become more unglued in the ten years since Masuzawa wrote her essay. Thoroughly critiqued by anthropologists, culture is now everywhere. Even law has "gotten" culture.[28] Culture both makes us whole and keeps us in bondage. And it also continues to be ambiguously related to religion. Together, perhaps, law, culture, and religion appear to keep naturalistic explanations at bay and preserve a space for "values," while enabling social engineering. Culture may also contain those embodied aspects of religion rejected by the Reformation, keeping them at arm's length in a place where they are subject to change without offending the separation of church and state and the free exercise of religion. The language in court filings in the Texas case moves uneasily among different accounts of what is wrong with the Yearning for Zion ranch as a place to raise children. A "pervasive system of belief"? A culture? Forced underage sex masquerading as "spiritual" marriage? Cultural pathology, or, bad religion?

For legal purposes, characterizing a practice as cultural, rather than religious, is arguably a useful way to avoid appearing to place legal restrictions on religion. It is a way of rhetorically taking religion offline, constitutionally speaking. "Religion" then can be reserved for what is good while culture can be good or bad and regulated accordingly. Calling something culture can also enable a disturbing lack of attention from scholars of religion, as Jonathan Z. Smith pointed out in his essay on the Jonestown disaster.[29] (Thus many have also insisted, for example, that female circumcision is to be understood to be cultural rather than religious.)

In U.S. law, it is the distinction between opinion and act that has most often permitted the regulation of unpopular religious practices, polygamy among them. Indeed, the Mormon practice of polygamy provided the Court with one of its first opportunities to define the meaning

---

[28] This is not just in the sense that legal anthropology is an accepted subfield within law. But culture itself is a category for law in contexts beyond the family. Some criminal jurisdictions recognize a cultural defense, that is, one can plead that "my culture made me do it," and some legal scholars are redefining law as culture. Paul W. Kahn, *The Cultural Study of Law: Reconstructing Legal Scholarship* (Chicago: University of Chicago Press, 1999).

[29] Jonathan Z. Smith, "The Devil in Mr. Jones," in *Imagining Religion: From Babylon to Jonestown* (Chicago: University of Chicago Press, 1982).

of religion for the purposes of interpreting the religion clauses of the First Amendment.[30] In 1879, in *Reynolds v. U.S.*,[31] the Supreme Court defended the lack of constitutional protection for Mr. George Reynolds's religiously motivated practice of plural marriage, asserting that constitutional protection for religious freedom was limited to opinions, while acts were punishable by law. Confirming the conviction of Mr. Reynolds on a charge of bigamy under anti-Mormon legislation passed in the Utah Territory, the Court announced that "polygamy has always been odious among the northern and western nations of Europe, and, until the establishment of the Mormon Church, was almost exclusively a feature of the life of Asiatic and of African people."[32] "Polygamy," the Court said, "leads to the patriarchal principle, and which, when applied to large communities, fetters the people in stationary despotism."[33]

The 1879 Court refused to condemn as prejudicial the trial judge's charge to the jury that

> ...you should consider what are to be the consequences to the innocent victims of this delusion. As this contest goes on, they multiply, and there are pure-minded women and there are innocent children – innocent in a sense even beyond the degree of the innocence of childhood itself. These are to be the sufferers; and as jurors fail to do their duty, and as these cases come up in the Territory of Utah, just so do these victims multiply and spread themselves over the land.[34]

The Supreme Court then, like the State of Texas today, was worried about the "culture of polygamy" – an insidious and infectious disease-like phenomenon that looms over women and children like a monster from a horror movie.

The Supreme Court's opinion/act distinction, a distinction that enabled the legal reform of Mormon religious practice and the admission of Utah to statehood in the late-nineteenth century after the Church

---

[30] Utah was a territory at the time and the First Amendment prohibitions applied to laws of Congress that governed the territories. This is in contrast to state laws, which would not be subject to the religion clauses until the mid-twentieth century. See footnote 8 in this chapter.

[31] 98 U.S. 145 (1878).

[32] 98 U.S. at 164. For a discussion of *Reynolds* in the context of the rise of U.S. imperialism and the articulation of a mission of "civilization," see Nathan B. Oman, "Natural Law and the Rhetoric of Empire: *Reynolds v. United States*, Polygamy, and Imperialism," *William & Mary Law School Research Paper* no. 09–43, online at http://ssrn.com/abstract=1560015 (accessed May 30, 2011)..

[33] 98 U.S. at 166.

[34] 98 U.S. at 167–8.

renounced its religious "acts" – the practice of polygamy and communal economics – remains fundamental to U.S. religion clause jurisprudence.[35] Its vitality faltered only briefly in the twentieth century. In 1972, the U.S. Supreme Court affirmed the constitutional right of Amish parents to withdraw their children from high school, although doing so was in violation of state compulsory schooling laws, and to teach them instead the premodern skills of housekeeping and farming.[36] Supported by the expert testimony of John Hostettler, a leading scholar and activist on behalf of the Old Order Amish community, the Court admiringly quoted from Hostettler's Amish history, beginning with the observation that, "The history of the Amish sect [begins] with the Swiss Anabaptists of the 16th century who rejected institutionalized churches and sought to return to the early, simple, Christian life de-emphasizing material success, rejecting the competitive spirit, and seeking to insulate themselves from the modern world."[37] Full of respect for their simple life and strongly affirming the rights of parents with respect to "religious training," the majority opinion in the *Wisconsin v. Yoder* case makes clear that what is characteristic of really religious people is that their religion and their culture are coextensive: "Broadly speaking, the Old Order Amish religion pervades and determines the entire mode of life of its adherents." The "culture" of Jefferson's yeoman was ironically protected in the *Yoder* decision as religion. In *Yoder*, the comprehensiveness of culture seemed beneficial to children, perhaps at a time when such a culture seemed to be fast receding.[38]

But the Court's opinion/act distinction formed in *Reynolds* was imperiled only for a moment. *Yoder* has had no successors.[39] While the law in all states permits home schooling, that schooling is state-regulated

---

[35] And also to religious freedom law internationally, although differently expressed.

[36] *Wisconsin v. Yoder*, 406 U.S. 205 (1972).

[37] 406 U.S. at 210. For an account of the use of anthropological testimony in the *Yoder* case, see Rebecca French, "*Wisconsin v. Yoder*: An Anthropologist Shapes a Supreme Court Decision," in *Law and Religion: Cases in Context*, ed. Leslie C. Griffin (New York: Aspen, 2010).

[38] Justice Douglas, in dissent, however, complained that no one had asked the children whether they wanted to go to high school. 406 U.S. at 241–50.

[39] *Yoder* is, however, cited in custody cases for the proposition that courts cannot usually limit religious teaching by parents and cannot choose between parents on the ground that one parent teaches religious belief in illegal practices, unless there is an immediate threat to the child's health. See *Shepp v. Shepp*, 906 A.2d 1165 (Sup Ct. of Pa.): "Where, as in the instant matter, there is no finding that discussing such matters constitutes a grave threat of harm to the child, there is insufficient basis for the court to infringe on a parent's constitutionally protected right to speak to a child about religion as he or she sees fit." 906 A. 2d at 1174.

and Americans have largely drawn back from wholehearted approval of the romance of insular communities implied in Chief Justice Warren Burger's opinion for the majority. Not all religious people are the Amish. Indeed, perhaps even the Amish are not the Amish in the *Yoder* sense. Religion as coterminous with culture, and therefore to be protected as such, has proved to be a dangerous legal idea. In 1990, in an opinion denying constitutional protection for the use of peyote by the Native American Church (*Employment Division v. Smith*, 494 U.S. 872 [1990]), the Court returned to and reaffirmed the opinion/act distinction made in *Reynolds*.

Culture is now divisible again, legally speaking, and Mormon religion, as all religion, is thereby subject to an "extreme makeover" by the government just as it was in the nineteenth century. Now we can protect FLDS culture insofar as it is like our imagined Amish community – and condemn it insofar it is "odious." Commentators mocked FLDS women on YouTube for their "creepiness." While Texas largely lost its battle in the courts concerning removal of the children from the ranch, the broader effect of U.S. law on the phenomenology of religion in the United States is evident in the aftermath of the raid. Many of the FLDS families were required to attend parenting courses. Furthermore, Linda Smith reports that during an October 2008 debate about polygamy and child protection at Fordham University, two audience members who identified themselves as polygamous men submitted the following questions to the debaters:

> As a fundamentalist Mormon (polygamist) dad who is absolutely against abuse, and who will not give up polygamy, what would you suggest as far [as] creating an environment where abuse can be reported without being fearful of being prosecuted for bigamy? There are many like me who want abuse to stop, but not plural marriages among consenting adults. There are already many eyes in plural communities who will report abuse should their consenting adult relationships not be put in jeopardy. In a nation where gay marriage is becoming legal, where killing an unborn child is legal – why can I not live my beliefs as long as I 1) do not commit incest, 2) do not marry a child, 3) pay my taxes (not live off the "system"), 4) do not marry someone against their will, 5) AND I – Love, respect, honor and take care for all of my family 6) AND allow them, to make their own choice to live the same lifestyle or not.[40]

---

[40] Smith "Kidnapped by the Land II," 65.

In points 1 through 6, these men sum up the obligations of Americans and the popular conditions of American "religious freedom" today: no child abuse, no freeloading, no coercion, family solidarity – and free choice for children. FLDS men claim the same rights as gay couples. Here we can see the negotiation of religio-legal norms by Americans, norms that are not easily summed up in formal constitutional terms. This is not a story of religion being free from law. It is the story of the legal shaping of religion to make it fit for Americans.

III. CONCLUSION

The mainstreaming or acculturation of American religions occurs, and has occurred throughout U.S. history, effectuated in part by many encounters with law, formal and informal. The defining and disciplining of religion are accomplished by tax authorities; military, prison, and hospital chaplaincies; zoning and building code authorities; food regulators; school boards establishing school dress codes; and the court of public opinion. As new religions enter the United States, they are disciplined by normative systems, and over time come more and more to resemble the prototype Protestant denomination – worshipping on Sunday, financing themselves through volunteer donations, supplying religious education to children through Sunday schools, developing specialized chaplaincies to serve hospitals and the military, creating seminaries to produce an educated clergy, and ... bringing up their children to choose for themselves.

The global religious field is increasingly a formally disestablished one, as all religions spread everywhere and as religious authorities lose control of religious monopolies, but the United States is in some ways distinctive in its disestablishment. There is a sense in which the United States has neither a state nor a church – and has never had either. The founders envisioned a government of limited powers and rejected the state churches of Europe. The United States is also distinctive in the absolutist nature of the pronouncements with respect to religion in the First Amendment. Most countries continue to manage religion formally through the bureaucracies of former religious establishments or through offices of religious affairs that explicitly decide what counts as religion and what does not count as religion. Most also formally and explicitly announce in their constitutions or fundamental laws that the extent of freedom for religious practice is limited by the norms of the society.

336 Winnifred Fallers Sullivan

Franklin A. Presler, in his *Religion Under Bureaucracy*,[41] traces the legal management of the South Indian temple from the time of the pre-colonial kingdoms through independent India. King and temple before the British, as he tells it, enjoyed a reciprocal relationship in which the temple provided legitimation to the king while the king provided a kind of oversight to the temple, intervening when necessary to settle disputes and providing patronage to ensure a steady income. Temples provided the kings a model of kingship. With the advent of colonial rule, a series of regulatory regimes succeeded, some of which were in competition. These included tax authorities and local and imperial agencies. Those have since been followed by a government ministry dedicated to the management of religious foundations, now called the Hindu Religious and Charitable Endowments Board. Presler shows how bureaucratic management of the temples, whether under the British or under the subsequent independent government of India, has shifted the goals and changed the nature of the temples. Bureaucracies become interested in standardizing the product, regularizing financial records, and ensuring qualified leadership. Through the writing of regulations and inspections by government bureaucrats, religion is produced that will serve the needs of the government and the government's ideology of equality and civility in a new way. Religion arguably goes from being a rival of government to being a creature of government, although religious persons, now out from under religious authorities, also use such transformations for their own purposes.[42]

It is not only the Texas DFPS that is interested in protecting and reforming religious culture in the United States. With the deconstitu-tionalization of religion in the United States, American law and legal institutions – federal, state, and local – are increasingly recognizing Americans, indeed all persons, as essentially religious – or "spiritual" once again. In myriad standards, rules, regulations, and proceedings, religion is being defined, standardized, homogenized, and made acceptable for government support. Being religious is now more and more under-stood in the United States to be part of being human, not something that

---

[41] Franklin A. Presler, *Religion Under Bureaucracy: Policy and Administration for Hindu Temples in South India* (Cambridge: Cambridge University Press, 1987). See also Arjun Appadurai, *Worship and Conflict Under Colonial Rule: A South Indian Case* (Cambridge: Cambridge University Press, 1981).

[42] Much the same story can be discerned in the last chapter of Talal Asad, *Formations of the Secular: Christianity, Islam, Modernity* (Palo Alto, CA: Stanford University Press, 2003).

sets you apart. Religion is being naturalized. As it is being naturalized, it is becoming a part of the domain of government in new ways.[43]

Recognizing both law and religion as plural and cultural shifts the reference to the human. The other competing models today seem to be nature and the will to power. That is, either law, religion, and culture, are simply adaptations of the human species for survival or they are at the service of whoever has the will to shape them. Theories of both law and religion founded in the natural order abound, while political theology is being reborn. From what place might we stand to recognize the children of Yearning for Zion as human? While the legal regulation of religious life in the United States continues to some extent to be structured by constitutional language, turning attention to the ways in which such regulation is also now negotiated on the ground is essential to understanding the new legal phenomenology of religion in the United States.

Select Bibliography

Asad, Talal. *Formations of the Secular: Christianity, Islam, Modernity.* Palo Alto, CA: Stanford University Press, 2005.

Bowen, John R. *Islam, Law and Equality in Indonesia: An Anthropology of Public Reasoning.* Cambridge: Cambridge University Press, 2003.

Cover, Robert M. "The Supreme Court, 1982 Term – Foreword: Nomos and Narrative." *Harvard Law Review* 97, no. 4 (1983): 4–68.

Gordon, Sarah Barringer. *The Mormon Question: Polygamy and Constitutional Conflict in Nineteenth Century America.* Chapel Hill: University of North Carolina Press, 2002.

Howe, Mark de Wolfe. *The Garden and the Wilderness: Religion and Government in American Constitutional History.* Chicago: University of Chicago Press, 1965.

Llewellyn, Karl N. and E. Adamson Hoebel. *The Cheyenne Way: Conflict and Case Law in Primitive Jurisprudence.* Norman: University of Oklahoma Press, 1941.

Maine, Henry Sumner. *Ancient Law.* New York: Cosimo, 2005 [1861].

Presler, Franklin A. *Religion Under Bureaucracy: Policy and Administration for Hindu Temples in South India.* Cambridge: Cambridge University Press, 1987.

Rosen, Lawrence. *The Anthropology of Justice: Law as Culture in Islamic Society.* Cambridge: Cambridge University Press, 1989.

Sullivan, Winnifred Fallers and Robert A. Yelle. "Law and Religion: Overview Article." In *Encyclopedia of Religion.* Edited by Lindsay Jones. 2nd Edition. Detroit: Thomson Gale, 2005. Vol. 8: 5325–32.

---

[43] See Winnifred Fallers Sullivan, "Religion Naturalized: The New Establishment," in *After Pluralism*, ed. Courtney Bender and Pamela E. Klassen (New York: Columbia University Press, 2010).

16   Sexing religion

R. MARIE GRIFFITH

Sex has been a fundamental descriptive category in religious studies for centuries. It is difficult, in fact, to imagine a subject that has played a greater role in shaping the conceptual frameworks that have dominated this field. The subject of sexual relations has been pivotal in accounting for something called "religion" in human experience, in generating curiosity and producing analyses about religious others, and in establishing boundaries between Christianity and other religions. The history of academic religious fascination with sex is a shifting and complex one, to be sure, and it has perennially had to contend with suspicions that its purveyors might turn out to be furtive libertines or voyeurs. But there is no missing the centrality of this subject in the genealogy of theories that have dominated the modern study of religion.

Recent decades have, nonetheless, witnessed a steep rise in the number of works devoted to sexuality in religious studies, generated by considerably different concerns and questions than their predecessors. This upsurge has been part of a larger trend throughout the humanities and social sciences, where, for nearly a quarter-century, questions about sexual identity, orientation, desire, and embodied practice, along with inquiries into legal proscriptions and protections, have proliferated. Scholarly publishing in the study of religion, as well as the conference programs of learned societies such as the American Academy of Religion and the Society for Biblical Literature, illustrate the prominence of such research in the discipline. But not all who work on sexuality are aware of the field's complex inheritances; still fewer of us have probed the implications of these inheritances for current research agendas. This chapter analyzes the history of religious studies by tracing the history of sex in the discipline, considering the stakes of sexuality for assorted scholars and their work. The discussion then shifts to the more recent sexual turn in religious studies, its continuities and ruptures with the past, and its relation to the wider public that religion scholars hope to engage.

I. SEX AND THE MAKING OF RELIGIOUS OTHERS

The earliest modern interpreters of religion theorized that sexual desire was the ground of religious experience and expression. This idea, which predated Sigmund Freud, was developed in particular in the vast literature devoted to phallic worship. (Freud drew on this work in shaping his own theories of religion as sublimation.) Attention to phallic imagery and claims for its deep significance emerged in nineteenth-century histories of religion, such as Lydia Maria Child's *Progress of Religious Ideas Through Successive Ages* (1855). Other influential volumes devoted to the notion of religion's origins in phallic worship included Hodder M. Westropp and C. Staniland Wake, *Ancient Symbol Worship: Influence of the Phallic Idea in the Religions of Antiquity* (1874); Hargrave Jennings, *Phallic Worship: A Description of the Mysteries of the Sex Worship of the Ancients* (1880); and Robert Allen Campbell, *Phallic Worship: An Outline of the Worship of the Generative Organs, as Being or Representing the Divine Creator, with Suggestions as to the Influence of the Phallic Idea on Religious Creeds, Ceremonies, Customs and Symbolism – Past and Present* (1887). All presumed phallicism to be near-universal in ancient religions.[1]

Far from being exclusively modern, however, this interest in sex and religion has pervaded the history of Western Christian thought from antiquity, shaping in particular how Christian leaders have imagined the religious practices of adversaries and identified heretics. What the historian David Frankurter has neatly summarized as "the fantasy of ritual as potential moral reversal" – meaning the ritual practices of religious rivals being described in pornographic terms – characterized the anti-Gnostic polemics of ancient Christian writers such as Irenaeus, Epiphanius, and Augustine. Through a repetitive "litany of perversions and reversals," the church fathers insisted upon the orgiastic promiscuity

---

[1] Lydia Maria Child, *Progress of Religious Ideas Through Successive Ages* (New York: C. S. Francis, 1855); Hodder M. Westropp and C. Staniland Wake, *Ancient Symbol Worship: Influence of the Phallic Idea in the Religions of Antiquity* (New York: J. W. Bouton, 1874); Hargrave Jennings, *Phallic Worship: A Description of the Mysteries of the Sex Worship of the Ancients, with the History of the Masculine Cross: An Account of Primitive Symbolism, Hebrew Phallicism, Bacchic Festivals, Sexual Rites, and the Mysteries of the Ancient Faiths* (London: n.p., 1880); Robert Allen Campbell, *Phallic Worship: An Outline of the Worship of the Generative Organs, as Being or Representing the Divine Creator, with Suggestions as to the Influence of the Phallic Idea on Religious Creeds, Ceremonies, Customs and Symbolism – Past and Present* (St. Louis: R. A. Campbell, 1887).

and perversion of the Gnostics in terms that Christians took for granted until the twentieth-century discovery of Gnostic and Manichean writings clearly contradicted such lurid accounts. Even then, old habits died hard among historians of Christianity. Midcentury writers such as Hans Jonas, notes Frankfurter, seemed to find the idea of Gnostic sexual libertinism so captivating that they "suspend[ed] the critical sensibilities" that such polemics demanded. Jonas himself sensationalized Gnostic dissipation as an important antecedent to medieval Satanism.[2]

This preoccupation with the sex lives of cultures outside one's own was not limited to the history of Christianity. Scottish ethnologist John Ferguson McLennan's influential 1865 work *Primitive Marriage* made much of the "general promiscuity" that pervaded what he and others called "savage" cultures, past and present. McLennan proffered the evidence for this claim in a single footnote: wife lending among the Keiaz, Kandyans, and Mpongme; "disregard of conjugal fidelity" in Caindu, Cascar, and Cumana; the "licentious wantonness among the women of Patan, against which the men had to adopt measures of self-protection"; the "incredible" immorality, short marriages, "frequent divorces," and "unsettled concubinage" were all vivid instances of "savage indifference as to marital purity."[3] (McLennan referred readers wishing to learn of "similar or worse" practices to a lengthy list of travel accounts by European adventurers in mysterious Asia.) As anthropological historian George Stocking has described McLennan's effort, "In the absence of any ethnographic evidence for a primitive state of general promiscuity, a mélange of ethnocentrically evaluated departures from the Victorian cultural norm served as proof of its possibility." McLennan was especially fascinated by what he understood to be the common practice of female abduction by the savage man, who would compel any woman he desired "to accompany him by blows, ending by knocking her down and carrying her off." McLennan's descriptions of the supposed savage practice made clear, as Stocking observes, that "primitive marriage was in his mind little more than 'rape'."[4] Moreover, McLennan's detailed account illustrates the salty thrills found in the sexual and religious practices of others and in the telling of them.

[2]   David Frankfurter, "Ritual as Accusation and Atrocity: Satanic Ritual Abuse, Gnostic Libertinism, and Primal Murders," *History of Religions* 40, 4 (May 2001): 368–70.
[3]   John F. McLennan, *Primitive Marriage: An Inquiry into the Origin of the Form of Capture in Marriage Ceremonies* (Edinburgh: Adam and Charles Black, 1865), quotes from 175 ("general promiscuity"); 176 ("disregard of conjugal fidelity" and "licentious wantoness"); 177 ("frequent divorces" and "unsettled concubinage"); and 178 ("savage indifference").
[4]   George W. Stocking, Jr., *Victorian Anthropology* (New York: Free Press, 1987), 202.

Nineteenth- and early twentieth-century anthropologists and others interested in the religion of "primitives" or "savages" in the contemporary world invariably dwelt at length on sexual matters. University professors and amateur researchers – the line between them was by no means sharply drawn and there was considerable influence between the two grounds – presumed religion not only to have originated in sexual passion (undifferentiated by the savages themselves) but also still to be animated by it. Otto Augustus Wall's *Sex and Sex Worship (Phallic Worship)* (1919) expressed the widely held view: "All religions are based on sex; some, like the ancient Egyptian, Greek, and Roman, or the modern Brahmanic worship of Śiva, very coarsely so, according to modern civilized thought; others, like the Christian religion, more obscurely so." Thus did the scholar – in this case, a celebrated American physician and professor of pharmacology ("pharmacognosy") – invoke sex both as the origin of all religion *and*, in its varied forms, as the criterion for distinguishing between primitive and advanced religions.[5]

These writers projected the crosscultural confidence exemplified in 1922 by James Ballantyne Hannay, a noted Scottish chemist and producer of artificial diamonds who also dabbled in the sex symbolism of various religions. In Hannay's understanding:

[A]s all religion, and especially the Christian religion, is founded on the idea of the creation of life by the two sexes and symbolised by the actual organs involved in reproduction, writers have found great difficulty in selecting language in which to tell the truth about the all but unreadable Hebrew scriptures – the natural shyness of Northern nations about any public reference to sexual matters being a ban to a clear open exposition of the true contents of the Hebraic Scriptures and their later "revelations."[6]

To Hannay and likeminded inquirers, the connection between religion and sex could not be clearer. Some viewed this relationship in evolutionary terms, using it to prove the superiority of Christianity over its primitive antecedents and its modern savage rivals; others were quite ready to interpret Christian devotional practices through a sexual lens, often with the clear aim of provoking the pious.

Freethinkers, for instance, who opposed all religion, including Christianity, as not merely childish but categorically oppressive, used

[5] Otto Augustus Wall, *Sex and Sex Worship (Phallic Worship)* (St. Louis: C. V. Mobsy, 1919), 2.
[6] James Ballantyne Hannay, *Sex Symbolism in Religion* (London: H. A. Oakeshott, 1922), vol. 1, 5–6.

this connection to advance their project of critical debunking. Theodore Schroeder, a lawyer and founder of the Free Speech League, spoke for many of the like-minded in this regard:

All religious experiences, in the special sense in which revival converts use those words, consist in the misinterpretation of an unidentified sex-ecstasy, founded upon the disturbances of the sexual nerve-centres as in adolescence, and ... this sex-emotion thus misinterpreted, certifies to the inerrancy of whatever doctrine is in the mind of the experiencing individual associated with that misinterpreted sex-ecstasy.

Religious emotion, in this view, was unconscious eroticism mistaken for a divine encounter. Schroeder's many writings on what he called "the erotogenesis of religion" applied the theory to a diverse array of groups that included Mormons, Christian Scientists, Shakers, black Pentecostals, and white evangelical Protestants. A case that especially fascinated him was that of the tormented sex educator Ida C. Craddock, who compared her own mystical sexuality to that of St. Teresa of Avila. Throughout, Schroeder argued that Christianity's denial of its own erotic origins was to blame for its "genuine phobias against normal sexuality," and he hoped that a more scientific, rational worldview would undermine the superstitions of Christian belief altogether.[7]

Writers put the religion-sexuality paradigm to a variety of uses in this period, some making a case for the advances marked by Christian morality over other religious systems, others arguing for Christianity as one manifestation of erotic obsession among many. While those with varied axes to grind forged claims about the sexual content of some if not all religions, scholars more sympathetic to religion worked to undermine this view, which they saw as reductionist and even ludicrous. In his 1898 Gifford lectures, published in 1902 as *The Varieties of Religious Experience*, William James disparaged "the fashion" common among certain writers in his day "of criticising the religious emotions by showing a connection between them and the sexual life." In James's view, "few conceptions are less instructive than this re-interpretation of religion as perverted sexuality." He continued:

It reminds one, so crudely is it often employed, of the famous Catholic taunt, that the Reformation may be best understood by

⁷ Theodore Schroeder, "Religion and Sensualism as Connected by Clergymen," *American Journal of Religious Psychology and Education* 13, 1 (1908): 28; Theodore Schroeder, "The Erotogenetic Interpretation of Religion: Its Opponents Reviewed," *Journal of Religious Psychology* 7, 1 (January 1914): 31.

remembering that its *fons et origo* was Luther's wish to marry a nun:- the effects are infinitely wider than the alleged causes, and for the most part opposite in nature. It is true that in the vast collection of religious phenomena, some are undisguisedly amatory – e.g., sex-deities and obscene rites in polytheism, and ecstatic feelings of union with the Saviour in a few Christian mystics. But then why not equally call religion an aberration of the digestive function, and prove one's point by the worship of Bacchus and Ceres, or by the ecstatic feelings of some other saints about the Eucharist?

Dryly noting that consistency would require religion to hinge "just as much upon the spleen, the pancreas, and the kidneys as on the sexual apparatus," James concluded, "the whole theory has lost its point in evaporating into a vague general assertion of the dependence, *somehow*, of the mind upon the body."[8]

As the study of religion took shape as a set of overlapping academic fields in the early twentieth century, James's skepticism took deeper hold. Although Freud and his successors continued to scrutinize the link between religion and sex, fewer scholars continued to argue for sex as religion's primary originating cause. But sex did not disappear. In the academy and in the pews, Christians often remarked upon the sexual lewdness and license they imagined to be rife in non-Christian religions, especially the religions of India. In his chapter on "Brahminism" in the popular 1901 work *Great Religions of the World*, for example, the English diplomat and historian Sir Alfred Comyn Lyall maintained that sexual-religious practices constituted one of the distinguishing markers between Christianity and Hinduism. "We know" the religion of Jesus, Lyall wrote, to be "the highest and purest faith in the world," whereas Indian religion "is unlimited and comprehensive, up to the point of confusion; it is a boundless sea of divine beliefs and practices; it encourages the worship of innumerable gods by an infinite variety of rites; it permits every doctrine to be taught, every kind of mystery to be imagined, any sort of theory to be held as to the inner nature and visible operation of the divine power." The "morality, public and private," of the Indian people might be improved, Lyall hoped, by increasing European, Christian influence. In the meantime, Indians were much like pagans in pre-Christian societies. "There are passages in Augustine's *Civitas Dei*, describing the worship of the unconverted folk among whom he lived, the deification of every natural object and even of physical functions, that might

---

[8] William James, *The Varieties of Religious Experience* (New York: Penguin American Library, 1982), 10, 11–12n.

have been written yesterday by a Christian bishop in India." Educated readers would have known of Augustine's outraged accounts of Roman pagans dedicating human genitals to the gods, as well as of Priapus's role in pagan marriage rites, "upon whose huge and beastly member," wrote the Bishop of Hippo, "the new bride was commanded (after a most honest, old and religious order observed by the matrons) to get up and sit!"⁹ Contemporary Indians were as religiously sex-obsessed as ancient pagans in the imaginations of many modern Christians.

This belief in the hedonism of South Asian religions persisted in the early canonical works of religious scholarship. James Hastings's *Encyclopaedia of Religion and Ethics*, published in the first decade of the century, noted "two bodies of extremists" among Indian worshipers whose practices were "grossly licentious." Such groups he described as "the Vāmachāri or Vāmamārgi, 'the left-hand' sect, which follow the teaching of the Tāntrik literature, and the Kaulas or Kaulikas, following the Kalua Upanisad." The "foul orgies" of these groups had received full description elsewhere, Hastings was relieved to say, so they "need not be further discussed here."¹⁰ In 1913, Crawford Howell Toy, a professor emeritus at Harvard, cited Hastings and other scholars favorably on the subject of sex and South Asian religion in his *Introduction to the History of Religions*, the fourth volume of Morris Jastrow's comprehensive *Handbooks on the History of Religions*. After a lengthy description of phallic cults in early primitive religions, Toy concluded that the only continents where phallic worship survived into the present day were Africa and India. The Yoruba and Dahomi peoples exemplified "the best example of a half-civilized phallic cult," in which phallic worship "is accompanied by the usual licentious rites." But Toy dismissed the identification of phallus worship as religion on the grounds that such rites "are expressions of popular appetite, and it does not appear that the cult itself is otherwise religiously significant." Primitive men and women were *naturally* prone to license and freely satisfied their basest appetites. "The promiscuity that obtains in many savage communities before marriage," Toy write, "is a naïve unreflective animal procedure." The subject of sexual "license" was so important to Toy's study that it had its own entry in the index. Intrigued by tribal attempts to control this lewd behavior, Toy projected the Victorian identification of marriage with coercion onto indigenous peoples, noting that among

⁹ A. C. Lyall, "Brahminism," in *Great Religions of the World* (New York: Harper and Brothers, 1901), 81, 83, 102; Augustine reference in Lyall, *Great Religions of the World*, 83.

¹⁰ James Hastings, *Encyclopaedia of Religion and Ethics* (New York: C. Scribner's Sons, 1908), vol. 2: 492.

the lower tribes, "marriage is merely the assignment of a given woman to a given man."[11]

As for modern India, Toy emphasized that phallicism remained "pronounced and important" and included "rites of unbridled bestialism." He cited the riotous South Asian spring festival of Holi as evidence of this depravity, adding that the harvest festival of one Indian religious community (the Ho community of northeastern India) "is a debauch." The association of sex worship with the religion of South Asia was so firmly established in Western scholarship by this time that Toy was able to observe casually that "Çaktism, the worship of the female principle in nature as represented by various goddesses," was "often accompanied, naturally, by licentious rites." Such rites included incestuous relations. "In orgies in India and elsewhere," as he put it, "no repulsion appears between persons of the same family." Notably, the scholar did see some survival of sex worship and "phallicistic cults" even in contemporary Christianity – at least of the non-Protestant varieties that exemplified "ignorant piety." He means Catholics: Toy's example of phallic survivals referenced those who sought "the aid of a Christian saint" for such benefits as fertility.[12]

Sex also featured prominently in higher religions for Toy, who argued that the sexual disciplining of women was a characteristic of the most advanced and sophisticated peoples. "The sentiment of chastity is a product of the highest civilization," Toy averred. "In many savage and half-civilized tribes the obligation on a woman to keep herself pure is not fully recognized," and sacred prostitution held an important place in many ancient religions:

> Reports from all over the savage world testify to the prominence of sexual intercourse in the lower forms of human life. Folk-stories are full of coarse details of the practice. Popular festivals are often characterized by gross license. To lend a wife to a guest is in many places a recognized rule of hospitality.... Early man seems in this regard to have obeyed his animal appetite without reflection, so far hardly differing from the brutes.

But in Toy's mind, the ascending evolutionary trajectory was clear:

> License, starting at a time when sexual passion was strong and continence was not recognized as a duty or as desirable, found entrance

[11] Crawford Howell Toy, *Introduction to the History of Religions* (Boston: Ginn and Company, 1913), 163, 161, 632, 77.
[12] Toy, *Introduction to the History of Religions*, 163, 95, 168, 180, 175.

into various social and religious customs and institutions, accommodating itself in different places and periods to current ideas of propriety. Appropriated by organized religion, it discarded here and there its more bestial features, adopted more refined religious conceptions, its scope was gradually reduced, and finally it vanished from religious usage.

While admitting that the precise details remained unknown, Toy nonetheless conclusively affirmed modern people's "emergence from savage conditions" and steady sexual maturation "under the influence of ideas of morality and refinement."[13]

The French sociologist Émile Durkheim, one of the most influential theorizers of primitive religion and of religion generally, took as a given the view of savage sacred sexuality held by European and North American scholars. "In all the lower societies, sexual union is," Durkheim wrote, "endowed with a quality of religiousness." Following the genealogy established in the nineteenth century by the widely read scholar of ancient Mediterranean religions, William Robertson Smith, Durkheim's core theory of "collective effervescence" assumed as fundamental the religion/sexuality nexus in primitive societies:

> The effervescence often becomes so intense that it leads to outlandish behavior; the passions unleashed are so torrential that nothing can hold them. People are so far outside the ordinary conditions of life, and so conscious of the fact, that they feel a certain need to set themselves above and beyond ordinary morality. The sexes come together in violation of the rules governing sexual relations. Men exchange wives. Indeed, sometimes incestuous unions, in normal times judged loathsome and harshly condemned, are contracted in the open and with impunity. If it is added that the ceremonies are generally held at night, in the midst of shadows pierced here and there by firelight, we can easily imagine the effect that scenes like these are bound to have on the minds of all those who take part.[14]

The prominent twentieth-century anthropologist Victor Turner likewise "found resonance in the notion of ritual as that point when humans launched themselves into varying degrees of amoral enthusiasm," writes David Frankfurter, above all, sexual abandon.[15]

---

[13] Toy, *Introduction to the History of Religions*, 517, 72, 520, 521.
[14] Émile Durkheim, *The Elementary Forms of Religious Life*, trans. Karen E. Fields (New York: Free Press, 1995), 319, 218.
[15] Frankfurter, "Ritual as Accusation and Atrocity," 368.

Mircea Eliade, the leading theorist of the history of religions school for most of the twentieth century and an influential professor of religion at the University of Chicago, inherited and further developed the identification of sex and religion in primitive cultures. But in Eliade's view, civilization had lost more than it gained when sex lost its sacred dimension. *"Homo religiosus"* – the primordial religious human being – experienced mystery, grandeur, and "ultimate reality" in sexual activity, while moderns were aware of nothing but bodily sensation:

> Psychoanalysis and historical materialism have taken as surest confirmation of their theses the important part played by sexuality and nutrition among peoples still at the ethnological stage. What they have missed, however, is how utterly different from their modern meaning are the value and even the function of eroticism and of nutrition among those peoples. For the modern they are simply physiological acts, whereas for primitive man they were sacraments, ceremonies by means of which he communicated with the force which stood for Life itself.

The "normal tendency of the primitive," Eliade emphasized, was "to transform his physiological acts into rites, thus investing them with spiritual value." This interpretation fit with Eliade's larger critique of modern civilization and his longing for a lost faith and innocence; as he wrote in the last sentence of *Patterns in Comparative Religion*, "the *real existence* of primitive man was not the broken and alienated existence lived by civilized man to-day." Modern people, estranged from cosmic meaning, had genital sex; primitive people had sacred sex.[16]

Eliade continued throughout his scholarly life to linger on the topic of primitive sex. Writing the first and longer of two articles for the "Sexuality" entry in the *Encyclopedia of Religion* (1987), Eliade described additional sexual rites, from sacred orgies among the Aranda and Kunapipi to a Chinese Taoist sect's rule for *coitus reservatus* with scores of partners in a single ritual event. Some of Eliade's more shocking revelations included an Irish king's rape of a female horse, which was then killed, hacked to pieces, and boiled to a broth in which the king bathed – and which he drank. (This rite, said Eliade, was a reenactment of "mythical intercourse between a mortal and a god in animal form, through which a transfer of power takes place.") Eliade's colleague at the University of Chicago, Ioan Culianu, described a series of equally

---

[16] Mircea Eliade, *Patterns in Comparative Religion*, trans. Rosemary Sheed (New York: Sheed & Ward, 1958), 31–2, 456 (emphasis in the original).

unusual practices in the second article, "Sexual Rites in Europe." His examples included a Russian Orthodox dissenting sect (the Skoptsy, or "castrated") that mutilated their genitals and chopped up the breasts of pubescent girls to ingest for communion. Others were more approachably sexier, such as the various adaptations of Indian Tantric practices, the Black Mass, and the "erotic delirium" famously suffered during the Renaissance period by sexually repressed French nuns. Culianu, a specialist in Gnosticism, sexual magic, esotericism, and the occult, closed the article with a discussion of Aleister Crowley and the erotic practices of Satanic clubs. "Sexual Rites in Europe" made no reference to the bedroom activity approved by church authorities, nor the doings of the common brothel or bathhouse, much less any practice in which women were other than submissive. Instead and quite clearly, the rubric "sexual rites in Europe" signified an alluring underworld of eroticized violence and transgressive rebellions.[17]

Although ambivalence about sex persisted in religious studies, Eliade and those influenced by him presented a more positive – even romanticized or celebratory – view of religious sexuality that would become mainstream in the discipline. Another University of Chicago professor, Wendy Doniger (formerly Wendy Doniger O'Flaherty), wrote extensively about sexuality in Hindu mythology and ritual practice in her first book, *Asceticism and Eroticism in the Mythology of Śiva* (1973), and many later works as well, notably *Women, Androgynes, and Other Mythical Beasts* (1980). This scholarship received accolades in the North American academy, but it generated passionate controversy among Indian (and some Western) critics who objected to what they saw as the distorted hypersexualization of Indian religions by Western scholars, whom they accused of neocolonialism. Jeffrey J. Kripal, one of Doniger's students, was particularly a target for such denunciations after the publication of his book, *Kali's Child: The Mystical and the Erotic in the Life and Teachings of Ramakrishna* (1995).[18] While the intricacies of this conflict of interpretations (still alive and raw at this writing) are too extensive to elaborate fully in these pages, one paradox is especially relevant here: while Doniger, Kripal, and others have seen their

[17] Mircea Eliade, "Sexuality: An Overview," in *The Encyclopedia of Religion*, ed. Mircea Eliade (New York and London: Macmillan, 1987), vol. 13: 184–6; Ioan Petru Culianu, "Sexual Rites in Europe," in *The Encyclopedia of Religion*, ed. Eliade, vol. 13: 186–9.
[18] Wendy Doniger, *Asceticism and Eroticism in the Mythology of Śiva* (New York: Oxford University Press, 1973); Wendy Doniger O'Flaherty, *Women, Androgynes, and Other Mythical Beasts* (Chicago: University of Chicago Press, 1980); Jeffrey J. Kripal, *Kali's Child: The Mystical and the Erotic in the Life and Teachings of Ramakrishna* (Chicago: University of Chicago Press, 1995).

interpretations of Indian religious sexuality in highly positive terms – even as a critique of the Western Judeo-Christian tradition – their critics have accused them of a depraved sex obsession, refocusing the controversy on the neurotic fixations of Western scholars themselves. As younger generations of scholars of South Asian religions attempt to chart new ground, many find themselves trapped by presumptions that they too are Orientalists, deploying descriptions of sex in order to create lurid and titillating images of religious others, however attractive and compelling these scholars intend such accounts to be.[19]

Respected interpreters of primitive religions, however, could write graphic and prurient descriptions of erotic religion mostly without fear of censorship. The dirtier these practices were, after all, the more outlandishly exotic they would seem, safely distancing them from the normal lives of modern readers. (Anthropologists such as Ruth Benedict and Margaret Mead, it should be noted, wrote in a very different vein and aimed to broaden Western readers' views about the diverse sexual moralities across cultures.) We now know, of course, that many modern intellectuals and scholars had their own complicated sex lives and that more than a few were more attuned to the reputed decadence of Aleister Crowley or Oscar Wilde than the modesty enjoined by polite convention. Elites in Britain and the United States had populated underground nightclubs such as London's Cave of the Golden Calf, while distinguished Protestant theologians such as Paul Tillich partook of the illicit pleasures available in subterranean New York and other urban playgrounds.[20] There would have been much to explore had the religion scholar's eye turned back to the sex practices of his or her cultured companions, but decorum mostly guarded against such inquiries. Whether performing as the classicist specializing in curious antiquities or the scientist bluntly cataloguing bodily instincts, religionists managed to evade critical examination of their own sexual practices.

---

[19] One of the most influential critiques is Rajiv Malhotra, "RISA Lila – 1: Wendy's Child Syndrome," which was posted online on September 6, 2002, at http://rajivmal-hotra.sulekha.com/blog/post/2002/09/risa-lila-1-wendy-s-child-syndrome.htm (accessed June 29, 2010). A fuller account, with contributions from a variety of observers (Indian and non-Indian), is *Invading the Sacred: An Analysis of Hinduism Studies in America*, ed. Krishnan Ramaswamy, Antonio de Nicolas, and Aditi Banerjee (New Delhi: Rupa, 2007). Doniger and Kripal have issued numerous responses to these criticisms; see especially Kripal's website devoted to this topic: http://www.ruf.rice.edu/~kalischi/ (accessed May 26, 2011).

[20] Philip Hoare, *Oscar Wilde's Last Stand: Decadence, Conspiracy, and the Most Outrageous Trial of the Century* (New York: Arcade, 1997); Hannah Tillich, *From Time to Time* (New York: Stein and Day, 1973).

II. SEX AND RELIGION CLOSER TO HOME: THE WESTERN MAKING OF CHRISTIAN INSIDERS

Those who did study Western religions, in particular Christianity, continued to avoid writing about sexuality at all. Anglo-American historians of Anglo-American Christianity, most of them male and all of them trained by male scholars, hardly saw the subject as within their purview. Like the early Puritan chroniclers concerned to chart the land's providential role, most American church historians well into the 1980s focused their research and writing on Protestant Christian doctrine, ministers, and institutions, preserving belief in their significant (and largely beneficent) influence on society, government, and culture. Avoiding sexuality as a relevant topic in religious history – at least Protestant religious history – made sense to this view of the field; the topic's absence, that is, was authorized from the very start. In his 1844 volume *Religion in America*, Robert Baird's sole mention of sexuality came as a defense of Presbyterian purity:

> [A]lthough painful cases of immorality in ministers have occurred, yet we know of no case in which it has been overlooked; we know no case in which either drunkenness, licentiousness, or any similar offence, has been proved against any minister, or been notoriously true with regard to him, without leading to his suspension or deposition from office.... As it regards the private members of the church ... the cases are certainly rare in which any such offence as falsehood, drunkenness, fornication, or adultery are [sic] tolerated in any church member. Discipline is so far preserved in our churches, that it would be a matter of general reproach if any congregation allowed the name of a man of known immoral character to remain upon its list of communicants.[21]

There was no mention of conjugality or adultery in the church historian Philip Schaff's widely read 1855 account of American religions, *America* (except for a knowing aside about the "refined immorality" of the Jesuits) or in Methodist minister, historian, and novelist Edward Eggleston's 1901 *The Transit of Civilization from England to America in the Seventeenth Century* (only a footnote quoting legal proscriptions against "common swearing, simple fornication, prophaning the Lord's Day and the like").[22]

---

21   Robert Baird, *Religion in America* (New York: Harper & Brothers, 1844), 240–1 (slightly revised 1856 version, 479).
22   Philip Schaff, *America: A Sketch of the Political, Social, and Religious Character of the United States of North America, in Two Lectures, Delivered at Berlin, with a Report*

In 1942, Edmund S. Morgan, a newly minted Ph.D. in history, broke the taboo. In "The Puritans and Sex," published in the *New England Quarterly*, the twenty-six-year-old historian demonstrated that the early New England colonists held a highly favorable view of sex within monogamous marriage, and if their legal proscriptions against fornication and adultery were harsh, severe punishments were rarely inflicted. "Here is as healthy an attitude as one could hope to find anywhere," noted Morgan of the minister John Cotton's positive view of conjugal relations. Nor was Cotton an exception, for his represented "the views of the New England clergy, the acknowledged leaders of the community, the most Puritanical of the Puritans," as well as the attitudes and expectations of Puritans in the pews. Morgan, who would become an eminent historian of early America, aimed to redeem the Puritans from a half-century of popular caricature for their allegedly dour ways, not to start a historiographical tradition of inquiry into sex and religion. Still, coming six years before the first of Alfred Kinsey's soon-to-be-infamous reports on American sexual behavior, his historical inquiry into sex among the nation's Anglo-Protestant forebears was an important milestone.[23]

One might suspect that Morgan's mentor, the highly regarded scholar of colonial New England, Perry Miller, was behind this trek into Puritan sexual practices and attitudes. With fewer details but more evident merriment than his former pupil, Miller loosened things up further in *Errand into the Wilderness* (1956), as he drolly reveled in the 1679 report of Increase Mather and his assembled synod on the corruption then afflicting the colonies:

> Under the eighth head the synod described the sins of sex and alcohol, thus producing some of the juiciest prose of the period: militia days had become orgies, taverns were crowded; women threw temptation in the way of befuddled men by wearing false locks and displaying naked necks and arms "or, which is more abominable, naked Breasts." ... In 1672, there was actually an attempt to supply Boston with a brothel (it was suppressed, but the synod was bearish about the future).[24]

Read Before the German Church Diet at Frankfort-on-the-Maine, Sept. 1854 (New York : Scribner, 1855); Edward Eggleston, *The Transit of Civilization from England to America in the Seventeenth Century* (New York: D. Appleton, 1901), 197, n. 11.

[23] Edmund S. Morgan, "The Puritans and Sex," *The New England Quarterly* 15, 4 (December 1942): 592–3.

[24] Perry Miller, *Errand into the Wilderness* (Cambridge, MA: Harvard University Press, 1956), 8.

Miller obviously enjoyed this bit of urbane sexual raillery, but it was about as far as his writing would go. Nor did others, until much later, take up Morgan's and Miller's lead and pursue sex as a topic more thoroughly among the Puritans or other American religious groups. The tacit, widely shared assumption was that sex was not fit for respectable research.

The subject of family relations, which gained traction in the 1970s, touched directly or indirectly on sexuality, and here historians began to write somewhat more frankly about sex. John Demos, analyzing family life in the Plymouth colony in *A Little Commonwealth: Family Life in Plymouth Colony* (1970), commented briefly about the colonists' views of adultery and marriage, concluding that the people there "do seem to have maintained a 'double standard' of sexual morality," in which rules and penalties for women were much harsher than those for men. Philip J. Greven, having taken an interest in premarital sexual behavior in earlier work, devoted a substantial section to "Femininity, Masculinity, and Sexuality" in *The Protestant Temperament: Patterns of Child-rearing, Religious Experience, and the Self in Early America* (1977), where he took an emphatically Freudian view of early American sexual relations. European historians were making detailed studies of Christian sexuality in Britain and Western Europe, exemplified in works such as Lawrence Stone, *The Family, Sex and Marriage in England, 1500–1800* (1977) and Natalie Zemon Davis, "Ghosts, Kin, and Progeny: Some Features of Family Life in Early Modern France" (1977).[25] By this time, scholars of women's history were coming into their own and beginning to direct the historical conversation in new directions. Some, such as those scrutinizing the Salem witch trials or other gendered persecutions in American religious history, brought sex more intentionally into discussions of the past, as a topic that could shed important light on women's disempowerment at the hands of Christian pastors, theologians, and husbands. But rarely did male church historians consider sex a focal point for their studies, an inattention that persisted well into recent decades.[26]

---

[25] John Demos, *A Little Commonwealth: Family Life in Plymouth Colony* (New York: Oxford University Press, 1970); Phillip J. Greven, *The Protestant Temperament: Patterns of Child-rearing, Religious Experience, and the Self in Early America* (New York: Knopf, 1977); Lawrence Stone, *The Family, Sex and Marriage in England, 1500–1800* (New York: Harper & Row, 1977); Natalie Zemon Davis, "Ghosts, Kin, and Progeny: Some Features of Family Life in Early Modern France," in *The Family*, ed. Alice S. Rossi, Jerome Kagan, and Tamara K. Hareven (New York: Norton, 1978).

[26] Ann Taves, "Sexuality in American Religious History," in Thomas A. Tweed, ed., *Retelling U.S. Religious History* (Berkeley: University of California Press, 1997), 27–56.

The old scholarly and popular practice of finding sexual promiscuity and depravity in the rituals of despised (or desired) religious others thrived amid this otherwise stubborn silence, however. Notably, critics, almost all male, showed particular interest in female sexuality – women as dupes and victims, sinners and whores. Protestants had long charged Catholics with secret vices inside the convent, and sensationalist – and completely fictional – nineteenth-century narratives such as *The Awful Disclosures of Maria Monk* (1836) confirmed this erotic fantasy.[27] A century later, eminent intellectuals, among them John Dewey, Albert Einstein, Bertrand Russell, and McGeorge Bundy, praised *Nation* associate editor Paul Blanshard's *American Freedom and Catholic Power* (1949), which claimed, among other things, that the recruitment of girls into Catholic convents involved bodily techniques to "sublimate the libido in passionate religious devotion." Blanshard's evidence, taken from an 1834 devotional manual republished under the Archbishop of Baltimore's imprimatur in 1927, sounded awfully risqué to Protestant ears, as it urged girls to make a vow of chastity with explicitly sexual imagery. "On the Vow of Chastity," the manual warned, in language pervasive in nineteenth- and early twentieth-century Catholic devotionalism, " ... you ought to live, breathe and pant for your Celestial Spouse alone." Blanshard added a few more salacious items and concluded by quoting the manual's description of what he called "the climax of the experience," which was the "union with Him, so intimate, naked, simple, sweet, and so perfect that nothing can be added to it.... Oh holy inebriation, which in the holy commerce of prayer transports a soul into the cellars of divine love.... Drink and be inebriated, my beloved."[28] Blanshard's 1958 revised edition further amplified the sexual dangers of Catholicism, pointing out "the ever-present peril of homosexual attachments" in the convent and the physical mortifications imposed on girls who "feel strong sexual desire." Blanshard invoked "modern science" for appraising most girls attracted to the convent as "mentally abnormal," that is, queer. Sex, violence, and abnormality were snugly intertwined in this influential imagining of modern American Catholicism.[29]

---

[27] Maria Monk, *Awful Disclosures, by Maria Monk, of Hotel Dieu Nunnery of Montreal* (New York: n.p., 1836).

[28] Paul Blanshard, *American Freedom and Catholic Power* (Boston: Beacon Press, 1949), 70–1. On Blanshard's favorable reception among Dewey, Einstein, Russell, and Bundy, see John T. McGreevy, "Thinking on One's Own: Catholicism in the American Intellectual Imagination, 1928–1960," *Journal of American History* 84, 1 (June 1997): 97–8.

[29] Blanshard, *American Freedom and Catholic Power* (1949), 71, 73.

But Catholics were no less adept at this game of sexualized insult than their Protestant counterparts. In his celebrated 1950 volume *Enthusiasm: A Chapter in the History of Religion*, the Anglican-turned-Catholic priest and historian Ronald Knox reviled the "obsess[ion] with sex-consciousness" of American revival movements, which he compared to pre-Christian paganism and equated with the eugenically motivated sanctioning of communal marriages by John Humphrey Noyes's Oneida Perfectionists.[30] Decades later, the conservative Catholic journalist and popular historian Paul Johnson made a point of discrediting a number of modern intellectuals, most of them Protestant in heritage if not affiliation – and in any case standing in for Protestant modernity – with bawdy tales of their licentious, sex-addicted private lives. The "sexual obsessions" of men from Jean-Jacques Rousseau, Henrik Ibsen, and Leo Tolstoy to Ernest Hemingway, James Baldwin, Kenneth Tynan, and Edmund Wilson made for gripping prose, whether or not one agreed with Johnson's premise that their "self-immolation on the altar of sex" (as he described Tynan's life) cast suspicion on the virtue of their intellectual and artistic contributions, and by extension on all of modernity.[31]

Johnson's antimodern, anti-Protestant screed was compromised when, shortly after the publication of *Intellectuals*, his long-time mistress publicly revealed not only her own identity but the long-married Catholic Johnson's sexual preferences, including his fondness for sado-masochism. (Gloria Stewart noted that spanking was "a big part of our relationship. I had to tell him he was a very naughty boy.") Johnson's reputation was (briefly) tarnished by the scandal, but he recovered soon enough, receiving the Presidential Medal of Freedom from U.S. President George W. Bush in 2006 and, in 2009, accompanying his close friend Margaret Thatcher, former British prime minister, to visit Pope Benedict XVI in Rome. The very old battles continued to be fought using charges of sexual indecency to discredit religious enemies.

Sex remained a powerful instrument for provoking outrage against religious outsiders, among them the fundamentalist Christians living with David Koresh in Waco, Texas; the Mormon wives occupying polygamous communities in Texas, Arizona, and Utah; and the Muslim suicide bombers said to be lured by promises of sex with virgins in the afterlife. Media attention to the very real horrors of sexual abuse has

---

[30] Ronald A. Knox, *Enthusiasm: A Chapter in the History of Religion: With Special Reference to the XVII and XVIII Centuries* (Oxford: Clarendon Press, 1950), 570.

[31] Paul Johnson, *Intellectuals* (New York: Harper & Row, 1988), 327; Christopher Hitchens, "The Rise and Fall of Paul 'Spanker' Johnson," *Salon*, May 28, 1988, online at http://www.salon.com/media/1998/05/28media.html (accessed May 14, 2010).

often focused on groups deemed to be "cults," and collective fantasies
about what may be going on inside them have repeatedly justified police
intervention and the presumption of guilt. Military operations in recent
years have likewise been justified in the language of sex and sexual rescue, as when American leaders pointed to women's sexual oppression
as a compelling reason for waging war in Iraq and Afghanistan. Fear,
violence, and mutual recrimination appear to be among the inevitable
components of the long association of religion and sexuality in Western
imaginations.

III. THE REDISCOVERY OF THE SEXUAL BODY

Meanwhile, following the first American edition of Michel Foucault's
The History of Sexuality, published as three volumes in 1978, the 1980s
witnessed a new flourishing of research into religion and sexuality
within religious studies.[32] This boom occurred as part of a much longer
trajectory in the discipline in which categories of gender, race, class, and
the body were coming to the fore. Yet the study of sex seemed to offer
new promise, the hope that innovative exploration of something so fundamental to human existence and experience as sexual desire or behavior would generate new critical perspectives on religion. For historians of
Christianity, formative texts included John Boswell, *Christianity, Social
Tolerance, and Homosexuality: Gay People in Western Europe from the
Beginning of the Christian Era to the Fourteenth Century* (1980); Judith
C. Brown, *Immodest Acts: The Life of a Lesbian Nun in Renaissance
Italy* (1986); and Peter Brown, *The Body and Society: Men, Women, and
Sexual Renunciation in Early Christianity* (1988).[33] Sexuality had a *his-
tory* – or rather *histories* – these works proclaimed, and its multifarious
social and political functions were inescapably bound up with religion.

Throughout the 1980s and 1990s, other subfields in the study of religion took up the challenges posed by Foucault and by theorists of gender and sexuality. Feminist theologians and ethicists, inspired by Mary

[32] Michel Foucault, *The History of Sexuality, Vol. 1: An Introduction*, trans. Robert
Hurley (New York: Vintage, 1990); *The History of Sexuality, Vol. 2: The Uses of
Pleasure*, trans. Robert Hurley (New York: Vintage, 1990); *The History of Sexuality,
Vol. 3: The Care of the Self*, trans. Robert Hurley (New York: Vintage, 1988).
[33] John Boswell, *Christianity, Social Tolerance, and Homosexuality: Gay People in
Western Europe from the Beginning of the Christian Era to the Fourteenth Century*
(Chicago: University of Chicago Press, 1980); Judith C. Brown, *Immodest Acts: The
Life of a Lesbian Nun in Renaissance Italy* (New York: Oxford University Press, 1986);
Peter Brown, *The Body and Society: Men, Women, and Sexual Renunciation in Early
Christianity* (New York: Columbia University Press, 1988).

Daly, Audre Lorde, and Adrienne Rich, began writing extensively about sexuality, with the explicit aim of freeing women from patriarchal strictures and developing more satisfying models for sexual ethics and sexual relationships. Queer theorists made a similar move for gay, lesbian, and transgendered persons. Scholars of Asian religions worked to dismantle the Western ethnocentric depictions of Oriental lasciviousness while offering their own commentaries on a wide variety of sexual formations. Sociologists and historians gave close attention to the sexual specifics in particular religious traditions, while comparative work explored similarities and differences in sexuality across religious lines. So too did scholars in disciplines outside religious studies turn to sexuality. The *Journal of the History of Sexuality* began publication in 1990, and articles by a multidisciplinary range of scholars, including scholars of religion, have appeared there. A consistent point held fast in this varied scholarship: whatever else sex may be about – love and pleasure, the desire to procreate, and the desire to be desired – it is always also about social power and discipline in its many visible and invisible forms.

The greatest outpouring of scholarship in religious studies on sexuality has been since 2000. New archival collections and resource centers, both within and outside institutions of higher learning, have helped make such work possible. These include the Lesbian, Gay, Bisexual, and Transgender Religious Archives Network (LGBTRAN), a project of the Chicago Theological Seminary that serves as a resource center and information clearinghouse; the God and Sexuality Conference (GSC), an annual academic meeting on religion and sexuality held at Bard College; the Feminist Sexual Ethics Project at Brandeis University; the Center for Lesbian and Gay Studies at the Pacific School of Religion; the Carpenter Program in Religion, Gender, and Sexuality at Vanderbilt University Divinity School; and the Religious Institute on Sexual Morality, Justice, and Healing in Norwalk, Connecticut. Major foundations, universities, and scholarly societies now regularly award fellowships to work on religion and sex. The study of sexuality has evidently come of age within the discipline of religious studies. If an interest in sex and sexuality has been with us all along, the most dramatic recent change has been to see sex move back toward the center of religious studies, becoming again one of the chief categories of critical inquiry.

The roots of that shift are, in large part, cultural and political, As the movement for gay rights developed, sexual minorities challenged scholars and religious leaders alike to rethink what had been taken for granted about the intersection of sexuality and religion. Much interest in sex and the study of religion emerged among scholars eager to scrutinize the historical origins of supposedly timeless prohibitions against homosexual activity and same-sex love. This context helps to explain the initial urgency of the study of sexuality in the study of religion as well as its ongoing flourishing. Just as the women's liberation and the civil rights movements helped inspire new scholarly research on women's history and on African American cultures, so too the movement for sexual freedom of many sorts – particularly, the rights of gays, lesbians, transgendered persons, and other ostensible sexual "minorities" – stirred the movement in queer studies in religion. One of the crucial questions probed by scholars who wish to "sex" religion, above all, pertains to the interrelationships among particular sets of sexual rules and the cultural norms, religious sanctions, theologies and cosmologies, and political regimes in which they are enacted. This broad way of thinking about the politics of sexuality has yielded a range of important theoretical contributions to the study of religion across many subfields.

While it is impossible to cover the full landscape of issues treated under the rubric of sexuality and religion today, broad patterns have emerged to suggest at least six bodies of work across diverse subfields in religious studies. The first sets out to prove (generally through textual criticism of scripture or theological reflection) that religious traditions contain serviceable resources for honoring same-sex partnerships and transgendered persons. A second attempts, by means of historical investigation, to show that religious restrictions on sexual activity have historically been looser than they are today, with the implication that an informed historical eye will uncover fluid living arrangements that may serve as exemplary models for contemporary religious people. A third body of scholarship scrutinizes negative portrayals of sexuality in religious traditions and offers analytic frameworks for understanding these in relation to culture and society. A fourth area of inquiry concerns sexual violence within religious traditions, particularly against women and children, in both historical and contemporary contexts, while a fifth explores the responses of various religious groups to the global sex trade. Finally, a literature has commenced in the study of American religious history and American law that appraises conservative religious groups (above all, evangelical Protestants) and their attempts to legislate particular sexual norms in public institutions.

These varied lines of inquiry have generated a set of interrelated conversations that have begun to make significant theoretical contributions to the study of religion in both its historical and contemporary dimensions. Attention to the historicity of sexual rules and practices has enhanced the field's long history of wrestling with the fluidity and variability of religious traditions across cultures. Analysis of the braided relationships among religion, sex, and law leads to larger questions about religion and politics or modern ways of conceiving religion's relationship to the state. The complexities and limits of liberal notions of religious tolerance, pluralism, the meanings of globalization, and human rights rise into view through examination of these issues, sharpened by close consideration of past and present debates over sexual purity, morality, and power. All of these investigative trails lead back to one of the most vexatious problems of the study of religion, which is the question of how to define and theorize its very subject, religion, with the precision, sophistication, and care needed to make ideas count to the many public constituencies for whom religion is a pressing matter, even more so when associated with sexuality.

Urgent questions, political and theoretical in nature, have brought us to this place. Unlike the work of earlier theorists of religion or scholars of religion in the latter half of the twentieth century, contemporary research takes place in a media world where sex is ubiquitous and where the boundaries between public and private are shifting more rapidly than ever before. Our age is also one characterized by polarized arguments about sex that have come to be called the "culture wars," so that sexual issues are debated relentlessly and publicly in a wide array of religious, juridical, and political settings. All too regularly, moreover, we learn of new atrocities in which trusted religious leaders have been unmasked – as hypocrites and criminals – either for sexually abusing children in their care or for protecting those who do, for consorting with prostitutes, or for sexually harassing their subordinates. Sex may have been the obsession of many eras before our own, but sexuality has become in our times a unique lens for viewing the intricate dynamics of religion and society. What books, films, and art are publicly accessible to us; how we talk and think about puberty, pregnancy, breastfeeding, and childrearing; what our schools teach children about science, health, and the body; how our medical, educational, and penal systems regulate sexuality within their institutional settings; and above all, how we relate to one another in public and private: nearly every encounter in our culture, in other words, is affected by how sex and religion have been understood in relation to each other over time. Indeed, the contest for authority to define sexual norms and to control sexuality has illuminated in new ways the social and psychological power of religion in the public sphere and at the nexus of private and public life.

Select Bibliography

Brooten, Bernadette J. *Love Between Women: Early Christian Responses to Female Homoeroticism*. Chicago: University of Chicago Press, 1996.

Doniger, Wendy. *The Bedtrick: Tales of Sex and Masquerade*. Chicago: University of Chicago Press, 2000.

Ellingson, Stephen and M. Christian Green. Eds. *Religion and Sexuality in Cross-Cultural Perspective*. New York: Routledge, 2002.

Engelstein, Laura. *Castration and the Heavenly Kingdom: A Russian Folktale*. Ithaca, NY: Cornell University Press, 1999.

Frankfurter, David. *Evil Incarnate: Rumors of Demonic Conspiracy and Satanic Abuse in History*. Princeton, NJ: Princeton University Press, 2006.

Hanegraaff, Wouter J. and Jeffrey J. Kripal. Eds. *Hidden Intercourse: Eros and Sexuality in the History of Western Esotericism*. Leiden, Boston: Brill, 2008.

Jordan, Mark D. *The Invention of Sodomy in Christian Theology*. Chicago: University of Chicago Press, 1997.

Machacek, David W. and Melissa M. Wilcox. Eds. *Sexuality and the World's Religions*. Santa Barbara, CA: ABC-Clio, 2003.

Schmidt, Leigh Eric. *Heaven's Bride: The Unprintable Life of Ida C. Craddock, American Mystic, Scholar, Sexologist, Martyr, and Madwoman*. New York: Basic, 2010.

Urban, Hugh B. *Magia Sexualis: Sex, Magic, and Liberation in Modern Western Esotericism*. Berkeley: University of California Press, 2006.

17 Constituting ethical subjectivities

LEELA PRASAD

On an April evening in 1999, in Sringeri, a small town in South India, the retired schoolteacher Meshtru[1] and I walked together on our way to our homes after the lively celebrations of the Rama's festival.[2] We stood to chat at the street corner where our paths would part. "It went really well!" I said. Meshtru's family, with whom I had become friendly over the years of my research in Sringeri, had been publicly thanked for sponsoring the evening's festive activities. "It went well, yes, this *service* to Rama!" he acknowledged. Amid nods and goodnights to familiar passersby, he narrated this experience. I still had my tape recorder on from the music performance I had been recording at the celebrations we had just attended.

---

[1] *Meshtru* is a colloquial Kannada word adapted from the English "schoolmaster." Kannada is the language spoken predominantly in the southwestern Indian state of Karnataka. The conversation took place in Kannada and was sprinkled with words from English. I retain English-language words in italics in the translations from Kannada that I provide in this chapter.

[2] Ramanavami is "Rama's festival." Rama is the crown prince of Ayodhya, whose beloved wife Sita is abducted by Ravana, a demon king. The story – of Rama and Sita's fourteen-year exile into the forest, the war with Ravana, and the recovery of Sita and Rama's subsequent rule with the challenges posed by Sita – is told in the great epic of the *Ramayana* and in its countless variants, which are etched prominently in the narrative landscape of India. The epic is at the vivid center of many Hindu worship practices, pilgrimages, festivals, and discourses on ethics. In Sringeri, the festivity commences on the ninth day (*navami*) of the Kannada New Year, which occurs in late March or early April, the day on which Rama is believed to have been born, and concludes ten days later with a celebration of his coronation upon his return with Sita to Ayodhya.

I am grateful to the organizers and participants of the 2008–9 "Moral Worlds and Religious Subjectivities" seminar hosted by the Center for the Study of World Religions at Harvard University, where I presented portions of this chapter and received helpful suggestions.

Meshtru: My father was initiated into the great Rama Tāraka Mantra[3] by the previous guru.[4]

My father lived a good long life; not once did he come to depend on others.

He died peacefully, chanting "Rama, Rama...."

He dedicated a good part of his life to serving in the temple of Sharada.

But when he was dying, he said, "Despite the wealth we once had, today I am reduced to not having money even to have my corpse carried when I die."

My brother assured him that God would take care of everything.

I'm telling you this to illustrate how the results of good service accrue.

Because of my father's service to the goddess, we got some money and were able to meet the expenses for the cremation and the ceremonies.

Whatever the hardship, every year at that time [of the annual observance], funds materialize.

This can only be [understood] as a result of the service he performed for Sharada. God doesn't come and tell us what to do and when.

It's ultimately our actions, our service to the divine, that brings good fruit. Somewhere in some previous life, there may be good that we have done – but only if we possess great knowledge can we identify the fruit of that good action!

Who was I in the past, who am I today, and who am I going to be? Such questions can only be answered by someone with great knowledge.

---

3 The Rama Taraka mantra is the following meditative invocation of the victory (*jaya*) of Rama: "Sri Rama jaya Rama jaya jaya Rama." The chanting of this mantra is believed to enable one to cross (*taraka*) the turbulent ocean of worldly existence. See Diana L. Eck, *Banaras: City of Light* (Princeton, NJ: Princeton University Press, 1983), 332–3, for a section on how Hindu sacred literature discusses the power of this mantra at the time of death.

4 Sringeri is famous for its temple to Sharada, the Hindu goddess of learning and the arts, and its twelve hundred–year-old monastic center (*maṭha*) believed to have been established by the philosopher Shankara in the eighth century CE. It has since then been headed by an unbroken lineage of gurus. The Shankara maṭha is historically known for the role it has played in interpreting Hindu codes of conduct known as the *Dharmashastras* for lay and royal audiences who have consulted it for advice on a wide range of social, personal, and legal matters. There is, in Sringeri, as a result of this background, a high regard for the maṭha's gurus and monastic life in general, and an ubiquitous reverence and affection for the goddess Sharada.

Is it possible for all of us to be like Chandrashekara Bharati?[5]

It was not possible to look at his face directly; his radiance was so powerful, like [that of] Śiva himself –

Leela: So I've heard. My father has told me about him. He had seen him.

Meshtru: He used to walk toward the temple with his hands folded and with eyes focused on the ground.

I was in the eighth grade then and would accompany my parents to have his *darśan* [the seeing of a divine image or person]....

I remember how he used to enquire after my mother's mother, "How is she? Her eyes used to give her trouble, is she okay?" and so on.

He used to hold women in high esteem, likening them to the divine mother, to Sharada.

Students who used to live in Narasimha gardens [where the gurus reside] tell us that they saw this happen once with their own eyes.

There was also a priest in the temple at Kigga [a nearby town]; he too told us about this episode:

Many years ago, there was this highly placed engineer.

He did not have any children.

He had just finished doing elaborate *pūjā* [worship] to the *Shivalinga* [an iconic image of śiva], and along with his wife, he went to take *darśan* of the guru, Sri Chandrashekara Bharati.

So when he was climbing the steps [that lead to the area where the gurus reside], Chandrashekara Bharati opened the door, and said – nobody else heard him – except the engineer:

"You base man! Have you come here also? A mother is the very image of the divine – you've abandoned your mother and you've come here, seeking *darśan* of god, seeking *darśan* of the guru."

"*Hanh?* Base man!"

"Can there be anybody more base than you?"

These words, spoken softly, were heard only by the engineer.

He was shocked.

He fainted and dropped the plate with fruit that he was carrying.

When he recovered his senses, he insisted on seeing the guru, but the guru had retreated into meditation and could not be seen.

The engineer was adamant to the point of threatening, "I will jump into the Tunga River," but he was persuaded not to and the couple went away.

---

5 Sri Chandrashekara Bharati was the guru during the years 1912 to 1954.

Meshtru went on to describe how the engineer immediately went to Mumbai (formerly Bombay), where his mother lived by herself, and he told her, "If you want your son to live, you must come and stay with me and let me take care of you." "Which mother will have the heart to refuse such a plea by her child?" Meshtru commented. A few years later, the engineer brought his wife and the two children that they now had, along with his mother, to Sringeri. He sought the guru's *darśan* and was able to meet him this time. Smiling, the guru observed, "So you've come with your wife and children and your mother. May the goddess shower her abundant blessings on all of you." That's how, said Meshtru, people with true knowledge are, what their meditation and penance yield: they *know* the fruit that accompanies an action.

I begin this chapter with this story (whose analysis I will return to shortly) because such narrations – in their spontaneity, their every-dayness, their assumption of other presences, and their moral imagination – have persuaded me to adopt an experience-centered approach to the study of ethics. As I explained in my earlier work:

> [E]xperience-centered approaches can vivify and challenge the study of ethics, which usually overlooks the crucial role of oral narrative and everyday practice in shaping moral being. Such a perspective would privilege how people engage with precepts and tell us something about the dynamic ways in which individuals not only imagine and live out their ethical worlds, but convey this imagination to others.... [T]he ethical process is one of gathering and unfolding manifold impressions – that are enlivened through emotional engagement.[6]

At the heart of such a mode of inquiry is "the subject," who is

> at once a product and agent of history; the site of experience, memory, storytelling and aesthetic judgment; an agent of knowing as much as of action; and the conflicted site for moral acts and gestures.... Yet subjectivity is not the outcome of social control or the unconscious; it also provides the ground for subjects to think through their circumstances and to feel through their contradictions.... Of particular concern ... are the inward reworkings of the world and the consequences of people's actions toward themselves and toward others.... [T]his arena is precisely where the moral comes into view....[7]

---

[6] Leela Prasad, *Poetics of Conduct: Oral Narratives and Moral Being in a South Indian Town* (New York: Columbia University Press, 2007), 226.

[7] João Biehl, Bryon Good, and Arthur Kleinman, *Subjectivity: Ethnographic Investigations* (Berkeley and Los Angeles: University of California Press, 2007), 14–15. See especially Paul Ricoeur, *Oneself as Another*, trans. Kathleen Blamey (Chicago: University of Chicago Press, 1992).

At the same time, there are contexts that make it difficult to identify a singular or stable subject. For instance, Hindu worship *(pūjā)*, in its basic form, considers both the deity and the devotee as the very objects to be transformed through the self-conscious cultivation of a relationship as divine guest and ideal host. The transformation, enacted through the paradigm of hospitality – that is, the deity is the supreme guest to be treated with reverence, love, and care by the devotee – creates new subjects with possibly very different subjectivities (with specific desires, capacities, affinities, affective states). These subjects then become reciprocally accountable to each other. The sixteenth-century Kannada poet-saint Purandara dasa reminded his favorite deity, Panduranga (affectionately called Ranga), that obligatory mutuality was the very basis of their relationship. He sang: "To not be deluded by body, mind or wealth, that is my oath, Ranga; to still my mind in you, that is your oath" *(tanu-mana-dhanadalli vañcakanā dare yanage āṇe, Ranga/ manasu ninnali nilisadiddare ninage āṇe)*. Ultimately, Purandara dasa claimed, "you and I, we are *both* bound by the oath of devotees" *(yanagu ninagu ibbarigu bhaktarāṇe).*[8]

A theme that recurs in Hindu devotional poetry is that of inside/outside, the thresholds of which elude the devotee as he or she attempts to cross over into the inside. Through another prevalent metaphor, the devotee moves from one subject state to another, in restless waves of bewilderment, ecstasy, pangs, or dejection, in the ultimate hope to rest this oceanic struggle in the reposeful state of nonsubjectivity, when the devotee merges with the beloved deity. David Shulman and Guy Stroumsa thus say, "Indeed, whenever we speak of transformation, we need to ask: How much of the person, or the self, is present at any point? Which part becomes transformed? Is one part more real or said to be more real than another? Is there some systemic level of the person that constitutes a whole?"[9] In the context of Sufi practices and discourses in Pakistan too, Katherine Ewing finds that "... the experiencing subject is a non-unitary agent (perhaps better described as a bundle of agencies) who – in part through the experience of competing ideologies and alternative

---

[8] I transcribe these lines from an oral rendering by the Hindustani vocalist Nachiketa Yakkundi, who learned the song from his teacher, Pandit Basavaraj Rajguru. The translation is mine. The full text of the song in Kannada can be found in S. K. Ramachandra Rao, *Purandara Sahitya Darshana* (Bangalore: Directorate of Kannada Culture, Government of Karnataka, 1985).(Personal communication, Yakkundi.)

[9] David D. Shulman and Guy S. Stroumsa, eds., *Self and Self-transformation in the History of Religions* (New York: Oxford University Press, 2002), 9.

discourses – operates with the potential for critical distance from any one discourse or subject position."[10] Yet, it is critical to understand that what all these perspectives highlight is that ethical subjectivity is *not* just a multitude of disparate subject positions that emerge independent of each other, but is context-sensitive, interconnected, and historically aware in the present with a vision of the future.

In my work, an experience-centered approach to ethics has entailed attending to such seemingly mundane things as a conversational recounting about bargaining at the vegetable market, acts of cooking or stitching, a daily offering at a shrine, or a commute to a workplace. It has also meant paying attention to "extraordinary" events, such as a dance drama performance or a ritual ceremony, which can be potential sites and sources of moral reflection, transmission, and aesthetic self-exploration. Street-corner conversations or orientations of worship are not, until recently at least, what studies of ethics have usually turned to in order to construct theories of ethics. Yet, it is in the everyday that our clay is shaped, and it is in the everyday that we fashion our continually emerging personhoods. Ethical theorization abounds both in what we mark as "ordinary" life and in "extraordinary" events like performance – although the boundary between the everyday and the extraordinary is porous and contextually drawn. Further, as my own work and that of others have pointed out, to exclude phenomena like visionary experience, divine mediation, or dream communication from the realm of ethical inquiry is to wish away a vital and creative source of moral knowledge and well-being from the lives of many individuals and communities. It is also useful to remember that these phenomena are far from being distanced from historical, economic, and social processes. On the contrary, they engage them quite thoroughly, even providing us a necessary corrective to monocular views of historical and economic experience.

In this chapter, I turn to three aspects of lived experience that illustrate processes of moral engagement and exploration: stories, routines, and performance. I separate these aspects only for heuristic purposes, for, in daily life, they commonly flow into each other, as when a routine practice becomes the subject of a narration, or the performance of a narrative is a routine practice for a storyteller.

---

[10] Katherine Pratt Ewing, *Arguing Sainthood: Modernity, Psychoanalysis, and Islam* (Durham, NC: Duke University Press, 1997), 5.

I. STORIES

Let us return to Meshtru's recollection that began this chapter. Why did Meshtru tell me this story in the first place? My simple remark that the Ramanavami celebrations had gone well called up unintentionally the concluding part of the event in which Meshtru's family had been profusely thanked for their sponsorship of the day's activities. Rather than view this as public encomium for the family, Meshtru gently redirected my attention to his family's "service to Rama," his father's devotion to Rama, and the lifelong service his father had rendered in the Sharada temple. As Meshtru understood it, although his father's good acts had not resulted in material benefits, he had had the greater fortune of a peaceful death with the words, "Rama, Rama," on his lips.

The larger ethical puzzle that Meshtru explicitly articulated was one that I recognized as a long-standing moral quandary in Hindu philosophy and daily life: Beyond knowing generally that "good service yields good fruit," how do ordinary people like us correlate specific acts and their consequences? The question took Meshtru to the figure of a particular Sringeri guru, one who was known to read with ease and insight the ordinarily inscrutable moral map of acts and consequences according to which our lives are said to unfold. I expressed my eagerness to listen, as here was a story of our family's guru, about to reach me through a channel other than family history. The "highly placed engineer," despite having performed the customary *pūjā(s)* – good acts, in one sense surely – was reprimanded by the guru in words spoken softly (were these articulated at all, or were they sensed by the engineer, I wonder?), and possibly also through the act of not being available for *darśan* (which would have amounted to a considerable disappointment and even given occasion for reflection on one's actions) for a breach in duty toward his mother. The norm (reiterated in Hindu commentarial and prescriptive literature, epic narrative, and daily lore) that duty to one's parents precedes *pūjā* and *darśan* – staple expressions of Hindu religious experience – is affirmed in this account also. Although there is only so far I can go in asserting Meshtru's intentions at the time he recounted the narrative, I find myself seeing a thematic continuity between the narrative about his father in which the sons care for him and the one about the engineer. Was the former functioning as a normative tale in relation to which the second would be judged? Personal experience becomes entwined with story that is in public circulation. (Does the public domain erase the privacy that was reported as a characteristic of the original communication –

that is, the admonishment was "heard only by the engineer" – so that the account has now become a public exemplum?)

What is clearer to me is that a broader cultural text, whose normative premises Meshtru and I may not have exactly shared but with which we were both robustly familiar, subtextually emerges in the intersubjective experience of Meshtru's telling and my listening. That is, we share a tacit awareness across many dimensions: (a) this is a moral mandate that aging parents should be cared for by their children (especially by sons); (b) a "true" guru will show the right path even if in a harsh manner; (c) a person such as *this* guru (who can see past, present, and future with clarity) embodies moral authority; and finally, (d) closure for the engineer can come only when he corrects his error and returns to Sringeri to seek – and gain – the *darśan* that once eluded him.

I draw on another story from Sringeri to illustrate how narrative provides the ground to express and explore ethical subjectivity. The monastic environment and the verdant seclusion of Sringeri, until the tourist boom exploded in the 1990s, used to attract itinerant renunciants (*sannyāsis*) who would visit Sringeri families for alms (*bhikṣā*). Sringeri families, even today, irrespective of caste and economic resources, make concerted efforts to provide alms to renunciants as enjoined by Hindu scriptures. Residents affectionately recall the idiosyncrasies of particular renunciants, some of whom were regulars, such as the nicknamed "banana swami" [holy man], who collected extra bananas from various shrines (where they would have been brought by devotees) and gave them away to children who could recite this or that verse.

The story I reproduce is about one such renunciant (*sannyāsi*) who lived in Sringeri for a few months. My landlord, Ramachandra Bhattru, shared it with me during a conversation at his home. Ramachandra Bhattru and his wife Amrutamba are both public school teachers, and I had many insightful conversations with them about my research. Ramachandra Bhattru is one of the most articulate and enthusiastic participants in the cultural and social life of Sringeri; in fact, it was he who had publicly thanked Meshtru's family during Ramanavami that year. I excerpt this story from a set of stories he told me that evening about Sringeri's visiting ascetics.

> There was one swami who used to visit our home.
> He would have been about twenty-six, twenty-seven years of age.
> Very radiant. He'd wake up at 2:30 or 2:45 in the morning and bathe, and until 10, he would meditate.
> You know what he'd do here?

You know this wheat flour, right? He'd roast it.

In the water from the river, he would mix the flour by putting it in a glass of water, and he'd drink two glasses of that everyday.

I didn't know that he did this, until Ramaswamy (a neighbor) told us, "Look at what's going on, this poor swami.

Who knows, perhaps he feels obliged if he seeks alms, and so look at what he's doing."

"*Tcha-tcha*, how can we let this go on? Let's go and tell him [to eat in our homes].

Let us take on the task of serving him one meal day each. He can seek *bhikṣā* [alms] from one home each day, and he can have his meal in our homes."

They conveyed this to the swami.

And he started to come.

You know, there's nothing compared to the human will, nothing, that's what this little story is about.

So he came.

We had readied ourselves, the meal was served and over with – after all, his food is all bland, just boil vegetables and lentils together, boil some rice, that's all.

He held a *karta* [the shell of a coconut].

He would eat, wash his hands, and move on.

Once a week in this manner he would come to our home.

Three or four months passed this way.

One fine day, I was standing here in the evening, just the way I was when you came.

He came. "Bhattre, I will not come for *bhiksā* from tomorrow, okay?" he announced.

What was I to make of that?

Could we have committed some impropriety? I racked my mind.

I asked, "Swami have we inconvenienced you in any way? Have we erred in the cooking?"

For us, feeding a *sannyāsi* [renunciant] – feeding a thousand people – and providing *bhikṣā* for one swami bring the same merit for a householder, there is that much merit in that act. "We have been gladly carrying on an ancestral tradition, believing ourselves fortunate; how can you do such a thing to us? Why? Have we caused you any trouble? Would you like something changed? Would you like me to bring your meal to where you will be? I can do that."

But he said, "It's nothing like that. I just feel sleepy when I eat."

He repeated slowly, "I feel sleepy when I eat."

"*Arre! Everybody* feels sleepy after eating, what is this that you're saying?"

"True, but it disturbs my spiritual practice."

And he stopped coming.

We assumed that the swami had gone to some other town, but he returned two months later.

"I've given up food altogether," he said.

"What do you do? Do you eat wheat flour again?"

"No," he replied.

"I drink a decoction of pipal leaves around noon."

Pipal!

Leaves of the pipal tree – leaves!

He said he'd put some leaves of the pipal tree in his mouth around noon.

Then, he'd chew them well and drink water from the Tunga [the local river].

That man – even after eating regular meals – even a half-hour's walk tires us – but that man, *puttu-puttu-puttu*, that's how *he* would walk.

He was twenty-seven-years old.

Just once a day.

Drinking a decoction of pipal leaves.

"Nothing happens if you forego food, Bhattre,"[11] he'd say.

"*Nothing* happens, but the mind doesn't agree, that's why we eat four times a day."

"You feel thirsty because you *want* to drink water. It's because you *want* to drink water that you feel thirsty."

"That desire should go," he said.

"You believe, 'I feel hunger.' If you believed instead, 'I don't feel hunger,' then?

"You will certainly *not* be troubled."

I used to see him around here for a year. Drinking that same decoction.

He used to wander around here.

And then, the elder guru said, "Go – go to Badri,"[12] and he sent him. So he went – and he's now in Badri.

---

[11] *Bhattru* is modified to *Bhattre* when used as a form of address.

[12] The philosopher Shankara is believed to have established four monasteries in India in the eighth century CE. Badrinath, or Badri, in the Himalayas is the northern center, while Sringeri is the southern. Shankara hagiographies narrate that he "disappeared" into the Himalayas from Badri in his thirty-second year.

Sannyasi-householder interaction is expansively treated in various *Dharmashastras*[13] notably the *Sannyasa Upanishads* (philosophical expositions on renunciation), and backed by an ambience in Sringeri that idealizes this interaction. Yet, in Ramachandra Bhattru's account, the details of this relationship and its everyday manifestations ultimately have to be worked out intersubjectively, through dialogue, trial and error, and reciprocity. In this case, there is an interesting commingling of compatible values in the decision of the young renunciant, who progressively moves from (a reluctant) compliance with one domain of shastric injunction (that stipulates that renunciants seek alms) to another domain that focuses on the purpose and goal of the very state of renunciation (*sannyāsa*). Ramachandra Bhattru's remark "How can you do this to us?" reflects the stress that the young renunciant's actions create within the ascetic-householder system.

Ramachandra Bhattru's telling reinforces several ethical discourses that he and I are familiar with and have been taught to admire even if we do not practice them in our paths of life. We have been taught to respect a *sannyāsi*, we are able to acknowledge the difficulties of that way of life, and we are more or less aware of the fragilities associated with that system. Yet, Ramachandra Bhattru's metanarrative comment ("this is about the human will") takes the story to a place where the distant injunctive becomes personally relevant: it is about the play – or the struggle – and exercise of the human will. In the young renunciant's journey, we see him struggle in pursuit of an ideal. He starts off, at least from where we first meet him, by consuming wheat flour. After doing a little bit of conventional *bhikṣā*, he soon switches to a pipal decoction. This is interesting. Why did he pick the pipal, when, after all, there are numerous types of trees in Sringeri? It is not lost on me as a listener that the pipal tree – known as *Ashwattha* in Sanskrit and many Indian languages – is highly symbolic in Hindu and Buddhist sacred literature and worship. (It is said that the Buddha obtained enlightenment under the pipal tree, and I have seen countless Hindu shrines under pipal trees in metropolises and rural

---

[13] The Hindu codes of conduct, the *Dharmasutras* and the *Dharmashastras*, are vast, normative compendia, collectively referred to as the shastras in everyday parlance. They have been compiled by different authors approximately between 500 BCE and 400 CE. The *Dharmashastras* discuss a staggering variety of topics relating to social and religious conduct, law, and righteousness. The *matha* has traditionally specialized in interpreting these diverse treatises. The term *shastra* comes from the Sanskrit root *shas* (to instruct) and can contextually mean rule, precept, or law, for example. The *shastras* have come to exert enormous influence in the cultural and literary thinking of early India, which can claim shastras on virtually all areas of life, from sexuality to statecraft.

towns alike.) The pipal tree's various parts, particularly the leaves and the bark, have medicinal properties in Ayurveda – but I did not ask specifically, and my attempt to understand the renunciant's final choice must now fall back on the sacred and healing aura of the pipal. Another unstated visual image adds to the ethos of the narrative: the journey to Badri is reminiscent of the one that Shankara, renunciant exemplar, himself had made when he walked a thousand miles from South India.

What is interesting to consider is how the narration closes the gap between rules of renunciation, on the one hand, and the renunciant's desire to be free, even of biological needs, on the other. He rejects one aspect of the system of *sannyāsa dharma* (that is, that food must be collected only through alms seeking) in order to uphold a larger goal of the same system through his commitment to the ideological root of the system: the goal of *freedom*.

Meshtru's narration is a discourse about how to construct relationships (between people, between acts). Ramachandra Bhattru's story is about a young renunciant's struggle to understand and gain control over his subjectivity in the light of renunciation. Both stories accomplish their moral work in the ordinary settings of casual conversations, one on a street corner, and the other on the small balcony of a home on Sringeri's main street. Conversationally shared stories are ubiquitous across the world; they (re)construct oral histories of a place, an event, or a family; they contain reflections on the environment, on the human body and consciousness, they describe realities and visions, they are remembrances. This vivacity makes it possible to hear the moral heteroglossia of human life that keeps elastic and contextual the notions of the normative. As narrations ponder issues of self and society, human and divine relations, or some luminous moment of a life, they capture the improvisational quality, the ambivalence and the struggle, and the give and take between the individual and the collective that characterize our everyday lives. Why do some ordinary encounters, as in the story that Meshtru shared, resonate for a long time, in unexpected places, and in new ways (possibly with alterations in intention, significance, and affect accompanying the changed context)? The concept that explains aesthetic resonance is the Sanskrit *dhvani*, a principle of poetics that was first enunciated by the celebrated critic Anandavardhana in his ninth-century CE treatise *Dhvanyaloka. Dhvani*, which was subsequently explored by centuries of Sanskrit literary critics, is "suggested meaning" signifying something not designated through language but only evoked, sensed, or experienced in context by an empathetic (they would say "cultivated") audience. As experiences find their way into narratives, and are expressed in dialogue, "the question of 'moral meaning' becomes a zone of exploration for both the narrator and the listener(s) in different ways."[14] Mikhail Bakhtin, explaining what he calls the "tertiary" nature of all dialogue, says that "the word is a drama" that includes implied interlocutors; in addition to the speaker and the listener, there is a third actor (an idea, a person, a place, a past, for example) who shapes speech.[15] Theories of narrative developed in folklore studies have proposed sophisticated methods for context-sensitive oral-narrative analysis. An attempt to understand conversationally shared stories as ethical acts would lead us to ask, Why this story, why now? What voices, what ideological presences, and which sensory modalities are being serviced in this telling? When all is said, what remains unsaid or unsayable? How do we trace narrative rapport or its absence? Indeed, why and how is someone moved by a story?

II. ROUTINES

In February 1999, the Balch Institute for Ethnic Studies in Philadelphia (now the Historical Society of Pennsylvania) opened its doors to the first exhibition in the United States on Indian American life, focusing on the Greater Delaware Valley. I had worked for two years as the guest curator, doing ethnographic work and conceptualizing the exhibition. An associated project was to produce a video documentary and a catalogue that would accompany the exhibition.[16] Bobby, an aspiring theater artist, whose parents had migrated to the United States when Bobby was three years old, was among the many younger Indian Americans in their twenties with whom I had spent time during my ethnographic work. He agreed to be videotaped in an open-ended group conversation among "second-generation" Indian Americans. The conversation had veered toward their high school years, and they began trading memories about how they had negotiated, sometimes for the first time in their lives, the coming to terms with having an "Indian background" (about which they were themselves unsure, being both at the same time "Indian" and "American") in milieus that did not comprehend, let alone support, such a formulation. And then Bobby said, about growing up in New York:

14 Prasad, *Poetics of Conduct*, 184.
15 M. M. Bakhtin, *Speech Genres & Other Late Essays*, trans. Vern W. McGee, ed. Caryl Emerson and Michael Holquist (Austin: University of Texas Press, 1986), 122.
16 Leela Prasad, ed., *"Live Like the Banyan Tree": Images of the Indian American Experience: An Exhibition at the Balch Institute of Ethnic Studies* (Darby, PA: Diane, 2006).

And I can recall things like not wearing slippers anymore, to go get milk from across the street. I really liked wearing my *chappals* you know, it was fun, and I was used to it, and then I decided it wasn't.

As a matter of fact, my Mom looked at me one day, and she said, "Go get milk." I said, "OK, give me a second, I need to put on my shoes."

And she said, "What...?? Just go get the milk!"

I said, "No, I need to put on my shoes."

And ... she's really smart ... we were not very close.... I wish we had talked about it, but we didn't. We were just silent.

I got up, put on my shoes, and walked out. It was a little decision.

I sacrificed something and I did plenty, plenty more.

And ... those are the kind of things that – you know.

I would walk out, I would have the shoes on, but I would still get shit. So what was it?

Or being [in] line in the store where there is an Indian man working, and not wanting to be identified with that man, so, god, so ... walking by the store, and making strategic decisions as "it's too crowded, there are kids my age.... I'll wait." I'd go round the block one more time to see if they've left. Going to buy certain things to see if no one else is at the counter, go up, make purchase, and leave.

All kinds of things. Little things. Those are the ones.... I don't know about the macro, but the micro really hurts the most.[17]

The routine acts of buying milk and slipping one's feet into *chappals*,[18] comfortable in one context, become loaded with ethnic cargo that turns unwieldy and ungainly in another context. *Chappals* became markers of an Indian ethnicity, of racial and cultural difference, or at least so it seems initially. But, as Bobby discovered, wearing shoes instead did not help him "blend in," nor did it protect him from racism. *Chappals* for me may remain "slippers" for others. There is recognition from the others in the group that this dilemma is a familiar one. A young woman participating in the conversation later referenced Bobby's "small sacrifice"

---

[17] Leela Prasad and Uma Magal, co-directors, *Back and Forth: Two Generations of Indian Americans at Home* (Philadephia: Balch Institute for Ethnic Studies, 1999).

[18] *Chappals*, generally flat slippers, are a characteristic and popular form of footwear in everyday life in South Asia. *Chappals* are not only practical to wear in South Asia's climatic conditions; their ubiquitous use has also created a colorful and varied *chappal* marketplace.

as "the *chappals* example." She went on to describe a family that had taught their daughter to be "very comfortable about being Indian." She explained that this girl would have probably told people "right when she was six years old" that "I'm Indian, these are *chappals*, we Indians wear them...." Yet the neatness of this self-narrative is undercut by a fundamental paradox: the sense of belonging is also a sense of alienation, because the price of being identified as Indian is to be tagged as "other" by a majority population. Additionally, subjectively speaking, the task of being many things, not only Indian (or "South Asian," as is the term more commonly used in the United States), becomes more complicated as one's networks and belongings grow and change. The unexceptional practice of buying milk is also fraught in Bobby's reminiscence. The identification with the Indian man at the counter is perhaps not in itself a problem, but the image in between is – the image of the stereotype of the crude Indian immigrant in every convenience store (an image that is ridiculed in shows such as *The Simpsons*) is an image a teenager's peers would know well. At the time of the making of the video documentary, Bobby, Mika, Shivani, and the others who participated had acquired enough distance from these experiences to construct a narrative about them, but nonetheless, the "micro really hurts the most." One might thus begin to consider how ordinary acts become imbued with ethical significance, or more generally, how routines and daily practices (spanning the visual, the material, and the sensory) speak of and embody a moral imagination and actor.

Back in Sringeri, when I mentioned to a mementos store owner in the early months of my fieldwork that I was learning more about the areca crop than I had expected to – the crop's diseases and fertilizer problems – he expressed surprise, saying, "But in these parts, agriculture is our culture." I came to appreciate the meaning of this remark as I followed people through their agricultural routines. The night-long shelling of the harvested areca nuts, an activity that is undertaken in groups for weeks and is characterized by conversation, food, and tea, generates a vivacious sociality that comments on Sringeri senses of place, mutuality, and norms. A *pūjā* that takes place in areca groves when lightning strikes a palm or when new saplings are planted express the perception that the human condition, inevitably unfolding in a field of inscrutable moral forces, is something that needs to nurtured through sacred auras. The smearing of courtyard floors with "black paste" made from areca is understood simultaneously as organic conservation and as the creation of auspicious everyday-use space. The shared re-thatching of storage sheds with areca fronds, with its accompanying leisure activities, is a process that reinforces the necessity of reciprocal commitments and the pleasure that can be gained through them.

One could also turn to another register of everyday routines: cooking. Typically injunctive, normative, and grounded in the local but ultimately concerned with the translocal sense of "well-being," food talk in Sringeri not only taught me how to cook this or that delectable dish, but also demonstrated how food itself is imagined as an ethical system whose central intertwined idioms are appropriateness and belonging, with its own aesthetics or politics. Furthermore, such a system can be known and learned only through immersion in the "seeing and doing" orientations that are part of everyday living in which proximity and sustained engagement are possible. Moral knowing and the ability to intuit or express it are just as powerfully acquired through what I have called literacies of practice.[19]

Daily routines can also provide the ground for rigorous self-cultivation. Anthropologist Saba Mahmood writes that women who participate in the women's mosque movement in Cairo are enjoined to take up the responsibility of living by a moral code of conduct that best aids in each woman's discovery of the "divine plan" for her life. The internal cultivation of piety is to be sustained by external markers of religiosity, by a range of bodily disciplines ("ritual practices, styles of comporting oneself, dress, and so on"). Reporting a conversation that takes place in a mosque in which Mona, an experienced woman, advises a younger woman, Mahmood says, "when Mona links the ability to pray to the vigilance with which one conducts the practical chores of daily living, *all* mundane activities – such as getting angry with one's sister, the things one hears and looks at, the way one speaks – become a place for securing and honing particular moral capacities." It is through infusion into daily practices that the desire to pray becomes "a part of [their] condition of being."[20] Even in the more specialized context of Haitian vodou as practiced in New York, we learn that spirits intuit and enact situations that reflect predicaments of practitioners. This vigorous and candid enactment, which is conducted jointly by spirits and practitioners, bristling with the tensions and contradictions of lived experience, does not position itself *outside* of daily routines and resources; rather, vodou drama unfolds through everyday acts such as conversing, quarreling, feeding, singing, marrying, and joking, and in thus "over[ing] so close

---

[19] Prasad, *Poetics of Conduct*, 18.
[20] Saba Mahmood, *Politics of Piety: The Islamic Revival and the Feminist Subject* (Princeton, NJ: Princeton University Press, 2005), 124–6.

to the social ground," they are able to empower practitioners to resolve their moral dilemmas.[21]

Everyday routines, rhythms of ordinary life, tend to go unnoticed, but in truth, they are what philosopher Paul Ricoeur would call "traces" that resonate in the present with the deep presence of the past, affecting both how we imagine that past perhaps in changing ways and how we see the present as bearing a relationship to it.[22] When I asked women in Sringeri how they had learned this or that practice, I often got the answer (mirrored in my own experience), "What is there to teach? It's all there in the family." Or, "this is how my mother did it." While on the one hand, these phrases close the formal project of meaning making and moral seeking, they say something valuable about how practices and ways of being are suffused with a sense of "this is auspicious, this is correct," and one learns these through experience.

III. PERFORMANCES

If stories and routines display a continual drama of negotiation, experimentation, and cultivation that characterizes ethical subjectivity, certain performance genres explicitly stage the makings of "a proper life." In Sringeri, performance and ethics meet in an oral tradition called *āśīrvāda* (ceremonial blessing) that frames and answers the question, How ought one to live? At the end of an event such as a marriage or a housewarming, a brief ceremony of no more than thirty minutes invariably takes place in which a priest or a scholar extemporaneously delivers a "speech" in Kannada that begins by offering thanks to hosts and guests. He praises the hosts for their well-performed duty and turns to the principal function of the speech: moral exegesis and instruction on everyday conduct. *Āśīrvāda* speeches are intertextual and carefully structured so that the ethical significance of the event is brought out through a map of scriptural citations. Typically, to achieve this, they annotate *dharmashastric* injunctions, abstract stories from the epics and other narrative traditions, and, when appropriate, they refer to local history.

A translated excerpt from an *āśīrvāda* that was delivered by Vinayaka Udupa follows. Vinayaka Udupa specializes in Purana scholarship and has taught at the Sanskrit school in the *matha* (monastery) for thirty years. Many people in Sringeri had directed me to him, as he

---

[21] Karen McCarthy Brown, *Mama Lola: A Vodou Priestess in Brooklyn*, Comparative Studies in Religion and Society (Berkeley: University of California Press, 2001), 254.

[22] Paul Ricoeur, *Time and Narrative*, vol. 3, trans. Kathleen Blamey and David Pellauer (Chicago: University of Chicago Press, 1988).

is considered one of the most erudite and eloquent scholars in the area. In this *āśīrvāda*, which he delivered at the end of a ritual dedicated to Rudra, a form of Śiva, for prosperity and well-being, Vinayaka Udupa creates a vision of ideal conduct by answering the question: In what manner can the most appropriate life be led? Vinayaka Udupa opens the *āśīrvāda* with a Sanskrit verse from the Rig Veda (1.89.8).

Om
bhadraṃ karṇebhiḥ śṛṇuyāma devā
bhadram paśyemākṣabhir yajatrāḥ |
sthirair aṅgais tuṣṭuvāṃsas tanūbhir
vy aśema devahitaṃ yad āyuḥ ||

[Om. O Worshipful Ones, may our ears hear what is auspicious.
May we, who worship, see with our eyes what is auspicious.
May we, who sing your praise, live our allotted span of life in perfect
   health and strength.] (Translation mine.)

After reciting this verse, which he does not translate, Vinayaka Udupa provides an exegesis in Kannada of portions of the verse. I have translated his exegesis into English.

Vinayaka Udupa:
Now,
Birth has been conferred on us.
Ishvara [God] has bestowed this body with all the senses.
Thus I have ears.
For what purpose should we use our ears?

bhadraṃ karṇebhiḥ śṛṇuyāma devā

That which is fit to be heard, that is "Veda."
Therefore, we must hear only that which is meritorious.
One should never listen to that which is evil.
That is the meaning.
That is why – when you worship,
why is it that you ring the bell? So that other sounds do not fall on
   our ears.
You sound the gong, you blow the conch, if you ask what the *inten-
tion* of this is: it is that no inauspicious sound must reach our ears
   at that time.
Only sounds that are auspicious must keep being heard.

bhadraṃ karṇebhiḥ śṛṇuyāma devā
So one must use the ears to listen to worthy thoughts only.

Then,
bhadram paśyemākṣabhir yajatrāḥ |
One's eyes must always see the image of God.
So it is said.

The worthiest of images – of gods, of gurus – these are the sights that
we must always see and rejoice in, that is the meaning.
bhadram paśyemākṣabhir yajatrāḥ |
sthirair aṅgais tuṣṭuvāṃsas tanūbhir
We use this strong and sturdy body of ours to praise the *paramatma*
[supreme soul] and to serve him.

...tuṣṭuvāṃsas tanūbhir
vy aśema devahitaṃ yad āyuḥ

Whatever our lifespan may be, we should use all of this [the senses
and the body] to seek God in a fit and worthy manner.

The sections that follow the excerpt given here lay out the moral orientations necessary for a householder in the conduct of his or her daily
life. Primary among these are understanding the right place of worldly
possessions and desires, remembering the interdependence of creatures,
and acknowledging one's inability to act without divine will and grace.
Udupa then directs the *āśīrvāda* to its summing statement: In a world
that is filled with choices of forms to worship, one should recognize that
all beings and forms are permeated by a single supreme self, Ishvara, the
root substance of the universe. And it is this Ishwara that listeners are
encouraged to worship; Rudra is a manifestation of Ishvara. But the body
and the senses have to be readied for this recognition of Ishvara's all-ness
to happen – this insight of the opening statement becomes the ground on
which the rest of the *āśīrvāda* is developed. Thus the well-known peace
invocation (*shanti patha*) is invoked to convey that one should ideally
make one's body the receptacle of auspicious sound, sight, and thought
in order to be able to perform "right action" (duty). Just what constitutes "right action" becomes the impelling question of the *āśīrvāda*, and
the often-repeated Kannada phrase *mada beku* (ought to) delineates the
approach to right action.

Audiences listen avidly to *āśīrvāda* speeches. Variations of the
reflexive statement "this is the meaning" keep audiences tuned into the
injunctive mode of the *āśīrvāda*. I learned that the tradition's oral poetics
point to an aesthetic of propriety that governs a speech's evaluation: only
when all elements of the speech are aligned – credibility of the speaker,
a broad historical familiarity with the subject, choice of allusions, style

of delivery, and a right balance between a sensitivity to the context and a distance from mundane details of the event, for instance – is the *āśīrvāda* speech deemed morally persuasive.

To what extent we are persuaded and persuade in ethical dialogue is a coming together of the aesthetic and the moral, which flow into and out of each other. The stories we hear, absorb, or (re)tell; the routines and material practices of our everyday life; and the performance traditions we engage: ultimately, these all suggest the ways and the terms in which our ethical subjectivities – relational, embodied, and imaginative – emerge and grow.

Select Bibliography

Burkhalter Flueckiger, Joyce. *In Amma's Healing Room: Gender and Vernacular Islam in South India*. Bloomington: Indiana University Press, 2006.

Cohen, Richard A. and James L. Marsh. Eds. *Ricoeur as Another: The Ethics of Subjectivity*. Albany: State University of New York Press, 2002.

Cruikshank, Julie. *The Social Life of Stories: Narrative and Knowledge in the Yukon Territory*. Lincoln: University of Nebraska Press, 1998.

Erndl, Kathleen M. *Victory to the Mother: The Hindu Goddess of Northwest India in Myth, Ritual and Symbol*. Oxford and New York: Oxford University Press, 1993.

Gold, Ann Grodzins. Coauthored with Bhoju Ram Gujar. *In the Time of Trees and Sorrows: Nature, Power, and Memory in Rajasthan*. Durham, NC: Duke University Press, 2002.

Mills, Margaret A. *Rhetorics and Politics in Afghan Traditional Storytelling*. Philadelphia: University of Pennsylvania Press, 1991.

Narayan, Kirin. In collaboration with Urmila Devi Sood. *Mondays on the Dark Night of the Moon: Himalayan Foothill Folktales*. New York and Oxford: Oxford University Press, 1997.

"'Honor Is Honor, After All': Silence and Speech in the Life Stories of Women in Kangra, Northwest India." In *Telling Lives in India: Biography, Autobiography, and Life History*. Edited by David Arnold and Stuart Blackburn. Bloomington: Indiana University Press, 2004, 227–51.

Shulman, David and Guy S. Stroumsa. *Self and Self-Transformation in the History of Religions*. New York: Oxford University Press, 2002.

18 Neo-Pentecostalism and globalization

MARLA F. FREDERICK

> ... I'm not going to let you stand here by yourself, Bishop, let you carry
> this load alone. Last night, my wife and I spent a lot of time.... We spent
> a lot of money to come here. Y'all know (looking at the crowd) we spent
> a lot of money to come here." ["Yes!" replied the audience.] "And, um,
> last night, the Lord told me in light of all that I've seen; my wife and I
> agreed to write you a check to the Potters House for $10,000.

With this act of generosity from a member of the audience, Dallas-based
Pentecostal Bishop T. D. Jakes lifted his hands and walked back and forth
across the floor of the stage. The announcement had come seemingly as a
surprise, a spontaneous gesture in the midst of the bishop's plea to his audience for financial support. Bishop Jakes's comments were directed toward
the primarily American donors gathered together that morning in Soweto.
The need he spoke of was specific. South Africa, like other African nations,
is experiencing a crisis of clean water. Women and children walk miles
to collect water from polluted streams. Those in remote areas of South
Africa, like persons located in similarly isolated regions of India and other
countries of the "developing" world, are in a quandary. "If you don't drink
it, you die. And, if you drink it, you die," in Jakes's words. Added to this,
the HIV/AIDS epidemic has devastated many in the country, especially
in neighboring Swaziland, the second stop on the bishop's tour. The HIV/
AIDS pandemic has left countless children orphaned and thousands of others without sufficient medical attention or even proper medical diagnosis.
The work of responding to this crisis, Jakes insisted, should come from the
Christian church. The same people who come to Africa and other "developing" areas of the world preaching the "good news" of salvation ought to
be vested in transforming the society, not simply in saving souls:

> People come in all the time to our country and to other countries
> and draw big old crowds. They pass out conversion cards and they
> leave. You know, they don't feed anybody; they don't clothe any-
> body; they don't build anything for anybody and they just go back
> and say, "You know, we had thousands. Thousands came!" [rolling

his eyes back in jest] "Oh, Bless God, it was just ... and when the Spirit got to falling...." [Jakes continued the jest with his own conclusion.] [When the Spirit got to falling,] people were hungry and naked; and their children were sold into slavery; and the women were still being raped and sodomized; and the children were running behind bushes for fear of their lives; and we go back home and think we did something for God! ... It's more to it than that.

Jakes's message this morning was unlike the calls for self-help, personal empowerment, and prosperity for which he is best known. It was not about salvation from sin. He was not preaching a thinly veiled rendition of the prosperity gospel. He issued a simple and straightforward plea on behalf of South Africans in need, directed to Christians in America. The generous donor quoted at the opening of this chapter was made no promise of riches or special blessing in return to him and his family if he would but "sow a seed." The only promise was that water would be provided and HIV/AIDS screening offered. The meeting at which this donor rose to speak came just prior to the final worship service at MegaFest International organized by T. D. Jakes.

Between October 6 and October 11, 2008, more than nine hundred men and women from Dallas, Texas, Richmond, Virginia, Montgomery, Alabama, Brooklyn, New York, Seattle, Washington, and other cities and towns across the United States boarded aircraft for the fifteen-hour trip to Johannesburg. For months, Jakes had been advertising on TBN, TV One, Daystar, and other religious television stations for his viewers to join him on a journey to South Africa. This was an experience they did not want to miss, he promised. Nearly one thousand people responded, from every corner of the United States, the Caribbean, and England in order to meet in fellowship with those with whom they had previously been connected only via satellite. The event itself, planned by the offices of T. D. Jakes, was a two-day festival held in an open-air stadium in Soweto, where evangelists preached to standing-room-only crowds. African American and South African musicians offered ministry in song. Vendors sold books, music, jewelry, clothes, and home decor in large exhibit halls to the rear of the arena. In adjoining buildings, volunteer doctors and nurses from T. D. Jakes's ministry and local medical teams offered free health exams, including HIV/AIDS screening. These services came under the umbrella of MegaCARE – an effort to intervene in the health and environmental crisis facing South Africa during the MegaFest events.[1]

---

[1] According to its website, MegaCARE "links the Potter's House with local governmental, NGO [nongovernmental agency], and faith-based partners to bring relief to parts of

Megafest International is emblematic of the power of media technology to create and sustain international religious communities at the
crest of the new millennium. The weekend itself offers a microscopic
view into the breadth of the international communities created via televangelism. In its inaugural year of 2004, Megafest drew over 140,000
men and women to Atlanta's Convention Center. With added satellite
distribution to prison populations and to persons in other countries,
Megafest "has reached more than 700,000 people around the world,"
the organization claims in a press release.[2] The 2004 conference was the
culmination of two prior major conferences that Jakes's ministry had
sponsored independently. The conferences "Woman Thou Art Loosed"
and "Man Power" were each promoted as addressing issues specific to
the social, psychological, and religious experiences of women and men.
Having established these two conferences as his signature annual events,
Jakes's ministry decided to join forces and create an occasion that would
encapsulate the entire family, male and female, under one roof. The first
Megafest was the realization of this vision.

Just prior to the concluding day of worship at MegaFest International
in South Africa, Jakes requested a meeting with the international guests,
the vast majority of whom had traveled with him from the United States.
We met in a large concrete auditorium adjacent to the outdoor arena.
As was the case with earlier sessions, the meeting began with a praise
and worship service followed by a message from Bishop Jakes. He laid
bare his vision for the conference, considered its successes thus far, and
looked to the challenges ahead. But he especially wanted to emphasize
the urgent need for financial donations. The meeting with Jakes that
morning serves as an entrée into thinking about the ways in which the
popular presence of black Pentecostalism influences and is influenced by
the realities of globalization and media technology.

I. OTHERWORLDLY PENTECOSTALS?

The study of black religion (and of black Pentecostalism in particular) has
consistently raised the question of religion's agency in society.[3] One of

Africa where medical and community assistance is most genuinely needed." Online at
www.megafest.org/megacare.php (accessed June 3, 2009).

2 Online at http://www.megafest.org/newsroom.php (accessed June 3, 2009).
3 For a recent historical analysis of this tension in black religious studies between accommodation and resistance, see Barbara Dianne Savage, *Your Spirits Walk Beside Us:
The Politics of Black Religion* (Cambridge, MA: Belknap Press of Harvard University
Press, 2008).

the classic presuppositions of this scholarship has been that Pentecostal practices represent otherworldly and compensatory modes of being in the world. Within the matrix of black religious studies, Pentecostalism has been viewed as falling short of an engaged political and economic challenge to social structures.[4] Critics of this view, however, among them Oberlin College Professor of Religion Albert (A. G.) Miller, have called this deprivation model of Pentecostalism into question. Howard University Professor Cheryl Sanders, likewise, has emphasized the resilience of black Pentecostals in resisting the lure of middle-class assimilation patterns.[5] These scholars point out that black Pentecostals have often worked among poor blacks and that they have embraced African forms of worship that were both kinesthetic and emotive. This type of religious experience demonstrated for Sanders that black Pentecostals were in some ways more engaged qualitatively with the poor than the many in the black middle class who moved away from poor communities and whose worship patterns more commonly resembled the austerity of modern Protestant worship styles.

The popular turn in recent years toward a decidedly neo-Pentecostal practice has introduced important alternatives to classic Pentecostalism. Embracing some of the expressivity as well as the basic theological tenets of classic Pentecostalism, yet leaving behind much of its doctrines and regulations, neo-Pentecostals have introduced more open and capacious interpretations of Pentecostalism. One of the most striking differences is the extent to which neo-Pentecostals embrace the material opportunities of consumer culture (fine cars, lavish homes, designer clothing) explicitly as signs of God's blessings, whereas classic Pentecostals warned against and rejected what they viewed as "worldliness" and its consequences.[6] Still, as seemingly easy as classic Pentecostals were to identify, neo-Pentecostals are much more elusive. Neo-Pentecostals move within

---

4   Hans A. Baer and Merrill Singer, *African American Religion: Varieties of Protest and Accommodation* (Knoxville: University of Tennessee Press, 2002).

5   A. G. Miller, "Pentecostalism as a Social Movement: Beyond the Theory of Deprivation," *Journal of Pentecostal Theology* 4, 9 (Fall 1996): 97–114; Cheryl J. Sanders, *Saints in Exile: The Holiness-Pentecostal Experience in African American Religion and Culture* (New York: Oxford University Press, 1996).

6   According to ethicist Jonathan Walton, neo-Pentecostals have three interrelated ecclesial and cultural features: (1) "Neo-Pentecostals have their finger on the pulse of society," often blurring "the line that for Pentecostals traditionally separated the sacred and the secular"; (2) For "neo-Pentecostals, the value system of the culture industries supplants traditional social mores"; (3) "Neo-Pentecostals emphasize personal experience over communal concerns and even doctrinal authority." Jonathan Walton, *Watch This! The Ethics and Aesthetics of Black Televangelism* (New York: New York University Press, 2009), 79–80.

traditional Pentecostal structures as well as within established independent, nondenominational structures. Furthermore, and most strikingly, neo-Pentecostalism has emerged from within traditional mainline denominations as well as from classic Pentecostalism. The presence of organizations such as the Full Gospel Baptist Fellowship as well as the increased presence of Pentecostal-like practices (speaking in tongues, faith healing, and ecstatic worship) in Baptist, Catholic, Methodist, and Presbyterian congregations and communities has compelled scholars to reconsider the ways that Pentecostalism operates in the world.

The Soweto meeting brings to the fore compelling questions about the intersection of religion – in this case specifically, neo-Pentecostalism – and globalization. How does something as seemingly local and indigenously American as "black Pentecostalism" reshape itself on the world stage? What presumptions of class status give way as American religious practitioners interact with their counterparts from other countries? What becomes of the American inheritances of race in the global context?

To anticipate my arguments, I reconstruct social class on a global scale, as understandings of America as a "developed" and "first world" nation are measured against understandings of other countries as "developing." These ideas effectively reify class differences internationally and suppress them intranationally, remapping those within the United States, even the poorest populations, as well off in comparison with the majority of the rest of the world. Moreover, these global revisions of class – in which relative economic standing is measured in international, not national, terms – reshape conversations among religious practitioners about the expectations and requirements of the Christian faith. The question is no longer whether black Pentecostalism is engaged (meaning locally engaged), but rather how – and where – it is engaged globally. Having accumulated some degree of wealth in the United States, a number of black neo-Pentecostals have gone on to focus their Christian service work on the "care" of individuals around the world, especially in light of the HIV/AIDS epidemic. This focus on care sidesteps structural critiques based on the sociopolitical histories of race and economic exploitation in the region (there was no talk of the colonial, racist, or international origins of social distress in contemporary South Africa at the Soweto meeting) and instead turns to the efficacy of global capitalism, religiously inflected, as the medium of care.

The contemporary paradigm of service and care takes into serious consideration the social and economic capital of the religious practitioners involved as a means of social engagement. The international guests at MegaFest *worked* – in the strong sense that neo-Pentecostals mean by this word – not so much through their physical labor in the region but rather by means of their ability to support the local economy and contribute monetary resources to local relief efforts. This helps explain the double nature of the church-sponsored trip itself. T. D. Jakes's presence in South Africa was both "missionary" work in service to South Africa and "vacationary" and recreational work in service to the American guests. Anthropologist Bayo Holsey has written about diaspora tourism in Africa as a means of connecting black Americans, separated historically from Africa by the trans-Atlantic slave trade, with a real and/or imagined homeland; at the same time, this type of tourism yields financial benefits for the host communities.[7] Similarly, anthropologists Brian Howell and Robert Priest have explored the development and significance of short-term missions (STMs) undertaken by Protestant Christian church communities. In the years after World War II, with the increased travel of Americans generally to new places, these one-to-two-week trips, according to Howell, have gradually taken the place of older, long-term models of Protestant Christian missions.[8] Priest's research in Peru suggests that the primary reason for such travel is "economic not religious." "These groups are not bringing a Christian faith that currently is present in the United States or Europe but is absent in Peru," he writes. "Rather, these groups travel from materially wealthy Christian communities to partner with Christian communities that are often numerically and spiritually as vigorous as their own, but which are, by comparison, materially poor."[9] T. D. Jakes's MegaFest International was a combination of diasporic tourism and a modified short-term mission project, with participants primarily pouring money into the local economy and contributing further toward the outreach efforts already established by Jakes.

II. FROM PROSPERITY TO CARE: BLACK PENTECOSTALS AS WEALTHY PEOPLE

Even as the heat of the South African sun scorched our arms and faces, most of those gathered remained focused on the messages being presented on stage in song and sermon. During the inaugural day of

[7] Bayo Holsey, *Routes of Remembrance: Refashioning the Slave Trade in Ghana* (Durham, NC: Duke University Press, 2008).
[8] Brian Howell, "Roots of the Short Term Missionary 1960–1985"; online at www.roundtripmissions.com/rethinking-missions (accessed June 27, 2010).
[9] Robert J. Priest, "Short Term Missions as a New Paradigm," in *Mission After Christendom: Emergent Themes in Contemporary Mission*, ed. Ogbu U. Kalu, Peter Vethanayagamony, and Edmund Kee-Fook Chia (Louisville, KY: Westminster John Knox Press, 2010), 96.

MegaFest International at the Nasrec Center in Soweto, thousands of us sat listening to a succession of charismatic speakers. Cordoned off by a line of ushers, American guests sat up front in white plastic chairs neatly aligned in long, extended rows. Behind us sat thousands of South Africans in similar white chairs or upon raised bleachers. The standing-room-only crowd extended outward to those who stood alongside the railings or sat in the cusp of overarching trees. We arrived early Saturday morning by busloads and stayed late into the afternoon. The sermons were offered by the American preachers Bishop T. D. Jakes, Pastor Paula White, and Bishop Noel Jones, as well as Ghanaian Bishop Mensa Otabil and Bishop John Francis from the United Kingdom.

While varying elements of the "prosperity gospel" that scholars have come to associate with the rapidly growing neo-Pentecostal movement found expression in the sermons, it was there in measured proportions. Paula White, the only white American speaker on the rostrum, at one point told her story of sowing a $1,000 seed offering into the ministry of T. D. Jakes when she was poor (having launched a yard sale to come up with the money) and gave her narrative of subsequent financial success as testimony to the power of seed faith giving. White went on to explain that while the international media are fixated on the global monetary crisis, in fact such a "crisis" was merely a "shifting" in the atmosphere. God was reordering things, transferring the wealth of the wicked to the righteous.[10] Such messages were not common at MegaFest International, however. To the broader conference, a message of hope and possibility in the midst of struggle seemed preeminent, while the message to the Americans in the sequestered auditorium off from the main stage was one of social responsibility to those who are less fortunate. Arriving in South Africa in the midst of the financial meltdown of virtually all glob-ally linked capitalist markets, the tone of this particular neo-Pentecostal gathering directed sobering attention to persons who struggle under the weight of poverty and disease.

This move toward care amid a debilitating international market speaks to the changing face of neo-Pentecostalism in the second decade of the twenty-first century. The theology of prosperity has been under growing criticism by theologians and church people in the face of the home mortgage crisis and of escalating unemployment. This shift has

---

[10] For a broader history of the prosperity gospel in African American religious com-munities, see Milmon F. Harrison, *Righteous Riches: The Word of Faith Movement in Contemporary African American Religion* (New York: Oxford University Press, 2005).

been evident in the thinking of Jakes himself. Sociologist Shayne Lee, in his 2005 study of Jakes, described the preacher as a business-savvy prosperity minister.[11] Subsequently, however, Lee has revised his judgment to take into account that Jakes "more recently ... has been critical of the excesses of prosperity theology."[12] Speculation about the motivations of the change include the fact that Jakes has already made his personal millions of dollars as a prosperity preacher; his ongoing public discussions with intellectuals and critics of the prosperity gospel, such as Cornel West; the mounting media skepticism about prosperity preachers as a result of national news exposés; as well as Jakes's own desire to appeal to more mainstream, middle-class audiences. According to social ethicist Jonathan Walton, this change in Jakes's message represents the historical circumstance that Jakes was raised up as a minister in the tradition of classic Pentecostalism rather than in the Faith Movement, which was more heavily influenced by broader mind-over-matter trends in nineteenth- and early twentieth-century American New Thought.[13] According to Walton, Jakes has always been a chameleon, changing colors among the various theologies he carries with him from his diverse theological upbringing. A self-help emphasis marked by dogged labor and spiritual renewal (with a touch of New Age optimism) has long been the hallmark of Jakes's ministry. His ascension as an international figure was facilitated by the proliferation of communications media, including television, radio, and Internet outlets (that is, tdjakes.com, thepottershouse.org, and streamingfaith.com), as well as social media interfaces such as Facebook, Twitter, and Myspace that have connected disparate groups of Christians around the world to his message of hope and abundance. Over the years, the message has paid off. Jakes has published over thirty books, including thirteen best sellers; he has written and produced two movies, *Woman Thou Art Loosed* and *Not Easily Broken*, both of which addressed relationship issues among African Americans; and he was named by *Time Magazine* in 2005 as one of the "25 Most Influential Evangelicals" in the United States. Although his church in Dallas is predominantly African American, his audiences include whites, Latinos and Latinas, and Asians within the United States, and his media outlets reach diverse constituencies around the globe.

[11] Shayne Lee, *T.D. Jakes: America's New Preacher* (New York: New York University Press, 2005).
[12] Shayne Lee and Phillip Luke Sinitiere, *Holy Mavericks: Evangelical Innovators and the Spiritual Marketplace* (New York: New York University Press, 2009), 59.
[13] Walton, *Watch This!*, 107–10.

While some might think of the contemporary language of "care" as a devious alternative linguistic and theological strategy for extracting resources from faithful followers, such a view does not do justice to what scholars of religion Donald. E Miller and Tetsunao Yamamori describe as the growing presence of progressive Pentecostals throughout the 1990s.[14] These new Pentecostals are interested in an "integral" or "holistic" gospel that engages firsthand with the plight of the poor on issues such as health care, nutrition, and housing.[15] According to Miller and Yamamori, "... as Pentecostals have become upwardly mobile, better educated, and more affluent, they have begun viewing the world differently. Pentecostals no longer see the world as a place from which to escape – the sectarian view – but instead as a place they want to make better."[16] The shift in the language of Bishop T. D. Jakes is reflective of this type of engagement with the world. It also carries forward an older tradition of international engagement among black Pentecostals. David D. Daniels III, a scholar of global Christianity, highlights the importance throughout the twentieth century of the overseas initiatives of the Church of God in Christ (COGIC), the oldest and largest black Pentecostal organization in the country. Daniels argues that "as a U.S. black–led organization, COGIC illustrates the mission-in-reverse movement wherein the people of color as former mission targets spearhead their own missions around the world."[17] Likewise, Clarence E. Hardy III notes that black Pentecostals of the early twentieth century, pushing against the limitations of race, did not see their "'destiny as bounded by the limits of the United States but rather forged identities within a more globally inflected Christian faith."[18] "In their quest to escape (white) man-made divisions," Hardy continues, "black religionists reached for the world beyond the nation's borders and as they did, new conceptions of the divine emerged that would convey the materiality of the divine."[19] Race became a central theme in how these African American Christians imagined their global religious commitments. While issues

14 Donald E. Miller and Tetsunao Yamamori, *Global Pentecostalism: The New Face of Christian Social Engagement* (Berkeley: University of California Press, 2007).
15 Miller and Yamamori, *Global Pentecostalism*, 42–3.
16 Miller and Yamamori, *Global Pentecostalism*, 30.
17 David D. Daniels III, "'Follow Peace with All': Future Trajectories of the Church of God in Christ," in *The Future of Pentecostalism in the United States*, ed. Eric Patterson and Edmund Rybarczyk (New York: Lexington, 2007), 178.
18 Clarence E. Hardy III, "From Exodus to Exile: Black Pentecostals, Migrating Pilgrims, and Imagined Internationalism," in *Religion and Politics in the Contemporary United States*, ed. R. Marie Griffith and Melani McAlister (Baltimore: John Hopkins University Press, 2008), 214.
19 Hardy, "From Exodus to Exile," 226.

of race emerge in Jakes's explanation of his work in Africa, the nature of his appeal to the Americans gathered was based primarily upon their economic privilege compared to the underprivileged status of many South Africans, not their shared history as victims of racist colonialist encounters.

The "care" offered by Jakes at MegaFest International reflected the central theme of his message of American responsibility within the context of South Africa's poverty. During the week, as tour buses took us to museums and shopping outlets, we were also driven past shantytowns to witness firsthand, albeit from the security of our air-conditioned buses, the plight of the country's poor. We were taken to South African museums in order to establish some historical and cultural context for the social and political conditions of the country. Jakes intended this, clearly: in his plea, he asked that those present understand themselves and their mission within a broader framework of the world's social and economic struggles. He wanted first to disrupt traditional understandings of "Africa" and then to use what we had learned on the trip as grounds for pleading the case for South African relief. We were wealthy in comparison to most South Africans, as we had learned looking out our bus windows and moving through the nation's history gathered up in museums.

While the dominant image of Pentecostals among scholars and pundits has been of persons on the margins of society, the neo-Pentecostals who traveled with Jakes to South Africa were successful middle- and upper-class people. Many were teachers; there were several ministers among the group; and government and civil service workers and businessmen and businesswomen were well represented. It was this constituency that Jakes wanted to appeal to, as both middle-class people and as *Americans*. Speaking to them as Americans, Jakes needed to disrupt their preconceived assumptions while at the same time ensuring their physical comfort. He joked with them during his message that he had kept his promise. "I told y'all I wouldn't have you sleeping in tents," a comment that was greeted with great laughter and applause. "I know you. I know your limits. I know how far to push you. You've got to be gradual about this missionary thing," he laughed, moving his hands back and forward in slow gestures. Bringing a group of Americans to the continent of Africa, many for the first time, required thinking through prior assumptions about the infrastructural development of Africa in order to dispel misconceptions. While speaking to those gathered, Jakes asked whether he could do a brief simulcast to those viewing back in the United States. During the live feed, he communicated to the audience not only the joy and excitement of the event, but also the fact that everyone who had traveled to South Africa was safe and sound.

The hotels at which we were staying served as further testament to Jakes's promise to ensure his travelers' comfort. While the conference itself was held at the Nasrac Center in Soweto, the hotels in which guests stayed were located in Johannesburg's upper-end region of Sandton City. We stayed at a range of three- to five-star hotels, encircled by fine restaurants and the shopping area at Mandela Center. This mall, comparable to America's high-end retailers, housed stores local to South Africa, but sprinkled among them were Western upscale classics such as Louis Vuitton, MontBlanc, and Cartier. From Sandton City Shopping Centre, we were within walking distance to our respective hotels, although those most ideally situated stayed at the five-star Michelangelo Hotel attached to the mall. In the evenings, we dined together at hotel restaurants or at restaurants near the mall.

To embark on this journey with Jakes, it was evident that the travelers had to be financially stable. Packages ranged from $5,000 to $7,000 U.S. Everyone seemed to have a story to tell about why and how he or she came to South Africa. I met Jasmine during a break one afternoon in a hotel lobby. She had traveled along with her mother, Evelyn, from Atlanta, Georgia. Single, under forty, with no children, Jasmine had recently finished legal work on a major bank merger and was now contemplating a change in careers. Treating her mother to MegaFest International (and to a Mediterranean cruise the following week) was her way of relaxing from the stressful demands of the year. Joking about the money that she had spent on the excursions and reflecting on her desire to secure a different type of employment in the near future, she said that knew one thing for certain: "I have got to keep Evelyn up to the lifestyle to which she has grown accustomed!" While Jasmine was one of the wealthier travelers, others were also relatively secure in their careers. Bishop and Mrs. Reid were enjoying the fruit of their burgeoning Pentecostal ministry in Texas. Having studied under Bishop I. V. Hilliard, a well-known prosperity minister from Houston, Bishop Reid told me that he used to struggle financially in his ministry until he learned from Hilliard how to raise an offering. Since then, he has been a faithful member of Aaron's Army, the circle of financial partners who support T. D. Jakes's ministry. This was his and his wife's second trip with Bishop Jakes; they had taken an Alaskan cruise with him a couple of years earlier. Olivia, another traveler, was a college administrator; Julia was the director of services for her local department of social services. Most of those who had come along had saved for the trip and treated the time away in South Africa as a vacation. Dianne and Joy were celebrating their fiftieth birthdays. Longtime high school friends from South Carolina, the two had run half-marathons together to stay in shape and committed themselves to making sacrifices in order to afford the trip to South Africa.

Jakes's message was geared toward these faithful. They were members of the black American middle class, not independently wealthy, but relatively comfortable. It was Jakes's goal to help them understand that in comparison to the impoverished people they would see in South Africa, they were wealthy. As he brought the issue of clean water to the fore, Jakes explained to those gathered, "It's hard to get Americans to understand about water, because most people have access to clean water.... And, our poor people, the people we call poor in America, are not really poor. They are inconvenienced.... Now, y'all know, our poor people got cable!" This last comment struck a cord with many and the audience roared in laughter, while Jakes concluded, "even if you got it in yo' baby's name."

Jakes's commentary on and criticism of America's poor, though effective in the moment, highlights the extent to which American class differences are flattened on the international stage. It shows the capacity of neoliberalism – the political and economic theory that maintains deregulation, free markets, and free trade as guarantees of global human flourishing – to make class distinctions seem fluid and unreal (though such distinctions are in fact exacerbated and entrenched under neoliberalism) while at the same time employing sickness and pain as a new template for mapping the world.[20] Jakes's ability to weave comedic relief into serious discussions is partially what makes him a popular and sought-after preacher. Yet his tone that morning was serious as he petitioned for relief by juxtaposing American poverty with poverty around the world:

> When we start talking about poverty in other countries, we're talking about dirt floors, twelve to fifteen people living in a nine-by-twelve space. We're talking about no plumbing, no plumbing at all, none. And, picture this, a nine-by-twelve area, no plumbing, ten to twelve people living in that one space, very little food, adverse situations and circumstances, and then you're talking about walking miles in many areas [to get water].

[20] For further discussion of the economic conditions created under neoliberalism, see David Harvey, *A Brief History of Neoliberalism* (New York: Oxford University Press, 2005); and John Rapley, *Globalization and Inequality: Neoliberalism's Downward Spiral* (Boulder, CO: Lynne Rienner, 2004).

This is the picture of poverty that Jakes wanted his constituents to see, not the American vision of poverty. Those gathered, he insisted, had the capacity to intervene.

The tour buses that shuttled us back and forth from the conference site to various tourist venues around the city had taken us by places of dire poverty. One day, we rode on two buses by shantytowns on our way to the Hector Pieterson Museum, which is devoted to the history of the struggle against apartheid. Later in the day, it became evident that the two buses had taken slightly different routes. Our bus driver had insisted that the shantytowns were not safe and he refused to allow us into the neighborhood and off the bus. Those riding in the other coach, however, were permitted to stop in the towns and to see children there. "We held one little baby," explained one of the women who had stopped by a day care center. As were the other members of the tour, she was taken by the size of the day care center and the shape of the homes, made of tin and stucco. Tires were laid atop of the houses to keep the roofs from blowing off in high winds, their tour guide explained. The toilet was a large hole dug in the ground just a short way off from the community. Children ran around barefoot in the dirt. The tourists took pictures before making their way to the museum.

Jakes's comments aimed to place all of this in context. It was evident from our journey that the contrast between the two nations – the United States and South Africa – was sharp. The American donors, possessed of a new sense of their relative prosperity compared to the suffering of the poor in other areas of the world, ought to respond generously to the needs they saw around them. Jakes was clear that he needed their help. "I'm going to give you a chance. I'm going to ask you to sow a seed in an offering this morning." He wanted to do more than save souls; he wanted to build water wells and provide HIV/AIDS care. The costs were high:

Now, raising an offering in an atmosphere like that [speaking of going out on the main stage before South Africans] ... if I raised the kind of offering that I needed to raise to meet our budget, I would lose all credibility. It cost us a little over $7 million dollars to do this. Seven million. And, to raise it, first of all, I don't know that we could raise it even with as many people as we had out there, because even the middle-class people who are coming don't make the kind of money that those of us who struggle in the U.S. make. And, so I don't have anybody to ask but you. And, I need you to help me to meet this budget. And, without you it can't be done.

The interplay that Jakes offers here between what he can ask his American donors and what he can expect from South Africans is telling. Aware of the privileged status of the Americans, Jakes suggests that his "credibility" is on the line. The only way he would be able to meet the costs of flying members of his staff to South Africa, renting the facility, staging events, organizing the health clinic, establishing water wells, and paying the speakers and musicians was to ask the "wealthy" American donors (meaning the Americans who now understood they were wealthy) who had traveled to South Africa. One could solicit an offering in South Africa, but not as one might back at home. "Yes, we are going to raise an offering in the service today, but we really can't *go at* an offering. *You* know what I mean," Jakes said, tongue in cheek.

> If you've got to raise $7 million in any country, you've got to go at it. You've got to get anointed and talk in tongues and roll your eyes back up in your head and get a prophecy. If you've got to get to $7million ... it takes a lot of $10 bills to raise $7 million. [great laughter] "Bless God, I'm standing with $20." You know how people come running up with $20 and you trying to raise $7 million, you say, $20?! ... But, I'm 'a tell you something, we're doing good. We're doing well. We're going to get it done. I need your help.

Jakes's candor and the playfulness in raising an offering are telling, but how one sees the exchange depends on where one is standing. Scholars, usually writing from an outsider's perspective, often think of Jakes and his ministry as being crass and materialistic, whereas those participating are more often than not aware of the game involved and accepting of it. They are in on the joke. There is a budget; there are expenses; there are needs to be met – and raising the offering in a playful spirit allows the minister to reach the goal. "You know how we do," Jakes had said. The audience laughed. He was well aware that they knew that the appeals for money back home in the United States are often outrageous. But he acknowledged that something was different about the stage in South Africa and the people gathered there. Those coming with him from the United States represented American money and power. Those gathered in South Africa represented the developing world to which Jakes wanted to minister. He asked Americans to give sacrificially.

III. DISRUPTING NATIONAL BOUNDARIES

The morning event with Jakes was also about disrupting notions of national boundaries related to health care and disease. While Jakes spent

a significant portion of his message relaying to Americans their privileged position, he also wanted to interrupt any ideas of Africa's health
crisis as being separate and distinct from America's. From the predicament over clean water supplies to the epidemic of HIV/AIDS, South
Africa and its people had more in common with America than not. This
was also Jakes's border-bending message.

One of the issues that has most preoccupied the study of globalization
and neoliberalism from the start has been the presumption of Western
dominance in the transmission of economic, political, and social ideologies. Anthropologists pushing back against the notion of Western unilateral domination have begun to explore the ways in which messages
are bilateral. In other words, as much as one message might give the
appearance of domination, the fact is that contact changes both giver and
receiver, albeit within the context of unequal power and wealth. This
idea is true in the production and distribution of religion internationally
as well. As religionists reach beyond their geographical borders, they not
only influence the cultures and communities in which they enter; they
change too. It is evident that Jakes's interactions with the rest of the
world have significantly influenced his theology. His gradual, increasing
involvement in health care and his deepening concern over HIV/AIDS
and clean water supplies in poorer countries followed several international trips. Jakes even now has a blog entitled "Around the World with
Bishop Jakes." This articulation of a new black neo-Pentecostal ethic in
Jakes's ministry is telling because it points to these very issues of acculturation and transformation illuminated by scholars.[21] His reflections in
Soweto reveal a pastor trying persuasively to convince other neo-Pentecostals of his vision of outreach to the world.

During the service, Jakes was clear that the pandemic of HIV/
AIDS experienced in South Africa was directly connected to America's
own HIV/AIDS crisis. He was also clear that the circumstances under
which persons acquire the disease matter less than the reality of the disease. As he encouraged us to visit the MegaCARE center that had been
opened in the back of the stadium, Jakes set to work dispelling some
commonly held myths, the very first being the myth of HIV/AIDS as a
disease primarily devastating the African continent. He talked about the

---

[21] In his study of African religion in the United States, Jacob K. Olupona argues for what
he terms "reverse missions" in the United States whereby African Christians feel
themselves called to minister to "the lost" in the global North, mainly Europe and
the United States. Such changes point to the multiple ways in which religious narratives are flowing. See Jacob K. Olupona and Regina Gemignani, *African Immigrant
Religions in America* (New York: New York University Press, 2007).

distressing prevalence of HIV/AIDS in the United States. Jakes was not simply trying to educate black Americans on the "African crisis"; by identifying the problems of both the United States and South Africa, he was highlighting the global interconnectedness of the issue:

> We have a common problem between our country and this country as it relates to HIV/AIDS, and, uh, it's certainly been a horrendous issue in this country. And, unfortunately, in our country, the numbers are escalating all the time and this is a totally preventable disease. It is totally, absolutely preventable, and yet many, many people are losing their lives because of HIV/AIDS.

Pointing to the success of the MegaCARE facilities in South Africa even over the short weekend, Jakes told the audience that in those three or four days, four hundred people had been tested; 20 percent of them were found positive. Because of this Christian initiative, HIV/AIDS need not be a death sentence. One young man was engaged to be married when he tested positive for HIV, Jakes reported. This announcement brought muted applause, followed quickly by criticism from the bishop. "That was a polite clap, but if he were getting ready to marry *your* daughter," he declared as the audience's applause grew much louder, "you would want him to know" his HIV status.

These public announcements were important and timely. But it was the way that Jakes spoke to the audience about their own sexual habits that neutralized any presumptions of American superiority as being the "enlightened" or virtuous nation. Jakes wanted not only to challenge self-righteous fulminations about how "sinners" behave in comparison with "saints," but by doing so, also to challenge misconceptions about how people in "develo*ping*" societies behave versus people in "devel-op*ed*" societies. His comments began with criticism of the church's silence on HIV/AIDS:

> Historically the church has been quiet about [HIV/AIDS] because it's tied to sex and it's tied to morality and it's tied to theology and it's tied to behavior, and it makes people uncomfortable.... Preachers have trouble talking about sex. But, what we can't say is killing us.... Just giving people rules doesn't bring righteousness. You have to balance your ideals, which is what we preach – we preach our ideals – against reality, which is our experience. And in reality, people fall short of the glory of God.... We had a generation where we could fall short of the glory of God, get up and repent and start our lives all over again. And now we're Missionary Price, and Evangelist

Such-a-Much, and Bishop Willy Wonder, but before we were Freeky Freddy, Jumpin' Jimmy, and Silly Sally. And some of us still haven't crossed over all the way. We're still kind of teetering back and forth. ... Just because you are poor doesn't mean you should die.... We always want to investigate how somebody got infected, but I tell you, there is no "good" AIDS and "bad" AIDS, no "good" HIV and "bad" HIV. It's just a disease. You know, it's just a deficiency. Don't try to make it something else and become self-righteous, because, you know, truly. If you be honest, if we would just be honest, there but for the grace ... [great applause]. There but for the absolute grace of God. You can act funny all you want to. You can turn up your nose and look at me all silly. If it were not for the very grace of God.... And I guarantee you that there are people in this very audience who had to take a cocktail this morning ... people living with HIV all around you....

By locating the possibility of HIV infected persons within the very audience of Americans sitting in their places there before him, Jakes at once neutralized the presumption that the Americans had come to save the poor dispossessed "others" who were infected. There was commonality and communion in the struggle to fight HIV/AIDS across nation-state boundaries.

Jakes had warned that he had some "challenging" words for the group, which included a statement about why he switched from preaching an abstinence-only theology that included a deafening silence on the use of condoms. His own ideas changed, he related, after he realized that married couples in his church used condoms because one partner was HIV positive while the other was not. He also mentioned the fact that more and more young people born with HIV were coming of age and preparing to get married. These realities altered his thinking on how to talk about sex. It is not just a gay disease, he cautioned:

The majority of people in this country who are HIV positive come from heterosexual relationships. In our country, HIV is spreading rapidly amongst black women, black women. Highest percentage of new cases of HIV is happening amongst black women. It is the taboo subject that we do not talk about and what we don't say is killing us.

Linking the plight of South Africans with AIDS to that of black women in the United States, Jakes made a case for disrupting national boundaries in the analysis of and fight against HIV/AIDS. As heterosexuals in

South Africa are dying from AIDS, so are black heterosexual women in the United States. He mentioned an incident where one woman in the United States had stood up after a presentation and wondered why he was so concerned about Africa. "We have our own problems right here in the United States," he recounted her objection. But it was his realization that nations are inescapably linked together that changed his mind. An HIV/AIDS crisis affecting large populations of people in Africa has implications for people in the United States, and vice versa; similarly, a water crisis affecting poor countries in Africa and other parts of the Southern Hemisphere will eventually become a water crisis for the Northern Hemisphere. By invoking the interconnectedness of the struggle against HIV/AIDS, without assigning blame, Jakes could be seen in part as setting himself against historic accounts of the disease that indiscriminately castigated poor and disadvantaged countries as the origins of the global AIDS pandemic. Paul Farmer's work in Haiti describes how such erroneous but ideologically powerful narratives about the country worked to further undermine that its social, political, and economic prospects.[22] While Jakes operated from the point of American privilege, most obviously concerned about the transmission of AIDS in the United States, he recognized that the potential for its spread as well as for its abatement rests with Americans as well as with Africans.

IV. ON THE MEANING OF RACE IN BLACK NEO-PENTECOSTALISM

Jakes's mission that morning was to draw a distinction between class in the United States and class in South Africa while simultaneously holding in tension the interrelatedness of the two countries. The first objective convinced the audience of their philanthropic resources (you will never be as poor as they are, however poor you think you are), while the second gave them reasons to share their resources (we are responsible for each other). Jakes's focus on class distinction versus racial solidarity is telling. While Pentecostalism has always represented itself as an interracial and multicultural movement, early black Pentecostals offered theological as well as social justification for taking race-specific measures and positions. And yet while one heard cries of "Up you mighty race" from pan-African nationalist Marcus Garvey nearly a century ago, the complexities of the twenty-first century render race a muted point of solidarity in the

---

[22] See Paul Farmer, *AIDS and Accusation: Haiti and the Geography of Blame,* 2nd Edition (Berkeley: University of California Press, 2006).

discourse of popular international neo-Pentecostal movements. Jakes mentioned the salience of race as a matter of personal conviction in his engagement in South Africa, feeling "uniquely connected" to Africa's soil. But race was not the focus of his collective call to action:

> Maybe I shouldn't say it, maybe it isn't politically correct, but there is a different feeling for me as a *black* man to know that as atrocious as slavery was, when I look at where the boats took me, and I go out in the bush and see that I could have been.... I could have been runnin' round with twenty people in a nine-by-twelve space, stacked up, defecating in a corner. I feel connected. I'm not saying other people don't feel connected, I know you do, but I feel uniquely connected because my roots run into this soil.

Whether what was politically incorrect here was bringing up race in the first place or expressing gratitude for not having to "run around" in tight living quarters or having to defecate in a corner of his home is hard to tell. What is clear is that Jakes invoked race as a means of explaining his *personal* convictions. He pondered the expediency of sharing these private thoughts as a black man while speaking to the blacks gathered along with whites, as well as with members of other racial groups listening via satellite. It was for those others that he acknowledged, "I'm not saying that other people don't feel connected; I know you do, but I feel uniquely connected because my roots run into this soil." To the extent that the majority black audience wanted to identify with his sentiment, they could; but this was not the focus of his call. Bringing up race in the narrative of slavery and then comparing the deplorable living conditions of some blacks in South Africa to the experience of blacks in the United States, Jakes's remarks could be viewed as politically incorrect. But the point is that he made a clarion call to everyone in the audience as well as those watching via satellite to give money based upon their *class status* as Americans, not on their race. In this way, those who had traveled with Bishop Jakes to South Africa entered upon the process of what Daniels identified as COGIC's "transfer of wealth from rich countries to poor countries."[23]

Scholars for years have exposed the Pentecostal history of racialized inclusion, given the availability of the Holy Spirit to all of God's believers as manifested in the Azusa Street Revival of 1906 in Los Angeles. They have also criticized Pentecostalism for its passive resistance to structural oppression. Yet the media-oriented nature of the message of contemporary neo-Pentecostals has led to the deemphasis on race. Jakes

[23] Daniels, "Follow Peace with All," 181.

in South Africa, though speaking to the predominantly black audience present there, was not addressing himself to a predominantly black public sphere. Cameras recording our meeting, capturing the details of his message, eventually sent his words abroad. It was this larger audience to which Jakes was consistently speaking. Focusing on class as opposed to race makes it possible to call for resources from this broader public to be invested in the cause of Africa.

V. BLACK NEO-PENTECOSTALISM AND THE WORLD

The presence of Jakes in South Africa with MegaFest International raises important questions about race, class, and nation, at the same time that it challenges understandings of black neo-Pentecostal engagement in the world. First, it opens up a conversation about how Pentecostals themselves understand their influence in the world. Miller and Yamamori make clear that while progressive Pentecostals are engaged firsthand with the amelioration of poverty through support networks and care facilities, they most often do not contend with the structures of oppression at the root of such conditions. Instead, "the Pentecostal ethic is very similar to the Protestant ethic," they write, "namely, it produces people who are honest, disciplined, transparent in their business dealings, people who view their vocation, humble or elevated, as a calling by God that warrants commitment."[24] In the end, they conclude, "Pentecostals seldom challenge the equity of the financial arrangements within global capitalism. Instead, they have been willing to work at pecking their way up the ladder of the capitalist economic system, even if the overarching effect of that system is to keep large numbers of people in poverty."[25] What is interesting about Jakes's lack of commentary about the problems of capitalism is that MegaFest International took place in the midst of an economic downturn that sent economies around the world into a tailspin. Yet no mention was made of the devastating effects of free-market economic policies around the globe. If under such stark and undeniable circumstances fundamental questions about the nature of capitalism are not asked, what type of future criticism may be expected? Does the increasing financial success of black neo-Pentecostals who have a place at the economic table by practicing the ideals of the Protestant ethic ensure their unquestioning loyalty to the "financial arrangements within global capitalism"?

[24] Miller and Yamamori, *Global Pentecostalism*, 165.
[25] Miller and Yamamori, *Global Pentecostalism*, 183.

At the same time, how might we come to understand the ways in which the Pentecostal calling not only to work diligently, but also to give sacrificially to the care of individuals, might signal a different type of engagement? In other words, can we still talk about the economic individualism of Pentecostalism without also talking about how philanthropy, very often at high levels of financial commitment, is expected of its members? This reallocation of resources by everyday neo-Pentecostal practitioners, who are generally not independently wealthy, invites us to think more broadly about the social engagement of men and women as religious practitioners. There is not only a politics of political protest, but also a politics of economic investment to be considered. How and where one spends money are fundamentally political decisions, whether made consciously or unconsciously. Unconscious spending often leads to the maintenance of the status quo; conscious, strategic, and organized spending (or withholding), on the other hand, can be as transformative as the Alabama bus boycotts and the success of the civil rights movement. Understanding neo-Pentecostalism in the years ahead – its social activism, political investments, and social influence – will require following the "money trail" of religionists and the institutions they fund.

The second observation to be made about MegaFest International and the meeting with Bishop Jakes in Soweto is that these events challenge us to think more broadly and inclusively about the shape and meaning of what is historically described as "black religion." As ministries such as Jakes's become ever more global, ever more detached from a geographically situated public, the question arises of whether their (inclusive) discourses will influence the ways in which traditional black church leaders and congregants think about their work in the world and their solidarity with a black public sphere. Will the globalization of neo-Pentecostalism have local consequences, transforming the identity of black American Pentecostals?

Furthermore, if black religion is known for its opposition to structures of (primarily racial) oppression, what do we make of a tradition that increasingly disengages from public discussions of race? According to religion scholar Sherman Jackson, "The central preoccupation of Black Religion is the desire to annihilate or at least subvert white supremacy and anti-black racism."[26] Distinguishing "Black Religion" from "African American religion" by pointing to the many

---

[26] Sherman A. Jackson, *Islam and the Blackamerican: Looking Toward the Third Resurrection* (New York: Oxford University Press, 2005), 29.

cases in which black religionists were "devoid of any racial preoccupation," Jackson suggests that "waging war against white supremacy and anti-black racism has not been an integral feature of *all* religion among Blackamericans. As such, 'Black Religion' and 'African-American religion' must be understood to connote two distinct, though interrelated, realities in Blackamerican life."[27] The expansion of neo-Pentecostalism via media outlets offers it a more inclusive community of viewers. Its public is changing. As black Muslim Americans, who are the focus of Jackson's work, have sought to make sense of the growing presence of immigrant Muslims from the Middle East among them who are reshaping the discourse of traditional Nation of Islam discussions of race, so too are black neo-Pentecostals, who take their message beyond the confines of black American congregations, rethinking race. Jakes's move toward class is indicative of this change. The move from racial solidarity as the impetus for social and political engagement toward class *privilege* and success within capitalism as the grounds of social responsibility speaks to these changing dynamics. Not only does such a move allow Jakes to convince those in the predominantly black American audience meeting with him that Sunday morning, it also allows those in the viewing audience of various racial and ethic backgrounds to feel connected to the causes he advocates. Race-specific language in this instance might have marginalized other populations willing to give.

Finally, Bishop T. D. Jakes's work in South Africa falls within a spectrum of debate about what is really needed in Africa. Scholars have long challenged the history of American and African American benevolence toward Africa for its paternalistic presumptions about the incapacity of Africans to care for themselves. Similar criticism is leveled today against relief efforts in Africa that offer financial aid without at the same time empowering African nations to create and sustain the political, economic, and social infrastructures needed for success. The increase in short-term Christian mission projects likewise raises questions about who such trips are meant to benefit: the missionaries or the people among whom they visit? MegaFest International finds a place within the larger discussion of mission work in the United States and abroad. With the increase of short-term mission projects organized by churches, particularly evangelical and Pentecostal ones, what new questions arise about the exchange of resources, ideas, and theologies across borders? Increasingly, scholars are thinking about short-term mission projects as events that serve the interest of those traveling as much as, if

---

[27] Jackson, *Islam and the Blackamerican*, 30 (emphasis in the original).

402   Marla F. Frederick

not at times more than, the communities in which they serve. But this
will not be the last word on this question.

The pace of scholarship on the African American church has not
kept pace with real changes occurring every day in African American
communities. Scholars have identified the role of social activism in black
churches, but the rise of the prosperity movement and the influence of
international and global connectivity on how black Protestant churches
function remain open topics. The influence that T. D. Jakes's ministry
has had around the world is undeniable. His books have sold millions
of copies in the Caribbean, South Africa, Latin American, the United
Kingdom, and Australia. At the same time, the influence of the world on
his ministry is likewise profound. Just as in the case of Malcolm X's *haj*
to Mecca or Martin Luther King, Jr.'s pilgrimage to India, the potential
for personal religious transformation within the context of international
dialogue is real. Bishop T. D. Jakes's movement onto the international
scene, regardless of how skeptical one might view his aims and inspira-
tions, says much about the changing nature of black Pentecostalism.

Select Bibliography

Baer, Hans A. and Merrill Singer. *African American Religion: Varieties of Protest
and Accommodation*. Knoxville: University of Tennessee Press, 2002.
Harrison, Milmon. *Righteous Riches: The Word of Faith Movement in
Contemporary African American Religion*. New York: Oxford University
Press, 2005.
Harvey, David. *A Brief History of Neoliberalism*. New York: Oxford University
Press, 2005.
Jackson, Sherman A. *Islam and the Blackamerican: Looking Toward the Third
Resurrection*. New York: Oxford University Press, 2005.
Lee, Shayne. *T.D. Jakes: America's New Preacher*. New York: New York
University Press, 2005.
Lee, Shayne and Phillip Luke Sinitiere. *Holy Mavericks: Evangelical Innovators
and the Spiritual Marketplace*. New York: New York University Press, 2009.
Miller, Donald E. and Tetsunao Yamamori. *Global Pentecostalism: The New
Face of Christian Social Engagement*. Berkeley: University of California
Press, 2007.
Rapley, John. *Globalization and Inequality: Neoliberalism's Downward Spiral*.
Boulder, CO: Lynne Rienner, 2004.
Sanders, Cheryl J. *Saints in Exile: The Holiness-Pentecostal Experience in African
American Religion and Culture*. New York: Oxford University Press, 1996.
Savage, Barbara Dianne. *Your Spirits Walk Beside Us: The Politics of Black
Religion*. Cambridge, MA: Belknap Press of Harvard University Press, 2008.
Walton, Jonathan. *Watch This! The Ethics and Aesthetics of Black Televangelism*.
New York: New York University Press, 2009.

19 Religious criticism, secular critique, and
the "critical study of religion": lessons
from the study of Islam

NOAH SALOMON AND JEREMY F. WALTON

Over the past several years, a number of scholars have diagnosed a crisis
in the field of the study of religion. Unlike previous debates within religious studies, this recent crisis has focused not so much on the object of
study but on both the relationship of the researcher to his or her subject
and the nature of research we as "critical scholars of religion" should
conduct. Institutional and professional anxieties over the legitimacy of
the field of religious studies within the broader academy have intensified the urgency of this debate. Above all, the dividing line between scientific scholarship and metaphysical speculation is increasingly drawn
around the ill-defined notion of critique. As José Cabezón has cogently
observed, "It is our commitment to a project defined ... in terms of criticism, methodological rigor, theory, self-awareness and so forth – that
we believe gives us ... the wherewithal to clarify the opacities and to
unmask the misrecognitions that are [supposedly] endemic to the first-
order discourses and practices of religion that are constitutive of both
our object and our Other."[1] The establishment of something called the
critical study of religion, as opposed to theological assertion or parochial apologetics, has become the primary justification for the place
of scholars of religion within the academy. Indeed, our at-times obses-
sive emphasis on the *critical* nature of the study of religion has even
threatened a sort of intellectual patricide within the discipline itself, as
a variety of contemporary scholars have argued that the very founders of
Religionswissenschaft were insufficiently detached from their object of

[1] José Ignacio Cabezón, "The Discipline and Its Other: The Dialectic of Alterity in the
Study of Religion," *Journal of the American Academy of Religion* 74, 1 (2006): 28.

The authors would like to thank Rosemary Hicks, Juliane Hammer, and the American
Academy of Religion, which offered the forum where some of the seeds of this chapter were
first planted; New York University's Religious Studies Program, which offered a stimulating
and collegial space in which to write this piece; and Professor Michael Foat of Reed College
for the chance encounter.

study, engaging instead in the culpable attempt to promote theological visions under the guise of cold objectivity.[2] Ironically, however, while we have come to valorize disinterested and critical scholarship, the term "critical" itself within the concept of the critical study of religion has not been subject to the very interrogations that it demands. Instead, a boundary war has erupted in which scholars have organized into opposing camps on either side of a dividing line between what is said to be an "insider" versus an "outsider" approach to the study of religion. This insider/outsider debate, hinging on the professional value of criticality, has affected scholarship on Islam – our subfield within the study of religion – in two distinct ways. On the one hand, overweening interest in maintaining the criticality of academic inquiry has distracted attention from the myriad ways in which Islam itself embeds and articulates disciplines of criticism. On the other hand, the so-called critical distance and objectivity of scholarship has often functioned in the post-9/11 context as a smoke screen for *deeply interested* polemics against Islam and Muslims, and often participate in deeper logics of Islamophobia. Our contribution seeks to offer a way out of these seemingly intractable impasses by destabilizing the self-evidence of the distinction between insides and outsides to religions in general and by showing the ways in which the study of Islam in particular can highlight unexpected formations of the relationship between religious devotion and criticism.

I. THE CONTOURS OF THE DEBATE: THE INSIDES AND OUTSIDES OF CONTEMPORARY RELIGIOUS STUDIES

In the interest of establishing clear intellectual boundaries and professional identities, scholars of religion have forwarded two basic arguments. The first of these is represented by Robert Segal, who argues for the privileged purchase that the "disinterested" observer, preferably viewing his object of study from a safe distance, has on the production of knowledge about religion within the modern academy. For Segal, a certain type of scientific, even biomedical, objectivity defines the ideal relationship that the scholar of religion should establish with his object of

[2] See Steven M. Wasserstrom's insightful volume, *Religion after Religion: Gershom Scholem, Mircea Eliade and Henri Corbin at Eranos* (Princeton, NJ: Princeton University Press, 1999); and Russell T. McCutcheon's *Manufacturing Religion: The Discourse on Sui Generis Religion and the Politics of Nostalgia* (New York: Oxford University Press, 1997).

study. In a recent contribution to the *Journal of the American Academy of Religion*, he argues the following:

> The most apt metaphor for the modern study of religion is that of diagnosis. It is not that religion is an illness but that the scholar is like the doctor and the religious adherent like the patient. Just as the patient has the disease but defers to the doctor's diagnosis, so the adherent has religion but defers, or should defer, to the scholar's analysis. The scholar, not the believer, is the expert. *The scholar's medicine kit contains what the believer lacks: theories.* In religious studies, as in medicine, the doctor knows best.[3]

For Segal, then, it is the individual who has not been infected by affective or ideological attachments to the subject at hand who is best able to comprehend and explain it.

In contrast, a second cadre of religious studies scholars advocates an alternate position, the mirror image of the first. For these scholars, the outsider has an epistemological disability in his study of religion because he is prone to reproduce categories that are tied to his own religious and intellectual worlds and which are thus essentially inappropriate to the unique world of the religion he studies. This position does not argue that one needs to be a practitioner of the religion in question in order to comment on it, but rather that one needs to shed his or her own intellectual baggage and come to approach the religion "on its own terms." A prominent representative of this school of thought is the Qur'anic scholar Jane Dammen McAuliffe. In a recent contribution, also to the *Journal of the American Academy of Religion*, entitled "Reading the Qur'an with Fidelity and Freedom," McAuliffe argues that in order to understand the Qur'an, we must divest ourselves of our Protestant-infused hermeneutics and thereby approach more closely the "true" meaning of the text. She writes: "Frequently misunderstood and misrepresented, the Qur'an deserves to be read on its own terms, rather than filtered through the genre categories and reception history of another scriptural tradition."[4] Elsewhere in her article, McAuliffe uses even stronger language when she writes that only certain scholars are able to "let the Qur'an speak to its contemporary North American and European contexts with *fidelity and freedom.*"[5] Thus, in contrast to Segal, for whom critical scholarship

---

[3] Robert A. Segal, "All Generalizations Are Bad: Postmodernism on Theories," *Journal of the American Academy of Religion* 74, 1 (2006): 158 (emphasis added).

[4] Jane Dammen McAuliffe, "Reading the Qur'an with Fidelity and Freedom," *Journal of the American Academy of Religion* 73, 3 (2005): 615.

[5] McAuliffe, "Reading the Qur'an," 630 (emphasis added).

necessarily requires exteriority, McAuliffe argues that good scholarship is impossible without the achievement of a unique mode of interiority.

While the approaches to the study of religion that Segal and McAuliffe uphold seem to be in utter opposition to one another, it is important to note that they in fact share the same presuppositions about the relationship between religious identity and knowledge. Both participate in the same discursive field, simply taking opposite positions therein. Regrettably, however, the very terms on which this field has been established remain unquestioned. Both scholars distinguish sharply between modes of inquiry (and by implication subjectivities as well) that they understand as interior to religious traditions and those that they understand as entirely exterior to them. The most immediate problem with framing scholarly inquiry into religion in terms of this insider/outsiderparadigm is that it reifies the very categories (believer, non-believer, Muslim, Christian, and so on) that much recent sociological scholarship in the study of religion has successfully problematized. If the purpose of much thick description of the past few decades has been to complicate the category of "the believer," "the Muslim," "the Christian," and so on, and thereby, to demonstrate the diversity of subjectivities that lie behind these hegemonic, seemingly common-sense labels, why then in conversations about method do we tend to resurrect problematically vague and monolithic categories such as insider/outsider? Another serious problem, beyond the simplistic construction of the categories themselves, is the very line that divides them. What makes someone a believer or a member of a faith community and what makes someone not so? What life experiences, confessional commitments, and ritual practices qualify one as an insider, and which prohibit an individual from inclusion? Are "insider" and "outsider" categories that we must inhabit permanently or can we move creatively between them? Most importantly, should scholars attempt to adjudicate these questions of religious identity and belonging, thereby becoming arbiters of orthodoxy? Our own research experiences with faith communities and devout individuals have clearly shown us the difficulty of maintaining such rigid distinctions. Nonetheless, both Segal and McAuliffe seem to insist upon them. We are left to wonder what the intellectual and political consequences are of maintaining such an approach to the study of religion.

To move forward, we might productively ask, What constitutes the "critical" in each scholar's endeavor within the critical study of religion? For Segal, criticality necessitates resuscitating a high Enlightenment equivalence between the physical and social sciences. Ignoring the past fifty years of critiques of both the physical *and* the social sciences, put forward by scholars as diverse as Thomas Kuhn, Bruno Latour, and

Michel Foucault, Segal argues that scholars of religion are capable of a disinterested scientific objectivity. Further, the very terms of Segal's engagement are in and of themselves problematic and evince a misunderstanding of the interventions of the postmodernist scholarship he claims to debunk. For postmodernists such as Foucault (whom Segal cites as the inspiration for much of the literature he finds so troublesome), the issue is not one of the "really real" of religion versus a distorted facsimile that scholarship has manufactured. Rather, they are interested in interrogating the notion of authentic, pretheoretical social facts in the first place, including religion. For Segal's ideal diagnostic scholar, the facts of religion are logically prior to the intervention of scholarship itself. Just as the doctor is uniquely able to recognize disease, only the scholar of religion's expertise is able to capture religion without distorting it. Therefore, this biomedical logic of diagnosis excludes any attention to the manner in which scholarship actively constructs the category of religion – the key postmodernist point. Segal caricaturizes postmodernism as solely concerned with individual scholarly bias and thereby misses the true innovation and importance of its intervention: the critique of an authentic objective category of the social in the first place.

While postmodernists do not argue for a notion of social objects that precede inherently biased analysis (and thus are odd targets of Segal's indignation), Jane McAuliffe does, and is therefore a fair target for Segal's skepticism. McAuliffe agrees with Segal concerning the existence of something called "really-real religion," but in contrast to Segal, McAulliffe worries that this authentic religion is always threatened by the distorting effects of theorists bringing their own cultural baggage to bear on scholarship. McAuliffe's advocacy of discussing Islam or the Qur'an on "its own terms" relies on the logic of an authentic, pretheoretical religion in distinction to one constructed by Western scholarship.[6] However, the notion of authentic Islam, or any other religion for that matter, is difficult to maintain, since the issue of what "its own terms" are, as McAuliffe's work in other places clearly shows,[7] has been greatly contested over the

---

[6] One might compare McAuliffe's approach to that of Talal Asad in Chapter 1 of *Genealogies of Religion: Disciplines and Reasons of Power in Christianity and Islam* (Baltimore: Johns Hopkins University Press, 1993). Both argue that there is an underlying Protestant logic in the way we study Islam and conceive of religion more broadly. Yet, for Asad, the recognition that Protestantism underlies assumptions that scholars make about religion does not lead him to go searching for a more "native" or "authentic" paradigm. Rather, he is interested in the question of how *any* attempt to construct a category of religion – post-Protestant, "Islamic," or otherwise – is necessarily involved in regimes of authorizing discourses.

[7] Jane Dammen McAuliffe, "Introduction," in *The Cambridge Companion to the Qur'an*, ed. Jane Dammen McAuliffe (Cambridge: Cambridge University Press, 2006), 1–22.

centuries, even within the tradition itself. To claim that "the Qur'an deserves to be read on its own terms" assumes (and indeed helps to solidify) the existence of a stable orthodoxy that is not historically or sociologically verifiable. Here we have an example of an odd disconnect between the conclusions of scholarship and the second-order conversations about theory and method that are conducted parallel to it. This kind of hermeneutics, which assumes a fixed inside and outside to Islam, obscures the vitality of the Islamic tradition itself and how that which constitutes that tradition has been not only a great object of debate but a product of cross-civilizational exchange that belies any attempt to view the understanding of the Qur'an as a bounded process of internals and externals. One might ask, to look at the present day, are the Qur'anic hermeneutics of a reformist scholar such as Abdolkarim Soroush, which rely on a deep engagement with Western philosophy, an example of talking about the Qur'an in terms that are not its own, or rather is his work merely one node in a long path of attempts to identify what is important and relevant about the Qur'an for contemporary life? Indeed, it is precisely the borrowing of terms and texts that are not "Islam's own" that has characterized intellectual movements throughout Islamic intellectual history. The notion of there being insides and outsides to the study or elaboration of the Qur'an is an orthodox fantasy.[8]

In summary, then, to juxtapose these two approaches to the study of religion, Segal holds that theory protects the legitimacy of religious studies from the distorting effects of religious commitment, while for McAuliffe disciplinary legitimacy relies on fidelity to authentic religion itself. But what if there is no endangered species to be protected, no "really-real religion" to be distorted by either overly attached believers or culturally encumbered scholars? Perhaps religion is always the product of a creative symbiosis of insiders and outsiders, populated by individuals who cannot simply be placed into the rigid categories of believer and unbeliever, just as the scholarly community contains theories and individuals who cannot be so easily placed into an either/or schema in terms of religious belonging. If this is the case, then religion is neither an object to be redeemed by theory nor an authentic truth to be protected from theory's detrimental incursions. Rather, the contours and contents of religion are always matters of debate on the part of a multitude of individuals: scholars, believers, and those who count themselves as both.

[8]   See Dimitri Gutas, *Greek Thought, Arabic Culture: The Graeco-Arabic Translation Movement in Baghdad and Early 'Abbasid Society (2nd–4th/8th–10th Centuries)* (New York: Routledge, 1998).

II. DESTABILIZING THE "CRITICAL" IN THE
CRITICAL STUDY OF RELIGION: LESSONS
FROM TWO CONTEMPORARY THINKERS

The recognition that religions are eclectic products of influences from across a broad range of historical and environmental contexts should not distract attention from the fact that religions themselves are often greatly concerned with establishing clear boundaries and elaborating the authorizing discourses that maintain them (as Michael Satlow argues in Chapter 6 of this book). That said, scholarship, whether the scholar conducting it considers herself a believer or not, must attend to the processes by which these boundaries are drawn, and not just by concerned believers but by secular scholars trying to define the category of religion or religions themselves. These boundaries are always the result of processes of debate and criticism. There are no self-evident scriptures, as all scholars of religion know so well. Thus it seems that instead of defending the critical study of religion as a secular privilege, we need to think more critically about the relationship between religion and criticism itself.

Two scholars who engage the topic of criticism from very different angles are Michael Warner and Talal Asad. For Warner, the concept of critique and, more specifically, critical reading practices maintains a suspect exclusivity over scholarship as a whole. In his article "Uncritical Reading," Warner brings to the surface myriad reading practices that much contemporary scholarship disdains precisely because these practices seem to lack a desirable "distance" from their object. Warner points out that this commitment to objective distance is beholden to a liberal concept of the subject, which assumes that interest and affect, on the one hand, and reasoned criticism, on the other, are mutually exclusive. For Warner, such an assumption elides the multiple ways in which reading and subjectivity intersect in both critical and uncritical fashions. The hegemony and exclusivity of the liberal subject in contemporary scholarship is also the target of a key intervention by Talal Asad. For Asad, however, the issue is not the juxtaposition between critical and uncritical readings in an attempt to address the relevance of the latter, as it is for Warner. Rather, Asad seeks to explore the foundations and disciplines of nonliberal modes of criticism, specifically those that emerge within the Islamic tradition.

In "Uncritical Reading," Warner calls for us to denaturalize what we mean by "critical reading" both through querying what turn out to be "the rather elaborate forms and disciplines of subjectivity we practice and inculcate"[9] as academic readers and by turning attention to the multiplicity of reading practices that do not rely on liberal modes of critique. He refers to these latter modes of engagement as uncritical reading. He asks:

> But what if it isn't true, as we suppose, that critical reading is the only way to suture textual practice with reflection, reason and a normative discipline of subjectivity? If we begin to understand critical reading not simply as the coming-into-reflexivity of reading, but as a very special set of form relationships, then it might be easier to recognize rival modes of reading and reflection on reading as something other than pretheoretically uncritical. The most obvious candidates for such a program of "uncritical" reading are various styles of religious reading, but they are not the only ones.[10]

By highlighting the textual practices and subjectivities of "uncritical reading," Warner succeeds in parochializing "critical reading" itself. The term "critical," then, ceases to be simply an adjectival modifier to "reading" (or, by analogy, "the study of religion"), but forms the name of a very distinct discipline. Like all other disciplines, critical reading has a history and, indeed, emerges only *through* history. Further, critical reading is more like uncritical reading than its proponents may be willing to admit: it also relies on embodied and affective technologies to achieve coherence. Indeed, before critical reading can imagine itself as universal and transcendent, it must develop within specific institutional contexts (for example, the academy) with their characteristic pedagogies and modes of professionalization (which, as those of us who have spent much of our adult lives in universities know only too well, are most often the result of the vagaries of institutional culture rather than the hypothetical pristine rationalities of the classical academy). Critical reading is, then, ideological and contingent rather than natural and inherent. Finally, Warner argues that the privileged distanciation between scholar and object of study upheld by "critical reading" does not maintain a monopoly on "reflection, reason and ... normative discipline(s) of subjectivity." Rather, "uncritical" reading practices, such as devotional recitation, are equally reflexive and dependent on discursive rationalities of their own. The "uncritical" is then not merely the dark penumbra of the critical.

---

[9] Michael Warner, "Uncritical Reading," in *Polemic: Critical or Uncritical*, ed. Jane Gallop (New York: Routledge, 2004), 16.
[10] Warner, "Uncritical Reading," 16.

Anthropologist Saba Mahmood, whom Warner cites approvingly in his article, draws attention to devotional reading practices that are both uncritical in Warner's sense and engage in highly reflexive, deliberative disciplines. She demonstrates that the women who are part of the Cairene mosque movement she studies are not simply mimicking established orthodoxies but are in fact engaged in pedagogies and styles of argumentation that are at once deeply reflective *and* rely on devotional sensibilities (and thus cannot be thought of as critical in the Enlightenment sense of the word). She writes, "any kind of skilled practice requires a certain amount of reflection and deliberation on the specific mental and bodily exercises necessary for its acquisition ... conscious deliberation is part and parcel of any pedagogical process, and contemporary discussions about it cannot be understood simply as a shift from the unconscious enactment of tradition to a critical reflection upon tradition."[11] Warner and Mahmood clearly show us that religious modes of engagement are not different from critical modes of engagement in that one is theoretical while the other is doomed to be pretheoretical. But pretheoretically uncritical is precisely what scholars such as Robert Segal assume their object of study, religious practitioners, to be. ("The scholar's medicine kit contains what the believer lacks: theories.")

What would the fate of religious studies be if we were to abandon the axis of distinction that locates critical theory on one side and pretheoretical practice on the other? The attempt by scholars such as Segal to quarantine the scientific, disinterested study of religion from that which they understand to be incurably *interested* scholarship, based on emotional attachments and submissive adherence to authority, seems to rest on the assumption that theories are the unique prerogative of scholars. Yet, Segal's imperative of disinterestedness – the watchword of critical reading and research – emerges, somewhat paradoxically, as an interest in its own right. It relies on a model of secular criticism that assumes the religious subject to be incapable of the reflexive engagement necessary to produce good scholarship. But if we seek to question the self-understanding of secularism as entailing the separation of religion and politics, religion and society – as much recent scholarship has succeeded in doing – and examine the ways in which the secular in fact reforms religion to produce a particular normative category thereof, how might we rethink related terms such as "secular criticism," "critical

[11] Saba Mahmood, *Politics of Piety: The Islamic Revival and the Feminist Subject* (Princeton, NJ: Princeton University Press, 2005), 54.

distance," and the kind of insider/outsider logic on which this criticism bases its authority?

Questions such as these have inspired Talal Asad throughout his oeuvre. We have introduced Warner and Asad as complementary critics of the notion of the critical itself, but it is crucial to acknowledge the distinctions between their arguments as well. As his broader work on affective mass publicity and counterpublics demonstrates, one of Warner's principal scholarly interests is to destabilize the hegemony of the liberal public sphere. Above all, he takes issue with Jürgen Habermas's apologetic argument for the liberal public sphere of early modernity[12] by noting the multiple, affective dimensions of contemporary publicness in European and American contexts. For Warner, then, criticality as a discipline is by definition a feature of *liberal* publics and persons; uncritical reading practices, on the other hand, correspond to nonliberal counterpublics. Although Asad is also deeply skeptical of the liberal public sphere, he is more squarely concerned with the contingent relationships among secularism, power, and critique in contexts outside of the Euro-American heartland of liberalism. By examining postcolonial contexts in which liberalism, secularism, publicness, and governance are differently hinged to one another, Asad achieves two key interventions. First, his dissection of the postcolonial laboratories of liberalism succeeds in highlighting the disciplines of power that undergird liberalism in all its contexts, even those Western ones in which it maintains an ersatz naturalness. Next, Asad's decoupling of secular liberalism and public political discourse allows him to explore the constitutive practices and political possibilities of other, nonliberal modes of criticism, particularly those that emerge within the discursive tradition of Islam. His essay "The Limits of Religious Criticism in the Middle East: Notes on Islamic Public Argument" offers a telling demonstration of religious criticism that is at once nonliberal, public, and potently political.[13]

In his discussion of activist, anti-establishment *'ulama* (traditional religious scholars) in contemporary Saudi Arabia, Asad unpacks the distinctness of Islamic ways of admonition (couched as *nasiha*, or advice). Here, Asad argues for a concept of public religious criticism within Islam that is distinct from critique in the Enlightenment, which is "inhabited by individuals aspiring to self-determination and dispassionate judgment,

¹² Jürgen Habermas, *The Structural Transformation of the Public Sphere: An Inquiry into a Category of Bourgeois Society*, trans. Thomas Burger (Cambridge, MA: Massachusetts Institute of Technology Press, 1989).

¹³ Talal Asad, *Genealogies of Religion: Disciplines and Reasons of Power in Christianity and Islam* (Baltimore: Johns Hopkins University Press, 1993), 200–36.

whose moral foundation is universal reason."[14] This Islamic public criticism is founded on the notion of submission to God, the *cultivation*
of a certain set of passions or virtues (moral rectitude, bodily integrity,
patience, love of God and the Prophet) that makes valid critique possible, and a form of reason that is particular to Islam and thus certainly not
universal in the Enlightenment sense of the word. So, through Asad we
come to understand that secular liberalism is not the only perspective
from which criticism emerges.

Let us look at how Asad conceptualizes this Islamic mode of public
criticism, which he equates with the concept of *nasiha*, in contrast to
liberal critique:

> [*Nasiha*] reflects the principle that a well-regulated polity depends
> on its members being virtuous individuals who are partly responsi-
> ble for one another's moral condition – and therefore in part on con-
> tinuous moral criticism. Modern liberalism rejects this principle.
> The well-regulated modern polity – so it argues – depends on the
> provision of optimum amounts of social welfare and individual lib-
> erty, not on moral criticism. The primary critical task, according to
> political liberalism, is not the moral disciplining of individuals but
> the rational administration and care of entire populations. Morality,
> together with religious belief, has become essentially a personal
> matter for the self-determining individual – or so the liberal likes
> to claim.[15]

While liberalism is of course also a moral project,[16] one that seeks to preserve the sanctity of individual autonomy, the specific moral criticism
that Asad is unpacking through the concept of *nasiha* seeks to subordinate the individual to an order that is at once religious and social. As he
writes, "Since the objective of *nasiha* is the person who has transgressed
God's eternal commands, its normative reason can be regarded as a
repressive technique for securing social conformity to divinely ordained
norms...."[17] By bringing the practice of *nasiha* in Saudi public religious
criticism to our attention, Asad outlines a mode of engagement with
and of religion that, while certainly not *disinterested*, can in no way be
thought of as prereflexive, pretheoretical, or precritical.

---

[14] Asad, *Genealogies of Religion*, 220.
[15] Asad, *Genealogies of Religion*, 233.
[16] One need look no further than John Rawls's classic *Political Liberalism* (New York: Columbia University Press, 1993) to understand the deeply moral dispensation of liberalism.
[17] Asad, *Genealogies of Religion*, 232–3.

III. ISLAMIC PUBLIC CRITICISM: SOCIAL CRITIQUE IN VERSE

To illustrate the uniqueness of Islamic modes of criticism in ethnographic detail, let us take the religious commentary that has recently arisen on the issue of urbanization in Sudan, a problem that has become so acute in recent years that few have remained silent on its implications. Unlike in the Saudi Arabia that Asad studies, the religious criticism that is most audible in the Sudanese public sphere often appears in poetic verse, commonly put to music, rather than in the writings of *'ulama* and new Muslim intellectuals (though Sudan is not bereft of the latter either). This genre of poetry, which in classical Arabic is called *qasid*, is referred to as *madih* in Sudan, as it is evocative of the panegyric tradition (*madh*) of prophetic praise poetry due to its Islamic content. Those *madih* that marshal social criticism are referred to as *madih al-islah al-ijtima'i* (*madih* of social reform). Through this category of poetry, a mode of criticism that relies on "securing social conformity to divinely ordained norms," as Asad characterizes *nasiha*, also unfolds. Indeed, one informant likened *madih* of social reform to the much-studied genre of Islamic legal *responsa* literature, referring to one poem as a "musical *fatwa*" (*al-fatwa al-musiqiyya*).

One poet who dealt explicitly with the moral dimensions of urbanization was the Sudanese Shaikh 'Abd al-Rahim Muhammad Waqi' Allah (d. 2005), known by the nickname al-Bura'i. Al-Bura'i was interested in the moral threats (dissolution of the family, shirking of responsibilities to home and tribe, neglect of ritual duties) that arose due to massive population displacements caused by the disruption of Sudan's entry into the global economy. Al-Bura'i was among the twenty-first-century Sudanese shaykhs who benefited most from the urbanization of the Sudanese population: the distinctive shape of his life could not have occurred in any other era, as his name and fame were carried from his rural home of Kordofan to the capital and then back to all corners of Sudan due to the massive influx of peoples to the capital as a result of war, famine, and underdevelopment. Yet he also recognized the dangers of urbanization. Take, for example, his poem, "The Return, Oh Forgetful One!" (*al-'awda ya nasi*).[18] This poem discusses the displacement of the Sudanese population to urban centers and abroad, which began in the 1980s and picked up pace in the early 1990s due to economic collapse. The poem

---

[18] The term *nasi* in Arabic could also be translated as "my people," but "forgetful one" is probably what al-Bura'i intends here.

counsels return to one's home country or village. It begins: "The return, oh Forgetful One: do it before death comes/staying put is the best thing to do."[19] The reasons that al-Bura'i counsels his listeners to return have nothing to do with the economic and social problems that have emerged as a result of the abandonment of the outlying states, uneven develop-ment, and the overcrowding of the capital; rather, they result from the moral threats that arise from the migration of (primarily male) popula-tions from rural areas in pursuit of economic opportunity. In this poem, al-Bura'i laments that so many Sudanese men have abandoned their fam-ilies for economic rewards.[20] In so doing, they shirk their responsibili-ties to their parents, children, and wives;[21] and their absence often leads their wives into sins such as infidelity.[22] Indeed, villages nearly aban-doned by young men were a common phenomenon that dotted the rural Sudanese landscape in the early twenty-first century and for many raised the specter of a complete meltdown of social norms in the way in which al-Bura'i feared. In addition to the moral duties to the family that were interrupted by urban migration, al-Bura'i bemoans the neglect of ritual duties caused by the displacement of individuals from the pious contexts of home life. Al-Bura'i writes:

There is benefit and blessing to those who are staying put, for our prayers are constant and at the right time. Staying put is the best thing to do.

[But if you provide to your family] clothes and the needs of the house *(kiswa wa mu'na)*, it is guaranteed you will go to heaven *('ind allah madmuna)*.

While aid and development agencies often spoke of the dangerous eco-nomic stakes of urban migration and uneven development, here al-Bura'i was reminding his listeners of the significant *moral* and *religious* stakes at issue as well.

Further, it is important to note that al-Bura'i's religious criticism in verse was not only aimed at a morally lax society but also intervened into intra-Islamic debates extant in Sudan concerning the relationship

[19] Translated from the cassette: al-'awda ya nasi (recorded by awlad al-bura'i, Umdurman: al-ruumani li-l-intaj al-fani wa-l-tawzi').
[20] "And how many have gathered money for themselves, following their own suspicious desires. Thus staying put is the best thing to do."
[21] "And so many people have left their homes and neglect their pregnant wives. Thus staying put is the most important thing."
[22] "The silly fools [who leave their homes] are punished, because at [their] house[s] men are coming one after another."

between piety and urban citizenship. Returning home, as al-Bura'i coun-
seled, also meant rejecting the new geography promoted by the Islamist
government of Sudan. In the new millennium, the government promoted
a novel urban Islamic sensibility, as average Sudanese were pulled in
like magnets to Khartoum because of emerging economic opportunities
(due principally to the exploitation of oil reserves). Al-Bura'i, however,
returned to a valuation of place based on different criteria, promoting a
rural moral geography, even if it meant economic hardship.[23] In doing so,
he marshaled a potent public argument, rooted in disciplines of piety,
that destabilizes the necessary relationship between individual autonomy and criticism assumed in the liberal subject of critique.

IV. ISLAM, DOGMA, AND CRITIQUE
IN A POST-9/11 CONTEXT

The relationship between pious sensibilities and practices of criticism
is not only a matter of concern within identifiably Islamic political
contexts such as Saudi Arabia and Sudan. Recent media spectacles surrounding the problematic concept of blasphemy against the Prophet
Muhammad vividly demonstrate that questions of religion, politics,
and criticism are objects of intense debate, speculation, and anxiety for
Muslims and non-Muslims alike. The pitch and frequency of conversations about "blasphemy" and "Islam" have certainly intensified in the
overwrought post-9/11 political context, prompting a crucial question:
How does Western fascination over Islam's supposed tendencies toward
rigidity and dogma serve to fix a more general antinomy between Islam
and criticism? And, in a parallel vein, why is it that the liberal value
of unfettered criticism – the principle that no object should be ipso
facto quarantined from criticism – cannot recognize Muslim reactions
to insulting depictions of the Prophet as acts of criticism in their own
right? Why do secular liberals construe the protests of public Islam as
necessarily *uncritical* acts of mimicry, dogma, and intolerance – and,
hence, as threat and outrage? As we have just demonstrated in our treatment of Islamic public criticism, the position of the liberal subject is not
the only one from which criticism can occur. Yet liberals themselves
deny the plurality of critique. Here, in a context that expands far beyond
the academy itself, the relationship between religion and criticism, and

---

[23] For a discussion of the concept of moral geography, see Engseng Ho, *The Graves of
Tarim: Genealogy and Mobility Across the Indian Ocean* (Berkeley: University of
California Press, 2006), 94, 121, 190–1.

the foreclosures inherent in maintaining a strict opposition between the two, bears the weight of exceptional political consequences. Moreover, these political consequences are especially acute for Islam and Muslims. This is above all due to the fact that the past decade has witnessed the progressive categorization of Islam as the most "religious" religion – that is, the religion most incompatible with the dictates of political liberalism.

These myriad tensions surrounding the relationship among liberalism, Islam, and criticism were vividly highlighted in 2005 when the Danish daily newspaper *Jyllands-Posten* published twelve caricatures of the Prophet Muhammad, sparking diplomatic objections, protests, and boycotts on the part of Muslim governments, organizations, and individuals worldwide.[24] A variety of scholars have argued recently that liberalism fails to comprehend the nature of the injury that Muslims experienced because of the cartoons.[25] More to the point for our purposes, however, is the fact that secular liberal commentators seemed incapable of recognizing the moral, religiously based criticism that Muslims marshaled in response to the cartoons *as legitimate criticism in the first place*. Secular liberals insisted that Muslims upset by the cartoons simply did not understand the proper modes and means of democratic citizenship and toleration. Rather than take Islamic moral criticism seriously, they took shelter in the unproblematic dismissals inherent in such accusations as dogma and inflexible orthodoxy. Most ironic of all, because of their unreflective assumption that Islam and dogma are synonymous (and, concomitantly, that Islam and criticism are mutually exclusive), they fail to recognize the ways in which even the Prophet himself can become an object of debate for contemporary Muslims.

To consider one salient example, in recent years Hasan al-Turabi, the Muslim intellectual and former ideologue behind the Islamist regime in Sudan, has surprised many by publicly making an argument that the Prophet erred on matters not explicitly related to the conduct of

[24] The Danish cartoon controversy is only one recent instance of a political event centering on questions of free speech and depictions of the Prophet Muhammad. For discussion of a more recent example, see Jeremy F. Walton, "Who's Afraid of the Free Speech Fundamentalists? Reflections on the *South Park* Cartoon Controversy," online at http://therevealer.org/archives/3950 (accessed April 28, 2010).

[25] Webb Keane, "Freedom and Blasphemy: On Indonesian Press Bans and Danish Cartoons," *Public Culture* 21, 1 (2009): 47–76; Saba Mahmood, "Religious Reason and Secular Affect: An Incommensurable Divide?" *Critical Inquiry* 35, 4 (2009): 836–62; Talal Asad, "Reflections on Blasphemy and Secular Criticism," in *Religion. Beyond a Concept*, ed. Hent de Vries (New York: Fordham University Press, 2008), 580–609.

religion.[26] Taking an interpretation of the well-known *hadith al-dhubab*
as the basis of his argument, al-Turabi claimed that although it is essential to follow the Prophet on matters of religion, modern science is capable of legitimately abrogating certain aspects of the Prophet's advice not
directly related to religion. *Hadith al-dhubab* reads as follows: "If a fly
has fallen in any of your vessels, dunk it in all the way, and then take
it out. For [while] in one of its wings [you find] disease, in the other is
its cure."[27] In a recent interview with an American researcher, al-Turabi
recapped his argument as follows:

> The Prophet was not a doctor. Anyone can be a doctor.... *Hadith
> al-dhubab* probably isn't a true *hadith* but even if it is true, the
> Prophet doesn't know [about medicine]. What he teaches you is a
> medicine of morals (*Tibb al-khuluq*) and a medicine which cures the
> soul (*Tibb al-nafs*).[28]

In spite of the instructions offered in this *hadith*, al-Turabi argued that
biomedical advancements have clearly shown flies to carry disease-
causing bacteria, and, therefore, the Prophet erred in this instance. It
is important to note, however, that al-Turabi's argument did not derive
solely from an attachment to empirical scientific inquiry (though this
was certainly an aspect of his intervention); nor was he championing
reason over revelation. Instead, his argument relied on modes of reasoning based on the logic of *sunna*, which indeed requires emulation of
the Prophet. Where al-Turabi *differed* from his more conservative critics
was simply on the definition of this emulation (*ittibaa'*). Importantly,
al-Turabi's very criticism of the advice offered in *hadith al-dhubab*
depended on yet another set of *hadith*. In these *hadith*, the Prophet
argued that on matters in which he did not have expertise, Muslims were
free to consult those who possessed superior knowledge.[29] Al-Turabi's

---

26 See al-Amin al-Haj Muhammad Ahmad, *Munaqisha hadi'a li-ba'd afkar al-duktur
al-turabi* [A Calm Debate on Some of the Ideas of Dr. al-Turabi] (Saudi Arabia: markaz
al-saff al-aliktruni li-l-taba'a wa-l-nashr wa-l-tawzi' wa-l-'i'lan, 1995), 95–8; and
Abdelwahab el-Affendi, "Hassan Turabi and the Limits of Modern Islamic Reformism,"
in *The Blackwell Companion to Contemporary Islamic Thought*, ed. Ibrahim Abu
Rabi' (Oxford: Blackwell, 2006), 145–60.
27 "idha waqa' al-dhubab fi ina' ahadakum falyaghmasuhu kullu thumma layatarrahu,
fa-inn fii ahad jinahihu shifa' wa fi-l-akhir da'." (Sahih al-Bukhari, "kitab al-tibb,"
5336). (All *hadith* translations that follow were rendered from the Arabic texts offered
in the extremely useful hadith encyclopedia at the Saudi Ministry of Islamic Affairs
website, online at http://hadith.al-islam.com/.)
28 Personal interview of Hasan al-Turabi, 2006.
29 The most famous of these *hadith* is one regarding the pollination of date palms. In this
account, the Prophet offers advice to his people about how to attain the best yield from

intervention caused deep offense to Sudanese Sufis (to take one example), who often uphold the doctrine of the absolute infallibility (*'isma*) of the Prophet. For other Muslims, who argue that the Prophet would not misguide believers, al-Turabi's disregard for him fell under the concept of *shatm* or *sabb al-rasul*, insult of the Prophet, an act that has legal consequences within the tradition of *fiqh* (Islamic jurisprudence); for some scholars, this act even constitutes unbelief (*kufr*) or apostasy (*ridda*).[30] The very contentiousness of this debate clearly shows that moral criticism, piety, and the discursive traditions of Islam are bound together in multiple ways that are impossible to comprehend on the basis of a strict juxtaposition between criticism and pious devotion.

V. CONCLUSION

On the basis of our itinerary through questions of *nasiha*, Sudanese devotional poetry, and debates over the advice of the Prophet contained in the *hadith* traditions, we have seen that liberalism does not hold exclusive purchase on critical reasoning. Perspectives that are both pious and critical exist comfortably within the scope of Islam. Furthermore, through our discussion of the contemporary politics of "blasphemy" and Islam, we have demarcated some of the political and conceptual limits of liberalism itself. As we saw, liberalism's insistence on the identification between religion and uncritical dogma – which is especially acute in the case of Islam – results in a failure to recognize creative, nonliberal syntheses of devotion and critique as legitimate. In this respect, liberalism has emerged as a parochial idiom in its own right, one which is not entirely free of the affective and irrational attachments that it so vociferously disdains. Once the "critical" epithet of our discipline is historicized and provincialized, neither Segal's call for diagnostic theorization exclusive of all affective attachments nor McAuliffe's romance of the authenticity of religious texts prior to Western scholarly intervention is tenable.

While problems of belief and criticism seem to be the definitive bugbear of the contemporary study of religion, perhaps the scholar of

---

their palms, but after following his advice, their harvest fails. The Prophet responds: "[I]f it is something from your material world, [in fact] you are more knowledgeable [about it than I am]. But if [it is] matter of religion, [then you must defer] to me" (*musnad ahmad*, 12086).

[30] For a discussion of *shatm* and *sabb* within the legal tradition, see L. Wiederhold, "Shatm (a.)," in *Encyclopaedia of Islam*, 2nd Edition., ed. P. J. Bearman et al. (Leiden: Brill, 2010); online at http://www.brillonline.nl/subscriber/entry?entry=islam_SIM-8898 (accessed August 1, 2010).

religion can take solace in the fact that such dilemmas are not exclusive to our field. Indeed, in disciplines as diverse as anthropology and comparative literature, the criticism of limits and the limits of criticism are the constant refrains of theoretical debate.[31] If these tensions are more extreme in the case of the study of religion, this is partially because religion itself – and Islam in particular – has become the placeholder for many of the anxieties native to contemporary liberalism. But this is precisely why the study of religion is uniquely important to the academy as a whole. For through its lens, the dilemmas of the contemporary moment come into focus in nuanced and unexpected ways.

Select Bibliography

Habermas, Jürgen. *The Structural Transformation of the Public Sphere: An Inquiry into a Category of Bourgeois Society.* Translated by Thomas Burger. Cambridge, MA: Massachusetts Institute of Technology Press, 1989.

Ho, Engseng. *The Graves of Tarim: Genealogy and Mobility Across the Indian Ocean.* Berkeley: University of California Press, 2006.

Keane, Webb. "Freedom and Blasphemy: On Indonesian Press Bans and Danish Cartoons." *Public Culture* 21, 1 (2009): 47–76.

Mahmood, Saba. "Religious Reason and Secular Affect: An Incommensurable Divide?" *Critical Inquiry* 35, 4 (2009): 836–62.

Warner, Michael. "Uncritical Reading," 13–38. In *Polemic: Critical or Uncritical.* Edited by Jane Gallop. New York: Routledge, 2004.

---

[31] For anthropology, see James Clifford and George E. Marcus, eds., *Writing Culture: The Poetics and Politics of Ethnography* (Berkeley: University of California Press, 1986). For comparative literature, see Susan Gubar and Jonathan Kamholtz, *English Inside and Out: The Places of Literary Criticism* (New York: Routledge, 1993).

Index

Abraham, 94, 148
Alles, Gregory D., 97
American Academy of Religion, 9
Amish, 333–4
animism, 93, 210, 214
Ankersmit, F. R., 104
anthropomorphism, 74, 308, 312,
    316
Aquinas, Saint Thomas, 246
Arendt, Hannah, 84
Aristotle, 172, 242
Arkush, Allan, 201
Asad, Talal, 3, 18, 209, 286, 409, 412
asceticism, 266
Asoka, 159–60
Assmann, Jan, 271
Augustine of Hippo, Saint, 177, 339,
    343–4
authority, religious, 41, 90, 111, 113,
    120, 134, 142–3, 147–8, 322

Bacon, Francis, 233
Baird, Robert, 350
Bakhtin, Mikhail, 372
Bamba, Amadou, 311
bar mitzvah, 146
Barth, Karl, 236–8
Barthes, Roland, 311
bat mitzvah, 146
Beecher, Henry Ward, 299, 301–2, 306
Bell, Catherine, 140
Benedict XVI, Pope, 65, 354
Benedict, Ruth, 349
Benjamin, Walter, 101–2
Bennett, D. M., 19, 26–31, 33–4
Bhagavad Gita, 266

Bible, 30, 213, 219, 222–3, 234, 246,
    301
Blanshard, Paul, 353
Blavatsky, Madame Helena, 33
Bloch, Maurice, 41, 118–20, 122–3,
    125
Boas, Fraz, 210
bodhisattva, 12, 260, 262–6, 269
Bodhisattvabhūmi, 264
Böhme, Jakob, 190
Bollas, Christopher, 100, 102–3
Borges, Jorge Luis, 207
Bourdieu, Pierre, 273, 279, 283, 285
Brahmā Net Sūtra, 258, 270
bricolage, 133, 136
Buddha, 5, 151, 154, 157, 159–62, 188,
    258–68, 370
Buddhism, 151, 154–63, 165, 188–90,
    203, 257–71
    and nationalism, 259, 262
    Golden Legend, 262
    Great Vehicle, 258, 260
    Indian, 267
    Japanese, 259
    Jōdo, 261
    Korean, 261
    Mahayana, 263, 265, 267–9
    meat eating, 268
    Nichiren, 261, 264
    Nikaya, 258, 263–4
    notion of Two Truths, 261
    Pure Land, 264
    self-immolation by fire, 261, 266
    Shinshu, 261
    Sinhala, 160
    Tamil rebellion (2009), 259, 271

Buddhism (*cont.*)
  Tantric, 259, 269–70
  Tibetan, 262
  Vietnamese, 261
  Vinaya, 267
  warrior-monks, 260
  Zen, 259, 266
Burger, Justice Warren E., 334
Bush, George W., 186–7, 354

Cabezón, José, 403
Cambell, Robert Allen, 339
Catholicism, 2, 5, 40–1, 63–4, 75,
    86–7, 90, 100, 103, 142–6,
    149, 220–2, 247, 283, 285,
    342, 345, 353–4
Certeau, Michel de, 100
Chakrabarty, Dipesh, 101–2
Chang, K. C., 114–15, 123
Child, Lydia Maria, 29, 339
Chopra, Deepak, 289
Christianity, 3–5, 7–8, 22–4, 27, 30,
    40–1, 44–6, 48–50, 63, 85, 88,
    95–7, 99, 116, 130, 134–6,
    138, 145–6, 152, 154, 165,
    177–8, 187–90, 211, 213–14,
    220–3, 232, 234, 236, 240–1,
    243, 246–7, 257–60, 264,
    289–91, 305–6, 310–11, 333,
    338–45, 349–50, 352, 354–5,
    380–1, 384–5, 387–8, 395,
    401, 406
Church of God in Christ, 388, 398
Cicero, 130
civil rights movement, 103, 357,
    400
Clarke, James Freeman, 29
Clement of Alexandria, 189
Clinton, William Jefferson, 191
Collingwood, R. G., 49
colonialism, 39, 85, 154–5, 165,
    221–2, 336, 384, 389
Comstock, Anthony, 27–8
Confucianism, 7, 114
Corbin, Alain, 51–4
Cotton, John, 351
Crowley, Aleister, 348–9
Culianu, Ioan, 347–8

Dalai Lama, 257, 262
Damasio, Antonio, 303
Dancy, Jonathan, 171
Daniels, David D., III, 388
Danish cartoon controversy (2005),
    417
darśan, 86, 100, 213, 224, 362–3,
    366–7
Dead Sea Scrolls, 147
demons, 75, 124–5, 137, 259–60,
    265–6, 269
Demos, John, 352
Dennett, Daniel, 175–6
dharma, 159, 261–2, 265–6,
    271, 371
Dharmashastras, 370
Dickens, Charles, 93
Dīpavamsa, 260
Dolar, Mladen, 215, 228
Doniger, Wendy, 348
Douglas, Mary, 53
Dubuisson, Daniel, 8
Dürer, Albrecht, 309
Durkheim, Émile, 59–63, 67, 80, 111,
    113, 346

Eck, Diana, 224
Edwards, Jonathan, 190
Eggleston, Edward, 350
Eliade, Mircea, 111–14, 117, 121–2,
    178, 347–8
Elias, Norbert, 275–6, 285–6
embodiment. *See* religion: and the
    senses
Emerson, Ralph Waldo, 20–1
Encyclopedia of Religion, 97,
    135, 347
Enlightenment, 5, 29, 93, 131, 199,
    232–4
epistemology, 4, 6, 9, 11, 46, 98, 104,
    179, 232–3, 248–52, 405.
    See religion: the study of:
    and epistemology
Erasmus, Desiderius, 275
ethnography, 51, 193
Eucharist, 46, 86, 100, 134, 220, 305,
    343
Ewing, Katherine, 364

faith, 94, 169, 177–8
Fanwang jing (Brahma-Net sutra), 267
Farmer, Paul, 397
fascinans, 92, 188, 190
Fenn, William Wallace, 24
fiqh, 145, 419
First Amendment (U.S. Constitution),
    321, 332, 335
First World War, 188, 236
Fitzgerald, Timothy, 18, 174, 176
flag veneration, 62, 313
Flanagan, Owen, 71–2
Foucault, Michel, 100, 148, 355, 407
Frankfurter, David, 340, 346
Free Religious Association, 20, 24
Freedberg, David, 297
freethought, 27, 30, 34, 341
Freud, Sigmund, 339, 343
Friday Apostolics (Ghana), 221–4, 228
Fries, Jacob Friedrich, 100
Fuller, C. J., 213–14, 225–6
fundamentalism, 257, 260, 262, 271
    Islamic, 36, 54
    Sinhala Buddhism, 260
Fundamentalist Church of Jesus
    Christ of Latter Day Saints,
    324, 326–30, 334–5

Galgani, Saint Gemma, 127
Geary, Patrick, 63
Geertz, Clifford, 1, 13, 99, 117–18,
    123, 126, 132, 298
ghosts, 75–6, 93, 124–6, 128
Gibbs, Robert, 197
globalization, 4, 154, 358, 382, 384,
    394, 400
Gnosticism, 115–16, 121, 339–40
Gold, Daniel, 102
Gourevitch, Philip, 191
Graeber, David, 65
Greenfield, Lauren, 307–9
Greven, Philip, 352
Griffith, R. Marie, 283

Haberman, David L., 86
Habermas, Jürgen, 412
Haidt, Jonathan, 71
halakah, 131

Hall, David D., 281
Hanh, Thich Nhat, 257, 262
Hannay, James Ballantyne, 341
Hartshorne, Charles, 249
Harvey, John W., 189
Hebrew Bible, 145, 147
Hegel, G. W. Friedrich, 210
hermeneutics, 138
Higginson, Thomas Wentworth,
    19–34
Hinduism, 5, 8–9, 24, 97, 143, 154–5,
    213–14, 223–6, 229, 265–6,
    270, 311, 336, 343–4, 348,
    364, 366–7, 370
Hirschkind, Charles, 37, 54–5, 228
HIV/AIDS, 380–1, 384, 392, 394–7
Hobbes, Thomas, 29
holy, concept of the, 85–100, 102–4,
    190
Holy Spirit, 213, 222, 290–1, 398
Homer, 207
homo religiosus, 98, 112, 347
Hume, David, 21, 29
Hutcheson, Francis, 21

icons, 137, 139–40, 213, 258, 269,
    311, 314, 316
images, religious, 213, 217, 224, 227,
    296–7, 311
    and aesthetics, 21, 154, 156, 161,
    201–3, 247, 313–14, 317, 363,
    365, 371, 379, 394
    and place, 302
    and the somatic present, 301, 305
Immaculate Conception, 75
Incarnation, the, 213
Ingersoll, Robert, 31
Inman, Thomas, 29
Inquisition, the, 46
inter-religious dialogue, 152
Islam, 2, 4, 24, 36, 54–6, 131, 135–7,
    142–3, 145, 152, 186, 277–9,
    284, 288, 297, 311, 320, 401,
    404, 406, 408–9, 412–20
    and urbanization, 414
    fears of, 404
hijab, 277–9
isnad, 145

Islam (*cont.*)
  law, 131, 145
  medieval, 145
  Muslim immigrants in Europe, 36
  Shi'ism, 136
  Sufism, 189, 364, 419
  umma, 55

Jackson, Michael, 192–3, 196, 204
Jackson, Sherman, 400
Jakes, T.D., 380–2, 385–402
James, William, 31, 95, 99, 102, 178,
    190, 249, 342–3
Jastrow, Morris, 344
Jay, Martin, 97
Jesus, 23, 30, 41, 65–6, 85–6, 88, 90–1,
    94, 96, 100, 103, 138, 188,
    213, 220, 240, 297, 300–1,
    308–11, 314, 327
jihad, 135
Jonas, Hans, 115–16, 120–1, 340
Jones, Bob, 302
Jonestown, Guyana (1978), 331
Judaism, 133, 137–8, 146–7, 196–201,
    203–4, 320
Jude Thaddeus, Saint, 173
Jueguan lun, 266
just war, concept of, 259–60, 265

Kaaba, 143
Kandinsky, Wassily, 70
Kant, Immanuel, 7, 92, 94–5, 99–100,
    172, 176, 201–2, 247–52
Kaufman, Suzanne, 63
Keane, Webb, 218–19
King, Martin Luther, Jr., 402
king, kingship, 46, 151, 156–62, 269,
    336
Kopytoff, Igor, 62, 81
Koresh, David, 354
Korsgaard, Christine, 171
Koyré, Alexander, 121
Kripal, Jeffrey J., 101, 348
Kristensen, W. Brede, 236

Lankāvatāra sutra, 268
Latour, Bruno, 210, 406
Leach, Edmund, 40

Lee, Shayne, 387
Legge, James, 7
Lehrsätze, 200, 202
Leibniz, Gottfried, 233
Levinas, Emmanuel, 197–8, 200, 203
Lévi-Strauss, Claude, 136
Lévy-Bruhl, Lucien, 216
Lincoln, Bruce, 33
lived religion, 212, 281, 297, 299, 305,
    317, 323
Locke, John, 43
Lofton, Kathryn, 195
Lourdes, 63–4, 84, 103
Luther, Martin, 44, 309, 343
Lyall, Sir Alfred Comyn, 343

MacIntyre, Alasdair, 132, 180–1
Mack, Hans, 308, 314
magic, 6, 40, 58–60, 80, 82, 157, 160,
    270
Mahāvamsa, 260
Maheśvara, 270
Mahmood, Saba, 375, 411
Maitreya, 260
Malcolm X, 402
Mâori, 204–5
Māra, 260
Marduk, 121
Marett, R. R., 93–4
Margaret of Città di Castello,
    Blessed, 91
Marion, Jean-Luc, 100
Marx, Karl, 61, 210
Mary, Mother of God, 64, 75, 84, 103,
    220–1
Masuzawa, Tomoko, 18, 330–1
Mather, Increase, 351
Maurice, F. D., 7
Mauss, Marcel, 42, 61, 310
McAuliffe, Jane Dammen, 405–8
McCutcheon, Russell, 18
McDannell, Colleen, 63, 223
McLennan, J. F., 340
McLuhan, Marshall, 223
Mead, Hirini Moko, 205
Mead, Margaret, 349
Mecca, 148, 402
meditation, 165, 281, 289, 362–3

MegaCARE, 381, 394–5
MegaFest International, 381–2, 384–6, 389–90, 399–401
Mendelssohn, Moses, 197, 199–203
Merleau-Ponty, Maurice, 301–6, 311, 314–15, 317
metaphysics, 211, 219, 232–3, 239, 242, 245–6, 248, 259, 403
Miller, Albert G., 383
Miller, Daniel, 215
Miller, Donald E., 388
Miller, Perry, 351
Minaksi, 225, 229
missionaries, Christian, 154, 165, 222, 258, 385, 389, 401
modernity, 3–4, 18, 48, 54, 109–10, 113–16, 121, 123, 131–2, 134, 153, 211–12, 220, 234, 247–8, 354, 412, *See* postmodernism
criticisms of, 112, 115
enchantment/disenchantment, 1–2, 31, 48, 109
versus premodern, 6, 47, 109, 114–15
Mohism, 124
monasticism, 62, 151, 159–65, 188–90, 257–61, 265–8, 271
Monier-Williams, Monier, 7
Morgan, Edmund S., 351
Mormonism, 133, 145, 323–5, 330–2, 334, 342, 354
Moses, 66, 131
Mubarak, Hosni, 56
Muhammad, 66, 416–19
Müller, F. Max, 11, 20
Muslim Brotherhood, 55, 228
mysterium tremendum, 92–3, 96, 98
mythology, 29–30, 137, 258, 269, 348
reconceptualized as narratives, 137

Nag Hammadi gospels, 147
Nāgārjuna, 263
nasiha, 412–14, 419
Nation of Islam, 401
National Socialism, 97, 236
Needham, Rodney, 45
neoliberalism, 391, 394
New Testament, 138, 246

Newton, Isaac, 233, 248
nirvana, 60, 188, 190
Novak, David, 199
Noyes, John Humphrey, 354
numinous, 75, 90, 92–8, 103, 190
Nussbaum, Martha, 172–3, 176–7, 179

Obeyesekere, Gananath, 100
O'Connor, Flannery, 86
Olcott, Henry Steele, 33–4
Old Testament, 145–6
orientalism, 154, 349
Orsi, Robert A., 127, 173–4, 176, 220–1, 283, 297–9
Otto, Rudolf, 7, 86–8, 90, 92–100, 102–3, 177–8, 183, 188–91, 203, 207, 236, 249

Panduranga, 364
Panksepp, Jaaik, 72
Parker, Theodore, 20
Peirce, Charles Sanders, 204, 210, 219
Pels, Peter, 214
Pentecostalism, 221, 283, 380, 382–6, 388–90, 394, 397–402
Perry, Bruce, 328–9
phallic worship, 339, 344–5
Phillips, Mark Salber, 131–2
Philo, 138
philology, 152, 156
photography, 296, 307–9, 311
Pinney, Christopher, 224
Pio of Pietrelcina, Saint, 142
Pius IX, Pope, 75
Plato, 71, 102, 197–8, 232
polygamy, 30, 324–5, 330–4
postmodernism, 169, 407
Potter, William, 24
presence, 65, 73–5, 212–29, 301, 304
and spiritual beings, 60, 77, 79, 143–4, 210–11, 214, 217, 292
Presler, Franklin, 336
Preus, J. Samuel, 210
Prosperity Gospel, 221, 381, 386–7
Protestant Reformation, 131, 135, 152, 221, 331, 342
Protestant/Catholic polemics, 5, 41, 146, 149, 220, 342, 345, 353

Protestantism, 5–7, 40–1, 114–16,
    135, 146, 149, 152, 168,
    173, 178–9, 209, 211, 220–1,
    223–4, 232, 236, 350–54, 385,
    399
  and Biblical criticism, 152
  Calvinism, 218
  crypto-Protestant, 211
  liberal, 18, 33, 97, 168, 232, 236–7
  Lutheranism, 233, 236, 309
  neo-orthodox, 238
pūjā, 143, 213, 226, 362, 364, 366, 374
Puritanism, 350–1
  and sexuality, 351

Quakerism, 211, 220
Qur'an, the, 51, 66, 137, 152, 405,
    407–8

race, racism, 154, 211, 216, 384,
    388–9, 397–402
Rahner, Karl, 247–8
Rahula, Walpola, 257, 260
Rama, 360–1, 366
Rawls, John, 180
reason, 27, 177, 202, 233–4, 247–8,
    305
  as religion's other, 177, 233–4
relics, 63, 139–40, 144, 213
religion
  and emotions, 49, 52, 71–2, 87, 94,
    124–6, 183, 202, 293, 342
  and law, 319–23
  and media, 227
  and memory, 101, 138, 148–9, 151,
    159, 283, 363
  and political liberalism, 36, 39, 41,
    44, 50, 53, 56, 409, 412–13,
    416–19
  and privacy, 44
  and relationships, 97, 297, 299
  and senses, 36–55, 139, 210, 223,
    228, 248, 250, 296–311, 318,
    362, 374, 377–8
  embodiment, 42, 190, 283, 303,
    305–6, 310, 313, 378
  and sexuality, 358, 397
  and spirituality, 71, 195, 251,
    257, 289–90, 308, 336
  as ultimate reality, 245– 247, 347
  defining of, 39, 63, 114, 116–22,
    131, 136, 210, 297
  in the contemporary world, 1, 287,
    341
  legitimization of, 125
  material, 139, 151, 209–15, 217–24,
    226–9, 299, 305–6, 313, 317
  meanings of, 7, 17, 36–40, 58, 82,
    110, 166, 209, 248, 408
  natural history of, 29
  the study of
    "primitive religion," 6, 33, 40,
      95–6, 98, 114–15, 117, 121,
      123, 146, 211, 216, 220, 320,
      340–1, 344–7, 349
    and epistemology, 43, 92, 104,
      236, 241, 247–50, 253, 303
    and postcolonialism, 155
    and psychology, 90, 111
    and relationships, 304, 375
    and Victorian anthropology, 37,
      40, 210, 214, 301, 340, 344
    as sui generis, 67, 90, 95, 97, 178,
      244
    belief-centered approaches, 136
    cognitive approaches, 40, 74,
      76–7, 81, 132, 210, 216–17,
      303, 310
    comparative, 24, 30, 96, 152, 216,
      235–6
    critiques of essentialism, 155
    epistemic bracket, 84
    evolutionary frameworks, 29–30,
      40, 71, 76, 82, 93, 110, 116,
      120–1, 123, 128, 210, 216,
      341, 345
    history of, 8, 85, 152–3, 177, 210,
      232, 405
    insider/outsider debate, 11, 404,
      406, 408, 412
    philosophy of religion, 2,
      235, 243
    pluralism, 25, 45, 166, 319, 358
    reductionism, 67, 117, 153, 156,
      165, 175
    religious "field," 280–1, 285, 294,
      335
    sympathy versus suspicion, 19

Reni, Guido, 301
Ricoeur, Paul, 376
ritual 225–7, 347–53
    versus belief 39–43, 118–29
Robertson Smith, William, 40, 346
Rosen Georg, 189
Rosenzweig, Franz, 100
Ruel, Malcolm, 41
Rumi, 188–9
Rwandan genocide, 191

sacred and profane, 42, 59, 63
    sacralizing/desacralizing, 62
Said, Edward, 154
Sanders, Cheryl, 383
sangha, 261
Santner, Eric, 101
Saranankara, Valivita, 160–3
Sarārthadīpanı, 160, 162
Satlow, Michael L., 274, 409
Saussure, Ferdinand de, 214–15, 219,
    222
Schaff, Philip, 350
Schleiermacher, Friedrich, 94, 178,
    231–2, 234–7, 239–43, 245–6,
    248–51, 253
Schmidt, Leigh Eric, 54
Schroeder, Theodore, 342
science of religion, 31–2, 34
scriptures, 30, 139, 145, 147, 152, 155,
    158, 226, 258, 409
Second World War, 155, 259, 261, 385
secularization, 36, 285–6, 320
    laïcité in France, 39
    secular "field," 286
    secularism, 18, 32, 34, 42–3, 284,
        286–7, 411–12
    secularity, 47
Seeskin, Kenneth, 199
Segal, Robert, 404–8, 411, 419
semiotics, 215, 218–21
September 11 (2001), 142, 152, 186,
    277, 404, 416
Seven Spires Monastery, Chiang Mai,
    151, 157, 159
Sharpe, Eric, 96
Shils, Edward, 131–2, 147
Short Creek, Arizona (1953), 325
shrines, 63–4, 98, 143, 365

Shulman, David, 364
Simmel, Georg, 61
Śiva, 154, 270, 348, 362, 377
Slingerland, Edward, 175–7
Smith, Adam, 21
Smith, Jonathan Z., 98, 102, 120–2, 331
Smith, Linda F., 328
Smith, Wilfred Cantwell, 17, 19, 23,
    25, 32, 37
Söderblom, Nathan, 84, 87, 104
Sontag, Susan, 190
Soroush, Abdolkarim, 408
Soubrious, Bernadette, 64, 75, 84
spirits, 12, 75–6, 101, 114, 124, 211,
    213, 375
Stout, Jeffrey, 132, 179–80
Strousma, Guy, 364
stūpas, 269
Sullivan, Winnifred Fallers, 282
śunyatā, 266
Supreme Court (U.S.), 321–3, 331–4
    Employment Division v. Smith
        (1990), 334
    Reynolds v. U.S. (1879), 332, 334
    Wisconsin v. Yoder (1972), 333–4
Suzuki, D. T., 266
symbols, 40, 62, 86, 132, 217, 219,
    268, 296–9, 302, 305–6, 309,
    315–16, 338

taboo, 59–61, 64–5, 67–9, 73, 75, 78–9,
    81, 357
Talmud, 205
    Babylonian, 139, 197–8
    Palestinian, 131
Tambiah, Stanley, 100
Taylor, Charles, 36–7, 44–5, 47–8, 50,
    287, 303
temples, 151, 224–6, 269, 336, 361–2,
    366
Teresa of Avila, Saint, 342
Tetlock, Philip, 64–5
texts, religious
    canon formation, 139, 142, 145–7,
        151, 160–1, 344
    composition and performance of,
        163
    consitiutive power of, 159
    critical post-textualism, 152–3, 156

texts, religious (*cont.*)
    efficacy of, 160
    historical critical reading of, 138,
        233
    modern practices of reading, 153,
        408
    textual communities, 163–6
    textual practice, 153, 156, 161, 166,
        410
theodicy, 193
theology, 8, 19, 94, 98, 100, 152, 168,
        170–1, 173–4, 176–7, 183–4,
        197, 222, 230–4, 236–53, 287,
        386, 394–6
Theosophy, 33–4
Thomas, George F., 32, 187
Tiele, C. P., 236
Tillich, Paul, 349
Tilokaraja, King of Chiang Mai, 151,
        156–9
Torah, the, 131, 145, 197, 199–203
Toy, Crawford Howell, 344
tradition, religious, 131–3, 136, 142,
        155, 166
transcendence, 36, 45, 60, 71–2,
        112–13, 191, 212, 247–8, 250,
        299
*Treatise on the Great Perfection of
    Wisdom*, 259
Troeltsch, Ernst, 7, 236
Turabi, Hasan al-, 417
Turner, Victor, 346
Tylor, E. B., 29, 93, 210–12, 214–20,
        222

Unitarians, Unitarianism, 20, 29
Upanishads, 370

Valerius Maximus, 130, 149
Valliere, Paul, 135–6

Vatican, 2, 145, 148
    Second Vatican Council, 145
vegetarianism, 268
violence, 5, 31, 127–8, 149, 152,
        258–69, 271, 276, 279, 348,
        353, 355, 357
    and terrorism, 276–7, 279
Vishnu, 154
vodou, 375

Waco, Texas (1993), 325, 328, 354
Wall, Otto Augustus, 341
Walton, Jonathan, 387
Waqi' Allah, Abd al-Rahim
        Muhammad, 414
Warner, Michael, 409–12
Watt, Douglas, 72
Weber, Max, 41, 109–10, 113–15, 119,
        121, 123, 125, 228
Weiner, Annette, 63
Weltecke, Dorothea, 46
West, Cornel, 387
White, Paula, 386
Whitehead, Alfred North, 237,
        249
Williams, Raymond, 274
Winfrey, Oprah, 194–6, 308
Winnicott, D. W., 100, 102
Wittgenstein, Ludwig, 47
World's Parliament of Religions
        (1893), 20

Yamuna-ji, 86, 97
Yearning for Zion, Texas (2008),
        323
YouTube, 334

Zaidman, Nurit, 64
Zemon Davis, Natalie, 352
Zohar, 137, 145

19650531R00260

Printed in Great Britain
by Amazon